IJESHAS AND NIGERIANS

AFRICAN STUDIES SERIES 39

OTHER BOOKS IN THE SERIES

IJESHAS AND NIGERIANS

The Incorporation of a Yoruba Kingdom 1890s–1970s

J. D. Y. PEEL

Charles Booth Professor of Sociology
University of Liverpool

CAMBRIDGE UNIVERSITY PRESS

CAMBRIDGE
LONDON   NEW YORK   NEW ROCHELLE
MELBOURNE   SYDNEY

Published by the Press Syndicate of the University of Cambridge
The Pitt Building, Trumpington Street, Cambridge CB2 1RP
32 East 57th Street, New York, NY 10022, USA
296 Beaconsfield Parade, Middle Park, Melbourne 3206, Australia

First published 1983

Printed in Great Britain at
the University Press, Cambridge

Library of Congress catalogue card number: 82–23660

British Library Cataloguing in Publication Data

Peel, J.D.Y.
Ijeshas and Nigerians. – (African studies series; 39)
1. Ijebu (Nigeria) – History
I. Title   II. Series
966.9'2   DT513

ISBN 0 521 22545 0

CE

Contents

Maps

Tables

Figures

Preface

I hope that in writing this book I have constantly kept in mind my greatest obligation: to the Ọwa, the chiefs and the people of Ilesha, for all the help, encouragement and hospitality they showed to an uninvited stranger, who had set himself to work on a history of their community. It was constantly borne in on me during the course of fieldwork how much Ijesha value their past, seeing it as a resource and inspiration for their present projects. A valued informant, the late Chief Daniel Gidigbi of Ifofin quarter, seemed to speak for many when he said, commenting on what the twentieth century had brought to Ilesha, that literacy was valuable since 'it would not let history be lost' (ẹkọ ko jẹki itan ṣọnu mọ). While this study is also addressed to an 'academic' audience with more theoretical concerns – ethnographic, sociological and historical – I have tried to write an account which literate Ijesha can read with interest and perhaps with pleasure, conveying some sense of the achievements of the personalities and groups who have shaped their history over the past century. It has been a history of boisterous controversy and of recurrent conflicts, some of which remain alive to this day, so I can only hope that my account, even if it does not please all parties entirely, is at least judged by Ijesha to be fair-minded.

It is a great sadness that, in the decade which has elapsed between the start of the project and final publication, many of the elderly men who were so generous with their time and their knowledge of Ilesha, have passed on. Particularly I had hoped to be able to present a copy of this book to the Ọwa, Agunlejika II, whose advice and support I enjoyed throughout the project. In dedicating it to him, I also have in mind several other chiefs and elders, both of Ilesha and of the district communities. Selection of a few names is invidious, but I feel I must record my particular indebtedness to Chief J. O. Malomo the Agbayewa, Chief S. A. Ataiyero the Aṣireyun, Chief S. Akinola the Sawẹ, Chief Baṣemi, Chief J. O. Fadahunsi, Chief J. M. Ajayi-Obe the Lẹmodu, Chief I. A. Owolabi the Ọbaodo, Chief S. O. Thompson the Ọlọni, Hon. M. I. Ekundare, the Revd D. B. Esan, Mr E. A. Fajemisin and other members of the Fajemisin family, Mr S. A. Apara and other members of the Apara family, members of the family of Chief J. D. E. Abiola, several members of the Ogedengbe family, Chief A. O. Fadugba, several members of the Haastrup family, Chief E. O. Ayoola, Alhaji S. A. Famuyide, Mr R. A. Awobiyi, Mr D. Aluko-Kupoluyi, Mr D. D. Layinka, Chief S. A. Ogundiya and Mr J. Awomolo.

I am grateful to the Social Science Research Council for grants to support two periods of fieldwork in Nigeria, in 1973–75 and in 1979. During both periods of fieldwork I enjoyed the support and generous hospitality of the Department of Sociology and Anthropology at the University of Ife, headed by Professor A. A. Akiwowo. Among academics in Nigeria Dr T. O. Odetola, Dr Carolyne Dennis, Professor and Mrs B. O. Oloruntimehin, Professor O. L. Oke, Professor Robin Horton, Professor Bolanle Awe, Professor R. O. Ekundare and Dr Karin Barber have been generous with help and advice. I have particularly benefited from discussions with Dr Deirdre La Pin about the nature of *itan*, as well as from her practical expertise in recording them. I would also like to acknowledge by name the Ijesha students who worked with me on the 1974 Household Survey: Messrs T. A. Ajayi (of Ibokun), A. F. Jegede, J. A. Ojo, R. A. Oyesile, O. Fadipe, J. O. Odeyemi, L. O. Amigun (of Ikogosi-Ekiti) and Jide Adedoyin. It was fun working with them and they incidentally taught me a great deal.

In the later stages, I have derived great benefit from comments made by Gavin Williams, John Dunn, and Michael Crowder on drafts of various chapters. My colleagues at Liverpool have been helpful in many ways, but I would especially like to thank Pepe Roberts, Julian Clarke (who contributed a great deal directly on the rural surveys in 1979), and Paul Francis. Mr Alan Hodgkiss and the staff of the Cartographic Unit of the Liverpool Geography Department deserve my thanks for the handsome maps. Most of all I express my sincerest gratitude to my wife Jenny, and our children David, Timothy ('Tokunbo – *eleyi l'o bi n 'Ileṣa*) and Francis, for putting up with the travails I have imposed on them during the production of this book.

Upton, Wirral   J.D.Y.P
March 1982

Note on orthography

In writing Yoruba names I have mainly followed the convention of spelling them as they are most commonly spelled in the sources and in English-language texts. This means that tone-accents and subscript marks (as in ẹ, ọ, ṣ) are not normally used. Consequently I have written of 'Ilesha' and the 'Ijesha' rather than of 'Ileṣa' or 'Ijeṣa' (still less of 'Ijẹṣa', which is how the name of the people is frequently misrepresented). There are some consequent inconsistencies – Oshu and Okesha, but Ilase and Isokun, all involving the sound ṣ – but this is how I found them most often spelled. If one man styles himself 'Alhaji' and another 'Hadji', why not respect their practice rather than go for phonetic consistency and write 'Alaji', which is how in both cases it would be most often pronounced? In any case, pronunciation varies considerably throughout Yorubaland, and between speech of the more and the less travelled and educated. If I wanted to be absolutely faithful to the speech of ordinary Ijesha I would be writing 'Uleeṣa' for the name of the town!

Where I have used Yoruba words (common nouns) and expressions in the body of the text, I have followed the standard practice with the use of non-English words in an English-language text and written them in italics, with such diacritics as are routinely used (i.e. subscript marks, but not tone-accents except where these seemed critical). Titles are also written in italics (but with capital initial letters), since it is important that the reader should be able to distinguish them from personal names. In place of a glossary, I have listed and defined the most important and frequently used Yoruba words and concepts in the index.

Abbreviations

ADO	Assistant District Officer
ASR	*African Studies Review*
AG	Action Group
CEA	*Cahiers d'études africaines*
CJAS	*Canadian Journal of African Studies*
CMS	Church Missionary Society
CSSH	*Comparative Studies in Society and History*
DO	District Officer
IDC	Ijesha Divisional Council
IGS	Ilesha Grammar School
IPU	Ijesha Patriotic Union
ITPA	Ijesha Tax-Payers' Association
IUDC	Ilesha Urban District Council
IUL	Ibadan University Library
IWP	Ijeshaland Welfare Party
JAH	*Journal of African History*
JDS	*Journal of Development Studies*
JHSN	*Journal of the Historical Society of Nigeria*
JRAI	*Journal of the Royal Anthropological Institute*
JRGS	*Journal of the Royal Geographical Society*
LBA	Licensed Buying Agents
NA	Native Authority
NAI	*National Archives, Ibadan*
NCNC	National Council of Nigeria and the Cameroons (after 1962, National Council of Nigerian Citizens)
NGJ	*Nigerian Geographical Journal*
NJESS	*Nigerian Journal of Economic and Social Studies*
NNDP	Nigerian National Democratic Party
NPC	Northern Peoples' Congress
NPN	National Party of Nigeria

NYM	Nigerian Youth Movement
PRO	Public Record Office
PWD	Public Works Department
RAPE	*Review of African Political Economy*
ROF	Reformed Ogboni Fraternity
SWJA	*Southwestern Journal of Anthropology*
UAC	United Africa Company
UDC	Urban District Council
UPGA	United Progressive Grand Alliance
UPN	Unity Party of Nigeria
UPP	United People's Party
WAV	*West African Vanguard*

Ni Iranti

Ọba Alaiyeluwa Peter Adeniran AGUNLEJIKA II
Ọwa-Obokun t'Ilẹ Ijẹṣa
1966–1981

1

Introduction

Books, especially when a decade has elapsed between conception and execution, have histories of their own and often can hardly be considered as the formed products of their authors' original intentions. This study of the Ijesha, and more particularly of Ilesha, their main town, was originally conceived in terms of two genres of work in African studies, which were certainly more fashionable in the early 1970s than the early 1980s.

It was to be the case-study of the incorporation of a people, who once had formed a 'society' – that is, a distinctive and fairly autonomous social and cultural system, which in this case also corresponded to a state – into a wider society, in this case Nigeria. The focus of such a study would naturally fall on such things as the extension of social relations over a wider area, the interaction of various peoples so incorporated as 'ethnic groups', and concomitant changes in individuals' identities and the effects of all this on their social life 'at home': in sum, on that 'increase in social scale' which the Wilsons highlighted as far back as 1945.[1] This perspective was commonplace in studies of social change in West Africa by the 1960s, whether they took it as a central problem (cf. Cohen and Middleton's *From Tribe to Nation in Africa: Studies in Incorporation Processes*)[2] or used it as a source of explanation in particular fields (e.g. Horton's theory of religious conversion).[3] In fact my initial interest was that, having already completed a study of religious innovation as an aspect of social change among the Yoruba,[4] I wanted to undertake a more total analysis of the process of social change in a substantial Yoruba community, and that, in a basic respect, demanded to be viewed as a process of incorporation. 'Incorporation', however, is a way of approaching historical problems, rather than a knock-down solution to them. As a complex process, how are its various strands – economic, political, cultural etc. – phased in relation to one another? What explains its differential impact on different regions or sectors, and what are the consequences of these differences? What are the bases of integration in the emergent, wider units? How is it apprehended and responded to by those caught up in it?

This last group of questions leads to a second genre within which this

1

study was conceived: the study of local-level politics, or of national politics as seen from the grass-roots, or of centre/periphery relations.[5] This genre, much more a product of the late 1960s, was proposed as a fusion of anthropology and political science, or rather as an anthropological correct-ive administered to political science, for views of national political systems that were too influenced by the self-images of mobilizing nationalist parties or the bland categories of political modernization theory.[6] While the concept of 'political systems' was intended to be sufficiently universalist to permit genuine cross-national, cross-cultural comparisons to be made, the emphasis now was on the input to them provided by indigenous political cultures and local structures. This brought real gains in our understanding of the forces determining African politics at the national level, as well as serving to demystify certain notions, such as 'tribalism', which were widely used to explain African politics in popular discourse. Yet somehow the promised fusion of the two levels of analysis did not come to fruition as a new paradigm for studies in the way envisaged, for the political sociology of West Africa in the 1970s veered off in quite another direction.

Again, the movement of ideas moved closely in step with – let us not say 'reflected' – the movement of events in the world. Marxism had hitherto exercised only small influence in writing in English on African societies, but now it suddenly seemed highly relevant, particularly in the form of 'dependency theory'. This had largely been worked out on the Latin American situation – Samir Amin had already written in similar terms about West Africa but he only now became widely translated – and now it spoke forcefully to the disappointment of those high hopes for Africa's stability and development which had been entertained at political independence.[7] Now it seemed that the critical determinants of change in African social structures lay not in things internal (let alone local) or cultural, as had been the faith implicit in political nationalism's assertion of African autonomy, but in things external and structural. Africa lay in the zone of peripheral capitalism: this was the prime and essential fact about her situation, the source of what was salient and distinctive about her social forms, particularly as they existed at national levels. Rather paradoxically, some older concepts and debates of social theory came back into favour. So 'state' tended to replace 'political system' and African realities came to be discussed in terms of such old problems as the relations of state and civil society.[8] Class analysis, haltingly begun back in the 1950s and used in an *ad hoc* way in several studies by American political scientists in the 1960s (e.g. Richard Sklar[9]), now became the main instrument for the explanation of post-colonial political forms.[10] It was not so much that the previous decade's emphasis on the need for new concepts, expressive of African cultural realities, simply gave way to older, universally applicable con-cepts, but that though older conceptual forms were used, they had to be infused with a new specific content. This was how Africa's stubborn novelty was to be reconciled with some perennial theoretical questions and

2

the ultimate need for a common language to talk about all societies. Hence the debates over such concepts as political class, the comprador or petit bourgeois state, African and lineage modes of production.

This period has also brought constant attention to a related area which is highly pertinent to the present study: the periodization of African history. The old, pre-nationalist, view may be put, with only slight exaggeration, as follows. African 'history', as an object of academic study, was held to begin with the creative intrusion of outsiders and especially with the establishment of the colonial order. Anthropologists were consigned to the realm of African 'pre-history' and indeed, the strong tendency of their practice had been to timeless constructions which were of little evident historical point. By the early 1960s two related intellectual developments occurred to change this. Firstly, the new African history, which soon became the strongest of all the humanistic disciplines in the African universities, had as its project the history of African peoples, rather than the achievements of Europeans in Africa.[11] Secondly, within anthropology there was a great awakening of historical interest[12] and several anthropologists of West African societies, such as M. G. Smith,[13] G. I. Jones,[14] Lloyd,[15] Bradbury[16] and Horton,[17] produced important historical work. That this was reciprocated by historians, despite the shadow which anthropology passed under in African universities on the grounds of its being a colonialist science, was due largely to a decisive re-periodization of African history which now took place. As Ajayi, the doyen of the Ibadan history school, put it in an influential essay, colonialism should be seen as merely an episode in Africa's history.[18] To thus de-emphasize the place of colonial annexation was to assert the importance of the links between the pre-colonial past and the realities and aspirations of contemporary Africa. That was part of the essential spirit of nationalism. But a further revision was soon on the way. Whereas nationalism had called into question the over-riding importance once given to the colonial epoch, now it came to be asked whether political independence, so lately gained, really itself marked so significant a historical divide. Obviously this shift of vision had its roots in the same circumstances which made dependency theory plausible. It did not mean, however, a simple return to the older periodization, for the insights (and substantial historiographical achievements) of the nationalist period could not be gainsaid. The colonial period got renewed attention, but was now seen much more as the outcome of links between Europe and Africa stretching back a long way into the past. The continuities between the present and the pre-colonial past now appeared, not only (and perhaps not most importantly) as purely indigenous cultural forms, but rather more as forms which were shaped by external contact and so in some sense pre-adapted to the intensification of links which came in the late nineteenth century. Many studies of pre-colonial states now found they had critical conditions of existence in external trade routes as well as in indigenous ideas about, say, sacred kingship. An 'African mode of production', constituted along these lines, was asserted to exist.[19] While all this, in a general way, was just what dependency theory would suppose, little of it was achieved as an application of dependency theory as such. Indeed the most impressive monument of this phase – Hopkins' *Economic History of West Africa* (1973), which for the first time presented a modern interpretation of West Africa's economic history in the *longue durée* – was rather hostile to both Marxism and dependency theory.

Periodization must be a central problem in any sociological history – that is a history which takes as its object the transformation of social structures – even if it is often a concealed one. Those who are historians *de métier* are more likely to address it directly, but it cannot be avoided by sociologists, since significant historical periods depend on a typification of societies (or of socio-cultural forms) and it is within some typification of society as a whole that sociological explanation of particular phenomena or practices must ultimately be set. Indeed, single categories like 'capitalist', 'industrial', 'colonial' or 'Muslim' society are too often and easily used as if they provided sufficient conditions for, say, some particular kind of deviancy or institutional conflict. But actual societies do not require to be classified exclusively within one typology or range of types (say that based on mode of production in the Marxian scheme) or to one of their sub-types or transitional stages between them. Potentially useful types cross-cut in all kinds of ways that cannot be theoretically predetermined. Only if this is acknowledged are we able, returning from types to periods, to undertake a study of an incorporation process without prejudging how social change is phased in different spheres, and how change in one sphere relates to change in another. 'Penetration of capitalist relations of production' may thus be one part of our story, but it is not assumed to be the essence of the story, for other strands of change, such as conversion to world religions and the imposition of new forms of political control, not only have their own dynamics, but may provide some of the conditions for change in the economic sphere as well as being influenced by it.

This is one area where this study has to reject the presuppositions of Marxism because they oversimplify, foreclosing on issues which need to be kept open. Another, which turns out to involve some related questions, is furnished by dependency theory. For all its plausibility as a stark delineation of the major ways in which the world system has come into being, dependency theory, if taken seriously, rather devalues studies of local communities set in the zone of peripheral capitalism. For it teaches that the historically significant features of the contemporary third world are due to the character and extent of capitalism's penetration and that significant variations and relations between different areas of the periphery are due to the differential penetration of capitalism. Anthropology, in so far as that is a study of small-scale or 'traditional' societies located in this periphery, is decisively marginalized, for much of its most distinctive subject matter sinks to being of merely residual importance, at most a matter of the form or the dress rather than the content of significant social relations. Besides the strong ethical or practical grounds for rejecting such a Eurocentric view of the world – for example, the crushing fatalism it seems to counsel about the capacity of societies in the periphery to help themselves – there is the major intellectual difficulty that there is vastly more variety in the characteristics and responses of the periphery than seems to be allowed for within the terms of dependency theory.

The main hope among Marxists for a correction of the over-simplifications of dependency theory has been for a theory of the 'articulation of modes of production', which would give a more realistic account of the mutual conditioning of indigenous pre-capitalist and capitalist modes of production. To this new role for anthropologists, within the Marxist programme for a total social science, the French Marxists addressed themselves, with fresh characterizations of indigenous modes of production and of the interplay of indigenous and capitalist modes.[20] And where they have, in pursuance of these objectives, contributed to certain traditional foci of debate in the study of West African societies – for example on the relations of kinship and political institutions, the nature of state structures and their economic foundations – they have provided significant bearings to the first part of this study which deals with the pre-colonial Ijesha kingdom. None the less, in spite of achieving substantial empirical studies and opening up new questions, the French Marxists seem to have failed in their major theoretical objective: to demonstrate that historical materialism could provide the categories, where other schools such as neo-classical economics or the substantivism of Polanyi's school had failed, for a coherent general theory of social formations and their transformation.

This has especially proved so in areas which bulk large in this study: culture and politics. The intellectual currents of the 1970s, precisely because they were so inclined to reduce them to the status of effects of economic or structural conditions, in the end compelled a clearer recognition of where in the explanation of social structures or an account of social change, cultural and political conditions must play a central part. Dependency theory, in its early days, was the most reductionist of all. An example may be drawn from the major empirical application of it to Africa, Colin Leys' *Underdevelopment in Kenya*. Faced with the problem that whereas the 'real' elements of social relations in Kenya (in his view) are classes, differentiated in terms of their various relations to external capital, a good deal of the manifest social relations – and predominantly so in the field of politics – revolve around ethnicity and patron–client ties, Leys relegated 'tribalism' to the realm of ideology, a set of notions encouraged by the colonial authorities and later the national bourgeoisie and a thing that 'initially develops out of, and feeds on, the real development of antagonistic classes'.[21] Not surprisingly, neither the actual past history of the Kikuyu or the Luo, nor their perceptions of it, 'the past in the present', figure at all prominently in Leys' account. One need not dispute most of what Leys says about the effects of tribalism, nor with *some* of the conditions (uneven development of different ethnic groups), which he adduces to explain it. But effects have to be produced through human agency – unless the Marxist, when scratched, is to turn out as teleological as any functionalist – and Leys does not show that uneven development *per se* provided *sufficient* conditions for tribalism. It is, after all, a phenomenon more of some African countries than others, and of some regions of peripheral capitalism, such as Africa, more than others. Rather, uneven development worked on and was to some extent shaped by prior identities, cultures, and social relations; and the charge of teleology can only be refuted if the patterns of action which are to be explained can be affiliated to actors' intentions as well as their situations. To insist on this is not to deny that the same external circumstances may in fact evoke similar responses from actors of diverse histories and cultures. But it is to assert that we need real histories of men acting and that their collective responses to being brought into the capitalist world economy must be seen as moments in *their* history as well as moments in the history of the capitalist world economy.

The problem for the French Marxists was quite different. Far from trying to reduce out politics and cultures, they tended – despite a tendency to fall right out of Marxism into technological determinism[22] – to appreciate all too well the role that ideological or cultural conceptions, or specifically political relations, played, in pre-colonial Africa as in all non-capitalist societies, in constituting 'relations of production'. It followed that they tended to use 'mode of production' in fact as a label for the social ensemble, rather than, as in most classical Marxism, for that part of the social ensemble, or 'base', which served to explain such 'superstructural' features as the kind of religion or political system a society had.[23] Some ingenious formulations were devised to save the theoretical terminology ('domination' vs. 'determination'; kinship, religion etc. 'serving as' relations of production etc.); but the obvious implication was that analysis of politics, religion, kinship etc. were as 'serious' a part of any adequate account of social change as economics and that the manner of their interaction, in any particular society, must be a matter for open enquiry, rather than the known consequences of a universal model of society.

This may, perhaps, be conceded fairly easily in the case of non-capitalist, pre-colonial societies of West Africa. Does it also hold for capitalist societies, and so continue to hold for West African societies as they have become increasingly penetrated by capitalism since the early nineteenth century? Much of the case for 'domination' by the non-economic rested on a contrast between non-capitalist societies – a contrast also made by some non-Marxists such as Polanyi, who saw 'economic determinism' as peculiarly a doctrine for societies where market exchange had triumphed.[24] The general issue is too vast to be taken on here. But one point is worth making: how unjustified it would be to resolve the issue for partially-capitalist West Africa (or any region of peripheral capitalism) on the grounds of some supposed essential trait of capitalism as such. It would fly in the face of a widespread recognition, among Marxists and non-Marxists alike, of the autonomy and saliency of politics in contemporary Africa. From different theoretical perspectives, this has been variously expressed: the 'primacy of politics',[25] the 'overdevelopment of the state',[26] concepts such as 'political class'.[27] This study of Ilesha will have occasion to point out instances where attempts to interpret political phenomena, such as parties, as corresponding to pre-formed socio-economic forces – a kind of reduction common in sociological and Marxist accounts of European politics – are utterly mistaken. Political activity seems to be *the* major mode of society's self-realization, in a stronger sense in Africa than is the case in many other societies. It is conditioned, not just by the structure of the state, but by attitudes and identities brought to the political arena by the members of local communities.

So, a certain irreducibility, if not saliency within the social formation, of the political sphere, seems common to both pre-colonial kingdoms and the contemporary national societies of West Africa. This gives rise to the question of whether this is because they are the similar but independent effects of some similar circumstances, although different modes of production prevail in the two cases, or because of a direct continuity of some kind. This question itself requires a study of greater historical depth than I originally conceived: a study of incorporation which focussed especially on the growing political links between a local community and the Nigerian state, and which took it for granted that the imposition of colonial rule marked the decisive turning point. Instead the pre-colonial period had to be treated as more than just a baseline for change, but fully as a historical object, a form of society with its distinctive processes and dynamics. In addition, this past needed examination as possibly having a deeper relevance than that of being a mere anterior state to the present, or an object needed to provide evidence of the conflicts and contradictions which had begotten the present, as it is for historical materialism. There the past is really 'another country' in relation to the present. To the extent that the past is in fact the 'same country', that is, that there are significant continuities between the human past and the present of an area, it is because the identities, social ideals, models for action which are employed in the present are drawn, at least in part, from that past. In other words I am concerned with 'the past in the present', with the continuing role played by a people's history in shaping its present, and not just with that past as a baseline for social change, and I am led to call into question that tendency to the ultimate reduction of history as a 'mythical charter', a mere form of ideology, where, once again, functionalist anthropology and structuralist Marxism find common ground.

YORUBA ETHNOGRAPHY AND IBADAN HISTORY

So far I have said little about the implications for this study of its Yoruba location, though it follows from the preceding argument that considerations which arise from local history and ethnography are no less crucial to a study of incorporation than global processes such as capitalist expansion. A cultural area as large and diverse as the Yoruba – now some fifteen million people or so, spread over more than 50,000 square miles – has called forth a literature both substantial and wide-ranging.[28] Moreover, to an extent that has occurred with few other African peoples, it is a literature deeply influenced by Yoruba self-conceptions and contributed to in large measure by Yoruba themselves.[29] Any sociological history of a Yoruba community, in which particular attention is paid to political concepts and actions as the main vehicle for the community's self-realization, must situate itself with regard to two groups of writings within the corpus: Yoruba ethnography, largely achieved by a series of expatriate social anthropologists, and the monographs on Yoruba history produced mostly by Nigerian scholars of the University of Ibadan.

Three features of Yoruba ethnography particularly demand attention. Firstly, it is an odd circumstance that this large body of literature, touching so many different institutions and communities, does not include any single work of substantial length, whether a monograph or group of articles, which presents an account of the social structure and culture of any one Yoruba community with the detail and in the holistic way considered characteristic of social anthropology. However much the over-easy assumption of functionalist integration might be criticized (and justly), exercises of this kind do provide the needed base for a sustained enquiry into the manner in which different elements of social structure condition one another as well as for their comparison and explanation. Instead, studies have focussed on single institutions or aspects of Yoruba life – Ifa divination, the role of women, local politics, the cocoa economy, kinship, religious independency – and moved to comparison between communities on that basis. The resultant tendency to fragmentation has tended to be reproduced, necessarily, in such general surveys of Yoruba ethnography as those of Krapf-Askari and Eades.[30]

A second feature has been the problematic character of the unit of study, where ethnographic practice has in two ways been affected by the ethnic self-conceptions of the Yoruba. It is evident that as an ethnographic category 'Yoruba' refers to a grouping of peoples, with many shared traits and some common traditions, it is true, but exhibiting great internal variety. In a strict sense, there are no such single entities as 'Yoruba religion', 'the Yoruba pattern of settlement' or 'the Yoruba political system', if the reference of 'Yoruba' is to all the people who *now* know themselves by that term and who are referred to as 'the Yoruba-speaking peoples' in the literature. While anthropologists are very conscious of the variety and in some cases, notably Lloyd's, have urged the use of the Yoruba category as a framework for comparison,[31] the pull to generalize at a pan-Yoruba level has been strong. Above all the growth of an extended concept of 'Yoruba' as a modern *ethnic* category – it originally only referred to the Oyo sub-group – seems to have given backing to its use as an *ethnographic* entity. From the authors of the 'Report on the Yoruba, 1910'[32] to contemporary academic historians it has been Yoruba scholars who have been most concerned to assert Yoruba unity, at both ethnic and ethnographic levels.[33] There seem to me to be two compelling reasons for keeping those levels distinct. One is that otherwise the real historical process by which groups like the Ijesha have *become* ethnically Yoruba during the course of this century will tend to be obscured. The other reason is that a just appreciation of the real interdependence of institutions in any actual Yoruba community or locality will be corrupted if observations about its particular features are 'filled out' by inferences drawn from the fact of its being 'Yoruba'. 'Yoruba society' cannot be more than a socio-logical lowest common denominator, the label for a bunch of the cultural traits which occur more frequently in the area; it may usefully serve to distinguish the area's salient features from similar areas such as those designated 'Akan' or 'Igbo'; but it does not denote a real, concrete unit for sociological analysis.

What, then, is the proper unit of study? Here again Yoruba social concepts have been important, neatly supplying the convenience of a discrete and bounded entity for sociological analysis. The Yoruba term *ilu* is most typically taken to refer to those large nucleated settlements ('towns') considered so distinctive of Yorubaland; with the same reference, a more sociological translation might be 'community', the emphasis being less on size than on the quality of social relations. Also, since there is no distinct term to refer to the political units of which these towns or commu-nities are the centres, *ilu* can be rendered 'state' or 'society'. An *ilu*, then, a 'town' surrounded by territory worked by farmers who belong to the central institutions of the *ilu*, seems to furnish a satisfactorily bounded and discrete unit. Of course, divergences in settlement patterns and politi-cal structures from this simple model have been noted, above all by Lloyd; but I would like to suggest that their implication runs much further than he allows, since the *ilu*-centred kingdom remains fairly and squarely his unit of analysis. If, in this study, much of the narrative seems to rest on the same assumption, it is more for reasons of convenience than theoretical conviction. For while the *ilu* or kingdom focussed on its town capital may serve well enough for some purposes, it does not have that discrete and bounded character which goes with our concept of 'a society'. In that precise sense, perhaps a single unit of study cannot be determined at all. For Ilesha, like other such *ilu alade* or 'capital towns', should really be seen as merely one, politically fairly autonomous level of a hierarchy of commu-nities. By community I mean a relatively enduring focus of collective action, distinguished, in the Yoruba context, by possessing the necessary organizational facilities, namely a ranked set of chieftaincy titles. An *ilu* falls short of being a complete unit of analysis in two directions. Below it stand smaller settlements, which vary in the extent to which they provide the facilities of a community for their residents and can aspire to stand independently of larger towns. The view from the countryside or the political periphery of the larger *ilu* has tended to be grossly neglected in Yoruba ethnography. On the other side, even a substantial kingdom like that of the Ijesha falls some way short of sociological self-sufficiency: there were higher or rival communities which competed for access to the resource flow of the region; these exogenous resources, both human and material, gave point, we shall see, to the internal politics of kingdoms and communities; there was a circulation of population, both voluntary and involuntary, between *ilu*; and there were institutions such as some cults, which transcended *ilu* boundaries. In other words, a regional analysis is also needed.

A third feature concerns the model of the *ilu* itself that has dominated Yoruba ethnography. The influential writings of Lloyd, in particular, portray the town as a federation of lineages, whose representatives govern the town as a council of chiefs under a king drawn from a royal lineage; the politics of the town is essentially lineage conflict.[34] Only a short acquaintance with Ilesha made this picture seem awry. At first it just seemed an empirical issue, the old problem of the variety of Yoruba political forms; for Ilesha has a great many titles, and important ones, which do not belong to lineages. But the fundamental objection is conceptual. By basing his theory of political forms on the sources of elite (i.e. chiefly) recruitment, rather than on the intrinsic character of political roles or relations, Lloyd achieves a reductionism analogous to that offered by those Marxists for whom politics is only a screen through which class interests express themselves.[35] In Lloyd's case, politics is reduced to kinship, for the rules of kinship are treated as producing forms (i.e. the lineages) anterior to and determinative of politics. In neither case is serious attention paid to the very forms of politics itself, which in the Ijesha case means largely the system of chieftaincy titles, which are differentiated in rank, function and relationship to 'constituencies' based on residential, kinship or occupational groups. Corollaries of the model are found widely, even in authors who might not wish to adopt the model's assumptions. Law, for example, while concentrating on the politics of Old Oyo, is equally reductionist about titles, treating them as no more than the recognition of power otherwise derived, through lineage, personal prowess or fortuitous circumstances.[36] It also produces an unrealistic account of Yoruba kinship. In the standard descriptions of Yoruba institutions, kinship is typically treated *before* politics, as if the constitution of descent groups followed simply from the operation of kinship rules. In fact, as will be seen at points in the account to follow, kinship and politics cannot be separated like this. It is not that kinship norms such as agnatic descent, adelphic succession, *per stirpes* inheritance etc., have no effect, but that the outcomes in the field of kinship are also shaped by such 'political' facts as where people find it expedient to live or to farm, or which individuals in a genealogy have held chieftaincy titles.

'Ibadan history' has provided another, quite distinct, critical reference point to this study, especially pertinent to Chapter 5 and the whole of Part II, where the main principle of presentation of material is chronological. This body of scholarship represents a major achievement of Nigeria's nationalist intelligentsia, based above all in the country's premier university, and their distinct viewpoint is expressed in both the selection and the treatment of themes. Prominent here are the sources of cultural modernization and their shaping of the educated elite (Ajayi's and Ayandele's studies of missionaries and their early converts),[37] pre-colonial states, especially those whose traditions are more relevant to the post-colonial states (Adeleye on the Sokoto Caliphate and Oloruntimehin on Segu in Mali),[38] patterns of colonial overrule and the place of local elites (Atanda, Afigbo, Igbafe and Asiwaju on Oyo, Eastern Nigeria, Benin, and the western Yoruba divided between British and French rule respectively),[39] the formation of the Nigerian state (Tamuno, Anene),[40] and the institutional means of the nationalist elite's rise to social dominance (Omu on the press; Adewoye on lawyers and judicial institutions).[41] The coherence of the underlying intellectual programme is as impressive as is its systematic execution.

Any intellectual tradition rests on some assumptions which are merely implicit and therefore undefended, and focusses itself on open areas of concern. Ibadan history has tended to assume the inevitability of the educated elite's place as the guiding element of Nigerian society, closely related to, though not identical with, its political class. At times critical of the political class, members of the intelligentsia have also been ready to assume the responsibilities of political and bureaucratic office;[42] and, while there has been criticism of how the educated elite has played its role in Nigerian society,[43] the criticism has not extended to any conception of a different kind of elite in sociological terms. The history they have written has tended towards a sort of Whig history, an account of how the fittest representatives of the African people – mediators and modernizers – have risen within the bounds of the colonial society. Typically the modern educated elite itself is not much in the picture – it, after all, is holding the camera – but the central theme is none the less the elite's social ancestry, where contradictions of continuing relevance require to be resolved. The contradictions arise from the modern elite's descent from two distinct groups, each of which it partly identifies with and partly rejects: the indigenous pre-colonial political class, which mostly came to provide a link in the colonial hierarchy, and the expatriate colonial elite (to which may be added Christian missionaries). As Africans, the nationalist elite made its claim against the expatriate cadres of the colonial period, and as educated people they made their claim against the chiefly leaders of local communities: each group was drawn on to provide the instruments by which the other was discredited; nationalism was a kind of Hegelian synthesis to the colonial order. Small wonder that Indirect Rule, which entailed such a complex triangle of mutual attraction and antipathy between the three forces – the chiefs, the colonial administrators, and the rising elite – and where, for a time, the elite found itself in opposition to both sides of its ancestry, has furnished such an essential terrain for Ibadan history.

However, some degree of ideological 'unmasking' only has point as a preliminary to an evaluation of the intrinsic qualities of Ibadan history, and particularly (for the purposes of this book) its studies of local Yoruba communities. In being so emphatically political and cultural in its foci of concern, Ibadan history does stand diametrically opposed to dependency theory and Marxism, whose own weaknesses were argued to lie precisely in their inability to handle local forms of politics and culture. What is needed to bridge this gulf is a rounded, non-reductionist history of the transformation of social structures. In fact, Ibadan history's reluctance to be socio-logical, or to engage at all closely with what the social anthropologists have had to say about Yoruba society, is systematic, though it has been much less marked among some of the more senior members of the school (e.g. Ajayi and Ayandele) and among several of those who have worked mostly on the nineteenth century (e.g. Akintoye, Awe).[44] The unsociological character of those Ibadan histories which deal with the transformation of local communities shows up sharply in the manner in which they deal with both the indigenous social organization and socio-economic change. The former is usually presented in an opening chapter as a sort of backdrop, thereafter not to intrude very much on the narrative; the latter tends to come in, usually as a penultimate chapter on 'economic and social changes', slotted in before the conclusion, which is likely to be a profit-and-loss account of colonialism's impact on the area.[45] Both tend to have a taken-for-granted character, as if the really interesting problems lie elsewhere. Indigenous social institutions are presented in a normative manner, as if the colonial notion of a stable 'Native Law and Custom' had taken deep root, and harmonious, rather than conflictual, aspects of social relations are stressed.[46] Social and economic change is treated as a cata-logue of achievements whose occurrence and social source are unproblem-atic, and is related to the well-being of the community as a whole rather than to particular sectional interests. A striking feature is that, whereas it has become commonplace among economic historians of Africa at large to stress the crucial role played by particular local agents in developing cash-crops,[47] the basis of economic prosperity, Ibadan history has tended to focus on colonial economic policy, the provision of infrastructure, the role of commercial outsiders.[48] All these features are related. In fact new social

12

and economic initiatives, as will be shown in the Ijesha case, stem from the desires for freedom or self-aggrandizement of particular sectional interests within the community, and are not to be appreciated or explained unless the community itself is seen as much in terms of its internal divisions of age, sex and status etc., as of its shared values. The reluctance to see the issue in these terms seems to arise from the spontaneous way in which an elite will portray a community it represents: as a collectivity which presents a unified face to the outside and to higher political levels, behind its proper leadership. As a corollary, the elite's relations with other non-elite sectors of the community will not seem especially problematic, and its relation to the former, chiefly elite will be one of natural succession, rather than of a continuing, structured opposition. It is as important to understand how plausible a representation this is, granted the structure of modern Nigerian society, as to draw attention to the limitations it imposes on a properly sociological history. The Ibadan historian who has most broken from these assumptions, E. A. Ayandele, has done so in significantly related ways: in an attack, swingeing even to the point of unfairness, on the educated elite's role in modern Nigerian history;[49] in a pioneering study of the social character of slavery in pre-colonial Nigeria;[50] and in an account of politics in a colonial Yoruba town – Ijebu Ode, not his own community – which does not disguise the boisterous and far-reaching character of conflict within the community.[51]

The weakness of the 'Ibadan history' treatment of change in Nigerian communities over the colonial period is, then, a double disjunction of elements that need to be analysed in their interplay: of indigenous institutions from social and economic change; and of the social sphere generally from political history. It is easier to make these criticisms than to propose a really satisfactory manner of uniting these elements. It is not just a matter of making use of 'sociological' data, oral testimonies and life-histories, or the techniques of social anthropology to recover more of the experience of the unlettered majority who have had less to say for themselves in archival documents but whose motives and actions lie mutely behind, say, columns of statistics indicating the rising volume of the export trade or the proportion of Christians recorded in a census. There needs to be the theoretical occasion to make use of such material, in relation to an account of the events of political history.

I have already argued for the advantage, in giving an account of the incorporation of an African community, of giving a central place to those institutions and actions that we call 'political'. It is not a complete or universal truth that politics is the main form of a community's self-realization, as different societies vary in the saliency and scope they give to politics, but it does hold rather strongly for the Yoruba communities in Nigeria. Here I do not differ from what I believe is implicit in the character of Ibadan history. But politics does become a very two-dimensional thing if it remains unrelated to its sources in and outcomes for other spheres – in

13

economic life, kinship, relations between age and sex categories, religion – where a more pervasive struggle is enacted among individuals, social categories and associations to tap or to wield power. This does not imply any one-way reductionism of politics to some 'real' base, since the pursuit of all other goals in the public or political sphere is deeply marked by the political forms and concepts that are available. In Nigeria, the formal political sphere, besides being an arena where many other conflicts may be most decisively resolved, has prestige because it is the point at which a community mobilizes its resources to make a bid for resources from outside, from the regional resource flow and from the state. A recurrent theme of this study will be the links that exist between the changing ways in which Ijesha have organized themselves to tap the resources of this external sphere, and the forms of social differentiation and conflict within the community.

A further problem, evident enough in the disjunction of political history and the analysis of social structure and processes of socio-economic change already noted in several of the Ibadan histories, is how material should best be organized to present an integrated account. It is notoriously difficult to combine structural analysis and narrative history, and the sociologically-inclined historian may be inclined to join the sociologist with a simple interest in describing 'social change' in moving away from the straitjacket of chronology altogether and organizing material in terms of a series of themes running parallel.[52] But too much that is essential to a proper sociological history would be lost that way. If sociological explanation must always in the end involve the explanation of actors' choices in contexts that are historically specific as well as structurally constrained, then to abandon a chronological framework is to impoverish the proper initial description of what is to be explained. It is not merely that these objects of explanation, in effect historical conjunctures or aspects of them, are usually unique combinations of social circumstances, but that (i) part of that uniqueness is their particular position within a sequence of such conjunctures and that (ii) the actors' responses to their social and historical context are governed in good measure by their ongoing assessment of this sequence of conjunctures, that is, their society's history. Here there operates that 'past in the present'.

The minimum target of a chronological approach is to make sense of the connexions between events in time. A sociological historian who thus opts for a chronological framework has to set himself against quite an established tradition within sociology which disparages 'events' as a superficial and ephemeral kind of data compared with 'structures' and 'processes', which are taken as a more essential reality.[53] Events – a riot, a strike, a succession dispute, an election, a witchcraft accusation – are used as 'symptoms', indicators of the pressures, structural contradictions that lie 'beneath'. Expository use may be made of them in this vein as in the kind of 'social drama' analysis brilliantly practised by Gluckman and his disciples.[54] But events are more essential data than this, and cannot be distinguished from structure or process, as 'light' to 'heavy' data in the way that is often implied.[55] For it is only through events, large or small, with all their tiresome historicity, that social structures can be realized: events are the very empirical constitution of social structures. A grand event – like the Ilesha riot of 1941 – may indeed be treated as symptomatic of various structural conflicts of the society; but equally importantly it helped to *make* social structure, not least because of the role it came to play as part of the 'past in the present' in men's minds and thus in the ongoing constitution of social relations.[56]

Finally, a few words of introduction about Ilesha and the Ijesha. Ilesha is a town of roughly 180,000 people, the historical centre of a region about the size of an English county, whose inhabitants number up to half a million. In 1952 it was the ninth largest Yoruba town, larger than any town in Northern Nigeria except Kano or in Eastern Nigeria except Onitsha. Among the ten largest Yoruba towns it has the distinction, shared only by Ile Ife, the sacred centre of the Yoruba, of having existed on its present site and with its present basic residential structure for several centuries. Most of the larger Yoruba towns (Ibadan, Ogbomosho, Oshogbo, Iwo, Abeokuta, Oyo) do not, in their present form, predate the nineteenth century. Likewise the pattern of rural settlement, in terms of the identity and location of most villages and small towns of any size, goes back before the upheavals of the nineteenth century.

Though the Ijesha clearly fall well within the Yoruba ethnographic category and share the legends of Ife dynastic origins, they only came to consider themselves 'Yoruba' in the course of the twentieth century, taking on a name once borne by one of their historic enemies, the Oyo or 'Yoruba proper', lying to their north-west in the savannah. Ilesha was the capital of a forest kingdom which saw itself equally closely linked to the non-Yoruba Benin kingdom to the south-east. In fact the Ijesha adoption of the Yoruba identity, though apparently 'traditional', has proceeded parallel to the adoption of other, obviously 'modern', identities, as Nigerians and Christians or Muslims. Today nearly all Ijesha claim to be Christians (the substantial majority) or Muslims.

Ilesha has always played a prominent part in the affairs of its region. Situated roughly midway between Old Oyo and Benin, on a trade route between them, twenty miles inside the forest, it was able to extend a fluctuating hegemony over neighbouring communities, to the north and east especially, and grew steadily over several centuries. In the nineteenth century, it was at first unable to resist the power of Ibadan, Oyo's successor, and was in 1870 sacked for the first time in its history. Much of the northern part of the kingdom has been lost permanently to Oyo settlement. However, it became the leading power of the alliance of smallish kingdoms called Ekitiparapo which eventually fought Ibadan to a standstill by the 1880s, and found itself incorporated into the Lagos Protectorate as a substantial administrative centre. The vicissitudes of its later administrative history will be considered at length in later chapters.

Because of these involvements, Ilesha found itself in the forefront of social change in the colonial period. It was one of the earliest Yoruba areas to adopt cocoa as a cash-crop, and Ijesha found a definite niche for themselves as cloth traders in other parts of the wider region. The consequent prosperity began to affect Ijesha life-styles and aspirations on a substantial scale from the 1920s: iron-roofs, sash-windows, bread and tinned sardines, bicycles and cars, education to the secondary level and beyond, and by the 1950s, electricity and piped water in Ilesha. A major trunk road runs through Ijeshaland, and most substantial communities in the district are linked to Ilesha by tarred roads. Indeed, few areas of rural Africa can be as prosperous or as attuned to the wider world as Ijeshaland is. The number of Ijesha who are graduates must now run into thousands, and Ijesha are well to the fore in modern, bureaucratic occupations in the Nigerian sphere. Ilesha itself is still predominantly a town of farmers, traders of all kinds, small craftsmen, and employees of government institutions. Because of its many secondary schools (which together took nearly 10,000 pupils in 1976–77), Ilesha's population profile shows a bulge in the years of school attendance, but, owing to the lack of local job-opportunities for the educated, most of its allegiant population is absent for much of its economically active life. The only large-scale industry is a brewery, established in 1978; but the inhabitants of the town do include two large traders who, by popular reputation, are millionaires.

Ijesha politics has always had two faces: an 'interior' face, concerned with the allocation of reward and access within the local system, and an 'exterior' face, concerned with maximizing Ijesha gains from the regional system and, latterly, the Nigerian state. Over the period considered in this book, five phases may be distinguished: (i) pre-colonial rivalry within the regional system of independent states; (ii) a phase of defensive response to the pressures of colonial overrule; (iii) a politics of 'improvement' (*atunluṣe*) from the 1920s, concerned with securing advantage within the colonial framework; (iv) from the late 1930s, a politics of nationalist mobilization running into (v) a politics of communal rivalry whether by means of political parties or not, directed to securing development goods within the arena of the Nigerian state. Virtually all Ijesha are interested in what they consider to be 'development' (*idagbasoke*), nor are their definitions of it all eccentric by international standards. Politics, as a collective activity, is about securing it, and about managing the distribution of advantages that political success brings between individuals and groups within the community. What is so striking is that, while the material ends of politics are so contemporary, the framework of action within which they are sought should show such continuity with the past. The Ijesha have, as it were, chosen to make their history relevant to their politics. How and why this should be so is the central question of this study.

16

Part I

The pre-colonial kingdom

2

The regional context

Ijeshaland lies in the Yoruba-speaking country of south-western Nigeria, around the upper reaches of the Oshun, Shasha, and Oni rivers which flow south and south-west to the Lagos Lagoon, some hundred miles away. It is undulating country, much of it lying around 1,200 ft above sea level, but rising from 800 ft in the forests of the Oni valley in the south to around 1,700 ft in the hills around Imesi Ile to the north and well over 2,000 ft in the spectacular ridge which today forms its eastern boundary with Ekiti. Irregularly over the whole country rise steep inselbergs, mostly wooded but sometimes presenting smooth, nearly sheer sides of grey granite, extrusions of the igneous rock which lies below the typical red laterite soils of the surface. Annual rainfall is heavy, of the order of fifty to sixty inches, occurring mostly from late March to early November, with peaks in June and September.

Its location in the forest, but adjacent to the savannah, has been the most important geographical parameter of Ijesha history. Though there is evidence that human settlement in some parts of the deep rain forest to the south is ancient,[1] the general movement of Ijesha settlement seems to have been from the drier and more open northern parts of the forest southwards. Ilesha, situated more or less in the centre of the two Ijesha Divisions (now called Obokun and Atakunmosa Local Government Areas) was probably founded about the early sixteenth century, but it was apparently not the earliest centre of the kingdom.[2] The foundation traditions of the Ijesha, as of the other major kingdoms of the region, take the form of a dynastic migration from Ile Ife, the sacred centre of Yoruba mythology. The first five or six rulers of the dynasty are associated with places other than Ilesha, particularly in and around Ibokun, some fourteen miles to the north.[3] The major civic deity Orisa Onifon seems to have a clear provenance across the Oshun to the north-west of present-day Ijeshaland. To this day Orisa's priest, the chief *Baloro* at Ibokun, plays a significant role in the installation of the *Qwa* and in the great annual festival-cycle of Ogun at Ilesha. In its earlier days, before Ilesha came so greatly to outstrip all other Ijesha settlements in size and power, it seems the kingdom may have been more of a federation, with the *Owa* a kind of *primus inter pares*. This is suggested by the nominal presence of the heads, styled *Ogboni*, of three small but ancient Ijesha towns – Ibokun, Ijebu-jesha and Ipole – among the most senior grouping of Ilesha's chiefs (the six *Agbanla*).[4]

This northern connexion remained important even after Ilesha's foundation. The founding ruler, Owaluse, is said to have come from Oyo (his mother's town) to claim his throne from Owari, a usurper, and at least one titled lineage (*Başemi*) claims to have come from Oyo with him.[5] The Revd Samuel Johnson wrote that the town-layout of Ilesha, so striking in its regularity, was modelled on that of Old Oyo[6] – and while this cannot be confirmed (the site of Old Oyo being hardly excavated), such a cross-reference between the traditions of different towns must be considered strongly indicative of a connexion of some kind. Ilesha traditions hold that the site of Ilesha was already occupied by scattered settlements of an aboriginal population, the most important being identified with today's Okesha, the long street running west–east along Ilesha's spine, whose leader is regarded as the forerunner of the *Obanla*, the senior non-royal chief of the town.[7] Owaluse and his followers, we may presume, settled at the Western end of the Okesha ridge, where the land opens and rises slightly, the site today of *Oja'ba* (king's market) and the *Afin* (palace); and whereas the *Afin* entrance is nowadays (and it would seem, logically) at the east, so that 'palace' and 'town' face one another, tradition holds that in Owaluse's time the entrance faced away from Okesha, being by Chief *Odole*'s official house at its north-western corner, towards Oyo. This is a tradition which, as far as I can see, has no specific importance as a charter for contemporary social claims or arrangements; we must infer that it indicates, at the least, a genuine recollection of an early northern affinity of the kingdom.

The later sixteenth century saw a decisive shift, however. The pivotal figure of the dynastic traditions is not Owaluse but his successor Atakunmosa, who is said to have relocated the *Afin* entrance to face east, and is associated with Ijesha expansion to the east and south. He is said to have sojourned in Benin, and is recorded in Benin traditions referring to the late sixteenth century (as 'Atakumarha') as well as in those of Akure, forty miles to the south-east, where he is considered an ancestor of the ruling house;[8] and as late as the 1890s *Owa* Ajimoko I was claiming jurisdiction over Akure on the grounds that Atakunmosa had set the boundary between Ijesha and Benin on the far side of Akure.[9] In the late nineteenth century a cairn, ostensibly marking a shrine over his grave, was shown to travellers near Iperindo, on the road south from Ilesha towards Ondo,[10] an area still known as Igbo Atakunmosa. Though it was opened up for cocoa-cultivation as an area of apparently virgin forest in the 1950s, the pioneers turned up the broken pottery and grindstones of earlier settlement, and there are traditions of an ancient kingdom of Osi which Atakunmosa overthrew.[11] A number of titled lineages at Ilesha claim to have come with Atakunmosa from Benin, such as *Oṣodi* (a titled priesthood, whose name seems to be of Edo origin), and *Eejigbo* and *Bakinna* (heads of small lineages in Itisin quarter, which up to the last century was charged with taking messages from the *Ọwa* to Benin and entertaining Benin messengers in Ilesha).[12] The major title at Ilesha linked with Benin, however, is the senior non-royal lineage title of the town, *Ogboni*, whose first bearer Oludu is said to have come from '*Igbo Bini*' (lit. 'Benin Forest')[13] and remained the customary patron of Benin nationals at Ilesha, just as Chief *Ọdọle* was of Oyo nationals.

It is not easy, in our present state of knowledge, to do more than produce plausible speculation about this turn to the south-east in the late sixteenth century, but it seems certain that it needs to be set in the wider context of inter-state relations over the whole region. The temporary eclipse of Oyo power by that of Nupe in the Niger valley to the north around the middle of the sixteenth century might have had the effect of reorienting the Ijesha southwards.[14] Ryder, writing from a Benin perspective, sees internal disturbances within several Yoruba kingdoms to Benin's north-west as drawing Benin in, enabling the last of its warrior rulers, Ehengbuda (with whom Atakunmosa's name is linked), to range right into Ekiti.[15] Ilesha, however, remained independent, between Oyo and Benin: Benin traditions claim no control over it, while those of Oyo specifically record that the Ijesha repulsed Oyo attempts, at about this time, to extend its sway into the forest.[16] The Ijesha seem now to have stabilized their north-western frontier with Oyo, Oshogbo on the far bank of the Oshun being an Ijesha outpost and Ada a border town where both the *Ọwa* and the *Alafin* of Oyo had rights.[17]

The basic geopolitical situation of Ilesha, as it was to be for the next three centuries, was becoming defined. Ilesha lay almost exactly halfway between Old Oyo and Benin, on virtually the shortest route between them: too far from Benin to be controlled by it, and protected by the forest from the cavalry which was the mainstay of Oyo power. It seems to be generally true in West Africa that the earliest significant trade and travel outside the immediate locality was stimulated by the differences between the products of different ecological zones, running from the coast inland through forest and savannah to the edge of the desert. Important markets and centres of power grew up at critical points near the boundaries of these ecological zones; and Ilesha, just twenty miles or so within the forest, was well-placed to control the exchange of products from the forest and coast for those of the savannah. The markets of Omirinmirin and Oke Ibode just south of Oshogbo, are well-attested for the late eighteenth and early nineteenth centuries, and there is no reason to suppose their like did not exist much earlier.[18] But for the reorientation of Ijesha interests to the south in the time of Atakunmosa an additional circumstance must be sought. It may be provided in the new presence of European traders – first Portuguese, later

Dutch and English – at Benin.[19] In the late sixteenth and early seventeenth centuries Benin supplied not so much slaves to European traders as ivory and cloth, much of it produced in her northern hinterland; while the major imports were again cloth, beads and, above all, metal. The last of these, with its strategic importance, is likely to have been crucial.

The strongest explicit evidence is supplied by Akure traditions recorded in the 1930s, which concern the ruler *after* the one linked with Atakunmosa. These refer to a trade in guns, salt and iron between Benin, Ilesha and Ilorin. And while this has a nineteenth century flavour to it, they also tell how the Akure ruler sent to borrow cutlasses and axes from the *Owa* of Ilesha, as well as from the kings of Owo, Ondo and Ise-Ekiti and how he fought with these others over the borrowed tools.[20] Whatever the precise significance of these unusual details, a close relationship with Ilesha, hingeing on a trade route involving the flow of iron between Benin and the interior, is clearly implied. These Akure traditions are strongly corroborated by the evidence of Ilesha's ceremonies. The high point of the civic religion of Ilesha is the festival of Ogun, god of iron – actually a festival cycle in which the major royal ancestors are commemorated as well as other deities of civic importance (notably Orisa Onifon and the smallpox deity, known in Ilesha as Olode, 'master of the town'). Another feature of the organization of religion in Ilesha is that whereas the cult of most other major divinities is the responsibility of a titled priest, Ogun has no such single priest but is possessed directly by all the major secular chiefs, who have shrines to him in their houses. He is, as it were, everyone's god, and was far more often mentioned as 'the family god' than any other *orisa*, Ifa alone excepted, in my 1974 Household Survey.[21] Though Ogun is a 'pan-Yoruba' deity, the prime centres of his worship are all in eastern and south-eastern Yorubaland – while the main indigenous locations of iron mining and smelting lay in an arc in western Yorubaland, from Ilorin through the New Oyo area down to the Awori country.[22] Places like Ejigbo and Ogbomosho in this area remained one source of iron for Ilesha into the late nineteenth century and at least one of the blacksmith titles (*Agbatayo*) claims an Oyo origin.[23] Throughout eastern Yorubaland 'coastal iron', contrasted with indigenous iron from the Oyo area, was found up to the end of the nineteenth century.[24] It is evident that the sacralization of iron went furthest in these areas where it was most needed – the forest, as Denis Williams rightly suggests[25] – and where it was hardest to come by, a situation transformed by the appearance of a new source of supply, through Benin. The blacksmiths of Ilesha are organized under chiefs of whom the senior is *Sajowa*, drawn from the same patrilineage as Chief *Ogboni*, and whose name is very likely derived from the Bini title *Osazuwa*;[26] and it is the feast of Oludu, the *Ogboni*'s first ancestor, which brings Ilesha's Ogun festival-cycle to a close – a public prominence accorded to no other non-royal lineage. Ogun in Ilesha is important as a god of agriculture, as well as of war, since iron was so vital to the exploitation of

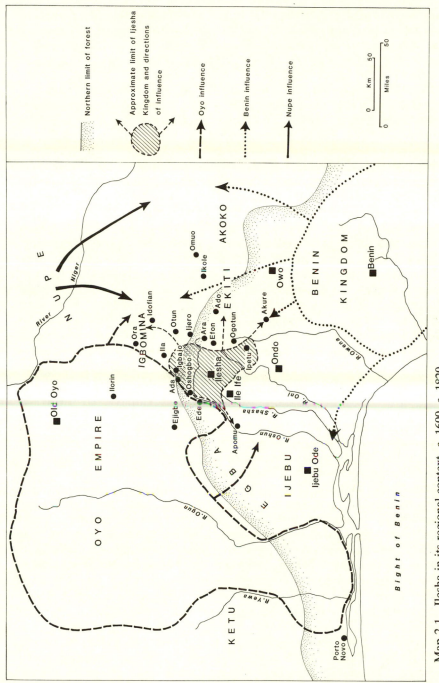

Map 2.1 Ilesha in its regional context, c. 1600–c. 1820

23

the forest environment. An *oriki* of Ogun from Ire-Ekiti, his major cult centre, expresses his character throughout the region succinctly:

> Ogun, alada meji, o nfi ọkan sa 'ko, o nfi ọkan ye 'na
> Ogun, with two cutlasses: one for tackling the farm, one for clearing the road[27]

The steady local thrust south into the forest which perennially occupied the Ijesha was thus facilitated by the new supplies derived from the Benin trade.

From the time of Atakunmosa it also becomes possible to discern something of Ilesha's relations with other neighbouring kingdoms. Her influence was most persistently directed towards the smaller Ekiti kingdoms to the east. *Itan Ilẹṣa*, the most substantial of the local printed histories, also has Atakunmosa travelling round Ekiti, establishing town-walls (*odi*) at Oye and Omuo and intervening in the politics of Ikole (all towns in the more open country of north-eastern Ekiti); he is also said to have besieged Ora, in Igbomina.[28] An *Ọwa* of the seventeenth century, Oluodo, is said to have rebuilt Ilesha's fortifications with the reluctant help of neighbouring rulers, mostly of Ekiti.[29] It looks like a fluctuating hegemony, with Ilesha making occasional incursions, perhaps called in by local political allies or involved (as occasionally in the early nineteenth century) through the local connexions of individual Ijeshas, and sometimes taking tributes or slaves. Some towns in Western Ekiti appear to have been definitely brought within the Ijesha kingdom for at least some time before the mid nineteenth century: Ogotun, for example, had an *onile* (patron-chief) at Ilesha in the person of the *Risinkin*,[30] while sons of at least some chiefs at Efon Alaye were sent, at some time before the nineteenth century, to serve as *ẹmẹsẹ* (messengers) at the *Ọwa*'s court.[31] Ilesha's size and steady growth from the sixteenth to the nineteenth centuries indicate that she must have been a powerful magnet in the whole zone between the spheres of Oyo and Benin. Again, the evidence from titles seems very suggestive. Many Ekiti towns have titles, typically born by quarter-heads, whose names are not derived from the names of their quarters, but are clearly borrowed from Ijesha titles which are so derived – and they are, too, overwhelmingly the non-lineage titles of *military* chiefs, who would be the prime bearers of Ijesha influence in the area.[32] Conversely many titled lineages at Ilesha have clear traditions of descent from free immigrants from other towns: *Loro* and later *Salosi* and *Sawẹ* from Ondo, *Risawẹ* from Ora, *Saloro*, *Aruwaji* and *Ṣapaye* from Ado-Ekiti, *Ṣegbuwa* from Efon or perhaps Ijero, *Ẹjẹmọ* from Owo, *Sọrundi* from Ikole, *Arapatẹ* from Aramoko. A similar picture emerges from the traditions of lineages without titles, which are mostly smaller and of later arrival in Ilesha: Akure, Efon Alaye and other towns of Ekiti or the southern forest region predominate.[33]

More obscure is the character of Ilesha's relations with the communities that lay due north. Igbajo, some twenty miles north, was linked closely with Ilesha in its traditions of origin and was, up to the late nineteenth century, regarded in Ilesha as a tributary Ijesha town – though it seems that this control could only be sporadically exercised. Beyond that, in the savannah, lay Igbomina, an area of small towns whose suzerainty was contested by the Oyo-Yoruba and the Nupe. But it seems that on occasion the Ijesha ranged this far too. Ilesha traditions of interest in Ora are matched by the traditions of another Igbomina town, usually under Oyo control, Idofian, 'then [the reference seems to be to the eighteenth century] named Igbonisi Ijesha because the Ilesha men used to harry these people'.[34] This presents problems, since it is hard to imagine a forest people like the Ijesha operating effectively in a zone where the dominant powers relied on cavalry. But it does square with persistent Ilesha traditions that, on at least two occasions in the eighteenth century, the Ijesha were embroiled in war with the Nupe.[35] They were active in Igbomina in the late eighteenth century, and are said to have attacked, and been defeated in Ilesha itself. There is an intriguing but faint possibility that it may be linked with a trade in kola nuts from the forests south of Ilesha to the savannah.[36] By the mid nineteenth century, Ilesha was so involved with things closer to home, or at least no further north than Igbajo and the neighbouring towns, that her earlier involvements in Igbomina had quite lapsed.

There remains the enigma of Ilesha's relations with Ife – which are merely an aspect of the greater enigma of Ife itself. How is the evidence of Ife's former glory – its magnificent artefacts and its unique place in Yoruba myth and legend – to be reconciled with the fairly modest role it has played in the last few centuries? For Ife was far closer – just over twenty miles to the west-south-west – to Ilesha than any other major kingdom. Yet when Oyo founded Ede, perhaps in the early sixteenth century, in the forest north of Ife, it was as a protection against the Ijesha, not the Ife. And when, somewhat later, but well before the nineteenth century, a disappointed contestant for the Ife crown left with his followers to found a new settlement barely eight miles away at Ifewara, he was already in Ijesha territory.[37] Ife tends to appear in Ijesha traditions as a sort of sanctuary, where a prominent man might retire to, from factional struggle in Ilesha;[38] or as a place where sons of the *Qwa* might be sent and from which they might be called to rule; or as a source of ritual specialists like Chief *Eṣira*, head of the crown-makers and worshipper of Odua, in sum, as a place of sacred prestige, rather than as a serious political rival or a place to be raided or dominated.

There may be an oblique representation of what happened in Ilesha's own foundation legend which, as Yoruba foundation legends go, has some unusual features. According to it, Obokun, the *Qwa*'s ancestor, is the youngest son of Oduduwa Olofin and, alone of all his sons, volunteers to go and fetch sea-water to cure his father's blindness. On his return he asks for his portion but is told that all the crowns were given to his elder brothers. Instead he is given a sword, *ida ajaṣe* ('sword of conquest') and told to seize his heritage from his brothers. Later he returns to Ife to perform his father's burial rites. His patrimony is claimed to begin from the square still known as *Ẹnu Ọwa* ('the Owa's approach') in front of the *Afin* of Ife itself; and the *Ọọni*, the ruler of Ife, is said to descend from a custodian left behind. This story is exceptional in that it does not just seek to legitimize some local hegemony on the basis of Ife origins, but appears to make sweeping claims against Ife itself. It seems quite unnecessary to sustain Ilesha's case in twentieth-century land claims against Ife (which in any case it antedates). May it perhaps be more plausibly seen as the expression of a real historical phase – the displacement of Ife by Ilesha as the predominant power in this part of the forest belt from the late sixteenth century onwards?[39]

BASES OF STATE POWER

What, then, were the keys to power in that rivalry between the various kingdoms of this area, large and small? A successful state was one which (i) controlled trade routes and attracted traders to itself, (ii) dominated its neighbours militarily, and (iii) increased its population at the expense of its neighbours. These three strands were linked, but are not equally prominent in the most direct evidence we have, the traditional histories. Typically, they make the least explicit reference to the factor of trade which in my account above has played the major role in explaining the historical geopolitics of Ilesha. Markets undoubtedly existed in a number of the subordinate towns of the Ijesha kingdom, but the major ones – to judge from the few references – were those located on the *frontiers* of the kingdom, and that located at the very centre, *Ọja'ba*. In the nineteenth century, when the volume of long-distance trade had undoubtedly increased and involved new commodities like palm-oil and guns, the importance of Iperindo (on the road south to Ondo, the major route for military supplies),[40] Oke Ibode (towards Oshogbo)[41] and Itagunmodi (towards Ife) is clearly attested.[42] The Iperindo–Ondo route seems to have eclipsed the other south-eastern route, that leading through Ipetu via Akure to Benin. Oke Ibode (though founded as a settlement earlier) seems to have developed as a market after the destruction, sometime in the 1820s, of Omirinmirin, situated 'on the banks of the Oshun' (*eti odo Ọṣun*), where Hausa, Oyo, Ekiti and others had met to exchange salt, antimony (*tiro*), natron (*kaun*), cowpeas, cloth and mirrors.[43] There is no evidence that the *Ọwa* had administered trade through chiefs or royal slaves though undoubtedly the military authorities in the late nineteenth century made direct arrangements for the supply of guns and munitions.[44] Trade seems to have been conducted by private individuals; but we cannot say how far these were Ijeshas, rather than citizens of other kingdoms, since the present fame of Ijeshas as traders within Nigeria does not definitely go back beyond the 1870s. The *Ọwa* and his chiefs benefited from trade because of the tolls they levied and the presents they received as patrons and protectors, and, while always anxious to attract traders, were unwilling to allow markets to be set up where these levies could be avoided. Hence the location of Oke Ibode ('Tollgate Hill'), whose chief or *Loja* was an appointed member of the royal lineage,[45] a mile or two back from Omirinmirin; and hence the fact, as Apara put it, that 'sons of the great Ilesha chiefs' built houses at the market itself.[46]

Levies on trade were one of the main material pillars of power within any kingdom. Competition between kingdoms to control trade and markets within the whole region was a major source of inter-state conflict. The endemic warfare of nineteenth-century Yorubaland, which left hardly any kingdom unaffected, was unleashed by a dispute over Apomu, an important market-town on the borders of the Oyo, Ife and Owu kingdoms and one that had earlier been the target of Ijesha predations.[47] In fact the control of trade and warfare reciprocally conditioned one another. Trade-revenues did not require royal or official participation in trade; being levies on the trading process from outside, a directly *political* intervention in it, they merely presupposed the rulers' political, that is military, domination of the area; and in their turn they contributed to the military capacity of particular rulers. For they put resources into the hands of leaders who, through redistribution, could ensure the loyalty and increase the size of their followings.

Here we come to the third policy objective: the increase of population. To outstrip rival communities in size was both the efficient cause and the product of military success, and it was also the measure of success in rivalry between political actors within the community. Population increase, human fertility, was a fundamental value of Ijesha culture: one strove to have one's town and household 'full'. *Itan Ilesa* begins its account of Atakunmosa's legendary journey to Benin by telling how, considering that the town 'was not as full as he wanted', he looked for suitable magic.[48] This took the form of a horse – apt symbol of military power in the north, to which Ilesha had been oriented – which was made to swallow certain herbs. It was led off towards Benin, past Erin and Ipetu, and where it died, beyond Akure, it was buried as a powerful charm (*esi*) to mark the limit of Ijesha influence. *Owa* Ataiyero (1902–20), the last *Owa* who was entirely loyal to the old ways, used to send his messengers to the market to assess how many women had babies at their backs; if unsatisfied, he would order medicines to be made for burial beneath the gates of the town to rectify matters.[49] For it was the supreme responsibility of the *Owa* to ensure, by both mystical and practical means, this basic condition of the community's survival and success.

Consequently, in the scanty memorials of past rulers contained in the traditional histories of Ilesha, two sorts of information stand out: wars fought, and titles and quarters founded. Ilesha's recorded traditions, compared with those of all other Yoruba towns, are notable for the care with which the foundation of new quarters, the evidence of population growth, is attributed to particular rulers.[50] The militarily successful *Qwa*, like Atakunmosa and Oluodo, are especially credited with the foundation of new quarters. Atakunmosa is said to have founded Idasa quarter with his and his chiefs' slaves, as well as the small (and now defunct) quarter of Isape for royal slaves, a sort of overflow from the *Afin*; and the office of *Babaileoke*, or head of the royal slaves, is also said to have been Atakunmosa's creation.

In addition to these involuntary immigrants were those who migrated freely to Ilesha. Some of these – those of high status in their places of origin or those accompanied by a following – would be given titles, and thus a fixed place in the town's government. By the early nineteenth century, as several lineage histories collected in the 1974 Household Survey showed,[51] there were many immigrants who received no such official recognition: they might initially seek the *Qwa*'s or a chief's patronage but the open title-system in most quarters offered a path for the energetic and capable to achieve recognition. Two proverbs indicate Ilesha's openness and eagerness to absorb these immigrants:

> *Alejo nla şe onile kanrinkanrin*
> A powerful stranger pushes the householder aside

> *Ijeşa ọmọ alalę igbajoji*
> Ijeshas, more welcoming to strangers than to their own sons

The most common story attaching to immigrant titled lineages is that their founder was a member of some other town's royal lineage who, having failed in a succession struggle, decided to migrate with his people to Ilesha, where the *Qwa* received them warmly. When the places of origin of these immigrant lineages are linked with the *Qwa*'s reign when they arrived, they fall into two groups. There are those from the great regional power centres of Oyo and Benin: mostly not large lineages, typically associated with a ritual office (like *Qwa*'s medicine man, *Başemi*, from Oyo) or a specialized function (like the lineages of Benin origin in Itisin), they are said to have 'accompanied' an *Qwa* (either Owaluse or Atakunmosa) back to Ilesha. They are thus perhaps more a symbolic expression of Ilesha's material or ritual dependence on their places of origin than evidence of any substantial population movement. The other, far larger, group of immigrant lineages is quite different: coming from places lower in the regional hierarchy (like the small Ekiti kingdoms) or at least no higher (like Ondo), with their arrival spread over many reigns, they seem to represent a clear case of migrants attracted to a power centre which, because of its strategic location, success in war and wealth, offered better opportunities for self-advancement. We know little (since the evidence would tend to be in the histories of other towns) about what population Ilesha may have lost to other towns, though its steady physical growth up to the foundation of the last traditional quarter, Iroye, probably in the

1850s, suggests that any loss cannot have been great.[52] It must have been the more shocking – for the traditional histories record the details of their names[53] – that when Ibadan began to operate as a continuous military presence in Ijeshaland in the third quarter of the nineteenth century, many Ijesha warriors deserted to become 'war-boys' (*ọmọ ogun*) in the following of great Ibadan chiefs, and participated in the enslavement of their former compatriots to Ibadan. Ilesha itself was sacked for the first time in its history in 1870 and its population largely dispersed. A decade later the *Ọwa* Bepo, in the first direct testimony of an Ijesha ruler, protested to the British about the enslavement of his people and bitterly described himself as merely 'now King of grass and wood'.[54]

What were the implications of this pattern of relations between states and communities for political identities within the region? There were, of course, many shared cultural features among the peoples of the region – similarities of language, social institutions, religious cults etc. – but, while a common identity nearly always presupposes a high degree of shared culture, there may also be much shared culture between peoples with bitterly opposed collective identities. The traditions of Ife dynastic origins which the Ijesha share with all their neighbours and contacts (the Nupe alone excepted) provided a certain idiom for inter-kingdom relations but did not imply a corresponding 'ethnicity', in the modern sense.[55] These traditions ran beyond the modern Yoruba area, as they embraced Benin; and the original Yoruba, the Oyo, were only one unit, though a large and powerful one, within this system. Indeed, it was *against* the Oyo that the Ijesha defined their own identity as a people most sharply,[56] no doubt because, though Oyo was culturally more akin to Ijesha in more ways than Benin was, the Ijesha were subject to much more constant military pressure from them. Old Oyo was a 'cavalry state', but, as a Yoruba poem put it 'the *Ọwa* has everything but a horse's stable'.[57] It is significant that they made so much of the materials provided by the protective forest environment to symbolize the distinction between themselves and the savannah-dwelling Oyo. At the border town of Ada, the palace of the *Alada* was roofed with *gbodogi* leaves on the Ijesha side, and with *bere* grass on the Oyo side. They prided themselves enormously on their national dish, pounded yam (*iyan*), in contrast to foods based on maize and guinea-corn, savannah crops favoured by the Oyo.[58] Even the gods seemed to adopt the food preferences of their regions of origin![59] One gets a complementary picture from the earliest European travellers who approached Ilesha from the north or west and drew their anticipations from their Oyo-Yoruba companions: 'a strange people, of bad repute among the Yoruba [i.e. Oyo], with a language somewhat difficult and liable to suspicion'.[60] They were forcibly struck by how different Ijesha seemed from Oyo, in the appearance both of the people and the town.

The distinction of identity between Ijesha and Ekiti was a good deal less precise. There was more of a common cultural base, though affected by the consequences of Ilesha's growth and hegemony over much of Ekiti. Nineteenth-century sources such as Johnson sometimes speak as if Ilesha was part of Ekiti, sometimes as if Ekiti was distinct from and opposed to Ilesha.[61] Certainly Ilesha acted as though Ekiti were part of its back garden, and was reluctant to allow early European visitors access to it.[62] Ilesha was the leading member of the Ekitiparapo ('Ekiti together'), an alliance to which some of the unambiguously 'Ekiti' states did not belong.[63] The Ekiti are sometimes defined in terms of their 'sixteen kings', and from most enumerations of them Ilesha is excluded.[64] However, it is probably mistaken to think of them as a determinate group of 'real' members. Rather 'sixteen kings' is another idiom for talking about inter-state relations within the region; and like an ego-focussed circle of cognatic kin, the membership of any list depends on its point of reference.[65] Ijesha versions of the origin of the dynasties of the region present their founders, all sons of Oduduwa, as cutting sixteen paths from Ile-Ife, and most of them are in fact 'Ekiti', since these small kingdoms to Ilesha's east were among the 'significant others' of her regional environment.[66] Since Ilesha became, between 1600 and the nineteenth century, the major power of this sector of the zone interstitial between Oyo and Benin, it was natural for the small kingdoms of Ekiti to look on Ilesha with some reserve, as not quite one of them.

So there emerged a regional hierarchy of communities, a growing differentiation between the many 'mini-states' which may be presumed the baseline political form of the region.[67] Competition for population, functional to both war and trade, lay at the heart of this differentiation.[68] In this zone where the military technologies of neither horse nor gun took root before the mid nineteenth century, it was the power of numbers of people which mattered. The growth of the regional hierarchy thus implied a flow of population, drawn to the more successful communities as traders, slaves or ambitious immigrants. When we come to deal with migration arising from distinctively modern stimuli, we must not suppose that it happened to a people sunk in some timeless stability or lacking a lively sense of the regional context of their actions.

3

The structure of the capital

Ilesha is a classic – though hardly a typical – example of that ethnographic celebrity, the Yoruba town: a large, nucleated settlement that is the centre of a kingdom and itself the primary residence of an overwhelmingly agricultural population.[1] Even when it was largely derelict owing to war, in 1886, Ilesha's population was estimated to be between 20,000 and 25,000 and a figure of up to 40,000 may be appropriate for the height of its growth before the sack in 1870.[2] Though this is not as large as the largest Oyo-Yoruba towns of the nineteenth century, its considerable size was not due, as theirs was, to very heavy recent immigration under the impact of the wars.[3] Some impression of Ilesha's singularity may be gained from a comparison with Kumasi, which was about the same size but capital of the far larger and richer Asante kingdom.[4] 'Town' seems a curiously flat designation for what kind of entity it was, and the unhelpfulness of the 'rural–urban' continuum, to which Yoruba towns are a kind of affront, is more indicative of *its* inadequacy as a framework of cross-cultural comparison than of the nature of a place like Ilesha. We do better to seek enlightenment from the overlapping, and culturally loaded designations of the Yoruba themselves.

Ilesha was definitely an *ilu*, a self-subsistent community; and since many other settlements in Ijeshaland are also, by general consent, designated as *ilu*, the privileged political status of Ilesha within the Ijesha kingdom can be expressed by describing it as *ilu alade* ('community with a crowned head'). Whereas *ilu* has a definitely social connotation, as the community of people who live in the town and farm its land, the term *igbooro* specifically refers to the built-up area, the 'town' (in a more European sense) as opposed to its farmland. Though *igbooro*'s prime referent is physical, it also has social connotations, since certain activities are specific to the built-up area where the main business of the community, as such, occurs. Hence civil disturbances arising from factional conflict, intermittent in the histories of most Yoruba towns, are known as *ija igbooro* ('town riot'). A further term, *ode*, takes us closer to the political character of the capital, both in itself and in relation to its subordinate territory. *Ode* means 'outside', sometimes 'the wide world', and is frequently, though not in fact in the case of Ilesha, used to describe the capital of a kingdom: Ijebu Ode, Ode Ondo. This reference seems closely akin to a usage that *is* found in Ilesha: the 'town' as against the *Owa*'s palace. Thus chiefs who have privileged access to the *Owa* are called *iwole* ('those who enter the house', i.e. the *Afin*), whereas the others are *t'ode* ('of the outside', i.e. the town). If the two idioms are indeed linked, it is indicative of an important political relationship: between the *ilu*'s status as the 'outside' of a king's palace, and as the 'capital' of a kingdom embracing subordinate communities. As will be repeatedly evident in what follows, the structure of the capital is built around two complementary elements: the *Owa* and the Ijesha people.

So much is, in any case, evident from the spatial layout of Ilesha. Its focal point is the *Afin*, set within its rectangular 51-acre grounds and surrounded by a high mud-brick wall, residence of the *Owa*, his personal staff and all manner of clients and dependants, location of the graves of the royal ancestors and the most potent shrines of the gods, judicial and political centre of the kingdom.[5] From the *Afin* radiated the seven roads that formed the armature of the capital's settlement and then ran to the frontiers of the kingdom. Ilesha's communal structure may be derived

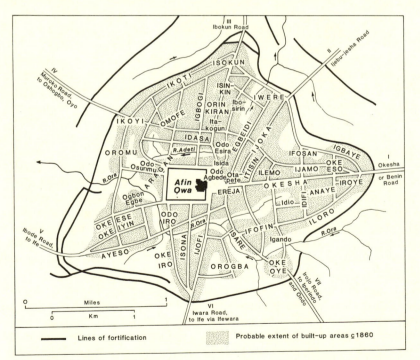

Map 3.1 Ilesha: quarters

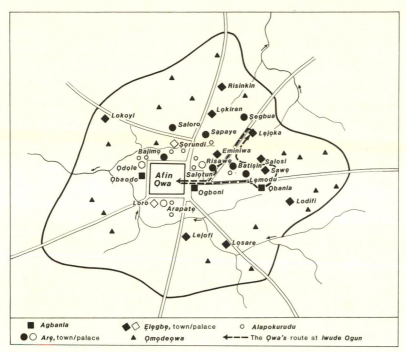

Map 3.2   Ilesha: chiefs' houses

from two coordinated principles: a spatial arrangement by quarters, and a political hierarchy of titles, both of which are focussed on the *Afin*.

THE QUARTERS

Ilesha is regarded by its citizens as comprising some forty *adugbo* (sometimes *ogbon*) or 'quarters', founded over several centuries until shortly before the sack of 1870.[6] These units exist for maintaining local order, their chiefs severally constituting the lowest-level judicial tribunals, and for meeting certain local needs, such as keeping the streets clean and in good repair. In the past they were the basic units of military mobilization and a major means by which the town authorities communicated with the population on issues of public importance. Typically each quarter has a local head whose title indicates his quarter (*Lejofi* of Ijofi, *Lorunyin* of Oke-Iyin, *Aloro* of Iloro etc.), presiding over a local council of chiefs, minimally six in number (*iwarefa mefa*) according to the local norm of the basics of communal government. Probably for this reason a quarter is sometimes described as an *ilu*, a social unit with a certain autonomy in running its affairs.[7] The young men of a quarter were organized under the *loriomo* (lit. 'head of young men') who was responsible to the chiefs of his quarter – an

33

arrangement that is akin to the age-set systems found in the Ekiti towns. In a society where inter-generational tension was, for reasons to be explained, endemic, the *loriọmọ* stood at a particularly crucial point of articulation, between those who took decisions and those who put them into effect.

The quarter was also constituted as a ritual community, and its physical focus was its sacred centre, the *akata*. This word appears not to exist in Standard Yoruba and was most helpfully translated for me by a quarter-chief: *ibiti a fi aṣẹ Ọwa si*, 'the place where we put the Owa's medicine/authority'.[8] Typically this was a spot at a cross-roads in the middle of the quarter marked by a particular tree. It is a sad loss that they were nearly all cut down when overhead electricity lines were introduced in the 1950s, and are now marked, if at all, by no more than a small raised stone roundabout. But when the quarter was founded, an *aṣẹ*, a specially prepared 'medicine' or sacrifice, was buried there imparting its power to the *akata* tree and the site became the scene of religious observances. Sacrifices were made there at times of need, such as an outbreak of fire or epidemic in the quarter, and at the annual occasion when, during the Ogun festival cycle, the quarter people went to take an offering and to pray at the *Afin* on a day related to the commemoration of the royal ancestor who founded the quarter. All these rites are now greatly fallen into desuetude.

What is here described is doubly a norm: over three-quarters of the forty traditional quarters, as they are now recognized, *do* have this structure; and this was the model upon which new quarters were established over at least 250 years up to the mid nineteenth century. But some of the most important *adugbo*, and especially the oldest ones, diverge considerably. Okesha and Ijoka, each stretching along one of the main axes of the town, and very large, have no traditions of foundation by an *Ọwa*: Okesha claims to be *the* original settlement, while Ijoka seems just to have grown from local immigration in Ilesha's earliest days.[9] Their heads, *Ọbanla* and *Lẹjọka*, have important titles in the government of the whole town, and their title-systems go far beyond the basic six – in Ijoka's case over fifty titles were claimed, which means a very high proportion of household heads must once have had them.

Other quarters, especially some near the *Afin*, are really accretions round or extensions of the houses of chiefs or ritual specialists closely linked with the *Ọwa*.[10] Thus Ereja consisted entirely of the houses of Chief *Alaye*, the priest of Orisa Onifon and others associated with that cult (*Ṣagbunrin, Ṣagbaṣẹ*); Chief *Agbayewa*, head of the *Alapokurudu* palace chiefs, an important ritual specialist; Chief *Ẹṣẹgba*, the senior diviner, and others associated with the cult of Ifa (*Asa* and *Lilẹrẹ*); Chief *Ariṣe*, head of the women chiefs of the town; to which is now added Idofin, an area which was traditionally distinct from Ereja proper, where Chiefs *Ogboni* and *Sajọwa*, the senior blacksmith, have their houses. Aragan, at the other side of *Afin*, is somewhat similar, comprising the areas round the houses of Chiefs *Odọle* and *Ọbaodo*, both senior chiefs; the street known as Odo Osunmu, residence of the royal wood carvers, which had its own craft-organization; and several other chiefs, including *Iba*, a royal herbalist, and *Bajimọ*, who plays a major role in the organization of the royal lineage. Several other adjacent small quarters have preserved a distinctive character: Odo Agbede, former home of blacksmiths; Odo Esira, where the royal beadworkers live; Isida, the area around the houses of the *Risawẹ* and the *Ọwa*'s physician, *Baṣemi*, both palace-chiefs; and, further out, Ilemo, around the house of Chief *Lẹmodu*, priest of Obokun. And scattered around this whole central area are the houses of minor titled diviners, blacksmiths, priests and junior palace-chiefs.

So from the mid sixteenth to the mid nineteenth century Ilesha grew from the bifocal core provided by the *Afin*, with its ring of ritual specialists, and Okesha and Ijoka, the aboriginal quarters: northwards across the Adeti stream along and between the axes of the Ibokun and Muroko roads, southwards across the Ora stream on three separate masses of rising ground separated by marshy and periodically flooded land, and to the east outwards from the spine of Okesha. Evidence from the chronology of founding *Ọwa* and the relative seniority of titles indicates a consistent pattern of settlement: new quarters were sited first outward along the axes of the seven main roads leading from Ilesha and then within the segments formed by existing radii of settlement. The quarter was laid out initially as a single street (hence, as Ijesha today describe it in English, the term 'street', corresponding to Yoruba *ọgbọn*, is often used as the equivalent of 'quarter'), land for the settlers' houses being marked out with a line of rope.[11] The standard account of quarter foundation holds that the *Ọwa*, seeing how the town is growing, invites his leading chiefs to settle part of their large households in a new quarter and sometimes adds a segment of his own; and, since the specialized functions clustered in the centre are for the town at large, arranges for a household each of *babalawo* (diviner) and of *agbẹdẹ* (blacksmith) lineage to be settled there too. Later on it might be extended with a second street cutting across at right-angles, or a parallel one laid out (as *Ọgbọn Titun Okeṣa*, or *Ọgbọn Okun* of Ijoka). Several of the early European visitors were particularly impressed by this layout, contrasting it with the hastily-settled Oyo towns from which they had come. 'Ilesha for its cleanliness, regularity, the width and straightness of its streets and the elevation for comfort of foot passengers far surpasses any native town I have seen in Africa,' wrote the Revd William Clark in 1857. 'Blocks of buildings could be distinctly marked out by the regularity with which the streets cut each other, thus preventing the town from presenting that confused mass of roofs so generally visible.'[12]

The quarter, rather than the lineage, was the major unit through which a man was 'placed' in Ilesha, the link between the household and the community at large. Its mutualities and services, its role as a unit of mobilization and control, were grounded in co-residence in a defined locality. The relations of the quarter were sanctioned by its establishment (*idasilẹ*) by a particular *Ọwa* and were not glossed in terms of descent. They were aggregates of households; and, while some lineages would be entirely limited to one quarter or regarded themselves as belonging essentially to one quarter, very many people would attend lineage meetings in other quarters than the one in which they lived. The larger titled lineages had members in many quarters and the great bulk of quarter titles were 'open', not restricted to any particular lineage. Within the spectrum of Yoruba towns, Ilesha's *adugbo* seem to resemble most closely the *idimi* of Ode Ondo and the *itun* of Ijebu Ode, where also the quarters/wards were the main units of the town's political structure; lineages were only loosely articulated with them and there was the flexibility produced by many 'open' titles.[13] Most other Yoruba towns are different. Those Oyo towns which were created by mass migration under the war conditions of the nineteenth century seem to have 'quarters' which are little more than the names of localities within the town, while it is lineages, strongly localized, which provide the direct means of representation at the political centre.[14] In the small but ancient Ekiti towns, by contrast, quarters and localized lineages are integrated into a single structure, the quarters represented at the centre by chiefs drawn usually from a dominant lineage within them.[15] The contrast with Ekiti is significant, since they most likely represent a kind of baseline from which Ilesha grew, a form which may be found in the smaller semi-autonomous Ijesha towns as well. It suggests that the distinctive quality of Ilesha's quarters was both a condition and a consequence of her steady and successful expansion as a community, their openness and flexible structure enabling newcomers to be incorporated.

TITLES, CHIEFS AND PEOPLE

The political articulation of the quarters to the centre took place through a complex system of titles, many of which had functions or attributes in relation to the community at large or related to lineage interests which crosscut those of the quarters and spread throughout the town. Title (*oye*; chiefs are literally 'title-holders', *ijoye* or *oloye*) is a publicly recognized status in the town's political structure, through which, on the one hand, the community's human and spiritual resources are summoned and, on the other, assets won by the community are redistributed. Because titles form a definite system, being fairly well fixed in relation to one another, an anatomy of that system promises the best way into an account of the regular pattern of Ilesha's politics. In saying this, I do not mean to suggest that the system was immune to manipulation, change or development. Indeed, it is impossible to give a satisfactory account of the structure without referring to some basic dynamics of political life. But titles were *not* infinitely flexible or merely labels for individual accumulations of

36

λπ   Qwa

AGBANLA ω Qbanla *OKESHA
(senior λ Ogboni Ibokun
elders) λ Ogboni Ijẹbu
         λ Ogboni Ipole
         ω Qbaodo

ARẸ   λπ Qdọle   ẸLẸGBẸ   ω   Lejọka*
(counsellors) λπ Risawẹ   (war-leaders) λπ Loro*
               λ   Saloro   ω   Lejofi*
               λπ Arapatẹ   ω   Lọkiran*
               λ   Lẹmodu   ω   Risinkin*
               λ   Bajimọ   λπ Sọrundi
               ω   Sẹgbua   λ   Salosi
               λ   Batişin   λ   Sawẹ* IJAMO
               λ   Şapaye   ω   Lodifi*
               λ   Salọtun   ω   Lọsare*
               ?   Emilaọtun   ω   Lokoyi*

ẸLẸGBAJI   ω Ejẹmọ Okeşa   QMQDEQWA   ω Bamura* IDASA
(junior   ω Risa Ijọka   (junior   ω Gbogi*
quarter   ω Risa Iro   quarter   ω Lọmọfẹ*
chiefs I)   ω Risa Ijofi   chiefs II)   ω Lufoşan*
               ? Qdọfin Ibokun   ω Lugbayọ* IKOTI
               ? Qdọfin Ijẹbu   ω Lifọfin*
               ? Qdọfin Ipole   ω Lẹmẹşọ*
               λ Eminiwa* EGBEIDI   ω Lemi* ISOKUN
               ω Risa Qrinkiran   λ Lanaye*
               ω Risa Isinkin   ω Lọrunyin*
               ω Risa Ijamọ   ω Lẹşẹ*
               ω Risa Idifi   ω Alọrọ*
               ω Risa Isare   ω Lewere*
               ω Risa Ikoyi   ω Lugbaye*
               as well as   ω Layẹşọ*
               junior chiefs   ω Saoye*
               in each   ω Loromu*
               quarter, six   ω Lorogba*
               or more in   as well as
               each. (Heads   junior chiefs,
               of most of   usually
               these quarters   making six
               are the   chiefs in each
               Ẹlẹgbẹ   quarter.
               chiefs.)

Other lines of chiefs, unranked relative to each other:
λπ ALAPOKURUDU (junior palace chiefs): Agbayewa, Ẹşira, Qsunmu, Başemi, Iba, Aruwaji (*ISONA), Oşodi, Ohunọrun, Şalua, Eniodi, Şedilẹ, Şinlaiye etc. not precisely ranked.
λ   ALAGBẸDẸ (blacksmiths): Sajọwa, Agbatayọ, Lukọsin, etc.
λ   BABALAWO (diviners): Ẹşẹgba, Pẹtẹ etc., ranked.
λ   AWORO (titled priests, not forming a clear group): Alaye (of Orisa Onifon) and others under him, ranked; Lioro (of Osun) etc.
ω   ISQGBA (women): Arişe, Risa Arişe etc., ranked.

Key
*   quarter-head (quarter named if not contained within the title)
λ   lineage title
π   palace title (iwọle)
ω   open title

Fig. 3.1   The Ilesha title-system

37

power from other sources: they presented their holders with definite possibilities and constraints and were certainly felt to have quite intrinsic properties.[16] They were culturally important because they were the form in which the community knew itself and continued to exist through all vicissitudes of personnel. When titles were vacant, the town was 'spoilt' (*ilu bajẹ*, as Ijesha put it); when Ilesha was restored in the 1890s, the refilling of its titles was both a symbol and the material means of its self-reconstitution.

Figure 3.1 presents the title-system in a summary form. The system has its origins in a simple linkage of function and authority to produce two grades of titles, which is the basis of the title-systems widely found in the small Ekiti towns which, I have suggested, may serve as a baseline for Ilesha's development.[17] There is a senior grade of 'elders', generically known as *iwarẹfa* and typically six in number, whose function is to direct the affairs of the community as a whole, though they will usually be drawn from the community's main quarter or lineage constituencies; and a junior grade of military leaders, generically known as *ẹlẹgbẹ* (leaders of bands or associations), who lead and represent the residential units of the town. In Ilesha the analogues of these two grades are present in the line of six senior title-holders, called *Agbanla* ('Great Elders'), and the *Ẹlẹgbẹ* line, also called *Ologun* ('war-leaders'), who are mostly the heads of the older quarters under the overall leadership of the *Lẹjọka*, head of Ijoka, the second largest and most ancient quarter. Whatever his position within the town's system, each such quarter-head also belongs to the *iwarẹfa* of his own quarter, as has been described above. Ilesha also shows some peculiarities, which arise, firstly, from the original way it was constituted as the Ijesha kingdom's capital; and secondly, from its expansion and the growth of the palace organization.

As to the first, Ilesha's *Agbanla* or senior grade of chiefs includes the heads of three district towns, which is perhaps the relic of an earlier 'federal' organization of the kingdom. Certainly, for at least a century, these *Ogboni*, as they are styled, have not been active as chiefs in Ilesha. The other three members are the *Ọbanla*, an 'open' title, titular quarter-head of Okesha, the aboriginal settlement, and now the chief representative of 'the Ijesha' as they are counterposed to the *Ọwa*; the *Ogboni*, whose ritual connexions with iron and whose Benin provenance have been described, but whose political role is to be a sacred mediator between palace and town;[18] and the *Ọbaodo*, an open title with no very distinctive functions. The creation of the *Ọbaodo* title, much more recent than the others, may have had the effect of underlining the *Ọwa*'s enhanced status, with the growth of his town, by removing him from the six nominal *iwarẹfa* of the community.

This basic two-tier system became greatly enlarged and diversified as Ilesha expanded. The *Afin* (palace) must from very early on have had titled officials. As its prestige grew, it attracted further ritual and craft

38

specialists and developed a wider range of internal functionaries, many of whom were accorded, unlike the chiefs of the town, privileged right of access to the *Ọwa*. These were the *iwọle* or 'palace-chiefs', headed by a chief, the *Ọdọle*, who, combining religious duties at the shrines of the *Afin* with a kind of chamberlain's role to the *Ọwa*, became a figure of the greatest importance in Ilesha's political life.[19] Some *iwọle*, the so-called *Alapokurudu* ('satchel-men') or junior palace-chiefs, remained fairly restricted to palace functions, while others (*Loro, Risawẹ, Arapatẹ, Ṣọrundi*) came to have, like the *Ọdọle*, important public roles, with very large lineages in the town. Then, as noted in Chapter 2, Ilesha also began to attract free immigrants, some just to settle in the quarters where they would be eligible for open titles, others being important enough to gain recognition by the award of titles which mostly became hereditary among their descendants. The *Ọwa* used these immigrants, who received their titles as his clients, to counterbalance the growing power of the quarters and their heads, the *Ẹlẹgbẹ* chiefs. The result was the line of chiefs called *Arẹ* ('Counsellors'), headed by the *Ọdọle*, though only a minority of them were also *iwọle*. Though many members of their lineages eventually came to live out in the ordinary quarters, rather than clustered round the *Afin*, these title-holders tended to stand outside the quarter organization, an alternative route through which opinion and support might be accumulated and redistribution of resources effected.

We may discern a series of rough correspondences in the political structure of the town – rough, because not all titles share all the other characteristics which tend to belong to their type:

Ọwa	The Ijesha
palace-chiefs (*iwọle*)	town-chiefs (*t'ode*)
hereditary titles (*oye idile*)	open titles (*oye ọmọ ilu*)
specialist and ritual roles	general and military leadership
immigrants	indigenes
lineages	quarters
Arẹ chiefs	*Ẹlẹgbẹ* chiefs

The rivalry of palace and town – which especially tended to flare up with the more militarily successful *Ọwa*[20] – also created exceptions to this set of structural opposites. Some groups of immigrants, whose leaders were given titles which became hereditary, must have been so large that they at once constituted quarters: thus the two separate groups of Ondo people who founded Odo Iro and Ijamo under the *Loro* and *Sawẹ* respectively, or the Ado people who founded Isona under the *Aruwaji*. The *Loro*, moreover, was both made an *iwọle* and placed in the *Ẹlẹgbẹ* line under the *Lẹjọka*, so that he could serve as the *Ọwa*'s 'eyes' within the body of military chiefs. This device became institutionalized in nearly all the newer quarters, in that most of their second chiefs or *Lọtun* were drawn from the *Loro*

39

lineage. This is said to have originated as a compromise when *Ǫwa* Ata-kunmosa and the chiefs quarrelled over the establishment of Idasa quar-ter, which the *Ǫwa* wanted to be headed by a son of his. As still more quarters were founded – some twenty-two under Atakunmosa's succes-sors – it became less and less possible for their heads to be represented directly in the higher counsels of the town through membership of the *Ẹlẹgbẹ* line. In similar fashion, as the town got larger, fresh immigrants made less individual impression and were less likely to gain recognition by being given senior *Arẹ* titles. Two new junior lines of chiefs came into existence, both associated with the quarters: the *Ẹlẹgbaji*, being mostly the lower chiefs of the older quarters whose heads were in the *Ẹlẹgbẹ* line, themselves headed by the *Ejẹmǫ*, second to the *Ǫbanla* in his capacity as chief of Okesha; and the *Ǫmǫdeǫwa*, who comprise all the chiefs of the more recent quarters, led by the *Bamura*, quarter-head of Idasa. Every year at the *Iwude* ceremony during the Ogun festival, the Ijesha are reminded of the contested relationship between them-selves and the *Ǫwa*, the great but overbearing symbol of their commun-ity's prowess, by a mock battle which takes place between these two junior lines of chiefs.

Each of these lines of chiefs, though their members might represent 'constituencies' which were to some extent rivals, had a quasi-corporate character. In the deliberations of the chiefs, for example when they met at the *Ogboni*'s house to choose a new *Ǫwa* or in their regular meetings to discuss the town's business which took place at *Okemẹsẹ*, the great courtyard of the *Afin*, the opinion of each line as a whole was sought, its senior chiefs speaking last on behalf of all. Redistribution of resour-ces from the centre, whether ritual things like kola or more substantial ones like tribute or installation fees, proceeded in a similar fashion: first to the leaders of each line and then from them to their juniors. While there were disputes about the exact order of precedence and sometimes changes in it, the principle of a rank order was clearly established and there was not much doubt for most of the time about what that order was, especially at the upper end where it was of most consequence. This method of representation and redistribution produced two definite consequences: the gradation between the ranks was not even, as those at the upper end stood far out ahead of those lower down; and, as a consequence, the leaders of lower lines tended to enjoy a higher stand-ing in practice than the lowest members of notionally higher lines. Both consequences can be illustrated, albeit in a rather exaggerated form, by the chiefs' salary scale established by the British early in this century, to compensate chiefs for the abolition of tolls, private judicial payments and other perquisites, shown below. As we shall see, the patronships of district communities, a major source of chiefly revenue and one that the British intended to replace, were very unevenly concentrated, among a handful of the most senior chiefs. The same principle is evident in the share accorded the *Qwa* in the division of any kind of tribute or revenue: he got the equivalent of the sum of what all other title-holders got, according to the adage 'the *Qwa* is one, the Ijeshas are one'. It had to be like this, since the higher the chief's status, the more claims there would be on him for redistribution.

AGBANLA		ARE		ELEGBE	
Qbanla	£168	*Qdqle*	£108	*Lejqka*	£96
Ogboni	£132	*Risawe*	£102	*Loro*	£90
Ogboni Ibokun	£18	*Saloro*	£20	*Lejofi*	£20
Ogboni Ijebu	£18	*Arapate*	£20		
Ogboni Ipole	£3	*Lemodu*	£20		
Qbaodo	£20	All other *Are* and *Elegbe* titles, each, £12.[21]			

Here we turn to the relations between chiefs and subjects. Ilesha belongs to that large group of African polities in which the title-holders are the representatives of particular bodies of ordinary people. Lloyd's general model of the Yoruba polity typifies these bodies or 'constituencies' as lineages, and holds that because the lineages are of equal status, the chiefs drawn from them must also be, 'though a formal ranking is unavoidable'.[22] As applied to Ilesha, however, the first of these propositions is over-simple, since even with lineage-titles, the 'constituencies' represented through them are much more diversely composed; while the second is false: the rank-order is very real, deriving from the manner in which constituency opinions and interests are aggregated. The greater chiefs embrace in their 'constituencies' not just their own lineage or quarter (plus, of course, a miscellany of other clients connected by all kinds of personal ties), but other chiefs inferior to them, especially within their own line, each with his own following. The 'downward linkages' of particular great chiefs vary considerably: the *Qbanla*'s constituency is structurally fairly simple, consisting of the largest quarter, Okesha. The *Ogboni*'s is highly complex, consisting of his very large lineage, the small neighbourhood of Idofin around his house, the blacksmiths and a number of titles, mostly at the lower end of the *Are* line, such as *Batisin, Salqtun, Sapaye* and *Emilaqtun*, which are said to be 'under' (*labe*) Chief *Ogboni*.[23] The *Qdqle*, besides the residents of Aragan and his own lineage, which included a number of chiefs in other quarters (*Sedile* in Itisin, *Mqniare* in Igbogi and so on), had a general responsibility for all the *iwqle* (inner palace) chiefs. The *Lejqka, Loro* and *Lejofi* each had their own quarters as well as the lower military titles; and *Loro*, in addition, had his large lineage from which sixteen *lqtun* of the *Qmqdeqwa*-led quarters were chosen. These ties, it can be seen, have a variety of sources: lineage, function, residence or historical association. The *Risawe*, for example, might hear cases that minor chiefs, not only in his quarter of Isida, but further out in his sector of the town, such as the *Eminiwa* of Egbeidi, had been unable to settle.[24] The *Sawẹ* (eighth *Ẹlẹgbẹ*, quarter-head of Ijamo) said that candidates for that title might make their approaches through the *Loro* (second *Ẹlẹgbẹ*, who shared with the Ijamo people a tradition of Ondo origin) or through the *Risawẹ* (second *Arẹ*; the first *Risawẹ* is said to have been half-brother to *Ọwa* Uyiarere, founder of Ijamo, and the first *Sawẹ*'s wife was a daughter of Chief *Risawẹ*).[25] For the ordinary man, of course, this gave a degree of political choice. Most people would, through their quarter, be members of an interest-group running up to the *Ọbanla* or one of the *Ẹlẹgbẹ* chiefs and also, through their lineage, potential members of the followings of the *Ogboni*, the *Ọdọle* or other hereditary title-holders, mostly in the *Arẹ* line. This made it necessary for title-holders to actively maintain their followings: their support, while inclined towards them by custom, was not automatic.

A further component of the pyramid of interest groups, already alluded to, was an important source of the status of the senior chiefs. The communities of the district each had a chiefly patron (*onile* or 'owner of the house', i.e. where their emissaries lodged at Ilesha) in the capital, through whom they sent customary tributes (*iwisin*) to the *Ọwa* and made any other kind of necessary representation, such as over disputes or over succession to their own headships. Not all senior chiefs seem to have been equally attractive as *onile*.[26] The *Ọbanla* and the *Ọbaodo* each had only one community to represent; and it was the hereditary, especially *iwọle* chiefs (*Ọdọle, Risawẹ, Arapatẹ*) but also *Ogboni*, or the military chiefs (*Lẹjọka, Loro, Lejofi*) who had the lion's share of this kind of patronage. This indicates the dual nature of the *onile*-system: an organ of representation for the powerless and of domination by the powerful. On the first score, those represented were concerned to get good access to the centre of things, the *Afin*, so that the most attractive patrons would be *iwọle* chiefs or a chief like the *Ogboni*; on the second, while all chiefs were concerned to dominate whom they could, it was the military *Ẹlẹgbẹ* who were most in a position to adopt as their clients communities who were brought and kept under Ilesha's sway by force of arms. So while the *Loro*, who qualified under both counts, was *onile* to at least eleven district communities, the senior chief of the capital, the *Ọbanla*, who qualified under neither, had only one.[27]

A striking metaphor was used by Chief *Agbayewa*, the head of the *Alapokurudu* or junior palace-chiefs, to describe the reciprocal quality of the relations between chiefs and their people.[28] The chief's *ọna*, he said, was also the subject's *ọna*. *Ọna* is the ordinary word for a way or path, and can also mean a 'line' of chiefs. The *ọna* of a chief was his 'means' to act as a chief, his income; for the subjects it was their path to the centre of things, which was also the avenue of personal advancement. The question we are led to ask of such a system of representative chieftaincy is: what held it in place? If the chiefs would be deprived of their *ọna* if their subjects turned elsewhere, what enabled them to dominate them to the extent they did?

42

The resources of a chief came partly from 'below', from his dependants, and partly from 'above', by virtue of his being an effective title-holder, that is of his having acknowledged dependants. Most of the senior chiefs, in addition to land they had individually inherited, had estates (*ilẹ oye* or 'title land') close to Ilesha, which were worked by the junior members of their households (including their slaves) as well as by free dependants who owed them annual presents of produce (*iwifọ*). A chief received gifts from all who needed his help or authorization, whether he was acting on his own authority or as the gateway to a higher authority. When district communities made their annual *iwisin* to the *Ọwa*, or made the payments customary on the installation of the head-chiefs, these went through their *onile* at the capital who retained a portion for himself. But these did not amount to very much in material terms: *iwisin* always took the form of foodstuffs, usually yams or bushmeat.[29] What was probably much more important than these regular payments were the occasional payments made by those clients who got into trouble or wanted some extraordinary assistance from their chief in affairs at the *Afin*. This is strongly indicated in the accounts of the disturbances in 1905 when the British were seeking to abolish tolls and chiefly 'bribes' (i.e. 'presents . . . customary from time immemorial', as Lagos Ijeshas then put it, mostly arising from the settlement of disputes), and when, it appears, certain non-chiefs had come to exercise equivalent political influence to the senior chiefs. The phrase *ba mi ṣe* ('help me to . . .') was used:

> as a Councillor, it is certain people come to you at your farm asking you for assistance in any matter at Ilesha. *Ba mi ṣe* . . . in every country means money – have you not been accepting it? . . . why then report and accuse the Owa and Council of receiving presents which the [British] Commissioner calls bribes.[30]

These are obviously payments in cash, not kind, and were of considerable value.

All these payments were essentially made for services rendered. On one occasion when I likened *iwisin* to tax (*owo ori*) since it did in fact stop being generally paid in the 1920s when tax became regular, I was corrected by some village chiefs who described it as *ẹbun* ('free gift'), payments made voluntarily by people in order to keep in touch with the centre.[31] The real point was not the lightness of regular payments but the reciprocity between chiefs and people. The bulk of the chief's constituents were those given to him by custom, depending on the character of his title. The closer to the centre it was, the greater the size of his constituency – those who had claims on him for patronage and from whom he could claim material support – and so also was his own body of *direct* dependants, his household. Clear evidence of this endures to this day, in that the size of lineages with hereditary titles in Ilesha corresponds to a nicety with the rank of those titles in the town's hierarchy. The royal lineage comprises 13.1% of the population followed by those of *Ọdọle* at 7.2%, *Ogboni* at 7% and *Loro* at 5.9%, while fifteen other titled lineages average 1.1% each (1974 Household Survey). The high levels of chiefly polygyny would ensure this effect. But while custom opens the way to a chief's effective power in a title, it does not absolutely secure it, despite the fact that in his installation the chief is told to put off his 'cloth of poverty' (*aṣọ oṣi*) since henceforth he will be rich.

Putting it in simple materialist terms, the chief managed to extract a surplus from two directions, each of them providing necessary conditions for the other. In order to realize the potential of his title to attract resources from higher up, the chief needed a large household of his own: without it his title land was of small value to him and he would be unable to be hospitable and open-handed in the way that was expected of him by his clients. But while a high degree of redistribution was necessary to maintain this following, it could not be complete: a certain proportion of the resources won by the labour power and/or weight of household members and clients had to be retained by the chief as a kind of capital for investment in the maintenance and extension of his position. Chiefs had a definitely leisured style of life to maintain and undoubtedly had a far greater enjoyment of luxury and prestige goods, such as imported cloth and higher-quality country-cloth, and it was regarded as a usurpation of chiefly prerogatives for commoners to wear them. By the late nineteenth century, at least, it was not uncommon for chiefs to have so much money, in the bulky form of bags of cowries, that many a chief set aside a small room in the recesses of his house as a treasury. Two reasons for the domestic advantages of chiefs (and other household heads) may be mentioned. Firstly, the institution of polygyny, despite its redistributive aspects, meant that young men – those whose farming and fighting muscle most built up the strength of chiefs – had to face a relatively long period of dependence and, under normal circumstances, married late. Usually, too, since girls were affianced in childhood, they had to perform several years' labour service for their prospective fathers-in-law. Secondly, the presence of domestic slaves, household members who were much less capable of putting pressure for redistribution on the household head, must have greatly weakened the bargaining position of sons, and so doubly helped to sustain the position of chiefs.

Still, even these negative sanctions ultimately led back to the chiefs' positive role as channels of the material proceeds of the entire community's successful interaction with its neighbours, through trade and war. Put another way, the social position of the political elite was very largely underpinned by the exploitation of outsiders. Traders differed from other categories of a chief's clients since, not being members of local households, their dependency was very great and there was no givenness in their relations with a particular chief. In the mid nineteenth century, chiefs (probably the *Ẹlẹgbẹ*) are said to have levied tolls of two cowries per traveller at each of Ilesha's seven gates.[32] Late nineteeth-century traders throughout Yorubaland lodged with chiefs and gave presents in return for board, lodging and protection. In the late 1890s a chief like *Lejofi* Esan, for example, acted as host to Ilorin traders, who stayed in his house for several weeks at a time and from whom he received cloth, tobacco, ostrich feathers and other gifts; if he received two cloths he would send one as a present to the *Qwa*.[33] It is evident that the *Lejofi*'s capacity to offer and to benefit from his patronage depended on the interstitial position he occupied between his people and the centre. He relied on his own people to provide the wherewithal of hospitality; and he also made sure, through the care with which he maintained good relations with the *Qwa*, that his capacity to offer patronage to his people at the centre was not impaired.

The other way in which the power of their people was mobilized to maintain the title system was more direct. The rewards of military success – booty and slaves (*eru*) – won by a citizen army organized under quarter-chiefs, was divided in such a way as to underwrite the established hier-archy. The exact details for Ilesha before the nineteenth-century upheavals are not available, but it is likely that something like the Oyo-Yoruba convention prevailed: one-third of captives to the *Qwa*, one-third to the chiefs, one-third to the ordinary citizen-soldiers.[34] So large a body of slaves belonged to the *Qwa* that in the 1890s any individual around the town who was not otherwise known would be considered an *eru Qwa*.[35] Ijesha traditions suggest that periods of successful war had a destabilizing effect on the relations between the *Qwa* and his subjects, producing tyranny on the one hand and rebellious reaction on the other; for the sudden accession of slaves through the centre will have encouraged those in political authority to ignore the claims of their ordinary constituents. Slaves are crucial to those in authority in a society where redistribution to free clients is in-escapable, since, being without outside kin of their own, their dependency is very great; and I have argued above that their presence was a key component of the domestic control exercised by all title-holders. But, from this viewpoint, slaves are a wasting asset: they tend to become assimilated to the status of ordinary Ijesha as they are drawn into the kinship system. Ilesha may have been a society which *required* to take in fresh slaves regularly in order to maintain the differentials of its political structure.[36]

Despite this marked political hierarchy and its related forms of social subordination – of slaves, of junior males, of strangers, of subordinate communities, to say nothing of women – Ilesha was not straightforwardly a class society.[37] In particular, it is profoundly misleading to call its chiefs an 'aristocracy', or a 'nobility' or an 'upper class', with the implication that here we have a social formation akin to European feudalism or perhaps, since we may compare the *ilu* to a *polis*, archaic Greece. There we may speak of a 'ruling class', implying that the political elite was grounded in a dominant class whose social position rested on its ownership of the key productive resource. In Ilesha, the main productive resource, land, was virtually a free good; the claim of *obas* and chiefs to be 'owners of the land' (*onile*) meant that they claimed the allegiance of the people who worked a territory, but, as we have seen, they had to work at winning and holding that allegiance. But social classes such as the medieval nobility or an ancient Greek aristocracy are more than categories of actors abstractly defined by 'relationship to the means of production'; they are real social entities, typically bounded against members of lower classes and operating techniques of social closure such as endogamy, consolidation of property through inheritance and a distinct class-culture. In this sense a 'dominant class' did not exist in Ilesha, not even in that category which comes closest to it: the entire body of male household heads. For that was not permanently closed to the 'under-class' of young men, nor even, in the longer run, to slaves; and women had their own line of chiefs under the *Ariṣe*. This peculiar combination of classlessness and political hierarchy derived directly from the manner in which the society was integrated, through the mobilization of 'people-power', to win external resources from the regional system. Polygyny, which was an aspect of this, meant that the property accumulated by the powerful was broken up among many heirs.

Some things remain to be said about the position of the *Ọwa* in the political structure of Ilesha. Rather than a simple harmony of interests between the *Ọwa* and the chiefs, there was much ambivalence in the relationship: each needed the other but also had to fight to preserve their own position against encroachment. The *Ọwa* could play off the rivalries of the great chiefs against one another and, as the title system shows, early *Ọwa* had given immigrants titles to set a check on the leading town chiefs. But the *Ọwa*'s position was vulnerable, especially towards the beginning of his reign. Since all members of the very large royal lineage (*ọmọba*) were eligible for the title in principle and the lines of chiefs, aggregated under their leaders, were responsible for choosing and installing the *Ọwa*, he began as the client of the most powerful chiefly interests of the moment; and was also greatly dependent on the existing *Afin* personnel.

Apart from the *iwọle* or palace-chiefs, the most important category here was the *ẹmẹṣẹ* or messengers, who would effectively be the 'hands' of the *Ọwa* in all his business throughout the kingdom, bearing the beaded staves (*ọpa ilẹke*) which symbolized his authority. When a substantial chief died, his family were obliged to send a number of his sons – it might be half-a-dozen with a great chief – to the *Afin* to serve as *ẹmẹṣẹ*. There would be several hundred or so serving at a time, organized in various categories under their own title-holders, the most important being *Lọmọdele* and *Lọtun Ẹmẹṣẹ*. This institution of *ẹmẹṣẹ* helped to establish links between particular lines of the royal lineage and particular segments of chiefly houses. Naturally the *ẹmẹṣẹ* were concerned to put to their own personal advantage the opportunities and the knowledge that their duties gave them; and the effective power of the *Ọwa* was thus again limited by the interests of his agents. One important official the *Ọwa* could make for himself: the *Babaileoke*, or head of the royal slaves, since his predecessor's would have died at his late royal master's funeral.[38] Even so, successive *Babaileoke* seem to have been able to institutionalize, like the major *iwọle* chiefs such as *Ọdọle* and *Risawẹ*, the power which flowed to them as organs of the centre, and here too the *Ọwa* himself confronted a political actor with a good deal of autonomy. By the nineteenth century the *Babaileoke* had become an *onile* for many rural communities, had acquired extensive powers in relation to disputed lands and was a major figure in the politics of the capital.[39]

But despite these checks, an *Ọwa* could usually look forward to the waxing of his power throughout his reign. By indirect means he could exercise a significant degree of influence in the filling of titles which fell vacant, even where they were 'owned' by a quarter or a lineage. As he learnt more about the workings of the *Afin* he became less dependent on its various sitting tenants. As he grew into his position, he would attract more clients of his own and his great chiefs would come to resent his growing independence of action. It was at this stage, on several occasions in Ijesha history, that the *Ọwa* with his following overreached himself to provoke a hostile reaction of the Ijesha. The last such occasion before the nineteenth century was a famous riot during the reign of *Ọwa* Bilagbayo: a son of the *Ọwa* seduced a wife of the *Lọọgan*, a quarter-chief of Okesha, triggering off a general insurrection, resulting in the death of a *Risawẹ* and the expulsion of *ọmọba* from the town.[40]

However much the chiefs sought to check the *Ọwa*'s power, they could not function as a political elite without it. They mediated between the *Ọwa* and their people, just as the *orișa* mediated between men and Olodumare, the Supreme Being. In many matters, such as the granting of land, custom prescribed that the *Ọwa* should not deal directly with his subjects, but only through his chiefs. But the power of that centre was a condition of their own social existence. In the foregoing account, most emphasis has been placed on the positive role of the centre as the point from which resources were distributed downwards. But Ijesha culture also recognizes, indeed emphasizes, its negative aspects too. A chief protected his people from the centre, and to that extent also depended on its negative qualities. The *Afin* was a mysterious and terrifying place, with its haughty *ẹmẹsẹ* and secretive *iwọle*, its forbidden dark recesses and its shrines of many sacrifices. The *Ọwa* rarely left it. The attitude of ordinary Ijesha towards him was of the greatest respect, but mingled with fear rather than affection. A corollary of the *Ọwa*'s responsibility to promote life, through the rituals he performed and the medicines he controlled, was his right to take it, judicially or in sacrifice. Human sacrifice was a regular practice until it was discontinued in the reign of *Ọwa* Bepo (*c.* 1875–92). The victims were slaves, but an unprotected stranger or anyone without a chiefly patron was at risk. The *Ọwa* was seen by the Ijesha as:

> a f'ọmọ rubọ ki yeye rẹ wa k'arufin ana
> he who sacrifices the child and requires the mother to come on the morrow to pray the sacrifice is accepted![41]

HOUSEHOLD AND LINEAGE

The foregoing account of Ilesha's politics has made frequent reference to two social institutions whose internal relations are largely played out in the idiom of kinship even if they are only partly governed by its norms – namely the household and the lineage. Something requires to be said about each of them.[42]

As the nuclear unit of the political system of the community, the household was a residential, rather than a kinship unit, though most typically its core was a patrilineage of short span. The same word, 'house' or *ile*, can be used for the building itself, the household or residential group, or any lineage based there, whether or not all its members also live there. Before the 1920s, when a trend set in for every married man to want to build his own house, households were much larger, embracing several married brothers or even cousins and more than one generation of adults. It would also appear that a much higher proportion of household-heads held quarter titles than is the case nowadays. Satisfactory reconstruction of household size or type for before the mid nineteenth century is made more difficult by the fact that the period of intensified warfare from the 1850s to the 1890s saw the appearance of what have been called *ologun* or warrior households, whose structure was provided less by an agnatic core than by a warrior's following, greatly inflated by large numbers of slaves.[43] These rather overshadow recollection of earlier household forms, though it is obvious that chiefs' households must always have had some of these features, augmented as they were with a plurality of wives, slaves and followers.

Ijesha recollections and the earliest reports of visitors agree that the Ijesha house differed considerably from those of the Oyo-Yoruba. Instead of buildings grouped round a large central space, the house was a complex of small linked courtyards called *akodi*; in the middle of each was a small impluvium, sometimes only a few feet across, enclosed by a covered colonnade off which led the rooms, perhaps six to ten per *akodi*.[44] Each *akodi* might house one section of the household – say one adult male and his wives, or all the descendants of a single senior woman – and nowadays estimates are often given of the sizes of ancestral houses in terms of numbers of *akodi*. Four or five *akodi* seems typical for an averagely large house, but larger numbers are mentioned for the more conspicuous warriors of the mid nineteenth century, such as the house of Fafisibe (seven *akodi*) in the then new quarter of Orogba.[45] And it was not only the households created *de novo* by particular warriors which were so large; under those conditions of chronic insecurity, agnatic kin stuck together, producing households as large as that of the Oluodo segment of the royal lineage, also at Orogba, which comprised twelve *akodi* in the mid 1890s, or the household of the sons of the *Loja Iwoye* at Ifofin, which is said to have sent seventy men to war in the 1860s.[46] Still, these very large concentrations did occur under circumstances fairly exceptional in Ijesha history and I think it fair to assume that many ordinary households, particularly before the wars, were of one or two *akodi* in size.

What sort of unit was the household? Here we must be wary of assuming – as writers of diverse theoretical persuasions seem to – that because households exist as definite residential and political entities and much of the economic activity of subsistence is organized through domestic roles, the household is to be viewed as a kind of nuclear economic unit, a single enterprise managed by its head as regards both production and consumption, in a 'domestic mode of production'.[47] The head, whether the senior resident male of the lineage or the warrior-founder, settled its members' disputes, represented their interests in the immediate public sphere (the quarter) and could certainly make *some* call on the members for labour and produce. But he was not, as far as I can tell, necessarily in the position of being the manager of a single enterprise or economic unit. It might come closest to this in small households with only one married male, and in warrior-led households as regards 'production' of slaves, booty and some trade-goods through the coordinated military manpower of the house – but this does not imply that subsistence activities of the household members were also so coordinated. Rather a household should be seen as a grouping of partially autonomous economic enterprises, co-resident and so politically unified under its head, whose relations evolved with the evolution of the domestic groupings involved and whose coordination only partly derived from the influence of the head. We need to look in turn at the positions of married males, unmarried males and women.

Fully adult (i.e. married) males farmed for themselves, with their children and personal dependants, even if (as was not necessarily the case, since land-rights might be acquired through their mothers) they farmed in the same locality as other adult members of the household. Of course co-resident agnates gave one another occasional help, and younger brothers and unmarried adult men might farm in close conjunction with a senior brother (especially one born of the same mother) or father. Younger boys worked wholly under the direction of their fathers, but their eventual move to partial, and then complete, economic autonomy was envisaged. None the less this autonomy was slow in coming, only being fully obtained at marriage. A fair proportion of the labour-time of a young adult, resident under his father's roof, would be given to his prospective father-in-law. Young men organized collective work-parties among themselves (*ẹbẹṣẹ*) to help one another discharge these obligations. Even when a young man had a plot of his own, he was still liable to contribute to large-scale tasks (bush-clearing, house-roofing etc.) under his seniors' authority.

Women were likewise differentially subordinated to authority within the household. Women were affianced before the age of puberty and married in their mid-teens. Except for unmarried girls and a few older women who returned to their father's household, moved to a house built by their sons, or were rich enough to have their own houses, the women of a household had married its male members and were ranked in seniority according to the length of their membership. General social respect for seniority, the influence of senior wives with their husband and the fact that young wives were more restricted by pregnancy and young children meant that more of the household chores devolved upon them. Though they did not undertake the major role in farming, woman did undertake light agricultural tasks (such as weeding), helped by processing farm products, and catered for the agricultural household. It was especially young wives who accompanied their husband to his farm hamlet (*aba* or *abulẹ*), receiving a share of the produce as recompense to feed them and their children. Older wives, who were not so likely to farm, might be supplied by their children.[48] In a sample of women economically active in the period before 1920, all but 14% had (as far as was remembered of them) avocations other than just being 'housewives' or going to farm with their husbands.[49] 62% engaged in trade of some kind, including much selling of cooked food, and 24% practised crafts, overwhelmingly weaving and dyeing of cloth. Much of this activity began as a kind of part-time extension of a woman's domestic role (e.g. the preparation of cooked food for sale), but as she grew older she might devote herself to it more full-time, using the cash proceeds to advance herself and her children. Weaving especially was done by older women.[50] All these avocations, even when they involved capital, raw materials or facilities supplied by the husband or through the household, were essentially distinct enterprises rather than aspects of a joint household enterprise managed by the husband. For example, relations between the enterprises depended on negotiated exchanges (which by the late nineteenth century often involved cash transfers) between all the parties rather than on the husband's allocative decisions, though he had a role in settling disputes between co-wives. The household's overall unity, then, was realized more as a small polity than a small economy.

Within the household the smallest social unit was a woman and her own children (*ọmọiya*). This is the point at which to start talking of descent, since here are present both the agnatic and cognatic principles. Descent was, in the first instance, agnatic: other things being equal, children belonged to their father's house, sons built houses or farmed on land to which they had claim through their father and were considered eligible for hereditary titles by virtue of descent in the male line from an earlier holder. The core of the typical household was a group of male agnates and, as throughout Yorubaland, the word for an agnatic descent group is *idile* (literally: *idi ile*, 'the stock of the house'). To this day the typical 'family meeting' (*ipade idile*) comprises, in the main, men and women who share agnatic descent from an ancestor two or three generations above the senior living generation. Nowadays they are likely to live in a number of separate households, not necessarily adjacent, but it is tempting to think that many of these groups are the descendants of agnates still co-resident just before the large households began to be replaced by smaller ones in the years around 1920.

The other main word for a kin grouping is *ẹbi*, for which the best translation is probably 'extended family', with its vagueness of reference; its root is *bi*, which means both to 'bear' and 'beget' children, and it frequently includes matrilateral as well as agnatic kin. The importance of the mother's side in Ijesha kinship has two principal sources: polygyny, and the position of women in their own *idile*.

Polygyny, whose political aspects have already been emphasized, distances children from their fathers and creates particularly close bonds between mothers and children, and among the children of one mother (*ọmọiya*). Property is divided in inheritance, not according to the number of children, but according to the number of wifely stocks (*idi*). The standard explanation given by Ijesha for why titles (in theory) rotate between different segments of a lineage refers, not to simple agnatic segmentation, but to the fact that the founding title-holder, being a great man, had many wives whose several sets of sons had equal claim on their father's title. When chiefs' houses broke up, or a segment was hived off as when a new quarter was founded, they sometimes did so on the basis of one wife's children going to live together, producing the phenomenon of small co-resident lineages whose apical ancestor (after whom the house is named) is a woman, but whose claim on the title is still agnatic.[51] The 'mother's side' was relatively more significant for the sons of great chiefs, since in their houses there would be more anonymity, to say nothing of jealousy and fears of sorcery, between rival segments. In the largest household of all, the *Afin*, sons of the *Ọwa* were by custom sent off to their mother's village to be brought up. This could also occur, more evidently as a result of situational pressures than as a norm, in the households of other great chiefs: a son of Ogedengbe, the hyper-polygynous warlord of late nineteenth-century Ilesha, was sent to grow up in Iperindo, his mother's village, since 'in his father's house nobody knew him' and there was dangerous rivalry between the children of different wives.[52]

Links established through the mother were the more important because of the fact that an Ijesha woman did not on marriage relinquish her membership of her natal lineage. A woman could continue to attend her natal lineage's meetings and inherit land and property through her father. Notable daughters of the lineage figure prominently in meetings and petitions about such lineage affairs as titles. Sometimes these rights and interests were transmitted from a woman to her children, and so to the members of another patrilineage. According to the 1974 Survey, 9% of respondents who owned land had some land from their mother's side. A higher proportion attended meetings of their mother's lineage, usually in addition to attending their father's, the ratio of mother's side to father's side attendances being 64 : 305. A number of reasons were given for attending mother's side meetings. Men notable in their own right might be prevailed on to attend, thus enhancing the political weight of their mother's lineage ('because I am an illustrious son of the family', said one respondent with no false modesty). A man might also attend for the opposite reason: as another respondent put it, 'I have no solid father's side.' Men who had chosen to live in the compound land of their mother's side would be likely to attend the family meeting there in addition (in most cases) to their paternal family meeting; men who had farmland from their mother's side were rather less likely to so attend. All these reasons are to do with the formation of political interest groups. Other reasons seem more affectual than utilitarian: one man loved his mother so much he could not 'lose her side', another's mother died young so he needed to represent her, another was the eldest son and had to represent his mother since she was old.

So the system yields various possibilities of matrifiliation. They arise from the workings of patrilineality in its specific Ijesha form, even though they produce ties which crosscut or supplement agnatic ties pure and simple; and they are facilitated by the existence of a residential framework, in the quarters, which has no basis in agnatic descent.

What, then, of the lineage itself? This word, 'lineage', carries such a burden of use in anthropology that it is hard to employ without being tendentious. In particular the basic feature of its being a group recruited on the basis of shared unilineal descent hints at its also being corporate and segmentary. In fact, 'lineages' have quite different sociological properties at the different levels at which they exist in Ilesha.

Nowadays lineages function at three main levels in Ilesha: those of very short span, two to three generations at most, which are co-resident in a single household; those of somewhat greater span, four to five generations at most, whose members are not co-resident in a single house but may well live adjacent to one another, and set up 'family meetings' to handle their joint business; and what Ijesha call 'chieftaincy families', groupings of all those considered eligible for the major titles, represented as lineages of usually six to ten generations back to the first holder. Their solidarity was evident in shared funeral rites, cult memberships, the possession and regulation of blocs of land where most of their members farmed and such practices as widow-inheritance from senior to junior brother. Most important of all, a small-span, co-resident lineage, where it was recognized as part of a larger 'chieftaincy family', gave its members access to title and some claim on the patronage of the current title-holder.

The large chieftaincy families or titled lineages – the four largest of which embrace about a third of the total population – only functioned very partially and intermittently as corporate groups. It is true they gave a definite identity to their members, often expressed in distinctive personal names, *oriki* (praise-names), cults and facial or bodily scarifications.[53] But their members lived dispersed in many quarters of the town and so lacked a facility for collective political action possessed by the smaller lineages localized as households within quarters (see Map 3.3). Their farmlands too

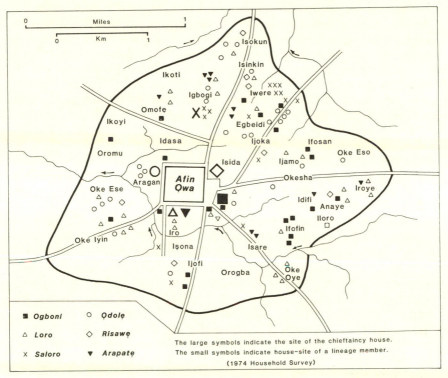

Map 3.3   Ilesha: lineage and residence

were scattered in many locations, this scatter being hardly less evident among members of the major segments of these lineages (Map 4.2, p.60). For in every generation some men got land in other ways than through inheritance of a portion of what was already recognized as land belonging to their lineage: from their mother's side, by fresh grant of vacant land by district chiefs or carved from virgin forest by the *Qwa*'s authority.

It has been suggested elsewhere that the major axis of conflict in Yoruba towns was lineage conflict.[54] At least in recent centuries, this can hardly be so with Ilesha's major titled lineages considered in their entirety. When title-holders were in conflict – say a *Loro* and an *Qdqle* – it does not follow that the entire *Qdqle* and *Loro* lineages would be involved. They would merely be one possible recruitment ground for each chief's following, whose exact composition would also depend on the title-holder's personal network of connexions and *ad hoc* features of the situation. Indeed, these large lineages were activated politically more as arenas of conflict among their own members than as solidary conflict groups in the arena of the town's politics. The largest lineages meet

53

infrequently and mostly because of titles. Lineages which have a number of titles – such as the royal lineage with its village-heads, or *Loro*'s with the *Lotun* of many quarters – meet to discuss their allocation: the *omoba* with the *Bajimo*, an *Are* chief who must be matrilaterally linked to the royal lineage, the *Loro* people with the *Yegbata* of Idasa quarter, the senior *Lotun*. All putative agnatic male descendants of the first holder of a title are eligible in principle to hold it, and succession contests bring the major segments (and sometimes fractions within them), to which they belong, into collision with one another. Despite an ideal of lineage solidarity, holding that a single candidate should be presented to the *Owa* and chiefs, this almost never happens with large lineages and major titles. Rather, rival contestants solicit support from powerful chiefs and other interest groups outside the lineage, who thus exercise much control over the outcome. A standard technique of competition is to impugn the descent of rivals and hence the legitimacy of entire lineages. The size and dispersion of the large lineages, and the fact that titles have, on occasion, been filled by other than agnatic descendants of earlier holders,[55] make this plausible.

The segmentary lineage, its structure produced by steady demographic increase handled according to particular norms of descent, is always something of an ideal. Ijesha lineages, at the widest level, are particularly divergent from the model, especially when compared with lineages in societies like the Igbo or Tiv. Demographic expansion is particularly uneven, being conditioned by which individuals and segments get titles, and thus extraordinary opportunities for increase of progeny. The genealogical representation of the lineage, especially at its upper end where major recognized segments unite as the stocks of 'sons' of the founding ancestor, is highly contested and repeatedly reconstructed. Larger segments may divide, smaller segments aggregate or hitch themselves to larger ones, the segments of recent title-holders seek to cancel out the claims of descendants of remoter holders. In this latter tactic, they are assisted by the fact that sons or grandsons of recent holders stand a much better chance than lineage-members more remotely descended from a title-holder of becoming chiefs. For they are likely to have fresher links with the *Afin*, with other chiefs and with other people who have an interest in the title in question. The same circumstance leads to the 'open' titles often in fact being filled with the close kin of recent holders, thus giving an extra focus to what are strictly non-titled lineages.[56] Thus lineages are produced by the politics of the town, and not just by norms of descent. Especially is this true of the royal lineage,[57] of whose politics more is to be said in the next chapter.

4

Town and district

It is a bias of Yoruba studies, not avoided so far in this monograph, that socio-spatial relations within the boundaries of the major political units, the kingdoms, are quite subordinated to relations within the capitals, each treated as a kind of point-source of power within its kingdom, and to relations between these point-sources, which make up the geopolitics of a wider region. Characteristically this bias is sustained by the dominant conceptions of Yoruba culture, which do emphasize the town-capital (*ilu* and *ode*) and present all the rest (all subordinate communities and 'rural' settlement and activity) as dependent extensions of it. In Ilesha itself, the contrast between the capital and the district around is summed up in the couplets *ile/oko* (i.e. 'house'/'farm'), or *ilu/ileto* (i.e. 'town'/'village') which has an identical reference.[1] But while this is fair enough for Ilesha's relations with those villages, otherwise called *aba* or *abule*, which were simply the farm residences of people whose *ile* (meaning both primary residence and lineage) were based in Ilesha, it is profoundly misleading in the case of a large number of subordinate towns. Places like Ibokun and Ijebu-jesha, which were not founded from Ilesha and are certainly considered by their own citizens to be *ilu*, are also classified as *oko* in an Ilesha perspective.[2] It is already well recognized in Yoruba studies that capital towns relate to subordinate towns with their own farmland as well as to settlements within the capital's area of farms, and Lloyd has proposed a useful typology of town/district relations which embodies different combinations of these variables.[3] But empirically the typological approach brings problems. Many Ijesha settlements are of a mixed or transient type, and their overall character should be viewed less as a 'social fact' than as the aggregate effect of whether their residents were primarily based there or in the capital. A greater difficulty is that it tempts us to see the overall pattern of capital/district relations of a particular kingdom at a particular time as the expression of a fairly stable cultural norm – the Ijesha this way and the Egba that, just as the Yoruba are said to have one settlement pattern while the Igbo have another. And this really pre-empts proper consideration of the object of our enquiry: capital/district relations as a product of constant development.

In setting a historical baseline we face severe problems of evidence, though in the case of Ijeshaland we are helped by a remarkable document: a manuscript entitled 'Towns destroyed by the Ibadans in the Ijesha country', written by Philip Jose Meffre, an Ijesha returned from slavery in Brazil who served as clerk and general go-between to the then *Qwa*, Bepo.[4] Though dated 1882, it would seem on internal evidence to give a picture of the settlements of the kingdom at a time some time before the upheavals of the middle of the century.[5] Nothing of this kind exists for any other Yoruba kingdom. It itemizes some 163 Ijesha settlements of all kinds, including some of what are now regarded as independent kingdoms such as Akure, Ogotun and Ido-Ekiti, organized by the seven roads: I Okesha, II Ijebu(-jesha), III Ibokun, IV Muroko, V Ibodi, VI Iwara and VII Irojo, each named after a quarter, subordinate community or market through which it runs. Over 80% of these settlement names are still extant – and very few present-day settlements of any size known to have existed before 1900 are missing – which argues for a high degree of continuity in the approximate location of settlements and provides us with a fairly stable framework for considering the evolution of capital/district relations; but little can be inferred from it about the sociological character of the settlements it itemizes. Oral traditions, collected in nearly 90 district communities, give much help, but they are much more fragmentary than those of Ilesha and have been greatly affected by competing communal self-aggrandizement this century. Something, too, can be inferred from the nature of contemporary links between villages and Ilesha, and of rural chieftaincy. But all this data needs evaluating in the light of twentieth-century relations between Ilesha and the district. Consequently, this chapter will lay less emphasis on giving an account of the 'traditional' (roughly pre-1870) state of affairs and more on trying to identify the enduring processes by which individuals and communities may move more or less close to Ilesha, and seek to exploit or escape relations with her. It is as well to be aware of the danger implicit in such a method: that some temporally or locally specific factors in the concrete history will get trimmed to accommodate the processes which seem to be most typical.

THE PATTERN OF RURAL SETTLEMENT

There is no choice but to start from today's disposition of Ijesha settlement, though it is both more extensive and more dense than it was before 1895. In the mid nineteenth century, Iperindo on Road VII, Igangan and Ifewara on Road VI and Oshu and Itagunmodi on Road V, except for a few hamlets beyond Ifewara, marked the limit of permanent settlement in those directions, as well as the arc running from Oshu via Iloba and Oke Osin on to Oke Ibode on Road IV. A region of uncertain extent, beyond

Oke Osin to the north-west and running up to the Oshun river, was abandoned under Oyo pressure in the 1820s.[6] Beyond the areas of settlement lay the virgin forest or *igbo dudu* ('dark bush') that marked the no-man's land between Ilesha and Ife to the south-west and Ondo to the south, the domain of the wandering hunter, the best kola trees and large game. Elsewhere, apart from the natural barrier of the high ridge to the east, settlements and cultivated land were found right up to the kingdom's frontiers in the more open north, and along Road I to the south-east.

If we leave aside the areas only opened up this century, Ijeshaland today falls into two zones, which correspond roughly (and not accidentally) with Ijesha Southern Division (latterly Atakunmosa Local Government Area) and Ijesha Northern Division (Obokun Local Government Area). The first of these contains Ilesha, and is the area in which farm lands held by Ilesha household heads overwhelmingly fall (see Map 4.2). Moreover, its settlements tend to be smaller in size than those of the second, more northerly area: according to the 1963 Census, 'Ijesha Southern' (i.e. all the Southern Division less Ilesha town) had 138,470 inhabitants, counted in 157 settlements, while 'Ijesha Northern' (i.e. all the Northern Division) had 177,428 inhabitants in 82 settlements. The real density of the farming population in the Southern area is in fact higher, since a sizeable proportion of it would be enumerated in Ilesha town. In both areas there are many very small settlements, mere handfuls of houses. Many of these, and in the Northern area most of them, are inhabited by tenant farmers who have migrated into the area this century, and so are irrelevant to a reconstruction of the pre-colonial pattern.[7] The inhabitants of the larger settlements of the Northern area, since their *ilu* are so much smaller than Ilesha, have less far to go to farm than Ilesha people and so have less need of farm hamlets. So we have a rural area sociologically closer to Ilesha, in the south, and another sociologically more remote, with settlements larger in average size. In the south, with which the discussion will be most concerned, settlement size is associated with settlement type – the smaller settlements being more likely to be *aba* (farm hamlets) of Ilesha people. But there are plenty of exceptions, and there is a fair degree of intermingling of the two polar-types of rural settlement, to say nothing of settlements which fall between.

All Ilesha men – that is, those who regard Ilesha as their *ilu*, have the mass of their kinsfolk there, hold their family meetings there, seek direct patronage from chiefs there and contest titles there – had access to farm-land, situated anything up to twelve miles away from town. As already mentioned, the major title-holders held large tracts just outside the town, worked in part for their own direct benefit by dependent male relatives and slaves; but other members of their lineages also had claims on the land, owing the chief small annual customary payments of produce (*iwifọ*); and other men might choose, and be able, to 'beg' land there, cultivating it on an annual basis and acknowledging the chief's rights by means of *iwifọ*. From oral evidence relating to early in this century, before farmland had

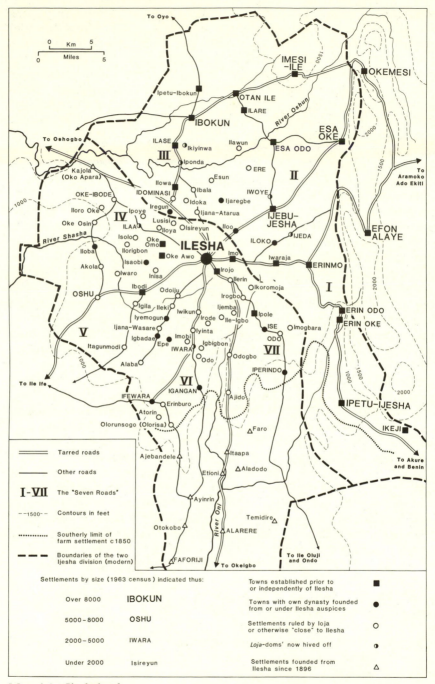

Map 4.1 Ijeshaland

58

acquired a cash-value or cocoa-growing was at all common, it seems that the use of title land near town might be attractive to a young man who had quarrelled with his father or who wanted to go it alone, and to stay in the town, perhaps as the client of the title-holder. But most farmland was held at some distance from the town, in tracts granted to a first settler by the *Qwa*, either directly or through the head of an existing rural community, and farmed by his descendants. Two further general points need to be made about the disposition of farmland. Firstly, there is a definite tendency for men who live in a particular segment of the town (defined in relation to one of the seven radial roads) to farm in the corresponding segment of the district (see Map 4.2). Secondly, members of the largest titled lineages may be found farming all over the district. This applies most strongly to members of the royal lineage, for a reigning *Qwa*'s sons were typically sent to their mothers' rural settlement, where they were given land, or else they acquired land in those particular rural communities (of which more will be said shortly) ruled by a member of the royal lineage as *Loja* or, sometimes, they got a fresh grant of land which their descendants inherited in the usual way. The royal lineage as such held no land except what was available in the grounds of the *Afin* for its current occupants, though of course the *Qwa* himself had extensive general rights over the allocation and use of land throughout the kingdom.

Rural houses of Ilesha people are either dispersed about the actual land farmed, or clustered in small hamlets round the house of a senior kinsman or first settler, or situated in village communities of a more enduring kind. The variety which characterizes much of the zone of Ilesha farm-settlement may be briefly illustrated from an area running out from three to eight miles from the walls of Ilesha along Road IV (Muroko).[8] Nowadays it contains over 50 distinct settlements, most of which are very small farm hamlets occupied by people who, even if they do spend more of their time at the farm, draw their claims from some Ilesha connexion. Nowadays many of the rural residents are in fact Oyo or Urhobo tenants of Ijesha owners. Most were established early in this century, some on the site of an earlier settlement abandoned in the wars to which the founder, having established his local connexions, was directed by local people; others were fresh settlement sites, whether or not local land claims already existed. The greater security of this century has probably encouraged a more dispersed settlement than existed before. The area includes largish tracts of lands long held by Ilesha titled families: the *Sawe* family has its main rural settlement (Aba Sawe) and at least three other hamlets set up this century by *Sawe* connexions (who include other lineages from Ijamo, the Ilesha quarter of which Chief *Sawe* is head); and two separate tracts, around Fagbore and Oke Osin, are held by members of Chief *Loro*'s lineage (or rather of segments of it). The area round Abebeyun – a hamlet which, being sited at a road junction, is on the way to something better – has been for long closely associated with the *Qwa*. In the late nineteenth century it is said to have been farmed by royal slaves under two

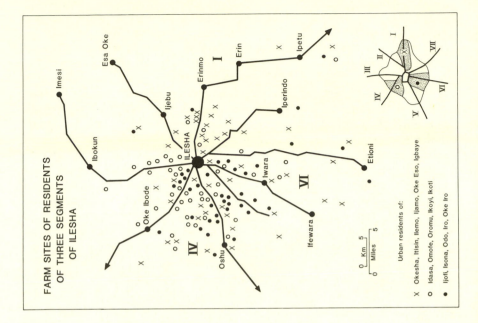

FARM SITES OF RESIDENTS
OF THREE SEGMENTS
OF ILESHA

Urban residents of:

X   Okesha, Itisin, Ilemo, Ijamo, Oke Eso, Igbaye

O   Idasa, Omofe, Oromu, Ikoyi, Ikoti

●   Ijofi, Isona, Odo, Iro, Oke Iro

0   Km   5
0   Miles   5

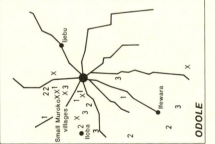

ODOLE

FARM SITES OF MEMBERS OF
THREE TITLED ILESHA LINEAGES:
OGBONI, ODOLE, LORO

Information from 1974 Sample Survey.
In each case the principal settlements of
which the chief is *onile* are marked.

The numbers signify the conventionally
recognised major segment ('ruling house')
of the lineage to which the respondent
holding land in that location claimed
to belong.

X signifies that while the lineage was
claimed, it was not possible to be certain
about which segment the respondent
was affiliated to.

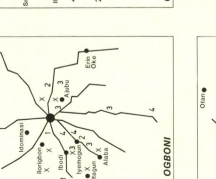

OGBONI

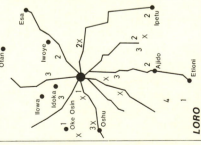

LORO

Map 4.2   Ilesha and its farms

60

bailiffs, Gbamohun and Loguniko, responsible to Chief *Babaileoke*, and in the 1930s was known as Aba Prince, because *Qwa* Aromolaran's eldest son, S.A. Adeniran, had a cocoa farm there; now the senior local man around is the descendant of an enterprising diviner who was granted land by *Qwa* Lowolodu (1893–94) and, with supporters from Ilesha, expelled the slaves to carve out his own farm.[9] Virtually all the foundation stories of these settlements indicate the founder's very close links with an Ilesha lineage with existing local land-rights or with a rural chief with authority to grant land, like the *Loja* of Oke Awo; and usually too they stress the founder's prowess, his capacity as a warrior or a diviner, his reputation as an *aladanla* ('a great man with the cutlass') or an *akikanju* (an intrepid, 'pushful' person), his preparedness to strike out on his own. Such small settlements are liable to shift their sites; they are highly personal, very often named after their founder (as Fagbore), his town title (Lotun, Lanaye) or his nickname (Aba Prince, Oko Babaibadan – 'farm of the old man who returned from Ibadan'). Such names are almost entirely missing from Meffre's list of 1882, which does not prove that such settlements did not exist then – merely that they were small and not regarded as permanent fixtures of the local scene.

But these hamlets exist among a small number, around twelve, of larger, more permanent settlements, most of which do figure in Meffre's list. These vary in their size, the attachment to Ilesha of their inhabitants, the time and circumstances of their origins, the completeness of their communal institutions and the nature of their political link with Ilesha. Four main categories can be distinguished.

Firstly, there are Oke Awo and Oke Omo, small secluded settlements of twenty to thirty houses, barely three miles from Ilesha, which have their own hereditary ruling houses, sets of *iwarefa* chiefs, distinctive cults and clear traditions of foundation from Ife independent of Ilesha.[10] Though they each paid *iwisin* to the *Qwa* through *Lejofi* as their *onile*, and used to organize collective hunts (*iwote*) to provide meat for the *Qwa* annually at Ogun, it is evident that their rulers were conceded by the *Qwa* to have extensive rights to grant land in the area, stretching for several miles away from Ilesha. Despite the close ties, by intermarriage and other, with Ilesha, Ilesha families do not, on the whole, live in these villages but in their own hamlets around.

Secondly, there are Ilaa and Isaobi, autonomous communities like Oke Omo and Oke Awo, but with traditions of foundation from Ilesha several centuries ago.[11] Ilaa claims to have been established by Atakunmosa after his return from Benin: there was a man farming there already, but Atakunmosa sent a son with powerful medicines who established a local dynasty. A shrine to Atakunmosa stands by the market. Isaobi, a smaller place and nearer Ilesha, also has its own dynasty and chiefs, as well as distinctive local cults, notably that of its founder Lejugbe, who came from Ife but via Ilesha; and the *Asaobi* shares a ritual link – the worship of Lejugbe – with the community's *onile*, the *Risawẹ*, whose first ancestor is said to have been reared in Isaobi. Small though Isaobi is, its chiefs are vehement that it is an *ilu*.[12] Whereas Ilesha people farm in the close vicinity of both communities, they seem more likely to have houses in the village, as against in nearby hamlets, in the case of Ilaa, where some of them hold village titles too. Even so, the core of Ilaa is 'Ilaa people'.

Thirdly, there is a group of five communities – Oke Ibode, Iloya, Isolo, Isireyun, Lusisi (Oko Igbo) – ranging in size from Oke Ibode, the largest settlement in the area with a population of 3,819 (including hamlets) to others which are hardly more than hamlets.[13] These were all more recently founded than the first two groups, but still well before the nineteenth century; and all are ruled by members of the Ilesha royal lineage who are styled *Loja* or else take their title from the place-name. But they vary greatly in composition and local identity. Two have no set of *iwarẹfa* chiefs and their *Lojas* are emphatic that they are not *ilu*: they are virtually farm hamlets – in one case virtually only for members of the *Loja*'s segment of the Ilesha royal lineage – and their residents look to Ilesha as their primary seat. The other three have local titles and a mixture of families who meet locally and who meet in Ilesha. In one of them, Lusisi (formerly Oko Igbo), the *Loja* claims that the title is restricted to his line of the Oluodo segment of the royal dynasty, and said that they held their family meeting in the village; and since none of that line has for generations been elevated to become *Ọwa*, it looks as if a purely local dynasty, as at Ilaa and elsewhere in Ijeshaland (e.g. Iwara, Iponda, Iwoye), is in process of formation.

Fourthly, there are three settlements – Oke Osin, Ipoye and Ilorigbon – which are definitely not transient hamlets but which have not yet achieved autonomy under their own chiefs.[14] All were founded well before the upheavals of the nineteenth century. Oke Osin, which since the 1920s has developed as something of a rural centre (primary school, market and churches) for the hamlets around, was founded in what must then have been the remotest bush in this direction by Logunaro, *Loro* of Ilesha and now recognized as the founding ancestor of one of that great lineage's major segments. He was directed to the land by the *Loja* of Oke Awo. The area was abandoned after the disturbances of the 1820s and 1830s and reoccupied later in the century under *Loro* Aoyo. Though members of several other Ilesha lineages farm hereabouts, its core is without doubt the lineage of *Loro* Logunaro, whose enlarged hamlet it is. Though local titles are named including an 'Ọlọsin of Oke Osin' they are not officially recognized in Ilesha, and the Logunaro family meet in Ilesha, at the house of its head, who is *Lọtun* of Iroye quarter. What is noteworthy here is how tenacious may be the Ilesha links of a lineage powerful in the capital, preserving the essentially *aba* status of a district settlement, despite settlers of other origins and the passage of many generations. Ipoye is also associated with a particular titled Ilesha lineage, that of Chief *Ẹṣira*, and its foundation story suggests that it is the site of lands initially granted to the first *Ẹṣira* on his arrival in Ilesha. From it and from three or four adjacent hamlets (e.g. Osugongo) there farm lineage members and others connected with the title, personal dependants or residents of Odo Esira quarter in town. But it would seem that despite these continuing links with Ilesha, there are enough people who are virtually permanently resident in Ipoye for there to have developed a local title system as well as a local cult: until the 1920s the people worshipped an *Oriṣa Upoye* as well as going to Owena, the major festival of Odo Esira. Its chief, however, is drawn alternately from two Ilesha lineages (Esira and '*Ọbanla*')[15] and is styled '*Balẹ*', a title unusual to Ijesha but common elsewhere, with the clear connotation of the head of a less than autonomous settlement. Finally, Ilorigbon, a small village of a dozen houses, with two tiny dependent hamlets of its own. Of considerable but uncertain antiquity – it claims to be older than Isolo and, like many settlements around, was desolated in the wars of the last century – it is the centre of an important cult of Ogun Lade. The festival is coordinated with the Ilesha Ogun festival, when the *Ọwa* sends down one of his *ẹmẹṣẹ* with an *ọpa aṣẹ* ('staff of authority') to Ilorigbon, and the community has a fitting *onile* in the *Ogboni* of Ilesha. The village includes Ilesha people, for whom it is a hamlet, as well as four families who meet here. The only local title – apart from Ogun Lade's priest (*aoro*) – is that of *Lọyin*, which does not carry the authority of a chief or the recognition of the centre, but is merely a coordinator of local wishes.

The local minutiae of the preceding paragraphs well exemplify three general points: (i) the variety of types of settlement and their connexion with particular ways in which those who farm in a locality relate to the centre; (ii) the spatial intermingling of these types; and (iii) the equal variety in types of process. Except at the outer edge of settlement, a community's territory had clearly designated boundaries (*aala*), usually coincident with a stream or some other natural feature. These were pointed out to the earliest settler by the *ẹmẹṣẹ* of the *Ọwa* and the chief of any existing nearby settlement who 'showed the land' to the newcomer.[16] Within the territory land was allocated by the chief of the local community or else of the founder's lineage (who might be an Ilesha chief); but before the twentieth century, intra-community boundaries (i.e. between the farms of its members) were far from being absolutely definite and permanent, owing to the rotational bush-fallow system of farming and the existence of plenty of spare land. The leaders of rural communities were always anxious to attract extra settlers, and the foundation of new communities arose less from any absolute land shortage than from the desire of powerful men to carve out a fresh sphere for themselves or to settle their slaves and followings.

It is evident that scattered communities existed prior to the emergence of Ilesha, and that those near the centre were absorbed or transformed as Ilesha expanded.[17] Several other such communities as Oke Omo and Oke Awo stand close to Ilesha – Ibodi on Road V, Irojo on Road VII, Imo on Road I – and it is significant that two of these gave their names to the roads. Their rulers are closely associated with specific local cults – *Ọlọja Ibodi* of Aramfe, *Arojo* of Osun, *Onimọ* of Ifa – and they were discreetly respected by the *Ọwa*, even though Ilesha out-settlement passed through and beyond them. With Ibokun, Ijebu and Ipole, earlier centres of the kingdom, Ilesha preserved closer ritual relations.[18] Ipole soon sank to a minor rural cult-centre, of Ogun and the *Ọwa* Owari; and its locality was eventually permeated by Ilesha farms and settlements headed by *Lọjas* from the Ilesha dynasty. This direction, Road VII, remained slow to develop and only became important in the nineteenth century: Odo probably belongs to the mid-late seventeenth century and Iperindo ('settlement of elephant hunters') which was the limit of Ijesha authority in the nineteenth century, was probably later.[19] By contrast with Ipole, Ibokun and Ijebu were sizeable and powerful enough for Ilesha not to be able to extend her farmland up to or beyond them, though it does seem, to judge from the close connexions of Iwoye, Ilawun, Esun and Ere with Ilesha,[20] that Ilesha people were able to push their farms and authority into a thin salient between them. In any case, the more open country to the north of Ilesha, where the earlier centres of the kingdom had lain, was probably already extensively settled. So Ilesha's expansion was directed towards the west and the south, along the axes of Roads IV, V, VI and VII. At the same time her prowess in trade and war enabled her to control Road I, at times as far as Akure, and the autonomous communities of the north and east as far as the marches of Igbomina and Ekiti. In this direction, the towns claim diverse origins – either from Ife directly or from the east or south – and, except for Erin, none of them has close ritual links with Ilesha.[21]

Ilesha's own urban growth, as she established her regional hegemony, led not just to a demand for farmland but to the establishment of settlements which tended over time to acquire some degree of autonomy, modelling themselves, as far as they could, on other semi-independent communities in the district. It is to Atakunmosa that tradition attributes the appearance of a new kind of rural community: one sent out by Ilesha and ruled by a member of the royal lineage as its *Lọja*. The first six of these are usually given as Iwara, Ikiyinwa, Iwoye, Ilerin, Isagbe and Iponda, of which Iwara and Iwoye were the most significant.[22] Iwoye's position, so close to Ijebu-jesha, rather suggests an attempt by Ilesha to keep check on its sister community, as perhaps Ikiyinwa does in relation to Ibokun, but tradition is not helpful with details.[23] Iwara, being a settlement in the forest to the south, an area with fewer established communities, was more indicative of the future. Over the next few centuries further *lǫja*-settlements were set up, preponderantly and increasingly in this direction, as has continued up to this day. Other new settlements in the south, datable to the seventeenth or eighteenth centuries, were established under a looser control from Ilesha, having their own local dynasties from an early stage. These all involved some immigration from outside Ijesha-land – Ifewara from Ife, Igangan from north-western Ekiti and Igbomina, Ise from southern Ekiti – their founders being characterized as either disappointed contestants for titles at home who asked the *Ǫwa* for land to settle or as hunters or warriors who performed some service for the *Ǫwa* and were rewarded with land for themselves and their followers.[24] It is evident that they were located at what at the time must have been the limits of farm settlement, and the Igangan tradition that its founder Babarake drove off scattered hunters from 'Ijamo' (i.e. Ondo) implies that it meant a definite extension and firming up of the always vague frontier in this direction.

So Ilesha expanded and the manner of her involvement in the district around became diversified. This prompts two related questions. Why and how did new communities evolve, largely among populations who began by farming from Ilesha? What is the significance in this of the headship of so many of these new communities by members of the Ilesha royal house as *Lǫja*? It should not be regarded as unproblematic that new communities were set up, even granted the existence of a firm cultural model in the concept of the *ilu* with its *iwarefa* chiefs. Why should the farm-settlements having no local chief not continue to exist in this form for ever? It is much more understandable that groups immigrant to Ijeshaland, with independent relations among themselves around an existing leader, should constitute a new *ilu*, like Igangan or Ifewara; but to the extent that membership of one *ilu* (including eligibility for titles) is generally regarded as inconsistent with membership of another, there is a problem as to how individuals could come to accept the ultimate costs of severance from a powerful community of origin to attain a more immediate status in a new, much smaller, emergent community. It is, to start with, a matter of individuals making the movement 'away and out', but it is a movement which can only be completed when, as the result both of such individual actions and of a local and central recognition of it as a social fact, a distinct community is constituted.

We would be on very slippery ground if we simply assumed the applicability of contemporary processes to the earlier phases of Ilesha out-settlement. A more direct line of argument serves to make their relevance clearer. The modern distribution of populations with clear Ilesha links, the long-term synchrony of Ilesha's growth as a town and her out-settlement, and the evidence (presented in Chapters 2 and 3) that Ilesha's own growth was largely at the expense of other kingdoms, especially to the east, make it very likely that both farm settlements and district communities grew largely as the result of out-migration from Ilesha to her farms. Since the original pattern, preserved as *ile/oko* in the categories of the centre, was for these settlements to be the farm-hamlets of a population whose primary base, their *homes*, lay in Ilesha, we must look for the source of the division within Ilesha's population between (i) those who, despite their dependence on labour carried out on farms up to a dozen miles away, continued to have their primary homes and identities in the town, and (ii) those who, despite their original membership of the same social units as the above, began to derive their identities from a district settlement.

Which sections of Ilesha's population, then, were likely to move out, to turn their secondary habitations into a primary home? The foremost category must have been slaves. As the discussion in Chapter 2 suggested, slaves were heavily concentrated in the hands of chiefly title-holders, who depended on food produced by them to sustain their role as urban patrons. Very many, perhaps the majority, were virtually permanent rural residents. Chief Ataiyero, the *Aṣireyun*, said it was customary when a new settlement was made, for the *Owa* to send 201 of his 'retinue' – that is, very largely his slaves – to join it.[25] Chief *Babaileoke*, let us remember, combined his duties as head of the *Owa*'s slaves with control of land that reverted to the *Owa*'s hands (e.g. land whose owners had died intestate or whose disputed ownership had led to murder), the overseeing of farms worked by royal slaves and the informal *onile*-ship of all rural communities that had not yet acquired a recognized local chief or a regular *onile* in one of the senior title-holders at Ilesha.[26] Gureje Thompson's Etioni, where cocoa was later introduced to Ijeshaland, was largely populated by his slaves who first grew food crops, and many of its present settlers are their descendants: if they could not return to their original homes, their lack of connexions at Ilesha would give them no incentive to do other than make a new home in the farms where they could acquire land and local standing. It is often said that slaves in Yoruba and other lineage-based societies became over time assimilated to their masters' families, an *eru* (slave) becoming an *omo* (son) within one generation.[27] While it is true that slaves and their descendants do become assimilated over time (i.e. their slave origin is forgotten), 'assimilation to their master's lineage' is a misleading way of describing what most likely occurred. The slave descent of people who claimed, and perhaps were accorded by outsiders, membership of a particular lineage (e.g. they would be known as '*omo Odole*' or 'one of *Odole*'s people') would be remembered very much longer within the various town-houses of the lineage, where matters of eligibility for title were principally decided. Lineages segment, and as they do, particular lines effectively lose claim on the title and ultimately hive off together. Most slaves would tend to integrate into Ijesha society as their line hived off from the central or title-holding lines of descent: a process both of whose aspects would be assisted by the predominant residence of slaves in the farm settlements. The growth of

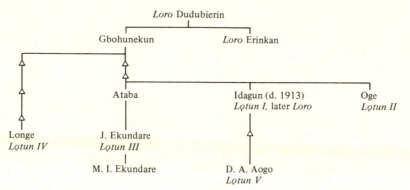

Fig. 4.1   A segment of the *Loro* lineage

Gbohunekun lost a contest for the *Loro* title to his younger brother Erinkan. He left his home at Anaye quarter with his people and set up in the bush to the south of Ilesha as a hunter. His brother found out where he was living and asked him to return to Ilesha. But the *Qwa* confirmed Gbohunekun in the land he had occupied with his people at Ajido (Road VII), where they lived for three generations. Around 1900 Ataba, who had fought at Kiriji, acquired houseland back in Ilesha, this time at Ifofin quarter, where his brother Idagun was *Lotun* (second chief in the quarter), later going on to become *Loro*. The lineage is now again Ilesha-based, at Ifofin, where four more of its members have been successively and to the exclusion of others *Lotun* since Idagun. Still its members farm at Ajido village, where other dependants live.
Source: Mr M. I. Ekundare, interview, 22 Dec. 1973.

these settlements into district communities was thus an aspect of the incorporation of slaves of alien origin.

  Slaves were not the only people who spent most of their time in the farm-hamlets, since agriculture was the predominant occupation of the entire adult male population. In addition it was usual, before the twentieth century, for any son of an *Qwa* to be reared in his mother's community, especially in the district – a practice confirmed by the dispersal of many *omoba* to safety in the district after the rising of the urban commoners against them in the time of *Qwa* Bilagbayo in the eighteenth century.[28] Standardly in the case of the *Qwa*ship, since contestants were meant already to be the *Loja* of a rural community, and commonly in the case of other titles, a new holder was said to be 'called from the farms' to take the title. Since those chosen for hereditary titles are usually not just *any* descendant of the first holder (i.e. apical ancestor) but someone closely related to a recent holder, those so called would in fact also be closely attached to an urban compound and inclined to attend family meetings there. And this suggests how the 'ruralization' of some lines of Ilesha origin could occur: through any of their members over several generations failing to get the title, so that the whole line drifted to obscurity, eventually reaching the point where, lacking good access to the front of power at the capital, they decided it was better to make their community in the district.

The same outcome might arise in another way: as the result of an unsuccessful contestant for a title deciding, whether in pique or from the calculation that he and his people could expect no help from someone they had opposed, to move out. Two lineage histories illustrate some of the possibilities. In the *Loro* history shown in Fig. 4.1, the process of 'ruralization' of Gbohunekun's descendants was arrested, perhaps just in time, by events in the late nineteenth century which caused much mobility and by the large number of town titles (the quarter *lotun*-ships) which served to sustain the capital connexions of *Loro* lineage members. The process went a decisive stage further in the case of the lineage whose greatest member has been Ilesha's great war-leader Ogedengbe (d. 1910), whose humble origins are always stressed in Ijesha accounts.[29] He was born at Atorin beyond Ifewara, which like Ajido lies in the zone where the limit of Ijesha farms had reached by the late eighteenth century; but according to family tradition, his ancestor had originally hailed, several generations back, from Ijoka quarter in Ilesha. No details of any lineage title were recorded and thus (if it had not been forgotten) one brake on the ruralization of the family, operative in the case of Gbohunekun's descendants, was missing. When Ogedengbe himself moved to Ilesha in the 1850s, it was as a virtual stranger, a young man on the make, seeking patronage there from Chiefs *Odole* and *Babaileoke*. Significantly, too, when in 1894 Ogedengbe clashed as an over-mighty subject with *Owa* Lowolodu, he proposed to withdraw with his people – in his case a vast following of slaves and soldiers from Kiriji – to establish his own settlement at Atorin.[30] Lowolodu resisted this, since it would have meant the instant creation of a powerful magnet to draw population away from the capital.

The decision to reside in and to claim a place as one's own – an aggregate of which decisions ultimately determines the accepted status of a settlement – is helpfully seen as a trade-off between the opportunity-costs of access to a regional power-centre and the relative independence of living in a smaller district community. The greater the regional power-centre was, the greater the resources which flowed through it but the more stratified was access to them. The opportunity-costs, therefore, varied according to each individual's standing in the political structure of the capital; and for many of those with poorer access, and a few who were dangerously eminent, it must have been more attractive to be a bigger fish in a smaller pond or even master of one's own pond. Thus the district communities grew. As they acquired, with permanent local residents, a communal structure of their own, their members also came to need, since Ilesha remained politically dominant, a new form of relationship with the capital. The characteristic phases of its evolution can be summarized thus:

(i) The rural dwellers are close enough to an Ilesha chief, recognized as his kinsfolk or dependants, to need no representation at the centre but through him. They pay no separate *iwisin* to the Owa, and the community has no *onile*.[31]

(ii) An exclusively rural core develops among those who live there. The settlement chooses a *lǫyin* and establishes links with the centre through the *Babaileoke*, though incipient, informal links may develop with some other town chief. The village people begin to commend themselves to the *Ǫwa* by making offerings each year at Ogun, Ifa or some other appropriate occasion.

(iii) Feeling they need a more authoritative local structure of coordination, they ask the *Ǫwa* to appoint a member of the royal lineage as their *Lǫja*. This will be done through Chief *Bajimǫ* at Ilesha, descended from the royal lineage on his mother's side, who is the intermediary between the ruling *Ǫwa* and all *ǫmǫba* in the district. Subsequent representation of the community (e.g. in litigation) will take place through the *onile* -chief.

POLITICS AND OUT-SETTLEMENT

If the impetus to permanent settlement in the farms came from the interests and decisions of various kinds of individual, what role did the central authorities play in shaping the emergent communities, especially through the institution of government by *lojas* of royal descent? The establishment view of the relationship was put by one *lǫja* in the form of a maxim:

Ibi ti oju Ǫwa ba s'okunkun si, l'oun fi ǫmǫ rẹ dodo si
Where it is dark for the eye of Owa to see, there he puts his son to rule[32]

In practice the *Ǫwa*, so far from being able to install whoever he wanted as his agent, was obliged to be more circumspect, in the face of local vested interests. Again, our only adequately detailed evidence comes from the last few decades, to which some of the factors that shaped these interests (e.g. greater rural security, progressive shortage of land good for growing cocoa) are specific, but it is none the less highly suggestive of the likely forms of earlier conflicts.

In 1944–45, *Ǫwa* Ajimoko II encountered local opposition to the man he proposed to appoint as *Lǫja* of Odoiju, a small settlement on Road VI.[33] There was in fact a division between those who lived permanently in the village and citizens of Ilesha who farmed locally, apparently under tenancies, and it was the former who opposed the *Ǫwa*'s nominee. The *Ǫwa* insisted to the District Officer that the general rule was that after a village had decided that it needed a *lǫja*, it approached him and that he, with the *onile*, had the sole right of appointment. The *onile*, the *Risawẹ* in this case, gave a more complex and realistic account of the procedure, stating that the *Ǫwa* 'consults the *onile* ... to assure security of office and welfare of nominee' – significant concerns! – besides investigating, with the help of Chiefs *Bajimǫ* and *Agbayewa*, the candidate's lineage, moral and physical condition, the attitude of the villagers etc. Similar problems occurred for the *Ǫwa* in 1953–54 at Itagunmodi on Road V.[34] Despite his selection of one Awokusibe as *Lǫja*, described as 'a real son of Itagunmodi', a local party under the *Lǫyin* (the village leader informally chosen without the *Ọwa*'s sanction) organized in opposition to him, even going to the point of claiming that non-natives (*sc.* of Itagunmodi) should leave the hearings of the dispute since 'they could not know the origins of the native laws and customs of Itagunmodi'. Paradoxically it was precisely as there emerged a *local* party, an interest group of those whose links with Ilesha had become attenuated, that the occasion arose for having a *lọja*, a local chief also recognized at the centre, and hence able to represent the community and to settle disputes authoritatively. No doubt too the *Ọwa* were also looking for occasions to establish this kind of control, being enabled to do so by the absence, among these small 'local people', of lineages powerful enough to claim headship of the community for themselves. Often the *Risa* title, typically the second title in the community, was possessed by a local lineage, such as the descendants of the first settler.[35]

But though they might turn to the centre for a local head, the village people had definite sanctions over him. A *lọja* quite lacked any regular power of coercion over his subjects and like any chief had to look to them and to his more personal dependants for the means to act as chief: he had to 'eat'. He had rights over land and over labour (particularly that of royal slaves in the area). But coming in as a stranger, he would, at the least, be dependent on local information; and an unwanted *lọja* could easily be kept ignorant of vital knowledge about land boundaries, the site of farms to which he was entitled (*oko oye*), even the identity of royal slaves. Several *lọja* and other 'princes' or *ọmọba* have told me sad stories of how a *lọja* may 'starve' and be constantly frustrated by the machinations of rivals well dug-in locally, if he does not have local, as well as central, legitimacy. And while a *lọja*'s contemporary concern is likely to be to collect the *iṣakọlẹ* he feels due to him from cocoa farms, it was equally necessary before the days of cash-crops for him to have the material wherewithal to sustain a chief's position, to be what a contemporary *lọja* called 'not rich, but with plenty of food'.

A further constraint on the *Ọwa*'s freedom of action in appointing *lọjas* derives from the interests of the members of the royal lineage itself. In principle, one is told, any *lọja*-ship may be held by any recognized *ọmọba*, without reference to a particular line or segment of the ruling house. Since the royal lineage is so large, this means that successive *lọjas* of a village might be *de facto* unrelated to one another, their common royal descent serving merely as a minimum qualification of appointment. In many cases this has in fact happened. Yet there is also a tendency for some *lọja*-ships to become, even if they were not always, the hereditary perquisites of particular branches of the royal lineage, thus tending to reduce the discretionary power of the ruling *Ọwa* over them. Figure 4.2, showing the *lọja*-ships held by the major lines of the two branches of what is now recognized as one of the four 'ruling houses' of the Ilesha dynasty, exemplifies some of the possibilities. Some *lọja*-ships (of Oshu, Ijana-Atarua, Ilerin, Isolo,

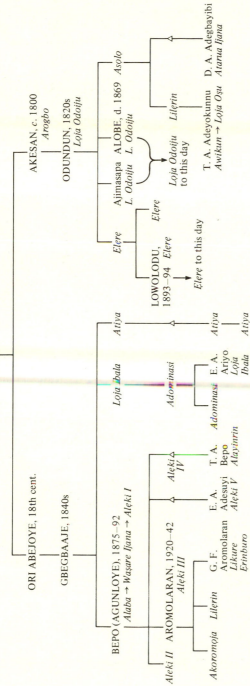

Fig. 4.2 Uyiarere ruling house and District *Loja*-ships

Notes: Names of *Ọwa* are in capital letters, titles of *loja*-ships in italics. The stemma is not complete as regards all agnatic descendants and it is likely some titles were omitted too.

'Uyiarere ruling house' is only a conventional grouping within the royal lineage, one of four, established when the chieftaincy declarations were drawn up in 1958–61. Effectively there are two separate groupings, those of Ori/Gbegbaaje and of Akesan/Odundun though each of these meets together infrequently. The degree of corporacy increases as the relevant lineage gets smaller – Bepo's descendants as a whole less than Aromolaran's. As far as the argument about how far the *loja* of a particular village is restricted to one lineage goes, the two *Lilerin* in the table can be considered as unrelated.

Sources: Chief E. A. Ariyo, interview, 8 July 1975; Chief E. A. Adesuyi, interview, 23 Dec. 1974; correspondence regarding Odoiju in ILE DIV 1/1 842, *NAI*, dating from its disputed succession in 1954–55; Chief G. F. Aromolaran, interview, 25 July 1979; Paul Francis, 'Power and order', pp. 198ff. on the *Atiya* title; Chief T. A. Adeyokunnu, interview, 7 Jan. 1974.

71

Ikoromoja, Alaba, Iloya etc.) seem genuinely open. Others seem loosely but definitely associated with a particular line (e.g. Idominasi, Ibala, Odogbo), whose members might come to have expectations regarding the title. Others are completely monopolized by one line, whether from the settlement's foundation (e.g. Ileki, Odoiju, Eyinta), or from some point in its history (e.g. Ere, Imobi, perhaps Oke Ibode). How is this variation to be explained; and what is its significance for our understanding of the evolution of relations between Ilesha and the district communities?

A ruling *Owa*, as far as he can, subject to the local constraints just described, will be especially prone to fill vacant *loja*-ships with his own close relatives. (The evidence of this for recent decades lies in the many close relatives of *Owas* Ataiyero, 1901–20; Aromolaran, 1921–42; and Ajimoko II, 1943–56, who are now found among the *loja*.) This is understandable: the *Owa* will be under pressure from his kinsmen to do this, he will be more likely to find them loyal and responsive to him and in so doing he will protect the future of his own line (*idi*) of the royal lineage. For *loja*-ships not only notionally qualify a man to be *Owa*, but also serve to validate as 'of royal blood' the close agnatic kin of the *loja* and hence to arrest the slide to obscurity of those lines of royal descent which have not for several generations produced an *Owa*. But by the same token, the other royal lines of descent are even more anxious, since less favourably placed, to maintain general recognition of their royal status by getting one of their members made a *loja* and will try to claim, if they can make it stick, that a particular *loja*-ship is 'theirs'. Thus in 1952 a member of the lineage of *Owa* Ponlose (none of whom had held the *Owa*-ship for nearly a hundred years) wrote angrily to a local paper against *Owa* Ajimoko II's creation of his cousin Adekolapo Haastrup as *Aloro* of Iloro Oke.[36] He claimed that Iloro Oke was founded by Ponlose's maternal grandmother, who had subsequently asked *Owa* Ojagodo to make him *loja* of it 'in his mother's land which was his own mother's personal property'. Subsequent occupancy of the *Aloro*-ship by members of Oluodo ruling house – the major segment to which the Haastrups belong – was explained as usurpation or as a favour specially granted by the Ponlose family. This claim is interesting precisely because it was unsuccessful, and reveals what kinds of factor might lead to the successful monopolization of a *loja*-ship, like those of Ileki or Ere.

The basis for a particular line claiming a community's *loja*-ship as its own lies in its members and clients effectively predominating in the possession of local lands. This might arise from a settlement growing from the *aba* of a particular *omoba* who later acquired a *loja*'s title in relation to it, as seems to have happened in a number of small settlements headed by *lojas* quite close to Ilesha (e.g. Ileki, said to have been founded as a farm-settlement by *Owa* Gbegbaaje, which his son Bepo moved to as its first '*Aleki*' after, apparently, being driven from Ijana Wasare for being overbearing);[37] or a particular royal line, perhaps as the result of one of their sons' long tenure of the *loja*-ship, might come to be so powerful and well-connected that members of other lines were effectively excluded. In settlements like Ileki it would effectively be impossible for an *omoba* from any other line to command authority locally; and, by a kind of common consent, their *loja*-ships are regarded as earmarked. It is evident that the Ponlose family did not achieve this kind of hegemony at Iloro Oke, its early likelihood being set back by the dispersal of their people during the wars. In general it would seem that the more heterogeneous the lineage affiliations of a settlement, the more likely would it be that the *loja*-ship remained truly open to any *omoba* appointed by the ruling *Owa*. A *loja* is both a local head and a representative of the community to the centre, and the actual practice regarding who is qualified is the contested outcome of two tendencies which work against each other. On the one hand, the local principle means that if a family is so dominant locally that it becomes identified with the community's corporate interests, the headship will become restricted to a local lineage, albeit one which may also be recognized as a branch of Ilesha's dynasty. On the other, representation is best secured by getting a *loja* close to the ruling *Owa*, whose own interests, as we have seen, coincide with this; but the principle of representation is only likely to triumph over the local principle if the local population is free of overriding connexions with one line of the royal house.

In other cases the effective creation of a local dynasty is less the product of a particular *omoba* line's being able to exclude *omoba* of other lines from the *loja*-ship, than an aspect of that community's own progress towards a further degree of autonomy. The ultimate stage would be the recognition of two mutually exclusive lineages, the royal dynasty of Ilesha and that of the district community, even though the latter's dynasty continued to claim descent from the *Owa*. Iwara, the senior *loja*-ship, and Ilaa have both long been of this type, while Iponda and Iwoye have graduated to it more recently. Though there are people in Ilesha, fully recognized there as *omoba*, whose nineteenth-century forbears are positively recalled as having been *Loja* of Iponda or Iwoye, both communities are now *formally* recognized as having their own ruling houses.[38] Iwara has been broken-off for longer, which perhaps explains why its traditions are so contradictory on the subject: for they combine a story of Iwara's foundation by a warrior Abereogun who came from Ife (which is a claim to absolute autonomy in principle) with a story, also told in Ilesha, that Ajila, the first *Awara*, was so rich and his people so numerous that, though invited to become *Owa*, he decided when he reached the town-gate of Ilesha that there was no point in his transplanting himself (which clearly implies the *Awara*'s original membership of the Ilesha royal house).[39]

The logical end of the process is that instead of being an *omododo* ('son of the inner courtyard'), the head of the district community becomes an *elu* ('companion' to the *Owa*, but also 'stranger') like such rulers as the *Apetu* of Ipetu-Ijesha or the *Tirimi* of Iperindo, to whom

the *Ọwa* accorded a greater degree of political autonomy. That this autonomy develops in close proportion as any *lọja* becomes separated from the
Ilesha dynasty, is implicit in a curious division sometimes made among the
lọja-ships. There are said to be those from which a man may be called to be
Ọwa, and those which, while equally requiring to be occupied by an
ọmọba, do not function as a gateway to the *Ọwa*-ship. Many actual *lọja*-
ships are not precisely or unanimously assigned to either category; and the
distinction seems to be notional or *post hoc*, rather than absolutely pre-
scriptive. What is most significant is the reason given for it: a *lọja* may not
go to be *Ọwa* if he is already an *alagbẹ*, head of a community which
possesses its own execution pit (*agbẹ*), over whose use the *lọja* has full
discretionary control. The distinction, then, serves to state and connect
two attributes of the properly autonomous community: its ruler has the
ultimate judicial sanction and should not have commitments elsewhere.

Is the distinction between Ilesha and its district one that we could call
'urban'/'rural' with its connotation of a separation of economic function in
which lie the seeds of fundamental social change? Clearly, there must be
more to 'urban' here than *merely* a marked concentration of population in
one locality. What is implied is a particular form of social life arising from a
distinct role within a societal division of labour.[40]

As far as the economic activities of subsistence are concerned, the
difference between Ilesha and its district was of degree rather than kind.
The work of most of Ilesha's male inhabitants was farming, and many of
these would have circulated between their houses in Ilesha and their farm-
settlements. The basic crafts – weaving, smithing, potting – were carried
out in quite small villages. Some villages in south-eastern Ijeshaland, like
Ikeji, specialized in the manufacture of mats woven from a kind of rush.
The casual detail of lineage and community histories suggests that some
rural markets – Muroko, Iwara, Odogbo, Odo – definitely existed well
before the upheavals of the nineteenth century.[41] These rural markets,
then as now, supplied the central Ilesha market with foodstuffs as well as
(in all probability) markets further afield with commodities like kola.

Ilesha's economic distinctness had its origins in its political domination.
There must, of course, have been a considerable in-flow of produce to
Ilesha to feed the substantial numbers of non-producers concentrated
there: title-holders, *ẹmẹsẹ*, personal dependants and hangers-on, as well as
the strangers and long-distance traders who lodged with chiefly patrons.
The great bulk of this must have come from the slaves and other
dependants of Ilesha-dwelling household heads working in the zone of
Ilesha's own actual farms, rather than from the semi-autonomous *ilu*. The
households of the capital, led by the *Afin*, also created a demand for such
specialized manufacturers as the wood-carving of Odo Osunmu, the skilled
crafts of Isona, and weaving and blacksmithing all over the town. Since
there is no evidence of Ilesha itself supplying the district or the wider

region with manufactured goods on any scale – cloth would seem the most likely – it seems that Ilesha was very much more a 'consumer' than a 'producer' town.[42]

What of Ilesha's relations with the semi-autonomous *ilu* of the district? Ilesha's direct levies do not appear to have been large. *Iwisin* was relatively light, as were the payments made when any district town's new chief was installed. Perhaps more important were the impositions of the *ẹmẹsẹ* or the payments made to the *onile* chief of Ilesha when cases went to the capital. What irked the larger district towns, which had ambitions for themselves, was not so much the scale of these levies but Ilesha's effective reservation to itself and its citizens of the opportunities provided by the wider region. Steadily, as Ilesha grew, their status was reduced. The *Ogboni* of Ibokun, whose installation once took place in his own town, later had to go to Ilesha to be installed; and despite his membership of the *Agbanla* line, Ibokun came to have an *onile* in the person of Chief *Arapatẹ* at Ilesha.[43] These towns were always alert to the possibility of throwing off Ilesha's control, whether through calling in outside powers or combination among themselves. In an episode known as *Ọtẹ Ẹlẹrun* ('The Palm-kernel Conspiracy'), perhaps in the 1830s, Ilesha was for several months blockaded by Ijebu-jesha;[44] and there was open conflict with Ibokun and Ifewara.

A final point concerns the cultural consequences of the division between Ilesha and the district. To call the district *oko* or 'farms' was to disparage it; to this day, throughout the Yoruba area, an *ara oko* is a rustic person, a yokel, someone remote from the prestige and connexions of the capital, unversed in its ways and in need of a patron there. Farms were associated with the status of slavery; it was the junior wives who followed their husbands to the farm, while the older ones pursued their commercial avocations where there was the largest market for their products. Such valuations of the rural are common in societies which have a rural/urban divide. But often the country dwellers, especially if they are to a degree encapsulated in a 'little tradition', respond to this disparagement (and the exploitation which goes with it) by asserting the positive value of their own way of life. This is a strong tendency in all peasant cultures, providing material for the ideology of peasant revolts. It is not absent from such West African societies as the Hausa, associated with the 'pagan' Maguzawa in contrast to the urban/literate/Islamic/elite strains dominant in that culture. But it is quite absent from the thinking of those Ijesha who are seen as 'farm people' by the centre. Instead, they aspire to the condition of those at the centre. When their relations with the centre become so attenuated that they start to consider the village as their *ilu*, they start to develop institutions (e.g. *iwarẹfa* chiefs) modelled on those of the centre. If the community prospered, they might eventually try to gain direct access to the regional system, demanding a beaded crown for their chief and asserting that his ancestor migrated from Ife. Communities, like individuals, did not believe that a lowly condition had to be permanent.

5

An age of revolution?

The three preceding chapters have each dealt with an aspect of pre-colonial Ilesha, without too much specification of exact period; and where change has been considered, it has been processes characteristic of the structure, rather than the unique course of the kingdom's actual history. To some extent this is forced on us by the patchiness of the evidence, as well as by expository convenience. But when we come to the nineteenth century, some attempt at a more transformational approach is both possible and essential to an understanding of Ilesha in the twentieth century. Some important developments of the twentieth century (e.g. cash-crop production) had roots in changing patterns of social relations running back into the nineteenth century, as well as in the impact of colonialism itself. The most challenging, and intractable, questions raised in the substantial and decent literature which now exists on the Yoruba wars of the nineteenth century concern the nature of the social and economic forms which accompanied them, which necessarily form the immediate baseline for any study of colonial incorporation. Indeed, it must not be forgotten that much of the residential and political structure described in Chapter 2 lay in abeyance between Ilesha's sack by the Ibadans in 1870 and its reconstitution in the late 1890s. Some passing reference has been made to social forms (e.g. 'warrior' households) perhaps peculiar to – or certainly more characteristic of – the mid and late nineteenth century,[1] and these need placing in a broader context. Finally, Ilesha's experiences in the nineteenth century – its turbulent civic history, its sack and its recovery, the exploits of its warriors and especially of its greatest communal hero, Ogedengbe – have had a powerful mythic significance for Ijesha and have been repeatedly drawn on in twentieth-century politics.[2]

Already in the 1840s and 1850s there were 'a great many' Ijesha freed slaves, living in the Colony of Sierra Leone, a sure indication of substantial Ijesha losses in the preceding few decades; and right up to the end of the century there was a similarly large number of repatriates from slavery in Brazil.[3] In fact it seems that the long-term equilibrium of Ilesha's relations with her neighbours, especially to the north, began to break up around

76

1820. There was open warfare between Old Oyo and its former tributary Ilorin, much of it taking place in the area immediately to the north-west of Ijesha territory.[4] Apart from direct incursions of the Ilorins, one of which was successfully repulsed by the Ijesha,[5] there began a steady influx of Oyo refugees to settle in the northern towns of the kingdom. A further source of pressure was the decision of the Oyo town of Ede to remove itself south of the Oshun, and thus into what had been Ijesha territory, to be safer against the Ilorins. Ijesha traditions name several wars in this north-western area, around 1822, which laid their farms waste (*ahoro*), drove the people back with all their possessions and saw many of them taken into slavery: *ọlọmọ ko mọ ọmọ, aya ko ri ọkọ mọ* ('parents knew their children no more, nor did wives see their husbands again') as one account put it.[6]

The pressure on her frontiers helped to undermine Ilesha's control over the larger subordinate towns. Oshogbo became effectively an Oyo town. The four northern towns of Igbajo, Ada, Iresi and Otan Aiyegbaju were lost forever, though their recovery remained a prime object of Ijesha policy for the rest of the century. Minor wars with Ibokun, Ijebu-jesha and Ifewara (to the south) all took place between the 1820s and 1850s. Ilesha is said to have invited Benin to help her in dealing with Ibokun, over an incident in the 1830s: a surprising circumstance, but perhaps a device to neutralize Benin's possible intervention on Ibokun's side at a time when her influence in northern Ekiti had lately revived.[7] A serious decline of security within the kingdom's borders is suggested by the source of a war Ilesha fought against Ifewara in the early 1850s: to avenge the kidnapping of Ijeshas returning from Lagos.[8]

A new phase developed when Ibadan, the new state sited in the forest that attracted 'war-boys' (*ọmọ-ogun*) from all over Yoruba country and was to come nearest to filling the vacuum left by Oyo's collapse, entered the scene.[9] After an early intervention on behalf of Ife and Ede raided by Ijesha from Oshu around 1829–31, Ibadan started to operate continuously across northern Ijesha and into Ekiti in the 1840s.[10] Ilesha maintained her independence, but her regional power shrank further: some Ijesha towns (such as Ibokun) became tributary to Ibadan, with Ibadan *ajẹlẹ* (official representatives) placed in them.[11] The first European visitors in 1858 found Ilesha itself in good order, its defences well-maintained, but its authorities intensely wary.[12] None the less Ilesha was still capable of military initiatives in pursuit of traditional objectives: in 1860–62, when Ibadan was occupied far away in the Ijaiye War, Ijesha forces subjugated Efon and Ogotun in Western Ekiti.[13] Emboldened by success here, the Ijesha then decided to try to recover Igbajo, the largest of their former subordinate towns in the north. Igbajo called Ibadan to her aid and the Ijesha, weakened by dissensions among the chiefs, suffered a severe defeat (1867). Ilesha itself now became Ibadan's prime target. A series of campaigns drew the noose tighter until finally, on 4 June 1870, the city

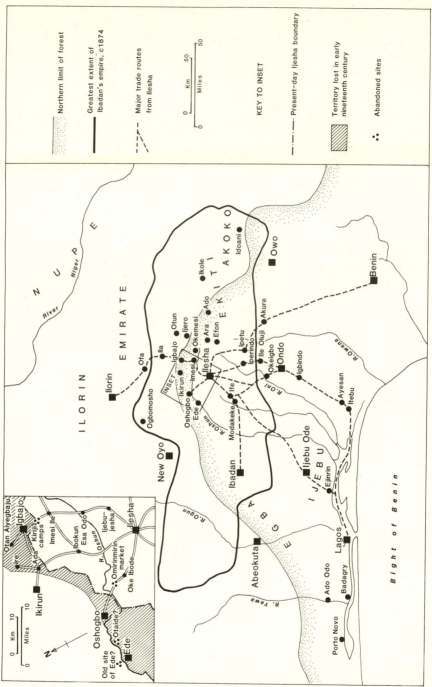

Map 5.1 Yorubaland in the later nineteenth century

Northern limit of forest

Greatest extent of
Ibadan's empire, c 1874

Major trade routes
from Ilesha

KEY TO INSET

Present-day Ilesha boundary

Territory lost in early
nineteenth century

Abandoned sites

78

was abandoned to the Ibadans by its defenders. A further humiliation followed: the *Owa* who was taken was accidentally drowned in the river Oshun on his way to Ibadan. The capture of Ilesha, 'being a town of great strength, both in its fortifications and in its able-bodied citizens', as Johnson was to put it, marked the high point of Ibadan's standing in the Yoruba country.[14]

The external warfare of this period was matched by a growing turbulence of Ilesha's internal politics. As far as I have been able to collect them, the traditions are fragmentary and somewhat mixed with fantastic details, but they do suggest that from the time of *Owa* Gbegbaaje (probably late 1830s) the routine struggle for mastery among the leading chiefs took more extreme forms.[15] The careers of *Lejoka* Danaija and *Lejofi* Alaka go back to Gbegbaaje's reign if not before.[16] Gbegbaaje is said to have died violently, perhaps through the contrivance of Alaka, who sponsored the next *Owa*, Ofokutu.[17] Subsequently Alaka's power and arrogance alienated him from the *Owa*, whose relationship with his *Odole*, Ariyasunle, grew closer. (Ariyasunle owed his own preferment as *Odole* to Alaka, who had a connexion with his mother; it is possible he was only matrilaterally linked to the *Odole* lineage.[18]) Ariyasunle connived at *Lejofi* Alaka's death – clubbed while prostrating to the *Owa* – with the help of a young kinsman of Alaka's, *Lokiran* Oruru. They next moved against *Lejoka* Danaija, who blew himself up in his house with gunpowder. Throughout the 1850s and early 1860s Ariyasunle's hegemony was unchallenged; it was he who hosted the European visitors of 1858 on behalf of the *Owa*.[19] There is a tradition that holds him responsible for *Owa* Ofokutu's death, by magical means.[20] Oruru and Ariyasunle fell out over the succession and Oruru, having backed a loser, was subsequently driven from Ilesha, eventually to find refuge in Ipetu, his mother's town. Ariyasunle's downfall was a consequence of the débâcle at Igbajo in 1867, for which he was popularly held responsible. The movement against him was promoted by a body of young warriors called *ipaiye*, their leader being one Ogedengbe.[21] A man of no very exalted parentage, born in the southern village of Atorin, Ogedengbe had come to Ilesha to advance himself and attached himself to the household of Jalaga the *Babaileoke*; later he had seen service, on occasion, in both the Ibadan and the Ilesha forces in various wars of the 1850s and 1860s, narrowly missing being killed by the Ibadans when they captured him at Igbajo. Ogedengbe and the *ipaiye* drove a wedge between *Odole* Ariyasunle and his allies by setting alight the others' houses and blaming him; they suborned women who drowned the *Odole*'s protests at a public meeting by shouts of *Ole* ('Thief!'). Ariyasunle left the meeting in anger and his people began to desert him; he killed himself and the *ipaiye* sacked his house.[22]

Before he died, *Odole* Ariyasunle is said to have uttered a famous curse. Casting aside the beads from his waist, he predicted that the Ijesha would never be united in one place until the beads were collected together; no elders would have authority over them, but only young boys; Ijesha would love each other abroad, but not at home.[23]

The point of this chiefly rivalry was far from entirely novel: to accumulate large personal followings and material resources and to exert influence at the *Afin*, the state's centre, each of these ends serving to sustain the other. It seems significant that it was *ẹlẹgbẹ* title-holders (*Lẹjọka, Lejofi* and *Lọkiran*), leaders of the community's military forces, and those who had close access to the *Afin* (*Ọdọle* and *Babaileoke*), who were foremost among the competing chiefs. But the great game was now played for much higher stakes and under conditions of greater uncertainty. The latter seems betokened by the heavy emphasis in the traditional accounts upon magical means: Alaka's downfall depended on the destruction of his protective charms by one of his wives; *Ọwa* Ofokutu made powerful *ẹbọ* (sacrifices) to rid himself of Alaka, and kept track of his chiefs by means of a medicine which turned him into a small boy who could wander unsuspected around their compounds; *Ọdọle* Ariyasunle's enemies destroyed his magical cloth (*aṣọ ogbo*), which was kept in a snail-shell and, expanding to full size in the sunlight, made its wearer impregnable! Unfortunately the traditions are less forthcoming about the secular instruments of conflict. One repeated detail is significant, however, for it indicates a new factor: guns.

Guns were hardly known in this part of interior Yorubaland before about 1840, though thereafter their use spread rapidly.[24] They would have come to the Oyo (including Ibadan) before the Ijesha. But *Lẹjọka* Danaija had enough gunpowder to spread round his house before he blew it up, and the *ipaiyẹ* are said to have captured Ariyasunle's store of muskets and used them against him.[25] Guns and powder, being costly, hoardable and derived from external sources, must, compared with earlier forms of weaponry, have tended to create a political gulf between those who could acquire them and those who could not, and enhanced the struggle for the means to acquire them. But still, the emergence of a new 'means of destruction' accentuated, rather than changed, old forms of conflict, since the *ologun* ('warlords'), as these rivals may generically be termed, continued to require large personal followings. Why was this?

Imports of weaponry had to be paid for. Is it fortuitous that the *Ọwa* in whose reign civil conflict began to take more extreme forms bears a praise-name, *Gbegbaaje*, which means 'one who possesses calabashes of money'? Since Ijesha traditions of this period contain so few direct references to economic life, inferences have to be made from more general circumstances of the region.[26] Essentially it was palm-oil, the staple of 'legitimate trade' at the coast once the outflow of slaves had stopped, which paid for munitions (and much else). Palm-oil production itself also created a heavy demand for labour, and hence enhanced the value of slaves in the interior. Whether states produced palm-oil themselves or levied it as tribute from others (as Ibadan came to do), the old cycle of military success and increase of population through the acquisition of slaves was still very much in force. By the mid-1860s Ilesha had lost many of her own people to slavery and much of the northern part of the kingdom had slipped out of her control. But the successful wars of the early 1860s against Efon and Ogotun must have somewhat replenished the population and presumably increased the proportion who were slaves. The level of exports needed in order to be able to import guns implies a higher level of exploitation than had been customary. The higher levels of slavery through Yorubaland, achieved by massive transfers of population – Ijesha to Ibadan and western Yorubaland, people from Ekiti and Akoko to Ilesha – strongly implies that this was taking place. As for direct evidence, we know that there were substantial royal farms worked by slaves, and the prominence at this period of Chief *Babaileoke*, head of the royal slaves, is suggestive.[27] Equally compelling is the indirect evidence: the nature of the opposition to the greatest chief, Ariyasunle. As before, chiefs could only participate in or contribute to Ilesha's power by maintaining large households. The levels of polygyny reported for the great chiefs – 240 wives for Alaka, 8,000 (*ṣile meji*!) for Ariyasunle – are, one presumes, greatly exaggerated, but make a point. The position of young men was particularly contradictory: the immediate instruments of any chief's power, they were drawn to the patronage of the powerful, but bitterly resentful of its implications. Their chances of marriage must have been reduced by the high levels of polygyny and their bargaining position reduced by the presence of so many slaves. No chief was more blatant in his ascendancy than *Ọdọle* Ariyasunle, and it was in the name of an age-based interest group – *ipaiyẹ* being a name widely found in Ekiti for the age-set of young men[28] – that Ogedengbe led the movement against him. The sack of a fallen chief's house was followed by a general redistribution of wives, slaves and property. Ogedengbe thus inherited one of Ariyasunle's wives, a sister of the *ọmọba* Arimoro, who was later to become one of his finest captains.[29]

In several ways all this represents a partial 'Ibadanization' of Ijesha political style, of which more was to come. Ibadan had been the first Yoruba state to adapt herself to the new conditions of political existence: palm-oil for guns, and a more thoroughgoing militarization of society through *ologun* (warrior) households than had been known before.[30] Ibadan was also distinctive in that the households which formed her residential and military base were unconstrained by the existence of a determinate title-system or an *Afin*. The contrast between a newcomer like Ibadan and an ancient kingdom like Ilesha can be exaggerated if they are seen as embodiments of contrasting sociological types (e.g. achievement versus ascription). Ilesha's political structure, with its non-lineage military titles, was fairly flexible, and the consequences of successful war and the incorporation of slaves had been several times evident in her civic history.[31] But still Ilesha was not Ibadan. The greatest chief of all, *Ọdọle* Ariyasunle, did not go to war, but was head of the *Afin* organization. Ilesha's politics still depended in good measure on the highly structured system of titles and not just on the shifting fortunes and alliances of the leading warriors. This was only to change some years after 1870, when the centre of Ilesha's politics moved to the war-camp at Kiriji, and those who, like Ogedengbe and many of his generation, had been to Ibadan to learn its techniques, assumed leadership of her affairs.

The 1870s were a low and chaotic period of Ilesha's history. They opened with more civil discord. Food was short during the siege and, according to Johnson, the ravages of Ogedengbe and his *ipaiye* in the town were so bad that many Ijesha households gave themselves up as slaves to escape from them.[32] After the *Qwa* had been drowned, Ogedengbe and the chiefs quarrelled over the succession, but both parties had to turn to their patrons at Ibadan, the real kingmakers. When his nominee was killed as a consequence of rivalries internal to Ibadan, Ogedengbe attacked Ilesha and expelled Oweweniye, the *Qwa* installed by Ibadan. Again an Ibadan army came to dislodge him and Ilesha was sacked a second time (early 1873). Ogedengbe now withdrew to the east, making his camp at Ita Ogbolu, and for several years operated as a pure freebooter, attacking Ibadan's tributary towns in Ekiti, even raiding far into Benin territory.[33] He attracted a large warrior following, kept himself well supplied with guns and came to enjoy the greatest reputation of any warrior in Eastern Yorubaland. Of the situation in Ilesha after his departure, little can be said in any detail, though for several years an *ajęlę* was stationed in Ilesha and tributes were levied by Ibadan.[34] Although a new *Qwa*, Bepo or Agunloye, was installed with Ibadan's authority around 1875, he must have ruled over the shadow of a town. Many titles were obviously unfilled for years, and it seems that, though Bepo tried to keep a token title-system going, he was sometimes unable to find eligible men for lineage titles and took whom he could.[35] Ilesha's population had shrunk, maybe to as little as an eighth of its former level;[36] many of its people who had survived the wars preferred now to live in the more secluded parts of the district, to the south. Though Ibadan had followed up its capture of Ilesha in 1870 with the capture of Igangan, Odo and Iperindo, it was not able to maintain its hold there, and that south-eastern corner of Ijeshaland grew in importance: as a refuge, as a source of food and, above all, as a strategic line of communication along which slaves, guns and other trade-goods could pass, down through Ondo to the Lagoon. This route was opened up, largely at the insistence of Glover, the British Governor of Lagos, in the early 1870s in order to have a link with the Yoruba interior that was not liable to be cut by either the Egba or the Ijebu.[37] It was to prove of vital importance when Ilesha and her allies in the Ekitiparapo were really to hit back at Ibadan.

The alliance against Ibadan originated in a spontaneous insurrection against the agents of Ibadan overrule, first at Imesi-Igbodo (Okemesi) and then in many other Ekiti and Igbomina towns (1878).[38] Contingents began to gather at Okemesi from throughout Ibadan's subject territories, including Ilesha, though Ogedengbe still held aloof, occupied as he was on his own account with a campaign against Idoani, in Akoko. Strenuous efforts were made by representatives of the Ekitiparapo Society, largely composed of Ijesha repatriates living in Lagos, to foster the alliance and to keep it well supplied.[39] Common cause was made with Ibadan's other enemies: Egba and Ijebu to the west, and, closer to hand, Ilorin. Their campaign began badly, however: after taking Igbajo, the Ekiti and Ijesha forces, with their Ilorin allies, were soundly defeated by the Ibadans at Ikirun. But they eventually regrouped in the hills north of Imesi-Ile, close to that contested zone where the forest yields to savannah and where the territories claimed by Ibadan and by Ilorin, by Ijesha and by the small Ekiti and Igbomina states came together. Here the Ekitiparapo camp was to remain throughout the long years of the Kiriji War, in fact till 1893, when they had fought Ibadan to a stalemate and the British intervened to bring the whole nexus of inter-Yoruba warfare to an end. By early 1880 Ogedengbe, a patriot at last, had joined the Ekitiparapo, his prestige and experience earning him, by common consent of the other *ologun*, the post of commander-in-chief.

The Kiriji camp of the Ekitiparapo became a substantial town, with a population that fluctuated seasonally but was estimated at 40,000-strong in 1886.[40] Its structure derived from the relations between the leading *ologun*, each with his following, and so this 'public' force, which certainly carried the aspirations for peace and freedom of the peoples represented there, was in fact an aggregation of private armies. There is little detailed evidence concerning the composition of any one warrior's following or the exact manner in which the leading *ologun* worked out some regular patterns of authority with one another. But it does not seem that there were 'national' contingents as such, though men who joined would very likely be drawn to a warlord from their own town. The Ijesha, for example, were not a unified contingent but went as the followers of Ogedengbe himself, Arimoro, Ogunmodede, Obe or whoever else they had some connexion with. The larger followings had something of a stratified command-structure: we read of Ogedengbe's 'under-baloguns', who would be subordinate captains within his following, rather than lesser *ologun* with followings of their own.[41] Many smaller *ologun*, with their followers, were there as independent agents, rather than as formal members of the personal following of one of the greater *ologun*. Control over personal followings (to the extent that these were not composed of slaves) depended on the capacity to supply them with guns, which in turn depended on having trade goods (notably slaves) and trading partners.[42] A warrior called Esan, for example, first followed his kinsman Gidigbi to war; he then acquired guns of his own, from the profits of trading in tobacco between Ilorin and the Lagoon ports (a route running conveniently through Ilesha and the Kiriji camp); and these guns, twelve of them, brought him a following of twenty men.[43] In battle the *ologun*, large or small, directed their own 'guns', though presumably under the direction of Ogedengbe as commander-in-chief. But Ogedengbe himself, despite his prestige and the size of his own personal following, did not stand at the head of a military bureaucracy. He was rather *primus inter pares* of the larger *ologun*, who had to carry the other leaders with him at their regular meetings. There were also general assemblies of the people at the camp, where strategic decisions were ratified.

Ibadan began its existence as a war-camp, an aggregation of the followings of *ologun* who only worked out a more-or-less stable pattern of relations among themselves – two major lines of non-hereditary titles, with promotion from the lower to the higher – over several decades of shared activity in war and peace. If Kiriji had become a permanent town, Ibadan is certainly what it would have resembled, rather than a transformed version of some Ekiti or Ijesha type of polity. Many of the leaders at Kiriji assumed Oyo-type titles – Fabunmi of Okemesi was *Balogun*, Ogedengbe *Seriki* (in theory a lower title than *Balogun*, denoting the leader of young warriors), Obe was *Bada*, Arimoro was *Aṣaju-ija* – but they were purely personal, not indications of positions in some fairly stable division of authority. Evolution towards a permanent Ibadan-type order was limited, not just by the break-up of the Kiriji camp, but by the fact that the *ọba* of the allied communities of the Ekitiparapo, including the *Ọwa*, continued as a kind of parallel authority and implicitly served as reminders of the former but unforgotten order. For most of the war *Ọwa* Bepo stayed at Ijebu-jesha or Esa-Odo, and the three leading Ekiti *ọba* (of Otun, Ido and Ijero) at Imesi-Ile.

Relations between Ogedengbe and the *Ọwa* were cooperative enough on the practical level; but Akintoye's picture of a cooperation fairly easily achieved, because of the necessities of the situation and a shared commitment to the goal of national liberation, does not entirely convince.[44] Of course the *Ọwa* and Ogedengbe were polite about one another to Europeans; but against the war-chiefs' description of the *ọbas* as their 'fathers', which Akintoye quotes to argue for their respect for traditional authority, must be set *Ọwa* Bepo's remark about Ogedengbe: 'young as he is, he is my father'.[45] No *Ọwa* would happily say that of a supposed subject, especially one who, like Bepo, felt his royal dignity strongly.[46] On this occasion Bepo even felt it expedient, presumably for fear of the soldiery, to decline to receive presents except through Ogedengbe's hands: a humiliating dependence. There was no doubt that Ogedengbe had usurped much of the *Ọwa*'s authority: for example, levying tolls on his own account.[47] Nor, after the war was over, did he yield at all easily to the authority of the *Ọwa*, as the next three *Ọwa* after Bepo were to discover.[48]

The wars and political upheavals were accompanied by profound economic changes. One of these – increased production of exports in order to meet strategic needs – has already been noted. In so far as these took the form of slaves (or such other 'collected' produce as ivory) they did not automatically affect existing productive relations, except to intensify the levels of exploitation, nor automatically to further commercialize the economy in general. But the chiefs required trading partners who took advantage of other opportunities to enlarge the market. Who were the traders? Many were former Ijesha slaves, who established themselves in Lagos or along the trade-routes, especially at two settlements in the eastern Lagoon: Itebu, an Ilaje town, and Ayesan, established in 1881 by Ijesha connected with the Ekitiparapo Society in Lagos, under the leadership of one Takuro (a name which means 'seller of palm-kernels').[49] These were terminal points of the 'Ondo road' from which commodities went by canoe to the great Lagoon market of Ejinrin and Lagos.[50] Then chiefs made use of their wives to sell their slaves and supply them with ammunition, and cultivated trading contacts and friendships in towns that lay along the routes to the greater regional markets.[51] Other important routes ran via Ife and Isoya through Ijebu to Ejinrin, to Benin through Ipetu and Akure, and to Ilorin – a route which seems to have received much stimulus from the fact that Ilorin was allied with the Ekitiparapo against Ibadan. The trade for which Ijesha have been famous in the twentieth century not only has its origins in these Ijesha responses to the opportunities of the 1860s and 1870s but is, as we shall see, quite precisely marked by these origins.[52]

The many references to traders in late nineteenth-century sources, and the range of trade-goods casually mentioned, make it seem likely that Ijesha society was being penetrated more thoroughly by market relations, though lack of evidence for the first half of the century makes this difficult to prove. The most direct evidence is that whereas Omirinmirin market, on the way to Oshogbo, which was abandoned in the 1870s, met only every sixteen days, its eventual successor nearby at Oke Ibode, whose range of commodities so astonished Clarke in 1858, met every four days.[53] Any increase in trade implies a population more dependent on cash incomes. In 1893, when the camp at Kiriji broke up, 'shortage of money' caused problems both for the small Christian congregation at Ilesha, since the people could not pay their class fees and the pastor was in difficulties, and for the town at large, since the soldiers, unpaid, were given licence to pillage the farms.[54] The best evidence for a widespread and novel importance of money at this period in Ilesha comes from personal names. Surnames born in Ilesha today are usually the personal names, often nicknames, borne by men active in the late nineteenth century, and very many of them (over 5% of the sample in the 1974 Household Survey) underscore the importance of money (*owo* or *aje*):

Fafowora	Ifa provides money to buy with
Fowowe	awash with money
Olowookere	a rich man is not a small man
Arowojobe	one who gets the money to eat stew
Owoeye	money is respect
Ajewole	money enters the house

and many more.[55] The demand for money incomes, which would have such sweeping effects in the early colonial period, was well established by the experiences of the nineteenth century.

The historical mainspring of these developments did not lie within any dynamic thrust of Ijesha society itself, but in the collapse of Oyo and the changing character of European trade at the coast, to which Ilesha had to respond. Though remote from the coast, Ilesha occupied a particular niche in a regional system of states which pivoted on relations with coastal points of trade, and her viability as a community depended on a certain level of success in appropriating resources circulating within this region. This was disrupted from the early nineteenth century, first by the pressure of Oyo refugees and then by the intrusion of Ibadan. The community's dependence on favourable external contacts became even more acute, in ways that could initially be more or less contained within the traditional political framework but eventually burst it asunder. The resultant rise of *ologun* households and the makings, in the Kiriji camp, of an Ibadan-style polity have been characterized as revolutionary.[56] They were certainly a sharper institutional break with the past than Ilesha had known for a very long time, perhaps since the development of the town's quarter structure; but these changes did not long survive the end of the wars which had begotten them. The *pax Britannica* destroyed the conditions under which large households of any kind could long survive,[57] and the 'traditional' title-system began to reassert itself even before then. When the warrior Obe died around 1890, his body being brought back from Kiriji for burial in his home quarter of Isinkin, the *Qwa* and his chiefs installed him as *Risinkin* – posthumously, so that the installation payments might serve as death duties and reduce his following. This gave rise to the saying:

> *Ijeşa nşeke, nwǫn fi oku joye*
> The Ijesha are hypocrites; they made dead men chiefs[58]

The real revolutionary force was the growing need of Ijesha of all kinds to make money, and the new values which accompanied it. The nineteenth century ended, therefore, with a political restoration, and with an economic and cultural transformation just gathering speed.

Part II

The kingdom incorporated

6

The Ijesha 'protected'

The Ijesha were not conquered by the British, neither did they willingly undergo incorporation into what became the Nigerian state. Rather they were manoeuvred by stages into the Lagos Protectorate and its successors (Southern Nigeria from 1906 and Nigeria from 1914), refractory to the demands of those to whom they conceded no right to demand and only gradually aware of the constructions that their 'protectors' put upon the relationship.

Yet, in two ways, their predicament was partly of their own making. From the 1880s and possibly earlier,[1] the British had been seen as a political resource which could be deployed by the Ilesha authorities in their struggle against the Ibadans, analogous to the other external powers which Ilesha had invoked earlier in her history. But as Britain became more directly interested in controlling the hinterland of Lagos, it became more and more impossible for Ilesha to impose her terms on the relationship. Moreover, Ilesha did not relate to the British as a unified agent, although this is how her response to the early colonial period is typically represented in the common traditions current in Ilesha today. As soon as the British had become a close, permanent and, as far as the Ilesha authorities were concerned, unwelcome presence, as they did with the construction of a District Headquarters just outside Ilesha in 1900, they were sought out as a potential ally by several of those political forces within the community that were opposed to the local establishment. So the theme of this chapter, covering the early years of the colonial period, is the interplay between the ongoing politics of the town, as they continued from the nineteenth century, and the stormy evolution of Ilesha's relations with the British.

The British came to intervene directly in Ijesha affairs in the 1880s, when the armies of Ibadan and the Ekitiparapo confronted one another in stalemate in the hills of northern Ijeshaland. The earliest European travellers, who had passed through the town in 1857–58, had been treated with the restrictive politeness that was customarily shown to important strangers. The most official of these visitors, D. J. May, was told in 1858 that the white man would be welcome to come and trade, build houses and teach the people, but that he could not travel eastwards to Ekiti.[2] An attitude of diffuse respect for European power, apparently conceived of as a force of disinterested benevolence, was evinced when the missionary David Hinderer visited Ilesha later that year. *Oibo Qwa, o ma gun, aiye gun rebete*, 'The *Qwa*'s white man has arrived, now the world will become straight', they sang in welcome to him.[3] Already there was a bridgehead of the European world in the town in the small group of 'Sierra Leonians', Ijesha returnees from slavery abroad, who came to play an important but ambivalent role representing the Ijesha and the British to each other. It was two of these, J. P. Haastrup and P. J. Meffre, who wrote on behalf of *Qwa* Bepo in 1882, seeking British intervention to secure the freedom of the Ijesha and Ekiti country from the Ibadans. A lion was wanted as a guarantor of peace, they wrote, and the Queen of England was that lion: 'Whatever she say I will do, only I want to be independent forever from the Ibadans; and without she comes as a Lion between us and checks the Ibadans, there will be no go in the matter.'[4] As the Lagos Government became more involved in the peace negotiations, however, British power came to be seen in a more realistic light. Haastrup wrote to Bepo in 1886, urging him to trust the Governor and his agents: 'those Ijeshas who are saying the white man will take the land are liars. Don't believe on those Ijeshas here who [are] continually telling you that if you allow the Governor to make peace, he will make you to abandon your fetish, free all your slaves and make you have one wife.'[5] These opinions had a fair groundswell of support among the ordinary Ijesha soldiers in the Kiriji camp, opposed to the concessions to Ibadan that the Governor's agents were urging; but most vehement of the 'hard-line' party were two repatriates, James Gureje Thompson who had been enslaved to Abeokuta, and a carpenter from Brazil, Abe by name, the special messenger of the Ekitiparapo Society in Lagos.[6] In 1886 a treaty was signed with Ibadan, both sides agreeing to break up their camps and the Ijesha reluctantly abandoning their northern towns of Otan, Iresi, Ada and Igbajo to Ibadan's suzerainty. The treaty of 1886 committed the Ijesha 'to endeavour in every legitimate way to promote trade and commerce and to abstain from dissension and acts likely to promote strife', and gave the Governor the right to arbitrate if further disputes occurred.[7] The only other treaty obligation which the Ijesha ever incurred, a few months later, was to abolish human sacrifice. What was ominous for the Ijesha in this latter Enactment, as the reference to 'all civilized nations and right-minded persons' in the preamble makes clear, was the cool assumption by the Lagos Government of the right to provide cultural directions to the independent kingdoms of the interior. The soldiery at Kiriji had not mistaken this tone.

In fact the 1886 treaty did not lead at once to peace, since the conflict in northern Ijeshaland was locked into a system of conflicts ranging over most of the Yoruba country. Ibadan and the Ekitiparapo's ally Ilorin were still at war, and it was not till 1893 that the troops finally dispersed from the Kiriji camp. That could only be effected when the Colonial Office yielded to commercial and other pressures both in Lagos and England and sanctioned a decisive general intervention by the Governor, backed up by military force, throughout interior Yorubaland. The conquest of Ijebu in 1892 by a British expedition – in which, incidentally, some Ijesha demobilized from Kiriji took part[8] – had a decisive impact on political opinion throughout the Yoruba kingdoms. In 1893 the greatest of them all, Ibadan, signed an Agreement putting itself under the Protectorate and accepted a British Resident with a garrison of the Lagos Hausas.[9]

The end of the wars revived political disorder in Ijeshaland. A large population began to redeploy itself from the centres of northern Ijeshaland where the war had drawn them. Ilesha itself was still a shadow of its former self, probably counting not more than 5,000 inhabitants.[10] Its title-system was largely in abeyance as many of its functions had been taken over by the command-structure developed in the camp by Ogedengbe. There could be no stability where titled office and the control of population did not correspond in relation to a regional centre, and this was not easily achieved. The reconstitution of the kingdom's capital was made more difficult by the death, in September 1892, of *Owa* Bepo, with whom Ogedengbe had achieved a working relationship throughout the long years of the Kiriji War. We know little enough about the politics which brought his successor Lowolodu to the throne in March 1893, but he and Ogedengbe were soon at loggerheads. Plans to restrain Ogedengbe and draw him into the government of Ilesha by conferring on him the title of 'Baba Okesha' (i.e. *Obanla*) came to nothing. The *Owa* did not have the means to exert any control in the district or to induce the demobilized soldiery to resettle in the capital. Throughout 1893 and early 1894 plundering and kidnapping at the hands of Ogedengbe's followers occurred widely in the district, and the *Loja* of Ijeda was murdered.[11] How directly Ogedengbe was behind this it is hard to say but the critical *Lagos Weekly Record* accused him of appropriating the revenues of Ilesha and adjacent towns.[12] Later he contemplated establishing himself with his followers at his natal village of Atorin, fifteen miles to the south of Ilesha, which Lowolodu opposed, reasonably fearing it would further suck away Ilesha's population. Ogedengbe's motives for such a secession are not entirely clear, though he may have found a precedent in Okeigbo, which Aderin of Ife founded with his warriors in the 1850s, barely twenty miles away and on a trade route south through the forest.[13] For it was less a sentimental attachment to his birthplace which recommended Atorin than its proximity to the Oni river, which could serve as an outlet to the Lagos Lagoon, free of the possibility of interference by the Ondos. Is it possible that Ogedengbe was governed by strategic considerations and, having delivered Ilesha from conquest by Ibadan, was anxious to keep it safe from the British? As recently as 1890, when the Kiriji War was all but over,

Ogedengbe had written to a Lagos trading contact, Seidu Olowu, who operated through Aiyesan and Itebu on the Ondo route, asking him urgently to send guns, since 'we don't like the white man to take our country at all'.[14]

The British, at least, took the threat to their incipient authority seriously. In June 1894 Captain Bower came from Ibadan and, with nine of his Hausa soldiers, arrested Ogedengbe at a public meeting in the presence of the *Owa*. Since over £1,500-worth of arms were later recovered from Ogedengbe's chief lieutenant Gureje Thompson, the lack of opposition is eloquent either of the awe in which British power was still held or of the uncertainty regarding British intentions. Ogedengbe was fined and exiled to Iwo, where he remained with his followers for over a year. Governor Carter came up to Ilesha in August to show support for Lowolodu and to assess the political situation. His characterization of the impotence of the *Owa*'s authority was scathing and indicates the lines along which the Lagos Government would later strengthen it as a component of indirect rule.[15] Some of the Hausa were stationed in Ilesha. But none of this was of much help to the hapless Lowolodu, who died mysteriously just three months later in the way that Carter had virtually predicted: 'if [a Yoruba ruler] makes himself unpleasant and tries to be independent [of his powerful subjects], he is promptly sent to sleep'. In Ilesha it is still said that Ogedengbe, by means of a powerful *aṣẹ*, 'spoke the fate of Lowolodu'.[16]

OWA AJIMOKO I

The new *Owa* was much more a man for the times, effectively chosen by the two major forces of Ilesha politics, the followers of Ogedengbe and those Ijesha who, as traders along the Lagoon, repatriates from slavery or possessed of some education, had links with the Ekitiparapo Society in Lagos. He was Frederick Kumokun alias Haastrup, who in his long life – he was now well over seventy – had fully shared in the tribulations of his country. Captured by the Ilorins in the 1820s he was sold into slavery and, by some means, later found himself in Sierra Leone, where he became a Christian.[17] Returning to Yorubaland, he traded along the Lagoon between Lagos and Itebu, where he had lived, dealing in salt and dried fish, and in strategic commodities that passed up the Ondo route to the Ijesha at Kiriji. Already considered the likely successor in December 1894 by Carter, it was reported to the Lagos Ijesha in March 1895 that 'they want no one else', and he was finally installed as *Owa* Ajimoko in April 1896.[18] The intervening year seems to have passed in consultations to ensure a working alliance of the major forces of the town – for there was not likely to be peace while Ogedengbe was still in exile – and to prepare a programme of restoration and development.

Restoration came first. Ogedengbe came home and was made *Obanla*, moving into the chieftaincy house in Okesha and settling the rest of his following, doubtless diminished by his exile, in a vast compound at Anaye, not far from those of his associates Thompson and Apara, who built next to one another in Iloro. His commitment to the town must have been increased by the paralysis which soon struck his legs and immobilized him for the rest of his days. In other ways time and peace aided the re-establishment of order: Arimoro, most prestigious of all the warriors after Ogedengbe himself, who might have been a serious rival to Ajimoko since he too was of royal descent, was too old and ill to contest, dying in 1899. He had settled with his followers in a large area of Lower Egbeidi, their houses surrounded by a stockade, and put himself behind Ajimoko.[19] Obe was dead already and his following largely dispersed. The next most prominent among the warlords, Ogunmodede, took the other major town title, *Lejǫka*. Other senior titles were filled with men of a warrior background who were personally closer to Ajimoko or might serve as counterweights to Ogedengbe, such as Lajiga the *Loro*, from whom the *Ǫwa* married a daughter, Gidigbi the *Ǫdǫle* and his kinsman Esan, whom Ajimoko raised to be *Lejofi* against Ogedengbe's wishes in 1897.[20] When Governor McGregor visited Ilesha in 1900 he found the reconstitution of the quarters in full swing, Ajimoko 'rearranging and laying out the town in square blocks, each little block [with] a headman who is held responsible for its condition', but 'creating a good deal of individual discontent' in the process.[21] None the less, he was sympathetic to a ruler who struck him as 'the most advanced of all the provincial chiefs' and as 'a man that will rule alone and not be directed by any inferior chief', as if in riposte to the Ibadan Resident's view, when he visited Ilesha in 1897, that 'the whole place wants knocking into shape'.[22]

But the primary task was to reassemble the town's population, which was still seen as absolutely fundamental to communal and chiefly prowess. There was a reflux of Ijesha from the markets and ports on the Ondo route to the Lagoon, of young men from Lagos, and generally of slaves.[23] The 1890s saw a general return of slaves to their homelands, which meant an overall movement of population back eastwards to the areas of earlier depredation, from Ibadan to Ilesha and Ekiti, from Ilesha to Ekiti, Akoko and beyond. The dispute which the *Ǫwa* had with the Resident at Ibadan in 1898 over three slaves of an Ibadan woman, who escaped home to Ilesha without redeeming themselves and whom he was forced to return, was thus of great symbolic importance.[24] None the less, Ilesha in 1899 seemed 'poor and depopulated';[25] and its outer quarters, small huddles of houses, were separated by zones of overgrown vegetation from the core of settlement. A real difficulty was revealed in the Travelling Commissioner's comment for November 1899: 'the villages under the Owa were called into Ilesha, in order to place them under their paramount Chief from whom they almost unanimously wished to break away'.[26] The cycle of communal success – population growth on the one hand, military mastery and control of trade on the other, each reciprocally conditioning the other – had been broken by the wars, and *Qwa* Ajimoko had the problem of starting it again. Ordinary Ijesha had small reason to go to any other kingdom, but most of them had links with a village or a district community, 'however dirty, sordid and out-of-the-way',[27] where they were most intimately known and where the business of subsistence was conducted. It was not at all clear what they, unlike the title-holders and their immediate followings, would gain from associating themselves, through residence, with the kingdom's capital. Ilesha's rulers needed to find some resources to attract, or sanctions to control, a dependent population.

One novel solution had already been canvassed among the Lagos Ijesha whose organ was the Ekitiparapo Society, a body whose *raison d'être* had grown rather thin since the end of the war. At the instance of C. A. Sapara-Williams, a lawyer of Ijesha birth who was to be the faithful champion of Ilesha's interests in Government circles for the next twenty years, 'it was proposed that the society be converted into an Industrial Company for the purpose of working Rubber in Ekitiland, a branch of the Scheme [being] to support the Ekiti government'.[28] These years were the height of the short-lived boom in the collection of wild rubber from the barely touched forests which stretched from Ijebu through southern Ijesha to the country beyond Ondo.[29] But we hear nothing more of this scheme, which was certainly beyond the organizational capacity of the Ekitiparapo Society or the Ilesha government. The resources of the forests were more easily exploited by individuals or at the most small groups of entrepreneurs, many of whom were in fact Ijebu.[30] Instead of organizing production themselves, the Ijesha authorities hoped to employ older methods of raising revenue from it, by making direct levies on those engaged in the rubber trade, especially through tolls.[31] Thus it was that the securing of frontiers, and the making and controlling of roads, were urgent preoccupations of the *Qwa* and his advisers.

In 1897 and 1898 Ilesha was visited for a few days by the Resident of Ibadan. On the first occasion he found it a terrible road from Ife, all through forest, and had occasion to warn the *Qwa* not to levy tolls on rubber not collected in places under his jurisdiction. A year later he found that the road greatly improved at the Ijesha boundary, and at Oshu, the first sizeable Ijesha community, he met a guard, wearing a grey uniform with red facings, and armed with a Snider rifle, whom the *Qwa* had sent to superintend road making.[32] Ilesha was as anxious to avoid the costs of her not having direct access to Lagos and the great markets of the Lagoon as she was to capitalize on her advantages *vis-à-vis* the further interior.[33] So when Governor McGregor in 1900 dilated on the importance of Ilesha's communications with Ibadan, *Qwa* Ajimoko countered with a plea for 'an independent road to Lagos' through Epe.[34]

The same concern was an important source of the systematic frontier policy which Ajimoko and his advisers soon put into effect. The strategic potentiality of the Oni river remained high in Ijesha thinking. 'A fresh effort [is] about to be put forth for the opening up of this desirable waterway to trade and commerce', reported the *Lagos Standard* in July 1896, 'the King of Ilesha recently enthroned has taken the initiative in devoting native and aboriginal labour to [it].'[35] In order to secure Ijesha control over it, Gureje Thompson with a company of his slaves and clients established a new settlement on the river, Etioni, in October 1896, nearly twenty miles south of Ilesha, well into the forest beyond the previous limits of Ilesha farms.[36] On the other side, where the loss of Ilesha's northern towns, now administered from Ibadan, still rankled, the problem was one of stemming a likely colonization of land south of the river Oshun by the dense Oyo populations of Oshogbo, Ede and Ikirun. Here, just south of the river at the deserted site of Omirinmirin market and barely three miles from the centre of Oshogbo, settled Peter Apara, who had supervised the machine-guns at Kiriji and accompanied Ogedengbe to exile at Iwo, and a friend of the *Owa*'s from when they had both traded on the Lagoon.[37] Later other men from the families of the warriors or the early Christians were to take cocoa-farms in this north-west direction. On the side of Ife, which posed less of a problem since its own population was still scattered, a kinsman of the *Owa*'s, Adeluyi, established an outpost of Ijesha territory at what became known as Alakowe, 'the place of the clerk'.

The eastern frontier presented opportunities rather than problems: as always in the past, it was an offensive rather than a defensive frontier. Benin's defeat in 1897 gave the *Owa* the chance to advance plausible, but resisted, claims over Akure.[38] The *Owa*'s grand design was that the interior Yoruba country should be divided into two realms, the *Alafin* to rule Oyo (including Ibadan), the *Owa* the Ekitiparapo, each 'having sole control over his own people'; but whereas 'the Alafin of Oyo and the Bale of Ibadan not understanding the modern civilized mode of Government, a Resident and an assistant should be placed to help to establish peace ... among them', 'Ilesha holding its own territories and being the key to the Parapo [and] understand[ing] also its method of proper selfgovernment, the Owa should be protected and strengthen[ed] to govern his towns and the rest of the Ekiti people.'[39] It was an audacious ploy thus to seek to predefine to Ilesha's advantage the role of the administrative official who was obviously shortly to be introduced, but it was not in the end successful. None the less, it might have seemed a step was taken in that direction when, late in 1899, Ilesha did become the seat of a Travelling Commissioner, Major W. C. Reeve-Tucker, whose brief was to cover the whole of the North-Eastern District, including all Ekiti. But Reeve-Tucker had been in Ilesha less than a year when he decided to abandon his original plan for a joint Ekitiparapo Council, in which the *Owa* would have been the leading figure. He had found that Ilesha's leadership was 'extremely unpopular' in Ekiti as a result of tolls and other impositions of the *Owa*'s agents and *emese*.[40] The *Owa* also kept up a prison, where he had detained the ruler of Ise after a dispute about a female slave, to the widespread consternation of other communities in the area.[41] Some contradictions in *Owa* Ajimoko's project to reestablish Ilesha as the dominant power of the region were becoming evident. The initial means he adopted – levying of tolls, discretionary control of subject communities and a general intervention in the activities of those hinterland peoples whose path to Lagos lay through Ijeshaland – required a staving-off of close British supervision of the area. When that became inescapable, the hope was to use the British as a political resource, getting them to define the political unit in such a way as to give Ilesha a privileged position within it. But once the British were directly involved in the affairs of the North-eastern District, the Ekiti kingdoms could present their own views as to the nature of the Ekitiparapo and the proper relations between themselves and Ilesha. It is hardly surprising that the modest political aspirations of the 'amenable' Ekiti found more favour with the imperial power than the aggrandizement of the Ijesha, 'a stubborn race, difficult to manage', as the administrators' stereotype soon had it.[42] Ultimately a more serious consequence of the Travelling Commissioner's presence in Ilesha was the close and increasingly critical attention given to political relations between the *Owa* and his own undisputed subjects.

A final aspect of *Owa* Ajimoko's programme remains to be considered: his cultural policy. Ajimoko was a consciously 'modern' ruler, in that he believed that the survival and prosperity of his kingdom depended, not just on external means such as the control of strategic resources or the successful manipulation of political alliances, but on the Ijesha being remade inwardly, that is on their being prepared to adopt a new culture. His committed Christianity – despite the annoyance his continued polygamy caused the Anglican clergy[43] – was a great part of this. He refused to perform many of the customary rites of kingship, having Chiefs *Babaileoke* and *Salua* to act for him instead, and even wore European dress on occasion, as when he went to Iloro Church, carried in a kind of rickshaw pulled by porters.[44] He invited the Methodists to establish a mission in Ilesha, calling on public labour to clear the site of the forbidden grove of Otapete for their church and their first minister, the Revd Hezekiah Atundaolu, became his 'Native Adviser'.[45] In all this he was assisted by a formidable lady, his daughter Adenibi (alias Mrs Isabella Macaulay), who had been a fully accredited local preacher in her Lagos circuit. Resident Fuller of Ibadan recorded his impression of them on his first visit in 1897: 'a shrewd and cunning old gentleman with a daughter who acts as his Prime Minister, from the amount of advice she gives him (generally good I should think)'.[46] Princess Adenibi supervised the school in the *Afin* to which chiefs were invited, under some pressure from the *Owa*, to send some of their sons.[47] Most of them were reluctant to do so, since the payoff of education for those not already predisposed in favour of the religious or cultural values associated with it was far from clear or certain. Ogedengbe sent none of his own, and it was only later, after long pleading, that he let the Revd

Oyebode at Iloro have one son to train, and Sapara-Williams in Lagos another. *Lejofi* Esan, who received his title very much as the *Owa's* man, angrily withdrew his son when he saw him being beaten by the schoolteacher. It was undoubtedly a prescient policy of the *Owa's*, but its main short-term effect was probably to strain his relations with his chiefs, just as his manifest disdain for the traditional supernatural sanctions of his office can only have weakened his authority in the community.

Ajimoko faced mounting opposition and conflict within Ilesha in the last eighteen months or so of his reign. Despite the frustration of the *Owa's* political ambitions in Ekiti, Ilesha's hold over the district communities of Ijeshaland had undoubtedly grown stronger, and with it the advantages of the *Owa* over other political forces in the capital. It was over the affair at Ise that Ajimoko fell out with his secretary Atundaolu, amid mutual accusations of abuse of power on the one side and disloyalty and corruption on the other, and drove him from Ilesha.[48] There were disputes between Princess Adenibi and other members of the *Owa's* household, which the Revd Oyebode was called in to mediate.[49] But more serious than these were his quarrels, of uncertain origin, with Ogedengbe the *Obanla* and Aduloju the *Ogboni*, the two senior chiefs. When Governor McGregor came to Ilesha in 1901 he was visited by the *Ogboni*, whom the *Owa* had fined £150 (an *enormous* sum) for failing to attend the opening ceremony of the Ogun festival, a sure indication of chiefly disaffection; and the paralysed Ogedengbe sent word asking for medical aid and protection from the *Owa*.[50] The Governor put it down to the *Owa's* age and ill-health having impaired his judgment, though the pattern of the conflict – chiefly resistance to the waxing of royal power – was quite in the normal run of Ijesha politics. But the British presence, to an extent which neither the Governor nor the Travelling Commissioner appreciated, was increasingly a destabilizing force, serving to bring resistance out, and thus to some extent undermined the preferred 'firm government'. For though the British liked to think of themselves as superior disinterested guardians, they had become a resource which parties in the town tried to call upon, and were thus drawn further into local political conflict. This new development had not gone far when Ajimoko died in September 1901, but his successor was soon to experience it in full.

OWA ATAIYERO: THE SOCIAL CRISIS

The new *Owa*, Ataiyero, a descendant of Ojagodo, was a more orthodox choice. But though a village-head, according to custom, he was not without a wider experience of the world, having spent some time as a slave in Ibadan and Ijebu before escaping to join the Ekitiparapo army at Kiriji. He reached the throne, despite his age of at least seventy years, through the sponsorship of Ogedengbe.[51] Maybe the other chiefs reckoned that such a man could not dominate them as Ajimoko had threatened to, though he lived to surprise them. Although his relations with Ogedengbe soon cooled,[52] the new *Owa* and the chiefs were in the main united in the political storms that were to occupy the first few years of his reign.

The Travelling Commissioner, with a small detachment of troops and a sizeable supporting labour force with all its dependants, was now well established at the station of Oke Imo, eight hundred feet up, overlooking the town.[53] Originally the Ilesha Council set up by McGregor with a dozen or so chiefly members (including one of the district *Ogboni*, a Christian and a Muslim), had met up here to much chiefly inconvenience and resentment; and even after a new council house had been built near the *Afin*, Oke Imo continued to grow as a force in Ilesha politics. With the passing of the Native Councils Ordinance in 1901, the British launched a much more definite policy to transform local administrative and fiscal practice.[54] This had two aspects. Firstly, tolls were to be commuted to an additional tribute from subordinate communities, set at £150 per annum. The *Owa* and chiefs complained that the sum collected fell short even of this inadequate compensation, and were incensed by the fact that the authorities at Ibadan and Abeokuta were still allowed to levy tolls.[55] Secondly a variety of customary levies, or 'irregular exactions' were to be replaced by the revenues, largely fees and fines, which would accrue to the Council sitting as a court, and from which salaries would then be drawn. This had an additional advantage, from the British point of view: it would oblige much more of the political and judicial transactions of the kingdom to pass through an arena where they would be subject to the supervision and intervention of the Commissioner. It was this which became the greatest focus of resistance since it radically undercut the discretionary power of the *Owa* and chiefs and made their authority clearly dependent on that of the colonial state. They tried to sabotage the new procedure by hearing cases 'secretly', receiving presents from supplicants and litigants whether individuals or subordinate communities in the customary way, and so depriving the court which the Commissioner wanted to set up as the keystone of the new order of both cases and revenue. In 1902–3 the Commissioner accused the *Owa* of making a proclamation that people were to come to him at the *Afin* rather than to the court at Oke Imo for the settlement of their disputes, and of refusing to raise labour for the new court-house that was to be built in Ilesha. And a whole series of complaints culminated in 1904, when the *Obaodo* and the *Loro* were each convicted and imprisoned for 'receiving bribes' in respect of cases which had come to them from Erinmo and Ipetu, towns of which they were the respective *onile*.[56]

Captain Ambrose, the Commissioner who made these policies peculiarly his own, came to see his task in the terms of a moral crusade: the *Loro* was 'a regular vampire'; there was 'persistent corruption among the ruling classes'; the chiefs were a predatory elite whose style of government was moulded by 'the past campaigns and successful raids of Ogedengbe'.[57] He was sustained in this by the new Governor, Sir Walter Egerton, a far more impatient and arrogant imperialist than his predecessor. But Ambrose had little idea of the difficulties into which his new proposals put the chiefs. Quite apart from the question of whether the *Owa*'s proposed stipend would in fact amount to an adequate compensation, the old system of 'irregular exactions' had been roughly gauged to reward differentially, according to distance from the political centre, all those who felt they had claims on the centre and who were in return the supports of the *Owa*'s authority throughout his kingdom. The rank of titles was adjusted to the resource flows they severally commanded, which came largely from stipulated sources such as communities attached to particular *onile* chiefs, and flowed out again to the title-holders' dependants. The system Ambrose proposed would, by outlawing 'bribes' and by diverting incoming resources to a common public fund, break those particular links between title-holders and their subjects which contributed a great part of the political integration of the kingdom; and it offered no guarantee that the new pattern of allocation would provide an alternative, graduated system of chiefly reward. Other chiefs had shared what the *Loro* received from Ipetu in 1904, and Chiefs *Risawẹ* and *Arapatẹ* 'openly stated they would starve if not allowed to take fees'.[58] A kind of levy which aroused the particular indignation of the Travelling Commissioner was the presents which the *Owa*'s *ẹmẹsẹ* received from supplicants in the district, known as *inihun* ('having a voice'). This may well have been regarded as irksome but, since they represented payment to the principal instruments of the *Owa*'s direct authority in the district, the Commissioner's attempt to remove them was hardly consistent with the declared British objective of maintaining Ilesha as the District's centre, let alone with *Owa* Ataiyero's conception of his royal office. The same went for the *Owa*'s right to take into the *Afin*, either as additional wives for himself or to pass on to his dependants, the wives of suicides or executed felons. This was one more element of the system of social control practised through the control of women by title-holders; and when Governor Egerton peremptorily declared it was to be abandoned, it could only be interpreted, whatever the actual numbers of women involved, as a significant blow at political authority. Perhaps most indicative of the *Owa*'s difficulties in maintaining his position in the face of Ambrose's policies was his insistence to the Governor at their heated palaver in March 1905 that he wanted tribute in yams, corn, etc. (by implication, not in cash) 'because people coming here get nothing to eat'.[59] For the *Owa* could still only function politically if he were able to feed his own large household as well as strangers, casual dependants and visitors to the *Afin*. There was, for reasons to be examined below, something of a crisis in agricultural production in these years, and the demand from Oke Imo and its personnel had further inflated food prices, rendering the value of the proposed stipend even more questionable. It would seem likely too that some district communities took advantage of the friction between the *Owa* and the Commissioner to neglect to send in their customary *iwisin* of tribute in kind.

The chapter of disharmony between the *Ǫwa* and the Commissioner grew steadily to a climax. In June 1904 the *Ǫwa* and chiefs sent a petition to the Governor, asking for Captain Ambrose's removal and pointing out that the only understanding that the Ijesha had had of the relationship was that the Commissioner should serve as an adviser, leaving the Ijesha to determine their own internal affairs.[60] But in February 1905 Ambrose received a 'Loyal Address', signed by over thirty people, many of them Christian or Muslim, and headed by none other than Princess Adenibi Haastrup.[61] It was fulsome in tone, referring to 'the benefit of your Worship's rule over us as from Imo Hill . . . daily descending, thorough and perfect redress to the poor, the oppressed and the afflicted for which Imo Hill is now to us not only a sacred palace but an object of adoration' and comparing his philanthropy to that of Sharp, Buxton and Wilberforce. This evidence of support within Ilesha may have strengthened the Government's resolve to take the drastic steps which ensued.

Governor Egerton arrived in Ilesha on 16 March and at once summoned the *Ǫwa* to visit him at Oke Imo.[62] The *Ǫwa* declined, asseverating that it was against Ijesha custom for an *Ǫwa* to leave his palace in such a way, but the Governor insisted, promising to send his travelling hammock down. The *Ǫwa* conferred with his chiefs and went the following day, bringing gifts which the Governor refused to accept. After this disagreeable overture, the *Ǫwa* complained of Ambrose's rudeness and high-handedness, his contempt for the customary prerogatives of the *Ǫwa*, his encouragement of insubordinate elements in the town against him, and of the inadequacy of his own material support. There could be no reactivation of the Council with the *Loro* and the *Ǫbaodo* still in prison. Governor Egerton reprimanded the chiefs for their refusal to cooperate with the Travelling Commissioner, yielding nothing on the requests for the release of the imprisoned chiefs or Ambrose's removal. He interrogated them on the drawing-up of last year's petition and warned them against the 'foolish advice of Lagos people'. The meeting reconvened the next day in the same spirit but on pettier issues and more personal grievances. Then, to general consternation, the Governor proposed that the *Ǫwa* should come on a visit with him to Benin, ostensibly to be shown its system of administration. There were desperate rumours that the *Ǫwa* might take his own life or even that Ogedengbe had counselled him to do so.[63] Chiefly intercessions with the Governor were to no avail: on 19 March four soldiers with hammock-men went to collect the *Ǫwa*, and with a large following crowd of his chiefs and subjects, he and the Governor set off for Benin. They camped the first night at Ipetu, where the *Ǫwa*'s people were told to turn back to Ilesha, and the *Ǫwa* went into exile where he was to remain for just over a month.[64]

These events caused great reverberations in Lagos among educated African opinion, whose major organs, the nationalist press and the unofficial members of the Legislative Council, were already considerable bugbears of the Government. Ilesha had always been of concern to them, since so many Ijesha had earlier followed the path of enslavement, liberation and subsequent involvement in commerce or the educated professions, like the members of the Lagos Ekitiparapo. The hopes they had entertained at Ajimoko's accession to see Ilesha restored and developed as an autonomous unit under British protection had been frustrated; and their own aspirations for respect and advancement within the colonial society of Lagos were increasingly threatened by the restrictive and segregationist policies that were now being pursued by the Government.[65] The struggle of Ilesha's rulers to maintain their autonomy became an exemplary case with them, and they put their skills and contacts at the service of the *Owa*. To Governor Egerton's vexation, Ilesha's case was raised directly with the Colonial Secretary in London by the Aborigines' Rights Protection Society, which queried not merely the conduct of officials but the whole legal basis of the Lagos Government's intervention in Ilesha.[66] Perhaps because it seemed to displace the local source of the troubles or because the educated nationalists of Lagos were disproportionately able to annoy and embarrass them, the colonial authorities were prone to attribute a quite exaggerated importance to the role of 'Lagos mentors' in fomenting the Ilesha troubles and tried to drive a wedge between them and the local rulers. So when Ataiyero returned from Benin, he was pressed by Ambrose in a private interview to sign a document declaring that he had not been treated as a prisoner at Benin (which he did not deny) and that 'he instructed no lawyer to fight with the Governor'. If the *Lagos Standard*'s report of it is accurate, the *Owa*'s reply to Captain Ambrose's direct question on this latter point was splendid:

> If Lawyer [i.e. Sapara-Williams] is fighting with Governor Egerton on my behalf, he is right, because Lawyer is my son. The ALAKE of Abeokuta is a king as I am but he has never been removed from Abeokuta by force and against his will. The OBA of Ilorin fought with British Government but he was not transported for it, he is instead in full enjoyment of his kingdom. A bombardment of Oyo was attempted by Capt. Bower but the ALAFIN of Oyo was never removed by the Governor of Lagos. The AWUJALE of Jebu Ode waged war with the Lagos Government, he was never deported or even threatened with transportation. And above all the King of Bida fought the English Government and killed TWO WHITEMEN but he was not transported; instead of his being removed, the British Government made friendship with him and treated him as a friend till he died. In my case I have not broken my treaty with the British Government, I have not stolen, I have not taken bribe nor have I broken any law of my country or your Government, yet I have been taken away from my country by Governor Egerton. No doubt this is the reason why LAWYER is fighting and will fight with the Governor for me. If all my children, as you say, at the other side of the Ocean (i.e. the Lagoon, meaning Lagos) are fighting Governor Egerton, no doubt it is because they see that I have been removed from my country without due cause.[67]

101

A wider appreciation of Sapara-Williams' efforts at Ilesha was expressed in a popular chorus, the basic form of which may still be heard sung at the Ogun festival:

> *Tani wipe a o ni baba? A ni baba, Lǫya Kirisi baba wa*
> Who says we have no father? Hey! We so have a father, Lawyer Chris is our father[68]

Yet it would be very mistaken to infer from this cooperation between the Ilesha chiefs and the educated Ijesha in Lagos that there was a unanimity of sentiment, either among educated Ijesha generally or within the whole population of Ilesha. The 'Loyal Address' is evidence enough of that and is confirmed by Ǫwa Ataiyero's complaint to Ambrose, that he 'has made detectives of his own people and chiefs and that he and these men have been upsetting everything'.[69] The truth was that British pressure on the Ilesha authorities was bringing to the surface a good deal of social conflict latent within the community. Moreover, as a result of social and cultural changes more generally afoot, there were emerging entirely new status-groups which were as yet ill-integrated in the social framework of the town. Ǫwa Ataiyero and his chiefs were in fact faced with a coalition of local opponents who were, to varying degrees, allies of the Travelling Commissioner on Oke Imo.

The most straightforward opponents were the heads of the larger and more autonomous subordinate communities, intent as always on loosening Ilesha's hold over them. Chief among them was the senior district *Ogboni* and a member of the new Council, the *ǫba* of Ibokun, whom the *Ǫwa* accused of 'insolence', perhaps because he insisted that his signature on the anti-Ambrose petition had been forged. Ambrose considered he was the only 'loyal' chiefly Council member, though the *Ogboni* of Ijebu was doubtfully so. Of other communities, whose heads had no seat on the council, we hear less; but Otan and Ipole had tried to throw off Ilesha's yoke a year or so earlier,[70] while Ipetu presented trouble, on and off, for years; and very widely there was foot-dragging on the payment of tribute. The British administration had the greatest difficulty in deciding how far to go in support of these small allies of convenience, for despite the moral gratification of championing the underdog, they still needed to maintain Ilesha as a regional centre.

But who constituted the opposition *within* Ilesha? A clue, but a misleading one, is provided by the high proportion of those with Christian or Muslim names who signed the 'Loyal Address'.[71] For it does not appear that the new religions as such had much reason to side with the Commissioner against the *Ǫwa*. True, Ataiyero was entirely loyal to the beliefs of his forefathers; but he did not actively hinder the practice or even proselytism of the new religions, and they, in turn, had everything to gain in practice from showing themselves loyal to the local establishment.[72] Rather it was attributes most contingently connected with the profession of

102

Christianity or Islam which brought a disproportionate number of their adherents into opposition to the *Qwa*, even where they tended to draw on their religion to justify it. The most complex and instructive case is provided by Ataiyero's most serious long-term critic within the town (though he was not a signatory), the leading Christian layman and a Council member: Peter Apara. He had been a key supporter of the Ajimoko regime and, according to the tendency of Ijesha politics, had gravitated into a camp of 'outs' as the new *Qwa*'s court became established. Others of this group were also estranged from the *Qwa*, none more than Princess Adenibi (who, to Ataiyero's justified annoyance, was still living in the storey house her father built in the *Afin* precincts, where she sometimes entertained Captain Ambrose to dinner *à l'anglaise*). One of the Muslim signatories, Bakare Orimogunje, also identified by the *Qwa* as one of his foremost opponents, was a cousin of *Qwa* Ajimoko's, who had wanted to make him a *Loja* and had granted the site for the Central Mosque at Ereja at his request.[73] *Qbanla* Ogedengbe himself stayed loyal to the *Qwa*, but his only reported contribution to the palaver of 17 March was hardly encouraging: on being asked by the Governor if he used to be a great warrior, he replied that 'he has some knowledge of war with the blackman but has never tried hands with the white man and cannot undertake to fight them'.[74] Two other signatories shared Apara's warrior and Christian connexions: David Ibidapo, son of the great warrior Obe and husband of Ajimoko's niece Aderinle, and Fariogun, kinsman and former companion of Arimoro.[75] But Apara and others also had more direct interests which inclined them to see some merit in the Commissioner. From his farm Apara supplied maize and cassava to the establishment at Oke Imo,[76] while yet another signatory, C. A. Lufadeju, worked as a carpenter there (at one time under the supervision of J. A. Thompson, eldest son and heir of Apara's friend Gureje Thompson).[77] For reasons to be explored more fully later, both cash-cropping and new crafts like carpentry were originally associated with the early Christians and their connexions. Several signatories were cocoa pioneers: Ibidapo, Fariogun, Lufadeju and also another of the Muslims, Abe Amodu, who went with Thompson to Etioni and later founded the nearby cocoa-village of Aladodo.

When Apara visited Lagos to report to the Ekitiparapo Society about events in Ilesha, he was closely interrogated by its members, who accused him of humiliating the *Qwa* and supporting the Commissioner.[78] This was an irony: that the Lagos members of the Ekitiparapo, who identified their cause with that of the *Qwa* as a common opposition to colonial arrogance, should find themselves at odds with their most prominent former member in Ilesha itself, who largely because of the attributes he shared with them was, if not an ally of the Commissioner, at least a definite opponent of the *Qwa*. Apara strenuously defended himself from the charge of disloyalty, but admitted he had urged the *Qwa* to accede somewhat to the Commissioner's demands. It appears that, apart from his personal and ideological antipathy to Ataiyero, it was chiefly over the manner of handling the Commissioner that Apara dissented from the chiefs. He had a much livelier sense of the power and permanence of the new order (*ọwọ wọn gun*, 'their reach is long', he would say of the British up at Oke Imo),[79] and felt that it had to be encountered with the techniques of the age, as Ajimoko had aspired to do, rather than with the mere reassertion of customary practice.

But Apara was not typical of the mass of opposition in the town, which came above all from *young* men. The 'detectives' or informers from whom the Commissioner got much of his information about the chiefs were youths for whom Oke Imo became a kind of Cave of Adullam. Bitter was the *Ọwa*'s complaint that they welcomed Ambrose back from his leave 'beating drums that he is the Lion of Ilesha and who can combat with the forest and hills?'[80] The most notorious of them was a man who signed the 'Loyal Address' as Israel Derby, but who is remembered today (with much wry affection, it must be said) as Dabi of Orinkiran, where at this time he practised as a tailor. He founded the first modern young men's *ẹgbẹ* and had a drummer, Aliyu, to beat provocative songs, such as:

> *iya l'aiye, Lejofi wọ 'wu ti mo wọ, iya l'aiye*
> what a miserable age, that the Lejofi wears the same clothes that I wear![81]

Since quality cloth, being a costly prestige good, had once been virtually restricted to title-holders and *Lejofi* Esan was known for the standard of his wardrobe, the force of this song, as social criticism, can well be imagined. These years, in fact, witnessed a major challenge to a cardinal element of the Ijesha social system: the control of young men and their labour by chiefs and by elders. Such had happened before, but this time the eventual result would be a permanent change in the relations between age-groups.

The essential mechanism of gerontocracy worked at the domestic level: polygyny and the custom of betrothing prepubescent girls to young adult males meant that a man married late, rarely before his thirties, remaining under the roof of his father and obliged to offer periodic labour-service and gifts over the years of his engagement to his prospective father-in-law; otherwise he might hope to inherit a wife on the death of a senior relative. The young man could only abbreviate the years of his dependency by earning some wealth himself; but there were few opportunities to do this in Ilesha that were not controlled by the chiefs. If he was not to seek his fortune outside, a young man typically had to swallow his impatience and serve his 'apprenticeship'. Now the British Protectorate had considerably changed the conditions of these practices. The abolition of tolls operated by chiefs, new commercial opportunities such as the rubber-trade, the introduction of new crafts not dependent on lineage transmission, and the availability of wage-employment around the establishment at Oke Imo, as well as the even greater opportunities in Lagos and along the railway, all provided young men with the opportunity to challenge the authority of chiefs and elders. Moreover the circumstances of the times must have meant that there were a good many young men who had never entered the traditional protracted betrothal, owing to their absence from town, and who thus had no spouse assured them, and since early adoption of the world religions was associated with out-migration, there would have been a good degree of overlap between this category and the Christians and Muslims. The chiefs moved to check them. When the Governor interviewed the Ilesha Muslims headed by Orimogunje, it was on behalf of them *qua* young men as much as *qua* Muslims that he spoke:

> People here do not like trade and whenever I speak truth in any matter, it is always irksome to them, hence they do not like the Mohammedans . . . I used to call the young men of the country to try to improve trade but when the Chiefs hear this they do not like it at all. . . . whoever tries to enlighten the people, he becomes their enemy . . . [They accuse him of being a 'detective' and of 'moving too near the Commissioner'].[82]

One way the chiefs might meet this challenge is illustrated in the case of Ojo Gangan, later *Ẹjẹmọ* of Okesha, who had acted as Ambrose's interpreter. The rubber-trade, after its near extinction through over-tapping in the late 1890s, was reopened under Ataiyero on a more modest scale, being controlled through the issue of licences, usually by the chiefs, for a fee. Ojo incurred the wrath of Ogedengbe (who was in fact his kinsman) by going directly to Oke Imo for a licence, and for this Ogedengbe had him flogged in open court; this was in 1908 and he did not dare return until after Ogedengbe's death two years later.[83] But there was not much local trade or employment that could be taxed or controlled in this way; and probably a good deal of the new cash incomes came from outside Ilesha anyway. But as it happened it was possible to impose on the primary item of expenditure and so the issue was joined – in the divorce courts!

The first charge on a young man's earnings was to get himself a wife. But he confronted a situation where most eligible women were betrothed or married (and, in addition, tended to be concentrated in the hands of senior men). There was thus a high level of seduction. Another of Dabi's songs put it with impudent clarity:

> *ilẹkẹ idi adelebọ, Dabi l'o ni*
> The beads round the loins of the newly-wed wife, they are Dabi's[84]

Overwhelmingly the business of the Ilesha Native Court at this period was divorce.[85] Few applications for divorce were turned down; and the Court's main practical concern was with fixing the amount of 'dowry' to be returned to the woman's husband by the new suitor. This was not, in fact, the amount of bridewealth which the husband had paid, but a form of compensation plus fine, graded according to the condition of the woman: £5 for a woman who had borne children to her husband, £7 10s 0d for a woman who had not yet, £12 10s 0d for a betrothed virgin. A contemporary fairly considered it 'a curious piece of legislation that has no parallel in the annals

105

of any Native State in the country',[86] and its terms were very severe indeed on the suitor. But this was not only because those who chose to challenge the marital arrangements that underpinned gerontocracy were to be made to pay for it. It was the Commissioner's scheme that court revenues would be the new mainstay of public finance; and to the extent that he had succeeded in reducing other sources of revenue, the *Owa* and chiefs were driven to make the most of what was permitted them. At one stage a divorce compensation of as high as £20 was intended; later on, around one-fifth of the appropriate sum went as court fees. The most serious consequences of the gerontocracy's control of women was that even more young men were driven to leave the country in search of a cash income as the means to independence. 'This law', wrote a perceptive correspondent, 'is working very fast against the morality of the people and is fast denuding the population of its younger elements'; but at the same time the challenge of the young men meant that 'husbands are beginning to find it impossible to control the actions of their wives'.[87] All observers, from the chiefs to the Commissioner, held that it was the departure of young men, especially from Ilesha itself, which caused a crisis in food-crop production, resulting in a serious famine in 1905; and 'scarcity of foods' remained a problem for some years to come.[88]

These conflicts had no immediate resolution, nor was the issue between the *Owa* and the Commissioner determined by the *Owa*'s short exile in Benin. Indeed, things seemed to get worse.[89] In July the imprisoned *Obaodo* fell grievously ill; and the outrage at Ambrose's severe treatment of two of his wives who disobeyed official instructions by taking him food in prison was compounded when the chief himself died. The *Owa* still refused to sign the document dissociating himself from the Lagos Ijeshas. Further cases occurred of chiefs settling disputes out of court, and, when his 'detectives' ferried news of these to the ears of the Commissioner, such was the apprehension at what he would do that first the *Arapatę*, and finally the *Owa*, escaped to Lagos. The *Owa* arrived in November, accompanied by virtually all his senior chiefs or their representatives, and shortly afterwards went with Sapara-Williams to complain to the Acting Governor about Captain Ambrose and the condition of Ilesha. Thereafter contemporary documentation, both in official papers and the Lagos press, abruptly tails off and we must infer that, with Ambrose's departure, the immediate irritant was removed.

OWA ATAIYERO: ACCOMMODATION WITH THE BRITISH

In the years that followed, the social conflict within Ilesha lost its saliency, with the removal of the political circumstances which had brought it to a head and the gradual transformation in the position of young men themselves. After his tribulations *Owa* Ataiyero moved into the ascendancy over all his rivals. His visit to Benin became, in retrospect, a triumph.[90] Princess Adenibi left town for good. Ogedengbe and *Lẹjọka* Ogunmodede both died in 1910 and their households were largely dispersed. The *Ọwa* is said to have rebuked the messenger who announced Ogedengbe's death in the words *aiye ti bajẹ* ('the world is spoiled') and to have responded: *mo j'Ọwa loni* ('I become *Ọwa* today').[91] Peter Apara was further isolated when C. A. Lufadeju, a leading signatory of the 'Loyal Address', accepted the title of *Lọja* of Ibala from the *Ọwa*: and from 1909, with the *Ọwa* somewhere behind it, he was embroiled in lawsuits over the land he had been granted at Omirinmirin by Ajimoko.[92] In his later years the *Ọwa*'s drummer beat his praise with these words:

> ẹniti a p'ero pọ lati fi gba ile nu, on naa l'o wa d'ọkọ wọn
> the one they meant to use as the broom to sweep the house clean, he has become their master[93]

But what was more conducive to his prestige than anything else was that Ambrose's successors learnt the lesson that they could not use the indigenous political structure of Ilesha as an instrument of regional government without sustaining it as a power centre and giving support and a good deal of discretion to its rulers. Since, however, neither party surrendered much to the other's vision of what was proper for the government of Ilesha, the outcome of the relationship was always strongly contested, especially on the Ijesha side.

A critical incident occurred in 1908.[94] The people at Ipetu, whose relations with Ilesha were always difficult, had refused to pay their tribute after they had been fined for some misdemeanour and the *Apẹtu* detained at Ilesha. At this, acting on instructions from the Colonial Secretary of Southern Nigeria, a force under Major Moorhouse, Acting Provincial Commissioner and an experienced trouble-shooter in this kind of situation, went to Ipetu (whose inhabitants fled to the bush on his arrival) and proceeded to pull down the houses of the followers of the known ringleader until he gave himself up. The Ipetus were then told that they were subject to Ilesha and that they must pay the fine of £95; the *Ọwa* and Council would decide on how those who had assaulted the *Ọwa*'s messengers would be punished. At Ilesha the *Apẹtu* and chiefs prostrated to the *Ọwa*, who forgave them. After this, it is hardly surprising that Commissioner Blair was pleasantly struck with the 'moderation' of the *Ọwa*. A similar episode, with an equally satisfactory outcome for the *Ọwa*, occurred with Imesi-Ile in 1914–15.[95] Its *Ọlọja* persistently aspired to wear a beaded crown, the symbol of political autonomy, but on the *Ọwa*'s word, Resident Ross of Oyo (under whose jurisdiction Ilesha by then fell) uncrowned him and insisted that he respect his tributary obligations towards Ilesha. The *Ọwa* took the opportunity to demand arrears of tribute since 1904 (when his humiliation by Ambrose must have emboldened the Imesi people), and the *Ọlọja*, on being found guilty in the Appeal Court at Oyo, was fined and required to prostrate to the *Ọwa* as overlord.[96]

107

But despite this support for the *Ọwa*, the British did not get any easy acquiescence for their schemes for Ilesha's future. The most sensitive area concerned Ilesha's most valuable natural resource: her forests. The Lagos Government had first enacted a Forestry Ordinance in 1897, to establish some conservation measures in the face of the devastation wrought to the great virgin forests of the interior by a few years of unrestrained exploitation of wild rubber trees; and Governor McGregor was pleased to report in 1900 that *Ọwa* Ajimoko seemed favourable to the idea of a forestry reserve.[97] For some years nothing further was done, but after 1906 the Ilesha Council did agree to a system to control rubber exploitation through the issue of licences – no doubt an acceptable measure since, as we have seen, it gave the chiefs some control over the producers.[98] But the Government's further hopes for acceptance of the Forestry Rules met with determined opposition. In May 1909 the Assistant Conservator of Forests reported to his superior 'with great glee' that the Ijesha had agreed to the Forestry Rules; but a few days later he found that they would not confirm it in writing in the Council minutes.[99] There then followed a long period of fruitless attempts to persuade the Council to accept the Rules, culminating in a meeting in November 1912, presided over by the Commissioner and attended by Forestry Department officials. The chiefs angrily said they would cut trees down when they liked, just as their fathers had done; and finally one of them indicated, with a pertinent gesture, that if any of the proposed Forest Guards intervened, they would have their throats cut. Peter Apara summed up the feeling by bluntly telling the officials to go elsewhere. Since he refused to apologize, this was construed as a grievous insult to authority and a written apology was subsequently demanded of the chiefs.[100]

The Ijesha chiefs' resolve to stand firm on their rights over the forests should be seen as part of a new anxiety over land which emerged in these years. Dennett, the Conservator of Forests, considered that the Forestry Ordinance, with its provision for declaring forestry reserves on land designated 'crown land', was suspected as a device for expropriating their land – a thing he further put down to advice from Ijesha in Lagos. But there were more fundamental reasons for the chiefs' concern. Though the fact was concealed by the language of custom in which the chiefs asserted their rights, their interest in the land was changing: for them it was no longer simply a territory with a resident population and a geopolitical potential, but also, for the first time, an economic resource which could yield a cash income and was in potentially short supply. Peter Apara, battling to retain his cash-crop farm at Omirinmirin from both Ijesha rivals and land-hungry Oyos from Oshogbo, must have been especially aware of this. There was no abrupt change of attitude, for much of the old paramount concern – for the political allegiance of those who occupied the land – was still evident in many of the boundary disputes which erupted in these years, with the Ifes over Ifewara and Araromi, and with the Oyos of

Iragbiji and Ede along the northern boundary.[101] But the Government now appeared to have its eye on vacant land in the southern forests, still relatively unthreatened by non-Ijesha settlement, and in the work of the West African Lands Committee, which began hearings in Nigeria in 1912 and was extensively reported in the Lagos press, the accent was very heavily on the commercial potential of land.

The spokesman of the Ijesha chiefs at the hearings was the *Risawę*, Omole Adedeji, a creation of *Ǫwa* Ataiyero's who had emerged as the strong man among them. He expressed anxiety at the Government's intentions as regards land, but said – a tactical concession, no doubt – that he did not object to a forest *reserve* provided no controls were to be exercised outside it. On land tenure itself, he stood on a simple presentation of 'custom': all Ilesha's territory is divided up as the lands of families, whose heads apportion land to family members who wish to farm; the land cannot be sold or alienated in any way, though a man might be turned out for wrongdoing; the heads of communities 'exercise no control over usage of land except insofar as they are the heads of families and manage their own land ... [and] as such are not in receipt of any money derived from land either for personal, state or tribal purposes'; and the land of a man who died childless 'would never revert to the head of the community unless he happened to be head of the family too'.[102] This was consummately misleading, since it made no reference at all to title land (*ilę oye*) or to *ilę Ǫwa*, lands which reverted to the *Ǫwa* and were managed by the *Babaileoke*, or to unallocated land, especially that lying towards the frontiers. But the motive of this account seems clear: to minimize the risk that the Government might capitalize on any indigenous principle of tenure that could be represented as 'public', 'crown' or 'title' land to declare that ownership of land was vested in itself. In this astute move, it seems probable that the Ijesha chiefs *were* given guidance by their Lagos friends, for the younger brother of Sapara-Williams, Dr Oguntola Sapara, also gave evidence, corroborating what the *Risawę* had said.[103] But if the Ijesha won this particular trick, the Government finally had most of its way on the forestry question: a system of licences and charges for felling was eventually introduced, to become a major source of Native Authority revenue, and a forestry reserve was set up – though since this was down at Ipetu the immediate deprivation to the *Ǫwa* and chiefs at Ilesha was minimal, and probably outweighed by the limitation it put on the opportunities of the *Apętu*.

It was unfortunate for Ilesha's future that it revived its reputation with the Government for being a trouble-spot just at this time, for with the amalgamation of Southern and Northern Nigeria clearly envisaged, Governor Lugard was undertaking an extensive review of administrative arrangements. 'The more I visit and enquire, the more chaotic does the condition of our administration in this Province appear', reported the Provincial Commissioner to Lugard in March 1913; 'the condition of ...

Ilesha ... in [its] relation to Government is deplorable ... you cannot get a carrier without a tremendous lot of trouble ... people won't sell foodstuffs to Government employees except at exorbitant prices ... the people are very out of hand'.[104] It was decided to abandon Oke Imo. And as if to humiliate what was now described in a secret despatch as 'the insignificant little district of Illesha [*sic*]',[105] in the new hierarchy of divisions and provinces Ilesha was put in Ife Division, its District Officer stationed at Ile Ife, under the overall authority of the Resident of Oyo Province. Ekiti was given its own Division, centred on Ado, in the Ondo Province.[106] The reorganization was, almost from the start, greatly regretted by the Ijesha since it pushed them further towards the political periphery, and it was to have far-reaching consequences for Ijesha politics for years to come. But there was nothing that the *Owa* and chiefs could do about it.

Needless to say, it did not improve relations between the Ilesha authorities and their new overlords, at Ife and Oyo. The old *Owa* took a stoically dismissive view of them. The last DO who knew him, Ward-Price, wrote that he resented having to deal with any European save his own DO, and would not be told by outsiders what was good for him and his people.[107] The Ife DO in 1916 complained of his 'general attitude of obstruction in all matters of progress';[108] he would not get the Ijesha to dig the *salangas* on which officialdom was so keen and did not want an agricultural instructor on cocoa-planting;[109] he objected to the revised Native Court system since sitting-fees were too low, and made no provision for the needs of minor chiefs and the *emese*;[110] plans for a separate court at Ipetu were resisted, and cases were still heard out of court; he even used his *emese*, in 1913 when trade was slack, to increase Ilesha's share of it by forcing Ekiti on their way to Oshogbo to sell at Ilesha.[111] Resident Ross actually contemplated having *Owa* Ataiyero deposed and tried to intimidate Peter Apara, whom he still considered to be a prime source of opposition, by having him taken to witness the execution of the leaders of the Iseyin uprising of 1916.[112] It is a comic measure of the desperation with which the government officers faced Ilesha that Ward-Price's predecessor, if the story is true, tried to discipline the Ijesha by pretending to possess occult powers and acquired the nickname *Baba Sango*.[113]

DILEMMAS OF INCORPORATION

Ilesha was thus incorporated into the structure of the Nigerian state. In the first instance this was a political process – a gradual, resisted but ineluctable loss of her sovereignty, which means above all the capacity of her rulers to make decisions regarding relations with neighbouring states and to control transactions across her boundaries. What were the implications of this political incorporation on the social incorporation of the Ijesha? In other words how far did political incorporation lead Ijesha to become more involved in social networks or institutions which ran outside Ijeshaland and the surveillance of Ilesha's rulers, such as by turning Christian or Muslim, starting to grow crops for external markets, or finding that their domestic social ambitions induce them to trade or seek employment outside? In a society constituted as pre-colonial Ilesha was, some degree of social incorporation had always existed, being an essential condition of its internal political order. But that very dependence on the proceeds of interregional trade under the economic and military conditions which developed in the nineteenth century itself drew the Ijesha and the other interior kingdoms into a complex of relations with themselves and the British whose contradictions were only to be resolved by political incorporation.

In considering the direct effects of political annexation, we cannot easily disengage the effects of the ending of the possibility of war with weaker neighbours (and hence the taking of slaves) from other 'economic consequences of the peace' – the abolition of tolls and the severe dislocation of tributary and judicial payments from subordinate communities – or the chiefs' loss of judicial autonomy. But the social crisis of 1902–05 was a severe one, indicating how much the supports of political authority had been knocked away. Slavery was very rapidly disappearing: Ilesha's own slaves, taken over the previous few decades from Ekiti and Akoko, had largely decamped, though some remained in the households of the leading ex-warriors. Ijesha who returned from slavery abroad could not be made to fill the gap, and young men generally could not be controlled. How then could the title-system, reconstructed with the town in the 1890s, continue to retain so much of the 'traditional' form (though rather less of its content) with its social base so severely fractured?

The title-system survived because the British wanted it to survive, and they could only effect that if they found a functional alternative to these abandoned or weakened supports. Tributary relations within the kingdom were restored, and much more was made to depend on the chiefs' judicial role, from which they derived both salaries and more informal sanctions over the other members of the community.[114] But still the balance within the hierarchy of titles was affected, since it was only the senior chiefs who were thus supported, and it was a support for which they were not beholden to more junior chiefs. Some redistribution to junior, particularly quarter, chiefs was virtually assured by the fact that the *Owa* and the senior chiefs still depended on communal labour, which was raised through them, for road-making and other public tasks; but that was made more precarious by the ease with which young men, who had to do the labour, could now leave Ilesha for outside employment or otherwise evade customary obligations. The clearest evidence of this lies in the fact that the *Afin*, which was severely damaged by lightning in 1916 and would traditionally have had the first call on public labour, remained dilapidated until Ward-Price arranged for its repair in 1919. The introduction of direct taxation for the first time in that year, while it was a decision taken by Government with no particular regard for the situation in Ilesha, provided the final answer to the main

111

problem which political incorporation created: how a local administration and basic local services were to be supported without the means which only an independent kingdom could employ. But in so doing, it decisively confirmed the growing change in the relationship between chiefs and subjects: political authority now rested on direct levies on the productive activities of its own subjects, rather than on levies on weaker outsiders, achieved through the mobilization of the chiefs' followers.

So far the emphasis of my argument has been on the effects of political incorporation. But in the difficulties to which the introduction of direct taxation at the local level provided an answer, aspects of the growing *social* incorporation of the Ijesha were both source and solution of the problem. It is hardly surprising that the young men welcomed the new commercial and employment opportunities throughout the Protectorate, since they permitted them to challenge or evade the system of social control which irked them; and the withdrawal of the support of their labour 'from below' made it necessary for the local administration to have additional support 'from above', through taxes levied by the State. Taxation itself could hardly have been introduced as smoothly as it was, if it had not been for the cash incomes, whether from trade or labour abroad or increasingly from cocoa-growing at home, which Ijeshas were already earning through entering the national and international economy. But if this incorporation was straightforwardly attractive to the young, it presented the chiefs with a dilemma, which was also the dilemma of the Ijesha social system.

Owa Ataiyero tends to be represented in current Ijesha views of their past as the consistent, thoroughgoing opponent of social incorporation in all its forms: and the prime instance of this, a paradigm of lost opportunity along with the abandonment of Oke Imo as the region's administrative centre, is held to be the way he, with Ogedengbe and the other chiefs, refused to grant land to let the railway come to Ilesha, on the grounds that it would enable their wives and children to be taken away! Whatever may have been said at public meetings about the likely effects of a railway, it could not be that *Owa* Ataiyero was *in fact* responsible for keeping the railway away, since the Government never seems to have considered routeing it through Ilesha.[115] (It did in fact go through Oshogbo, to which Ilesha was, by 1910, connected by means of a good motorable road.) Moreover, Governor Egerton reported that, at their stormy meeting in March 1905, the *Owa* did in fact ask him if the railway could be brought to Ilesha, and was told that produce would have to be headloaded to Oshogbo.[116] Nor were the chiefs averse to the development of such cash-crops as rubber, since it promised a revenue from licences, or to the establishment of European trading firms which paid rents, like the German firm Witt and Busch which set up locally late in 1904.[117] The chiefs were in a double bind: the limits which political incorporation put on customary sources of revenue forced them to embrace some aspects of social incorporation as providing alternative sources; but these in turn tended to make their political incorporation more complete, reducing them in the end to the position of dependants of the colonial state. As free men do, they resisted none the less. The paradox of their situation is shown most sharply in the case of Peter Apara. None had stood more positively for the benefits and necessity of social incorporation: his Christianity was a repudiation of the ideological autarky of the old Ijesha kingdom, and his introduction of cash-crops declared that economic self-sufficiency was no path to prosperity. Yet he received a singular tribute when he died in December 1922, an obituary note in the *Oyo Province Annual Report* which described him as 'one of the leading spirits in opposing every Government action and champion [of] the contention that the Ilesha people were independent of Government control and would manage their own affairs'.[118] We may also read it as the epitaph of an epoch.

7

Cocoa and its consequences

The kingmakers took their lead from the *Risawę*, Adedeji, and it was a friend of his, the *Alęki*, Aromolaran, who succeeded Ataiyero as *Ǫwa* in 1920. The succession was also contested by the late *Ǫwa*'s eldest son, Idaomi, who had traded and been influential in the town in the latter part of his father's reign, as well as by several literates: Lufadeju, the *Lǫja Ibala*, whom the *Risawę* was especially anxious not to see elected, and two or three members of the Haastrup family. But Aromolaran was chosen, apart from his amiable personal qualities and his links with the *Risawę*, precisely because, having always lived in a village, he 'had been kept out of the circle of those managing the district . . . [seemed to be] of no great strength of character and [was] nothing more or less than one of the people'.[1] The chiefs therefore felt he would be amenable to their wishes in a way that those literate or already acquainted with the *Afin* would not be. The election was the first in which the outcome had to be acceptable, as the chiefs well knew, to the DO, Ward-Price, even though he did not in fact exert himself to countermand their clear preference. Thus it was the first in which occupational and cultural groups, formally excluded from the selection process, sought to influence the outcome by appealing over the heads of the kingmakers to the Government's representative. So anonymous 'Ijesha Young Traders' wrote to the Resident asking him to 'not allow our big chiefs to persuade you in taking a bushman from whom we cannot know the head or tail of the government', while another group of 'Youngmen', apologizing that they could not come openly, wrote complaining that the chiefs

> like us to continue the old fashion and barbarous practices [which] do not allow
> us to get on in the town, so that we have to scatter through all other countries.
> We ask you to help us. They do not care if their town remain in bush for as
> much as they can get their chop, not caring for we the children. All of us like to
> see you put Adetona [Haastrup] into the position of Owa, for he can controle
> and he loves British Idea [*sic*] and understand what they [i.e. the British] want
> and what they do not want, for he has education.[2]

These pleas, in all their awkward vigour, certainly look back to the youngmen's grievances in 1904–05; but, with their frank acceptance of

Ilesha's dependence on the powers controlling the Nigerian state, they also look forward to the politics of 'improvement' (*atunluṣe*) which came to predominate over the next three decades, ultimately begetting nationalism as it existed at the local level. Ọwa Aromolaran, however, was to surprise these youngmen with his policies, just as he was to confound the DO's patronizing assessment of his character. For the keynote of his reign was very soon revealed as the alliance he forged with the 'enlightened' elements of the town, and especially the traders who returned to set up business in Ilesha in the 1920s, the core of the Young Ijesha Improvement Society (*Ẹgbẹ Atunluṣe*). An essential condition of this was the increased prosperity which Ilesha was now able to enjoy. The very name of the new Ọwa expressed the spirit of the age: *Aromọlaran* means 'we clothe our children in velvet'.

The basis of the new prosperity was cocoa. This crop, introduced through the spontaneous initiatives of local farmers with not more than a modicum of support from the Government (and that being restricted to its preparation for sale, grading and marketing), provided the means for a considerable diversification of the local occupational structure; and it not only opened up new sources of income but eventually made them less dependent on the old status-system, with important consequences for the social and political life of Ilesha. Its remoter effects, arising from the boost it gave to Government revenues and expenditure, were to attract more Ijesha to employment outside and thus to increase Ijesha awareness of their position within Nigeria; and will be the theme of the next chapter. Though cocoa first achieved striking effects in Aromolaran's reign, its origins lay well before and its spread continued well afterwards, presenting a process with a definite trajectory to it. For this reason we must step somewhat outside the framework of chronological stages suggested by the successive public ascendancies of particular personalities, movements, parties or conflicts to examine the character and conditions of this longer process as a whole.

THE TRAJECTORY OF THE COCOA ECONOMY

While the main outlines of the rise of cocoa-growing among the Ijesha are clear enough, a detailed picture of its extent and spread over time is hard to establish, since adequate time-series data are so hard to come by. Published data, relating either to the total volume of cocoa exported through Lagos or to acreage planted or tonnage graded in particular large areas (usually provinces, divisions or produce inspection areas), do not yield a precise picture of changes in the volume and value of production in relation to particular communities.[3] However, data from the 1974 survey of household-heads in Ilesha do produce a picture of the growth of cocoa-planting in the area which is consistent with other fragmentary or partial indications of Ilesha's cocoa production, such as Galletti *et al.*'s evidence that, before

115

Table 7.1 *Cocoa-planting by Ilesha residents*

	Decade							
	Pre-1910	1910s	1920s	1930s	1940s	1950s	1960s	1970s
No. of reported farms planted	20	23	32	18	25	19	13	4

1943, cocoa-planting in Ife-Ilesha peaked in 1930.[4] From what respondents in present enjoyment of incomes from cocoa-farms (whether farmed by themselves or by tenants) reported concerning when and by whom cocoa was first planted on their land, the profile shown in Table 7.1 emerges as to the spread of cocoa cultivation.[5] The 'natural history' of Ilesha's cocoa, then, is fairly plain: it began well before 1910, and the rate of its adoption accelerated to the end of the 1920s. In retrospect we can see that never has cocoa-farming been as rewarding, compared with other pursuits, as it was in the years before 1916.[6] The 1930s, when cocoa prices plummeted, recovering somewhat in 1936–37 (though not to the levels of the late 1920s), saw a lower rate of planting, but the rate picked up again in the 1940s, prices shooting up again in 1948 and remaining high into the mid-1950s. In 1974 nearly 54% of Ilesha's households derived some income from cocoa-farms, most of them first planted before the 1950s, and it seems likely that this proportion was higher in the recent past, since households with heads in their sixties were more likely to have income from cocoa than households with younger heads, the proportion falling off down to only 30% of household heads (a small number) in their twenties. It is also notable that these household heads in their sixties (i.e. born 1910–19) were more likely to enjoy farms in which cocoa had been first planted by their fathers than by themselves, whereas those in their seventies mostly enjoyed farms which they themselves had first planted, largely in the boom of the late 1940s.[7] Cocoa starts to bear about seven years after planting and continues to do so for a further twenty or more years, so the surge of production noted in the Oyo Province Annual Reports of the 1920s indicates the outcome of planting decisions taken right back to the beginning of the century.[8] By the late 1930s Margery Perham reported, presumably on the basis of what she learnt from the Agricultural Department, that Ilesha was 'the most productive cocoa-growing region in Nigeria'.[9]

Ilesha was thus one of the earliest interior kingdoms to see the large-scale adoption of cocoa. Dr Sara Berry has explained this precocity, similar to that shown by Ibadan, by the fact that both places, having been major participants in the wars, experienced high levels of virtual unemployment among demobilized soldiers at the coming of peace. They were thus 'more or less compelled to seek new economic opportunities' – hence cocoa, introduced from the oldest centres of its cultivation near Lagos through Christian networks, but rapidly taken up more widely in the community.[10] This is an attractive thesis and the association between heavy involvement in the wars and early adoption of cocoa is a real one, though in Ilesha's instance, at least, the strands linking them are rather more complex than Berry's account suggests.

The proto-pioneer was Gureje Thompson, a Christian and Ogedengbe's chief henchman, who settled, under circumstances already described, at Etioni, which became the first great centre of cocoa production.[11] But since he died in 1901, it was really his son, James Adegbola Thompson, who saw the enterprise through to fruition: around 200 acres under cocoa by the late 1930s, when one season's profits permitted the construction of the hand-some family house in Iloro quarter. Around 90 adults settled with Gureje, mostly his slaves, and later a string of kinsmen, friends and connexions joined the Thompson settlement. Before 1910 other settlements sprang up in the neighbourhood: Aladodo, a largely Muslim village, and, a secession from Etioni in 1908, Itapa, whose leaders were Daniel Kujembola, church-warden of St John's, Iloro, and uncle of J. A. Thompson, and Fariogun Fajemisin, an ex-warrior, Iloro church elder and later President of the Farmers' Association. A little later, certainly by 1906–09, a further focus of cocoa-farming developed to the west and north west of Ilesha, around Igila and the road to Igbadae, and on the Muroko Road, from Isolo to around Oke Ibode. Here the pioneer was Benjamin Adekusibe Haastrup, the *Asolo, Owa* Ajimoko's brother, who was connected both with the southern pioneers (Kujembola married his daughter) and with others who took up in the western and northern areas: David Ibidapo, son of the warrior Obe and brother of one of Peter Apara's wives, who started cocoa near Igila, married another daughter of the *Asolo's*, and the pioneer at Ilaa was Adeyokunnu, an *omoba* who had earlier lived in the Haastrup house in Lagos, where he had carried the young Benjamin Haastrup to school. Christopher Lufadeju, a fellow member of Christ Church Omofe with Ibidapo, planted cocoa on land he got from the *Owa* in 1906 in the same area. The character of the primary network of cocoa-planters is thus clear enough, and so is its very close relationship to the group who challenged *Owa* Ataiyero with the 'Loyal Address' to Ambrose in 1905. It soon began to diffuse beyond them, though very unevenly as between localities, perhaps depending a good deal on the character of its local sponsors. At Oshu, for example, a trader with Ayesan connexions, Ayomaya by name, was selling cocoa pods at 6d. each in 1913–14, but he found few takers, and large-scale adoption of the new crop did not occur there before 1918.[12] But in many places cocoa did soon diffuse beyond the Christian pioneers, suggesting that it soon came to meet a very general need. Evidence enough is that it was *Risawe* Adedeji, the chief most stalwart in supporting *Owa* Ataiyero's resistance to over-hasty cultural modernization, who declared in 1912 that 'we are all taking to the growing of cocoa and cotton and rubber'.[13]

Despite the prominence of several ex-warriors among the innovators it is not really satisfactory to see cocoa-growing as a direct response to demobilization. A good ten years elapsed between the rampages of the demobbed *ipaiye* in 1893–94 and the adoption of cocoa on any scale, and though it might be argued that this period twice saw the rise and fall of rubber (1895–97 and 1906–08) as an unsuccessful attempt to deal with the problem, the lens is not really sufficiently focussed on the individuals, rather than the general situation of the town, to permit us to determine whether demobilized soldiers, as such, were especially crucial. Many of them did quite other things, like trading or subsistence agriculture or the new crafts, in the immediate aftermath of the wars, which leaves their eventual turning to cocoa a different problem. What is undeniably true about cocoa is that it offered, rather than employment, a cash income in a community where cash incomes were increasingly, and in advance of many neighbouring communities, becoming a universal necessity. I have already argued that Ilesha's involvement in the forefront of the wars greatly stimulated the local growth of a cash economy.[14] Then the manner of colonial overrule created revenue problems for the chiefs and drove them to depend on cash fees and fines from their subjects on a greater scale than ever before. Marriage, where the young man's traditional obligation had been for labour service, was coming to require substantial cash payments. The power struggle between social categories and factions conducted under the new conditions of local British overrule and the economic opportunities now available throughout the Protectorate, further fuelled the demand for cash incomes. The political 'outs' no longer had to knuckle under or seek refuge elsewhere: they had the prospect of building themselves up at home through cash-crop production; and once they were so doing, it was impossible for the chiefs, despite the incomes they could still derive from their official positions and their judicial roles, to refrain for very long from joining them. And if the young men could abbreviate the period of their juniority by earning cash incomes abroad, those who had once depended on their labour for the maintenance of farms and public works had increasingly to find the wherewithal to pay people to do these things – and that without leaving home.

This spreading need for cash incomes could be met in various ways, of which cocoa cultivation (or indeed any kind of cash crop) was only one, which particular social categories variously found viable and appropriate to their situation. Now growing cocoa under the social and environmental conditions prevailing in Yorubaland had certain prerequisites: some working capital was one, but, as Berry puts it, 'the chief managerial requirement ... was the ability to mobilize and organise human resources'.[15] (The factor of land, granted the availability of these other two, was not an obstacle in the early decades.) This has the implication that the typical cocoa-pioneer was not a young adult, since only established household-heads could really begin to command adequate labour resources. In the

Table 7.2   *Changing age of men at first marriage*

Men born in	Proportion of age-cohort married, by age							Total no.	N.A.
	19	24	29	34	39	44	49		
1880s	0%	10%	24%	45%	60%	85%	95%	20	6
1890s	5%	10%	48%	70%	85%	100%	100%	40	4
1900s	5%	17%	53%	81%	91%	95%	97%	75	4
1910s	4%	35%	72%	91%	94%	99%	100%	85	7
1920s	7%	36%	78%	97%	100%	—	—	76	6
1930s	11%	28%	83%	94%	100%	—	—	54	3
1940s	4%	20%	90%	96%	100%	—	—	49	1

early years there was a critical relationship between the ages at which a man married, the real beginning of his independence and his acquisition of a dependent domestic labour force, and when he could start to plant cocoa. Table 7.2 shows how the age of first marriage, which now for several decades has lain in the late 20s for over half the male population, has come down since early in the century. Household-heads now in their nineties, that is men born in the decade after 1880, who were in their twenties in the first decade when cocoa was planted in Ijeshaland, the survivors of that generation for whom Dabi of Orinkiran spoke, got married for the first time over a wider period than has been the case since, over half of them spread between the ages of 30 and 44. The next two ten-year cohorts, those born in the period 1890–1909, show a different pattern: the most popular age for marriage now lies between 25 and 34, and around half are married by the age of 30. The trend continues for the next two cohorts, those born from 1910 to 1929, with the marriage-age tending to lie between 20 and 29, and around three-quarters married by the age of 30.

These figures, when seen in conjunction with data concerning the changing age at which men turned to planting cocoa, show how the opportunity-structure was evolving. As Table 7.3 shows, over half the cocoa-plantings reported by respondents born before 1909 were made by men in their forties, and less than a third by men before their forties, which strongly suggests a situation where most farm labour was domestic. A typical individual's history would be for him to marry around the age of 30, after a period in which he had traded or taken wage-employment outside Ilesha in order to raise capital, and to turn to farming a decade or so later, when his children were growing to an age when they could offer help on the farm and when he had perhaps managed to marry a further wife. With respondents born after 1910 a quite different picture emerges. If they did plant cocoa, they mostly did it in their twenties and thirties; but at the same

119

Table 7.3 *Changing age at which cocoa was planted*

	Age when cocoa first planted by respondent					
Men born	20s	30s	40s	50s	60s	All plantings
Before 1910	4	4	16	6	0	30
After 1910	11	10	5	3	2	31

time, the majority of this group (and the proportion gets larger the younger they are) enjoyed farms in which cocoa was first planted by their fathers who, it seems plausible to infer, conformed to the pattern of the older respondents. Though the age-cohort which inaugurated the shift did marry significantly younger than the immediately preceding one (53% compared with 72% married by age 30), the source of the change seems to lie less here – since the marriage-age had not fallen so low as to permit many men to have working-age children even by their thirties – than in the increasing availability of non-family or hired labour, which meant that the establishment of a cocoa-farm did not need to occupy such a definite place in the individual's life-cycle. Since the shift started to occur in the 1930s, it is likely that the wider economic environment played a part, by drastically reducing the trading opportunities which had drawn young Ijesha abroad in increasing numbers in the 1920s. But the earlier pattern of planting by older men continued to coexist with the new one into the 1940s and early 1950s, when many men who must have established themselves in trade outside Ijeshaland before 1930, returned to plant cocoa – the last really substantial group of Ijesha to do so – in those years of buoyant prices. They too now needed to employ labour on their farms, but for a different reason; not because their children were too young, but because they were much more likely to go to school.

The above picture of how cocoa-growing evolved is corroborated by the direct but fragmentary evidence concerning the labour supply. To begin with, and even when it was supplemented with other kinds of labour, the core of the farmer's labour force was the members of his own household, especially wives and children. Virtually all the cocoa-pioneers, committed Christians though many of them were, were several times polygynous and their wives, though not undertaking the central agricultural tasks, played a key role in running the agricultural household, helping to process farm products, etc.[16] Thompson kept three of his wives out at Etioni, and Fajemisin used to take two of his with him to Itapa – his sons recalled that up to the 1920s he had a regular labour force of around fifteen, on a farm which went to nearly fifty acres, mostly drawn from his household, with the addition of two or three family relations. From the age of six or so children weeded and headloaded; and though

120

Christian parents faced the dilemma of whether to sacrifice this labour for their children's education, they would be set to work during the school holidays. At least one informant owed his schooling and Christianity to the fact that at the age of nine he sustained an accidental injury which temporarily crippled him, disabling him for farmwork and enabling him to be sent to school.[17] No doubt for this reason, several Christians appear to have been among the first to seek out other sources of labour. But there was always non-domestic labour, even when much of the framework governing its use had a somewhat 'familial' character to it. Two forms were predominant before the 1920s: 'slaves' (*ẹru*) and 'pawns' (*iwọfa*).

Ex-warriors or their heirs were in an exceptionally favourable position to develop cocoa-farms to the extent that, despite the reflux of slaves in the 1890s, they still were often able to command the loyalty of 'slaves': men who for whatever reason preferred to stay in Ilesha and who needed their former master as a patron. These ties might endure well into the colonial period: Ajayi Obe was able, when he planted cocoa after 1911, to call on the labour of a handful of former slaves of his father, who had died around 1890. At Etioni they began by living in the same compound with Thompson and working under his direction; later they were allotted plots of their own and built their own houses but continued to give part of their time, usually the whole morning of the day, to their 'master', from whom they too in the end received cocoa seedlings.

The other source of labour, *iwọfa*, was an ancient and widespread Yoruba credit institution, and its general character in Ijeshaland does not seem different from what has been described for elsewhere.[18] The *iwọfa* or pawn is a person given by a debtor to a creditor who has lent him money, usually the child or junior sibling (*aburo*) of the debtor, who lives with the creditor and works for him, the service being the equivalent of interest on the loan, until the money is repaid in full, when the *iwọfa* returns home. As an institution it belongs to social contexts where regular opportunities for earning money incomes are limited, but where individuals are quite likely to encounter a sudden need for cash. Unfortunately I do not have data which show either the total pattern of *iwọfa* use early in the century or what proportion of cocoa farmers used them. But the *generalized* account given by informants is that the institution enjoyed a kind of final flourish before dying out for good in the course of the 1920s; and there is definite evidence concerning its use by some of the largest cash-crop pioneers. Outstanding in this was Peter Apara who, according to his youngest son, had the service of upwards of 40–50 *iwọfa* at times: people would come to borrow money from as far afield as Ipetu or Odo, sending a child as *iwọfa* for a loan of £2 10s 0d, or an adult for one of £5.[19] J.A. Thompson had them too, though on a much smaller scale, never more than ten, while Ajayi Obe sometimes had up to half a dozen; and in general their use, though fairly widespread, seems to have been in ones and twos. The suppliers of *iwọfa* themselves needed cash for purposes as varied as paying for medical or divinatory services, court fees and fines, trading capital, marriage and funerary expenses, even, at one time, the 10s 0d licences needed to tap rubber; and as the commercial economy, with cocoa at its base, advanced, they could turn to domestically less distressing ways of acquiring cash.

The permanent answer to the labour-problem was to employ wage-labourers, a practice whose origins can be pinpointed fairly precisely, though it is likely that day-labourers had been casually hired before then. Wage-labourers began to be employed on the Apara farm around 1917, when J.B. Apara, formerly a trader living at Oshogbo, took over its running from his father. The first paid labourers on Fajemisin's farm at Itapa were eight Urhobo for whom his son, then a teacher at Warri, arranged to come in 1924. J.A. Thompson was employing them by the early 1920s, mostly men from Ekiti, Akoko and Yagba. In 1921 it is reported that with so many Ijesha attracted to trade, their farms were kept weeded by hired labourers 'usually small boys [which probably means teenagers] from the Ekiti country', which implies a very widespread adoption of wage-labour.[20] By 1951–52, when the authors of *Nigerian Cocoa Farmers* conducted their survey, over half the labour on cocoa-farms in Oshu, one of their sample villages, was provided by hired labourers, a similar proportion to the average for a group of villages drawn from a wide sample of the Yoruba cocoa belt; and at Oke Ibode especially, another Ijesha village in their sample, farmers 'complained that they had very little assistance from their families'.[21]

In another respect too what first emerged in the 1920s has remained the case for the subsequent half-century: the dependence of Ijesha farmers for the bulk of their hired labour on non-Ijeshas from areas to the north and east, beyond the cocoa belt, where local incomes were lower. The Ekiti had originally predominated among them and were still common in 1952, though their numbers were then decreasing.[22] With the spread of education in Ekiti and the extension of cocoa cultivation eastwards, this trend has continued, and in 1974 the largest single category was 'Agatu', non-Yoruba from the region of the Niger–Benue confluence, followed by Oyo Yoruba from those savannah towns which abut Ijesha territory to the north and north-west or else from Modakeke. A further feature that had emerged by the 1950s and was pronounced by the 1970s was that, in sharp contrast to the earliest decade or so of agricultural wage-labour, a significant proportion of hired labourers, not far short of one-fifth of the whole, were Ijesha.[23] The reason for this is strongly suggested by the observation of *Nigerian Cocoa Farmers* that in 1952 local hired labour was particularly important near Oke Ibode. For that was, as it remains, an area where, owing in good part to the large number of Oyos who had acquired farms in the area, the pressure on land was greatest and the average holding especially small.[24] Here local Ijesha first turned to supplement meagre incomes based on small holdings by hiring out their labour locally, though twenty years later it appears that such local hired labour has become much more widespread.

The evidence of inequality in land-holding, linked to the employment of wage-labour, prompts the question of whether we can speak of the emergence of social classes grounded in differential access to agricultural resources, and acting as the basis of organized interest-groups. According to data collected by Galletti and his associates from six Yoruba villages (including Oshu) in 1951–52, around 50% of farming households held 14% of the land under cocoa, while 50% of the land was held by around 15% of households.[25] However, mere inequality in land-holdings might be interpreted in several ways. Unequal as cocoa holdings were, they were less so than acreages held for food growing where there was less propensity to use hired labour;[26] and that kind of inequality, far from being anything of a novelty, is quite consistent with customary practice, under which the amount of land worked or held for future use by a household was a consequence of the household's size and needs rather than of the absolute amount of land available to it. The social status and connexions of the household-head, which determined the size of his household, and not the amount of land he possessed, were primary. The same principles underlay the granting of large amounts of land to several of the cocoa-pioneers. Their earlier holdings of land might be slight or nil – Thompson presumably had claims on *Loro* chieftaincy land, Fajemisin had worked a plot of *Risawę* chieftaincy land near Ilesha on which he paid *iwifǫ* and might have taken up land at Iwoye where his father had been *Lǫja*, Ajayi Obe 'borrowed' land on Muroko Road from his kinsman the *Losi Ijamǫ* – but they had no difficulty in getting cocoa land, mostly virgin forest, when they wanted it. What mattered was *who* they were, in terms of their own or their fathers' personal prowess, social and kin connexions and so on, and hence their ability to command respect and a following; the skills and cultural advantages of Christianity, the possession of capital from trading or of 'slaves' left over from the wars all helped to set the land to work, but it was their social assets which really counted.

However, it might be argued that though the greater cocoa farmers acquired their land within a traditional framework of land-use, the consequence of their using it for cash crops and employing so much non-domestic hired labour on it was that a new kind of rural stratification, with definite implications for rural politics, emerged. But can we speak of a 'gentry', as Galletti *et al.* were tempted to do,[27] with its connotation of an enduring relationship between a rurally-based superior class, possessing a distinct life style made possible by land-rents, and largely endogamous, and a lower class of labourers and/or tenants? Those who possessed more land and who thus tended to employ more labour were not set sharply apart from the rest of the farming population by that fact. Hired labour was predominantly drawn from non-Ijesha who were not permanently committed to the local community, so that this class division was largely subsumed under an ethnic one, with important consequences which I will return to later; while the Ijesha who later hired out their labour were overwhelmingly small landed proprietors themselves. It was not too difficult, till the 1950s at least, for labourers who wanted to stay in the community, like the ex-slaves before them or like new Ijesha settlers, to acquire land, either outright or for small annual payments, which served to signify the grantee's acceptance of the local political leadership or of the continued ultimate ownership of the grantor. In most areas fresh land remained available and those who controlled access to it usually had more to gain from attracting political clients than from trying to compel substantial rents from tenants. Thus in the Etioni area, even Thompson's slaves, originally quite dependent on him, acquired farms on which they did not need to pay rents (*iṣakǫlę*), as they 'indigenized' and acquired local connexions.[28] So too with the many later Ijesha settlers in the area. Despite Thompson's undisputed local leadership, if he had pushed for the payment of *iṣakǫlę* he would have run the risk of alienating his local following and opened himself to unwanted intervention from the centre, for successive *Ǫwa* tended to look askance at the unofficial leadership exercised in outlying districts by those who refused to allow themselves to be co-opted through taking titles.

Rather different practices, giving rise to something much more like a *rentier* gentry, began to develop where land was scarce and where there were large numbers of aliens or 'strangers', in the area to Ilesha's northwest. Here too large farms were acquired by Ilesha notables, beginning with Apara at Omirinmirin. Some of the same trends occurred: for example, Ajayi Obe's former slaves eventually acquired farms on which they paid no rents to their patron, being regarded, as far as outsiders were concerned, as if they were of his lineage. But from very early on *iṣakǫlę* came to be required of other dependants – ex-labourers, Oyo settlers, even some *iwǫfa* who stayed on – who took up farms on land which Ajayi Obe, Apara and others claimed as theirs, but which was surplus to what they could work directly. The initial purpose of these payments was less to yield an income than to prevent the permanent appropriation of the land by people who, because they remained members of their own communities (which were mostly closer than Ilesha, such as Oshogbo), were not potential clients within the Ijesha political field. For this reason too, these tenants were not for many years allowed to plant cocoa or other tree-crops or to put iron roofs on their houses, since these could be taken as evidence of permanent rights over the land they were occupying. The Aparas (Peter, and later his son J.B.) had an additional problem since successive *Ǫwa* were alert to use this situation to weaken their base, and encouraged rivals, both Ijesha and Oyo, to bring lawsuits against them over the land.[29] Small wonder that J.B. Apara was the first person to draw up clear written agreements, that would hold good in court and not depend on verbal witnesses who were too easily suborned by powerful chiefs, specifying

124

exactly the work his labourers were to do and the terms on which they had been leased land to grow food for themselves.[30] Eventually many of these labourers left Omirinmirin and established a new village, just outside the Apara estate, on land granted by the *Lọjas* of Oke Ibode and Idominasi, which they called *Kajọla* ('let's be wealthy together'), where they were freer to develop themselves. Later, after 1945, J.B. Apara withdrew from running the bulk of the estate as a plantation and let most of it on 25-year leases to Oyo tenants who were allowed to plant tree-crops and on which they paid significant economic rents. Since it continues to be generally felt that Ijesha should not have to make more than fairly token payments on land they 'rent' from other Ijesha, especially on land used for food crops,[31] it seems likely that the transition from token to substantial rents, from *iwifọ* to *iṣakọlẹ* as it were, was facilitated by the fact that it was Oyo strangers who were involved, people against whom the social costs of a more purely exploitative relationship mattered much less than they would have done with Ijesha. Not all Oyo who farmed in this north-western area, especially round Lala (an almost entirely Oyo village beyond Oke Ibode), were the tenants of Ijesha, for many were in actual occupation of land when powerful Ijesha like Apara and Ajayi Obe moved in, and it was often largely fortuitous for them whether they encountered Ijesha who could make their claims to the land good, in force and in law. And while I have often heard Ijesha regret in a general way that so much Ijesha farmland (i.e. land within the Ijesha Divisions) is occupied by Oyos, there is no doubt that it could be expedient for Ijesha owners to encourage Oyo settlement. According to his son, Ajayi Obe gave the advice that it was wisest to accommodate strangers if there was land spare, since an Ijesha 'may become stronger than the children, especially in this civilised period ... if he gets money he may be able to bribe the judge'.

It thus seems that no single pattern – let alone a 'rise of the gentry' – serves to characterize how rural stratification developed under the impact of cocoa. Indeed Apara and Thompson exemplify two contrasting possibilities for what shape a stratum of large land-holders might take, though in fact we find a shifting mixture of the two, and there is no sharp social division between individuals who tend either way. On the one hand it might be a *rentier* class, controlling its land from the town where its members had other interests (chieftaincy titles, transport businesses etc.), maintaining a more purely economic relationship with strangers who cultivated the land or delegating management of a plantation to an agent. On the other it might be an elite of large farmers, employing labour but themselves active members of the local rural community whose natural leaders they were. In many ways it was the latter which was the real novelty, since it was a rurally-based elite whose leading members, despite their Ilesha origin, refused to take the chieftaincy titles which would have bound them to the centre – partly no doubt for the usually stated reason, that they were religiously compromising for Christians or Muslims, and partly as the expression of a more generalized disdain for the Ilesha establishment that they felt as men of *ọlaju* ('enlightenment').[32] These leading farmers, unlike the *rentiers*, were less a class divided from the smaller farmers, as Galletti's talk of 'gentry' and 'peasants' suggests, than the very elite of the farming class, and they led them as *farmers* against such class-opponents as trading middlemen rather than as members of district communities against the centre. None the less, the class divisions relevant to commercial agriculture were never purely 'economic', since membership of economic categories continued to depend so much on access to political resources, which in turn was a matter of ethnicity, lineage and urban status and contacts. This emerges clearly when we look at the two final aspects of the rise of cocoa which I want to consider: the Farmers' Association, and the eventual fate of the farming elite which emerged in the first generation of the cocoa economy.

The Farmers' Association had its origins in a friendship between one of the early cocoa farmers, a neighbour and cousin of Fariogun Fajemisin's, and a West Indian agricultural instructor, Ricketts by name, from Moor Plantation at Ibadan.[33] He arranged for the first demonstration of the fermentation technique of preparing cocoa for sale at Fajemisin's Ifofin compound in 1918, and by 1923 a circle of enlightened farmers using and advocating the wider adoption of the new techniques had organized itself under Fajemisin's presidency, which was to last for thirty years. Cocoa fermentation, producing a superior product on which a supplement was paid after grading, spread so quickly, at least among a significant minority of farmers, that by the late 1920s the Ilesha area was considered to produce a crop of particularly good quality.[34] But the main activity of the Farmers' Association was to act as a marketing organization, to enable producers to bypass the hierarchy of middlemen and sell directly, as a cooperative, to the European firms. In order to buy produce it needed capital, initially provided by the sellers' donation of an additional panful of beans for every hundredweight of cocoa they sold to the Association, later by members' subscriptions. But it remained chronically short of funds, with the result that it could not make cash advances on the same scale as the buying agents of the firms to guarantee a share of the crop and never succeeded in buying more than a small share, around 4% or so, of the total crop. Even then, as Galletti *et al.* pointed out,[35] a very high proportion of its cocoa was bought from a handful of members – the largest producers. For the smaller, poorer farmers could not afford to wait for the better prices they would eventually be paid by the Farmers' Association, just as they might not be able to invest in the labour of fermentation in order to secure the premiums paid for superior graded produce; and the general depression of incomes of the 1930s led to a decline in the volume of fermented cocoa produced as well as to a crisis for the Association's marketing arrangements, making it uneconomical for them to maintain several of their local branches.

The same pattern of strength and weakness emerges when we look at the Association's main geographical bases which lay in the recently settled south, where cocoa was first grown and where holdings were relatively large. Etioni, Itapa, and Aladodo provided the main support and their people predominated on the committee till well into the 1930s; to these were soon added communities to the south-west of Ilesha, ranging in an arc from Igangan and Iwara round through Igila, Epe and Igun to Ibodi, as well as places closer to Ilesha on the south, such as Ajido, Ijemba and Ilerin.[36] The densely-settled tract to the north-west of Ilesha, from Oshu round to Oke Ibode, where a good deal of land was farmed by Oyos and where Ijesha were most likely to hire themselves out as agricultural labour, was never so strongly for the Farmers' Association. Even the larger farmers in this area, probably because they were more of the *rentier* type, title-holders like Lufadeju or Ajayi Obe (*Lẹmodu* from 1913) or substantial traders and transporters like J.F. Longe or *Ọwa* Aromolaran's eldest son Adeniran, were not supporters of the Farmers' Association. But it did manage to establish branches, from the late 1930s, among several of Ilesha's subordinate communities (rather than farm-villages) to the north and east (e.g. Ibokun, Ilase, Erin Oke) where cocoa-planting started later.

Nevertheless, at least up to the 1940s, the Farmers' Association was much more important than the size of either its membership or its share of the market would suggest, since it was the principal mouthpiece of farming interests generally, especially in the main cocoa-growing areas. It led the lobbying for the construction of a proper road from the southern area – which until the late 1930s was only linked to Ilesha by tracks along which cocoa had to be headloaded. When Fariogun Fajemisin made this appeal directly to the Governor on his visit in 1933, he was told to turn to the Native Authority (NA); and when that came to nothing, the Association organized a collection from the villages to engage labourers to make the road.[37] The Etioni road was finally taken over by the Native Authority in 1942, but many more roads were still needed; in the late 1940s, the DO on tour remarked on the extensive network of 'cocoa-roads' in the area, created through such local initiatives.[38] Then again the Association repeatedly made representations about the high levels of tax and methods of tax assessment on cocoa farms, and later received the limp explanation given by the Superintendent of Cooperatives for the collapse of prices during the depression of the 1930s.[39] And when in 1930–31 there was a major wave of rural unrest about taxation – farmers armed with daneguns marched from Oshu to complain to the *Ọwa* and angry meetings were held at the Association's store at Ifofin – it was above all to Fajemisin that the DO turned to learn about the farmers' grievances and whom they hoped would be a restraining influence on them.[40]

But the most telling feature of the new farming elite which emerged in these years was its impermanency as a social force in and of the country-side. Its members' success as individuals, as well as its failure as a class, equally point to the continued dominance of the urban (*ile*) over the rural (*oko*). This was despite the fact that cocoa cultivation under British over-rule had held out the radical promise that, with major wealth for the first time being directly generated from agriculture and it now being possible to achieve wealth locally without holding title in Ilesha, a new social class might rise to dominance from the countryside. This promise was not realized. Quite apart from the various ways in which the members of the farming elite themselves qualified their aloofness from the institutions of the centre – for example, by building substantial houses in Ilesha, by patronizing churches and educating their children there and by making good use of personal connexions arising from 'traditional' status there – the system of Indirect Rule meant that the political masters of the capital retained important powers to dispose in the district. The leading cocoa farmers, especially in the south, were still something of an out-group, as if their association with the 'Loyal Address' of 1905 still mattered, despite *Qwa* Aromolaran's attempts to co-opt them. It is not surprising that it took them so long to get the infrastructural support they wanted from the Native Authority (which at this time meant the *Qwa* and his close circle of chiefly advisers), although its revenues were so dependent upon the taxation of cocoa-incomes.[41] True, many chiefs themselves now had cocoa farms; but their other interests ran counter and were paramount; money spent on roads might raise rural productivity and benefit them a little as producers, but it would have to be diverted from headings under which they benefited more substantially and directly as salaried office-holders. The same low priority was to be accorded to the provision of rural infrastructure by more sophisticated Governments in years to come. Indeed, despite the general rise in rural incomes and the new opportunities cocoa had brought, before 1920 especially, the urban, or rather anti-farming, bias of the opportunity-structure was reasserted. But the larger farmers, especially the Christians, were in an excellent position to exploit it for their children. To their genuine devotion to literacy and 'enlightenment' (*olaju*) as necessary concomitants of Christian profession was added the pragmatic attraction of education as the gateway to the commercial and bureaucratic careers whose rewards, recruitment and social importance expanded steadily from the 1920s. The profits of the farming fathers took the sons out of farming into professions remunerated from the proceeds creamed off agricultural production by the structures of trade and government. An obituary in a local newspaper in 1952 put the whole process in a nutshell: 'The late Daddy — was a big farmer, and used his modest enlightenment to give his children good education.'[42] There was thus no permanence in the composition of the rural elite, no emergence of a gentry there. The families themselves, to the extent that they have not been so successful as to lose all their sons and grandsons to employments in Lagos and Ibadan, have mostly retained social pre-eminence in Ijesha affairs, but it has been exercised by their members from other class positions.[43] At the same time

128

the continued importance of these families as interest-groups and points of attachment has greatly impeded the emergence of clear-cut oppositions between rural and urban class interests.

The natural lifespan of the cocoa-tree corresponds nicely with a human generation. The trees which a man plants in his prime and which begin to bear as his children grow up, enabling him to educate them, age with him. The sons of successful farmers are especially likely to move out of farming and perhaps to take employment for most of their lives away from Ilesha, and their father's farm is likely to be managed by a 'caretaker', typically a less fortunate friend or relative (who may well have a farm of his own) who owes them specified amounts in cash and kind. But they are often half-hearted *rentiers*, since marginal returns on efforts in other directions are so much greater, and it is a trouble to replant the farm, which gradually reverts to bush. This pattern does not hold universally, since many elderly Ilesha residents enjoy cocoa farms which were first planted by their fathers and where they must therefore have done some replanting themselves, but it *has* been the fate of most of the pioneer cocoa-farms, and its general effects are evident in the very low yields on Ijesha farms which Galletti *et al.* noted by the late 1940s, less than twenty years after Ijesha farmers had been singled out for special praise at what must have been the peak of their productivity.[44] They concluded that the age of farms was the most important determinant of yields. Fresh planting *was* still taking place then by Ilesha residents, but at a sharply declining rate, and increasingly we find the same phenomenon within Ijeshaland as within Yorubaland as a whole: a shift in importance from the pioneer areas and peoples to newer areas and peoples who came later to cocoa.

Since 1950 fresh cocoa-planting has chiefly occurred in the autonomous communities of the Northern Division (Ibokun, Ipetu, Ikeji etc.) and in virgin lands in the far south, beyond Iperindo and Etioni towards the disputed border with Ondo Division. Here substantial plots were sold by *Owa* Ajimoko II in the early 1950s to urban notables, members of the chiefly and political establishment of the day, who mostly did not plant the land themselves but leased it to migrant Oyo farmers who paid them *isakole*, after the precedent set by J.B. Apara. Many substantial new settlements, almost entirely inhabited by migrants from northern Yorubaland, such as Alarere and Temidire, came into existence. From about the same time determined attempts were made by successive *Owa* and by many *loja* to reinterpret their customary rights over occupants of land under their sway so as to yield substantial *isakole*.[45] These met with very variable success but we may presume – as indeed was alleged in the later 1950s – that immigrant strangers were most vulnerable.[46] While such rents doubtless made significant contributions to the incomes of a good many households in Ilesha, it cannot be said these *rentiers* have formed a distinctive stratum there, or that rents have approached in importance other means by which a surplus has been taken out of agriculture to sustain non-agricultural occupations and the position of the Ijesha elite.

THE COMMERCIAL HIERARCHY

In contrast to the farmers stood the traders, a complementary part of the developing commercial economy and a growing element in the composition of Ilesha's population, whether operating inside or outside Ijesha-land. The records of the Farmers' Association indicate ambivalent attitudes towards them; for while they note the 'bitterest opposition' of trading middlemen to the system of farmers' cooperative marketing, the Farmers' Association held discussions in 1929 with leading traders from the Young Ijesha Improvement Society (*Ẹgbẹ Atunluṣe*) about the possibility of establishing an 'Industrial and Commercial Bank' for Ilesha and joined with the Traders' Union of the town in opposing the establishment of Syrian traders in the late 1930s.[47] Traders formed most of the rising leadership of the town in the 1920s, and are quite outstanding among those whom elderly Ijesha today consider to be the most notable (*gbajumọ*) figures of Ilesha during their lifetimes.[48] 'Traders' (*oniṣowo*) is not a precise designation but refers to the whole hierarchy of occupational roles through which the produce of thousands of farmers reached its European purchasers and, in turn, manufactured goods imported by those same firms, as well as other local products, were supplied to consumers. Their dependence on the market to meet their needs increased *pari passu* with the advance of cocoa-production, the great motor of the Ijesha economy. Of the positive economic functions of this great multiplicity of traders, which essentially consisted of the bulking and bulk-breaking of commodities for a myriad of small-scale producers and consumers, there is little that needs to be added in a general way to the classic analysis of P.T. Bauer, though it must be said that his analysis lacks sociological realism to the extent that, taking something like a perfect market system as his baseline, he then asks why and with what effects 'restraint of trade' in its various forms crept in to spoil it.[49] In fact trade had always existed to serve the ends of the political elites who provided much of the occasion and conditions for it, this being ultimately no less true of the colonial period, even though colonial governments found it expedient to widen the arena within which 'restraint-free' trade could take place; while ethnic or communal solidarity, which enters Bauer's account as a further source of irrational restraint, has provided both motives and means to the development of trading institutions.[50] The commercial hierarchy, and with it the position of traders in the social life of the town, has been in constant evolution, and here our concern does not stretch beyond the epoch closed by the Riot of 1941, in which the antagonisms of traders were a crucial ingredient, and the Second World War, which greatly changed the conditions of the produce trade.

Of the system of trade before 1910 it is not easy to give more than an outline sketch.[51] Apart from the store of Messrs Witt and Busch, produce – at this period rubber, palm-oil, kernels and cotton, rather than cocoa – had to be headloaded in small quantities to markets where it could be sold and transported onwards in greater bulk. Before the railway reached Oshogbo in 1907, most produce had to be taken to the great market of Ejinrin on the Lagoon some 120 miles distant, or else to Ibadan, over 70 miles away, which the railway had reached in 1901. Ejinrin required an arduous eight- or nine-day round-trip, undertaken by young men travelling in convoys of friends for self-protection, acting independently and not as the agents of chiefs or their elders. Some larger traders also made this trip: one of the most famous, Ode Abugan, who used his personal connexions with *Owa* Ataiyero to 'help' people to have rubber-tapping licences issued around 1906–08 and got his trading capital that way, had six or seven porters taking rubber to Ejinrin with him. Farm produce and livestock for consumption in Lagos also went from Ilesha to Ejinrin.[52] In return they would buy such commodities as cloth, hardware (traps, locks, axes, knives, nails, cutlasses, bowls and plates), gunpowder, salt, sugar, and spirits, and these they would sell in Ilesha or hawk around the district. Even after Oshogbo ousted Ejinrin as the main external focus of trade, the same pattern continued for several years: young men collecting as much produce as they could carry, taking it to the place where it could be exchanged for a similar load of consumables, and returning to sell them, sometimes in certain favoured lines (e.g. palm-kernels one way, bags of sugar the other).

At this stage, with lowish levels of market production and consumption and little opportunity for bulking of produce in that part of the trading network controlled by Ijesha, because of poor transport facilities, the trading system was very little differentiated. From 1910 or so this began to change. A small group of older men, definitely senior to the unmarried young men who were active in the Ejinrin trade but often former Ejinrin traders themselves, and possessing some capital, began to establish shops in Ilesha, where they sold over the counter the same kinds of commodities which had previously only been sold in the market or hawked around – a sure sign of the population's increased power to consume imports. The chiefs were at first suspicious of this development, and, partly in response, it would appear, to pressure from women traders, forbade them from setting up their shops in Ereja by the market, and so they concentrated themselves in Orinkiran, on the axis of the Oshogbo road.[53] This occurred around 1911–13, the pioneers being S.A.K. Ilesanmi, E.A. Ariyo (who had started in the Ejinrin trade in Ajimoko's reign with £2 10s 0d capital from his mother, and set up the shop with capital of £200), and two other ex-Ejinrin men, both at Okesha, S.A. Osobu and Aluko Dugbe.

At the same time, there grew up between 1909 and 1918 at Oshogbo a group of Ijesha traders, partly catering to the market needs of its resident population, which included many migrants, labourers and clerks but partly carving out a new, higher niche in the trading hierarchy, by selling cloth for further distribution in a wide region around Oshogbo as well as over the counter, and buying produce collected by smaller traders for resale to the European firms. Ijesha traders were well placed to perform this latter role at Oshogbo since an increasing share of the produce sold there came from Ijeshaland and they could use their own social contacts to attract custom. When these men – J.F. Longe (Longe Faloyo), James Oginni, J.A. Fadugba, and others – moved back to open stores as the agents of the buying firms in Ilesha in the early 1920s, as the ever-increasing volume of cocoa grown in Ilesha and improved transport on the Oshogbo–Ilesha road made it economically feasible, the main features of the trading hierarchy as it was to be for several decades slid into place.[54]

Let us follow the produce as it passed up the hierarchy from farmer to firm.[55] The great bulk of produce was sold by farmers to 'middlemen', 'pan-buyers' or *onigba*, men who went round the farms buying cocoa in smallish quantities by measure. Only a small minority of farmers sold to the cooperative stores or in larger amounts to larger traders higher up the hierarchy. These 'middlemen' then sold by weight to 'scalemen'. These were larger traders, operating in a recognized marketing centre, initially at Oshogbo and the central market in Ilesha, but by the late 1920s also at several places closer to the farms, such as Oshu. Access to the scales was not open, but controlled by local Produce Traders Associations. Membership required personal sponsorship and a subscription, so that each association resembled the title-holders of a community in being a cluster of the relatively privileged, focussed round a resource whose scarcity was not just the effect of economic forces. Working capital was needed too, both to maintain a small produce-store and to make cash advances to the middlemen who made them in turn to the farmers. These traders at the scales in turn sold to even larger Ijesha traders, the elite of whom were commission agents of the firms, who would arrange for sufficient quantities of produce to be collected by lorry and taken to Ilesha, where it would be graded by officials of the Produce Inspection Department. A young trader with ambition and capital – like for example J.O. Fadahunsi, who began at the scales in Oshu in 1927 and became an agent of the United Africa Company and later the Union Trading Company in the 1930s – could take a greater share of the value added to the produce in its progress up the hierarchy by chartering a lorry to take his own cocoa (as well as that of any other trader who was prepared to let him transport it) directly to Oshogbo, where the firms' European chief agents supervised buying throughout the entire area.[56]

In the early 1920s there were upwards of a dozen firms buying cocoa – Russell, Miller Bros, John Holt, African and Eastern Trade Corporation, Paterson and Zochonis, G.B. Ollivant, Société Commerciale de l'Ouest Africain, J.H. Doherty and so on – though the rigours of competition had reduced them to a handful by the mid-1930s, the United Africa Company

(UAC, formed by amalgamation of several of the others in 1929) and John Holt leading the field. Crucial to the system of trade was the capital which each buying firm made available through its principal agents, the larger African traders, at the beginning of the buying season, and from which they in turn made cash advances to their suppliers lower down the hierarchy. To become a buying agent, a man needed two acceptable guarantors and capital enough to make a deposit with the firm – but there was never any shortage of applicants since the firms' capital gave such an advantage to their agents, who could draw on it to make advances lower down the hierarchy, over 'independent' competitors without this resource. In addition to his trading profits, the agent received a commission on produce he bought for his firm and sometimes a small salary or retainer as well, in addition to any rents he might receive on buildings let to the firm. But since the firms were absolutely dependent on their agents for access to producers, the trader-agents, despite the periods of their indebtedness, were very much their own men. An agent who was energetic, well-connected locally and able to use his extra-economic status to attract business, was much sought after, and the expression which one sometimes hears of a big trader (say, J.D.E. Abiola) that 'he brought John Holt, AETC and J.H. Doherty to Ilesha' is not too far-fetched. As a result, relations between agents and firms were flexible. A really big trader like Abiola might act as the agent of more than one firm, provided he paid deposits to each one and repaid their several advances in the form of appropriate quantities of produce. Since the firms made individual arrangements with each agent as regards commission, retainer and cash advance, and kept the details strictly secret, it could be advantageous, as each firm offered its own buying prices and changed them periodically on instructions from head office throughout the buying season, for the trader to be able to shift the incoming supply of produce from one firm to another as appropriate. Moreover, Ijesha traders were quite prepared to shift from one firm to another, if they could get improved terms for their agency.

The firms also needed retail outlets on the merchandise side. Here they made substantial sales, especially in cloth, from their main stores in places like Oshogbo and Ibadan, selling to various types of smaller trader, some of whom (like the Syrians, or larger women traders) would resell much of their purchases to even smaller traders, as well as to such traders as the Ijesha *oṣomaalo*, who would hawk merchandise around small rural communities. But they also needed bulk outlets in substantial population centres away from their stores, and so they adopted a system of agencies parallel to the one for produce-buying. The conditions under which individual traders served as agents on the merchandise side were equally varied and again credit played an important role, taking the form of advances of goods. By the 1930s the range of products sold had greatly expanded: enormous quantities of cloth were sold (that decade seeing the virtual collapse of domestic manufacture of the rough cotton cloth called *kijipa* for

133

household members' common use); building materials such as corrugated iron sheets and cement for the new Lagos-type houses which the large traders had made fashionable; new convenience foods like those great staples of the Nigerian petty trader, condensed milk and tinned sardines, or wheat flour (Ilesha's *third* bakery was opened in 1939 by E.A. Lufadeju, son of the *Lǫja Ibala* and a former salesman of the German firm of G.L. Gaiser).[57] It was possible for a trader to be involved both in buying produce and selling merchandise, and not necessarily for the same firm, since each agency, governed by its own conditions, was a distinct operation. While it might be an advantage for a trader to combine them, in that customers on one side might be put under some obligation in respect of the other, there were managerial and accounting difficulties in involving oneself in too many separate agencies. The lure of additional credit was attractive, but most traders settled for one firm and one side. In general, the largest trading fortunes were made on the produce-buying side, where *cash*-advances were made and which was most involved with that activity which really seemed to promise the traders their El Dorado: transport.

Until after the First World War Ilesha was linked to Oshogbo (through which her produce went by rail to Lagos) by a lorry service, initially provided by the Government, later by the firm of W.A. Dawodu, Egba merchants at Oshogbo. But from 1918, there was an extraordinarily rapid increase in transport owned and operated by Ijesha traders. A decade later, upwards of two dozen Ijesha seemed to have owned lorries – their picturesque names, 'Rio', 'Laker', 'Denbigh', fondly recalled today – and several of the biggest traders had sizeable fleets: J.D.E. Abiola and Asaolu Osue are each said to have had twelve, J.F. Longe owned six and shares in another four.[58] S.A.K. Ilesanmi and his friend Jegede Ogboni owned one jointly, but broke up because they couldn't agree whose house it should stand in front of when not in use, for 'it was a glory in those days'. To his other enterprises Abiola added an agency in motor parts with the firm of Weeks. The opportunities for motor transport were greatly extended when, in 1923–25, the Government joined Ilesha to Akure and Benin on the one side, and Ife and Ibadan on the other, by means of tarred Trunk 'A' roads.[59] Almost at once much produce started being taken directly to Lagos instead of to Oshogbo (thus precipitating a crisis for railway revenues), an innovation in which Ijebu lorry-owners were to the fore.[60] Ijesha owners, at least in the mid-1920s, were more concerned with the shorter routes, to Ibadan via Ife, Ondo and Oshogbo, where the increased demand for transport, now going beyond the marketing of export-produce to involve a much greater circulation of people and commodities between the major Yoruba towns, seems to have been outstripped by the supply. In 1925 Ijesha lorry-owners responded warmly to a suggestion of their Ife counterparts to join in setting up a tariff of minimum charges – in fact to hold charges at what they had been in 1924, when market conditions were tending to depress them – on these routes; for, it was claimed, costs of oil and spare parts were so high and passengers, necessary to meet running expenses, were too thinly spread, owing to the rapid increase of lorries on the road.[61] However, when J.A. Fadugba on behalf of the whole group published some intended 'Fare Regulations for Motor Vehicles', threatening fines for infringements up to 'withdrawal of licence by Government' for a third offence, he got a stinging retort from the DO at Ife demanding that it be withdrawn.[62] Transport remained a very risky enterprise: vehicle breakdowns, the supply of parts and shortage of skilled mechanics were one set of problems, but equally serious were the managerial difficulties of supervising drivers and controlling costs.

From 1930 the Depression decimated the ranks of lorry-owners; few had the prescience of Asaolu Osue, who got out of transport in 1929, and the large fleets were, for a few years, obliterated. One day in 1931 Abiola was devastated by the news that no less than seven of his lorries were broken down and, when his problems were compounded by a serious illness, virtually withdrew from transport. Fadugba fared even worse – 'today is a desperate day to me', he wrote in his diary on 30 August 1932, 'being the first time I ever offer my wearing apparel for sales in order to repair my lorry' – and he was soon forced entirely off the road. Significantly he started taking a much closer interest in his cocoa-plantation near Ibodi,[63] as a number of other traders were doing – J.F. Longe, for example, who had bought land beyond Iwaro which he planted with cocoa, *gbanja* and plantains,[64] and could visit conveniently by car to supervise his labourers. These men were not farmers of the stamp of Thompson or Fajemisin. None the less, as the Depression passed over, it became clear that transport linked with produce-buying was still the route to the greatest local fortunes. By the late 1930s, the field was dominated by one man, Aromolaran's eldest son, Prince S.A. Adeniran or 'Awe *Owa*', who was the principal agent of UAC (then the largest firm in the market) and ran a fleet of twelve lorries on his own account; and the two outstandingly rich men whom Ilesha has produced since the Second World War, I.O. Ajanaku and Lawrence Omole, also made their fortunes this way, moving from a base in produce into transport.

The wealth, prestige and influence of traders in the town, and especially of their transporter elite, was a new phenomenon of the 1920s. Previously traders, operating on a smaller scale, had been strangers, women, or men at an early stage of their life-careers – or else Ijesha pursued trade, as Frederick Haastrup had, outside Ijeshaland; now it was an activity pursued at home by mature men of standing, on a scale which might lead to the largest cash incomes in the community. The largest farmers probably earned between £500 and £1,000 in good years, but Abiola at his height might make up to £2,000 annual profit on his produce-buying alone.[65] The *Owa*'s total income is hard to estimate, but the Resident described him in 1931 as 'not in need of money but not well off', while most ordinary chiefs, as we shall see, were by the late 1930s under great pressure to augment their meagre incomes by selling land over which they had customary rights.[66] The wealth of the larger traders, compared with that of the primary producers, is striking, but we do not explain it by merely passing it off as 'exploitation'. To the extent that trade went with transport, that was a function which provided an essential condition of production for distant markets, and which had been one of crucial importance for economic development throughout West African history. It is not easy to argue that the trading sector as a whole got more than it earned of the total product's cost to its European buyers. The point is rather the vast gap between the incomes of the mass of ordinary traders – the *onigba* foot-slogging it round the farms, the *alatę* at the motor-park with her head-tray of small items – and the trading elite. This was a consequence of the commercial system itself, in which the movement of produce from geographically dispersed producers towards its eventual purchasers needed to be combined with its bulking; and the firms' provision of credit to finance the system inevitably produced a steeply stratified hierarchy of traders. There was no comparable necessity inherent in the structure of agriculture that there should be large and small farmers, and the actual inequalities here mainly arose from the distribution of what might be called the 'social assets' of individual farmers in the community.

THE TRADERS IN THE COMMUNITY

At this point, however, we must turn to look at the traders in the same way, as members of a social community rather than just as elements in an externally oriented commercial system. There are two aspects of this which merit attention here. Firstly, the particular social assets they brought to trading were crucial to how they performed their economic role. Secondly, they were influential in Ilesha, not so much because of their wealth itself, but because of how they spent it; and this must be related to aspirations that underlay their life-histories, played out against a changing historical context. Let us begin by looking at the background to some individual trading careers.

All the large traders of the 1920s had a background of outside travel or residence outside Ilesha, though this does not especially distinguish them from very many of their contemporaries who left Ilesha to trade or labour in the years before 1910 and who returned to settle down and farm. Several of the cocoa-pioneers also had such a background of outside travel and trade, but when they came home there was not much for mature men to do but farm; and even after the new commercial opportunities opened up, there were not *many* opportunities on the higher rungs of the traders' hierarchy, while pan-buying was not an activity for one who had come home to settle. The substantial traders we have been considering, then, were mostly a decade or so younger than the cocoa-pioneers, born in the 1870s or 1880s. They mostly spoke little English, though many of them were self-taught literates in Yoruba and could keep simple accounts. Virtually all became Christians (a few, Muslims), though not usually as a result of schooling, and many were staunch supporters of their churches, though were rarely as religiously active as the leading cocoa-pioneers. A minority had more unusual backgrounds, bringing them into closer contact with Europeans and with spheres beyond farming and trade, and giving them skills and ideas of a more far-ranging kind. The early careers of three of them may be summarized:

J.A. FADUGBA. Born 1870, son of a warrior at Kiriji and grandson of a Chief *Arapatẹ*, he left home against his parents' wishes with an Egba trader to whom he became attached and who educated him to Standard 5. At Abeokuta he mixed a good deal with Europeans, who gave him a prize for his skill as an interpreter, and took employment with the Forestry Department, at Olokemeji and Jebba (Northern Nigeria). He added to his savings with petty trading and eventually took to trading full time, becoming an agent of Gaiser and later McIver at Oshogbo before he moved back to Ilesha in 1921, as agent for Miller Bros.

J.D.E. ABIOLA. His father Eso was in no way outstanding but his grandfather, *Lọkiran* Oruru, was one of Ilesha's warlords, active in the 1860s. Born *c.* 1877, he left town around 1904 and went to the North as a labourer. In 1906, he learnt tailoring at Iseyin and, in 1908, he worked as a labour contractor on the railway at Aro Station, Abeokuta. Around 1914, at the suggestion of a European superior, he went as a contractor to Port Harcourt, then in the earliest years of its construction. 1916–18 he was overseer on contract to the PWD on the Oshogbo–Ilesha–Akure road, continuing on other road contracts in the West till 1929. He learnt photography. In 1920 he established his produce-buying business, agent for John Holt and others, in Ilesha.

J.S. OGINNI. Born *c.* 1878, his father Ogunseitan being a first cousin of *Ọdọle* Ariyasunle, greatest of the pre-1870 magnates. He was a convert of the Revd Atundaolu, the pioneer Methodist, and became steward to one of the Commissioners at Oke Imo. From 1909 he worked as a tailor at Oshogbo and later opened a shop there, finally moving into produce (agent for Russell, and then John Holt) and transport, and re-establishing in Ilesha in 1926.

These brief biographies, besides documenting the genuine sense in which they were self-made men, getting some assistance from adventitious helpers, it is true, but not basing their fortunes on material assets inherited from parents, still raise the question of whether their descent and home social connexions were relevant to their success as traders in Ilesha, by helping them to find guarantors, raise loans, acquire land for stores in suitable locations, attract customers or control employees. The evidence – the close relations of several of the largest traders with major title-holders or political figures and with each other – is circumstantial but suggestive. The connexions are often spontaneously remarked upon by informants giving accounts of their careers. Figure 7.1 shows how J.D.E.

Abiola, the biggest trader of the 1920s, was through his mother related both to another of the larger buying agents, E.A. Ariyo, and to the *Owa* himself and his son Adeniran, the biggest trader of the late 1930s. Through his father he was kin to D.M. Anjorin, doyen of Ijesha traders at Ilorin and first Patron of the *Egbe Atunluṣe*;[67] more remotely linked, via Anjorin's mother, to another whole nexus going back to another of the mid nineteenth century warlords, *Obaodo* Obojo, one of whose sons, Onigbogi, held the *Obanla* title from 1910 to 1926; and his younger half-brother, G.O.E. Aduroja, after starting as apprentice to another famous early, but unrelated, trader, Aluko 'Olowo Ijero', passed on to the tutelage of Anjorin, kept a shop as agent for Paterson and Zochonis and bought produce for Prince Adeniran, before achieving success as transporter (32 lorries) in the 1950s and taking the same open title, *Lejoka*, which his brother had occupied. But did these links really matter much – not all traders, at least, seem to stand in the middle of such a nexus as did Abiola; or conversely were there not many close relatives of title-holders who lived lives of obscurity? This is so: pre-existing social ties of this kind were strictly neither necessary to, nor, more certainly, sufficient for success. But they furnished a field of possibilities, social assets which could be exploited: they put a man in the way of things. Thus, when cocoa started being produced in quantity around Ibokun in the late 1920s, it was Abiola, and then Adeniran and Ariyo, all of them with Ibokun connexions going back several generations, who were able to establish links with local suppliers there. Abiola stood surety for his cousin Ariyo with John Holt and for Prince Adeniran with UAC. I.O. Ajanaku, whose transport business emerged during the Second World War to become the largest enterprise any Ijesha has ever created, was a cousin of E.A. Ariyo through his mother and married Adeniran's daughter, and started his career as a produce clerk for Ariyo. (It may not be quite accidental that he too, along with his cousin J.F. Olojo of Egbeidi, another trading magnate of the interwar years, is a direct agnatic descendant of another of the great warlords of the last century, *Lejoka* Danaija.) Kinship and title, obligation and power, were the two main coordinates of the system. Title itself, of course, no longer gave the opportunity to make direct levies on trade, and being a chief was still felt to be incompatible with conducting trade; but proximity to title, and hence likely membership of an influential social network, made a man attractive as a patron or contact, someone whom it was worth establishing relations with, even for purposes unconnected with trade. Prince Adeniran's exploitation of his unique status to consolidate his business in the late 1930s, as will be described in Chapter 9, provides the classic case of this. Kinship, on the other hand, the residue of past connexions, enabled a man to make claims for a fresh connexion in a new sphere; and while it was neither necessary nor sufficient as the basis of such a claim, it could have definite results. Ijesha kinship ideology, while never so binding as to exclude promising outsiders, did predispose people to expect

138

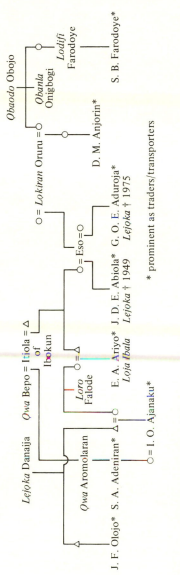

Fig. 7.1 Some connexions of J. D. E. Abiola

Source: additional information regarding these relations derived from interviews with: Mr S. B. Farodoye, 7 Aug. 1974; Chief E. A. Ariyo, 8 July 1975; Chief G. O. E. Aduroja, 20 Aug. 1974; Mr I. O. Ajanaku, 24 May 1975; Chief D. L. Ajayi at Ibokun, 14 July 1975.

139

that the personal qualities and connexions of a previous generation would, and should, be reproduced in its descendants.

What drew men into trade was that it promised the resources necessary to fulfil their ambition for personal success, which was to attract a following and to exercise influence through spending money and controlling opportunities. The wider normative patterns of social life, which engendered these ambitions, permeated and set limits to the businesses, *qua* economic enterprises, which the traders set up.[68] Though they were in competition with one another, large traders were expected to sponsor others (e.g. by standing surety for them) who would be their rivals – in a sense being able to do this *was* success and not to do it would, paradoxically, weaken one's standing as a trader. For the nature of competition in this society meant that commercial success was fostered by buyers being able to offer more than simple cash in exchange for produce. It depended on 'credit' in a broader sense than the cash advances made available by the firms, in fact on a general 'social credit': a proven reputation for being able and prepared to give help and assistance, materially and in other ways, to those who wanted them. In some cases generosity might tip over from being the foundation to the destruction of an enterprise – at least two traders abandoned shop-keeping for more wholesale forms of trade because they found it impossible to prevent relatives helping themselves to stock.[69] The same critical balance was clearly of concern to the traders who joined the Reformed Ogboni Fraternity (ROF), a form of freemasonry whose rapid spread after its introduction in 1934 shows how much additional bonds of obligation were sought by traders as a hedge against the vicissitudes of the Depression. 'Members of the Fraternity', says the Constitution, 'are in duty bound to one another in distress, to succour in adversity, against danger; and to be charitable under all circumstances without being plunged into debt by the demands of fellow members.'[70] The 'social credit' which a trader required belonged to him personally, not to his enterprise or to any particular agency he might have, since it depended in good part on his extra-economic status in Ilesha; and what made a successful enterprise was the individual trader's ability to manipulate a whole network of relations centring on himself. For these reasons, and because a trading enterprise was only one possible means to an individual's realization of his life-goals, the enterprises themselves – albeit proclaimed to the world under a nice durable blue enamel sign reading 'John Holt of Liverpool' or some such – were transient. A son did not inherit a business, but a father's reputation and the social ties he established with it, to make of it what he chose.

Though the emphasis in the preceding paragraphs has been on the continued relevance of both traditional ideals of personal success and social connexions rooted in past relationships to the new traders, they seemed to themselves and their contemporaries to be bearers of a new way of life. It is fitting to call the 1920s something of a Jazz Age in Ilesha – and not just because of the gramophone records which Fadugba was forced to sell when the party was over in the early 1930s.[71] Trading profits and debts soared to unprecedented levels, bringing with them increased litigation to alarm many older traders: Fadugba recorded in his Diary how Jacob Jegede, a trading partner, 'cursed [his] generation in the open market'.[72] So much of the age seems epitomized in another entry, which casually notes that on one day in 1923 he had £216 in cash in his safe and £670 in outside credit, acquired an additional wife (one of several who came in the years of his prosperity and deserted him when he was flat broke in the Depression) and was summonsed.[73] The large traders scrambled from one agency to another: Fadugba added to his shop and store for Miller a further store for the Hamburg Nigeria Co. in 1926, but in 1927 we find them suing him along with J.F. Longe and J.S. Oginni for recovery of funds; and in 1930 he opened another agency for John Holt. The possibilities of consumption rose equally dizzily: Fadugba's gramophone was nothing to the electrical generator which Abiola installed in his Omofe house and from which he planned to light neighbouring Christ Church. Further downmarket the pace-setters were the younger *oṣomaalo* traders whose societies – *Ẹgbẹ Amuludun*, 'we make the town agreeable', *Ẹgbẹ Ayẹba*, 'we honour the king' – held dances around Christmas and would turn out at major social occasions, and who popularized such items as sash-windows for houses or 'Rudge' bicycles.

The new levels and styles of consumption themselves betokened significant shifts in social relations which became evident in the 1920s. Though the aspirations which underlay them were hardly new – to be an independent man, head of one's own household, with the accoutrements of personal prowess such as fine clothes and fashionable consumer goods – the fact that they could be so much more widely attained had real effects. Households became smaller as more men built houses for themselves, instead of remaining under the roof of a senior relative from whom they might one day inherit its headship; and Ilesha began to assume something like its present-day appearance as these new Lagos-type, sometimes storeyed, iron-roofed houses replaced the old low compounds of linked *akodi*. This tended to the loosening of Ilesha's political integration, especially at the lower levels; for as households multiplied in number, a smaller proportion of their heads were involved in the town's government through taking titles in the quarters, thus compounding the effects of the quarter-chiefs' decline since the introduction of taxation and their loss of official judicial duties.

Now in this situation lay potential seeds of conflict between the large traders and the chiefs. For the traders were not just leaders of cultural fashion; they exerted an active influence which was measured in the same coinage as chiefly rank, in the allegiance of numbers of followers. In a way analogous to that of the chiefs, their influence was expressed through several channels: their own personal social networks, their economic activities and, very importantly, their leadership within localities of the town.

The extreme timidity shown by the anonymous 'Ijesha Young Traders' in 1920 was very soon left behind as it was realized that something of a leadership vacuum had developed in the town, with the decay of the lower reaches of the chieftaincy system, and the emergence of new spheres of economic and social activity in which the chiefs had little competence or control; and the larger traders were best able to fill that vacuum.

The *Qwa* and chiefs did not initially welcome this, any more than they welcomed the emergence of substantial farmers and leaders of new communities in the district who refused to be co-opted through the title-system; and they used their powers to try to curtail the traders' opportunities. Fadugba wrote on behalf of the traders to the *Qwa* in 1924 complaining at the *Qwa*'s order to remove all buying-scales from the villages. He noted their presence in villages elsewhere in Yorubaland, asking to know 'why then is Ilesha refused to give free trade to the Town and *Villages* alike?'; and referred to the disagreeable reception that traders had got when summoned to the *Afin*, 'sorrowful to hear the Chiefs using abusing language and did not allow us to say a word'.[74] But it was futile for the chiefs to pursue this negative policy against the clear trend of the times, and in any case, there were ways in which they could cut in on the commercial economy. Many of them controlled land in the town and, with the increased demand for land for commercial premises as well as for houses, started to demand a cash price, instead of the customary offerings of kola, gin and a ram.

Qwa Aromolaran, however, had the astuteness to see that a much more positive relationship could be established with those whom the commercial economy had made wealthy and influential outside the title-system. He set about this in two ways: cooperation with the traders as a whole in a programme for Ilesha's communal advance (*atunluṣe* or 'improvement') and the consolidation of a dominant political coalition around himself, its members including both traders and chiefs of conventional stamp. As to the former, the *Qwa* appreciated that the traders, especially the literate ones, had the measure of the times more than anyone else, while they realized that, because of what the *Qwa* was in the eyes of both the Government and the mass of the population, the communal projects dear to them could not go forward except in his name. The resultant political programme will be considered in Chapter 9. Here our concern is with how the *Qwa* achieved the coalition which put it into effect.

The *Qwa*'s principal means, which he deployed with consummate finesse, was a personal network focussed on himself and the chieftaincy system. He needed, firstly, a strong personal link with the larger traders, which he affected through the friendship of his eldest son, Awe Adeniran, with J.D.E. Abiola. Adeniran was not educated, but he became a Christian and had some training as a tailor, and Abiola took him under his wing in a general way: he joined the circle of 'enlightened' traders, and built a large storey house (*pẹtẹsi*) in the fashionable style at Isokun, just inside the old town wall on the Oshogbo road. But chieftaincy had the central role to play since it was a means to establish mutual obligations between the *Ọwa* and men raised to title from diverse backgrounds, and could serve as a kind of curb on those chiefs.

Now the role requirements of a trader, who had to be active in pursuit of his business, and of a chief, who was obliged to attend regularly at the *Afin* and to be generally available at his chieftaincy house, were still considered more or less incompatible; and today's practice of giving purely honorific titles to important people who continue to pursue their occupations, even if away from Ilesha, was scarcely conceived. It is said that the *Ọwa* wanted to give Abiola the *Ọbanla*-ship, when its holder Onigbogi died in 1926, but Abiola declined; 'in those days a chief didn't do any work'.[75] J.A. Fadugba, who was less close to the *Ọwa* than Abiola, is said by his son to have refused (or perhaps to have refused to contest) his lineage's title *Arapatẹ* when it fell vacant in 1929, on the grounds that it was a 'means to tie his hand'.[76] But in 1934 Abiola did finally join the chiefs as *Lẹjọka*, the senior *ẹlẹgbẹ*. Why did he change? Partly, no doubt, it was because the Depression had largely overthrown his business, and the title, with the judicial powers that went with it, would be a way of restoring his fortunes. But apart from this circumstance, title was attractive as the culminating embodiment of the life-goal of the trader, which was simply the aspiration of Ijesha in general, namely to exercise influence over other people's lives in his community; and it was a means to achieve this that was more fitting to old age than running a business, with its ceaseless agitation. The cash sought by the trader was always principally a means to this end, rather than personal consumption or the enlargement of the enterprise itself; and even the items of conspicuous consumption, above all those grandiose residences, Abiola's 'Elephant House', Fadugba's 'Lion House', were essentially public declarations of prowess and means to accommodate a large personal following. Almost the most poignant entry in Fadugba's diary, made when he was experiencing the most bitter poverty and desertion by his dependants, is one which records how pathetically uplifted he was when one of his sons predicted that one day all the land in his compound at Iroye would be built over.[77] A different concern for the future weighed with Abiola, foremost of Ilesha's local historians: when his affairs had sunk low in the early 1930s, he felt, said his son, that he never would be remembered if he did not become a chief.

Ọwa Aromolaran responded with discrimination to the eagerness of the larger traders to take titles.[78] To give titles to some traders would bind them to the chiefly establishment; but it was also important not to ignore the claims of men who were not traders, since *they* did not feel their eligibility was *ipso facto* any less and they might be less feared as rivals by established chiefs. Apart from the general resentment that the exclusion of

143

non-traders might create, there were powerful lineage interests which might not have a wealthy trader as their favoured representative, and it was wise for the *Ọwa* to pay some attention to their preferences. He would also need to settle personal political debts, arising out of his own election, and in any case the power which a title conferred would tend to be politically safer if it lay with a personal friend of the *Ọwa*. Aromolaran's political expertise lay in the manner in which he reconciled these personal interests with the integration of a community threatened by the emergence of wealth and power formed outside the title system.

So what we find is that *some* traders, but especially those personally linked with the *Ọwa*, received titles. J.D.E. Abiola, of course, was the most obvious choice, being made *Lẹjọka* in 1934. His two predecessors, who had brief tenures, were both candidates of a 'traditional' stamp – Falomo had been an *ẹmẹsẹ* of the *Ọwa*'s and Ologuro a farmer from Ajido – and they were preferred to traders, D.O. Agbeja and Ode Abugan respectively. Around 1933, Adedeji was replaced as *Risawẹ* by his brother, Komolafe Adedigba; he too was a trader, with an agency for John Holt, and an *Atunluṣe* member, but the most compelling reason was that he had helped Aromolaran 'both physically and financially', no doubt along with his brother, to get the *Ọwa*ship in 1920.[79] He was preferred over Gureje Asogbe, a man of similar status but smaller as a trader, despite the other chiefs' preference for Asogbe and the sentiment that lineage titles should not be monopolized by one descent line. It was of no small consequence that the *Ọwa* at this time enjoyed a status as Sole Native Authority under British overrule, which gave him an extraordinary, diffuse and not clearly bounded disposing power over Ijesha affairs. The *Arapatẹ* title, vacant in 1936, went to a modest produce-buyer who had been at Oshogbo, Aogo, who was recommended by the respect he had always shown chiefs and *ẹmẹsẹ*. Other traders were less successful. The other top hereditary *iwọle* title which fell vacant in these years was *Loro*; and though a variety of popular traders aspired to it – Alege of Iwere, Ben Ajilore of Iroye and J.F. Longe – Aromolaran selected for it a man of little 'modern' experience, but a friend of the influential *Risawẹ* and well connected (cf. Figure 7.1), Idaomi Falode. J.F. Longe was compensated for this disappointment by being made *Asọju Onigbagbọ* (the Christian representative on the Native Court, which was at this time the virtual equivalent of a chieftaincy) on the death of C.A. Lufadeju in 1933. But his friend J.S. Oginni, the *Atunluṣe* Chairman, failed in 1935 in his bid for the biggest prize of all, the *Ọbanla*-ship, against a 'traditional' candidate, Ogedengbe's grandson Ogunmoyesin.[80] In advancing him, the *Ọwa* made a gesture towards that considerable body of people who shared relationships through the great warrior and which, despite the fragmentation of his household in 1910, was still a potential interest-group in the town. We must not forget, for example, that many of Ogedengbe's former *ipaiyẹ* had achieved a modest dignity as junior quarter-chiefs, and that sentiment if not strong personal connexions would lead them to appreciate that, though the *nouveaux riches* were getting titles, Ogedengbe's grandson was not neglected. Perhaps most important of all was that by Ogunmoyesin's elevation the *Owa* bound to himself the charismatic prestige of Ogedengbe, the greatest historical symbol of Ilesha's communal prowess.

Through these means Aromolaran effected two things. The first was that he headed off the threat to the town's integration posed by the emergence of a group of men, wealthy and influential in new ways but set apart from the chiefs. The second was a corollary of this, though perhaps less of a conscious object of policy. Whereas the tendency of early colonial rule was to the opening of local economic opportunities, the powers accorded to the chiefs, and especially the *Owa*, under the political dispensation of colonialism, were used, especially after the co-optation of the traders, to make economic opportunity significantly more dependent, not just on inherited socio-political assets but on direct relations to the local power structure of the day. In fact, Aromolaran succeeded only too well in binding the wealthy and the titled into a joint establishment; for a reaction was provoked where it was not expected, among the smaller men who were incidentally excluded, with explosive consequences which will be treated in a later chapter.

8

The discovery of Nigeria

'Nigeria' began its existence as a pure expression of imperialist political will. To say this, of course, is in no way to deny the profound continuities in culture and feeling which connect the pre-colonial societies of the area which became Nigeria and Nigerian society of today; but it is to insist that the emergence of a Nigerian *society* be considered as a sociological problem. Though 'society', in one of its most common uses, means a system of social relations corresponding to a state, the existence of a state does not guarantee that such a system of relations must exist. The Nigerian state, actualized in its major features in Lugard's amalgamation of 1914 and confirmed with the introduction of direct personal taxation in 1919, had significantly constrained Ijesha action and shaped the opportunities to which Ijesha responded, yet for over two decades it existed as an entirely alien reality. And for Nigeria to exist as an entity to which Ilesha belonged, and was not just subject to, it required more than for the pressures of the state to become more intense or for more people to enter new social relations dependent on it. Rather, Nigeria needed to be appropriated into the thinking of the Ijesha about their situation, to be 'discovered' or made subjectively their own, by those who had been forcibly or unknowingly incorporated into it. How this happened is an important historical question, since on it depends our understanding of the nationalist movement which began to reach inland from its Lagos origins in the 1930s and swept up the rising political leadership of Ilesha in the late 1940s.

For the Ijesha, a new and distinctively *Nigerian* realm of social relations opened up in two dimensions: in the 'supra-Ijesha' realm of new roles created by the Nigerian state, especially bureaucratic office and other kinds of employment in state bodies; and in the 'extra-Ijesha' realm of new opportunities taken up by Ijesha outside Ijeshaland. Two kinds of mobility, social and geographical, are involved here, and they were very closely linked. Few went 'up', at least in *new* ways, without also going 'out' for a significant period of their lives. This migration played a decisive role in making Ijesha think of themselves as Nigerians, and it produced the apparent and oft-noted paradox that Nigerian-ness came with an *increased*

146

rather than a diminished ethnic consciousness, both as Yoruba – itself a new identity too – and as Ijesha.[1] The same period saw another form of identity-shift which relates, though in no simple way, to the entry of Ijesha into wider social relations on the Nigerian state: the conversion of the great bulk of Ijesha to one of the world religions. Quite apart from the dependence of both Christianity and Islam on agencies external to Ijeshaland, they can only have consolidated Nigerian-ness by providing Ijesha with new personal identities linked to a wider cosmos than that marked out by Ogun and Obokun. The theme of this chapter is the linkages between mobility and identity.

PATTERNS OF MIGRATION

Though the migration we are to consider has as its most general condition the capitalist world economy as mediated through the colonial state, we cannot separate it sharply from pre-colonial forms of migration and it would certainly distort our understanding of its local sources and meaning to do so. Our account of 'traditional' society included many references to the migration of strangers to settle, of movements of colonization into the forests and of oscillatory movements of longer or shorter duration within the Ijesha sphere. Short-term migration is less likely to have left much record in oral tradition, but the movement of young Ijesha to grasp the opportunities of Ibadan and the Lagoon trade-routes in the mid nineteenth century shows that it is unacceptable to draw a simple distinction between a pre-colonial migration of population to settle and a colonial migration of labour, as Samir Amin has done.[2] The basic idea of going 'out' of the local social system to get the resources to later go 'up' within it arose within Ijesha culture, combining with the opportunities of the early colonial period to produce the conflicts described above in Chapter 6.

It is not easy to present a fairly precise account of the volume and type of out-migration as it has changed over the past few decades. In what follows, the data was derived from the 1974 survey of household-heads and is of two kinds: personal migration histories by men who had returned home, and check-lists of absent family members as of that time. Since over half the household-heads were over sixty years old, and nearly a quarter over seventy-five, this yielded a good deal of information about the structure of Ijesha out-migration back to 1914 or so. Questions were also asked about respondents' fathers' migratory experiences, as far as they were known, but so many 'no-answers' were recorded from the older respondents that the data do not do much more than confirm the qualitative impression derived from written sources and casually-collected family histories, that there were many Ijesha in the late nineteenth century who ranged in warfare over north-eastern Yorubaland, endured periods of slavery in Ibadan or Abeokuta, or travelled as traders up to Ilorin and Bida, or along the Lagoon as far west as Porto Novo. As with the discussion of the cocoa

147

economy in Chapter 7, the aim will be to present the whole trajectory of migration up to the present, rather than just the structure of migration as it was when it began to produce the changes of consciousness which are our main focus of interest.

The age at which migration occurs ranges, in the vast majority of cases, from the late teens to the early thirties, the age of departure having tended to come down over time, so that the occupational data presented in Tables 8.2, 8.4 refer, on the whole, to what Ijesha out-migrants were doing some 20+ years after their decade of birth. Thus, even if the first two age-groups were considered rather small to be reliable, and provided that household heads are not too untypical of the rest of their age group in their migratory experience,[3] the data do yield a clear picture of the structure of out-migration as far back as the decade 1910–19. Two things are outstanding about the years before 1930: the very high proportion of males who *did* migrate out before returning home to settle down; and the high proportion of them who migrated to become *oṣomaalo* traders: 80% of migrants born 1890–99 (i.e. men who would mostly have been leaving Ilesha in the decade after 1915) and still well over half of Ijesha migrants two decades later. Tables 8.1 and 8.2 do not, however, give a full picture of migration after 1910, since, as Table 8.3 confirms, a good proportion of those aged 55–64 (born 1910s) have not yet returned home to settle, as the great majority can be expected to do. In the absence of direct evidence about the migratory experience of Ilesha residents who are not household heads, we have to make an estimate of the proportion of each age-group overall which has migrated at some time; but this gives 74%, 75% and 76% for those born in the 1910s, 1920s and 1930s respectively.[4] In other words, a high proportion of Ilesha's male population, very steady at around three-quarters since early in the century, has moved outside Ijeshaland to find employment for a significant period of their lives. In 1974 the proportion of absentees reached a peak among those aged 25–34, but was still up to a quarter among those aged 55–64.[5]

The occupations of these migrants tell a great deal about Ilesha's changing relationship with the rest of Nigeria. Table 8.4 continues the story implicit in Table 8.2. The extraordinary preponderance of *oṣomaalo* among Ijesha ex-migrants born before 1920 (which means among actual migrants down to the 1950s, at least) has been replaced, first by a move into other kinds of trade (in the age-group born in the 1920s) and then into 'clerkly' occupations, claiming half of all migrants born in the 1940s. With 32% of those born in the 1950s already employed as 'clerks', and 38% of them still being educated, this proportion is likely to rise a good deal further in the future. Ultimately this was the fruit of farming earlier in the century, savings invested in education either by parents for their children or by the Government, in its great programme of educational expansion from 1955, funded from agricultural surpluses, reaching through to secondary and tertiary levels in the 1960s and 1970s.

Table 8.1   *Former migration of heads of households, by age-group*

Age-group	Never-migrant	Former migrant	Total
Before 1890 (85+)	9 (24%)	29 (76%)	38
1890s (75–84)	17 (23%)	56 (77%)	73
1900s (65–74)	15 (18%)	69 (82%)	84
1910s (55–64)	28 (35%)	52 (65%)	80
1920s (45–54)	31 (42%)	43 (58%)	74
1930s (35–44)	36 (56%)	28 (44%)	64
1940s (25–34)	11 (52%)	10 (48%)	21

Table 8.2   *Occupations as migrants of formerly-migrant household-heads*

Age-group	Oṣomaalo	Other trader	Clerkly	Craft/ manual	Total
Before 1890	20 (69%)	5 (17%)	2 (7%)	2 (7%)	29
1890s	45 (80%)	3 (5%)	3 (5%)	5 (11%)	56
1900s	51 (74%)	7 (10%)	7 (10%)	4 (6%)	69
1910s	29 (56%)	7 (13%)	10 (19%)	6 (12%)	52
1920s	14 (33%)	13 (30%)	10 (23%)	6 (14%)	43
1930s	9 (32%)	6 (21%)	9 (32%)	4 (14%)	28
1940s	1 (10%)	1 (70%)	7 (70%)	1 (10%)	10

Notes: The predominant or longest-lasting occupation is taken when more than one was reported. 'Other trader' includes produce-buyers, contractors and transporters. 'Clerkly' includes all occupations for which a degree of literacy is essential: clerks, teachers, printers, clergy, police, etc. 'Craft/manual' is predominantly tailors, carpenters, bricklayers, drivers, rarely unskilled labourers.

Table 8.3   *Rates of migration among male members of Ilesha households, by age-group*

Age-group	Ilesha residents	Absent family members	Total	Absentees as % of total
1890s (75–84)	87	3	90	3%
1900s (65–74)	108	8	116	7%
1910s (55–64)	120	42	162	26%
1920s (45–54)	150	99	249	40%
1930s (35–44)	191	258	449	57%
1940s (25–34)	150	401	551	73%
1950s (15–24)	291	219	510	43%

Notes: 'Absentees' means all those males noted by household heads as 'family members' (ọmọ ile), i.e. those who have a recognized place in the household should they choose to come home, but normally resident outside Ilesha at the time of enquiry (July–September 1974). With the native Ilesha residents, they constitute what might be the total 'allegiant population' of Ilesha. Non-Ijesha residents of Ilesha recorded in the Household Survey are excluded.

149

Table 8.4   *Occupations of male migrants, by age-group*

Age-group	*Oṣomaalo*	Other trader	Clerkly	Craft/ manual	Full-time education	Total
Before 1900	1	1	0	0	0	2
1900s (65–74)	2	2	0	2	0	6
1910s (55–64)	14 (39%)	10 (18%)	7 (19%)	5 (14%)	0	36
1920s (45–54)	14 (15%)	27 (39%)	31 (33%)	10 (11%)	2 (2%)	94
1930s (35–44)	20 (8%)	59 (24%)	120 (49%)	44 (18%)	3 (1%)	246
1940s (25–34)	22 (6%)	54 (14%)	206 (53%)	64 (16%)	44 (11%)	390
1950s (15–24)	3 (2%)	24 (12%)	64 (32%)	23 (12%)	74 (38%)	199

Table 8.5   *Educational levels of migrants, by age-group*

Age-group	None	Primary 1–3	Primary 4–6	Some Second-ary	School Certi-ficate	Profess-ional	Univer-sity	Total
1910s	29 (74%)	0	7 (18%)	0	1	1	1	39
1920s	32 (34%)	10 (10%)	32 (34%)	0	9 (9%)	5 (5%)	7 (7%)	95
1930s	60 (24%)	10 (4%)	89 (36%)	5 (2%)	38 (15%)	22 (9%)	25 (10%)	249
1940s	39 (10%)	5 (1%)	159 (40%)	14 (4%)	117 (30%)	26 (6%)	33 (8%)	393
1950s	15 (7%)	0	83 (38%)	51 (24%)	59 (27%)	6 (3%)	2 (1%)	216

Note: In the last two age-groups, allowance must be made for the fact that a significant proportion is still in full-time education.

Table 8.5 shows this decade-by-decade advance in migrants' levels of education. The 1910s age-group, the last in which *oṣomaalo* was the dominant occupation, is around three-quarters lacking in even primary education. The next two age groups (i.e. those who would have been passing through primary school mostly in the 1930s and 1940s), have only about a third with no education, a third who reached the upper primary levels and, in the case of those born in the 1930s, over a third who achieved some kind of post-primary education. A marked jump occurs between them and the next age-group, no doubt the consequence of the educational expansion of the 1950s. Over 40% of these have some post-primary education, and since this is a group, aged 25–34, 11% of whose members (Table 8.4) were *still* being educated, this proportion will rise even further. What is interesting, when the data for migrants' occupations and educational levels are compared, is that, though the shift towards 'clerkly' occupations *roughly* corresponds (as it has to) with the rise in educational levels, the major shift in occupations seems to come a decade earlier (between the age-group born in the 1920s and that of the 1930s) than that in education (between the 1930s group and

Table 8.6. *Place of residence of migrants, by age-group*

Age-group born	Ibadan	Lagos	Other Yoruba	Non-Yoruba south	Kano	Rest of north	Out-side Nigeria	Total
Before 1910	2 (17%)	0	8 (67%)	2 (17%)	0	0	0	12
1910s	10 (24%)	3 (7%)	20 (48%)	0	1 (2%)	7 (17%)	1 (2%)	42
1920s	24 (24%)	19 (19%)	33 (34%)	1 (1%)	6 (6%)	12 (12%)	3 (3%)	98
1930s	56 (22%)	70 (27%)	69 (27%)	13 (5%)	13 (5%)	26 (10%)	8 (3%)	255
1940s	77 (20%)	145 (37%)	81 (21%)	9 (2%)	25 (6%)	38 (10%)	19 (5%)	394
1950s	51 (21%)	75 (36%)	63 (26%)	10 (4%)	8 (3%)	11 (5%)	0	238

Note: This includes Yoruba areas in Kwara state and the Republic of Benin (Dahomey), as well as in Oyo, Ogun, Ondo and Lagos states. 'Ibadan' includes locations in the rural parts of Ibadan division as well as Ibadan city.

Table 8.7 *Place of residence of migrants, by occupation*

Occupation	Ibadan	Lagos	Other Yoruba	Non-Yoruba south	Kano	Rest of North	Out side Nigeria	Total
oṣomaalo	12 (16%)	6 (8%)	25 (33%)	1 (1%)	7 (9%)	25 (33%)	0	76
Other trader	48 (26%)	27 (15%)	50 (27%)	9 (5%)	23 (12%)	29 (16%)	1 (1%)	186
clerkly	95 (22%)	197 (46%)	73 (17%)	15 (4%)	16 (4%)	25 (6%)	4 (1%)	425
Craft/manual	25 (17%)	49 (33%)	48 (32%)	5 (3%)	8 (5%)	13 (9%)	0	148
F.t. education	24 (20%)	25 (20%)	48 (39%)	3 (2%)	1 (1%)	2 (2%)	19 (16%)	122

that of the 1940s: an indication either of an extension in 'higher' bureaucratic posts or of an inflation in the level of education required for entry.

One final aspect of the changing structure of Ijesha out-migration remains to be considered in this preliminary overview: its destination. The older age-groups, as Table 8.6 shows, were mostly found in Yoruba-land, but fewer in Ibadan and its environs elsewhere, and fewer still in Lagos. This pattern, as Table 8.7 indicates, is closely linked with the occupational structure of Ilesha's migrants. The *oṣomaalo* originally predominated, but as this form of trade declined, Ijesha moved into other occupations and became more concentrated in the greater urban centres, Ibadan and Lagos. Lagos overtakes Ibadan as the main destination for the age-group born in the 1930s (where clerkly occupations also take the lead), a circumstance which began to occur, by inference, in the 1950s;

and its predominance is even more marked among those born in the 1940s. Whereas the *oṣomaalo* in their heyday, as we shall see, were scattered over a very wide range of communities in Ibadan Division, and in Ilorin Province and other rural areas, mostly of the savannah, those absent from Ilesha in 1974 were considerably more concentrated in a few centres: Ife claimed the most (47), followed by Ilorin (41), Oshogbo (36), Abeokuta (15), and Akure (12). Except for Oshogbo, for so long a commercial magnet for Ijesha, all these places, like Lagos and Ibadan, are state capitals and/or university towns.

These related changes in the occupations, destinations and educational levels of Ijesha migrants are but aspects of one underlying trend: from an involvement in a wider society that was fairly incidentally Nigerian – in that their activity was only remotely and indirectly conditioned by the colonial state – to one which was quite essentially and evidently so, because it was the Nigerian state which had played the major part in providing the migrants both with their marketable qualifications and with much of their employment. But though we here contrast the fathers who were *oṣomaalo* with the sons who are salaried employees, it was in the experience of the *oṣomaalo* that the seed of a wider-than-Ijesha identity was planted.

OṢOMAALO

An *oṣomaalo* (which is a contraction of a phrase meaning 'I will squat down until I'm paid') is a trader who sells cloth on credit by hawking it on foot round small towns and villages, typically giving three months to pay. *Oṣomaalo* trade is an activity for which the Ijesha are celebrated – virtually exclusively so[6] – throughout and beyond Yorubaland. Its origins are somewhat mysterious, for there is no agreement as to just when, where or by whom the name was coined, but the most frequently cited names of its pioneers, men such as Oginni Odole, Awe Ajanaku, and Ode Abugan, suggest the years around 1910.[7] They were the sons of men active as warriors or Ejinrin traders at the end of the nineteenth century, and what they did was to extend and adapt Ijesha trading practices in areas which Ijesha had already come to know. Ode Abugan, after a varied early career, literally made a name for himself from the novel form of trade which he developed round Igbara Odo in south-western Ekiti, selling cloth on a year's credit: *Abugan* means 'one who gives away bundles of cloth'. But he was 'not quite an *oṣomaalo*', in his son's view. From the responses of one or two of the oldest ex-*oṣomaalo* in the 1974 survey it appears that the *oṣomaalo*-trade partly grew from the old Ijesha trading links with the Lagoon markets and that for a few years the trade to Ejinrin coexisted with the *oṣomaalo* trade which displaced it as an avenue of advance for young Ijesha, though the Ijebu Waterside area (and as far west as Cotonou in French Dahomey) remained an area worked by Ijesha, now increasingly as *oṣomaalo*; and this too suggests a date of around 1910 for the earliest true *oṣomaalo*. By 1920 the *oṣomaalo* trade was well established in the Ijesha opportunity structure and it was most associated in these years with the Ilorin area, made newly accessible by the railway which had sealed the doom of Ejinrin's great market but already a significant focus of Ijesha trade in the late nineteenth century. An *oṣomaalo* who began at Ora, east of Ilorin, in 1919, said that the Ijesha met there 'Yoruba' traders who sold cloth without credit, suggesting that this commercial speciality of the Ijesha was relatively new, coexisting with older forms of trade.

In order to get a clearer picture of the individual *oṣomaalo* career, some 34 *oṣomaalo* from the larger sample of household heads were reinterviewed, using a loosely structured schedule of questions about the course of their careers; and what follows is a composite 'portrait' based on these interviews. The *oṣomaalo* left home in his early-to-mid twenties. The average departure age for those born in the 1880s was 26.7, and since this gives a departure date of roughly 1911–14 we must here have a section of almost the first wave of *oṣomaalo*. The departure age drops to 24.6 and then to 20.8 over the next two decades and then, for those born in the 1910s, rises again to 22.5, almost certainly an effect of the constricted economic opportunities of the early 1930s.[8] (1935–36, *Ọdun Jubili*, on the other hand, was reported by several *oṣomaalo* as an especially good year.)

Two thirds of the *oṣomaalo* had farmed first, sometimes under the eye of a father or senior brother ('like a slave', said one), sometimes with a plot of their own, but always finding it a relatively unrewarding career compared with their contemporaries. (Only one, a man born in 1904 who had had two years of primary education, had planted any cocoa.) The early motives for departure were clear:

> In those days you only farmed to eat – there was no wealth in it. Trade was the thing to make you rich ... (man born *c*. 1888)

> we saw how those of our age-mates who were *oṣomaalo* were doing, how they bought Raleigh bicycles, how they got married, how they wore fine clothes ... and it was that which gave me the idea to go and be an *oṣomaalo* ... (man born *c*. 1889)

Whereas real conflict with their senior relatives was reported by two of the thirteen born before 1900, those born later, especially those who left in the 1920s, often reported positive encouragement, including small gifts of money as trading capital, from their parents. For by that time it had become an approved career-line in Ijesha life. The 1920s saw several of the earliest successful *oṣomaalo* return home in glory – like Awe Ajanaku from Ikare, who set up a cloth store in Adeti Street in 1928–29; and the social activities of the *oṣomaalo* societies in the town, as already noted, proved to be powerful magnets.

Since the trade involved a peculiar expertise, the young entrants 'followed' an established *oṣomaalo*. In rather striking contrast to what has been noted in at least one other Yoruba trading diaspora, only a minority of them followed senior agnatic kin.[9] Of the 34 cases, 17 followed non-kin (12 being slightly senior 'friends', 5 'masters' – *ọga* – selected in some other way), 6 senior brothers, 5 other senior agnatic kin and 6 maternal kin. The standard pattern was for the young man to serve an 'apprenticeship' of around three years, being 'freed' at the end of this period and receiving a small sum for his own trading capital. Only a small minority – mostly men older and more experienced, or already owning a significant capital – considered they had not entered this apprentice relationship but merely accompanied a friend or relative. About two-thirds took some capital with them which they entrusted to their master: mostly well under £10, though one respondent, going in 1918, took £30 which he had earned as an army-driver in the Tanganyika campaign. At the beginning this money was mostly earned from the sale of farm produce or by labouring; later on it more often came from parents as a gift. The amount of the lump sum they received at the end of the apprenticeships related to what they had come with – a man who had come with nothing being given, perhaps, £2 10s 0d for his service – but was clearly also affected by other, informal considerations. One respondent had taken £2 10s 0d with him to his uncle, and got £20-worth of outstanding bad debts to start him off on his own!

The trade itself went like this. The *oṣomaalo* bought cloth from wholesale dealers in Ibadan or Lagos: many spoke warmly of the generous credit, help and lodging they got from the *Kọraa* (Syrians) at Ibadan. Buying at Lagos gave access to a wider and more fashionable range of cloth but, since it involved greater capital expenditure, only the richer *oṣomaalo* tended to do it. Those *oṣomaalo* who worked around Ilorin, the area most favoured in the early years, used the railway as the link to their supplies. Most *oṣomaalo* based themselves in villages or small towns, close to their customers, and they made their sales on foot, trudging round the locality. Christmas, the Muslim *Ilẹya* (Id-el-Fitr) or more local festivals were the best times to make sales. A price and a time for payment were concluded and noted in a book against the customer's name – virtually all *oṣomaalo*, despite their lack of education, at least for the first few decades, acquired a basic literacy to this end – and the money was collected three months later. At least, this was the ideal: in fact a wonderful folk-lore exists among old *oṣomaalo* about this essential mystery of their trade: the collection of debts. And since it relied much more on bringing moral and social pressures to bear on the debtors than on strong-arm tactics or the judicial power of the state, it must be set within the broader question of the social relations among the *oṣomaalo* and between them and their non-Ijesha hosts.

When Ijesha first entered a place as *oṣomaalo* they lodged with a prominent local man or even the *ọba* or *balẹ* of the place, giving him presents and seeking his advice as to where to trade. Such reliance by stranger-traders on chiefly patronage was, as we have seen, the age-old pattern throughout the region. Later, as the numbers of *oṣomaalo* grew, they would choose one of themselves, usually the longest resident, as their president:

> *Eniti a ba l'aba, l'a npe ni baba*
> Whoever we encounter in a village we call our senior

When the numbers got very large – say the 150 *oṣomaalo* said to have been based on Bida in the late 1920s, or the 90 based on one Ibadan rural market-centre in the 1930s – regular meetings were held at fortnightly intervals. The Ijesha took lodgings in small groups about the town and, though a small minority of the most settled and successful might build houses and lodge other *oṣomaalo*,[10] they never favoured living in *sabo*-type concentrations, set apart from the local people.

Debt-collecting procedures seem to have varied a good deal from place to place, though they usually involved the support of both local powers and other *oṣomaalo*. In the remoter villages the back-up of the chief could be crucial. One respondent, who said he was almost the first Ijesha to move north-east into Igbira and Igara country, said that the chief, to whom he had presented cloth, schnapps and matches on his arrival, would send his drummer and a Native Authority policeman to accompany him on visits to the houses of recalcitrant debtors; and he added that when he moved to the area of Ubiaja (northern Edo), the absence of this kind of local authority made his trade difficult. In areas where *oṣomaalo* were more a regular part of the scene and where the *oṣomaalo* and their customers shared a greater range of common cultural understandings, such as the Ibadan farms, the influence of local 'elders' generally, especially those with whom the *oṣomaalo* lodged, was useful in bringing moral pressure to bear on defaulters. The most general gambit was to try to shame the debtor into paying: by 'squatting' at the entrance to his house – the *oṣomaalo* would help one another by taking it in relays to do this – or by turning up at a festival or family occasion to embarrass him before kinsmen and friends to whom he wanted to appear as an honourable and creditworthy person. Bluff and juju could also play a significant role. An amazing story was told about how the local *oṣomaalo* at Ikare all attended a funeral ceremony at the house of one debtor, and put a spell on him so that he was forced to dance before the house till his clothes were all dirty; while once at Ijesa-Isu (Ekiti) the *oṣomaalo* threatened to pull the clothes off the *egungun*, thus making the chief responsible for their deaths, until he put pressure on the defaulters to pay. Cruder tactics, like laying in wait for the debtor to pour dirty water over him, were also used, though most *oṣomaalo* expressed disapproval of them; and while local courts were sometimes used, the *oṣomaalo* tended to distrust them too. But of course, it was the 'guile and guts' (*ogbọn ati aya*, as one man put it) of the individual *oṣomaalo* which set this social machinery into motion; and there were always lots of debts that could never be collected.

The importance of the resident community of *oṣomaalo* to its members seems to belie the very individual character of the trade itself. For even if *oṣomaalo* worked closely together – three friends, say, or two brothers, helping one another sell or collect debts – their cooperation stopped short of a commercial partnership. It was only more than a one-man show to the extent that *oṣomaalo* had apprentices or, in some cases, wives to work with them. These undoubtedly represented under-remunerated labour, and one respondent remarked that it was when his wives left him to trade on their own and he could get no more apprentices that he finally decided to pack it in and retire. Though it was several times said that Ijesha loved one another more abroad than at home, relations between *oṣomaalo* were equivocal. Despite the vital social support of his fellows in the locality, real success in the trade *did* depend on the *oṣomaalo*'s discovering market imperfections and exploiting them to the exclusion, as far as possible, of others. A new line of cloth or an unworked local market could not in any case be kept secret for very long, especially from apprentices. A proverb quoted by one of them sums up what every *oṣomaalo* knew: that in the end he had to look out for himself in the trade:

> *Adiẹ o fibi gogoro han ọmọ rẹ*
> The hen does not show her back to the chicks!

The careers of *oṣomaalo* (cf. Table 8.8) are ample proof of their restless search for new markets; and they also tell us much about the changing character of the trade, and with it, of Ijesha relations with their neighbours. Unfortunately only a partial explanation of why the *oṣomaalo* chose to go where they did can be attempted, in the absence of detailed, comparative information about social and economic conditions in the areas which received them. But what initially stands out from the total list of trading locations mentioned by ex-*oṣomaalo* is how preponderantly they were drawn to areas of Yorubaland outside the cocoa belt, especially to the northern savannah areas: of 312 trading locations, 21% were in Ilorin Province, 13% in the rural parts of Ibadan, 18% in Oyo or Oshun Divisions, 11% in non-Yoruba parts of the savannah (around Bida, Pategi and Lokoja), 10% in north-eastern Yorubaland (Kabba Province, Igbomina, Ekiti and Akoko). Of these, only Ibadan and some parts of Oshun Division lie within the cocoa belt; and the great bulk of the remainder lie outside it to the south or west (Ijebu with Waterside, southern Egbado and the Badagry area reaching into Dahomey). The *oṣomaalo*'s kind of trade presupposes a social context where, despite a demand for consumer goods like imported cloth, purchasing power is too low and sporadic and the population insufficiently concentrated to permit fixed retail outlets. This seems to hold most strongly for the savannah areas of Yorubaland, where few cash-crops were grown and where the remittances of labourers (including many who went to work on cocoa farms) were the main source of money. But the case of Ibadan shows that still the cocoa belt might present

156

Table 8.8 *Careers of selected early oṣọmaalo*

Year born	1920	1930	1940	Year home
1884	[Ejinrin trader] Ilorin → Ikorodu → Abeokuta, Sagamu, Igbobini →			1946
1884	[carpenter] Ijebu Waterside → Ibadan, Ijebu → Ado Odo →			1972
1885	[army driver] Ilorin → Ila → Bida area, Ijebu →			1950s
1885	Igbara Odo → Ilorin area → Ibadan farms →			1951
1886	[eṃẹṣẹ] Ilorin → Ire (Oshun) → Ijebu area →			1942
1889	Ilorin → Bida area → [produce buyer]			
1890	Ilorin → Abeokuta, Eruwa, Ijebu, Ibadan farms →			1950s
1890	Ilorin area → Bida → Ijebu → [produce buyer]			
1890	Igbomina → Yagba → Ijebu →			1941
1895	Ilorin → Ilobu (Oshun) → Akoko, Igbira, N. Edo →			1965
1897	Ilorin → [produce buyer] → Ibadan, Ijebu Igbo, Abeokuta →			
1897	[labourer at Ibadan] Okeiho → Ilorin →			1963
1899	Porto Novo, Ilorin, Ibadan → [shop at Ilesha] Ikare → Yola [trader] →			1974
1900	Ibadan → Abeokuta →			1955
1901	Aramoko, Ilorin → Ibadan, Ijebu, Kabba, Ilonin → [shop]			1947
1902	Igbomina → Ijebu, Waterside, Ibadan → [shop]			1950s
1903	[eṃẹṣẹ] Oshogbo → Ibadan farms, Oshun → [transporter]			1969
1904	Ilorin → Ila, Oshun, Ibadan → [trader] →			1943
1904	Cotonou → Akoko → Ibadan farms →			?
1905	Ijebu Ode → Ikere (Ekiti) → Bida →			1959
1905	Bida → Iwo, Oshun area →			1951
1905	[produce buyer] Oshogbo → Ilorin →			
1906	Ibadan farms → Abeokuta, Ijebu, Ekiti, Ibadan →			1956
1907	[petty trade] Ogbomosho, Ibadan, Akoko →			1960s

Note: Unless otherwise specified, the occupation pursued before departure was farming, and after return, farming or retirement.

157

opportunities. Cocoa incomes were highly seasonal too, of course; but the striking fact is that the Ibadan rural population should buy from stranger-traders, at the higher prices which inevitably came with the granting of credit, rather than from markets in Ibadan. It seems to indicate not just the relatively low and seasonal incomes of those farmers who lived in the Ibadan villages, but also a certain remoteness from the central institutions of their *ilu*. One respondent implied this when he said that it was only in villages that a *man* could go round with a bundle of cloth on his head, yet not feel shame! For both categories of the *oṣomaalo*'s customers – the *ara oko* as well as the *ara oke*, so to speak[11] – shared a situation of relative political peripherality and cultural disadvantage: circumstances which, as the Ijesha were aware, underpinned a certain ascendancy they had over their customers.

This comes out most clearly when we consider how the trade developed. Ilorin lost its early overwhelming popularity as a target-area for the *oṣomaalo* and by the 1920s Ibadan had come well up among new entrants to the trade. At the same time older men began to move to fresh areas. Questioned about the decision to move, ex-*oṣomaalo* spoke, of course, of the trade being 'spoiled' as the area became saturated with newcomers; but they also referred to a growth in the sophistication of their customers. One man said he would only stay in a place for four or five years, since collecting debts got difficult if you were too well known. Another said he worked at Ejidongari via Ilorin while the people were still 'unenlightened' (*oju wọn ko ti la*) and then moved up to Nupe country. The same theme – that the *oṣomaalo* needed to have the edge of *ọlaju* ('enlightenment' or sophistication) over his customers – arose in another case, where a decision to move on from a town in eastern Ekiti was explained thus: 'when they became as sophisticated as us, it was no seller's market any more' (*nigbati oju nla bakanna ọja ko ta mọ*).[12]

But there were in fact two possible responses. One was simply to find yet unexploited areas for the same kind of trade. So from Ilorin and Ibadan, *oṣomaalo* moved into the Oshun and Oyo areas which lie between them, and they pushed out north and east to the limits of Yoruba country and beyond, especially to Nupe. But they also moved down to Ijebu, and here the character of the trade tended to change; for Ijebu was close to Lagos and relatively wealthy, and the people did not yield much in *ọlaju* to anyone.[13] Here turnover was great, profit margins smaller and credit was for shorter periods: many Ijesha traders were known as *aradoṣu* ('sell by the month', instead of the usual three months). Though only a small minority made this latter transition, it was an indication for the future of the Ijesha trading diaspora. For, with the general spread of cash incomes and a greater concentration of the population, fixed retail outlets began to take over from the kind of commercial institutions developed by the *oṣomaalo* and the whole pattern of trading opportunities became enlarged and diversified. The Ijesha, with their region-wide commercial experience, were well placed to respond to

158

Table 8.9   *First and final trading locations of selected oṣomaalo*

	First Locations					Final locations
	Up to 1920	1920s	1930s	1940	Total	all periods
Ilorin area	25	11	8	5	49	5
Ibadan area	5	12	8	2	27	6
Oshun/Oyo	1	9	4	5	19	23
Kabba, Ekiti, Akoko	2	5	4	2	13	8
Abeokuta	—	4	1	—	5	3
Egbado, Dahomey	9	3	2	2	16	1
Ijebu	3	2	2	2	9	13
Non-Yoruba (north)	3	3	4	4	14	8
Non-Yoruba (east)	3	1	1	1	6	2

Note: Data drawn from larger sample in Household Survey, but only in cases where information on both times and places was sufficiently detailed. 'Final location' means the last area an *oṣomaalo* traded in, and only applies in those cases where the trading career involved a move from one major area to another.

this, just as their regional involvements in the late nineteenth century had contributed to the *oṣomaalo* movement.

What of the *oṣomaalo* themselves? Most of them spent several decades in the trade – thirty years was the average for seventy-six cases of men born before 1910. When asked what the aim of the successful *oṣomaalo* was, they said it was to get married, build their own house and see their children educated. They had maintained close links with Ilesha, returning once or twice a year, and on their final return, most settled down to farm, typically growing food crops with some cocoa for cash. Of all the ex-*oṣomaalo* in the sample, 72% were farming or in retirement, 17% were in various forms of trade, 8% were practising some kind of craft (from cycle-repairing to gold cap embroidery) and 4% were herbalists or religious specialists. Yet they saw themselves as having occupied a significant place in Ilesha's history. The *oṣomaalo* trade, said one old man proudly, 'was God's blessing to help build up the Ijeshas' after so many of their people had been lost in the wars with the Ibadans. But perhaps the most far-reaching effect of the *oṣomaalo* was on Ijesha self-awareness, for their experience enabled them to rephrase that sense of the regional hierarchy of communities and of their own place in it, which Ilesha had always had, in terms more relevant to the emerging economic and political field of Nigeria.

EDUCATION AND ETHNICITY

But the major part in shaping Ijesha perceptions of this hierarchy in such a way as to make a Nigeria-focussed politics possible was played, not by the

159

Table 8.10 *First occupations of the educated: (i) men born before 1920, (ii) men born 1920–29*

	Primary 1–4 (i)	Primary 1–4 (ii)	Primary 5–6 (i)	Primary 5–6 (ii)	Any Secondary (i)	Any Secondary (ii)	Total
Trader	13	7	10	9	—	1	40
Crafts	7	3	1	—	—	—	11
Driver	4	1	1	—	—	—	6
Clerk	5	2	11	2	2	2	24
Teacher	—	—	2	1	2	5	10
Total	29	13	25	12	4	8	91

Note: Data from sample of household-heads.

oṣomaalo, but by those of their contemporaries who had passed through enough of the educational system to enable them to become clerks and teachers. This influence began right back when, compared with the *oṣomaalo*, they were a small proportion of the age-cohort. There was, as Table 8.10 shows, a fairly steep drop-out rate among those who entered primary education, and by the late 1930s only a minority of those who completed Primary VI were becoming teachers or clerks. In fact, as the numbers of educated increased, we find occupations once the preserve of the modestly educated (such as driving or new crafts like carpentry or tailoring) being taken by the relatively uneducated and more education being demanded of the most essentially literate professions. None the less the whole system remained as strongly geared in this direction.

The contribution of the educated, which runs as a theme continuously through the narrative of the next three chapters, lay partly in defining what the ends of political action should be, and partly in providing much of the means to pursue them. The first of these was derived from the broader social experience of a working life spent in one or another colonial bureaucracy, the latter from the specific skills that this work presupposed or created. Since the overall numbers of relevant individuals are so small, it is really impossible to synthesize a 'typical' career, as was done for the *oṣomaalo* from the Sample Survey data. It is more instructive to present a handful of exemplary, but actual careers of men who came as individuals to play politically significant roles in the town.[14]

E.O. AYOOLA. Born *c.* 1895 at Oshu, where father farmed and held a minor cult title connected with *Loro* lineage. After father's death he continued farming under his senior brother but with a friend was attracted to the Methodists, leading to his becoming a Christian (1914) and starting school (1916). 1918 to Wesley College, Ibadan, to train as a teacher.
1923 to Ago Iwoye (Ijebu) as teacher. 1929 back as teacher to Oshu. 1931 to Ibadan (Agbeni). 1934 to Ilesha as Headmaster of the leading

Methodist school, Otapete. 1938 resigned when yet another transfer was proposed and 1939 founds the first independent school in Ilesha, Temidire, which he heads till his retirement.

Active in *Ęgbę Atunluşe* and as an educated member of the Council's Advisory Board (1940s). Elected Councillor 1950, losing his seat with other AG members when the NCNC swept the board in 1955.

S. AKINOLA.   Born *c.* 1896, of Chief *Sawę's* lineage. Partly through influence of a Christian neighbour, Osungbohun, a carpenter, goes in 1904 to St John's Iloro and so 'grew up a Christian', under the Revd Oyebode. 1914–19 at St. Andrew's College Oyo to train as teacher.

1920 as teacher to Okeigbo. 1921 to Idoani. 1924 to Oshogbo. 1932 to St Jude's Ebute Metta (Lagos). 1934, travelling teacher, Benin Province. 1935, Owo. 'No future in it save for Church ministry', so 1939–43 he traded at Owo. 1943 back to Ilesha to deal in timber and machinery.

1940s active on the Advisory Board and as representative on Council. 1951–54 one of the two first elected Members of the House of Assembly at Ibadan, joining AG. 1959 takes his family title *Sawę* and active as one of the most educated chiefs.

J.M. AJAYI-OBE.   Born 1898, grandson of the great warrior Obe. 1911 sent to live with father's brother Ibidapo, an early Christian and member of Omofe Church (CMS). After Standard VI, attends two years at Ibadan Grammar School.

1919 to Ibadan as tax-clerk. 1921 court-clerk at Ilesha. 1926 produce buyer with UAC. 1934 salesman and storekeeper for John Holt. 1968 retires but keeps his own store.

1930s–40s active in *Ęgbę Atunluşe* and on Advisory Board. Member of the NCNC caucus from late 1940s, elected Councillor 1950, serving for most of next fifteen years. 1968 takes father's title *Lęmodu.*

I.A. OWOLABI.   Born 1910, of lineage of *Arojo* of Irojo, but at Wasimi, the early Christian settlement in Iloro, under influence of father's aunt, an active Christian. Educated at St John's to Standard V.

1926 selected to train as teacher under the Revd Mackay at Oshogbo. 1928 teacher at Ilesha (Christ Church, Omofe), where Chadwick, ADO, noticed him on Empire Day and invited him to be his typist/messenger. 1935 District Clerk, Ilesha. 1948 to Benin as First Class Clerk. 1949 to Ilesha as Treasury Clerk. 1951 to Oyo as District Clerk. 1954 to Ilesha as Chief Clerk. 1957 to Ibadan as Exec. Officer. 1958 Oshogbo. 1959 Exec. Officer, Oyo, till retirement in 1968.

1954–71 Apena of ROF at Ilesha. 1968 wins open title of *Lǫkiran* and in 1972, *Ǫbaodo*.

E.O. FAJUYITAN.   Born *c.* 1913 to a Christian father, of *Ogboni* lineage. 1919 was one of seven boys who started Oke Ese Methodist School, transferring 1923 to Otapete where he read Standard VI.

1934 teaching at Sagamu. 1937 at Oshogbo. 1938 at Otapete again as Assistant Head. Left teaching after his 8-year bond was up, owing to poor salary, and in 1942 became a produce-examiner, being posted around the Western Region. He also kept a bookshop and ran a taxi for a while. 1953, fed up with transfers, he returned to teaching as Headmaster at Oshu and later Oke Ese. 1955 made Schools Supervisor and in 1968 Manager of Ife-Ilesha Local Schools Board. 1973, after retirement, President of Grade 'B' Customary Court.

Active member of Nigerian Youth Movement in late 1930s and of the 'Peace Party' after 1941 Riot. 1952–55 Councillor.

These serve to bring out several features of the bureaucratic career and its consequences. It rested on formal education to at least Primary V or VI and preferably some form of secondary education, and for practical purposes at this time this implied not just Christian profession but close and continuous involvement in church and mission institutions. Ilesha had no secondary school of its own before 1934, and, except for a mere handful of Ijesha who went on to grammar school in Lagos, Abeokuta or Ibadan, Ijesha relied most on what were the two premier institutions for training mission teachers: St Andrew's College, Oyo, (CMS) and Wesley College, Ibadan. Between 1902, when it took its first Ijesha students, and 1935, some 34 Ijesha passed through St Andrew's; Wesley College, between 1907 and 1934, took no less than 48, twelve of these being from Imesi, the great centre of Methodist activity in northern Ijeshaland.[15]

These institutions fashioned their students into what may be advisedly termed a Yoruba elite. Before the 1920s or so, very few Ijesha considered themselves to be 'Yoruba' at all – this being a term applied only to Ilesha's historic adversaries, the Oyo. One may still occasionally hear the word being used in this restricted way by elderly, uneducated people.[16] It is entirely explicable why it should have been the educated who played the major part in introducing the widened meaning of 'Yoruba', to include the Ijesha. 'Standard Yoruba' – based on the Oyo dialect – was the language they were taught to read and write and which was used in public worship in the church; and it was the missions, especially the CMS, whose key manpower institution was St Andrew's, appropriately sited at Oyo, which had set that standard.[17] Yoruba consciousness was a major by-product of the concentration in institutions like St Andrew's of the young men, drawn from all over Yoruba country and beyond, who would use that language as the medium of instruction in school and church. This Yoruba-ness had a dual aspect: it unified the extended category of Yoruba speakers against other language groupings and thus gave extra subjective reality to the Nigerian context which had brought them together;[18] and it defined a regional framework within which different communities could compare one another – though now increasingly by criteria of communal prowess set by the ever more influential 'educated elements', by an 'elite' which saw itself as the bearer of 'enlightenment' (*ọlaju*) to its home communities.[19] The early career pattern of the teacher or clerk, where movement up was associated with frequent transfers from one place to another, but mostly within the Yoruba language area, further served to emphasize both Yorubaland as a cultural universe and the relative situations of communities and areas within it.

And this hierarchization of communities was much more underscored in their experience than in that of the *oṣomaalo*. Their personal advancement was manifestly through a hierarchy, and was often critically dependent at some stage or another on contact with a patron or sponsor at some strategic higher level – a fact to which the fading portraits of people like H.L. Ward-Price, Ife DO and later Resident of Oyo, or the Revd Oliver Griffin, sometime Methodist Superintendent, that you sometimes see hanging in the parlour of a retired public servant, bear mute witness. The individual's advance in his profession symbolized the hierarchy of the locations to which he was posted: Oshu to Otapete, Idoani to Oshogbo to Lagos. Their careers suggested to them how much the advance of communities, like that of individuals, might now depend on having good relations with the higher founts of power in the colonial state. It was a lesson which, from the 1920s, their non-educated fellow townsmen were willing to learn: *ọlaju* became a general value rather than the badge of a troublesome minority. The very negative view of the colonial state held by the old chiefly leadership before 1920 became a positive one: the state was there for what could be derived from it. And for this educated sons of the town were needed, to serve as guides and, ultimately, patrons for the community in the higher reaches of the Nigerian state.

The very rapid triumph of this view at Ilesha was greatly eased by two more local circumstances. One, the ideological triumph of Christianity in the community at large, will be considered shortly. The other is the fact that there never developed any sharp divide between the educated in the bureaucratic hierarchy and the uneducated who predominated among traders. Though relatively few of those not educated beyond Standard IV went into clerkly occupations, they virtually all retained the Christianity which had been associated with their education; and even the over-whelmingly uneducated *oṣomaalo* – who in nearly all cases did become Christians or Muslims – had respect for the values linked with education, and wanted it for their children. On the other hand there was a significant number of the best educated, as three of the careers summarized above testify, who, after some years as a clerk or teacher, moved back into the sphere of trade, where their literate skills enabled them to play important leadership roles – for example, as secretaries or spokesmen of such bodies as the Produce Traders' Union which appeared in the 1930s. Their careers suggest three reasons why. Firstly, the frequent transfers expected of a teacher or public servant became increasingly irksome as a man reached social maturity and wanted to be able to exercise influence in his home community. Secondly, trade might offer greater monetary reward than a salaried post. This was especially so in the late 1930s. The Depression had led to severe reductions in the salaries paid by both government and missions. By 1936–37 trade was markedly picking up again, but salaries remained depressed. Mission salaries were the lowest and tended to remain so since the missions were torn between paying more to their staff and engaging more staff; and the great popular predisposition to conversion of these years strongly inclined them to do the latter. Thirdly, there was in several ways a convergence of the spheres of trade and bureaucracy. On the one side there were new market needs – for example for books and the impedimenta of education – which could be most readily met by traders with some education. On the other the Depression had produced a smaller number of larger firms, which required a greater variety of storekeepers, accounts clerks etc. – occupations which led easily to independent trade; and there came about a greater government supervision of trade, even more so under the conditions of the Second World War, which again led to salaried posts closely linked with the trading hierarchy. The most significant of these latter were produce-examiners, whose job, in addition to the salary, yielded an excellent knowledge of the produce trade, contacts with producers and considerable opportunities for graft. It was the ladder by which a number of solid post-war trading careers were made. In these ways trade and the bureaucracies, which initially presented themselves as career alternatives (though the vast bulk of those who directly entered the former did so because they had not the means to enter the latter) drew closer together.

CONVERSION TO CHRISTIANITY AND ISLAM

Virtually all Ijesha are now adherents of either Christianity or Islam and a large majority of them (88%) were already so by the time of the 1952 census.[20] The 1974 Sample Survey gave the following breakdown for religious allegiance in the town:

Anglican	30.2
Methodist	11.7
Apostolic	15.1
Other Aladura	14.4
African Church	6.3
Roman Catholic	3.8
Other Christian	4.7
All Christian	86.3
Muslim	11.5
Other/No answer	2.3

Since the world religions, virtually by definition, are vehicles of a wider-than-local consciousness, and the most influential general theory of conversion to them in modern Africa has been one which relates to it the widening of the range of social relations,[21] it is all too easy to rest content with this as a sufficient account of religious change.[22] So, fundamental though this perspective is to our present concerns, we should be careful not to ignore other types of religious change (e.g. developments within the 'traditional' religious repertory) or the extent to which conversion to the world religions has other sources than 'increase in social scale'.

The range and diversity of Ilesha's old religion belies any characterization of it as *purely* the cosmology of a closed and static society. While there was much there that was highly specific to particular localities and lineages, the major deities were of 'pan-Yoruba' type and many quite local cult-figures were refractions of them.[23] The ensemble of cult traditions tends to indicate a constant incorporation of outside elements (as well as diffusion from local centres), and hence establishes the system's capacity to respond to social change in other terms besides a growing saliency of the Supreme Being as preached in the world religions. Two examples serve to establish the continuance of this traditional adaptiveness into this century. Firstly, though *egungun* or masked ancestral spirits play a very small part in Ilesha's traditional religious repertory, a number of them were introduced in the 1890s by powerful chiefs, and used as vehicles of their prowess.[24] These *egungun* were almost as alien to *Ijesha* religion as Jesus or Mohammed – mostly of Oyo or northern Ekiti origin, as their speech indicated. Secondly, the pressures and epidemics of these years, interpreted as the products of witchcraft, led to an extensive outbreak of sasswood ordeals, with horrendous results. This use of sasswood (*ọbọ*), administered by societies called *ẹjẹgbẹ*, appears to have been indigenous around Ikeji and Ipetu and in adjacent parts of Ekiti, and spread widely in south-eastern Ijeshaland in response to the most frightening external visitation of all, the influenza epidemic of 1918.[25]

This, however, was the last outbreak of its kind, and just over a decade later, in 1930–31, it was a Christian idiom, in the Aladura, which answered to such popular anxieties. Behind this lay a process of fifty years in which the symbolism of the world religions had grown in appeal for Ijesha seriously concerned with coming to terms with the powers implicit in the wider world. Ogedengbe had lived and died a 'pagan', but back in 1885 a visitor had commented on the 'hundreds and hundreds of Mohammedan charms', which festooned his warrior's hut at Kiriji.[26] (His chief adversary, Latosa the *Arẹ* of Ibadan, was already a practising Muslim.) At the same time Ogedengbe was prone to a staunch scepticism about some of the standard military magic of the day. There is a nice Cromwellian wit to a saying of his:

Igọgọ igi nla ni baba irẹta; ojugun mejeji titẹ mọ ọna ni baba afẹẹri
The stem of a big tree is the best charm against bullets; to make haste on your two legs is the best invisibility-magic![27]

He shared Muslim and Christian antipathy to the practice of human sacrifice, coming into conflict with *Ọwa* Bepo on the issue. It was in this climate predisposed to moral and cosmological change that the agents of both world religions sought to win converts.

There had been Christians in Ilesha – returnees from Sierra Leone – as early as the 1850s and, after the CMS had sent George Agbebi as scripture reader, a small congregation was formed, given support by *Owa* Bepo, and endured through all the vicissitudes of the war years.[28] More returnees and a steady trickle of local converts had built up a congregation of around 300 by the early 1880s;[29] but the pattern of future advance only became clear in the favourable conditions of Ajimoko I's reign: a second CMS church was established at Omofe in the northern part of the town in 1896, the other major mission, the Methodists, began work from Otapete, and, above all, the outreach to the district communities began.[30] Between 1896 and 1914 Christians of either Anglican (CMS) or Methodist affiliation came to be found in virtually all Ijesha communities of any size.[31] By 1920 these churches had been joined in Ilesha by the Roman Catholics (1916) and the African Church (1917);[32] and the distribution of the Anglican and Methodist churches within Ilesha gave a complete local coverage around the quarters of the town which finds clear expression in the spread of their adherents today.

The determined evangelism of those years – the public preaching in markets, the missionary tours of active church members, the whole network of persuasion conducted within households and neighbourhoods – could not have had its effects without the spontaneous and impersonal influence of circumstances. We should not forget how very few full-time church personnel there were. The CMS never employed any European missionary in Ijeshaland (if we except Mackay's influence from Oshogbo) and from his arrival in 1896 into the 1920s there was only one Anglican clergyman: the Revd R.S. Oyebode, an Ibadan man, pastor of St John's, Iloro. He was aided by a handful of catechists – men such as J.A. Babatope at Iperindo, E.J. Oke at Ijebu-jesha or J. Opadina at Christ Church, Omofe. The Methodists, not long after the short and stormy ministry of Hezekiah Atundaolu, put their Ilesha circuit (which originally ran far beyond Ijeshaland) under a European superintendent, but they were locally as reliant as the Anglicans on unordained workers like J.T. Laleye, who opened up Imesi-Ile for them. Of great importance too was the small but growing number of teachers, many of them untrained, who provided much general local leadership and were greatly prized by the local Christian groups. The essential task of this personnel was to channel the tide that was running in their favour.

In the early stages of what soon became a quite indigenous process, external connexions figured vitally. At Ipetu, for example, the Revd Oyebode, travelling down to Ondo one day in 1906, stopped to ask in the market-place if there were any Christians in the town.[33] He was directed to the house of Oriade, a local man, where a small group was already meeting. Christianity had been introduced by Odubajo, an Ijebu rubber trader back in the boom of 1897, who had collected the first converts before he left. The local people began to learn their ABD, getting further help from a literate customs-clerk sent by Ajimoko I and later finding leadership in Solagbade, an Ekiti man who operated the first sewing-machine in the town. Oyebode brought the whole group under his supervision, arranging for Babatope, a few miles away at Iperindo, to come and prepare them for baptism. Elsewhere, local people usually played a greater role in the process, women as well as men, returnees as Christians from outside. Before 1900 these people were very often 'from the farms of slavery',[34] often at Ibadan; later Abeokuta and Lagos are frequently mentioned, at this time probably locales of unskilled labour as much as of trade, and we are almost certainly dealing with a consequence of that exodus of young men in search of new opportunities that was noted above in Chapter 6.[35] They would gather a few people around them, meeting in a member's house. Acquiring basic literacy in Yoruba, through *Iwe ABD*, was a vital part of Christian socialization, since without it there was no baptism. Soon land would be acquired for a church building, a token of at least minimal acceptance by the local chiefs, and the much-desired teacher sought – the larger villages, whose Christian congregations originated round about 1905, tending to get them about a decade later. By 1920 most congregations were institutionally complete, locally headed by senior male and female members, a *Baba Ijọ* and an *Iya Ijọ*, no longer exotic implants but indigenous institutions which, more than any other locally, revealed and interpreted a wider world.

Why were people drawn to Christianity? Though case-histories of the circumstances (the 'how' of conversion) may be very illuminating because of their concrete detail, motives (the immediate 'why' of conversion), at least in the form of reconstructed accounts, are often hard to elicit and harder to interpret in the light of broad theories of religious change. The 1974 Survey produced some sort of data on not far short of 300 individuals said to have been the first person in the respondent's family (whether the respondent himself or not) to have become a Christian or a Muslim convert. Just under 20% of such Christian conversions took place outside Ijeshaland.[36] It is easy to suppose how out-migration might serve to estrange a person from a religion much of whose meaning and power had to do with the concerns and environment of home, and in very many cases the fact of migration was mentioned as if it was a sufficient explanation of conversion.[37] But this cannot explain their eagerness to propagate their new religion at home or their ability to persuade others there. Here too the commonest accounts were quite unhelpful as to reasons, let alone explanations: 'everyone was joining, so I joined' or 'he [respondent's elder brother] wanted to be moving with his friends, who were Christians' were typical. More instructive, but essentially similar was the response which specified the crucial Christian contact: a man on whose farm he went to cut planks, the girl he wanted to marry, the master from whom he learnt

167

carpentry. So often was the Revd R.S. Oyebode mentioned in this regard that his description as 'verily and truly the Apostle of Ijeshaland' in the Anglican Centenary History seems entirely justified.[38] Other common answers like 'because of civilization (*nitori ọlaju*)' or the appeal of Christian liturgy or life-style, really indicate no more than that by then Christianity had become a mass movement, able to assign meaning because it was deemed to possess power.

So what gave rise to the attribution of power? The most obvious answer, itself strongly suggested by many responses, is the missions' control of education. The argument would run that the Government's perception of its and society's manpower needs led it to step up its education provision, through the missions, in the 1920s; popular demand for education grew because of its consequent rewards; and the missions, as purveyors of that education, were rewarded with converts.[39] But it is much too simple an account. The great bulk of early converts – those who set the tide running in Christianity's favour – did not go to school; and here it was Christianity's links with literacy (through *Iwe ABD*) rather than with formal education and qualifications which mattered. The reciprocity between them was so constant that a priority of motive is impossible to determine, as in the remark of that respondent who said of his father: '[he became a Christian] after buying a book called ABD and studying it. The end of it was his conversion'. Since formal education was, of course, valued for its occupational consequences (so that boys, in the early years, were much more likely to be sent to school), it is the more remarkable that as many as 37% of the pupils at Otapete Methodist School in 1927 were girls.[40] The Methodists made a distinctive contribution to girls' education with their Homecraft Centre, set up under Mrs Ludlow, a medical missionary, in 1935 and here it was a whole 'enlightened' way of life, ranging from hygiene to reduce infant mortality to new homecraft skills, as well as marketable qualifications, which was associated with Christianity.[41] The same is more generally true. There were the new crafts – tailoring, carpentry, bricklaying – whose early diffusion was along Christian networks. For decades after its foundation in 1912 Wesley Guild Hospital, with its out-stations, provided by far the most important source of modern medicine for the Ijesha. And surely no agricultural extension service was ever more successful than the demonstration plot of cocoa, oranges, plantains and other crops which the Revd Oyebode maintained at the back of Iloro parsonage.

But even when our conception of the 'power' of Christianity is extended to a wider 'cultural capacity', that still falls short of explaining the extent of Christian success in Ilesha.[42] In some other Yoruba towns, after all – for example Oshogbo, just twenty miles off – Islam won many more converts, despite a similar balance of cultural advantage between the two world religions. But since conversion was never solely a matter of acquiring certain techniques or beliefs, associated with one religion, but also one of joining a body of people, the power of a religion must also be seen in an aspect no less real for being quite contingent to it: its pull as a political force, as measured in the numbers, status and connexions of its leaders and adherents. The Ijesha thus also assessed the churches and the Muslim body in political terms: to be resented as tending to sever part of the community from the authority of its chiefs, or drawn in as a new accession of people and resources for the community, or treated as a reservoir of possible social allies. So it followed that both religions should be given their own spokesman (*asoju*) on the Council, as set up in 1900, to sit alongside the chiefly representatives of lineages, quarters or communities, and that each congregation, in addition to its professional leaders, should set up its leading laymen as 'chiefs' within the group. The epithet of praise most often used of church pioneers in the Centenary History is *akikanju*, a 'pushful' or intrepid person, which is so often also applied to the founders of new settlements in the district. In order to advance the church Oyebode used to press chiefs and other influential people to let him have a child or two to live with him in the parsonage and so be 'trained', which so closely replicates one of the ways in which the *Owa* and chiefs established social bonds between one another; and how Oyebode was used by the village congregations when they were in local difficulties as an intercessor with *Owa* Ataiyero clearly recalls the *onile* relationship. It is difficult not to believe that the particular success of Anglicanism was due in good measure to the political skills of Oyebode, exercised with cumulative effect over the thirty-two years of his ministry in Ilesha.

In the terms of Ijesha culture, the two aspects of the power of the Christians – their cultural capacity and their strength in numbers – would run closely parallel. Local people, and especially their chiefs, feared Christianity might harm the community in two ways: by interfering with the cultivation of those spiritual forces which controlled the local environment, and by alienating people from local chiefly authority. A characteristic sequence of events seems to occur. As the Christians grew in numbers and confidence, it came to a point – usually, in the early colonial period, about half-a-dozen years after the new religion first found a local foothold – that a phase of persecution (*inunibini*) occurred.[43] The form itself was symptomatic of Christianity's political as well as cultural challenge to the local order of things: young Christians refusing to perform their customary labour obligations to the community through the chiefs where these involved support for pagan cults, and encountering a hostile response. At Idooko 'we would not help them serve the *orisa* Osun'; at Ilase 'the Christians flatly refused to help the pagans (*awon Keferi*) with the *orisa* house or the work of the house of Olokun, whom they worshipped'; and at Ibokun there was a whole series of incidents from 1913 to 1922 involving refusals to weed the path to a sacred grove, to help repair the house of the important local *orisa* Ita or to participate in the annual hunt to provide meat for Omiran, the *orisa* of Ibokun's main ritual specialist, the *Baloro*.

The authorities responded appropriately: at Iponda the path to the church was obstructed by the 'town's medicine' (*aṣẹ ilu*) and at Ipetu the Christians were sentenced to perform disagreeable tasks like conveying to the bush the bodies of smallpox victims. Even in Ilesha itself, whose size, advancement and relative heterogeneity ruled out this kind of thing, at least at this period, Christians were widely unpopular, being in some quarters held responsible for epidemics such as the influenza through their neglect of the old spiritual precautions. It was not simply the growth in Christian numbers which ended these confrontations between the adherents of these essentially local deities and a Supreme Being preached in the language of a wider world. Rather this growth was itself an aspect and an effect of the evident growing incorporation of the localities in wider social ties. A religion whose import had initially seemed to be to weaken a community by undermining its relations with the local spiritual powers and alienating its people from their local leaders, increasingly seemed able to augment it by providing resources and contacts to enable it to deal with a wider world. By the 1940s the spread and influence of the world religions had reached the point that they were more easily considered an aspect of the entire town's character, rather than a distinct political grouping within it, and separate representation of them on the Ilesha council of chiefs through *asọju* was abandoned. Significantly, it was from the Muslim community, which by then must have been conscious that it was likely to remain a minority, that the only protest is recorded.[44]

It is instructive in other ways to compare the growth of Islam with that of Christianity.[45] It seems certain that Islam arrived in Ilesha about the same time as Christianity, and in much the same way: the oral traditions of Ijesha Muslims hold that the pioneer, Seidu Ogun, returned from Lagos in the 1860s. Their political representation went back to the time of *Ọwa* Bepo and 'a mosque with six priests' was noted in 1894.[46] Like the Christians, they experienced a surge in Ajimoko I's reign, and by 1905 they claimed 200 adult male adherents (40 being recent converts) in Ilesha and its farms – which suggests that their total following was of the same order as that of the Christians. Oyebode's letter of 1906, while commenting with satisfaction on the 'rush to learn to read and write from various motives', which was bringing new adherents to Christianity, also notes that Islam was making a spurt and implies that the Muslims were adopting some Christian missionary techniques.[47] As with the two main churches, there is some residential concentration of adherents round early mosques and the residences of early converts, this being especially marked round Iwere (Oke Ola) and Upper Egbeidi.[48] Even the intransigence of the young Christian converts of these years towards their chiefs was paralleled by the Muslim claim that they 'are no more under obligation to lift their cap or prostrate to any person, king or chief'.[49] Like the Christians, too, they were greatly dependent on young male returned migrants for their early adherents, though not of the same provenance: Lagos and Abeokuta are less prominent than Epe (a highly Islamized town on the Lagoon), Ilorin and the non-Yoruba North.

But there is an even more significant difference between Muslims and Christians which shows up in the place of conversion of their early adherents: a much higher proportion of Muslims than Christians (43% to 20%) joined *outside* Ijeshaland.[50] Since Muslims were no more prone to migrate than Christians, the inference to be drawn is that the Muslims were less successful than the Christians in adding home converts to the returnees who formed the basis of their early congregations. Why so? The overall reason is likely to be that the cultural power of Christianity was backed by a more effective organization for propagating it – none of the non-Ijesha *alfa* who served the Muslim body acquired anything like the connexions and influence which Oyebode did[51] – and was not counterbalanced by the crucial advantage which the Muslims enjoyed in such places as Ibadan or Ijebu Ode. This was that Islam had arrived there a generation or so earlier than Christianity and had thus been able to acquire sufficient power as a *political* force, in numbers and in contacts, to offset the appeal of Christian conversion on other grounds. For the world religions conferred such definite religious identities, rooted in the social ties of a local congregation, that subsequent movement between them has been remarkably small.[52] While either of them, in the Nigerian context, might serve as means of adaptation to a wider world, the choice of which is determined quite locally, by the balance of various powers possessed by either, which is historically quite contingent to them. Only one Ijesha community, Erin Oke, became predominantly Muslim, for such reasons. Even though so many Ijesha traded as *oṣomaalo* in mainly Muslim areas, it was the religion which seemed powerful at home which they overwhelmingly adopted. Indeed, since it was so bound in with the *ọlaju* on which they prided themselves, it may have played a role in defining the boundary between them and their customers.

The advance of the world religions is marked by a number of definite peaks, as Figure 8.1 shows. The first, confirming more casual impressions from documentary sources, falls in the reign of Ajimoko I. The second peak, 1910–14, linked with the establishment of many new congregations in the district and of new churches for both Methodists (Oke Ese) and Anglicans (St Peter's, Isona) in Ilesha, occurs in the years which saw the first outburst of *oṣomaalo* activity. The third, 1920–24, corresponds to the opening of *Ọwa* Aromolaran's reign, that period of prosperity when the large traders returned from Oshogbo and, in high hopes for the future, the Young Ijesha Improvement Society began its activities. The fourth, 1930–34, saw the onset of the Depression and found dramatic expression in the great Revival of Prophet Joseph Babalola. Each of these is a period in which some new phase or consequence of Ilesha's involvement in the wider world of Nigeria came about. The last brought a major new component to the religious life of the Ijesha: the Aladura churches.[53]

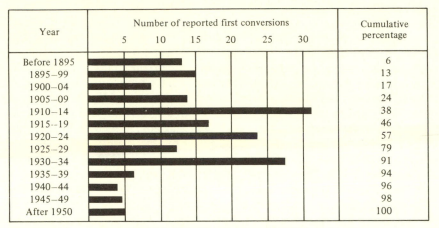

Year	Number of reported first conversions						Cumulative percentage
	5	10	15	20	25	30	
Before 1895							6
1895–99							13
1900–04							17
1905–09							24
1910–14							38
1915–19							46
1920–24							57
1925–29							79
1930–34							91
1935–39							94
1940–44							96
1945–49							98
After 1950							100

Fig. 8.1 First converts within families to a world religion, by year

Note: To these 178 cases, reported by respondents in the 1974 survey, should be added 33 more, which all fell before 1930, but cannot be included in the histogram because the time reference was too vague, being either 'before Babalola' (1930) or 'in the time of Oyebode' (1896–1927). They are, however, included in the cumulative percentages at 1925–29, since that is the latest when they could have occurred. In answers to the question, 'Who was the first person in your family to become a Christian or Muslim?', the relationships specified were nearly all very close: self, father, father's brother, senior brother, father's mother, etc.

As the Aladura movement in general has been dealt with at length elsewhere, the aim here will be to briefly assess its place and effects in the course of cultural change in Ilesha. An essential condition of its spread in the early 1930s was the rapid growth and public acceptability which Christianity enjoyed in the 1920s. Instead of chiefly persecution, Ọwa Aromolaran attended church. Now the Christians went on to the offensive; and their young men sang such songs in the streets as:

> Keresimesi ọdun de, ki l'Eṣu gbe Eṣu sọ s'igbo
> Christmas festival has come, whoever has an Esu let him throw it into the bush

which must have been highly demoralizing to the adherents of old ways.[54] The reference is to the main physical form taken by the *oriṣa* Esu or Elegba, formerly a very prominent part of Ijesha religion: a lump of pumice-like stone, set at the base of the wall just by a house's doorway.[55] You hardly ever see them nowadays, except at the title houses of chiefs or priests, and it must have been when it became popular to build iron-roofed Lagos-type houses in the 1920s that this most widespread and public token of the old religion started to disappear. Church attendance, adult baptisms and primary school enrolment went up by leaps and bounds.[56]

172

The dangers – for the existing church bodies – in this success were soon revealed when the Revival brought a further huge increase in the numbers of would-be Christians. The churches, whose professional manpower was very thin on the ground and which required an intensive socialization of their converts, were strained far beyond their organizational resources. New converts flooded in, and then out again into the Aladura churches.[57] For at the end of 1931 the leaders of the Revival affiliated themselves to the Apostolic Church of UK, whose missionaries established a headquarters at Oke Oye near the scene of the Revival and began organization and further propagation in the district. In this they were greatly helped by some former catechists of the older missions – J.A. Babatope, who had worked for years at Iperindo, being especially important, and largely responsible for the rural outreach of the Apostolic Church in that direction – and in some places by lay church leaders from Christianity's early days who came over, drawn by the 'spiritual power' of the prophet.[58] The manner in which the Aladura churches have built on early Christian foundations is also evident from individuals' religious histories: 43% of household heads of Aladura allegiance were formerly adherents of one of the older churches. The outcome has been that Aladura are now more omnipresent than any other religious agency. Hardly a hamlet, even in the outlying cocoa areas, is without one of their little church buildings; and in Ilesha, while there are some large central congregations, the typical one relates closely to the small neighbourhood it serves.

The Aladura success, both in terms of its own growth and as marking the climax of Ilesha's cultural adaptation to the fact of its incorporation, rests on an apparent paradox. On the one hand, it related to those mundane concerns of the individual whose treatment had been the popular strength of the old local cults; on the other, this was achieved with little diminution of the universality of its Christian idiom or, despite the tensions with the older churches, much deflection from the historical trajectory of religious change. It was a popular Christianity which served to sustain and strengthen the participation of ordinary Ijesha in the wider world. Consider what happened at the Revival itself. The young Ekiti-born prophet, Joseph Babalola, attached to a prayer-group whose local leader was Babatope, sanctified the water of the Ora stream that divides Isare and Oke Oye quarters as *omi iye*, the 'water of life'. People were drawn from hundreds of miles around: for a month or two Ilesha became a *Nigerian* Lourdes. They drank the water to cure their sicknesses, to enable them to bear children and to disprove the charge of witchcraft, and were enjoined to renounce the instruments of their old religion – great piles of which were handed in and burnt. But the means as well as the concern still touched deep local chords: less than a mile from the scene of the revival was the *Arojo*'s shrine of Osun where for centuries (and still today to a modest extent) fresh spring water was used as a medium to confer healing and fertility;[59] and it was not accidental that later in the 1930s a group called the *Olomitutu* ('cold water people') caused such a stir in the villages round Iponda – another historic centre of the Osun cult. None the less, despite the use of these locally affective symbols, it was to a new variety of Protestantism, very recognizable in European terms, that the bulk of the Aladura converts were drawn; and it was with that characteristic symbol of literate *ọlaju*, a school hand-bell, that Prophet Babalola banished the evil spirits and hastened many of the most local cults of the land into a final desuetude.[60]

9

Remaking the town

We now turn to new forms of collective political action made possible by the social processes examined in the last two chapters. Their keynote can be summed up in one Yoruba word: *atunluṣe* or 'remaking the town'. Often it is less vividly translated as 'improvement', and the main vehicle of this politics in Ilesha was an association originally known, in English, as the Young Ijesha Improvement Society, but colloquially and to this day, as the *Ẹgbẹ Atunluṣe*. The eyes of this society, founded in 1921–23, were firmly fixed on the place Ilesha had come to occupy in the hierarchy of communities in this part of Nigeria and its energies were devoted to advancing that place, within a colonial framework whose legitimacy it did not challenge. Only after the economic and cultural divide of the early 1930s, and then not solely as a consequence of local developments, did a political association emerge with a definitely nationalist aspect, the Ilesha branch of the Nigerian Youth Movement. By the late 1930s there was a greater variety of organized interest groups of an economic and political kind: the Farmers' Association (by then absorbed into the Cooperative Movement and consequently emasculated as much of a *political* force) was joined by bodies representing produce-traders and motor-transporters, occupations whose interests had often been represented by *Ẹgbẹ Atunluṣe* in the 1920s. This differentiation of organized interest groups was partly a response to the greater consolidation, at times almost tending to monopoly, of specific opposing interests in the economic sphere, and partly a consequence of the wider diffusion of the capacity to organize in the population. But also this diversity was an expression of the fact that, while organizations might set out to promote what were in their members' view simply the interests of the whole community, any such programme of 'remaking the town' had implications for the balance of power between existing or emergent interest-groups within it. This is not to suggest there is an easy equation to be made between political forces and social classes, for political forces might express transient interests, interests based on generation and locality, and combinations of class-fractions with any of these. Moreover, especially in a culture like this one, any grouping which attracts supporters

175

and consequently shows itself capable of exerting political influence, tends to become a new interest-group in its own right. Politics thus continually creates social structure and does not just express it. The third major body concerned to 'remake the town' that will be considered in this chapter – *Ẹgbẹ Ọmọ Ibilẹ Ijẹṣa* ('Society of Native Ijesha Sons'), founded in 1940 – shows this rather clearly. Its actions – culminating in one of the great set-pieces of twentieth-century Ijesha history, the Riot of 1941 – served both to show what sort of society Ilesha had been becoming over the preceding twenty years and to define for the future a pattern for the relations between the community and its leaders.

Since 'remaking the town' was essentially directed at improving Ilesha's relations with and position in the political hierarchy of Nigeria, something more must be said about its higher administration. As has been described in Chapter 6, Ilesha stopped being a major administrative centre with the creation of the new provinces in 1913–14. Thereafter it fell under the immediate authority of the District Officer, twenty miles away at Ife, and ultimately under the Resident of Oyo Province, nearly a hundred miles away by the roads of those days.[1] Within Ife Division all Ijesha territory formed one political unit or 'Native Authority' (NA) under the *Ọwa* at Ilesha, the others being Ife and Ila-Orangun; and juridically the *Ọwa* himself was 'Sole Native Authority' – presumed to consult with his chiefs and council-members (these all being chiefs with the addition of the Christian and Muslim *asọju*), but the sole channel of powers devolved by the colonial state and consequently possessed of large discretionary powers within the community at large.

The colonial state operated in two broad divisions:[2] the political and administrative hierarchy, and the specialist or technical departments. Officers of the latter – Education, Forestry, Posts and Telegraphs, Public Works, Medical etc. – were professionals, organized in departments under their own directors, ultimately responsible to the Lieutenant-Governors or the Governor, whose spheres of operation intersected with the political administration, but did not fall under it. Ilesha, for example, was the centre of produce inspection for a wide area extending to Oshogbo and Akure, and was usually the seat too of a Superintendent of Agriculture and a Divisional Engineer. As the sphere of their activities was circumscribed and centrally funded, they were usually less the object of attempts from below to influence them than was the politico-administrative structure.

The remit of the latter was potentially very broad indeed, but routinely its officers had two paramount concerns: courts and taxes. Ever since the colonial order had been imposed, the exercise of judicial authority had been the cutting edge of power at all levels of the political hierarchy: the DO could at any time preside over native courts, he heard appeals or transmitted them to the Provincial Appeal Court at Oyo, and at all times he received informal approaches from litigants. Struggles over the location of separate courts and over the control of court personnel were vital aspects of inter-communal and intra-communal political conflict respectively.[3] The form of revenue collection was equally important as a constituent of Nigeria's colonial order. As a whole the state was dependent, not on personal taxation, but on levies on imports and exports. But the key to the limited local autonomy upheld by Indirect Rule, was the personal taxation which, along with fines and certain licence fees charged locally, funded the treasury of each Native Authority. At Ilesha the treasury was situated in the *Qwa*'s palace and administered by a Treasury Clerk. The budget was subject to the DO's approval and was largely devoted to the salaries of the *Qwa*, certain stipulated chiefs, a small NA staff of clerks, policemen etc., and some local projects, such as minor roads and public works. The collection of this revenue, however, sharply distinguished as it was in the minds of Ijesha from traditional forms of tribute, was organized by the DO, using 'tribute clerks' (as they were misleadingly called in the 1920s) from his Ife headquarters, who were divided between the three Native Authorities under his charge. In addition to his small Divisional office staff (all of them Africans), the DO also had a handful of 'numbermen' or 'political agents', who acted as eyes and ears for him in the local communities.

At the crucial middle levels – where the European administration made contact with the subject African population – it was a tight little world in which bureaucratic procedures of appointment and promotion were strongly tempered by personal connexions and influence. Most employees moved from one job to another within the Division or Province; while they might come from anywhere in Yorubaland and included several Ijesha, it seems that, because of the location of the Divisional Office, sons of Ife and Modakeke were especially well represented among them. The flavour of things is well conveyed by a short account of the early career of J.T. Laleye, who became deeply involved in the events to be analysed shortly:

His father, a teacher, hailed from Ifewara (but the Ife side); his mother was Modakeke, his father's mother an Ijesha of Iperindo. On his father's death he stayed with a teacher at Omofe school, so he lived in Ilesha from 1919.

On leaving school in 1921, he was recommended to Ward-Price, the Ife DO, by his elder brother, tribute clerk for Ipetumodu (Ife NA) and chosen to be his Yoruba teacher and interpreter. When Ward-Price left, he served his successors in various office capacities, rising to be senior office messenger. In 1925 he resigned to work as produce clerk with A. Aderemi, the largest Ife trader, but was dissatisfied. Ward-Price, now Acting Resident of Oyo Province, took him on again as interpreter. In 1926 he became Assistant Court Clerk at Ilesha; he was already known to *Qwa* Aromolaran but went on the recommendation of S.B. Ige, the Treasury Clerk, an Ibadan man. Later on, he replaced the Ijesha Ajayi-Obe as Court Clerk at Ife, but the old *Qqni* Ademiluyi's practice of hearing cases secretly so alarmed him that he begged for transfer and was sent to a lower posting, as Court Clerk to Ipetu-Ijesha. Finally, in 1930, appointed Senior Court Clerk at Ilesha.[4]

Ilesha was always a problem to the Ife DO. Considered the 'richest and most progressive' of all the three Native Authorities in the Division and 'far more go-ahead than Ife' in 1925, it required closer supervision than it got.[5] This was despite the very favourable impression created by *Qwa* Aromolaran: 'a loyal supporter of the Government [who], most important of all, will always listen to advice ... all he does is sound ... [he] has the town well in hand'.[6] In 1928 a separate District Office was opened in Ilesha and an ADO was posted there. But the retrenchment forced by the Depression led to his withdrawal, and things slid further after Aromolaran had a stroke in 1931.[7] With monotonous regularity the Handing Over Notes now commented on the slowness and difficulty of tax-collection in Ilesha town (much worse than in the districts); and there began to be complaints that the court required 'constant supervision'. Ilesha would require a full half of his time, one Ife DO told his successor in 1933, until the ADO was again put there.[8] And apart from these routine problems, Ilesha seemed to throw up a lot of political difficulties: the forest reserve and Ipetu's relations with Ilesha gave much trouble; there was the turmoil created by the Aladura Revival, though with Aromolaran's tact and judgment that was smoothly handled, and then the 'cocoa agitation' against one of the tax clerks in 1931 which got close to the point of armed insurrection; there were continuous problems over Syrian traders who wanted to settle in the town; and in 1937 even an extensive outbreak of counterfeit coining.[9] Yet when Ilesha had an ADO, he was usually a newly appointed cadet,[10] and even the Ife DOs followed one another in such quick succession – twelve different men served in this capacity between 1929 and 1939 – that they could acquire little intimate knowledge of the area or its problems.

While the higher British authorities might be expected to be concerned about this, the very light and casual manner of Ilesha's administration was also of concern to many Ijesha. Some anonymous 'Sons of the Soil' wrote to the Resident in 1935: 'We beg to state herein that the now-a-days progress of a town depends solely upon the supervision of Political Officers. Therefore, we set of Ijesha people beg to state that Ilesha town from the origin is one of the recognized towns having no subordinacy to any other town in all her affairs.'[11] They stressed the inconvenience of administration from Ife and urged that a permanent officer be stationed in the town. Here we seem to reach a high point in the acceptance of the colonial order as the framework for communal advance. It was an assessment which underlay the programme of *Ẹgbẹ Atunluṣe*, the major organ of articulate public opinion in the town.

THE POLITICS OF 'IMPROVEMENT'

Ẹgbẹ Atunluṣe may be said to have definitely formed late in 1923, when it absorbed an independently existing 'Ijesha Home Union for Education'.[12] Meetings had been held, appropriately in Otapete schoolroom, since 1921, and there had even been unsuccessful attempts as far back as 1913 when 'we formed a society, we walled the wall of the school and only failed during the time the want of business took many members away from home'.[13] The 1920s, however, brought a stable constituency in Ilesha among the larger traders and produce-buyers who formed the bulk of the membership and in the expanding and now self-confident body of Christians. The society began as a self-consciously *Christian* body and, while they were not formally excluded, very few Muslims have been members to this day.[14] It was with *Ọwa* Aromolaran's support – his eldest son Adeniran became an active member – that they set about publicizing the society and raising money, with their objectives stated as: 'to see the general improvement of Ilesha and districts, with a view to place Ilesha under proper Administration [and] to build a school by the Owa's name'.[15] The latter goal was achieved with the establishment of Ilesha Grammar School in 1934, though the original conception had been somewhat different: an 'Owa's National Industrial School', intended to provide 'the industrial knowledge capable of maintaining the children of the soil apart from clerical pursuit'.[16] This emphasis is of interest, not only because of how markedly the opportunity structure and consequently the character of education has since shifted towards 'clerical pursuit', but because it shows the extent to which *Ẹgbẹ Atunluṣe* began from a resuscitation of *Ọwa* Ajimoko I's abortive programme of economic modernization.[17] In other ways, too, there was talk of reviving earlier projects aborted or neglected and now hopeless dreams: opening the Oni river for navigation down to the Lagoon or getting a railway line to Ilesha.[18]

There were direct personal links with Ajimoko's circle: G.O. Apara, a son of Peter Apara, was the first secretary, and Okunade Haastrup, a son of Ajimoko himself who had spent three years as a medical student in London, was the first chairman.[19] It was this Haastrup who, one day in 1916, had interrupted the proceedings of the Native Court to give what the DO considered a 'violently anti-Government' speech.[20] He had then advocated a government for Ilesha after the style of 'old' Abeokuta,[21] with its own revenues and a flag of its own, and the 'princes' appointed to rule subordinate towns; Ilesha was to cooperate with the other Yoruba kingdoms to oppose Government measures they disapproved of, like the Lagos water-rate;[22] there were to be plans for developments in education, hygiene, religion. He continued to advocate a much watered-down version of these aspirations to members of *Ẹgbẹ Atunluṣe*.[23] The Ijesha should have their own representative on the Legislative Council in Lagos, instead

179

of depending on the Member for Oyo Province. This direct representation was necessary to right the great historic wrong of 1914: Ilesha's separation from Ekiti. 'We are a subject race', he insisted;[24] Ilesha must be 'free from either Oyo and Ife, to be independent under the British flag and have our own District Officer.'[25] But it was difficult to see how the Ijesha could overturn the existing provincial system if they had to go to the Governor through the Ife DO and the formidable Resident of Oyo: 'Mr. Ross would try not to lose a part of the Province on whom he plays his pomp and the Government would of necessity be behind his government.'[26] So Haastrup advised the *Qwa* to send a secret delegation to the Governor. It was as part of this strategy that links were refurbished with the old Ekitiparapo society, which still existed in some form, in Lagos;[27] Dr Oguntola Sapara, Sapara-Williams' younger brother and himself a member of the Legislative Council, was invited to Ilesha and given the *Baṣemi* title;[28] and some kind of affiliation with Herbert Macaulay's Nigerian National Democratic Party (NNDP) was entertained.[29]

But none of this came to anything substantial and it may have helped cause the supercilious attitude which the colonial administration initially showed *Egbe Atunluṣe*.[30] Within a year or two, however, Okunade Haastrup withdrew from the society, and the big traders who then took over pursued politically less risky courses. Any delegations to Lagos went there to raise funds from migrant Ijesha for the secondary school project.[31] The zeal with which, say, they wrote to the Resident to wish him a good furlough or arranged a 'refreshment' in honour of the Prince of Wales' visit to Nigeria in 1925 suggests they were anxious to wipe away any tincture of disloyalty to the colonial state or involvement in Lagos nationalist politics.[32] They made representations about roads and local markets to the *Qwa* and chiefs and many of their leading members, as described in Chapter 7, established close personal connexions with them.[33] In turn the Ife DOs came round to take a much more favourable view of *Egbe Atunluṣe*'s activities.

None the less, 'remaking the town' involved direct attempts to change Ilesha's place in the hierarchy of communities as well as modifying its own culture and institutions. Each was a means to the end of the other.[34] The ambition to get the *Qwa* gazetted as a 'first class chief' – a nicety of grading introduced by the British – typifies a much broader programme (and no doubt *Egbe Atunluṣe*'s devotion to this symbolic crusade also usefully served to commend them to the *Qwa* in their more domestic projects). But it went much further. The doctrine that 'Ekiti commences from Ilesha'[35] still had much appeal. Indeed, the administrative reorganization of 1913–14 had made Ilesha's geopolitical objectives of the late nineteenth century seem newly relevant: get out from under Oyo ('a different nation with a different aptitude and government') in order to re-establish mastery over Ekiti. As for Ekiti, Ijesha aspirations were made plain in an Almanack issued for 1925, in which a portrait of the Ọwa was captioned:

Ekiti gbogbo ni ekute, Ọwa ni ese
All the Ekiti are rats, the Ọwa is a cat.[36]

The furore that this created among literate Ekiti can well be imagined.

These manoeuvres took place at a time when ethnic consciousness among the Ijesha and their neighbours was at a critical stage of development. The social experiences of migration and the cultural influence of the educated were gradually making the Ijesha think of themselves as Yoruba – and thus paradoxically take on an erstwhile designation of the Oyo at the same time as they sought administrative separation from them.[37] Both the consciousness of kind and the rivalry were expressed and encouraged by new pan-Yoruba institutions. The Reformed Ogboni Fraternity was one. Founded by a Yoruba clergyman and introduced to Ilesha from Ibadan in 1933, its lodges served to put groups of local elites in touch with one another throughout Yoruba county: and in Ilesha, as we shall see, it provided a means by which non-Ijesha employees of the Native Authority could establish ties of mutual obligation with prominent Ijeshas. Another was *The Yoruba News*, started in Ibadan in 1924, which extensively reported the doings of *Atunluṣe* members in Ilesha (who were obviously its major local source of information) and was a forum in which the elites of different towns could conduct their rivalries. The offensive Almanack of 1925 excited angry rejoinders from Ekiti correspondents in its pages, and arguments about the ceremonial precedence of the Ọwa and the *Ewi* of Ado-Ekiti.[38] Within the new, education-generated framework of Yoruba-ness, the fact of a certain ranking of Yoruba communities, in terms of their educational endowments, had to be admitted, though it was not accepted as unalterable. 'In education, civilization and competency', wrote Okunade Haastrup, 'at present the Egbas lead, the Ijeshas follow';[39] while an Ekiti contributor to the Almanack controversy angrily wrote to *The Yoruba News* that 'you Ijesha of nowadays want to crush the Ekiti underfoot, since they are not as enlightened as you'.[40] Each group's special sense of itself grew in reciprocal relationship with those of all its neighbours.

Here, local interactions on the ground, rooted in changing economic relationships, as well as the more geopolitical rivalry within the arena of the Nigerian state, also played a role in shaping ethnic identities. Ilesha's desire to get herself re-established as the centre of a large unit of administration, which should ideally be something like the old North-Eastern District, implied that, just as she should minimize her links with Oyo, she should emphasize those with Ekiti. This is the clear emphasis in the *Itan Ileṣa* of Abiola and his co-authors. Its most explicit statement comes, again, from Okunade Haastrup: 'as the time is getting higher and men growing wiser, all the Ekiti people like to be known as

Ijeshas', he asserted in a letter to the *Qwa*, especially those in Lagos. The Akures, in particular, do not want to be called Ekiti but to be greeted in the friendly Ijesha manner, '*Awe, kari o!*'; but if the Ijesha displays 'his pomp and pride as a better race' over the Ekiti who brings him cocoa to sell, then he will turn him away.[41] The trouble was not just that the Ekiti had quite other ideas and were in fact tending to develop their own identity within the administrative framework of Ekiti Division[42] but that, as Haastrup recognized, the definition of the Ekiti *as strangers* was something spontaneously tending to occur within Ijesha-land. There was more to this than some coincidence of economic specialization with distinctness of communal origin,[43] such as sometimes underpins African ethnicity;[44] nor did objective cultural differences matter much – they were minuscule in the case of the Ekiti and hardly decisive even in the case of the Syrians, who stood out most as a stranger group in Ilesha at this period.[45] The essential point is that whereas Ilesha had traditionally welcomed and *absorbed* strangers, there was a growing tendency to treat stranger origin as a permanent status attribute, in order to exclude strangers from access to resources now in short supply. The resources in question might be good trading locations (as in the case of the Syrians) or (as we shall shortly see at greater length) local bureaucratic office, but most often took the form of land: the general tendency of a period in which good cocoa land became progressively less easily available was for a clearer divide to be set between Ijesha-owners and stranger-tenants.[46] This became the pattern of a broader discrimination that the DO considered was practised in the Ilesha Native Court: 'the chiefs are far too inclined to differentiate between their own people and "strangers" who may be before them.' (1932).[47]

Of course, Ilesha courts were far from unique in showing this kind of bias. This mattered more and more as farms were cut further out into the bush towards the boundaries of each Native Authority's jurisdiction and became intermingled with farms established by men of another town from the other side. The problem had long existed on the north-west boundary with Oshogbo, but in the 1920s it became newly acute beyond Ifewara, along the boundary with Ife, where many new cocoa farms were being established. The precise location of the boundary might determine whether a farmer was liable to pay *iṣakọle* as a stranger or not, as well as to which Native Authority he should pay his tax, so it generated much concern at both individual and communal levels. The DO set to work and in 1932 produced a new boundary agreement, but instead of satisfying the Ijesha it merely added to their grievances about the administrative hierarchy.[48] Moreover, it added further cogency to the view put out by *Ẹgbẹ Atunluṣe*, that communal advance was critically dependent on educated leadership. That was why the Grammar School was needed. For, rightly or wrongly, it came to be believed that the

Qwa and chiefs were misled over the survey used and that the new *Qoni* of Ife, appointed in 1930, had exercised his sophistication on the DO to Ife's advantage.[49] (This *Qoni*, Adesoji Aderemi, had an excellent command of English and as the most substantial of the Ife traders in the 1920s was already well known to Abiola, Fadugba and the leading *Atunluṣe* members.) The point was driven home in the most effective way possible, if the following anecdote is true – and it is almost equally significant that it should be believed to be true. When preparations for Ilesha Grammar School to open were nearly complete, *Ẹgbẹ Atunluṣe* contacted a Lagosian clergyman, the Revd M.S. Cole, with a view to his becoming the first principal. He came to Ilesha and was warmly received, but on his way back was intercepted by the *Qoni* who prevailed on him to head Oduduwa College instead.[50] Ile Ife thus had its first secondary school in 1932, and Ilesha Grammar School had to follow two years later.

THE NIGERIAN YOUTH MOVEMENT

Ilesha emerged from the Depression a community profoundly out of sorts with itself. One major objective of the politically conscious – the establishment of the Grammar School – had been achieved, but others seemed far off: Ilesha had not achieved that place in the administrative hierarchy which its history and importance were felt to justify. *Qwa* Aromolaran, despite his sterling qualities, no longer seemed quite the ruler whom the times required, being outshone by the brilliant young *Qoni* of Ife; and his recurrent infirmity badly affected the town's administration.[51] Moreover a new political generation was emerging, impatient with what they considered 'the low state of affairs here and the failure of most of our projects and aspirations'.[52] These people, typically a couple of decades younger than the *Atunluṣe* founders, were now more active than they were in the town's economic life, supporters of the Produce Traders Union for the Ilesha Inspectorate Area and the Ilesha branch of the Nigerian Motor Transport Union, and they were also better educated, many of them literate in English and so open to the stirrings of nationalism in the Lagos newspapers. Their politics was less dominated by the advocacy of the undivided interest of Ilesha as a community against other communities, in two ways. On the one hand, their circle included some non-Ijesha and they referred much more to the interests of *Africans* against interests promoted by the colonial government. On the other hand, they were drawn into expressing (and hence also opposing) particular sectional interests within the community. Moreover, once this political ball had started to roll, other sectional interests within the community began to see advantages in joining in. This presented the original activists with a dilemma: whether to maintain their original goals by ignoring the claims of these sectional interests or to allow these new adherents to influence the content of the political programme towards projects more divisive of the community. In the event, each alternative was endorsed. The first new organization, the Ilesha branch of the Nigerian Youth Movement (NYM), held to its original goals but became ineffective in the politics of the town; while a handful of its members withdrew to take up a variety of locally more pressing causes in the *Ẹgbẹ Ọmọ Ibilẹ Ijẹṣa*. Nationalism's first appearance in Ilesha was thus deceptively fleeting.

The Nigerian Youth Movement had become, between 1936 and 1938, the leading nationalist group in Lagos – indeed it could be said to be the first truly *Nigerian* nationalist group, since Macaulay's NNDP had effectively limited itself to domestic Lagos issues, whereas the NYM seriously and persistently sought a constituency in the hinterland.[53] Closely linked to the NYM at that time was the *West African Pilot*, which Nnamdi Azikiwe first brought out in 1937 and immediately introduced to Nigerian journalism a new style of politically sophisticated and abrasive nationalism.[54] E.A. Fajemisin, a son of Fariogun Fajemisin and the chief clerk in the Ilesha office of John Holt, who became Secretary of the Ilesha NYM, joined through reading the *Pilot* – which he did furtively (for it *was* a very radical paper) until one day the European Agent, out of interest, casually asked if anyone had a copy.[55] The dozen or so members were mostly clerks or literate traders in their thirties and early forties, but Fadugba joined, and so did Richard Ogedengbe, a retired railway-clerk who became Chairman.[56] Vice-chairman, and later Chairman, was Hadji A.R.A. Smith, an agent for Paterson and Zochonis and at this time the only Muslim in Ilesha who was educated to the standard of his Christian compeers.[57]

Most of the NYM's national programme – extension of the franchise and Nigerian self-government, judicial reforms, equal economic opportunities for Africans, advance of Africans in the civil service, movement towards free and compulsory primary education[58] – did not, at this stage, directly translate itself into forms of political action at the local level, and here the NYM operated rather as a discussion circle. Indeed, when national leaders of the NYM like H.O. Davies, J.C. Vaughan or Ernest Ikoli visited Ilesha, it was complained to them that the NYM was 'all words'.[59] That was perhaps exaggerated since the NYM, through the *Pilot* and several of its leaders, was linked with a number of more specific areas of protest.

The most important of these was the agitation in 1937–38 against the attempt of the major European cocoa-buying and shipping firms, combining together as the Association of West African Merchants, to eliminate competition between themselves by fixing prices.[60] This would have frustrated certain of the strategies of their agents,[61] the African traders, and excited fierce resentment ardently fanned by the *West African Pilot* and the NYM leadership. Opposition to the 'Cocoa Pool', as it was called, never got to the point of the hold-ups achieved in the Gold Coast,[62] but was staved off by the appointment of the Nowell Commission of Enquiry. When thereafter the Kelly Committee was set up to consider its recommendations as they might affect Nigeria, its support for a greater role in marketing to be played by the farmers' Cooperative Societies alienated African trader interests and consequently the NYM. And in Ilesha, the leading role in presenting evidence to the Committee was played by a local NYM member, secretary of the local Produce Traders' Union, J.O. Fada-hunsi.

The NYM's national leaders were also involved in protests against colonial policy in a closely related area: transport. Early 1937 saw solid support in Ilesha for the 'strike' of transporters against the Government's decision to double licence-fees for lorries plying routes where they were in competition with the financially ailing Nigerian Railway. A young NYM activist named Obafemi Awolowo, also prominent in the Nigerian Motor Transport Union, headed a mission to Ilesha to rally support for the strike.[63]

When these issues receded somewhat on the national level, the Ilesha NYM turned its attention to more local concerns. Discussions drawn out over a year led in April 1940 to a document entitled 'Suggested Reformation of the Ilesha Native Court System and the Afin System and other relevant matters'.[64] Here they complained of procedural irregularities, particularly in relation to the Matrimonial Court, over which Lẹjọka Abiola then presided, and asked for greater supervision by the higher administration. Then they went on to ask for three chiefs to be designated as asọju-ọba or 'king's representatives', to sit daily at a set time at the *Afin*, 'in order that the complaints at one time rife in the town and districts that the Owa is always inaccessible may be removed and His Alaiyeluwa himself relieved of tiresome sitting over minor daily complaints'. Here the concerns of the NYM members were very much those that the DOs had been expressing about Ilesha's administration for several years. They also asked for a quarterly Council meeting, bringing the Ilesha chiefs together with heads of the district towns and representatives of sectional interests within the community, to be 'effectively established'. Here too they were closely in accord with official opinion, which had decided that an Intelligence Report should be compiled as the preliminary to a complete over-haul of the local administration.[65] This needed, felt the DO, 'to be adopted to modern conditions and modern progress, the voice of the progressive and literary [*sic*] members of the community will have to be represented owing to the influence wielded by them'.[66] One might well think it odd that detailed enquiry into the allegedly traditional system of political relations, bringing forth assertions of communal interest in the deepest language of custom,[67] was considered an appropriate means to this end; but the compilation of Intelligence Reports was a favoured activity in the Indian summer of Indirect Rule and the ambitious ADO was usually keen to set to work on one. But compared with those which had lately been compiled for nearly all the towns of Ekiti, Ilesha's was begun in a notably different way. The DO sought the help of 'a committee of impartial persons', drawn from different Ijesha communities and societies; and it was another leading member of NYM, a retired government clerk and trader called E.A. Ekunseitan, who coordinated their activities and early in November submitted a series of interim reports to the DO for his perusal.[68]

But the Report was never completed. It, and the NYM members who wanted to deal with the town's administrative problems through patient representations to the DO, were quite overtaken by events. Though in their definition of the problem the NYM view was close to the Administration's, they had already sounded one alarming note as regards the solution. Writing to the *Ọwa* back in 1939, they had advised that Ilesha's affairs might be better served if a native of the town were appointed as Council Clerk. Aromolaran responded by appointing a literate nephew of his, E.A. Adesuyi, to the post.[69] But this did not quell discontent with the Native Authority, particularly in its fiscal and judicial roles. Resentment at the employment of non-Ijesha began to reverberate more widely round the town, soon being compounded with other grievances. The catalyst was provided by a handful of literate men, some of them former government clerks, who had retired from service outside Ijeshaland. One such, J.B. Akinola of Ijoka quarter, wrote a reasonable letter to the ADO in December 1939 touching on that sensitive subject, taxes, and recommending that the Ekiti system of collection be adopted.[70] In May 1940 he wrote again, referring to a 'promise' made to him in March; but this time his theme was the need to employ natives in the 'Native' Authority. 'It is easier for an aborigine to know the dealings, feelings and interest of his people than a mere stranger who comes for his daily bread and pocket.'[71] All the highest NA positions at Ilesha, he claimed, were held by non-natives, though in other places like Ife preference was given to natives. Substance was given to this claim by the case of G.O. Akinwunmi, an Okesha man recently retired from his post as Treasurer of Ekiti NA – it was believed to the advantage of native Ekiti. Akinwunmi and Akinola were joined by S.O. Ademilola, a literate produce-buyer and Secretary of the Motor Transporters' Union.[72] Getting no satisfaction from an interview with the chiefs, they consulted J.S. Oginni, Chairman of *Ẹgbẹ Atunluṣe*, who advised them to form a society. Round about mid-July 1940 *Ẹgbẹ Ọmọ Ibilẹ Ijẹṣa* ('The Society of Native Ijesha Sons') came into being.[73]

THE RIOT OF 1941

The organization and procedures of the *Ẹgbẹ* differed markedly from anything known before, though its ethos certainly had precedents in Ijesha history. In its early, active, months it was loosely organized round a core of founder-members, who did not establish a hierarchy of offices but all contributed to the agitational work of writing letters to officials, getting up petitions and spreading the word among the population. There was no membership list, since all Ijesha were considered to be members of the society. To the already-mentioned founders were soon added Richard

Ogedengbe and J.A. Fadugba from the NYM, and it was Fadugba who soon came most to embody the *Ẹgbẹ Ọmọ Ibilẹ Ijẹṣa* in the public eye. It was of course a routine practice for associations of any kind, from churches to social clubs, to choose a senior person to serve as *Baba Ẹgbẹ*, partly to play the elder's role of mediating in disputes among the members and partly to serve as a link with the ruling circles of the community, who were typically set apart by their age from the predominantly youthful membership of societies, especially newly-founded ones. Such had been Daddy Anjorin's part in the *Ẹgbẹ Atunluṣe* in the 1920s. But here Fadugba's role was more decisive. Already around seventy years of age, he was well known in the town through his former eminence as a trader and an activist in the *Atunluṣe*. Not merely did he possess a mastery of English and an informed sympathy, more characteristic of a much younger man, with the currents of Lagos nationalism, but a personality, sharpened by experience, that was well suited to head a populist assault on local privilege. Vehement, forthright and proud, his desire to take a leading part in the affairs of the town had been thwarted by his bankruptcy, a personal catastrophe made worse by insensitive treatment from one ADO in the mid-1930s[74] and by the contrasting success of his erstwhile intimate, J.D.E. Abiola, the senior chief closest to the *Ọwa*. Thus it was that the social conflict which erupted in the late months of 1940 came to have the quality of an epic confrontation between two giants, the Lion of Iroye and the Elephant of Omofe.

The conflict developed on several distinct but interlocking fronts. The issue of the employment of non-natives merged into criticism of the Native Authority as such, for incompetence, corruption and oppression. A round of letter-writing, to the DO, the *Ọwa*, the Resident, even the Chief Commissioner of the Western Provinces in Lagos, occupied Ademilola and Akinola into August, but produced little response.[75] They then started to mobilize open support by informing Ijesha societies in other towns of their complaints, and by organizing a public meeting of the *Ẹgbẹ Ọmọ Ibilẹ* at Obokungbusi, the recently completed Council Hall in front of the *Afin*, on 24 August. The DO, though invited, declined to come; he had no previous correspondence and no knowledge of the society, he said.[76] They made their point, however, since at a Council meeting on 10 September attended by the Resident as well as the DO, the concerns of the *Ẹgbẹ* dominated the agenda. The Resident defended the financial position of the Native Authority but said that any complaints must go to the *Ọwa* in the first instance. Fadugba claimed that harm was being done to the NA by the non-natives employed there and asked that they be retrenched as Ijesha had been elsewhere. To this the *Ọwa* replied that it was the DO who had engaged S.B. Ige, the Treasury Clerk, but that the Treasury was in any case checked by two Ijesha chiefs.[77]

After this public meeting the crisis began to escalate rapidly. The *Ọwa* gave Fadugba permission to check the Treasury and, on 12 September, he also requested the DO for the *Ẹgbẹ* to be allowed to scrutinize the files and records of the Tax Office and Native Court.[78] It says a good deal for the ignorance and/or trust of the administration that this was so easily given. On 14 September, Ademilola, who had concentrated on the affairs of the forestry guards (who issued the licences for tree-felling which were a major source of NA finance), wrote to the DO asking for the Senior Conservator (in Lagos) to conduct an official enquiry.[79] Anxious to head off the direction events were taking, the *Ọwa* and chiefs wrote to the Resident on 16 September asking to be allowed to replace the non-natives in the NA, 'so that great confusion may not arise in our town', and tax-collection could get under way.[80] But the official line was politically unhelpful: Ijesha could be appointed to any vacancies, but non-Ijesha could not be dismissed without charges being proved against them. As the *Ẹgbẹ's* investigations proceeded, their complaints took a more definite form, and public suspicions grew as they were accorded the legitimacy of a sympathetic official ear. The *Ọwa* had good cause for concern: the focus of suspicion and complaint was moving inexorably closer to prominent Ijesha in the circle around him. In a series of meetings of *Ẹgbẹ Ọmọ Ibilẹ* representatives with the *Ọwa* and chiefs (one of them allegedly attended by 8,500 people) in October, all the old complaints were repeated, but the *Lẹjọka, Ọdọle* and *Loro* defended themselves from charges of peculation.[81] But still there was no resolution and at a further public meeting on 7 November, the antagonisms were nakedly expressed: *Lẹjọka* Abiola 'cursed those who would spoil the affairs of the town', while Jegede Lemodu, a prominent member of *Ẹgbẹ Ọmọ Ibilẹ*, responded with the accusation that 'Chief Lejoka was responsible for the great confusion as he never directed the people in the right way'.[82]

One set of grievances against the *Lẹjọka* arose from his Presidency of the Matrimonial Court.[83] The *Ẹgbẹ's* analysis of court records compared his term of office since 1938 with the *Ọdọle's* term from 1933 to 1936 and concluded that many more cases were outstanding, 'dowries' had often not been returned to divorced husbands, and the clerks were accused of procedural irregularities, inefficiency and petty peculation. But this probably mattered less than the more general responsibility which was felt to rest with *Lẹjọka* Abiola for the unsurpations and corruption shown by officers of the NA and those in the circle round the *Ọwa*. The essential symbol of this was the Reformed Ogboni Fraternity which Abiola had introduced to Ilesha and which aroused the deepest enmity of the *Ẹgbẹ*. 'Please, beware of all the *Bats* whenever dealing with our letters', warned E.A. Oke writing on behalf of the *Ẹgbẹ* to the Lagos Ijesha, 'for their society is the root of all the various and varied vices now operating in the town.'[84] Ademilola denounced it publicly at the meeting of 7 November as 'a separate Government ... which was spoiling the affairs of the town'.[85] According to a list of members drawn

188

up by the *Ẹgbẹ* the ROF included, besides the *Lẹjọka*, *Loro* Falode the Criminal Court President, Adedigba the *Risawẹ*, several district heads, the two Treasury Clerks and the Court Clerk, three leading members of the Public Works staff, the two NA forest guards, several leading *ẹmẹsẹ* (including Aromolaran's special favourite, E. Kayode), Prince Adeniran and other of the *Ọwa*'s sons.[86] It thus served to link, both substantially and in the eyes of popular opinion, the non-natives with the Ijesha members of the local establishment.

Of all the investigations conducted in October and November, that into the forest guards was most completely successful. Once the *Ẹgbẹ* declared itself publicly, complaints flowed in from villages in every corner of Ijesha-land.[87] The main illicit practices were refusing, unless bribed, to give receipts for fees paid by sawyers for trees felled, and allowing a group of favoured people, for sundry considerations, to fell trees without paying the fee. What had been going on for several years is tersely conveyed in many written testimonies sent in to the *Ẹgbẹ*:

> In 1935 [at Oshu] David Sawyer fell[ed] 5 Iroko trees for which he paid £15, and no permit, no recept given him. Each time of making the planks the Forest Guard demanded 3/6d., which cost 17/6d. Upon all 5 bottles of beer were demanded and paid to Forest Guard two legs of antelope @ 1/3d., each = 12/6., at each time of making planks.

> [at Ajido] S.B.I. [Treasury Clerk] received a case of dry gin from Alfred Fatuase for killing a young kole-agbe tree, this was given to prevent legal step and can be witnessed by J.B. and J.J., both of Isare Street, and this was given by S.A. [Forest Guard] and upon the whole Alfred was fined £1 in the court the second day.

It appears that the forest guards received far more from their illicit levies on sawyers and villagers than accrued to the NA from the felling fees due to it.[88] From lists of trees illicitly felled, it also seems that, while a good many people received some benefit here, the lion's share went to two men, both members of the ROF, who built up substantial timber businesses this way. The worst depredations occurred in areas where non-Ijesha sawyers, often men from Igbajo or Ikirun, were set up in camps deep in the forests. A senior official of the Forestry Department came to investigate on the spot – guides and bearers being provided by *Ẹgbẹ Ọmọ Ibilẹ* members – and concluded that the charges were justified. The two chief guards were dismissed, but extortion was felt to be so hard to prove in court that the others, though no doubt badly frightened, went free.[89]

These investigations into NA finances also contributed to another axis of conflict, already coming out into the open through the compiling of the Intelligence Report. For it became clear that the Treasury staff had been systematically docking portions of the small quarterly salary payments which the heads of district settlements had to come to Ilesha to collect.[90] When the *Asaobi* came to collect his quarterly 10s 0d he was told 'that the money has been used by Government and that [he was] late to come for the payment', while the *Olọtan* claimed S.B. Ige had deducted 4s 0d from his £2 17s 6d and in the third quarter was simply told 'there is no money in the safe to pay for it'.[91] Many other places, both villages sociologically close to Ilesha like Oshu or Ijemba and subordinate towns like Ipetu-Ibokun and Esa Oke, complained of the same. Mingled with their testimonies on this score were still more irregular exactions of the centre. Odo village alleged that an NA vaccinator, a close relative of the *Qwa*'s, had levied £17 16s 0d in cash, as well as quantities of schnapps, gin, beef and yams; while villagers on the Muroko Road complained of having been forced to clear a road to the cocoa farm of a son of the *Qwa*, without being either paid or compensated for damage done to their own farms. From September onwards letters streamed in to Fadugba and the other *Egbẹ Ọmọ Ibilẹ* leaders from bodies like the Ikeji Youth Improvement Union or the *Egbẹ Atunluṣe* of Ilare, or from individuals, expressing anger at the impositions of the centre, or what one Ibokun man called the 'wickedness, partiality, selfish of administration Ilesha done for our chiefs'.[92] The same message came from the Ijesha communities abroad which the *Egbẹ* had contacted: the Ijesha Union of Kano said that people there from Ibokun and Ijebu-jesha refused to join, on the grounds that Ilesha people treat them 'not as brothers but only as mere chattels'.[93]

Here it was not just the illicit levies of the last few years, but long years of administrative subordination and dependence on facilities sited in Ilesha as capital town, which rankled. It can hardly have been the intention of the *Egbẹ Ọmọ Ibilẹ* leaders, who were all Ilesha men, to be the vehicle for the interest of the subordinate towns against the centre, that age-old axis of Ijesha politics; but it was now so tied in with conflicts within the capital that they willingly took it on board too. *Tile toko* ('town-interest, farm-interest'), an expression of the solidarity of the whole Ijesha kingdom, became one of the *Egbẹ*'s slogans.[94] Late in November, delegates from the district towns were the main speakers at a mass meeting held at Lion House, Iroye, where the grievances of the villages, and the level of tax, rather than the employment of non-natives in the NA, were the main focusses of concern.[95]

By November, when the forest guards were dismissed, *Egbẹ Ọmọ Ibilẹ* was riding high. There is a certain note of hilarity in the way E.A. Oke replied to a puzzled letter from the *Qwa* asking the *Egbẹ* to forward its grievances in writing: 'we have no grievances whatever, what we are fighting for is (*a*) right, (*b*) liberty and (*c*) justice'.[96] But there was a danger of the momentum being lost. An attempted investigation of PWD accounts, with the DO's permission, was frustrated by the opposition of the District Engineer, an expatriate. The incident was not without its humorous side. When Ogedengbe and others got to the Engineer's office, they met his wife, who assured them her husband '*is such a most honest man*' and demanded to know their credentials. 'All these unexpected subjugations, humiliations and disrespects we had encountered from her. *Nolens volens* she was drilling us up and down the office to answer her questions one by one, standing with our hands at our backs like school children, so that we were happier to escape than when we entered there.'[97] On other fronts too, an impasse seemed to have been reached. The non-natives were still employed in the Treasury and Court, and no further prosecutions were intended. On the grievances of the district, the DO was awaiting completion of the Intelligence Report.[98] *Ẹgbẹ* members protested to the *Ọwa* in late December against his reported intention 'to pick out of your favourites', in the replacement of the dismissed guards.[99] But such was the sense of unease in the town that tax-collection was going very slowly indeed; and it was tax which provided the final spark.

The explosion came on 6 January 1941, which that year was the day of *Ibẹgun*.[100] This is the ceremony when, with the sacrifice of a dog to Ogun in the market-place, the Ijesha people put all evil behind them in preparation for *Iwude*, the climactic ritual of the Ogun festival cycle, when the *Ọwa* restores his compact with the Ijesha. The town was full of *oṣomaalo* and other Ijesha returned from abroad to hold their annual reunions. In the mid morning of that day Fadugba was called to the Tax Office at the instance of a household-head who had been fined for not paying his tax as assessed. The chief assessment officer was *Lẹjọka* Abiola, and a violent altercation took place between him and Fadugba in the presence of the other chiefs. Attempts were made to arrest Fadugba but, a scuffle breaking out among the people in the office, he left for Ademilola's house, nearby in Ereja, where he was arrested. News of this spread quickly round town and, when Ogedengbe and others appeared to ask for bail at the *Afin*, a crowd began to gather. Word was sent to the DO, twenty miles away at Ife; he came, found things quiet enough and left. No sooner had he got back to Ife than a further message summoned him again to Ilesha. It was now late afternoon and a large and angry crowd had begun throwing stones at the Treasury, despite the attempts of various *Ẹgbẹ* leaders to restrain them. When the DO tried to address them, he was manhandled and his baton taken. Later he interviewed Fadugba at home, finding him 'very excited' after being released by his supporters from the NA Prison. As darkness came on a mob formed again, and now began to go round attacking the houses of prominent members of the NA and other buildings. This continued till 3 a.m. on the morning of 7 January, and started again at daybreak. The DO was back again in mid-morning to talk to the crowd and agreed to hear grievances later in the day in the grounds of the Grammar School. A detachment of armed police with tear-gas was summoned from Oshogbo to back up his authority. Disorder continued sporadically in the afternoon – many people had come in from the villages – but by the morning of 8 January it was all over.

191

The damage showed a systematic pattern.[101] The houses of Prince Adeniran at Isokun and *Lẹjọka* Abiola at Omofe and Ijoka were the prime targets. At the Ijoka chieftaincy-house the staircase was chopped down, a wife's sewing-machine, gramophone and typewriter smashed, domestic animals killed, and at Omofe all his books and papers, as well as other fittings, were destroyed. Next came the house of Falode the *Loro*, with his car smashed; and the ROF Lodge was entered with crowbars and burnt. Lesser amounts of damage were sustained by the houses of three other sons of the *Ọwa*, of Ige the Treasurer and Laleye the Court Clerk, of Pa J.F. Longe, the Christian *asọju* on the Court, and of a minor produce-examiner; and by NA buildings. Nobody appears to have been either killed or injured – the victims had had good time to run for safety to friends' houses. In the event, therefore, the main judgment of the crowd lay clearly against powerful Ijesha in the circle of privilege around the *Ọwa*, rather than against the non-natives who were their clients.

The aftermath can be summarily told.[102] Eighteen men, including Fadugba were charged with offences ranging from inciting people not to pay tax to malicious damage, and given prison sentences of up to a year. A pall of bad feeling and an uneasy calm settled over the town. A 'Peace Party' was set up, composed of people from the NYM, *Ẹgbẹ Atunluṣe* and the Muslim societies, to tour the quarters, preaching reconciliation and seeking a basis for reform. The DO prepared a report on the causes of the Riot and in consequence the Council was greatly enlarged with representatives of junior lines of chiefs and the district communities, and an Advisory Board to include leading literate members of the community. But in the prevailing atmosphere this work of reconstruction could not get far. During the trial there were reports of men massing with guns in the villages if Fadugba were convicted; and while nothing positive came of this, there were 'movements' against 'loyal' chiefs in several subordinate towns.[103] The morale of the *Ọwa* and chiefs in Ilesha was so badly affected by the Riot that, in the DO's view, they were 'unable to take an intelligent interest in affairs for more than half an hour at a time'. Important titles, like *Ogboni*, *Risawẹ* and the heads of the two junior lines, *Ẹjẹmọ* and *Bamura*, which had fallen vacant, could not be filled. The junior lines (*Ẹlẹgbaji* and *Ọmọdeọwa*) were quite unresponsive to the suggestion that they might take a hand in tax-assessment to ensure its fairness.[104] Not surprisingly, since the senior extant title-holder in the *Ẹlẹgbaji* line, Bolaji the *Risa Ijọka*, was among those imprisoned, they were much more concerned to raise funds for the defence and the appeal. Government insisted that the Riot victims be compensated, but this again could make no headway while the eighteen men were still in prison:[105] in the popular view, the greater injustice of their imprisonment far outweighed the lesser injustice of the riot damage. The men were duly released; but ultimately it was *Ọwa* Aromolaran's death in mid-1942 which, by changing the key personnel at the centre, permitted institutional reforms to go forward. It was a sad end to a reign which had solid achievements to its credit. The old *Owa* probably had small personal responsibility for the misdeeds of those around him, and one is happy to note that he is exonerated in the collective memory of the town.

The central issue in a sociological account of the Riot must be why an event which was such a turning-point in the colonial history of Ilesha should be so 'traditional' in its form and so susceptible of representation in the idioms of the past. Chief Daniel Gidigbi, a skilled story-teller (*opitan*) who was the youngest of those sent to prison in 1941, gave a taped account of the Riot.[106] It began thus:

> The *Egbẹ Ọmọ Ibilẹ Ijẹṣa* did not come into existence idly, without a serious cause. It is when the king of the town abuses his status, when the chiefs ignore those under them, when they begin to treat their subjects in any way they fancy, when they take their farms from them; and when they are told, they pay no attention.
>
> It is at such a time that the Society comes to life. If things are not like this, if the town is going on well, everyone joins a society in his own quarter. But if a time of abuses comes about then those who live in Igbogi, in Omofe, in Isokun, in Iloro and Ifofin will join together in anger at the state of affairs, coming together and holding many meetings ... concerning the actions of those people, the chiefs and the king, to discover how to make them heed their advice.

This particular society is first typified in temporally unspecific terms, and related to a recurrent kind of social situation, marked by *aṣeju* (excess) and *ilokulo* (abuses) on the part of the powerful. Gidigbi went on to cite, 'within this class of things' (*inu ṣiṣe bẹẹ*), two earlier populist bodies: one called Gbagba, mobilized against a powerful palace chief, *Baekure*, who was killed and his house destroyed to prevent his influence over the king,[107] and Upaiye (i.e. *ipaiyẹ*), the group of young men who with Ogedengbe challenged the influence of *Ọdọle* Ariyasunle in the 1860s.[108]

The links between *Egbe Ọmọ Ibilẹ* and Ogedengbe are multiple and significant at several levels. First, there were the involvements of particular descendants of Ogedengbe. Two of his sons, Richard and Faleto Ogedengbe, were among the literate *Egbẹ* activists and a third member of the family, J.L. Ogedengbe, was imprisoned.[109] In the immediate aftermath of the Riot, *Ọbanla* Ogunmoyesin, J.L.'s father and head of the family, emerged as the only senior chief on the side of the *Egbẹ*. Secondly, there was the formal position that Ogunmoyesin held as *Ọbanla* (like his grandfather) in the town's political structure: head of Okesha quarter and thus the leading 'Ijesha' of the town in structural opposition to the *Afin*. His support of the *Egbẹ* was thus structurally appropriate though whether it would have come about without his personal connexions (which were apparently independent of it) it is hard to say. Thirdly, there were close ties of sentiment between the junior quarter-chiefs, the *Ẹlẹgbaji* and *Ọmọdeọwa*, strong supporters of the

Ẹgbẹ, and the great Ogedengbe. One has only to see these chiefs with their cutlasses and war-songs at the Ogun festival today to realize how much their style of chiefship was military; and in 1941 it is likely that among these chiefs there were still survivors of the good number of Ogedengbe's former *ipaiye* who were given these minor titles in the reigns of Ajimoko I and Ataiyero. Fourthly (and in part as a consequence of the last point), Ogedengbe was a potent symbol of the values which the *Ẹgbẹ* was asserting. This requires some elaboration.

There were two sides to the traditions of Ogedengbe which were relevant to the cause of *Ẹgbẹ Ọmọ Ibilẹ*. On the one hand, as in Gidigbi's account of Upaiye, he stands for an oppositional, populist stand in Ijesha political culture, the exploited and unprivileged rising up against the powers of the centre when they abuse their position. It was a war-song of Ogedengbe's time which the rioters sang as they attacked their enemies' houses:

> *A mo ka 'gbigbo m'ori igi o,*
> *Ogbigbo, aa wo bi eiye ti a fo, Ogbigbo!*
> We have caught the Bighead Bird on the tree,
> Bighead, we will see how the bird will fly, Bighead![110]

At the trial, this was tersely glossed by Asani, the Muslim *asọju*: 'by birds I knew they meant us [NA officials] – it is a song which means trouble'.[111] The weak point in the *Ẹgbẹ*'s case was that, in the name of the community, it was dividing the community and, in attacking the *Ọwa*, denying the symbol of its unity. This comes out as a persistent contradiction in Gidigbi's account; for he hovers between blaming the *ọba* and holding him responsible, and exculpating him by focussing the charge on the usurpation and bad advice of the chiefs.[112] The dilemma occurred to the rioters in action: they attacked the *Afin* because it was the central institution of their oppression, 'but others reminded them it was their *Afin* and that they should not touch it'.[113] But here was the other side of Ogedengbe's symbolic importance. He provided a resolution of the contradiction since he had gone on, from being a youthful divider of the town, to be its mature unifier and saviour. It was not forgotten that a basic condition of Ogedengbe's power as Ilesha's war-leader was that he had continuously reported and redistributed to his followers.

The content of the grievances that lay behind the Riot were much less 'traditional' than the form in which they were expressed. This is most obviously so with the grievances which first triggered the *Ẹgbẹ* – those of a handful of Ijesha literates against non-Ijesha employed in the NA – but these faded in importance as the protest movement gained momentum. The resentment of the district communities at their members' exploitation was itself no new thing at all, though the occasion for them now was provided by the new commercial economy, in the case of the forestry frauds, and by the forms of Indirect Rule, in the case of the illicit salary

194

cuts imposed on district chiefs. As both depended on Ilesha's local political hegemony, however, the solution was to pursue the old geopolitical goals, now newly activated by the compilation of the Intelligence Report.

But in the Riot itself, it was grievances generated within the capital against those who held power there which were paramount. All the leading members of Ẹgbẹ Ọmọ Ibilẹ, and all those imprisoned after the Riot, were men of Ilesha. Colonialism had here produced two contrasting sources of conflict, though they produced in the Riot a combined outcome.

On the one hand, there were economic opportunities more widely made available in principle, but then limited as a side-effect of the political framework of Indirect Rule. It is clear from the occupations of Ẹgbẹ Ọmọ Ibilẹ activists that, the four or five ex-clerks apart (and they, of course, were potential traders), they were in the main a 'petty bourgeois' group, intent on enlarging its commercial opportunities but frustrated by the concentration of privilege round the *Afin*, in some cases perhaps downwardly mobile.[114] Great must their bitterness have been to see two substantial timber businesses created by ROF members in cahoots with the NA forest guards. Prince Adeniran's unpopularity had similar causes.[115] By the late 1930s he had become the principal agent of UAC, with fifteen main buyers under him, and it was said that an understanding with the African manager of UAC at Oshogbo, an Ijebu named Olukoya, cemented by shared membership of the ROF, was behind this. Moreover, he used his influence to put pressure on other traders to sell to him at Ilesha instead of selling directly to the company's store at Oshogbo. He was thus able to take the 10s 0d difference in the prices offered for produce between the two places, on account of transport costs, and so to guarantee the viability of his transport business against smaller, less well-connected competitors. Small wonder that we find the Secretary of the Motor Transport Union (S.O. Ademilola) and several middling traders (J. Apoesho, J.O. Lagunju, Jacob Jalugbo) among the most active members of Ẹgbẹ Ọmọ Ibilẹ.

On the other hand, conflict also arose, not from new opportunities frustrated by the undergirding given by Indirect Rule to certain traditional office-holders and their close connexions, but from old rights set aside by new administrative practice. Two features of rule by 'Native Authority' – support of the Ọwa and senior chiefs from outside their community by the colonial state, and the creation of a small technical bureaucracy to perform tasks once undertaken by public labour – had deprived the junior chiefs in the quarters of much of their power and their function. Ọwa Ataiyero had seen the danger of this occurring over twenty years before, and the process had now gone much further.[116] The disaffection of the Ẹlẹgbaji and Ọmọdẹọwa was one reason for the poor record of tax-collection which Ilesha town had shown in the 1930s, for, in a community of Ilesha's size, they were a vital link in the chain between individual households and the *Afin*. It was noted by the DO in the immediate aftermath of the Riot, that these chiefs were a body of opinion absolutely solid in their support for *Ẹgbẹ Ọmọ Ibilẹ Ijẹṣa*.

The Riot then, must be considered in sociological terms a particularly 'impure' instance of collective social action, in which a variety of class-fractions, political status-groups and local communities combined forces against a local establishment. The ideology of community which sustained this combination of forces drew its critique from the Ijesha past, but it failed to take the real measure of the social divisions growing within Ilesha. Rather, the very image of community put forward tended to represent those divisions as a necessary and continuing part of it. *Tile, toko; Ọwa, awọn Ijẹṣa*; even, as one letter from the district to Fadugba put it, 'slaves and free-born sons, poor people and rich, strangers and natives'.[117] So the *Ẹgbẹ*, not representing a definite social force, could not effect more than a change of personnel: *Ọbanla* Ogunmoyesin and Fadugba, closely in touch with the junior quarter-chiefs, saw to it that their candidate, Ajimoko II, became *Ọwa* on Aromolaran's death in 1942. Thereafter, the *Ẹgbẹ*'s direct influence faded rapidly. The social group which really benefited was the more sober 'educated elements' who had been active in the NYM rather than in *Ẹgbẹ Ọmọ Ibilẹ Ijẹṣa*. The *Ẹgbẹ* cleared the way for them, but they would have come to the fore anyway, as they did in other Yoruba towns.

The major significance of the Riot was in the longer term, in what it contributed to the political culture of Ilesha. It showed that self-aggrandizement, even when it had the backing of the Nigerian state, could still be checked by the effective sanctions of the community. Ilesha would in fact see even greater inequalities of wealth and power emerge among her citizens in the next thirty years, but none the less a kind of implicit compact was struck between this privileged elite and the mass of the community. The old ideal of an answerable and redistributive leadership, symbolized in Ogedengbe, Ilesha's greatest communal champion, had a definite relevance. The elite was allowed to make the most of its opportunities, provided it showed communal responsibility by acting as effective community champions in the securing of development goods from the state. The Riot was thus a presence in the culture of party politics, and it was only when its lesson was forgotten, by a party elite which thought to rely on fraud and coercion rather than on the channelling of reward to its constituents, that it was recalled in practice.

10

The chiefs and the educated

The principal beneficiaries of the administrative reorganization which followed the Riot were the 'educated elements' of the town. Their star rose the quicker because Aromolaran's death caused a vacuum of power around the *Afin* and it takes time for any new *Qwa* to establish his grip over public affairs. Moreover this one, Alexander Adejomola Haastrup, a son of Ajimoko I who for forty-odd years had been *Lumobi* at Iwara, was already an old man and never matched his predecessor's political sagacity or strength of character.[1] Though he was Christian and modestly educated, and, being a Haastrup, might have seemed a fit symbol of educated 'enlightenment' (*ǫlaju*), he was not in fact their preferred candidate, but that of the *Ęgbę Qmǫ Ibilę*, the *Qbanla*, and the junior quarter chiefs, and of popular opinion generally. Both groups would have happily settled on the *Lumobi*'s son, A.L.O. Haastrup, a ship's chandler in Lagos and active in nationalist politics there, but he was reluctant to step in front of his father. The educated, and several groups of Ijesha resident in other places, petitioned the DO and Resident for someone 'literate, young, broadminded, progressive' and found the *Lumobi* 'devoid of [these] qualities'.[2] Of the other candidates, the front-runner was A.O. Ogunmokun, a commercial clerk in Lagos.[3] The young DO, Cox, who was on excellent terms with the leading educated elements, considered Ogunmokun the 'outstanding' candidate but, though he put a lot of pressure on the chiefs on his behalf, finally allowed *Lumobi* Haastrup's candidature to go through.[4] One factor which weighed strongly with chiefly and popular opinion against Ogunmokun was that he was known to belong to the ROF, and 'almost all educated persons are suspect as being either members or friends of the Fraternity'. Before the Riot, there had been much talk of the need for a well-educated *Qwa*, but this talk was now stilled. Peace in the town must come before progress, the DO advised the Resident; the new *Qwa*, Ajimoko II, acquired the praise-name Fidipote ('he who puts an end to strife').

This brief account of the succession already contains the three elements – the educated, the chiefs and the common people – whose changing

197

relationships form the theme of this chapter. The crudest essentials of the story can be shown diagrammatically thus:

The reign of Ajimoko II (1942–56) more or less covers the phase of Ilesha history in which the contest for social hegemony between the chiefs and the educated was worked out.

At its beginning all formal authority (and still enormous informal power) lay with the *Owa* and chiefs; and while the educated and traders had a growing influence because of the increasing importance of the commercial and educational institutions which they controlled, their role in public affairs was only advisory and they had no judicial functions (the Christian and Muslim *asoju* excepted). By the mid 1950s the educated had achieved political mastery of the town. This came in three main stages. In 1944, along lines which emerged as an informal necessity in the aftermath of the Riot, a new Council was constituted, with 107 members: *Owa*, 28 *Agba Ijeṣa* (senior town chiefs), 2 women and 6 quarter-chiefs from Ilesha, 58 district representatives (chiefs), and 12 representatives of the societies and educated.[5] The Native Authority was now designated as 'Owa-in-Council'. In 1949, in order to increase educated representation and to produce a less unwieldy body, the overall size was reduced to 78 – 48 chiefs, equally divided between town and district, and 30 educated councillors, likewise divided – and the NA designation changed again to 'Owa and Council'.[6] The councillors were now elected on a ward basis, instead of being nominated from societies after consultation with the DO. Finally, in 1954–55, when a two-tier system of local government was instituted – an Ijesha Divisional Council and an Ilesha Urban District Council (IUDC) – the elected councillors became an absolute majority: three-quarters or more of each body. As this process got under way, antagonism deepened between the chiefs and the educated councillors, reaching a high point in the years 1952–55. At the same time, as the councillors gathered more control over the community's affairs into their hands, they had to face a surge of popular opinion to the side of the chiefs. This provided a nasty but salutary lesson about the meaning of representation to the elected councillors, which bore fruit in the conduct of Ilesha's dominant political party, the National Council of Nigeria and the Cameroons (NCNC), after 1955.

The politically-active educated linked their communal aspirations closely with African nationalism. Invaluable as a mirror of their outlook was a newspaper called the *West African Vanguard*, published in Ilesha between 1951 and around 1960, which stated its guiding principles as: 'to foster unity in Ijeshaland, arouse the Ijeshas to political consciousness, place Ijeshaland on the Nigerian map and fight along with others for the emancipation and redemption of Africa and all other races of the world.'[7]

But nationalism, though a movement well supported in Ilesha, was none the less very 'underdetermined' by local forces. It is understandable that when nationalism began to make serious headway in the late 1940s, someone as immersed in locally-generated problems and concerns as the DO should feel able to discount what he called 'the distant rumble of irresponsible propaganda emanating from Lagos' and feel that, while 'the seed beds for anti-government propaganda [were] extended',[8] the seeds would not easily take root. But it did not greatly matter if the bulk of Ilesha's population was not strongly drawn to nationalism, provided that the educated, who were making themselves the masters of local politics, were so drawn. For as far as the local struggle between chiefs and the educated goes, the British inclined to the educated, even if what they deemed to be locally expedient sometimes prevented them from going as far as they wanted. None the less, their support for the educated was manifest in a famous confrontation between chiefs and educated in 1952–53, to be analysed below. The administrators got on well socially with the core group of educated councillors and in 1947 started holding 'Question Hours' in Ilesha and around the district in order to get 'in closer touch with the educated section of the population and the trends of their thought'.[9] The editor of the *West African Vanguard* from 1956, who was as versed as anyone in the rhetoric of nationalism, might attack the colonial power for 'economic slavery', but he did not also fail to temper it with praise for the 'Pax Britannica under which knowledge spread'.[10] This was the voice of the educated elite praising itself through praise of the British.

There was thus a certain disjunction as well as a linkage between 'nationalism', *qua* the national anti-colonial movement, and the local political tendencies related to it. These latter had, at least before the mid 1950s, a good deal of autonomy. Indeed, the Local Government Act of 1953 – one of the first measures of the Action Group Government of Western Nigeria – was more tangentially 'nationalist' than it seemed.[11] The chiefs were subject to attack – and the power of the state was used against them – less on the grounds that they were an instrument of colonialism than that they were the main obstacle to the educated conducting local affairs as they thought fit. Those who passed the 1953 Act were the select of the 'educated elements' throughout Yorubaland, and its roots were in their local experience. It was only when this issue was settled and party politics really got into gear after 1955 that the 'balance of determinations', as we may call it, tips over so that local politics becomes a series of mediated responses to conflicts generated at the regional and national centres.

Our immediate questions, then, concern the nature of the conflict between the educated and the chiefs, and its relationship to other forms of conflict within Ilesha. It is not at once obvious what *sort* of group, in sociological terms, either the 'educated' or, at this stage, the chiefs, were. On the surface it was a competition between rival political elites, one established and one rising; but more was at issue than a mere change of personnel since the educated could only come to power by changing the formal political structure. It was thus also a conflict of values, in which both sides made appeal to more broadly shared public values, such as the prowess of the community within the region and the adequate representation of the common people. The key value of the educated was, of course, *ọlaju* or 'enlightenment', linked both to education and experience of the wider world.[12] The strength of the educated lay not just in the fact that their *ọlaju* made them far more plausible as communal champions than the chiefs, but that, owing to migration and the spread of education, more and more people were becoming able to identify with them or consider them as role-exemplars. To the extent that the educated may be considered as a class (an issue that I will shortly return to), *ọlaju* may be seen as a class ideology; but at the same time, because it worked through encouraging social emulation and the wider acquisition of a certain 'symbolic capital', it militated against immediate class closure.

Because so much of the rivalry between the chiefs and the educated was for the control of symbolic values, the symbolic boundaries as well as the actual membership of the two groups were constantly shifting. This was often concealed by an image of the direct replacement of one *kind* of leadership by another used by members of the educated group. P.O. Famogbiele, headmaster of Otapete School and political aspirant, wrote an article 'A Challenge to Ijesha Chiefs', in which he seemed to argue that the chiefs were an entirely outmoded form of leadership, fit only to be replaced by the educated:

> In the old days chiefs led Ijesha in war 'to rescue Ijeshaland from becoming the footstool of other tribes in Nigeria'. Weapons were then swords and guns. 'But the modern weapons with which to fight our present enemies like Illiteracy, Bribery, Ignorance and all sorts of social corruption is Education'. Let them not spend money on obtaining titles but on educating their sons, who would return 'with progressive political and administrative ideas ... to assume reigns [*sic*] of Government.'[13]

T.M. Aluko, writing as an engineer on Ilesha's town-planning problems, could write briskly of 'old customs and traditions giving way to new and superstition giving way to enlightenment', and proposed a means by which the Native Authority (by then controlled by the councillors) could surmount a major obstacle to its plans by taking over all urban and peri-urban chieftaincy land.[14] But in legitimating this proposal by commending Atakunmosa's 'planning sense', as evident in the grid-pattern of Ilesha's streets, he implied that the NA councillors were perhaps the true heirs of the old leadership, and invited a blurring of the attributes of the two groups. In any case, on the other side already the most formidable chief of *Ǫwa* Ajimoko II's reign was Jacob Rosiji Turton, eventually OBE, *Risawę* from 1943 to 1952, a former clerk in the Lagos Secretariat. He could pen an artful memorandum, and proved a real adept at presenting the traditional claims of chiefship in modern terms. Along with I.B. Akinyele, later *Olubadan* of Ibadan, he represented Oyo Province in the old, non-elected Western House of Assembly (late 1940s), belonged to a whole variety of government advisory bodies and was with difficulty dissuaded from seeking election as one of the two Ijesha members to the first elected House in 1951.[15] Conversely, the educated representatives eventually tended to find something irresistible in the red *akun* beads and the appellation 'Chief', even though it was usually a purely honorific title. More was carried over in the style of authority than the educated critics of the chiefs had imagined, and it was an easy token of communal identification for the politician. T.M. Aluko's splendid comic invention, 'Chief the Honourable Minister', lies at the end of this road.

The conflict of the chiefs and the educated at the local level, linked with the rise of nationalist parties at state level, has also invited analysis in class terms. Writing in 1953, Lloyd discerned the rise of 'new economic classes' behind the local government reforms.[16] In view of the links between the local elites and the nationalist leadership, this category may be identified with the 'rising class' which Sklar saw expressed through the political parties,[17] particularly the Action Group, eventually becoming the so-called 'political class' of the 1960s.[18] But it is important not to succumb to a teleology which explains a phenomenon in terms of what it was to become. The first question to be posed is whether the conflict of these rival political elites, the chiefs and the educated, has its basis in an opposition of local class interests. The answer may be anticipated: only very partially so.

Who, then, were the educated, considered as a potential class rather than as a status-group? Table 10.1 presents data on men elected as councillors in 1950, who may be taken as typical for the whole period, since most of them had served as Council members nominated by societies before then.[19] The dominant occupational profile is clear: varying amounts of education, sometimes followed by a spell teaching, and then a career in trade, often as an agent for one of the large trading firms. The teachers would have been more numerous were it not for the transfers which kept taking them away from town; significantly, the three teachers in the list were either at Ilesha Grammar School (where they were not subject to transfer, as it was managed by *Ęgbę Atunluşe*, not a mission) or owner of his own school (E.O. Ayoola's Temidire).

The Second World War had brought changes of both personnel and structure to the produce trade.[20] Despite the shortages and a changed pattern of metropolitan demand (for palm-kernels and rubber, instead of cocoa), the war had not been too bad for trade. The Government took over the purchase of cocoa at a fixed price, burning surplus stocks – so here the African traders at least enjoyed a guaranteed (though limited) and

Table 10.1 *Characteristics of Councillors elected in 1950*

	Age	Education	Occupation
J.O. Fadahunsi	50	2 years Wesley College	Big trader, managing director IUTTC
J.J. Ibironke	50	2 years, SS	Transporter, agent for J. Holt
E.A. Lufadeju	38	Standard VI	Trader
L.O. Omole	35	Standard V	Depot agent, UAC
E.O. Ayoola	54	TTC	Headmaster
D.D. Layinka	40	Higher Elementary Certificate	Teacher, IGS
J.M. Ajayi-Obe	52	2 years, SS	Salesman, J. Holt
C.A. Fajemisin	38	Diploma in Agriculture	Transporter (later lawyer)
A.R.A. Smith	56	2 years, SS	Agent for Paterson & Zochoins
M.O. James	54	Standard VI	Tailor
J.M. Makinwa	50	Standard IV	Trading and mining
M.O. Owotumi	56	2 years SS	Trader
D.O. Osunloye	36	Higher Elementary Certificate	Teacher, IGS
M.M. Popoola	55	TTC	Letter-writer, farmer
S.A. Lamikanra	58	TTC	Trader (later pastor)
R.A. Awobiyi	35	Class 2, SS	Trader
J.A. Turton	44	3 years, SS	Credit Customer, G.B. Ollivant & Co.

Note: SS = Secondary or grammar school. TTC = Teachers' Training Certificate. IGS = Ilesha Grammar School. IUTTC = Ijesha United Trading and Transport Company.

predictable market. After the war the government retained its monopsony through a Cocoa Marketing Board and licensed firms or traders as its Licensed Buying Agents (LBA). An LBA required to have capital of £6,000, storage-space, adequate transport and 'experience'. These conditions, tough though they were, did enable African agents to move up the buying hierarchy as LBAs. In Ilesha the first breakthrough was made by the leading member of the educated group, the man who topped the poll in the 1950 Council elections, J.O. Fadahunsi. In 1947 he was appointed to the Cocoa Marketing Board and in 1948 was the leading figure in a private company, the Ijesha United Trading and Transport Company, along with eight other partners, which became an LBA. Another joint enterprise, Western Produce Traders Syndicate, was founded by Fadahunsi's nephew S.A. Famuyide in 1952. The opportunities for transport also developed during and after the war. C.A. Fajemisin, having been the leading light of a new Motor Transport Owners' Union (1942), organized another joint enterprise, the Ilesha Transport Company, in 1944, to run passenger buses between Ilesha and Warri, Ibadan and Ilorin.[21] But, on the whole, the success of these joint enterprises tended to be short-lived: they were plagued with managerial disagreements and divided responsibilities, and the most capable and energetic of the individual partners gave their best efforts to their own projects. Prince Adeniran, the giant of the late 1930s, was virtually retired from the trade by the end of the war. The main rising star was his son-in-law, I.O. Ajanaku, who by 1944 had abandoned produce for his fleet of twenty-four lorries, though he also bought shares in Fadahunsi's Ijesha United Trading and Transport Company. He was not greatly active in public affairs, but two others were: J.J. Ibironke, Fadahunsi's closest associate in IUTTC and perhaps the largest cocoa buyer in the late 1940s, and Lawrence Omole, Ibironke's able young produce clerk during the war, appointed manager of IUTTC in 1945. Omole soon left for his own agency with UAC, his uncle S. Akinola (active as a councillor for most of the 1940s) standing surety for him, eventually building up the largest produce business in the 1950s, which he combined with transport.

For a few years IUTTC was very much at the centre of things. It brought together a group of the most influential men in the town and its network ramified widely, meshing with that of the councillors and the educational elite of the town, around the Grammar School. Moreover it was seen, in the words of Lawrence Omole, as 'a kind of economic nationalism'. The capital-raising functions of bodies like IUTTC were closely linked with the political demands of their organizers and of the educated leadership generally. They led to the setting up of the Western Nigeria Development Corporation in the early 1950s, which made loans to indigenous businessmen who had long felt that expatriate banks and companies were unsympathetic to their applications. Omole, Ajanaku and several others in Ilesha were thus helped on their way. The class interest most clearly linked with the rise of the educated here was that of a local commercial bourgeoisie against colonial commercial institutions. But it also had local implications. Fadahunsi was forthright at a meeting of the Council's Executive Committee in 1947 in expressing his fears that the government intended 'taking off the middleman in the trade'.[22] If there was a *local* class-interest opposed to that of the educated traders here, it could only have been the farmers'; but that could hardly express itself at all distinctly, for reasons outlined in Chapter 7. The farmers' profits were being invested in educating their children for non-farming employment; and it was their communal, rather than their class interests, which these children would champion through the emergent structure of electoral politics.[23]

Nor can the chiefs be very easily seen as an agricultural interest, despite the importance of agricultural incomes to them. More and more of them were retired traders or clerks, just drawing some income from their own or others' farming like other retired Ijesha; so the occupational differences between them and the educated councillors were also in good part a function of age.

The interests which divided chiefs and educated councillors and led to bitter conflict between them were not of a straightforwardly economic kind – that is, interests which are constituted fairly independently of political relations and hence possibly determinant of them – but were themselves an aspect of the changing political structure. The kind of compact between chiefs and traders which *Qwa* Aromolaran had established was no longer possible. Ajimoko II could not incorporate the educated from a position of strength. The ultimate reason for this was that they had become indispensable to the whole system of Ilesha's activities and relationships. They were the essential communal champions in the regional environment, and played the crucial agitational role in securing a major political breakthrough in 1948: an Ijesha Division, entirely separate from Ife.[24] The business of the Council grew steadily more complex and technical, and was increasingly conducted by the handful of educated representatives. The majority of chiefs sat silently through meetings and depended on the educated to interpret and explain documents and correspondence.[25] Power in the community, and with it wealth and the ability to consolidate their interests further, flowed to the educated. All this was deeply mortifying to the chiefs, who determined to capitalize on the one major asset which could not easily be rationalized out of their hands, and on which the commercial and educational interests represented by the councillors made increasing demand: land. It was thus over land that the interests of chiefs and educated councillors came into sharpest collision.

CHIEFS, LAND AND TITLES

This was the period in which Ilesha really burst beyond the confines of its nineteenth-century walls and began to assume the pattern of urban geography we see today. In the centre of the town stores and shops of all kinds had spread from their original location along Adeti and out through Orinkiran along the axis of the Oshogbo road ('A line', in the house-numbering system *Risawę* Turton had just devised) to all around the King's Market and down Okesha ('B line'); and from Ereja roundabout, where the memorial pillar to Ogedengbe would eventually be girt around with banks and petrol stations, through Ereguru and past Igbo Ose, where Obalogun's shrine ended up as the cemented forecourt of a produce store, towards the Ife road ('F line'). A great deal of this land lay in the former precincts of the *Afin* or around the *ile oye* of senior chiefs, particularly the *Ogboni* and the *iwọle*. The other area of development – leaving aside the more dense settlement of the quarters with dwelling houses – lay just outside the old walls, which was the zone of chieftaincy farms. Here were concentrated the larger commercial establishments (IUTTC and Ajanaku's transport to the north, Omole's to the east), Government quarters and offices (to the west), schools and colleges, the old and the new sites of Wesley Guild Hospital.

Formerly, when land in all locations had been plentiful and the dominant

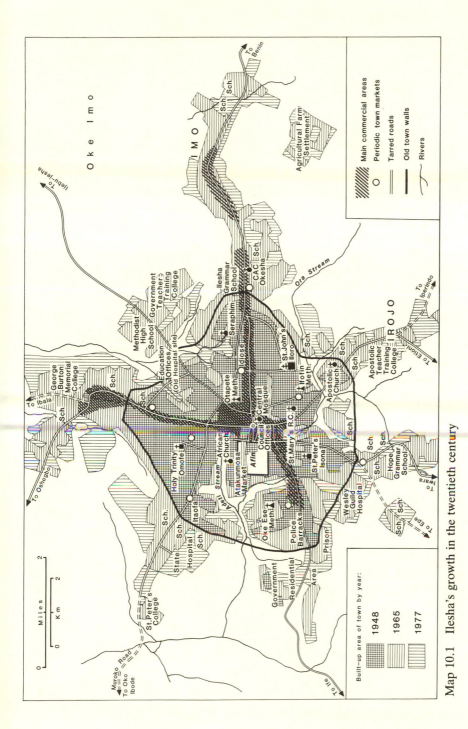

Map 10.1 Ilesha's growth in the twentieth century

concern of chiefs had been to attract subjects, only token payments had been made – and those to cement the social relationship between the incomer and his host. In the case of agencies like missions, they had approached the *Qwa* who 'directed' them to a chief with suitable land to bestow. In this way the Methodists had acquired their first hospital site just outside town on the Ijebu-jesha road from Chief *Ṣegbua*. Vacated sites simply reverted to the chief who 'owned' them. By the 1920s sites in particular places had begun to be sold for modest, but real prices, and the buyers, traders in the main, considered they were acquiring freeholds. There was a steady acceleration of the practice and the prices – land around the centre owned by Chiefs *Ogboni* and *Risawę* being in particular demand. Escalating site values and rents led, by the early 1940s, to sharp conflict and litigation between chiefly owners and the buyers.

On the one hand, many chiefs found to their chagrin that predecessors had alienated 'their' title land for a fraction of its present value, and even that present owners were deriving substantial incomes from it. They fought back with varying success:

> *Ogboni* Fapohunda (*c.* 1903–1941) had been persuaded by his son Seriki Ogboni, a trader, to let Jacob Arapate, another trader and Seriki's friend, build a house on *Ogboni* land in Idofin. Jacob eventually built 5 or 6 houses and let one to Compagnie Française de l'Afrique Occidentale for an annual rent of £35, giving £6 as 'present' to the *Ogboni*. His position was consolidated in the interregnum after Fapohunda's death, but the next *Ogboni*, Latunji (1944–58) wanted him off. However, Latunji settled for some payment as arrears.[26]

> *Risawęs* Adedeji (1900–1931) and Adedigba (1933–41) had let out buildings on *Risawę* land at Isida to John Holt. When J.R. Turton became *Risawę* in 1943, their children (who belonged to a different branch of the lineage from Turton) claimed these as their own property. Turton claimed one-third of any income as his own on the ground that the present titleholder enjoyed continuing rights in title land. The *Qwa* and other chiefs supported him, and the Resident upheld the claim.[27]

Similar problems arose with land alienated outside the old town.

> The Government Residential Area had been established on *Ohunǫrun* title land on the Ife road, and rents paid to the Native Authority. In 1947 the then *Ohunǫrun* demanded that it be paid to him. (A precedent for this shift was cited in the case of the CMS Bookshop, on *Lęmoǎu's* land in town). It was agreed that the *Ohunǫrun* should receive the rents from UAC and John Holt tenancies on the Government Residential Area, but the educated councillors objected, at least until 'land tenure rules' could be adopted. The DO suspended the issue.[28]

> In 1954 the Regional Government acquired from the Native Authority for £10,000 the old hospital site for a Teacher Training College. It had once been *Ṣegbua's* farmland, and the present *Ṣegbua* wanted £1,000 as comp-

ensation. Councillor J.J. Ibironke argued it would be a bad precedent to give the *Ṣegbua* anything, and the NA Executive Committee told him to approach the *Ọwa* for compensation.[29]

The concern of the buyers, consistently represented by the educated councillors, was to make sure that any land they 'bought' was thereafter free of any further claims from the chiefs. An imposing 'Resolution of the Ijesha Community' was passed on 8 October 1944 after a public meeting chaired by J.S. Oginni, Chairman of *Ẹgbẹ Atunluṣe*, and signed by leading literates as well as by members of *Ẹgbẹ Ọmọ Ibilẹ Ijeṣa*, *Ẹgbẹ Atunluṣe*, the Ijesha Literary Society, the two leading Muslim societies *Ẹgbẹ Killa* and *Bọrọkini* and the popular *oṣomaalo* society, *Ẹgbẹ Ayẹba*.[30] The presence of the Muslims and the *oṣomaalo* is clear evidence that this was not just the cause of an educated minority, but that there was a large actual or potential body of people with an interest in freehold tenure free from chiefly encumbrances. There was an additional reason, as the above cases show, why there was resentment against the chiefs. The corporacy of the lineage – that anthropologists' fancy! – was tried and found severely wanting: the chiefs did not spontaneously act at all as if they were the custodians of their lineage's or their quarter community's eternal and inalienable land-rights but as if they were quite free to treat title land as personal private property.[31] It was chiefs whose urban title land had already been largely disposed of, like Turton the *Risawẹ*, who argued for the inalienability of title land. Otherwise the legal indeterminacy suited the chiefs fairly well, and those with land in favoured areas pressed on with sales.[32] None was better placed than Aogo Falabonu the *Ṣọrundi*, whose title land stretched to the north of the town on the Oshogbo road, and who went ahead against the protests of other members of *Ṣọrundi* lineage.[33] There was, if anything, even greater resentment against the holders of non-lineage titles who made money from land-sales. Ogunmoyesin the *Ọbanla* fell out with the Okesha people over this, and it was a spokesman of *Ẹgbẹ Ọmọ Ibilẹ Ijeṣa* (of all groups, granted Ogunmoyesin's recent favour with them) who accused the *Lọkinran*, the *Ọbanla* and the *Lẹjọka* of pocketing the proceeds of land-sales, to their successors' impoverishment.[34]

Discussions in the Council and in its Land and General Purposes Committee to establish land tenure rules were drawn out into the 1950s but never reached a workable decision acceptable to both sides. The sale of land was necessarily accepted as a fact and past sales, notwithstanding the *Ogboni* and *Risawẹ* land decisions, were confirmed. Eventually the crux of the argument concerned the conditions and proceeds of sale, and hence the prerogatives of chiefs. In the case of hereditary titles, unviable schemes were put forward for land only to be sold with the consent of a majority of lineage members or of recognized heads of lineage branches (as if those were ever anything but highly contested); or the proceeds of sales to be divided among them. In the case of open titles, the councillors, playing the role of custodians of communal interests against the chiefs, proposed that

207

the proceeds should be divided in the ratio 25% to the chief, 75% to the Urban District Council. *Risawẹ* and *Ọbaodo*, rather piously regretting the sale of land, made a counter-proposal of 50:50, and a councillors' compromise figure of one-third: two-thirds went through. The *Ọbanla* protested to the end, but, as far as I am aware, the rules never became operative.[35] It remained possible for a living to be made by dealing in land.

The determination of the senior chiefs to make as much as they could while they could, must be seen in relation to the changing economics of chiefship. It was now becoming quite expensive to achieve one of the senior titles – in the 1940s several hundred pounds appears to have been normal, and contestants for the *Ọwa*-ship were by the 1950s laying out thousands, and required wealthy 'backers'.[36] This inflation occurred within a generation. Aromolaran, coming from his farm at Ileki in 1920, paid no more than £150 on becoming *Ọwa*, and is said to have helped Idaomi Falode, another farmer, with the wherewithal to make the expected gifts when he became *Loro* in 1929. The amounts paid varied from case to case, however, and when Ajayi Obe became *Lẹmodu* in 1913 he was required by Ataiyero and the chiefs to pay what was considered a sizeable sum for his installation: *ọgbọn ọkẹ* ('thirty bags') or £7 10s 0d.[37] But that was no more than an absolutely standard marriage payment; since then, marriage has got relatively much cheaper and chieftaincy a very great deal more expensive.[38] The increase in payments was linked with a change in their character. Previously, it seems, a candidate for a title was made acceptable by his social assets (e.g. character, performance in a lower title, closeness of connection with influential chiefs) rather than by his prior wealth, though if he *was* wealthy, he might be obliged, on 'joining the club', to transfer some of it to the existing chiefs, in such a way as to underwrite their ranking system. Inflation began when wealthy traders (like those in for the *Loro*-ship in 1929) started contesting titles. The old importance of social assets, often particularistic in character, tended to decline as the community got larger and more loosely integrated, and this was confirmed by the growing practice of people contesting titles after years outside Ilesha, so that they were not well known in the town. Cash, however, spoke a universal language of recommendation. It was unavoidable that higher levels of payment got built into the system, since candidates often went into debt in order to contest and needed to recoup from their anticipated shares from future contests. Whether the anticipation of proceeds from land-sales or from the possible acquisition of judicial powers played much part in first setting off the inflationary spiral, it is hard to say, though they certainly became an integral part of it. In sum, chieftaincy titles became investments, but rather risky ones.

The consequences were continuously evident throughout Ajimoko II's reign. He was much more the victim of the system than its architect.[39] Ajimoko himself must have paid well over £1,000 to get his crown. He is said to have paid £25 each to the *junior* chiefs, the *Ẹlẹgbaji* and *Ọmọdeọwa*. This greatly surprised them, since they normally received from the senior chiefs rather than directly but, as we have seen, they had an unusual political importance after the Riot. He even sent £50 to the DO, out of gratitude for having dropped his opposition, though this was returned![40] Opportunities to recoup were soon sought and by 1944, he was reported to be 'using his authority to enrich himself in one way or another'.[41] There were many complaints about the hangers-on at the *Afin* and the avaricious impositions of his *ẹmẹsẹ*.[42] Two major titles – *Risawẹ* and *Ogboni* – were vacant and presented opportunities. What Turton paid to be *Risawẹ* can only be guessed at, but it was probably substantial. The *Ogboni* contest was protracted, and went to a substantial trader, Samuel Latunji, retired from years in Dahomey.[43] The most significant aftermath was that three *unsuccessful* candidates, Falana, Layide and Onigbogi complained to the DO that sums of £165, £155 and £158 respectively had not been returned to them – only the successful candidate's offerings were meant to be taken – and Onigbogi proceeded to take the *Ọwa* to court. This kind of thing continued. When the *Lẹjọka* title became vacant in 1949 on J.D.E. Abiola's death, the contest was again drawn out and went to S.A. Falade, a retired agricultural officer.[44] But the *Ọwa* was accused of not sharing the money received from the candidates, and the case went against him in the Benin High Court when he sued for slander Asaolu Fowowe, an unsuccessful candidate who had declared publicly that he had given £430 to the *Ọwa* on the understanding he would be made *Lẹjọka*.[45]

These pressures on contestants had further knock-on effects. Urban and peri-urban land we have considered. But farmland also held out possibilities, particularly with the fresh post-war boom in cocoa-planting by strangers who were liable to pay *iṣakọlẹ* to the Ijesha owner. One *cause célèbre* concerned the farm at Bowaje, beyond Ifewara, belonging to the family of J.S. Oginni, the Chairman of *Ẹgbẹ Atunluṣe*.[46] An earlier dispute with local rivals had been settled in Aromolaran's time in Oginni's family's favour, supporting evidence having been given by Ajimoko, then still the *Lumobi*. Now Ajimoko took the case up again on the other side, and though the DO found against him, it dragged on into the 1950s. The prize was who should be declared 'landlord', to receive the tenants' *iṣakọlẹ*. No chief appears to have been under greater financial pressure than *Ogboni* Latunji, whose title had extensive land rights in villages of which he was *onile*, to the south-west of Ilesha. He had the additional problem that, having been absent for many years before his installation in 1944, he had great difficulty in knowing or establishing his full rights over tenancies established by his predecessor and against encroachments. In one village, Alaba, some of Chief *Ọdọle*'s people had got themselves well entrenched and, with some connivance from the *Ọwa*, were frustrating the *Ogboni*'s attempts to claim his dues.[47] This case went before the Executive Committee of the NA, and, as with the Bowaje case, showed up the *Ọwa* and chiefs in a poor light with councillors and people.

In view of the rising costs of getting titles, the uncertainty of their rewards and their declining real power, it may seem surprising that titles remained as important as they did. But until eclipsed by party politics in their intense phase after 1955, major chieftaincy contests were the form of political conflict into which most people were drawn, and no single episode of this period aroused greater passions or brought Ilesha closer to the brink of civil disorder than the *Risawe* contest of 1952–53. Chieftaincy contests tended to become vehicles for a whole series of significant social divisions to express themselves, as the individual contestants and their lineage segments sought to enlarge their wider communal support, and as other social groupings sought to strengthen their voice in the community through links with a successful candidate. They were also significant for a contrasting reason, precisely because a new kind of power, that of the educated councillors, was rising to overshadow the power of the chiefs, and that a new, steeper ladder of wealth and privilege was emerging. Against these trends the values – if not the practice – of chieftaincy enshrined a social critique: they were for the principles of the widest eligibility for office – any Ijesha could be the son of his father, the resident of a quarter – and a warning that leaders must not cut themselves off from their followers.

CHIEFTAINCY AND POLITICS: THE *RISAWE* DISPUTE

The political forms of Ajimoko II's reign showed a fluidity which was in sharp contrast to what had preceded them and what would follow: there was no longer any single strong centre of authority, such as Aromolaran had been able to provide, and conflict in the town was not yet absolutely dominated by the lines of political party. From 1951 to 1955 parties existed, but they were just one of several axes of conflict. Even the conflict between chiefs and educated, which has been singled out here because of its important consequences for the town's political structure, flared up in intermittent bursts, sometimes expressing itself through other kinds of conflict like chieftaincy contests, sometimes being displaced by conflicts between political generations, between town and district, or between individuals or factions aspiring to wield political influence.

It was a time ripe for political entrepreneurs. Although in the 1940s the active non-chiefly members of the Council were there as representatives (*aṣọju*) of societies or 'educated elements', the 'constituency' interest was often not very well defined in relation to specific issues, and the representatives were able to act as free agents in forming alliances or clientages. *Ẹgbẹ Ọmọ Ibilẹ Ijẹṣa* in particular, which had so recently expressed such precise interests, soon lost most of its character, to become not much more than the vehicle to promote the political career ambitions of its organizers. In fact it had split into two quarrelling factions by 1943, and the old hero Fadugba, disowned by one faction, went his own way.[48] Almost alone he spent his last years championing the cause of farmers who had not received proper compensation for damage done to their crops by the alluvial gold miners who were active in the area south-west of Ilesha.[49] Representatives came and went, and an effective speaker, like S. Akinola, might appear on the Council under different hats in different years. The most continuous and coherent grouping, steadily taking shape as the new political centre, was a circle of friends which met in E.A. Ekunseitan's house at Isokun and patronized the African Tennis Club. It had its origins in the NYM, many of its members formed a younger group in *Ẹgbẹ Atunluṣe* and its leading member was J.O. Fadahunsi.

Individual issues tended to produce *ad hoc* committees and spokesmen, bringing together different combinations of the politically active. The reception committee for Azikiwe, on his visit in 1946, was one such, leaving behind a small branch of the NCNC with Ekunseitan its Chairman and a younger man, R.A. Awobiyi, its Secretary. Other such issues included the renewed dispute with Ife over the boundary from 1947 to 1949, the agitation to secure Divisional status for Ilesha in 1948, and the canvassing of public opinion about Nigeria's constitution in 1949. These variously affected the political stock of those individuals who took them up and, to the extent that public opinion was dissatisfied with their performance, gave opportunities for new faces to come forward. The events of 1947–49, in particular, brought forth a new grouping, the Ijesha Patriotic Union (IPU), some of whose members formed an Ijeshaland Welfare Party (IWP), specifically over what they saw as the failure of Ilesha's representatives on the boundary commission to defend her interests.[50] But these bodies were less new social interests finding their voice in the political arena, than a new political generation launching itself on current issues of communal concern. 'Remember', declared the Secretary of the IWP, 'that the ... so-called irresponsible YOUTHS of TODAY shall become the famous, responsible historian [*sic*] CHIEFS, RICH and GREAT-MEN OF TOMORROW'.[51] The IPU drew its members from similar occupations as more established political groupings – traders mostly but with some teachers, but younger, mostly in their thirties; and it was the most abrasively nationalist in its tone.

It is indicative of the importance still attached to chieftaincy, that several disputes between the chiefs as individuals, sometimes arising from land-disputes and sometimes from apparently more trivial causes, created such public resonance. The greatest of these quarrels came to a head in 1949 and involved the *Ọwa* and Chief Turton the *Risawẹ*, occupying much of the Council's business for several months and on occasion disrupting it.[52] The young men of the IWP sided strongly with the *Ọwa* and the chiefs who wanted to discipline Turton, and the councillors (i.e. the older ones who represented *Ẹgbẹ Atunluṣe* or 'educated elements') had difficulty in restraining them. At one level 'there was nothing serious in it',[53] as one informant put it, but the trifling symptoms indicated the presence of a major conflict of values. *Risawẹ* Turton

211

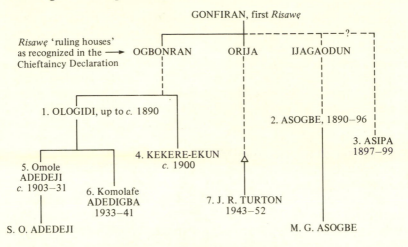

Fig. 10.1   Genealogy of *Risawę* families

Note: *Risawę* are numbered in order of title-holding from Ologidi, who is represented in most listings as seventh or eighth from Gonfiran. Before Ologidi, genealogical relations between title-holders (and even their relationship to the three
later-recognized 'ruling houses') are not clear or agreed. Continuous lines represent more or less real genealogical relationships, discontinuous ones notional but
generally agreed ones.

knew his own mind very well and did not hesitate on occasion to give
pointed advice to the *Ǫwa* on how he was to conduct himself. Though a
chief, his standards were very much those of the educated. He was thus
deemed by the administration to be a more appropriate representative of
Ilesha than the *Ǫwa* on bodies like the Oyo Provincial Council, where he
sat alongside the *Ǫǫni* of Ife and the educated Ibadan chiefs. The *Ǫwa*
must have felt himself quite upstaged by his *Risawę*. The *Risawę*'s fraterni-
zation with colonial officialdom – let alone Ilesha's communal rivals[54] –
raised further suspicions in the minds of the young IWP members, who
vehemently opposed the proposal that he should be charged with collecting
public opinion in Ilesha on the proposed new constitution for Nigeria.[55]

It was *Risawę* Turton's death on 15 May 1952 which unleashed the greatest
open conflict of Ajimoko's reign. As everyone in Ilesha anticipated, the
front-runner for the title was an elderly man, Michael Gureje Asogbe, who
had already twice contested unsuccessfully, in 1933 and 1943. He was a
trader of decent prosperity, a well-respected member of Otapete Methodist Church and of *Ęgbę Atunluşe*. After the death of his father Fasoyinu
Asogbe (*Risawę*, 1890–96), he had been sent to the *Afin* as an *ęmęşę*, and
was among that very first batch of sons of chiefs whom Ajimoko I had put
into school in the *Afin*. It very soon became clear that he was the man

212

whom Ajimoko II and the chiefs, with rare unanimity, wanted to install as the new *Risawẹ*.[56]

But his legitimacy was vehemently contested by the largest generally recognized branch of the *Risawẹ* lineage, the close relatives not of the late Turton but of Turton's two predecessors: Adedeji (*c.* 1903–31), and his brother Adedigba (1933–41). They argued that there were two 'houses': their own, named after Ogbonran, a famous early *Risawẹ*, and a much smaller group, usually named after Orija, which included Turton and his close kin. Their case against Asogbe had already been put by Turton back in 1941, writing effectively as the literate champion of both of these branches and in support of his own claim: Asogbe's father, though he served and was buried as a *Risawẹ*, was an interloper, installed by *Qwa* Bepo after the death of *Risawẹ* Ologidi because the wars had scattered all genuine sons of the lineage.[57] They said that this was also true of the next *Risawẹ*, Asipa (1897–99). Asogbe's people counterclaimed that they descended from a much earlier *Risawẹ*, Ijagaodun (genealogically represented as a son of the first *Risawẹ*, Gonfiran), though admittedly they had not enjoyed the title for many years in between.[58] Because the Ogbonran branch had held the title for so much a greater part of the past century than the others, they were able to muster much larger numbers to so-called '*Risawẹ* family meetings', thus adding plausibility to their claim that 'the *Risawẹ* family' – and according to one doctrine of Ijesha chieftaincy, it is families who 'put up' candidates for consideration by the *Qwa* and chiefs – disowned M.G. Asogbe. However, it is so common in chieftaincy disputes for rival families to impugn one another's descent, that Ijesha public opinion was not unduly impressed by this. In its view Asogbe had a much stronger argument: he could point to several ways by which his claim to be a genuine *Risawẹ* family member seemed to have been implicitly recognized by his rivals. His father (the later *Risawẹ*) was, so he argued, helped to marry by the mother of *Risawẹ* Ologidi of the Ogbonran line and used to send food to him during the Kiriji war. Later on, M.G. Asogbe himself had presented a case of gin to *Risawẹ* Adedeji on the latter's return from England in 1913 (and been asked for a further one!), and had provided several bundles of iron sheets, readily accepted by Adedeji, to re-roof the chieftaincy house. These were the kinds of practical mutuality which would be taken as telling evidence of kinship in an Ijesha court.

However, the issue was determined by external circumstances. The Ogbonran side had their own candidate, a son of Omole Adedeji's named S.O. Adedeji, a younger man who had served many years as a clerk and was Acting Treasurer of the NA. Within two or three weeks the battle lines had ramified right along several major fissures of Ijesha society. When the matter came before the NA Executive Committee on 13 June, there was a dual split: the *Qwa* and the *Ilesha* chiefs were strongly for Asogbe, announcing that the Ifa oracle had foretold a 'future prosperous tenure' for him; but the educated councillors strongly inclined to Adedeji.[59] The *district* chiefs, however, (the *Ogbonis* of Ibokun and Ijebu-jesha) aligned themselves with the councillors, even advocating (since they knew that together they formed a majority) the very uncustomary use of the ballot: 'modern things were being done today and this Committee should adopt modern method appointing chiefs'.[60] Despite the post-Riot reforms which were intended to bring forward district opinion in the Ijesha Divisional Council, the district communities were as aggrieved at Ilesha's hegemony as ever – indeed more so now, since the advent of party politics had held out new hopes for radical changes in their relationship with Ilesha. Throughout the later months of 1952, the only theme to rival the *Risawẹ* dispute in the pages of *West African Vanguard* was the grievances of the district towns against Ilesha.[61]

The councillors saw their support for Adedeji as part of a higher cause, the crusade for the triumph of 'enlightened' opinion. Fadahunsi, the leader of the councillors, was also Chairman of the Ijesha Higher Education Committee and of the directors of the Ijesha Press, publishers of the *Vanguard* (whose first issue came out two days before *Risawẹ* Turton's death and which found its first big cause in the support of Adedeji). Thick and fast came the metaphors of *ọlaju* in its pages. Let 'Light, Liberty and Service' be its motto; it was 'a light to lighten Ilesha and a glory of my people Ijeshas' to another correspondent; while a third saw that with education the 'veil is removed and the fetters of darkness and ignorance are broken and most naturally give way to the rays of light and hope, the spirit of progress and steady improvement for all and sundry'.[62] Lush was the language of vituperation of the chiefs. Why was it, asked an anonymous author in the *Vanguard*, that the Ijesha NA 'still dances to the tune of primitive drums'; and the chiefs were 'a conservative, frivolous and inconsistent aristocracy, whose utter selfishness, extreme self-assertiveness and great desire for personal self-aggrandisement has no compunction against following a course that is as unprogressive as it is unpopular'.[63] The educated made the mistake of talking so loudly that they only heard one another's voices; and they tended to monopolize the crucial channels of communication to the District Office. But still they knew that in any committee set up by the NA to 'represent' town and districts, chiefs and councillors, their opinion must prevail, since in that arena only the *Ọwa* and town chiefs were for Asogbe.

But in Ilesha at large the councillors' position was vulnerable. It was embarrassing that they should be, on this issue, in alliance with the spokesmen of district communities (opportunistic though the latter were) against the chiefly leadership of their own community; and communal sentiment in Ilesha swung strongly against them on other grounds too. They began to attract the characteristic opprobrium of an unresponsive political establishment. As one correspondent to the *Vanguard* put it, they were elected to report back regularly to their electors, not to 'function as ... Commandants of Battalions';[64] but they took decisions by themselves, neglected meetings and were disrespectful to the elders. Even more ominously it was asked, what had happened to the monies raised for the land case with Ife? The conduct of the senior councillors opened up again the split of political generations which had prevailed around 1947–49, but seemed healed when several of the younger IPU/IWP people had been elected councillors in 1950. For the councillors were not absolutely united for Adedeji: R.A. Awobiyi and D.O. Osunloye, younger men and both ex-IPU, were for Gureje Asogbe, and in June announced plans for the revival of the Ijesha Patriotic Union.[65] Osunloye (who was himself now headmaster of his own school, Orire Memorial) managed to strike a number of chords – Christian, customary and nationalist – in his plea to 'uphold the lawful authority of chiefs'.[66] The educated councillors, he argued, had forgotten to 'render unto Caesar':

> If you see how the literate Councillors treated the Chiefs, spoke to them and wrote articles in the papers to ridicule them, you would be ashamed of the kind of education those councillors got. Now it is wrong education if it makes you look down on your fathers [or teaches] that there is no other good custom besides Western culture.

But it was a new grouping, the Ijesha Tax-Payers Association (ITPA), which crystallized popular opposition to the councillors. The councillors had ambitious projects to develop Ilesha, in which better educational provision figured prominently, and were now permitted to levy additional local rates to do so. A Local Education Levy of 5s 0d was one of several proposed.[67] Ijeshas' natural sensitivity to increased local taxation was accentuated by the feeling that the councillors were intent on the systematic exclusion of the non-educated from influence. *Eniti ko ba kawe ko le joye baba rẹ* ('No one who is illiterate can take his father's title') was the doctrine attributed to them.[68] The populism of ITPA recalled the political stance of the now defunct *Egbẹ Ọmọ Ibilẹ Ijẹṣa*, and it does not surprise that some *Egbẹ* activists – J. Apoeso and E.A. Oke for example – were present when the *Risawẹ* issue was first taken up.[69] The key figures, however, were its President, S.A.K. Ilesanmi, a trader of Asogbe's generation, and its eventual Secretary, M.I. Ekundare, a young man with some secondary education who had been a clerk with the Motor Owners' Union but was now a shoemaker. Ilesanmi ranked very high in the estimation of respondents in the 1974 sample survey.[70] The qualities for which Ijesha admire him – time and time again he is called a 'gentleman', *ọmọluwabi* – themselves express a critique of patterns of elite behaviour emerging in the town, though not just from a traditional standpoint. His shop at Idi Ose market, just off Okesha, from which he sold cloth, was one basis of his popularity: he introduced new styles, was generous with credit, was unpretentious and affable. 'People liked him so much they'd invite him to their festivals.'[71] He had been a member of Iloro Church, where there was an *Egbẹ Ilesanmi* after him; later through his love of singing he was drawn to the Cherubim and Seraphim at Oke Eso, whose *Baba Ẹgbẹ* he became. His independent and disinterested judgment commanded wide respect. Though a founder member of *Ẹgbẹ Atunluṣe*, and hence a senior associate of such councillors as Fadahunsi and Ayoola, he was prepared to side with the chiefs against them over the *Risawẹ* issue; but he was equally forthright in his condemnation of the growing attempts by *Ọwa* and chiefs to demand *iṣakọle* from Ijesha farmers.[72] The ITPA started regular meetings at Ilesanmi's house at Idi Ose (which was, in fact, right next door to Gureje Asogbe's); and being situated half-way down Okesha, it was as if an unofficial *Ọbanla*, representing the common people, had come into existence as a counterweight to the new powers of the centre. Most significantly, the market-women of the town – to whom the reciprocities they enjoyed with traders like Ilesanmi and Asogbe meant more than the new values promoted by the councillors – were staunchly on Asogbe's side.[73]

The *Ọwa* and the town chiefs, despite the majority against them in the NA Council, were emboldened by their evident support in the town to press on with their intention to make Asogbe *Risawẹ*. This came to the ears of the DO who told them it would be 'wholly unconstitutional'.[74] None the less on 30 June, barely six weeks after Turton's death, Asogbe was installed as *Risawẹ* by the chiefs at the *Afin*.[75] That was the first ceremony, on a Friday; the *ije* ceremony when the chief, gorgeously clad, goes out in the town, was due for the third day. It was on the Sunday that Fadahunsi, the councillors' leader, heard at Iloro Church that Adedeji's people had performed their own installation at the *Risawẹ* title-house in Isida. On their way to see the DO, a group of councillors met a party of senior chiefs, including *Ọbanla* Ogunmoyesin and *Ogboni* Latunji, and their followers, dancing and singing war-songs.[76] A replay of the disorder of 1941 seemed all too likely. After an emergency meeting of the councillors in Otapete schoolroom, the Resident was requested to set up a commission of enquiry into the deadlock on the NA Council, which was now impeding other functions, such as tax assessment.[77] The *Ọbanla* and *Ogboni* were suspended without their salaries and the chiefs generally were told to return monies received from Asogbe pending an agreed solution. Another committee of the NA was set up which, because of its composition, was bound to recommend Adedeji.[78] The Tax-Payers continued to meet at Ilesanmi's, their support growing and the tone of their resolutions getting more exasperated. Asogbe's side won a moral victory in September when a deputation from the Council of Ijesha Societies in Lagos, largely composed of educated people, came to Ilesha, heard the opinions of all sides and strongly condemned the attempts of his rivals to rule Asogbe out:

Ọlọgbọn kan ko le tẹ ara rẹ n'Ifa, bẹni ọmọran ko le fi ara joye
As the wise man cannot initiate himself to Ifa, so the prudent man cannot install himself a chief.[79]

The DO temporized, though he clearly sided with the councillors. One must speculate a little as to the rationale of the eventual decision. The *Owa* had for several years back presented a weak image in the District Office files, and it was now part of the official wisdom that in this nationalist age, the educated elements were the real voice of public opinion. In any case, they were the chosen partners of the British in a peaceful process of de-colonization. On the issue in hand, there was the powerful and apparently disinterested voice from the grave of *Risawę* Turton, preserved on file! Moreover, *Owa* Ajimoko was known to be pliable. So – and this, too, is surmise – he was discreetly leant on throughout several months of seeming administrative inaction, until, by the extraordinary meeting of the NA Executive Committee on 22 January 1953, he had switched sides to the majority (carrying most of the Ilesha chiefs with him) for Adedeji.[80] When they heard, the ITPA wrote bitterly to the Resident warning 'the old man [i.e. the *Owa*] is now on the sure road to create confusion' and reiterating that Adedeji was 'not the choice of the people of the town'.[81] There was again delay, while more salvoes were fired by either side. But as Adedeji's triumph began to look more and more like a *fait accompli*, the issue shifted over to the question of the reinstatement of the suspended chiefs, where the councillors found it expedient to link up again with popular opinion. At a full meeting of the NA Council on 22 April, only two members – Councillors Awobiyi and Osunloye – still stood against the nomination of S.O. Adedeji; the Resident declared him to be the *Risawę*; and the *Obanla* and *Ogboni* were reinstated.[82] The outcome was a crushing personal blow for Gureje Asogbe, and he was rarely seen in public again.

This *Risawę* dispute can hardly be called typical of its kind, except as regards its broad genealogical conditions and the strategies of the most immediately interested parties. But its very untypicality makes it peculiarly symptomatic of this phase of Ilesha's history, set apart both from the days before chieftaincy disputes were affected by ideologically defined interests, as this one was, and from the time to come when party-political allegiance would overshadow all other forms of conflict. By 'ideologically' I here refer to the manner in which broadly conceived value-systems, such as the councillors' faith in education as the key to communal progress, were identified with particular candidates and so shaped the pattern of their support, instead of the fairly immediate, pragmatic or unrationalized inter-ests, mostly arising from personal connexions, which had hitherto almost solely governed the taking of sides in chieftaincy disputes. This did not just occur because political conflict linked to social change tends to produce 'ideology' in this sense, but because, with the growing mobilization of Ilesha's population to 'ideological' goals, this contest was played out in a much broader arena than chieftaincy contests usually had been. Con-sequently, a large number of people, who would once have been on the sidelines through lacking a direct personal connexion with the contestants, now felt they had a stake in the outcome. Indeed, 'ideology' was important enough in some cases to override what would have been 'normal' patterns of alliance, and produced surprising effects. While Fadahunsi, as the leading councillor, was strongly identified with Adedeji, his father-in-law, Ọdọle J.E. Awodiya, was the last of the senior chiefs to desert the cause of Asogbe.

The other striking feature of the *Risawẹ* dispute was the complete irrelevance to it of party-political divisions. Two rival parties, NCNC and AG, had been in operation for a year, and the two elected Ijesha representatives in the Regional House of Assembly at Ibadan, J.O. Fadahunsi and S. Akinola, had declared for NCNC and AG respectively. Party was a growing feature of town politics and within a few years would become all important. I wasted a good deal of informants' time pressing them about the party allegiances of actors in the *Risawẹ* dispute until once, having used the expression 'chieftaincy politics', I was firmly told that 'chieftaincy is one thing, politics is another'. Despite the fact that Fadahunsi (NCNC) was for Adedeji while Akinola (AG) was for Asogbe, this was for reasons unconnected with party; and the councillors' group in the dispute included AG as well as NCNC names. For a while in 1952–53 councillors and educated sympathizers of both national parties even combined to form an 'Ijesha National Party' to promote their shared values of local enlightenment;[83] and they were impartially condemned by the populist group of Tax-Payers (ITPA).[84]

But there is a point to this 'null hypothesis'. It serves to indicate what the next chapter will explore in depth: what a wholly different kind of division was introduced to Ilesha's politics by the exogenous force of party. The *Risawẹ* dispute also sheds crucial light on the NCNC's later mastery of Ilesha. While party did not contribute to the line-up of forces over the *Risawẹ* title, the Action Group seemed most likely to be its beneficiary. The core group of councillors (Fadahunsi, Ibironke, *et al.*) were NCNC, and the populist leadership of ITPA might have been expected to carry their rejection of them to the support of AG, especially since it was the AG parliamentarian who was their ally in the *Risawẹ* dispute. *Risawẹ* Adedeji was of known NCNC sympathies, while Guroje Asogbe's sons joined AG, eventually gaining recognition of their line, as 'Ijagaodun Ruling House', in the *Chieftaincy Declaration* approved by the Action Group government in 1961. But in fact it was the NCNC which came to draw its strength as a mass party from its incorporation of the bulk of the populist forces which first showed up in the *Risawẹ* dispute. It is no small tribute to Fadahunsi's political skill that he was able to repair the confidence put in peril in the *Risawẹ* dispute. The manner and consequences of this belong to an account of party politics.

11

Party politics

From the mid 1950s up to the military coup of January 1966, life in Ilesha was increasingly and at the end near-totally dominated by party political struggle. The rivalry of the two parties was not like that found in some other parts of Nigeria (e.g. the Tiv areas of the Northern Region),[1] where only one party had any real spontaneous local support and the conflict arose from the attempts of a rival party, based elsewhere but regionally dominant, to crush it. Both parties were substantially grounded within Ijesha society; the conflict, despite its external conditions, was the more severe because of the extent to which it was home-grown. Its violent climax was quite appalling to Ijesha themselves. Ijesha informants in 1973–75 almost uniformly spoke ill of oṣelu, 'politics', and many of those who only spoke Yoruba none the less often used the English words 'party' and 'politics' as if to renounce the legitimacy of these things which had once commanded so much local energy and commitment. Three specimen answers of respondents in the 1974 Sample Survey to the question 'What things have most held back the progress of the Ijesha?' convey what most Ijesha who had lived through it came to think of this period:

> awọn oṣelu l'o ba ilẹ yi jẹ, Ijẹṣa ko ṣe t'Ijọba
> the politicians spoilt this land – the Ijeshas didn't support the Government

> ija 'party' t'o kọja da ilu ru pupọ
> the former party struggles quite wrecked the town

> imọtara-ẹni-nikan, agidi ati oṣelu
> individual selfishness, stubbornness and politics

No academic study which takes it as a premiss that the values, beliefs and perceptions of the actors themselves are crucial to an adequate explanation of the phenomena in question can distance itself from these assessments. 'How was it possible?' is thus not just a moral concern of very many Ijesha but a question which can take us to the heart of the question of what kind of society Ilesha was, that it was vulnerable in the various ways we shall consider.

SOURCES OF PARTY POLITICS

Party conflict in Ilesha did not really begin until after the first elections (1951) which sent Ijesha representatives to Ibadan, where they became members of the two leading parties of the Western Region of Nigeria, AG and NCNC.[2] The NCNC, Nigeria's oldest nationalist party, had had a branch in Ilesha for upwards of five years, set up in the aftermath of Nnamdi Azikiwe's visit to Ilesha during his all-Nigeria tour of 1946.[3] J.O. Fadahunsi, who was to become Ilesha's political boss for the next decade or more, did not yet belong to the NCNC, though he was very closely associated with it through his friendship with E.A. Ekunseitan, its Chairman. Then there was Zik's Athletic Club, a popular recreational club which counted among its members a group of younger men, many of whom would later become active in party politics; several respected figures of the older generation (e.g. S.A.K. Ilesanmi) acted as patrons of it. Azikiwe had been the inspiration in the establishment of a number of clubs so called, throughout southern Nigeria in the early 1940s, to promote the cultural aspirations of modern-minded youths as well as to provide for their recreational needs. The Lagos leadership of the NCNC was also informally associated with Ilesha's communal aspirations through the continuing friendship of Fadugba with Ogedengbe Macaulay (son of Herbert Macaulay, the late founder of the NCNC), and Macaulay had given his support to the successful agitation to get Ilesha its separate Division in 1948.[4] The Haastrup connexion played a role here too.

As the lines of Nigeria's likely political development became clearer through the mid and late 1940s, the ethnic divisions nurtured in Lagos and other urban centres, especially between Yoruba and Igbo, grew in potential political importance.[5] A group of Yoruba nationalist activists led by O. Awolowo, most of whom had played some part in multi-ethnic political bodies like the Nigerian Youth Movement, founded an organization for the Yoruba, *Ẹgbẹ Ọmọ Oduduwa* (Society of the Sons of Oduduwa), first in London in 1945 and later in Nigeria in 1948. Its basic objective was consciousness-raising – 'generally [to] infuse the idea of a single nationality [i.e. as *Yoruba*] throughout the region'.[6] Though the Ijesha were probably no less spontaneously 'Yoruba' in their self-image than many other Yoruba sub-groups at this stage, they were not even initially enthusiastic about *Ẹgbẹ Ọmọ Oduduwa*. In April 1948 the *Ẹgbẹ* approached the NA Executive Committee for sanction to open an Ilesha branch, apparently with the support of *Risawẹ* Turton,[7] but Fadahunsi's response was cool. For the *Ọọni* of Ife's known role in the *Ẹgbẹ*, coming just at the time of the revived boundary dispute between Ilesha and Ife, strongly counted against its appeal to the Ijesha; and what really damned it in Ijesha eyes was a ritual performed to foster Yoruba unity, involving the sacrifice of five lambs in the name of five Yoruba rulers, the 'fingers of the Yoruba hand': the Ọọni of Ife, the *Alafin* of Oyo, the *Alake* of Abeokuta, the *Awujalẹ* of Ijebu-Ode and the *Ọba* of Benin.[8] The omission of the *Ọwa* seemed all of a piece with the colonial designation of the *Ọwa* as a 'second-class chief'. Ilesha's estrangement from *Ẹgbẹ Ọmọ Oduduwa* meant that her local political leaders were not among the men who founded the Action Group, which grew from it, in 1950 or attended its first conference at Owo early in 1951.[9] An AG delegation came from Ibadan and with the help of D.A. Ariyo, an activist in the IPU but not a councillor, held a public meeting. Their theme was that, under the new constitution, Nigeria's politics would focus on regions; Azikiwe had taken the NCNC to the East; and the Ijesha, as Yoruba, should opt for the party of the West. Fadahunsi told the delegates that if they had wanted the Ijesha to be for AG, they should have involved them in the initial planning of it. A number of people are reported to have joined the party after the meeting, but at this stage, they did not amount to much more than a scattering of individuals.[10]

The 1951 elections were based on a college of forty-three electors, literates chosen informally by quarter or village communities under the DO's supervision, sixteen from Ilesha and twenty-seven from the district according to the proportions of tax-payers.[11] Eight candidates put themselves forward, including some from the district, but, although the DO made it plain he would like one of them to be a district man, the two elected, J.O. Fadahunsi and S. Akinola, were both from Ilesha. The NCNC branch had stepped up its activity during the run-up to the election and claimed pledges from most of the candidates to declare for it. Fadahunsi and Akinola went to Ibadan where, amid many other Independents, they were furiously wooed by the two party organizations. Accounts now given of how and why they opted the ways they did are contradictory, but it was not surprising that they should go different ways or that Fadahunsi, in view of his past associations, should declare for NCNC.

Only after the election did the two parties seriously set about building popular support within Ilesha. But it was only in 1954–55, with the first real federal election and the prospects of a major local government reform, followed by local elections, that party-politics started to sweep all before it. Before a satisfactory account of local processes can be given, the political logic imposed by Nigeria's federal structure, which provided their wider environment, must be appreciated.

Structurally, party politics may be seen as the interplay of three major orders of institutions: a hierarchy of communities, a tiered administrative structure and a duality of parties.

'Community' itself is an elusive, though apparently indispensable notion in the explanation of Nigerian political behaviour. Post concludes his detailed study of the 1959 election by arguing that, instead of seeking an account of individual voting behaviour, we should rather seek the determination of communities' party preference, since community membership so strongly shaped individual opinion.[12] But there is a major difficulty with this view, as Dudley has pointed out.[13] 'Community' does not have a definite content, for it may be said to exist in some sense at several levels from the household through units like quarter, village or town up to entire ethnic groups. This means that we can never assume that any particular level of community has an automatic relevance to party preference. And that openness is extremely important here since different levels of the communal hierarchy are frequently found producing different aggregate preferences, producing a whole series of electoral minorities which also require explanation. If the 'communal' choice of the Yoruba was AG, we have to explain Ijesha attachment to the NCNC; if Ilesha was for NCNC as a community, what are we to make of the AG loyalties of certain quarters and villages? Any notion of 'communal choice', as a general principle to explain the preponderant party allegiances within the major regions of Nigeria, tempts us to seek other ways of explaining the preference of minorities and soon leads us deep into a thicket of unsatisfactory antinomies: individual/communal, interests/values, instrumental/expressive. In any case, particularly where there were fairly unified communal interests at local levels at the beginning of the period of electoral politics, communities were often content to follow their leaders into what *they* considered the appropriate party.

The concept of community, as such, implies a collectivity which appears to its sub-sets, right down to individuals, to be a vehicle both of common interests, and of common values, expressing the sentiment of community members, usually dependent on the possession of common symbols like language, that they belong together or share a 'consciousness of kind'. Each of these aspects possesses a degree of autonomy, but in general they provide sustaining conditions for one another: consciousness of kind justifies and facilitates the pursuit of common interests, and a stable continuity of interests helps build up the shared symbols through which consciousness of kind is realized. But it does not follow that, because the sub-units of a community share common interests *vis-à-vis* the outside, there may not be divergent interests within as regards the subdivision of goods jointly achieved. Precisely *that* is the key to Yoruba political complexity. Typically the division is both unequal and contested, right down to the most nuclear unit above the individual, the household. A community interest, at any level from household up to the Yoruba as an ethnic group, has to be represented by spokesmen drawn from particular sub-units, who thus gain advantages over other sub-units in the subsequent distribution of benefits acquired on behalf of the entire community. If the potential payoff seems to justify it and the opportunity is given, these other sub-units within the community (which are themselves lower-order communities) may find it advantageous to make common cause with the community's rivals at a higher level.

In order to make this analysis less abstract, we have to specify the notion of community more precisely in the terms of Yoruba culture. The Yoruba word which comes closest to 'community' in English is *ilu*, which is also the root of the Yoruba term for 'politics', *oṣelu* (lit.: 'the business of the *ilu*'). Concretely, however, *ilu* is a 'town' with its dependent territory including subordinate settlements, so no clear terminological distinction is made between, say, Ilesha as the capital and the 'kingdom' of Ijeshaland which by 1951 was for practical purposes coterminous with Ijesha Division.[14] Now the lower-order communities within an *ilu* like Ilesha/Ijeshaland which might dissent from the communal leadership because of a feeling that communally acquired resources might not be divided in their favour or even used against them, were of two quite distinct kinds. They might be aspirant *ilu* on their own account, such as the large district towns like Imesi-Ile or Ipetu, that is lower-order units with a very enduring character; or they might be groupings within the capital which, even when they do represent enduring lower-order units like quarters within Ilesha, are in fact rather more adventitiously in opposition to the prevailing political expression of their higher-order communal interest. But to oppose what is generally defined as a communal interest, *tout court*, is not a morally feasible position for a Yoruba politician to adopt, even if that is how his opponents will limn it. It is a premiss of Yoruba political culture that communities have undivided interests, and spokesmen of a dominant version of that interest will therefore deny that dissentient sub-units can be communities in the same sense. Opposition must therefore be accompanied by attempts to redefine the relevant community, typically by fixing it at a different level. The concept of hierarchy of communities itself remains a shared presupposition of all sides in this political argument. The logic of their respective situations led the two categories of dissentients to different responses. The major political voice of the *ilu* of Ilesha was NCNC. The larger subordinate towns which turned predominantly AG were following an age-old strategy: to move their communities up the hierarchy, making themselves the effective *ilu* for the representation of their interests at higher levels instead of Ilesha. The AG opposition within Ilesha could not do this, but made it their central argument that the Ijesha should see their interests as lying in a closer identification with a yet higher-order potential community, namely the Yoruba ethnic group as a whole.

Although by the 1960s it had become common to regard 'ethnic groups' like the Yoruba as the highest-order communities, no shared values of a 'specific cultural group'[15] can be considered as providing a *sufficient* explanation of alliances within the Nigerian political field. Rather, one key to explain how 'the Yoruba' *became* much more of a community over the years of party politics lies in appreciating how the tiered administrative structure affected the definition of communities. An interest-group tends to be formed, at any level below the state, wherever powers to accumulate and redistribute resources and to punish and direct activities are concentrated. States vary, of course, in how much they devolve these powers to lower levels and in how far powers of different kinds are linked and so concentrated at particular levels. In Nigeria in the early 1950s, two levels exhibited such a definite concentration of power. Firstly, there were the three Regions (West, East, and North), with their own elected governments, judiciaries and police forces, and statutory corporations; and the overall system of revenue allocation strongly favoured regional autonomy since it meant that most revenue was spent in the Region where it was generated. Secondly, these were the major units of local government. Their character varied a good deal within and between the Regions, depending on local political and settlement patterns, but for the Ijesha as throughout most of Yorubaland, it was the Council which corresponded to a Division. (The old Provinces, with their Residents, were done away with in 1953.) By the Local Government Act (1952), the very first measure of the first African Regional Government, the Councils enjoyed very substantial devolved powers: they assessed personal taxation and were allowed to retain most of it locally; they were empowered to raise a variety of local rates; they employed sizeable local staffs (including Local Government Police) and awarded contracts for a wide range of public works. Communal interest-groups variously sought to capture these regional and local power-centres or, if they deemed themselves to be permanent minorities, sought to dismantle them. And to the extent that these power-centres seemed to be permanent features of the political structure, they tended to consolidate those emergent communities which could hope to control them. It was thus in relation to the Western Region of Nigeria that the Yoruba completed their formation as a communal interest-group. In sum, a continual and unending process of mutual definition was (and still is) played out between the hierarchy of communities and the administrative structure.

Party was the essential catalyst in this process, for it was the means by which communal interest groups at various levels sought to capture or modify the administrative structure. Though a two-party system may seem the obvious and natural expression of a series of formed communal oppositions (e.g. Ilesha v. the district, Ijesha v. Ife), it came as an external fact, the product of a wider-than-Ijesha arena. It is a rather striking fact that the Yoruba within the Western Region were so much more divided between two parties than either the Hausa or the Igbo in their respective heartlands, but a convincing explanation in terms of some distinctive ethnic trait has yet to be found.[16] The historical accident that the Yoruba region, including Lagos, was the cradle and cockpit of pan-Nigerian political divisions, ensured that Yoruba communities were from the beginning presented with an effective choice in the organized political instruments for their aggrandizement. The complex mesh of inter-*ilu* and town/district rivalries yielded plenty of potential support for both parties. And the concentration of devolved powers at two distinct levels below that of the Nigerian state enabled both parties to dig themselves in against sanctions deployed against them at levels controlled by their rivals. Thus the NCNC's control of the powers of Ilesha Divisional Council enabled it to hold out for a long while against the hostile AG government of the Western Region; the local AG, based in certain Ijesha communities and a handful of Ilesha quarters, was sustained in its struggle by belonging to the ruling party at Ibadan; and minority interests in all Regions were helped along by their membership of, or alliance with, parties dominant in other Regions. Most West African countries slipped over fairly quickly to one-party rule during the period of nationalist mobilization and the early years of independence, and most of the mechanisms by which this was done were present in Nigeria.[17] The complexity of Nigeria's governmental structure as well as her cultural heterogeneity guaranteed that for the Ijesha party-conflict would be long-drawn-out and bitter.

As we move from structures to individual behaviour, that is, to the real site of explanation, the notion that solidary community interests govern party preference at once takes a severe knock. What impresses when we examine political choice in detail is how often very small communities – such as the small agnatic lineages of two or at the most three generations' depth which constitute the bulk of 'family meetings' in Ilesha – became politically divided right at the start. A few striking examples may be cited:

> E.A. Fajemisin was approached in the early 1950s by the people of Itapa village where his father had farmed, to press for the remaking of the Etioni road. NCNC had a small majority on the Council, so he declared for them the better to get it. In fact he was already inclined that way, having been chairman of Zik's Athletic Club in the 1940s. Later he was, for NCNC, Chairman of Ijesha Southern DC. His elder brother S.A. Fajemisin, a trader at Kano, was an early supporter of AG, attended the Owo conference in 1951 and urged Ijesha to support it as Yorubas. A younger brother, C.A. Fajemisin, joined AG in London where he was training as a lawyer 1950–54, and was later very active as a candidate and party stalwart, though he was defeated when he stood in his family's quarter, Ifofin, against M.I. Ekundare in 1958. B. Olowofoyeku, who was also training as a lawyer in London at the same time, later joined NCNC, partly through the offices of E.A. Fajemisin, to become Ilesha UDC Chairman in 1958.[18]

At least in leading families, the divergence of first cousins or half-siblings seems commonplace:

> Of Chief J.D.E. Abiola's children, his eldest son A.D. Abiola, produce examiner and contractor, supported AG, becoming chairman of a tax assessment committee when they took over Council in 1960. His brother Gabriel, clerk with the NA, was for NCNC, to which he drew his sister Mabel (Mrs Aluko), a teacher, who became secretary of the NCNC women's section.[19]

The most politically active of the Lufadeju family was E.A. Lufadeju, Councillor from 1950, who declared for AG and lost his seat in 1955, but was appointed to the AG caretaker Council in 1960. Other members of his family were NCNC: his brothers Gbadebo, who was the NCNC caucus's first choice for the *Ǫwa*-ship in 1957 and S.O. Lufadeju, a forestry official with the N.A. S.O.'s mother, Mrs Lufadeju, was at one time leader of the NCNC women's section. One of their sisters was wife of E.A. Ekunseitan, NCNC's first Chairman.[20]

D.O. Aluko-Kupoluyi belonged to AG from the beginning – indeed his Banuso Hotel was meeting place of the Ilesha Club in the 1940s, a social network which connected with AG as the African Tennis Club had with NCNC. Later he served as an AG agent. His half-brother E.T. Okelola (*Baba Onikoko*) was an NCNC stalwart and for a while party Chairman.[21]

In 1961 D.L. Ibidapo-Obe, railway-pensioner and AG field Secretary, brought charges against his neighbour, the secretary of NCNC for Isinkin quarter. His own first cousin J.M. Ajayi-Obe was Councillor for Isinkin and one of the top members of NCNC in the town.[22]

Variety in the influences which led to individuals' choices very often had their origins, for these men and women from important polygynous households, in links deriving from their mother's side. As far as I am aware, in none of the above cases did party sunder *ǫmǫiya* (children of the same mother). In other cases matrilateral and affinal connexions seem to have sustained party networks. *Ǫdǫle* Awodiya's compound at Ifofin, for example, linked the NCNC leader, Fadahunsi (who had married Awodiya's daughter) and its major organizer, Ekundare (whose mother hailed from there). A maternal link lay between S.A. Famuyide, NCNC councillor for Iwere and eventually one of the party's major figures, and his uncle, Fadahunsi. Pa J.F. Longe, on the other hand, was the focus of an AG network: his son, Daniel Longe, was an early member, as well as his two eminent sons-in-law, S. Akinola and E.O. Ayoola. Still, beyond the household with its resident members who were presumed to share a party allegiance determined by its head, there were few pre-given ties, whether of kinship or association, which compelled or prevented a particular allegiance. It may have been the case that party came so easily to cut across other valued ties precisely because it was not at first anticipated where it would lead, so was in many cases adopted rather casually. What we have to explain is how it went on to create such fierce commitments.

There are, however, some general tendencies behind the idiosyncrasies of individual choice. Since the existing core political leadership – reaffirmed in a mini-election to the Council in 1952 – was now clearly NCNC, and the NCNC also had some claim to represent itself as the real voice of Ilesha's communal interest, it is convenient to look at AG support as a deviant case. The AG did not arise from a distinct class or occupational base – with one significant exception, to be considered shortly – but tended to coalesce from a variety of groupings that happened to be, at this particular period, 'eccentric' – distanced in some way from the NCNC-inclined core group. This might come about in various ways: youth, passing disfavour with the existing political centre and, of course, belonging to a district community.

The AG drew less than might have been expected from a younger political generation.[23] As we have seen, one had emerged in 1947–49 to form the IPU/IWP grouping but, by the time the AG appeared on the scene, most of them had joined NCNC. Some of them did switch, for a variety of reasons, to AG – Ariyo, Osunloye, Omole somewhat later and Awobiyi much later – but others remained stalwarts of NCNC – L. Amokeodo, M.A.K. Eso and J.K. Dare. Somewhat overlapping with this group was another, with little or no prior NCNC involvement, which met socially at the Ilesha Club and the Banuso Hotel in the centre of town. They were younger than the NCNC-linked circle of the African Tennis Club (Fadahunsi, Ekunseitan *et al.*) and gravitated to the AG: men like S.O. Thompson, I.O. Ajanaku, D.O. Oguntoye of Imesi-Ile, Daniel Longe. But it must be stressed that these were rather fluid groupings, and do not provide a sufficient explanation of party membership.

The same has to be said about transient political 'outness'. In any Yoruba community we expect to find the family and favourites of the preceding *ǫba* to be rather thrust out in the cold by the turnabout which brought the new *ǫba* and his people to the centre. This had been the case with the Haastrups and their associates in the early years of *Ǫwa* Ataiyero's reign; and the close relation between the 1941 Riot, directed at the circle round *Ǫwa* Aromolaran, and the succession of *Ǫwa* Ajimoko II implies a similar situation. Despite the antagonisms between the *Ǫwa* and the educated councillors, the *Afin* was still a significant power centre and there were established links between the Haastrup family and the NCNC circles in Lagos. It is thus not surprising to find many members of the Aromolaran/Bepo family and others of the late *Ǫwa*'s circle turning to the AG. Prince Adeniran supported it, as did his son-in-law I.O. Ajanaku; two other Aromolarans, presumably sons, were party candidates in the 1958 local elections and F.A. Bepo (nephew) was forward in the AG from the early 1950s. Most of J.F. Longe's connexions were AG supporters, though, as we have seen, only some of J.D.E. Abiola's. The connexion is far from being perfect, since other circumstances, such as employment in the Native Authority or some subsequent quarrel or alliance, might affect party choice. The activists of *Ęgbę Ǫmǫ Ibilę Ijęṣa*, who played such a role in giving Ajimoko II his crown, and whom we might expect to be NCNC, do not seem to show a definite overall preference. In fact many of the *Ęgbę*'s activists, perhaps because their imprisonment had long disqualified them for public office, seem to have resented the mainstream NCNC leadership for having, as they saw it, taken over their populist inheritance. 'Ogbigbo politician' was a phrase used to castigate their opportunism, and it is hardly surprising that some of them found their last opportunity with the NNDP in 1964–66.[24]

What of occupation, that staple source of explanation for party-political choice? Here, teachers were the only group, according to the 1974 Household Survey, to show a markedly divergent preference from the community at large: in a community where around 60% supported NCNC, teachers were 58% for AG.[25] There would seem to be two reasons for this. Firstly, teachers were likely to be, from their training and work experience, the most advanced in a specifically 'Yoruba' consciousness, and so the most drawn to a party which clearly expressed it.[26] This was reinforced – since teachers were so influential in the national AG – by that party's particular respect for the teacher's ideal of *ọlaju*, which it put into effect in Western Nigeria's greatest piece of social legislation, the act establishing free primary education in 1954.[27] The few other links discernible between occupation or economic position and party seem to be less the cause than the consequence of the parties possessing power at particular levels of the state. Contractors (i.e. men dependent on small building contracts given out locally) were, according to the 1974 Survey, net supporters of NCNC in the same proportion as the community at large. Conversely, Ilesha's very largest commercial/transport magnates supported 'the government of the day', which until 1962 was AG: thus they assured themselves of substantial loans and continued government support. It was, among other things, Ajanaku's clear perception of these likelihoods that led him to AG support around 1950, though the loan he received was hardly crucial to him.[28] Omole – who may again have had other reasons, S. Akinola being his kinsman – was more decisively helped, leaving NCNC (of which he had been Treasurer) for AG. Other Ijesha AG supporters received loans too, though they did not make such successful use of them.

The final distinct source of AG support, in the district towns, did not become immediately evident, since their earliest educated representatives from back in the 1940s – men like S.M. Ogunjulugbe or C.O. Komolafe of Ipetu-Ijesha, E.A. Sajuyigbe of Ibokun and B.O. Orioke of Ijebu-jesha – tended to adhere to the NCNC. This was because the NCNC was a locally dominant alliance through which they could best hope to exercise influence; but within it they could be very trenchantly critical of Ilesha's domination of the district. AG support was initially concentrated in some of the remotest subordinate towns like Imesi-Ile and Esa Oke which were in many ways more akin to Ekiti. It was only after 1955, when the regional government at Ibadan seemed likely to stay in the hands of the Action Group, that NCNC lost its control of a large part of the district.

ELECTORAL POLITICS

A first public test of party – or at least of politicians identifiable by party – came in May 1952 when a small, still indirect, election was held to fill 9 vacant Ilesha councillors' seats.[29] Voting for the top 12, out of 27, candidates was as follows:

J.O. Fadahunsi NCNC   128
J.M. Ajayi-Obe NCNC   112

J.J. Ibironke NCNC	96
E.O. Fajuyitan AG	69
L.O. Omole AG	61
S.A. Famuyide NCNC	59
E.O. Ayoola AG	57
M.O. James AG	55
O.A. Williams NCNC	53
M.M. Popoola NCNC	48
E.A. Lufadeju AG	45
L. Amokeodo NCNC	44

The NCNC core group has lost none of the popularity it had enjoyed from before the days of party, and NCNC candidates overall claim some 60% of the votes. But a respected AG councillor might come well up the poll and, until 1955, when a new Council based on direct election to single-member constituencies took office, about half of the Councillors for Ilesha were in fact AG. From this we may infer that party had so little entered the electors' consciousness that the party complexion of elected bodies was purely a side-effect of the councillors' own choice of party. What, then, were the conditions under which Ijesha would vote for a party rather than for the other-than-party attributes of a candidate?

The electoral data show that rather different conditions governed local and parliamentary (whether federal or regional) elections. It was in the latter that party first appears to structure choice. Neither of the two candidates for Ijesha Division in the 1954 federal election was an Ilesha man: C.O. Komolafe (NCNC) was from Ipetu and J.A. Akinyemi (AG) was from Ifewara, both of them school teachers.[30] Komolafe won a decisive victory with 76% of the vote overall, rising to 81% in Ilesha itself; Akinyemi only took Imesi, Esa Oke, most of Ibokun, a handful of other northern towns and one ward of his own Ifewara.[31] The total poll, however, was very small (just over 12,500), which suggests that only the most politically aware were voting. The NCNC success – the greatest it ever won in terms of proportions of the poll – would seem due to two factors. Firstly, the AG had only just begun serious attempts at mobilization of support through campaign tours, and the NCNC could still capitalize on its head-start as the party known to the Ijesha and preferred by the most popular councillors, and so the fit vehicle for their higher representation. Secondly, Ijeshaland conformed to the general trend of this election, which saw the AG, despite its success in 1951, slip into second place behind the NCNC in the Western Region overall. The AG regional government had lost a good deal of popularity through additional levies for health and education schemes which had not yet borne fruit, and it had not yet been able to use patronage and administrative sanctions to curtail the appeal of its rival. Ilesha's participation in the winning side in this federal election, though it did not affect AG control of the regional government, did,

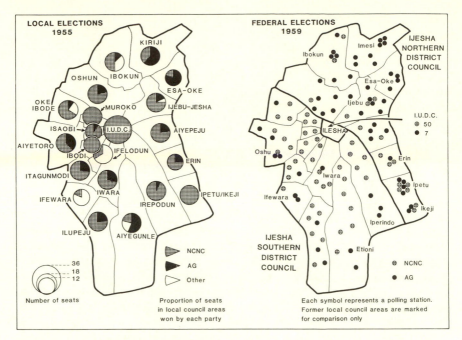

Map 11.1   Ijesha politics, 1955–59

however, considerably boost the prestige of the local NCNC. It encouraged Ijesha (or at least the people of Ilesha and the southern districts which were sociologically close to it) to think that their best means to success lay through the party in which they were influential overturning their rivals' control of the Western Region at the next opportunity (1956), rather than through abandoning the NCNC for what was still the party of Government at Ibadan.

The next contest came early in 1955, at the first elections under the new structure of local government, and they were the first at which local councillors were chosen through wards or constituencies by direct election. The old Native Authority Council, a single body to govern the whole Ijesha Division, was finally abolished.[32] In its place was a two-tier system, with powers divided between the Ijesha Divisional Council on the one hand, and an Ilesha Urban District Council (IUDC) with 24 local councils on the other. Members were elected to the latter (along with a small number of chiefs designated as 'traditional' members), and they in their turn nominated members to sit on the Ijesha Divisional Council. The distribution of seats in the new first-tier councils seems to show a marked polarization, three (Kiriji or the Imesi area, Esa Oke and Ifewara) going decisively AG, while the NCNC swept the board elsewhere, including Ilesha itself.[33] But this is deceptive. From the very partial voting figures

230

which are all that is available, relating to fifteen of Ilesha's electoral wards, it would appear that the elimination of AG representation from Ilesha's councillors was achieved with a significantly lower overall vote for NCNC candidates (65%) than had been achieved in the previous year's federal election (81%).[34] Why was this; and why were 'independent' candidates so strongly in evidence in this election?

This was a *local* election. Consequently the candidates were known to all the electors in their ward for all sorts of other things besides party: there might be many other grounds besides AG sympathies for voting against an NCNC candidate. A certain level of 'AG' support, higher than one would find in the impersonal conditions of a parliamentary election, is thus to be expected – quite apart from any consequences of AG's vigorous electioneering.[35] Direct elections at local level opened up new career opportunities for a wide range of people – many of them petty traders or contractors – of less education and lower status than the typical councillor of the preceding period. If a party's nomination (especially the NCNC's) were not to be had, either for his town quarter or his village, a man might still feel he could be elected on the basis of his personal qualities and connexions. Two were: Seu Arowojobe, a former teacher and goldsmith, and now a dealer in land, who had previously been a councillor for Ijebu-jesha in the old Council, but now wanted to represent his own Isida/Odo Agbede/Ode Esira ward in town and had to run against the official NCNC candidate under his own symbol, a lantern;[36] and S.B. Farodoye, a retired *oṣomaalo* and popular trader, son of a former *Lodifi* and well-connected enough to contest the *Ọbanla*-ship in 1958, who carried Idifi/Idio ward as an independent.[37] Both then declared for the NCNC.

These cases indicate both the limitations of NCNC organization as well as its substantial prestige as *the* Ijesha party. One source of this was local opinion's profound dislike of party-political conflict, which was widely seen as an exogenous force to divide the local community, and consequent eagerness to embrace one party as *its* party. Because the NCNC held the ground, and had done so well in the recent federal election, the AG had to take the electoral offensive, and its vigorous intrusions can only have further served to stamp it as an alien force. Hence, it would seem, the reluctance of many of those who were obliged to oppose NCNC candidates to stand as AG candidates. In the Ilesha wards of which we have full details, 'independents' (many of whom were or would become AG adherents) did better overall than declared AG candidates, getting 40% compared to 27% of the vote against NCNC opponents.[38] In rural Ijeshaland the weaker of the two major parties tended to win fewer seats than independents. The same phenomenon occurred in areas where the AG was considered to be the community party, such as Kiriji, for here its opponents used the 'independent' label to avoid branding themselves NCNC (i.e. as belonging to Ilesha's party). The most interesting case was Ifewara, J.A. Akinyemi's town, whose political logic was pointing ever more strongly to an AG takeover; here the break with their previous NCNC representation was effected by a bloc of candidates who contested as Independents and later passed smoothly into the AG. After this election, the delicacy of going 'independent' was no longer plausible: if one was not NCNC, one had to be AG.

The local elections of 1955 saw the origins of the NCNC's remarkable popular organization, though it was only fully realized afterwards, when the party had the responsibility for conducting local government. In mid 1954, in preparation for the election, M.I. Ekundare, the radical shoemaker of Ifofin quarter and former secretary of the Ilesha Tax-Payers Association, was appointed NCNC organizing secretary for Ijesha Division. Rather surprisingly, we find that as late as September 1954 at least some of the ITPA leadership, no doubt still distrustful of Fadahunsi and the NCNC councillors whom they had pitched against in the *Risawẹ* dispute, wrote from Pa Ilesanmi's to tell the DO they wanted to contest the elections as a separate party, with salt as their voting symbol.[39] But this plan was dropped and the populist tradition of the ITPA was brought by Ekundare to the NCNC.

The fact that the NCNC had hitherto had much less of a distinct local party organization than the AG was a positive advantage since it was not inhibited from taking on as its own the representatives thrown up more or less spontaneously by the quarters. Mistakes could be made, like the failure to endorse Arowojobe in Isida; but in very many cases the man who emerged as the NCNC candidate had several years of quarter responsibility behind him, like Ekundare at Ifofin or B.B. Makinwa at Lower Okesha, who had both served as clerks/secretaries to their quarter elders.[40] Makinwa also helped to get the representative for Upper Okesha, his cousin, O. Siyanbola, elected. Siyanbola was the son of a former *Ẹjẹmọ* of Okesha, who had just come back from Lagos to be a teacher at the Grammar School; the quarter people took him to see where public water-taps had been installed, near the houses of existing councillors, and urged him to be their representative.[41] In the run-up to the election many quarters met together to choose a representative in the same manner as in pre-party days. Thus the Electoral Officer received a letter from the people of Oke Eso, to say they had 'met under the *Akata* tree' and chosen R.A. Ajayi, the popular owner of a medicine store in the quarter, as their representative.[42] This was in December 1954, well before the election; but Ajayi duly carried the seat for the NCNC.

Mr Ekundare saw as the key to his organizational success the use of ordinary illiterate people as party agents: 'old and feeble men, market women, some younger boys'.[43] They were paid £10 a month to enable them to entertain and make small presents as they spread the word. The NCNC simply did not have the resources to make large gifts in cash, but their modest largesse was none the less effective, associated as it was with close personal contact. As one rueful AG activist put it: 'it was *iyan* [pounded yam] and *ẹmu* [palm-wine] which drew the Ijesha to the NCNC'. Many of these agents were not known as such to the AG, so that, again in Ekundare's words, 'votes came from the room, not just from the street'. They did not meet at the NCNC Secretariat in Okesha, but at Pa Ilesanmi's house and later at Prince Ademisoye's (a cousin of *Ọwa* Ajimoko's, a retired produce-inspector, who was party chairman in the late 1950s). People were encouraged to take AG money and to promise their votes, but, as a party slogan put it:

Ẹ gbowo ọlọpẹ, k'ẹ dibo f'akukọ; owo ara wa l'a nra
Take AG money and vote NCNC; it's our own money we're getting

Differences in party organization were related to differences which the parties presented of themselves and their opponents. Both parties used ethnic appeals. The AG sounded their Yoruba-ness, urging the Ijesha to join the party of their Yoruba brothers and attacked the NCNC leadership for its alliance with non-Yoruba. Party songs again:

O dẹru Isobo (2), Fadahunsi Ijẹsa o dẹru Isobo
He's become an Urhobo slave, F. the Ijesha an Urhobo slave

Or else, in an allusion to the NCNC symbol, a cock, Fadahunsi might be called *adiẹ Igbo* ('an Igbo hen'). Fadahunsi, wrote some AG Ijeshas from Ibadan, 'has severed Ijeshas from their next of kin in the Western Region by virtue of his Leadership in Ilesha and has sold the Ijeshas to the Eastern Region where he shared heavey [*sic*] amount from his Lord the Zik'.[44] The NCNC, on the other hand, emphasized its truly home-grown quality. Its party songs and slogans were played in the town to a distinctively Ijesha style of music and sometimes just seemed to celebrate their being Ijesha:

Elu b'elu şire, hin ya w'ọmọ Ijẹşa
Comrades sport with comrades, come and watch the Ijesha play

It was from a more local viewpoint that they stigmatized the alienness of the AG. In a neat allusion to the AG symbol, the palm-tree, the NCNC linked their rivals with the outcaste and the bush:

Inu igbo l'ọpẹ ngbe, a ki ikọle adete s'igbooro
In the bush lives the palm-tree, we don't build a leper-settlement in the town

From the mid 1950s the NCNC added a more definitely populist note to its major theme of local patriotism, and in the contrasted stereotypes of the two parties, the different level of ethnic appeal was compounded with an element of class. It is summed up in the sardonic addition which the NCNC made to the AG's party motto, 'Life More Abundant': *fun awọn ọga l'oke* ('for the bosses on top'). Fadahunsi alluded to this in a speech he made in 1955 opening the NCNC secretariat, and went on to say that the AG people only 'knew themselves' and did not care for the poor; 'when they

233

are using cars they will not care for the poor who have none'.[45] This theme
was often taken up, and it seems to lend support to Richard Sklar's class
explanation of party-political conflict in much of Western Nigeria.[46] The
Action Group, argues Sklar, represents the 'rising class' in Yorubaland –
strata distinguished by their wealth, control of commercial enterprise and
education, dependent on the growth of the capitalist economy and now
poised to take over the colonial state. In hitherto 'classless' communities this
class encountered popular opposition to its growing privilege, which took
the political form of support for the NCNC. Ibadan, Oyo, Benin and Ilesha
are cited as examples of the phenomenon. This differential class basis is also
held to explain key organizational differences between the parties: the AG
being an 'associational' party, relying on individual memberships and a
distinct, rationalized organization, the NCNC being 'communal', membership being mediated through belonging to a community and its organization
reliant on the community's own structures.

As a description, Sklar's account does capture some of the features of the
Ijesha situation. But it is seriously flawed, especially in its explanation. As
we have seen, on the gross level there is not much to differentiate between
the two parties as regards the class background of either their leaders or
supporters. It is not explained why Ilesha, in particular, should be such a
stronghold of such populist politics, granted the general Yoruba predilec-
tion for the AG. The comparison with Ibadan, where Adelabu's 'Mabolaje
Grand Alliance' took the town against the AG (becoming in effect the local
NCNC), is instructive but can be misleading.[47] Adelabu's party swept aside
the older, educated leadership provided in modern politics by a Christian
elite, which joined the AG in 1951, in the name of the chiefs and the largely
Muslim indigenes of Ibadan. There are parallels here with the line-up forces
in Ilesha between the chiefs and Ilesanmi's ITPA in 1952–53. But in Ilesha
members of the pre-1951 educated political elite (Fadahunsi *et al.*) remained
leaders of the local NCNC and managed to co-opt its populist elements.
Though the Ilesha NCNC made good use of popular cultural idioms, its
leaders were very sensible of the crucial importance of education to communal advancement and, this being an overwhelmingly Christian town, there
was little distrust of education as the perquisite of a religious minority.
Indeed it was Councillor Ekundare who, in the face of AG support for an
illiterate candidate for the *Lejofi* title in 1958, argued that 'we need educated
fellows who can serve the town successfully ... chiefs of sound education',
especially as lawyers would soon be appearing in customary courts; 'we do
not want "thumb-print it, Baba"'!⁴⁸ Perhaps the most significant contrast of
all is that whereas Adelabu drew support from anti-tax movements,[49] the
Ilesha NCNC managed to raise very high levels of tax for public development goods. The implications of this we shall shortly examine.

Still, how do we interpret the ideological equation of the NCNC in Ilesha
with the poor (lit. *mẹkunnu*, 'common people') and the AG with 'the rich',
and the undeniably 'communal' character of the NCNC? The essential

objection to Sklar's account is that, though it is that of a political scientist, it is too sociologically determinist. By this I mean that he treats political forms and conflicts too exclusively as the products of social processes taken to occur independently of them. The attacks of NCNC speakers on the AG as a party of 'rich men' do not mean quite what they seem. A 1958 editorial entitled 'Reject the Action Group' in the *West African Vanguard*, runs, in paraphrase and quotation, as follows:[50]

> It commends the skilful conduct of Council affairs. Areas under AG control, such as Ekiti, Oshogbo and Ife, lack amenities and the councillors enrich themselves. In the Ilesha AG 'we have our old loantakers who were at one time bus-owners, some of them still indebted to the regional loans board'. The AG is further typified as including 'retired future seekers who think they can make money in politics . . . social outcasts, rascals and trouble brewers . . . notorious burglars of 1940s fame. Some of them are now chiefs and in their shamelessness they can take up any job even with their beads on . . . old ne'er-do-wells. They have failed in their various callings . . . but [are] still optimistic of acquiring wealth if voted in.' Then there are the ambitious 'carpet-crossers', with no real interest in the AG. They are reminded of the disturbances of 1941.

Here, as elsewhere, it is not the wealthy as such or in general who are the object of criticism. There were, in any case, many prosperous traders and lawyers in the NCNC, and the party felt no need to excuse them. A party speaker *defended* the NCNC from an AG charge that it only comprised 'poor and irresponsible' people, and expressed the view that:[51] 'rich people and poor must cooperate so that poor people will be rich as well. Poor people will eat under rich people and they will satisfy [*sic*] . . . . they [have got] rich people among the members of the NCNC.' The riches that mattered, that drew NCNC criticism in angry *Vanguard* editorials, were not those 'spontaneously' produced by the market and the occupational structure, but those acquired directly through party access to the state. NCNC indignation was profoundly ambivalent, however, since they wanted to acquire state power for the same purposes of direct individual and communal aggrandizement. The most telling point of AG propaganda was that only through support of the governing party could the Ijesha help themselves. NCNC leaders were very sensitive to this charge and strove to rebut it, by arguing that AG leaders neglected their towns. Had S.L. Akintola, the AG deputy leader, managed to get the railway to *his* town, Ogbomosho, it was taunted;[52] and which town was bigger, Ilesha or Ikenne (Awolowo's home-town)?[53] The foregoing argument may be summed up thus: the two parties differed, to the extent that they did, in image, organization and policy, far less because of any primary distinction in the social bases of their support than because of the secondary consequences of what levels of the state they were able to command.

The grand aim of the leaders of the Ilesha NCNC, to promote the development of their town, was constantly occluded by a more immediate one: how to maintain and extend their party's control of local government against their AG rivals, not merely without possessing access to the resources and powers of the regional government, but with the sure knowledge that the local AG would draw on them to loosen their hold. None the less, even within a formal system of powers, determined by Ibadan, there were certain crucial latitudes. The most important concerned tax.

The 1950s, the years of nationalist mobilization and of growing party struggle, were a period in which individual incomes reached unprecedentedly high levels. Cocoa prices (i.e. prices paid to producers by the Marketing Board), rose almost every year from £23 per ton in 1944–45 to £194 per ton between 1954 and 1956, after which they tended to fall off, though the fall was not marked till the mid-season of 1960–61. The producer price index, a more exact guide to individual prosperity, shows a sudden jump from 26 to 71 between 1947 and 1948, and thereafter tended to rise steadily to a peak of 110 in 1960 (1959 = 100).[54] The rise in personal prosperity, with social aspirations sharpened by growing levels of education, was reflected at the public level: greatly increased government revenues and a determination to spend. As Figures 11.1 and 11.2 indicate, the revenues of both the Western Regional Government and of Ijesha local government rose steadily through the 1960s. Government spending locally reached unprecedented levels between 1954 and 1960, largely as a consequence of the Act establishing free primary education. That is why, in Figure 11.3, the proportion of local government funds derived from grants swells so markedly in those years. The benefits were felt widely by the contractors involved in the school-building programme, by the traders and artisans who equipped and provisioned the schools, and by the enlarged teaching profession, as well as by the parents who saw them as the means of their children's advancement.

Taxation, as such, is bound everywhere to be unpopular, and it must therefore be a concern of those who levy it to effect as satisfactory a trade-off as they can between the resentment of the taxed subject, on the one hand, and the support and/or control of subjects which may be secured by spending the revenue those taxes bring in, on the other. Not all subjects may be equally able to press their claims on the state, and not all taxation is equally visible or immediate in its impact and hence likely to arouse resentment. Two features of the prevailing taxation system are especially pertinent here. Firstly, the Nigerian colonial state and the regional government derived the bulk of their revenues in forms that were relatively 'cost free', in political terms: levies on imports and exports, and, from the 1940s, the difference between what the Cocoa Marketing Board received from buyers on the world market and what it paid the farmers. These accumulating surpluses gave an enormous fillip to the political capacity of the Government and its party, the Action Group. Secondly, the most 'politically expensive' form of revenue,

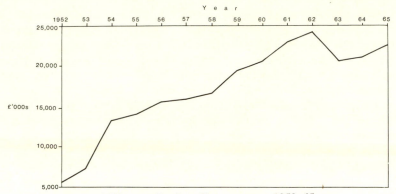

Fig. 11.1   Revenue of Western Region Government, 1952–65
Source: Western Nigeria Statistical Bulletin, vols. I (1959)–VIII (1966).

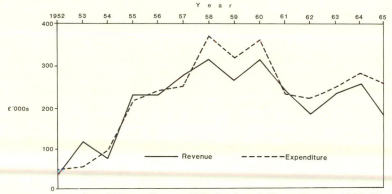

Fig. 11.2   Revenue and Expenditure of Ijesha Local Government, 1952–65
Source: Western Nigeria Statistical Bulletin, vols. I (1959)–VIII (1966).

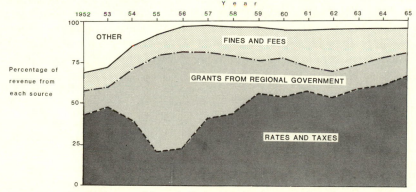

Fig. 11.3   Breakdown of Local Government revenue (all Western Nigeria) by source, 1952–65
Source: Western Nigeria Statistical Bulletin, vols. I (1959)–VIII (1966).

237

direct taxes on personal incomes, were assessed, collected and largely retained at local levels for the purposes of local government bodies.

Ilesha's NCNC leadership, therefore, had an opportunity – significant powers of taxation and hence control being vested at the local level – and a constraint – the fact that the taxes were highly visible and thus far from politically cost-free. Of the latter, they had already had a warning in the appearance of the Ilesha Tax-Payers Association during the *Risawẹ* contest of 1952–53, and revenues from local rates and taxes sagged badly, against the steady trend of the period, in that year (cf. Figure 11.2). In 1954 a proposal to tax women – as was already done in some other Yoruba areas – was dropped because it would be too unpopular.[55] Tax collection was late getting under way that year and the tax clerk, S.O. Makinde, complained that the NA police were not 'cooperative' over tax evasion; the members of the NA Executive Committee felt it necessary to advise them that 'they should not befriend [tax] offenders'. None the less, over the next few years, a great transformation was wrought, both in numbers of registered tax-payers and in tax levels. Between 1951–52 and 1957–58 the number of tax-payers went up by 49%, whereas in a number of other large Yoruba towns, such as Iwo, Ede and Ibadan, it actually went down.[56] By the latter year the NCNC councillors, zealous for improvements, had imposed education, water, electricity and general improvement rates, so that the total in Ilesha town was greater than in any comparable town – £4 8s 3d for a man assessed at £50 annual income, compared with Ibadan's or Abeokuta's £3 5s 0d or Ife's £3 15s 4d; even Ijesha rural rates, which at £3 1s 3d did not include anything for water or electricity, were higher than Oshogbo's at £2 14s 2d.[57]

How was this done? The local Action Group did not fail to make what it could of an apparently ideal political weapon. Why should Ilesha people pay more tax than Oshogbo or Ife; why should the rates be higher than what Prime Minister Awolowo had authorized, their spokesman urged.[58] But it availed them little: one group of petitioners against the rate rises of 1956 was denounced by Pa Ilesanmi and other leaders of the former ITPA as 'a handful of frustrated Action Groupers who, true to type, have been running a series of futile denigrating campaigns against the NCNC controlled Ilesha Urban District Council'.[59] The NCNC took especial care to explain the need for increased rates at fortnightly meetings of the councillors together with the *loriọmọ* – heads of the young men – of all the quarters, who passed things on to their quarter chiefs and people and kept them in touch with sentiment in the quarters. Tax was assessed in every quarter by a local committee, usually headed by one of the chiefs and with a majority of NCNC representatives.[60] Significantly, the chairman of the UDC Tax Committee was for many years Councillor Ekundare, who was also the chief architect of the party's grassroots organization. Of all the NCNC's projects, none gave more pride than the new Atakunmosa Market, established on a large oblong of land excised from the northern side of the *Afin* grounds, to replace the now over-crowded *Oja'ba* in front of the *Afin*. When the project was first mooted, AG leaders were scornful about it, asking how it was possible without the support of the government. But the site was cleared using unpaid public labour, recruited in traditional fashion through the quarters; an additional township improvement rate of 5s 0d was raised; and eventually the scheme qualified for a grant of £15,000 from the government at Ibadan. That this grant *was* made is an indication both of the competence of the scheme's preparation and of the extent to which, despite party-political pressures, the formal rules of the system were still operating in 1958, even when to the advantage of opposition-controlled areas.

But party competition was fast eroding these rules. We have just seen how the Ilesha NCNC, under the pressure of its situation, produced a regime remarkably responsive to the sentiments of ordinary members of the community: a genuine local democracy. But there was a more sombre side too. It also had to be particularly responsive to the interests of its own members within the community. They required consideration from their party in the face of their exclusion from the substantial patronage which the AG could offer to many of its supporters, even in an NCNC-controlled town. Under the judicial reforms instituted in 1954 with the prime object of putting the higher local courts (grades 'A' and 'B') into the hands of the educated, rather than the chiefs, the regional government appointed court presidents; and these were AG members.[61] It was AG members who received loans from the Western Nigeria Development Corporation, and they included a handful of the richest men in town. Possibly greater political consequences flowed from the distribution of many more small loans to many smaller folk. An NCNC member of Ilupeju Local Council 'complained bitterly [in 1957] on how loans were being distributed to Erinburo villagers, men and women, as a means of propaganda to win the people to the AG and to jeopardize the smooth running of existing NCNC Local Council'; and others agreed that 'such act is liable to convert some members of existing Council'.[62] The regional government selected a majority of AG members to make up the local Liquor Licensing Board from the names submitted by the Ilesha Council.[63] And so on.

The local NCNC used all its local powers to the full. Whereas up to 1954 contracts for things like road maintenance were awarded to AG as well as NCNC members, afterwards NCNC membership was essential.[64] Such 'nepotism and political jobbery', so AG leaders argued in a petition for the Council's dissolution in 1960, also involved the creation of unnecessary posts to create political support for the NCNC. 'All IDC officials [they alleged] have been converted into NCNC organizing secretaries.' There was a recrudescence of illegal tree felling, they further alleged: 'all Forestry officials are political agents of the NCNC [and] because they are their good boys, they wink at their excesses'.[65] By 1959, tax assessment committees were NCNC to AG in the ratio 4 : 1, and AG members were prone to complain of punitive assessments. AG councillors from district communities came standardly to complain of high levels of rates and taxes, matched by low levels of spending on local amenities; while the NCNC Chairman of the Divisional Council complained that the local assessment committees in AG-controlled towns like Ibokun and Imesi-Ile deliberately under-assessed their citizens' incomes.[66] The local AG redoubled their efforts to change the rules of the game or the frameworks within which the rules were applied. Responding to these pressures, the regional government tended to take more powers into its hands (as with regional income tax, introduced in 1957), it changed the units of local government to allow areas which the AG controlled to be autonomous (as with the creation of the new council areas – Urban, Northern and Southern – in 1958), and it became more ready to use its residual powers, for example to suspend NCNC-controlled councils altogether (as it eventually did in 1960). All this was made much easier by an extra-ordinary political advantage which the NCNC conceded to their opponents: they allowed the election of a new *Qwa*, already known to be a keen supporter of the Action Group.

Ajimoko II died on 18 October 1956. The ensuing contest was drawn out over six months, and Ilesha enjoyed, at least on the surface, a sort of long vacation from party politics.[67] It appears to have been a much larger initial field than in any recent contest for the *Qwa*-ship: 48 people in all, according to the *West African Vanguard*, of whom 18 were considered to be doing it mainly to keep the name of their line known for the future, and some 12 to be serious candidates. There was no shortage of educated candidates either: a pharmacist, an Anglican clergyman, at least two primary headmasters, the manager of the Pro Bono Publico Press, Lagos, as well as the usual *lojas*, by now often retired traders or produce-inspectors.[68]

The contest fell into two stages. In the first, the tide seemed to be running for Gbadebo Lufadeju, who had worked as a pharmacist in Jos, the son of C.A. Lufadeju, whom Ataiyero had made *Loja Ibala* and was later the Christian *asoju* on the old court. Generous gifts, it was said to the extent of several thousand pounds realized from the sale of properties, appeared to have won over the *Qbanla* and the other chiefly kingmakers; and he was not unwelcome to the leading figures of the NCNC political establishment. But Lufadeju was not widely popular: he was said not to have been sufficiently forward in public affairs and to be 'too cool for the Ijeshas'.[69] A large public meeting at the Obokungbusi Hall articulated these feelings so strongly that Fadahunsi was moved to dissociate himself from the charge that Lufadeju was his candidate. Other *qmqba* took the opportunity to get together and pass resolutions that Lufadeju was not really, despite his father's *loja*-dom, of royal descent.[70] Eventually, the Ijesha Divisional Council recommended to the kingmakers to withdraw their support.

240

The contest was now open again. The most likely family, that of the late *Qwa* Ataiyero, was divided against itself, rival factions putting up the young, educated *Aṣireyun*, Chief S.A. Ataiyero, and the popular son of one of Ataiyero's daughters, the Lagos printer Ladejola Oginni.[71] By March 1957 the winner began to emerge: A.O. Ogunmokun, an ex-UAC employee in Lagos, who had been the candidate of Fadahunsi and the young literates against *Lumobi* Haastrup back in 1942. Despite his known AG sympathies, Ogunmokun commanded wide support for several reasons. He had won great popular credit from the generosity and help he had shown to ordinary Ijesha, *oṣomaalo* and others, over many years, in Lagos, where he had also been active in the Council of Ijesha Societies.[72] His membership of the ROF – still a force to create personal alliances, even across the growing divide of party – stood him in good stead among many notables. Moreover, he was closely related to several leading figures of the NCNC who felt he would be constrained to moderate his AG commitment and (as Ogunmokun himself is said to have put it) 'be a father to all the Ijeshas'.[73] Ogunmokun's personal popularity and his good non-royal connexions outweighed the circumstance that he did not belong to a large or well-organized segment of the royal lineage.[74] His ancestor, in fact, was that ill-fated prince Odigbadigba who was Ogedengbe's nominee for the *Qwa*-ship in the chaos of 1871 and, becoming a pawn in the factional politics of Ibadan, was murdered by his escorts on his way there.[75] Ogunmokun, on becoming *Qwa*, acquired the praise-name Fiwajoye ('good character brought the title') and styled himself officially Biladu III, after a more remote and distinguished royal ancestor; but 'Ogunmokun' was how he continued to be known.

The political situation was not at all such as to encourage a strong AG sympathizer now to forsake those loyalties. The 1956 regional elections had reversed the AG's humiliating defeat at the 1954 federal election, when the NCNC had taken a majority of the seats from the Western Region. With 49 seats to 31 in the House now, AG control of the West was stronger than it had been after the 1951 regional election.[76] Both Ijesha seats had gone decisively to the NCNC, but the margin of the victory was not quite as great as it had been in 1954, especially in the rural areas:

Ilesha Central	*Ilesha Southwest*
B. Olowofoyeku (NCNC) 74%	J.O. Fadahunsi (NCNC) 61%
L.O. Omole (AG) 26%	J.A. Akinyemi (AG) 39%

There was every sign that the AG government at Ibadan was prepared to use its powers energetically on behalf of its local supporters. Another triennial round of local elections was due for early in 1958. The local AG was put in excellent heart by Ogunmokun's accession.

Qwa Ogunmokun's main weapon in the AG cause was chieftaincy. It

241

had come to seem in the past few years in Ilesha that chieftaincy had lost most of its political significance. *Qwa* Ajimoko, accepting his defeat over the *Risawẹ* title in 1953, had just gone along with the modern political establishment. A substantial number of chiefs sat on the Divisional Council as 'traditional members', but they voted with the elected councillors of their towns. Indeed, the Council had tended to encroach on the autonomy of the senior chiefs as 'kingmakers' by extensive discussion of disputed titles at the Lands and General Purposes Committee.[77] Nominations for senior titles were (after the Chiefs Law of 1957) passed, with the *Qwa*'s signature, to the Ministry of Local Government and Chieftaincy Affairs at Ibadan which confirmed them. Ogunmokun had two aims: to make sure that *his* nominees filled any fresh vacancies, and, making use of those norms of the chiefly order which stressed solidarity and obligation to the *Qwa*, to induce them to form a bloc of AG opinion, behind him, on the Council.

A number of senior titles were, or soon fell, conveniently vacant: *Sawẹ, Ogboni, Lejofi, Qbanla, Lẹjọka*. All were eventually filled by Ogunmokun's choices, and staunch AG supporters. Of these, *Qbanla*, being next only to the *Qwa* in seniority and an open title (*oye ọmọ ilu*), was of exemplary importance. The NCNC caucus met soon after *Qbanla* Ogunmoyesin's death early in 1958 and decided that of the three leading aspirants – Fadahunsi, Ibironke and Ajayi-Obe – Fadahunsi was the one they wanted: in effect he became the popular choice and the choice of the chiefs. This *Qwa* Ogunmokun would not have, and he soon found a very eligible candidate of his own in Ibironke, who severed himself from his political associates and declared for the AG. The inability of the *Qwa* and chiefs to agree led to a protracted wrangle about the selection procedure. Ogunmokun sharply rebutted the advice of the Local Government Adviser that the kingmaker chiefs (i.e. the leading members of the three senior lines, *Agbanla, Arẹ* and *Ẹlẹgbẹ*), having sounded out popular opinion through consultation with the heads of the junior lines (i.e. *Ẹlẹgbaji* and *Qmọdeọwa*, representing the bulk of the quarters), should meet and forward a name to the *Qwa* for his ratification; instead, argued Ogunmokun, the *Qwa* should meet together with the kingmakers in joint conclave, where he hoped the royal presence would overawe chiefly opposition.[78] Ogunmokun pushed his claims further, greatly to the annoyance of several of the senior chiefs, in a Memorandum which he circulated, which reviewed the titles' origins in often tendentious language and claimed the backing of 'tradition' for the strongest royal initiative: the *Qwa* 'has the right by tradition to select anybody whom he is sure will discharge the duties attached to [a] chieftaincy ... [the *Qwa*] is to the chiefs as a husband is to his wives ... has to be approached many times and persuaded, but where he is bent on his own course he is never molested or ridiculed'.[79] Eventually Ogunmokun played his trump card, which was not tradition but the sure support of the AG government at Ibadan. By January 1959 the chiefs and the *Qwa* were still deadlocked, so the *Qwa* proposed that *two* recommendations, one for Fadahunsi and one for Ibironke, be sent to the Ministry at Ibadan; 'the kingmakers did not make any comment'; and J.J. Ibironke was duly appointed *Ọbanla* of Ilesha.[80]

The *Ọwa* pressed his advantage. Compliant chiefs were favoured, recalcitrant chiefs pressurized. At least some chiefs are said to have been bound by a ritual in which, in the *Afin*, a lamp was lighted, a kind of medicine (*aṣẹ*) put by it, and the lamp was put out, with the threat that so would their light be put out in the land of the living (i.e. all their children would predecease them) if they broke faith. The then *Lọja Oṣu* refused to undergo this ordeal, and was told not to come to the *Afin* again.[81] The *Babaileoke*, who derived considerable revenues from his rights over certain categories of land, was frozen off from his position for opposition to the *Ọwa*. But as more senior chiefs loyal to Ogunmokun were appointed, it was impossible for their juniors not to fall in line. When Councillor Ekundare spoke critically at a Council meeting about the *Ọwa*'s claims for expenses, the *Ọwa* summoned Ekundare's father, the *Lọtun* of Ifofin quarter, and the old chief had to beg his son to leave politics.[82] Within a year or two, only two of the senior chiefs – *Ọdọle* Awodiya, Fadahunsi's father-in-law, and *Risawẹ* Adedeji, who paradoxically were both *iwọle* – continued to resist the *Ọwa*. Ogunmokun was so successful in inducing the chiefs to take the AG line that in 1959 the AG nearly captured the chairmanship of the recently elected Ijesha Divisional Council, despite the NCNC's clear majority of its elected members, since with the support of nearly all the 'traditional' members (the holders of designated major titles) the AG elected members, mostly representative of towns in Northern Ijeshaland, made up a bare AG majority. From this humiliation the NCNC was only saved by the chance death of the *Ogboni* of Ibokun a few days before the Council met.[83] Even on Ilesha Urban District Council, where the NCNC's majority was unshakeable, the traditional members eventually requested to be allowed to sit with the AG opposition.[84]

The local elections of 1958 revealed a definite erosion of NCNC strength throughout Ijeshaland.[85] The political units had again been changed. In place of twenty small local councils, which had never functioned well, were two larger District Councils, Ijesha Northern and Ijesha Southern, parallel to Ilesha Urban DC. Ijesha Divisional Council remained as a higher tier, but its political significance had declined, since it was only a precepting authority: rating and many services were carried out by the District Councils. This new arrangement both rewarded the district communities which had earliest voted AG by putting them outside many forms of Ilesha/NCNC control, and it created the administrative framework for further AG advance. Whereas in the federal election of 1954 the NCNC had carried 22 out of 30 polling stations in the Northern area, now 24 out of 32 seats went to the AG. The NCNC retained control of Ilesha Urban, with 29 out of 36 seats, but AG support was more substantial and widespread than this suggests, as it now got 37% of the overall vote. The AG breakthrough in several quarters was mostly achieved by the personal influence of locally resident big men, such as S.O. Thompson in Iloro or I.O. Ajanaku in Isokun. In the Southern area patterns of party support approximated to the Urban: NCNC got 24 out of 34 seats, with 58% of the vote. In some communities, like Ifewara, the AG consolidated earlier inclinations to their support; in others, villages followed the political preferences of their patrons, as the Thompson fief of Etioni voted for the AG candidate, while neighbouring Itaapa followed E.A. Fajemisin to the NCNC.

The treadmill of elections continued to turn with the consequence that party conflict bit deeper into the fabric of Ijesha life. Since the voices we hear tend to be those of the most politically active, it is difficult to gauge the precise extent of this. But we hear a crescendo of complaints about over-assessment of tax, the punitive use of sanitary inspectors, trumped up charges and judicial severity, hooliganism and abuse of party opponents especially at elections, discrimination on the basis of party in things as diverse as the levying of *iṣakọlẹ* or the granting of licences. Was it possible to avoid it, to be accepted as neutral? Political participation, as measured by numbers who voted, certainly increased greatly between the election of 1954, when 12,509 people voted, and the 1959 election, when the number of voters peaked at 58,129, but even that must fall a good deal short of the total possible.[86] But basic population statistics, against which these figures need to be set, are too unreliable for much to be made of these figures. More to the point is that local political organizers and activists, when questioned during fieldwork, seemed able to identify very positively the party identification of virtually every house in their neighbourhood. Detailed enquiries in a good many cases nearly always confirmed them, even though many heads of households then (1974) preferred retrospectively to record no party affiliation on the survey form. That preference must be seen in relation to two of the attitudes referred to at the beginning of the chapter: that party politics was a rotten thing, and that the Ijesha were unwise to oppose the party of government. But what the near universal identification of households by party means is that few public acts or achievements by individuals – getting a paid job, a licence, a title or a scholarship, appearing in a court case, expressing any kind of opinion about the affairs of the town – failed to get charged with party-political significance: to be interpreted as moments in the struggle between NCNC and AG. Families, churches, the multifarious social clubs which abound in Ilesha, were fractured by party or strove desperately to avert its corrosive impact. The oldest society of all, *Ẹgbẹ Atunluṣe*, was still in existence – it was the proprietor of Ilesha Grammar School, and counted many activists of both parties from Fadahunsi downwards among its members – and was buffeted into a kind of paralysis by party. In vain did its Chairman, D.A. Aderogba, recall 'the good but dark old days when politics was unknown';[87] the society's attempt to mediate between Ogunmokun and the NCNC councillors came to nothing. Rather, it found itself hard-pressed to prevent its own subversion: again its Chairman insisted it 'was a

Table 11.1   *Percentage of popular vote won by NCNC, 1954–60*

	1954 federal	1955 local	1956 regional	1958 local	1959 federal	1960 regional
Ilesha	76	65?	74	63	62	62
Ijesha North	69	[65]	?	[25]	37	34
All Ijesha Division	81	[73]	65	[63]	62	56

Notes: Figures in brackets indicate percentages of *seats*, which are given in cases where voting figures are not available, in order to give an impression of the general trend. The figures for *seats* naturally accentuate the dominance of the dominant party, since they were for single-member constituencies. The figures for the 1955 election in Ilesha represent only 15 out of some 40 wards. 'Independents' in the 1955 election are assigned to whichever main party was locally in opposition. 'Ijesha North' refers to all communities in the area which came to form Ijesha Northern District in 1958.

cultural society and he smelt danger and ruin to the society if politics was allowed in the Society which had so good a name'.[88]

Table 11.1 shows that the elections of 1959–60 followed a steady trend. In view of the dual pressure being applied on it – externally from the regional government and internally from the *Qwa* – the NCNC held its position in Ilesha very well, despite its progressive collapse in the Northern area. The regional election on 8 August 1960 precipitated the final crisis in the relations between the *Qwa* and the local council. It was a quieter election with a lower poll than in 1959, and produced the inevitable outcome of an even firmer AG hold on the regional government.[89] On 13 August the AG held a victory celebration at the *Afin* in which the *Qwa* openly participated and naturally there was much singing and dancing around the town, with the usual provocative songs sung outside the houses of leading NCNC-ers. On 15 August the Ilesha Urban District Council met in an angry mood. They banned all drumming and dancing in the streets of the town till the end of the month and passed a motion calling on Ogunmo-kun to abdicate, accusing him of a whole variety of charges from 'harassing Ijesha people with unnecessary exactions and annoying them with litiga-tion' to idolatry (!).[90] The AG opposition submitted to Ibadan a formal prayer for the dissolution of the Council and an enquiry into the manage-ment of its finances. The Council met again a week later to discuss Ibadan's letter, which stated that it had acted illegally in seeking to depose the *Qwa*. On these grounds it was dissolved, and a Management Committee appoint-ed, predominantly AG in its membership, which met for the first time on 8 September. By the saddest of ironies, Ilesha participated in the independ-ence of Nigeria less than a month after it lost its own elected local govern-ment.

POLITICS BY OTHER MEANS

Throughout the two years of its existence, the Management Committee did not have an easy task or win much popular acceptance. The four NCNC members appointed to it refused to participate and were soon replaced by AG members.[91] The tax assessment committees also had a built-in AG majority and their NCNC members refused to cooperate. Assessment went ahead none the less, but tax revenues began to fall. Stronger measures had to be taken against defaulters and prosecutions before AG judges became more common. With funds from the government some new projects were undertaken – such as extensive tarring of urban roads – but there were increasingly tight limits to what largesse a local government could channel from a government of its own party.[92] In any case, the first to be rewarded – for example, the contractors who were engaged to do the stone retaining walls and culverts for the new tarred roads – had to be AG supporters.[93] The cocoa price was falling and the government was finding it ever harder to meet the recurrent expenditure to which it had committed itself in the boom years of the mid 1950s, let alone undertake new projects.

But the Management Committee's regime fell for reasons entirely external to Ijesha politics. The story has been well told elsewhere so here need only be presented in summary.[94] Nigeria became independent under a federal government dominated by a coalition of the NPC (ruling party of the Northern Region) and the NCNC (ruling party in the Eastern Region). The AG leader, Chief Awolowo, had decided to go to the centre as federal Leader of the Opposition, leaving the party's deputy leader, S.L. Akintola, as Premier in the Western Region. A split developed in the party between those who, with Awolowo, wanted to push their opposition at the centre in a more radical fashion, and a 'regionalist' faction, led by Akintola, who wanted to join the federal coalition with the understanding that each party's hegemony in its regional base would be respected. Awolowo carried the party with him and it was voted to replace Akintola as regional Premier. In May 1962 a fracas broke out in the Western House of Assembly at Ibadan over the vote of confidence in the new Premier-elect and this eventually led to the federal government declaring a state of emergency in the West, suspending the regional government and appointing a federal Administrator in place of the Governor. In the months that followed two further blows befell the AG: the Coker Commission of Enquiry did much to discredit AG rule over the preceding decade and Awolowo was convicted and imprisoned on charges of plotting to overthrow the federal government. Akintola organized his faction of the AG into a separate party, the United People's Party (UPP), and, as it became clearer that he had the backing of the federal government, more and more AG parliamentarians joined it. When, from January 1963, the emergency Administrator was withdrawn, Akintola became

Premier of the West, heading a coalition of his UPP with the Western NCNC against the loyalist rump of the AG, who now formed the opposition.

At first there was much in all this to bring satisfaction to the Ijesha. In September 1962, the Administrator had restored the elected IUDC, dominated by the NCNC, and Babatunji Olowofoyeku, the able lawyer who was Council chairman as well as a member of the Western House of Assembly, could express satisfaction at the ending of 'two years reign of hardship, sufferings and agonies inflicted on NCNC supporters'.[95] When the regional constitution was restored, the *Ọọni* of Ife was replaced as regional Governor by none other than Chief Fadahunsi. Soon Olowofoyeku became Minister of Health in the UPP/NCNC coalition, *Ọwa* Ogunmokun became President of the House of Chiefs and C.O. Komolafe (the former federal representative for Ijesha Division) became Director of the Western Nigeria Development Corporation, that former cornucopia. Never had so many Ijesha been so well placed in positions of state power. But it was a hollow victory. Almost from the first the Council was facing financial problems: rates were slow being paid, there were not the funds to pay staff to chase up defaulters, the regional government was not making its contribution. By the end of the year the Council was living off bank overdrafts and the Electricity Corporation of Nigeria was proposing to disconnect the town for non-payment.[96] The NCNC was unable to repeat its earlier successes in creating willing tax-payers.

Further developments again depended on external political manoeuvres. Early in 1964 Akintola and his coalition partners decided to form a new party, the Nigerian National Democratic Party (NNDP) to fight the federal election due in December in alliance with the North's NPC. Consent had to be engineered at local levels, and this Babatunji Olowofoyeku set out to do. It does not seem that the Ijesha, however disillusioned they had become with political parties, should have felt they could lose much by supporting the NNDP, in so far as the issue was simply one of individual expediency or communal advantage. In fact the Council did 'declare its unflinching support and loyalty to the Regional Government' when asked to do so shortly after the NNDP had been formed in April 1964.[97] But in fact Ijesha opinion at large soon came vehemently to reject the new party. Overridingly this was for moral reasons, linked to the wider sense of identity that Ijesha had – even NCNC supporters who had tended to underplay it rhetorically – as Yoruba. Chief Awolowo had not been much liked by the Ijesha, but now in his imprisonment he acquired throughout Yorubaland an almost religious aura of a 'Suffering Servant' of his people, a man betrayed by his lieutenant, Akintola, a potent symbol of the Western Region's unfair treatment at the hands of the federal government. At this time no Ijesha politician acquired greater moral authority than the federal member for

247

Ilesha Rural, the Revd J.A. Akinyemi (who was also Principal of Ilesha Grammar School), for being one of the few AG parliamentarians to stay loyal to Awolowo.

The manner in which the NNDP was launched locally did little to recommend it. It appears that Olowofoyeku anticipated difficulties in winning the Ijesha over: though Attorney-General in Akintola's government, he was not among the first to announce his adhesion to the NNDP, until Akintola told the NCNC members of his cabinet they had got twenty-four hours to conform.[98] He had not found the party elders in Ilesha very enthusiastic about joining the NNDP at a meeting convened to discuss it at the Obokungbusi Hall, and the announcement of his becoming an 'independent', obviously a prelude to going over to the NNDP, came very abruptly, even if it was not entirely unexpected.[99] For there was already something of a split within the local NCNC, and it was one of these factions which became the kernel of the local NNDP. This divide went back to 1959, when Olowofoyeku and other party leaders had disagreed over nominations for the federal elections of that year.[100] Olowofoyeku had then found allies in a number of more youthful party supporters who felt that the party elders were not giving them their fair share of influence or reward. The thing was more or less patched up then, but the youths continued to regard Olowofoyeku as their patron, a lorry was bought for them, and they continued to meet at Olowofoyeku's house. This divide between 'elders' (*agba*) and 'youths' (*ọdọ*) merged into another, between two networks of councillors and party activists: some closer to Fadahunsi, on the whole but not exclusively a rather older group (e.g. Famuyide, Ekundare, Oriowo, E.O. Makinde, Ajayi-Obe), and some to Olowofoyeku (e.g. Amokeodo, J.K. Dare, M.A.K. Esho, L.A. Owolabi). This divide was far from absolute, but it continued to reappear over diverse issues.[101] In 1962 the party rather swung Olowofoyeku's way with the election of Lawrence Amokeodo as local Chairman, but in 1963 the NCNC Council passed a vote of no confidence in him.[102] It was in Amokeodo's house that the embryo local NNDP began to meet, while the NCNC loyalists met separately under E.T. Okelola (a former Chairman). Eventually, they started having joint meetings with the AG loyalists, and in August together formed the local branch of the United Progressive Grand Alliance (UPGA), the national coalition which was to oppose the NNDP in the elections due in December 1964.

When the NNDP did not receive any great spontaneous welcome from the Ijesha, sanctions began to be employed. Large bribes – in one case £5,000 and a Peugeot car – were offered to men who were considered respected opinion-leaders, like R.A. Awobiyi or Alhaji Famuyide.[103] A few 'scholarships' were offered to Muslims to enable them to make the Haj. The existing council was dissolved, as being too unreliable an instrument of NNDP control, and a new caretaker council was installed under the chairmanship of M.A.K. Esho, who had long served as NCNC councillor for Idasa quarter.[104] Its members, appointed by Ibadan on local NNDP nomination, were a real miscellany.[105] Only a handful of them had, like Esho, any municipal experience; a good many had been lower-level party activists, members of the 'youths' group; in the main they were of much lower status than the former elected councillors. Significantly, the most distinctive group was connected with transport, as drivers, motor charterers, transporters; this was because the parties, and the NNDP in particular, increasingly recruited their activists from *agbero* (i.e. men who touted business for drivers in the motor-park), whose occupational expertise made them good material for party thugs. There were also one or two teachers (including a newly-made Alhaji), the pastor of an Aladura church, a couple of Adeti cloth traders, a tyre dealer, a watch-repairer who was *loriọmọ* of Iroye, a photographer, a barber or two, a pools agent; here at last we find ourselves among the lower reaches of the 'informal sector'. Only one man of real substance – the magnate I.O. Ajanaku – appeared as a member of this council, but hardly in an active role. In sum, this was a local political 'elite' – if the term can be used – more purely dependent on office 'for chop' and thus less socially respected, than any hitherto. The petty careerism, taking its chances where it could, to which the NNDP was forced to appeal, produced effects which further undermined the council's chances of legitimizing its authority. For example, the chairman of the council's Health Committee was disturbed to learn that in Oke Iro quarter an NNDP councillor was levying bribes from the local people through the sanitary inspectors and party workers who served as his 'middlemen', paid so as to avoid trouble over their premises.[106] So ineffective was this council that a year later, in May 1965, another one was instituted, with less than half its members carried over from the former council, in an attempt to achieve the near-impossible: a body both respected in the town and committed to the NNDP's goals.[107]

Right from the beginning the NNDP made it clear that it was prepared to use the severest measures to cow the opposition to it. Premier Akintola might give pretty speeches reminding the Ijesha of the benefits they gained from having their people well up in the ruling party,[108] but his pithy threats are more readily remembered:

> *Awolọwọ fun ẹnyin Igbimọ Ileṣa ni rice pẹlu ẹja tutu jẹ, ṣugbọn emi o pa okuta wẹwẹ si rice fun yin jẹ*
> Awolowo gave you Ilesha councillors fresh fish to eat with your rice, but I'll feed you rice mixed with gravel![109]

Initially, the NNDP taunted their opponents for their impotence:

> *Ẹgbẹ Ọlọwọ ni k'a si maa ṣe, akukọ di irindin*
> It's the NNDP we should support, the cock [i.e. NCNC] has become a wingless termite.[110]

A famous incident occurred on the day Akintola and his Deputy-Premier, Fani-Kayode, arrived to inaugurate the NNDP in Ilesha, on 6 April 1964, which gave a foretaste of things to come.[111] The Premier's convoy, accompanied by lorries filled with armed party supporters, arrived from the east, so they had to pass between Ilesha Grammar School and Mr Lawrence Omole's headquarters as they entered the town. At this point they encountered a crowd shouting '*Ole! ole!* [thief! thief!] Go back! No Room!' and 'a free-for-all fight ensued between the Premier's entourage and the crowd, and cutlasses, matchets, clubs and broken bottles used'. It was inter-house sports day at the Grammar School (where the pupils, like their principal, were strongly UPGA in sympathy) and athletic javelins were nearly put to deadly use. The situation was saved by the intervention of a large detachment of riot police. For this the Revd Akinyemi was suspended for failing to maintain order at his school, though he was later vindicated by the commission of enquiry.

The NNDP thugs, sometimes given support by the Local Government police, roamed town and district intimidating open UPGA supporters. All the accustomed techniques of party pressure were deployed (licences and contracts withdrawn, charges trumped up, properties condemned by sanitary inspectors) to the full. The UPGA leaders were first dismayed by this, but soon they realized there could be advantages in purely nominal adherences to the NNDP, and started to sanction them. One of the first pressures the NNDP exerted was to threaten to withdraw their licences from the large traders who were Licensed Buying Agents. So Omole, who had figured prominently in the incident of 6 April, declared for the NNDP after discussions with his political associates; but everybody knew where his sympathies lay. A saying became common:

> Dẹmọ mo wa, b'o ri oju mi, oò ri inu mi
> I am for the NNDP; but you don't see my inside as you see my face.[112]

'The NNDP just *wanted* to be deceived', commented one UPGA supporter sarcastically.[113] The influx of purely nominal members produced much distrust and uncertainty, even paranoia, within NNDP circles. They might put pressure on a locally respected person like, say, I.O. Odeyemi, a trader who had been the elected NCNC councillor for Ijamo, to join the Council, although the quarter was already represented by A— J—, a driver and NNDP activist. But such men were as inactive as they could be and the NNDP core did not trust them. It did mean, however, that there was little the NNDP could plan or carry out without the UPGA leaders knowing about it. Frustrated again in their hopes to win Ilesha from within, they relied more and more on the powers of the state and the importation of the means of coercion.

Political action in 1964 was overshadowed by the federal election due in December, which UPGA (the AG/NCNC alliance) was convinced it would win easily in the Western Region. Intimidation and electoral fraud were so widespread in many parts of the Federation, however, that just before the election the UPGA leaders were moved to make the disastrous mistake of

250

announcing that their voters should boycott the polls. The boycott was variably observed, but in Ilesha the poll was low and the NNDP took all three Ijesha seats.[114] Despite this bitter setback UPGA had one last chance: the regional elections due for October 1965. The first half of the year saw something of a lull in open party conflict. The new NNDP-controlled Council hoped that the new State Hospital and the tarring of the Etioni road which Ijeshas in the government had secured would win some support. But UPGA was now recruiting its own thugs and with the tacit support of the majority of the population, they eventually proved more than a match for the NNDP. Carefully selected and given special training before taking up service, they assumed names redolent of sinister delinquent courage – Counterfeit, *Omiata* ('pepper sauce'), *Eruobodo* ('the river does not know fear'), Jungle Stay, *Efi* ('smoke') – and they included women. Thugs of both parties were very active both in Ilesha and the rural areas in the run-up to the election.[115]

The election was strongly contested in more ways than one. Election officials were under severe duress from the government on behalf of the NNDP, and UPGA had sometimes to use measures amounting to coercion even to get their nomination papers duly registered. On election day, 11 October, polling was heavy and the UPGA presence around the booths and counting stations sufficed to ensure that polling and counting took place in a fairly equitable way. The UPGA intelligence network was such that they knew of NNDP plans to store extra ballot boxes with the NNDP symbol of the Hand in party members' houses in Ayeso and Igando (Ifofin) quarters for later substitution, so that these attempts at rigging were largely frustrated. But returning officers were under instructions not to announce the results at the counting stations nor to give certificates of them to the candidates, but to take the results directly to Ibadan. This meant that, faced with the evidence of decisive UPGA victories, the government could simply announce false results. In Ilesha Urban West, Olowofoyeku's defeat was first announced on the radio, then, presumably on government instructions, a 'correct' result indicating his victory was put out on the regional radio station (WNBC). Of the four contested seats, only Ijesha Rural South, after a long delay, was announced for the UPGA candidate, S.O. Akinbolagbe. The official results for the other three seats gave NNDP candidates majorities of 78% (Ijesha Rural North: A.O. Awogboro, a lawyer son of the *Ogboni* of Ibokun), 71% (Ilesha Urban West: B. Olowofoyeku), 58% (Ilesha Urban East: O. Olaitan).[116] The unofficial UPGA figures (which differ as to totals of votes polled as well as the majorities), announced in the *Pilot* a few days later, gave UPGA majorities of 82% for O. Siyanbola in Ilesha Urban East, 68% for B. Sadipe in Ilesha Urban West, 86% for S.O. Ige in Ijesha Rural North and 86% for S.O. Akinbolagbe in Ijesha Rural South.[117] Wherever the exact statistical truth may lie, the only important fact is that UPGA believed itself cheated of a landslide victory and of its last chance to expel Akintola's government.

251

Now began a terrible ordeal for the Ijesha. From late October rioting and increased activity by the UPGA private armies which began at Mushin on the Lagos outskirts spread through the Yoruba interior and soon to Ilesha. The two hottest spots in Ilesha – the main thoroughfare, Okesha, and Isokun, where notables of both parties had houses and thugs were lodged – were nicknamed Somolu (after another Lagos suburb) and Mushin respectively. On 2 November, the rediffusion station at Ijamo quarter, symbol of government propaganda, was burnt down and the houses of several NNDP leaders looted.[118] People, including children on the way home from school, started carrying palm fronds – the palm being the AG symbol – or attaching them to their car bumpers, and those without this 'passport' were liable to be attacked by UPGA thugs.[119] Processions were banned but, on 8 November, twenty-six market women were arrested for publicly parading their opposition to the government.[120] Violent affrays and house-burnings were reported from villages such as Etioni, Isaobi and Irogbo.[121] The most frightful thing was 'Operation Wet It': party opponents or their cars were doused with petrol and set alight.[122] The police were virtually powerless to prevent the systematic operations of destruction which UPGA now carried out: senior officers of integrity had been removed by government pressure even on the Nigeria Police, while the Local Government police were by now too frightened (or too much in sympathy with party aims) to get in the way.[123] The chiefs – led by *Ọbanla* Ibironke, for Ogunmokun had died in July 1963 and the *Ọwa*-ship was still vacant – tried fruitlessly to organize meetings of reconciliation.

The last fury of all was unleashed by the arrest, on 8 January 1966, of sixteen UPGA notables on a charge of responsibility for the murder of an NNDP activist. Now UPGA went on the high offensive: night after night, in a systematic sweep, the houses of NNDP adherents were attacked and destroyed.[124] Even Chief Sir Odeleye Fadahunsi's own family house at Ilemo quarter did not escape, since as Governor he was popularly held responsible for the situation in the Region. Despite his mediating and restraining efforts, one fact only seemed to matter: 'he signed for Akintola'.[125] The mobs that carried out the house-burning were led by practised thugs but largely consisted of secondary school pupils. Each night decisions were taken as to which house would be next and the quarter people were carefully consulted as to the reputation of its owner. Thus, next to the house of R.A. Awobiyi (one of the 16 arrested) in Orinkiran, a house belonging to a female relative of an NNDP leader (known as *Mama Ijọba* – 'Madam Government') was destroyed, but the house opposite, owned by a lorry owner who was NNDP, was spared because the owner had gone to the court after Awobiyi's arrest to plead for him.[126] Even an active NNDP councillor might be spared the worst, if he were locally felt to be a decent man, like B.B. Makinwa of Lower Okesha.[127] As in 1941, popular violence was finely judged in its targets. Once the destruction started – and especially after the military coup which finally came on 16 January, to remove all restraints on the expression of popular anger – prudent NNDP-ers left town, often for Ilorin where the NNDP's coalition partner, the NPC, had been securely in power. Otherwise they ran the risk of being lynched or burnt to death when their house was attacked. It was an Igbo officer of the Nigerian Army, Captain Iweanya, who at the end of the month declared that all violence and disorder should cease, and that the Ijesha should sink their differences.[128] They were only too happy to comply and accept what the new military regime had to offer.

In retrospect, Ijesha political activists were profoundly ambivalent about the first Nigerian experiment in party politics, and its outcome. They seemed torn between regarding it as being of and yet not of their community, something familiar and yet incomprehensible, events outside the normal categories of their politics and yet representable in available idioms. On the one hand, they were often frank to the point of cynicism about the main-springs of political action, those motives of individual and communal self-aggrandizement and preparedness to use such means to those ends as the context (including the apparatus of the state) made available, and it was these which had led to the violence they were as sincere in deploring. On the other, the violence was seen as alien, a point often made by emphasizing the importation of thugs from outside. While it is true that some thugs were imported, and that such externally recruited thugs might go about their task with less compunction, in the manner of mercenaries, many were not; and in any case, the violence of the thugs was deployed to ends determined within the community. More fundamentally, the preparedness to use such negative sanctions from outside the community was an aspect of the same political culture which enjoined actors to look for external resources to forward their ambitions within it. It presupposes the hierarchy of communities which was such an age-old element of Ijesha political thinking, a hierarchy none of whose levels was fixed, and each of which opened up to a yet higher level of power and resources. Consequently even the terrible final months of the conflict did not entirely lie outside the categories of Ijesha historical understanding. More than the Riot of 1941 (though that had often been invoked as a warning), it was the civil disorders of almost exactly a hundred years before, culminating in the violent overthrow of *Ọdọle* Ariyasunle by Ogedengbe and his *ipaiyẹ* in 1867, which were apposite. The parallel of the thugs with the *ipaiyẹ* or 'war boys' (*ọmọ ogun*) was evident, as was the form of the revenge taken on those judged 'enemies of the people'.[129] The NCNC editor and activist Akindele Ojo found an easy nineteenth-century parallel to *Ọwa* Ogunmokun's use of his links with the powers at Ibadan to bring pressure on his political opponents at home.[130] When S.O. Ogedengbe, lawyer and NCNC committee member, found himself menaced by NNDP thugs armed with broken bottles while waiting to have his car tyre repaired, he was delivered not just by his own resolution but by the support of bystanders who asked the thugs if they did not know that this was the grandson of the great Ogedengbe?[131] Thus it was with a long glance into their past that the Ijesha cleared the way to a new phase of their history.

12

The present and the past

The end of what Nigerians sometimes call their 'First Republic' is a suitable place at which to close this narrative history. The period of military rule, which lasted nearly fourteen years, will probably turn out to be something of a divide in Ilesha's history. During it the Ijesha were more deeply and irrevocably affected by events and processes constituted at the level of Nigeria as a whole than ever before. Moreover by the 1970s the steady process of their incorporation seemed to have got to a point where the kind of history essayed here becomes inappropriate to its object. My treatment has rested on the assumption that Ijesha has still been enough of a 'society', despite its incorporation within Nigeria, for its history to be largely presented as arising from internal determinations. This assumption has become more strained for each succeeding decade. Henceforth, I suspect, Ilesha's history will require to be treated more as one would write a history of Liverpool or Port Harcourt: a history of a local segment of a national experience or of the working-out of wider forces in a local context.

The straightened economic climate of the early 1960s was not altered by the *coup*; indeed it worsened with the financial pressures of the Civil War (1967–70). When rural protests against taxes and the centres of local government broke out widely in the Western State of Nigeria in 1968–69, disturbances were only just averted in Ijesha South, which was, like rural Ibadan, an old but declining cocoa-growing area.[1] A few years later, in the early 1970s, Ilesha and the Ijesha faced entirely different prospects with the transformation of Nigerian public finances by oil.[2] The national oil economy affected Ilesha's sense of itself as a community in two major ways. Firstly, the phenomenal increase in oil revenues, coinciding with a marked decline in the cash-crop production of the region, made Ilesha, like all other local communities, much more completely dependent on the state for the resources needed for local services and development goods. Secondly, the state was able to extend its own activities, enormously increasing the numbers of people it educated and employed or enabled to be employed. As a consequence, trends of occupational mobility and migration towards the major cities, already well established among people like the Ijesha, were strongly reinforced. A profile of the outcome, by the mid 1970s, was presented in Chapter 8.

A question arises as to how these two consequences have combined to affect Ijesha patterns of thought and action, since they seem to have contradictory implications: the former tending to consolidate the community as an interest group *vis-à-vis* the state, and so ethnic/clientelist patterns of politics, the latter drawing Ijesha out of the community to a directly Nigerian sphere of relations, where occupation-based interests and class politics might be expected to become more salient. Of the decisive process of national class-formation in this period there can be no doubt; and many, many Ijesha must have participated as workers, state or company employees at various levels, employers or officials, in the diverse strikes, negotiations, pressure-group activities of all kinds that occurred to give shape to the evolving class structure. In its broadest sense, politics did not cease with the eclipse of the politicians (*awọn oṣelu*) or only take the form of communal and regional rivalry. However, in contrast to those who have interpreted this as evidence of a real shift of consciousness and action from ethnic or clientelist to class orientations,[3] I would argue that class and community should not be considered as antinomies but as coordinates in a single system of social relations, each providing conditions for the realization of the other. The movement to be discerned is not an 'emergence of class' but development of new forms of interplay between class and community as Ilesha becomes more dependent on the Nigerian state and as more Ijeshas move into the 'Nigerian' sphere.

The abolition of party politics in 1966 combined with the new financial dependence of communities on the state from the early 1970s radically undercut local political autonomy. Two centrally-appointed officials – a Council Manager to supervise local government services and a Divisional Officer with a more general responsibility for the order of the district – now ran affairs. A Council was reinstituted in 1973, but its members were nominated by Government, not elected, and they were right to think they had little power or responsibility.[4] The chiefs recovered some of their old prominence – a new *Ọwa*, Agunlejika II, a successful farmer educated to Standard VI who had been *Loja* of Oke Ibode, was installed in 1966 – but 'interpretation of Government policies to the members of the public' was clearly stated as their primary task, with 'performance of traditional functions' low down on the list.[5] In the absence of parties, several new societies such as the Ijesha Progressive Circle and the Ijesha Esquire Society came into existence, and *Egbẹ Atunluṣe* enjoyed a mild revival; they combined discussion of public affairs, fund-raising for local projects and informal representation to the administrators about Ijesha affairs.[6]

This appearance of a return to the political forms of Indirect Rule, however, can be deceptive. In this superficially depoliticized period, a much greater role came to be played in Ijesha affairs by Ijeshas living *outside* Ilesha, particularly in Ibadan and Lagos. The *Owa* and chiefs gave a lead by giving important titles to such 'external' Ijeshas – S.B. Bakare, a commercial magnate in Lagos, being made *Saloro* and T. Fagbola, a senior police officer, *Lokiran* – using their installation ceremonies as the occasion for reinforcing the claims of the home town in its absent 'sons of the soil'. These people – some big traders but more often professionals, lawyers, academics and civil servants – first figured prominently in the lists of 'leaders of thought' which the military administration drew up for consultation. In 1966 an Ijesha Planning Council in which 'external' Ijeshas played a major role, came into existence 'to foster the economic, educational, cultural and social advancement of Ijeshas'.[7] After its demise, an Ijesha National Affairs Council was set up, to bring together on a common platform all the Ilesha societies concerned with public affairs and the major societies of external Ijeshas – the Lagos Council of Ijesha Societies, and other Ijesha bodies in Lagos, Ibadan, Kano and Oshogbo.[8] Later they played an important role in shaping Ijesha response to the two major issues of the later 1970s: whether Ilesha should opt to join Oyo State (capital: Ibadan) or Ondo State (capital: Akure, coterminous with the old Ondo Province) when the Western State was to be divided in 1977; and the choice of party allegiance when civilian politics finally returned in 1979. In opting for a link with the Oyo rather than the Ekiti, the Ijesha rejected the major affinity of most of their history, as well as the inclination of the early 1920s and the late 1940s, when administrative reorganization had last been debated. Many factors were considered but two seem to have been decisive: Ijesha felt that, as they were fairly well placed in the Secretariat at Ibadan and had relatively higher levels of education than almost any other area destined for Oyo State, they could only lose by joining a new State which was taken to be the especial project of a circle of Ekiti intellectuals and politicians by whom they were distrusted. Moreover Ijesha traders, the successors of the *osomaalo*, had acquired substantial properties and businesses in Ibadan and were reluctant to put them at risk by setting an administrative divide between them and Ilesha.[9]

The 1979 election showed how far Ilesha's perceptions of its collective interests followed the prompting of external Ijesha opinion, echoed most consistently at home by the young, who had hardly known politics before 1966 and were largely destined, through education, for out-migration and employment in the 'Nigerian' sphere. All Ijesha constituencies returned massive majorities, higher than those in any election of the 'First Republic', for the candidates for the Unity Party of Nigeria (UPN), led nationally by Chief Awolowo.[10] UPN won a far greater share of the Yoruba vote, and was less successful in attracting non-Yoruba votes, than its AG predecessor. Locally, UPN derived from UPGA networks, its leader being Alhaji Famuyide (ex-NCNC), but most of its originators were former AG-adherents; its rival, the National Party of Nigeria (NPN), was largely,

257

but not entirely, drawn from old NNDP circles.[11] Ijesha were more relieved at not being sundered by party from the Yoruba at large and the State government at Ibadan than they were disappointed at seeing their party fail to win power at the federal level. Their overwhelming support for UPN represents the culmination of two linked processes: the adoption of Yoruba identity and the ascendancy of the values associated with 'enlightenment' (*ọlaju*). UPN's electoral symbol is a lighted torch (of the kind that used to signify 'school' on British road-signs) and its motto was 'Light over Nigeria'.

Informing these political choices is an assessment by Ijesha of their individual and communal situations grounded in an evaluation of their history. What follows is a synthesis of views expressed by respondents in the 1974 Household Survey to a series of questions, inviting open-ended answers, about the effects and conditions of social change during their lifetimes.

The amenities brought by the twentieth century were very much appreciated: *ile paanu* (iron-roofed houses) above all, tarred roads, piped water and electricity, schools and hospitals, the building-up of the town; all characterized as progress (*ilọsiwaju*) or development (*idagbasoke*), and having their deeper roots in the spread of enlightenment (*ọlaju*), the entire syndrome of values clustered around the world religions, especially Christianity, and education. It must be stressed that, overall, social change was viewed positively – the decline of old ways, as such, being much less regretted than Ijesha failure to take full cognizance of modern conditions of communal advancement. However, there was a good deal of contradiction in opinions expressed on this and in some instances evident misgiving about the lessons which history appeared to teach.

The most universally expressed discontent was over a general condition of the community, though it was often related to the grievances of individual situations, as of farmers who could not get labourers for their cocoa-farms, or traders and others who complained of a lack of local patronage. It was that the very current of social change, so ineluctable and in many ways so beneficial, was taking the bulk of the population in its active years out of the town. As one respondent put it, in reference to the system of tenement rating whose introduction was under discussion in 1973–74, Ilesha was 'a place with buildings and no people': the built-up appearance of the town was mocked by the absence of so many of its sons and daughters. There was universal conviction that *aiṣiṣẹ larin ilu* (lack of local employment) was the root problem, ironically aggravated by the very educational advancement on which Ijesha prided themselves. By far the most popular solution was: *ki Ijọba da ile-iṣẹ silẹ* ('let the Government establish a factory'). The corollary was, as one educated respondent put it, that the Ijesha must 'unite politically and support the government of the day', which was exactly what they did in 1979.

This 'solution' is seen in a clearer light when it is related to what respondents felt had been the main reasons why Ijesha had spoiled their chances in the past. The bulk of definite answers to the question, 'what things have most held back the progress of the Ijeshas?' fell into two main categories: general moral failings or specific historical errors of judgment as to how Ilesha's interests would best be served. In addition, and in a sense embracing both categories, was the sweeping condemnation of politics that I have mentioned. Four great errors were repeatedly mentioned, often in conjunction, since they were felt to share a common characteristic. All served to estrange Ilesha from the external connexions and higher sources of power: driving the Europeans from Oke Imo, and so depriving Ilesha of its role as a major seat of administration; preventing the railway from coming to Ilesha; expelling the Syrian traders from the town in the late 1930s; and, above all, supporting the opposition party in the 1950s. Even the abstract nouns denoting moral failings or states of mind are often codewords with a historical reference: 'stubbornness' (*agidi* or *orikunkun*) hints at 'opposition to the government of the day' (*alatako ijǫba*), as 'dark dispositions and ignorance' (*iwa okunkun ati aisimǫ*) indicate the attitudes of the chiefs who opposed the railway, the opposite of *ǫlaju*. The Syrians are paradigmatic of strangers, which a prosperous town should attract, just as sons of Ilesha are drawn to all manner of other towns. As one man put it succinctly:

> *isę ko si, alejo ko si, owo ko si*
> no work, no strangers, no trade

Another commented that it was strange that the chiefs opposed the railway 'as it would be used to take their wives and children away' since it was the lack of employment which the railway might have brought which was now taking the children of the town away. But what it remarkable is that two of these 'errors' had no real effect, or much less effect than was claimed for them. It appears to be a complete myth that the railway was in fact prevented from coming to Ilesha by the chiefs in Ataiyero's day.[12] Nor did Ilesha's loyalty to the NCNC, while it certainly caused some problems, demonstrably result in serious deprivation. The university, often cited in this regard, which many Ijeshas feel should have been theirs, was not sited at Ife just because of its AG support – most AG towns got no such prize – but because of the unique place of Ife in Yoruba sentiment and the unique position of the Ǫǫni of Ife in AG counsels. None the less myths matter; and the Ijesha political doctrine that the key source of power and resources lies outside is a powerful mythopoeic force.

The belief that the chief condition of communal advance is a favourable relationship to the state as a distributor of resources tends to sustain a clientelist view of class relations and ultimately an ethnic pattern of politics in the wider society. But at the same time Ijesha are more aware of *class*-hierarchy in society than they have ever been: of the *living* people they named as the most notable Ijeshas of their lifetimes, the two richest commercial magnates, neither of them a chief, were most often named and several respondents merely said, usually with a resigned shrug, *awǫn olowo* ('the rich'). There was also a very widespread tendency to blame the rich for holding back Ilesha's progress. But this was not at all in the way in which, in an industrial and capitalist society, the rich might be accused, in a strict sense, of exploiting the poor. Rather, as one elderly man, a retired carpenter and evangelist, put it:

> *Ijeṣa fẹran owo ju ilu wọn lọ. Awọn olowo Ijeṣa tara wọn nikan ni won mọ. Nwọn ko mọ ti talaka . . . Gbogbo Ijeṣa nilati jẹ ọkan: awọn ara-ile ko gbọdọ korira awọn awa ara-oko, ati olowo ati talaka*
> The Ijesha love money more than their community. Rich Ijesha are only concerned about their own affairs, and are indifferent to those of the poor . . . All Ijesha must be one: the townspeople must not hate us country-people, or the rich the poor

He was a native of Odo, on the Iperindo road, and the context of these remarks was the failure of a project to build a ceramics factory in that area. What is demanded of the rich – and of other categories who conceptually overlap with them: politicians (*awọn oṣelu*), 'external Ijesha' (*ọmọ Ijeṣa t'o wa lẹhin odi* or *n'idalẹ*), the educated (*awọn ọmọwe*) – is that they should associate themselves with the town, build houses and spend money there, and above all give it effective leadership in the competition of communities for the resources of the state:

> *Awọn akọwe ọdọmọde igbayi nilati gbiyanju lati bọ aṣọ iya kuro l'ara Ileṣa*
> Today's educated youngsters must try to take the cloth of suffering from Ilesha

> *Ki awọn ọmọ wa nlanla ki nwọn jiroro bi ilu wa yio ṣe tẹsiwaju*
> May our important sons advise us on how our town may progress

> *Ijeṣa t'o wa l'ẹhin odi ki nwọn maa sanwo ori n'Ileṣa k'a sọwọpọ*
> May the external Ijeshas pay their taxes in Ilesha so that we can cooperate

One implication of these criticisms that Ijesha at home express of external Ijesha is that out-migration puts some strain on communal loyalties and perhaps even that class interests and identities may come to erode them. Of the undoubted force of class relations in the 'Nigerian' sphere, others have written.[13] But the positive expectations which Ilesha residents have of external Ijeshas, especially wealthy and/or educated ones, also presume some fair degree of reciprocity. There is, of course, a great deal of evidence of the lively role that ethnic identities may play in the world of work where class is constituted, both in the informal sector of trade and petty commodity production, and in formal employment.[14] The Ijesha have certainly deployed theirs with a good measure of success. The whole *oṣomaalo* phenomenon is one instance; another is suggested by the perception reported in a study of migration from Iganna (a remote north-west Oyo town) that Ilesha people are considered to dominate jobs in radio and television.[15] Ethnicity is precisely the outcome of an alignment between two forms of competition: between individuals of diverse ethnic origins for jobs, contracts and opportunities in urban and national contexts, and

260

between their regions and communities of origin for favourable access to development goods distributed by the state.

Ethnicity, then, presupposes a system of class relationships, just as it helps to propel people into it. That at the level of political action ethnicity so largely eclipses class is defined in some quarters as a problem. The intellectual grounds for this is a model of social action in which the social system, itself the outcome of its relations of production, defines a definite pattern of real 'interests' which govern the actions of members of society. Concepts like 'false consciousness' will then need to be invented in order to reconcile (i) some show of explanation of why action is sometimes governed by other than these real interests, and (ii) the maintenance of the ontological privilege accorded to class-interests. The theoretical difficulties which then arise are too well known to be rehearsed here. It is better to abandon the narrow and unjustified conception of 'real interest' which gives rise to them. An interest, in its simple sense, is 'that which relates to or for the advantage of any one'.[16] It therefore contains an element of evaluation and relates, in the first instance, to individuals. There is the extra complication that the short-term and long-term interests of the same agent may not actually or apparently coincide. Consequently, interests, in so far as they really do guide action, cannot be considered as existing independently of strategies for their realization that are set within the agent's personal history and life-plan. A collective interest is an even more complex notion. Collectivities may certainly be said to have interests, but it is only the shared assessments of their individual members that can produce collective action to pursue them. Individuals may participate in many cross-cutting and even incompatible collective interests – that is, possibilities of advantage through the advancement of categories to which they belong – and in any society a variety of collective interests, of different kinds, may be activated in the appropriate contexts. But for a collective interest to be more than rather transient and situational, it needs to be grounded in a collective identity: the sense that a category of individuals may have that they 'belong together', in a diffuse and a long-term sense, and from which they derive, as individuals, a sense of *who* they are.

Now, identities are not derived from the structure of specific situations, but are brought to them, the precipitate of many past situations always themselves partly shaped by the assumptions and identities which past agents have brought to them. Identities which give rise to collective interests so salient that they dominate the overall pattern of political alliance and cleavage in a society presuppose a history: both in the sense of some temporal continuity in the identities, and in the sense of a possessed past without which no identity, other than those grounded upon sex and age, can be realized. How does a possessed past contribute so vitally to identity and hence to the possibility of action? It is not, as it has often been regarded by social anthropology, a mere 'mythical charter' conjured solely out of contemporary interest.[17] However much it may be reinterpreted, a possessed past, or the history active in the present, *is* a reflexion on a real historical process. By recalling to the living members of some social category the shared experiences and actions of their predecessors, the feasibility of future shared achievements is strongly suggested. The 'making of Ijesha history', as Fadugba put it, was thus an essential part of the future-oriented politics which *Ẹgbẹ Atunluṣe* began in the early 1920s.[18] At its simplest, the appropriate metaphor for such a possessed past is of a journey together: Obokun, with his followers and his sacred sword, making his way from Ife through Igbadae, Ilowa and Ibokun and eventually, in the person of his descendant, to Ilesha, is the archetype of all such histories. If there is no such actual continuity, the making of history and thus the realization of collective action to present ends is harder to achieve. Small Ijesha villages, anxious for development but frustrated by the discontinuities caused by past wars and constant out-migration, none the less produce a severely truncated form of communal history. 'A certain woman at Ife, lacking children, was told by a diviner to come to this place, and she bore our first *Lọja* ... the surface of the road linking us with Ilesha is not good, so that our sons and daughters do not build here': such was the gist of many village histories collected in 1975 and 1979.[19]

This analysis began with the rejection of the view that class interests and identities must be regarded as more 'real' than other kinds of interest and identity. Nigeria is normal, rather than exceptional, among human societies in that it is communities, rather than classes, which are able to generate powerful enduring identities and so to dominate the pattern in which interests are pursued in the public sphere. Indeed, as Max Weber commented in a well-known discussion of this problem, it is only in so far as classes become 'communities' that they are able to realize the collective pursuit of their interests.[20] Classes vary greatly in their capacity to engender in their members that sense of enduring common purpose which derives from having a possessed past. Upper-class groups are much better placed to do so since, in addition to the kind of class-specific history which is sustained by such means as genealogies and heirlooms, they can easily conceive of the history of the community which they dominate as *their* history, a history with a special space for the achievements of their class. The Nigerian elite, despite its relatively short history, has thus come to 'know itself' through its role in the nationalist movement, the self-creation of Nigeria. That precisely is one important aspect of the 'Ibadan history', which I briefly discussed in Chapter 1. Lower-class groups are much less well placed to possess their past as a class. It may be easiest where they enjoy a good measure of residential segregation and/or social separation from other classes in their community or society; but where they do not, as is still largely the case in Ilesha, their members will tend to derive their strongest identities from the community that they belong to. Thus, the dissatisfactions of the most deprived Ijesha, the farmers who live in villages, most typically give rise to demands for communal facilities – tarred roads, clinics and dispensaries, meeting halls to which to summon their absent educated 'sons of the soil' – and so feed into the communal and ethnic pattern of political cleavage which predominates in Nigeria.

History provides, then, an essential key to a sociological understanding of contemporary realities in Nigeria. The communal identities in which the most salient interest-groups are grounded go back in time, overrunning the bounds of those historical periods which might be derived from the dominance of particular forms of production or particular phases of class formation. The communal identities which were once oriented to tap into the resource flow of the region adapted themselves to a competition for resources distributed from a single embracing state. Even when such identities are strictly novel, as 'Yoruba' in its present extension is, they tend to be aggregates of longer-existing, lower-order communities, or constructed from the materials provided by a pre-existent political culture. (*That* one, indeed, was powerfully helped into existence by a historiographical *tour de force*, the Revd Samuel Johnson's *History of the Yorubas*, the very work which put the Ijesha on their mettle and led to the composition of *Itan Ileṣa*.) The products of this Ijesha passion to possess their past – ranging from the traditions handed down (and now often printed as pamphlets) by towns, villages, quarters and societies of every kind to the personal life-stories which old men are eager to recount – have been the most vital and revealing materials in the making of this study. Half their significance is lost if they are only seen as providing the means to a historian's reconstruction of the past, if the sociologist fails to appreciate how they enlarge – no, permit – a proper understanding to the present. Thus it is that this study of social change has also been so much a study of the past in the present.[21]

Notes

1 Introduction

1 Godfrey and Monica Wilson, *The Analysis of Social Change* (Cambridge, 1945).
2 R. Cohen and J. Middleton (eds.), *From Tribe to Nation in Africa: Studies in Incorporation Processes* (Scranton, 1970). Cf. the essays by E.H. Winter and T.O. Beidelman, R.A. Manners and S. Diamond in J.H. Steward (ed.), *Three African Tribes in Transition* (Urbana, 1967), or by the contributors to J. Goody (ed.), *Changing Social Structure in Ghana: Essays in the Comparative Sociology of a New State and an Old Tradition* (London, 1975).
3 R. Horton, 'African Conversion', *Africa* 41 (1971) and 'On the Rationality of Conversion', *Africa* 45 (1975).
4 J.D.Y. Peel, *Aladura: a Religious Movement among the Yoruba* (London, 1968).
5 Notable examples of the genre include (for West Africa) M. Staniland, *The Lions of Dagbon: Political Change in Northern Ghana* (Cambridge, 1975), J. Dunn and A.F. Robertson, *Dependence and Opportunity: Political Change in Ahafo* (Cambridge, 1974), J.N. Paden, *Religion and Political Culture in Kano* (Berkeley, 1973), N.S. Hopkins, *Popular Government in an African Town: Kita, Mali* (Chicago, 1972), H. Wolpe, *Urban Politics in Nigeria: a Study of Port Harcourt* (Berkeley, 1974).

   K.W.J. Post and G.D. Jenkins' *The Price of Liberty* (Cambridge, 1973) is rather different, being a political biography, but it does have the merits of a good local-level study, since it draws on Jenkins' unpublished Ph.D. thesis, 'Politics in Ibadan' (Northwestern University, 1965). Apart from Pauline Baker's rather less successful *Urbanization and Political Change* (Berkeley, 1974), on Lagos, it is the only such study dealing with the Yoruba.

   The kinds of disquiet to which these monographs were an answer were cogently expressed in two essays, by M. Staniland and J. Vincent, in Colin Leys (ed.), *Politics and Change in Developing Countries* (Cambridge, 1969).
6 G.A. Almond and J.S. Coleman, *The Politics of the Developing Areas* (Princeton, 1960) was the seminal work, D.E. Apter, *The Politics of Modernization* (Chicago, 1965) a culminating statement. None the less Apter's *Gold Coast in Transition* (New York, 1955) had broken new ground in looking at an African nation as a whole, and Coleman's *Nigeria: Background to Nationalism* (Berkeley, 1958) was a valuable and original work of synthesis.
7 S. Amin, *Neo-Colonialism in West Africa* (Harmondsworth, 1973). There had, of course, been left/radical writing – e.g. Thomas Hodgkin and Basil Davidson – but its theoretical character was eclectic rather than Marxist. The writings of A.G. Frank on Latin America, rather than Amin's (in French) on West Africa, were the key stimulus to anglophone Marxist analysis, drawing in the French Marxist anthropologists later: cf. introductions to

C. Leys, *Underdevelopment in Kenya* (London, 1975) or D. Seddon (ed.), *Relations of Production* (London, 1978). W. Rodney's *How Europe Underdeveloped Africa* (London, 1972), though not an especially original work, was a significant marker, since it brought together several strands: black/radical, academic historical and neo-Marxist. See the 'Bibliographical guide to the study of the political economy of Africa', by Chris Allen in P.C.W. Gutkind and I. Wallerstein, *Political Economy of Contemporary Africa* (Beverly Hills, 1976).

8 E.g. J.S. Saul 'The State in post-colonial societies – Tanzania', *Socialist Register 1974*, reprinted in his *The State and Revolution in Eastern Africa* (London, 1974); Colin Leys, 'The "overdeveloped" post-colonial state: a re-evaluation', *RAPE*, 5 (1976); John Dunn (ed.), *West African States: Failure and Promise* (Cambridge, 1978).

9 *Nigerian Political Parties* (Princeton, 1963).

10 The literature is vast and growing; but see R. Cohen, 'Class in Africa: analytical problems and perspectives', in *Socialist Register 1972*, I. Wallerstein, 'Class and class-conflict in contemporary Africa', *CJAS* 7 (1973), G. Arrighi and J.S. Saul, *Essays on the Political Economy of Africa* (New York, 1973), papers on Nigeria by Williams and Peace in E. de Kadt and G. Williams, *Sociology and Development* (London, 1974), R. Stavenhagen, *Social Classes in Agrarian Societies* (Garden City, 1975; originally published in 1969, this compares Mexico and Ivory Coast), R. Sandbrook and R. Cohen (eds.), *The Development of an African Working Class* (London, 1975), Part V of P.C.W. Gutkind and P. Waterman, *African Social Studies: a Radical Reader* (London, 1977), S. Katz, *Marxism, Africa and Social Class: a Critique of Relevant Theories* (Montreal, 1980), for a bibliography and general overview.

11 See the introduction by J.D. Fage to the 1961 printing of his modest but important book, first published in 1955, *An Introduction to the History of West Africa* (Cambridge), where he in effect pointed the way to a history of 'internal forces'.

12 Evans-Pritchard had both practised (*The Sanusi of Cyrenaica*, Oxford, 1949) and preached (*Anthropology and History*, Manchester, 1961) this for a number of years, but it was only taken up widely by social anthropologists in the 1960s. See especially I. Schapera, 'Should anthropologists be historians?' *JRAI* 92 (1962), 143–56; M.G. Smith, 'History and social anthropology', ibid., 73–85; I.M. Lewis (ed.), *History and Social Anthropology* (London, 1968). Most significant of all, both methodologically and substantively, has been the work of J. Vansina, especially *Oral Tradition* (1961; English translation 1965).

13 *Government in Zazzau* (London, 1960).

14 *The Trading States of the Oil Rivers* (London, 1963).

15 *The Political Development of Yoruba Kingdoms in the Eighteenth and Nineteenth Centuries* (RAI Occasional Paper 31; London, 1971).

16 The five papers collected as Part I of *Benin Studies* (London, 1973). This work was done as part of the interdisciplinary Scheme for the Study of Benin History and Culture, directed by K.O. Dike.

17 'A Hundred Years of Change in Kalabari Religion', in J. Middleton (ed.), *Black Africa: its Peoples and their Cultures Today* (London, 1970), 192–211, and 'Stateless Societies in the History of West Africa', in J.F.A. Ajayi and M. Crowder (eds.), *History of West Africa* (London, 1971), chap. 3.

18 J.F. Ade Ajayi, 'Colonialism: an Episode in African History', in L.H. Gann and P. Duignan, *Colonialism in Africa*, vol. 1 (Cambridge, 1969), 497–508. For a reassertion of the view of colonialism as *the* divide, see the chapter by A.A. Boahen, 'The Colonial Era: Conquest to Independence', ibid., vol. 2 (1970).

19 C. Coquery Vidrovitch, 'Research on an African Mode of Production', in D. Seddon (ed.), *Relations of Production* (London, 1978; originally in *La Pensée* 144, 1969).

20 C. Meillassoux, *Anthropologie Economique des Gouro de Côte d'Ivoire* (Paris, 1964),

P.P. Rey, *Colonialisme, Neo-colonialisme et Transition au Capitalisme* (Paris, 1971), E. Terray, *Marxism and 'Primitive' Societies* (New York, 1972), M. Godelier, *Perspectives in Marxist Anthropology* (Cambridge, 1977), esp. pp. 15–62.

21 Leys, *Underdevelopment in Kenya*, pp. 198–206.

22 E.g. as in Terray's reinterpretation of Meillassoux's Gouro material *(Marxism and 'Primitive' Societies*, pp. 95–106) or in Meillassoux's reworking of Turnbull's Mbuti material: 'The Mode of Production of the Hunting Band', in P. Alexandre, *French Perspectives in African Studies* (London, 1973), pp. 187–203.

23 Thus P. Anderson: 'The "superstructures" of kinship, religion, law or the state necessarily enter into the constitutive structure of the mode of production [in pre-capitalist societies] ... In consequence [they] cannot be defined but via their political, legal and ideological superstructures, since these are what determine the type of extra-economic coercion that specifies them': *Lineages of the Absolutist State* (London, 1974), pp. 403–4.

24 K. Polanyi, *Primitive, Archaic and Modern Economies*, edited by G. Dalton (Garden City, 1968), pp. 70–2.

25 H. Spiro (ed.), *The Primacy of Politics* (New York, 1966). No doubt he had in mind Nkrumah's famous slogan: 'Seek ye first the political kingdom.'

26 C. Leys, 'The "overdeveloped" post-colonial state', *RAPE* 5 (1976).

27 J. O'Connell, 'The political class and economic development in Nigeria', *NJESS* 8 (1966). The term 'political class' was particularly current among the social scientists at the University of Ibadan who produced the periodical *Nigerian Opinion* around 1964–66.

28 For publications up to c. 1975, see D.E. and C.M. Baldwin, *The Yoruba of Southwestern Nigeria: an Indexed Bibliography* (Boston, Mass., 1976), which contains 3,488 items.

29 The most indispensable work in the whole corpus – and an outstanding one by any criteria – is by a Yoruba: the Revd Samuel Johnson, *The History of the Yorubas* (Lagos, 1921; completed about 20 years earlier).

30 Eva Krapf-Askari, *Yoruba Towns and Cities* (Oxford, 1969) and J.S. Eades, *The Yoruba Today* (Cambridge, 1980). Still of value is Daryll Forde, *The Yoruba-speaking Peoples of Southwestern Nigeria* (London, 1951).

31 P. C. Lloyd, 'Political and Social Structure', in S.O. Biobaku (ed.), *Sources of Yoruba History* (Oxford, 1973), chap. 12; also, in practice, his *Yoruba Land Law* (London, 1962) and *Political Development of Yoruba Kingdoms in the Eighteenth and Nineteenth Centuries* (London, 1971).

32 Edited and introduced by A.G. Hopkins, *JHSN* 5 (1969), 67–100. It was written for the British authorities by H. Carr, O. Johnson (S. Johnson's brother), E.H. Oke, A. Edun, W.T.G. Lawson and C.A. Sapara-Williams (an Ijesha, on whom see pp. 94–102).

33 See, for example, *The Proceedings of the Conference on Yoruba Civilization*, 2 vols. (eds. I.A. Akinjogbin and G.O. Ekemode), held at the University of Ife, 26–31 July 1976.

34 P. C. Lloyd, 'The traditional political system of the Yoruba', *SWJA* 10 (1954), 'Sacred kingship and government among the Yoruba', *Africa* 3 (1960), and 'Conflict Theory and Yoruba Kingdoms', in Lewis, *History and Social Anthropology*, pp. 25–61. in particular.

35 'The political structure of African kingdoms', in M. Banton (ed.), *Political Systems and the Distribution of Power* (London, 1965), pp. 63–112; cf. p. 84: 'we take as our starting point [for a classification of kingdoms] the recruitment of the political elite ...'. This is in contrast to the principles advocated by Vansina (degree of territorial devolution), M.G. Smith (character of the administrative hierarchy) or Easton (degree of differentiation in political roles), here reviewed by Lloyd.

The inadequacy of this conception of Yoruba political structure was first clearly pointed out in a footnote by Niara Sudarkasa, *Where Women Work: A Study of Yoruba Women in the Marketplace and in the Home* (Ann Arbor, 1973), pp. 11–12. The fact that Sudarkasa herself worked in Awe, an Oyo town, makes it likely that the difference of interpretation does not arise from empirical variations between different Yoruba subgroups, such as the Oyo and the Ijesha, but from different theoretical models.

36 R.C.C. Law, *The Oyo Empire, c. 1600–c. 1836* (Oxford, 1977), p. 62: '[chiefs] were given senior titles in recognition of their power; political power did not derive from the possession of a title'. (For a critique of this view, Peel, 'Kings, titles and quarters', 225–7.) Law goes on (p. 63) to indicate the source of this view: a picture of Old Oyo 'as essentially a federation of lineages'.

37 E.A. Ayandele, *The Missionary Impact on Modern Nigeria 1842–1914: a Political and Social Analysis* (London, 1966); J.F. Ade Ajayi, *Christian Missions in Nigeria 1841–1891: the Making of a New Elite* (London, 1965).

38 R.A. Adeleye, *Power and Diplomacy in Northern Nigeria 1804–1906* (London, 1971); B.O. Oloruntimehin, *The Segu Tukulor Empire* (London, 1972).

39 J.A. Atanda, *The New Oyo Empire: Indirect Rule and Change in Western Nigeria 1894–1934* (London, 1973); A.E. Afigbo, *The Warrant Chiefs* (London, 1972); A.I. Asiwaju, *Western Yorubaland under European Rule 1889–1945* (London, 1976); P. A. Igbafe, *Benin under British Administration* (London, 1979).

40 T.N. Tamuno, *The Evolution of the Nigerian State: the Southern Phase 1898–1914* (London, 1972); J.C. Anene, *The International Boundaries of Nigeria* (London, 1970).

41 F.I.A. Omu, *Press and Politics in Nigeria 1880–1937* (London, 1978); O. Adewoye, *The Judicial System in Southern Nigeria 1854–1954* (London, 1977).

42 One might compile an impressive list of this public service. For example, from Southern Nigerian historians alone: state commissioners – Igbafe, Atanda, Omu, Awe, Folayan; federal commissioners – Adeleye, Adewoye; senator – Akintoye; vice-chancellors (in Nigeria a far from cloistered post!) – Dike, Ajayi, Ayandele, Biobaku, Tamuno.

43 E.A. Ayandele, *The Educated Elite in the Nigerian Society* (Ibadan, 1974), originally given as a University Lecture at Ibadan.

44 S.A. Akintoye, *Revolution and Power Politics in Yorubaland 1840–1893* (London, 1971), B. Awe, 'The Ajele system', *JHSN* 3 (1964) and 'Militarism and economic development in nineteenth century Yoruba country', *JAH* 14 (1973). Both bodies of writing have been invaluable in the context of the present study; see below chap. 5.

45 Thus Atanda, *New Oyo Empire*, chap. 6; Asiwaju, *Western Yorubaland*, chaps. 7–10; Igbafe, *Benin under British Administration*, chap. 10.

46 Thus Atanda, *ibid*., pp. 29–30, arguing against Lloyd's suggestion that conflicts between *Alafin* and chiefs might be the major cause of Old Oyo's downfall: 'the conflicts referred to were not likely to be as intense as imagined in a society where family ties, interlineage marriages, some measure of economic cooperation and other personal ties might cushion the impact of conflicts'. Compare the highly consensualist view of inter-state relations implied by the '*ẹbi* [family] theory of government' put forward by I.A. Akinjogbin, *Dahomey and its Neighbours 1708–1818* (Cambridge, 1967), pp. 14–17.

47 E.g. Polly Hill, *Migrant Cocoa-Farmers of Southern Ghana* (Cambridge, 1963); A.G. Hopkins, *Economic History of West Africa* (London, 1973), pp. 216–22; Sara S. Berry, *Cocoa, Custom and Socio-Economic Change in Rural Southwestern Nigeria* (Oxford, 1975), chaps. 2–3.

48 E.g. Igbafe's chap. 10 on economic change is quite explicit: 'Aspects of British economic policies in Benin'. Or Atanda, p. 215, introducing the topic of economic change: 'Firstly, the economic and social changes that took place resulted largely from development projects carried out by the central Government in conjunction with Native Authorities at the local level.' Asiwaju (*Western Yorubaland*, pp. 158 ff.) stresses the introduction of wheeled transport, roads and the railway, strongly recalling the emphasis placed on the transport revolution found in Allan McPhee's classic (but Eurocentric) *Economic Revolution in British West Africa* (London, 1926). Tamuno's *Evolution of the Nigerian State*, chap. 9, is quite explicitly focussed on the achievements of British administrators and

pressure groups, even when these had far less economic effect (e.g. The British Cotton Growers' Association) than those of illiterate local farmers.

49 Ayandele, *Educated Elite.*

50 E.A. Ayandele, 'Observations on some social and economic aspects of slavery in pre-colonial Northern Nigeria', *NJESS* 9 (1967). See too the more general contentions of his 'How truly Nigerian is our Nigerian history?' *African Notes* (Ibadan), 5 (1969).

51 'The Changing Position of the Awujales of Ijebuland under Colonial Rule', in M. Crowder and O. Ikime (eds.), *West African Chiefs* (Ile Ife, 1970).

52 As, for example, D. Brokensha *Social Change at Larteh, Ghana* (Oxford, 1966) or E.P. Skinner, *African Urban Life: the Transformation of Ouagadougou* (Princeton, 1974).

53 Thus, as it were speaking for a whole discipline of which he was a powerful though often unacknowledged legislator, Herbert Spencer: 'the denial of a Social Science has arisen from the confusing of two essentially different classes of phenomena which societies present – the one, almost ignored by historians, constituting the subject matter of Social Science, and the other class, almost exclusively occupying them, admitting of scientific coordination in a very small degree, if at all'. These are 'the structures and functions' of societies, and 'the phenomena of conduct', respectively: *Study of Sociology* (London, 1873) pp. 47, 58, further discussed in J.D.Y. Peel, *Herbert Spencer: the Evolution of a Sociologist* (London, 1981), pp. 158–65. A similar notion clearly underlies Marx's conviction that the key to understanding the movement of modern society lay in a 'base', lying beneath its 'surface' features.

54 E.g. M. Gluckman, 'Analysis of a social situation in modern Zululand', *Bantu Studies* 14 (1940), V.W. Turner, *Schism and Continuity in an African Society* (Manchester, 1957), especially the use made of the vicissitudes of Sandombu, or D.M. Boswell, 'Personal Crises and the Mobilization of the Social Network' in J.C. Mitchell (ed.), *Social Networks in Urban Situations* (Manchester, 1969).

55 F. Braudel, in his well-known essay 'Histoire et sciences sociales: la longue durée', in *Annales* 4 (1958), and in *The Mediterranean and the Mediterranean World in the Age of Philip II*, trans. Sian Reynolds (London, 1972; Fontana edn. 1975), pp. 20–1, distinguished three levels of history: an almost imperceptible movement of man's contact with nature, a history of social groups with long-term trends, and 'a history of events'. One may agree that the interrelations of these differently timed trends furnishes history with a grand theme. None the less Braudel (cf. his 1965 postscript, in *The Mediterranean*, pp. 1242–4) sees events conditioned by the larger trends without presenting any clear model of how the trends are constituted by events.

56 Cf. Emmanuel Le Roy Ladurie's splendid analysis *Carnival in Romans: a People's Uprising 1579–1580*, trans. M. Feeney (Harmondsworth, 1981).

2 The regional context

1 See Thurston Shaw, *Nigeria: its Archaeology and Early History* (London, 1978), pp. 45–51, 157–63.

2 On Ijesha chronology, J.D.Y. Peel, 'Kings, titles and quarters : a conjectural history of Ilesha. Part I : the traditions reviewed', *History in Africa* 6 (1979), 109–53.

3 On Ibokun, P.A. Francis, 'Power and order: a study of litigation in a Yoruba community' (unpublished Ph.D. thesis, Liverpool, 1981), chapter 2.

4 See pp. 38, 64.

5 On Oyo–Ijesha relations at this period, see the very thorough review by Law, *Oyo Empire* pp. 127–33.

6 Johnson, *History of the Yorubas*, p.22.

7 The most important collection of local Ijesha traditions is a history of over 200 pages by J.D.E. Abiola, J.A. Babafemi and S.O.S. Ataiyero, *Itan Ileṣa* (Ilesha, 1932). This was quite deliberately intended to rebut some of Johnson's account of Ijesha traditions – Johnson's

history being published in 1921. For evaluation of this and other local histories see Peel, 'Kings, titles and quarters, Part I', 111–13, and for a fuller account of the political context of its composition, see below chap. 9, pp.179–81.

8 J.U. Egharevba, *A Short History of Benin* (Ibadan, 1960), p. 33. On Akure, see S.O. Arifalo, 'An analysis and comparison of the legends of origin of Akure' (University of Ibadan, Dept. of History, unpublished undergraduate dissertation, 1966) and 'Pre-colonial Akure', in I.A. Akinjogbin and G.O. Ekemode (eds.), *Proceedings of the Conference on Yoruba Civilization* ... (mimeographed, Ife, 1976), vol. 1, pp. 154–79; also N. A. C. Weir, 'Intelligence Report on Akure District, Ekiti Division (1934)', CSO 26/10995 (*NAI*).

9 Akintoye, *Revolution and Power Politics*, p.226.

10 The Revd William Allen, 'Journal for 1878', in CA2/019 (CMS).

11 Mr E.A. Makinde, chief landlord of Alarere village, the first modern settlement in the area, interview, 17 Aug. 1979.

12 Chief Ṣedile and other Itisin chiefs (the *Batiṣin* title then being vacant), interview, 6 Aug. 1974.

13 This reference seems more likely than to the settlement called Igbobini in Okitipupa Division, as the *Ogboni* is also described as *ọṛẹ Ọba Ado* ('friend of the King of Benin'): Chief Bode Phillips, Aduloju II, Ogboni of Ilesha, interview, 1 Aug. 1974.

14 Law, *Oyo Empire*, pp. 37–9.

15 A.F.C. Ryder, *Benin and the Europeans* (London, 1969), pp. 14–15.

16 Law, *Oyo Empire*, p. 127, referring to Johnson, *History of the Yorubas*, p. 168. *Exactly* when this was is impossible to say: Law's suggestion that the 'Ijesha Arera' of Johnson's account may be linked with the name of Atakunmosa's successor Uyi*arere* seems strained.

17 On Oshogbo, see Johnson, *History of the Yorubas*, p. 156. He describes it as a reply to the Oyo settlement of Ede, which in turn was to prevent Ijesha molestation of traders going to the market at Apomu. Until the nineteenth century Ede stood *north* of the Oshun, which was here the Oyo/Ijesha boundary, not south of it as at present. On the details of the boundary, see Law, *Oyo Empire*, pp. 87–8. On Ada, see traditions reported in Atanda, *The New Oyo Empire* p. 7: here there were two ruling houses, one of Oyo, one of Ijesha descent, and they took it in turns to provide the *Alada*.

18 Omirinmirin market is described in *Iwe Itan Oko Apara* ('History of Apara's Farm'), MS. composed by J.B. Apara between 1939 and 1964 on basis of information from his father Peter Apara (*c.* 1847–1922), who established a farm-settlement on the site (University of Ife Library).For Oke Ibode, see W.H. Clarke, *Travels and Explorations in Yorubaland (1854–1858)*, ed. J.A. Atanda (Ibadan, 1972), p. 127.

19 Ryder, *Benin and the Europeans*, p. 98.

20 Weir, 'Intelligence Report on Akure District', referring to Igbogi, 22nd Deji of Akure.

21 In all, 518 family cults were mentioned, which involved 53 distinct *oriṣa*. Ogun was mentioned 136 times, followed by Ifa 131 times. As the god of divinition, Ifa is the most important pan-Yoruba *oriṣa*. After these two came Osun 42, Orisa Onifon (including other descriptions, such as Ogiyan, Obatala, Orisa Alaye etc.) 32, Obokun (the dynasty's founder) 21, Owaluse (Ilesha's founder) 15, Olojo 12, Oludu (*Ogboni*'s ancestor) 10, Obalogun (hunters' god) 9, Olokun 8, Orisa Asalu (worshipped especially by Chief *Loro*'s lineage) 8, Oduduwa 8, Owari (Owaluse's predecessor, an autochthonous figure) 7, Olode/Soponna 7, Sango 7, Oro-Oluodo (a powerful *Ọwa*) 6.

22 See the two maps in G.J.A. Ojo, *Yoruba Culture: a Geographical Analysis* (London, 1966), pp. 96, 171. For an overall view of 'the sacred iron complex' in Yorubaland, see Sandra T. Barnes, *Ogun: an Old God for a New Age* (Philadelphia, 1980).

23 Members of *Ule Agbẹdẹ* (Ogboni lineage) at Igando street mentioned these places as sources of *ẹṣọṛọ* (presumably smelted iron), interview, 23 December 1974.

24 See Sir William McGregor, 21 May 1901, in CSO 879/58/580 (PRO).

25 Denis Williams, *Icon and Image* (London, 1974), chap. 11.

26 *Sajǫwa* is said to be a more recent title than the Oyo-linked *Agbatayǫ*. Oludu is said to have had no male issue till he put kola for the blacksmiths at Ogun's shrine. The resultant child was given to *Agbatayǫ* for training and eventually became *Sajǫwa* (I. F. Opesusi of *Ogboni* lineage, interview 31 Oct. 1974). Another story is that *Sajǫwa* was a man from Idoka, a village to the east of Ilesha, who killed a man and ran to the *Ogboni* of Ilesha for sanctuary. The *Ogboni* adopted his son and gave him to *Agbatayǫ* to train (*Ule Agbǫdǫ* members). In both cases, the Oyo connexion comes first, but is surpassed by the later Benin connexion.

27 Quoted by Olu Akinyeye, 'Ogun – God of Iron', *West Africa*, 12 June 1978, 1127. This proverb is echoed in a saying about Ipole or Ilaje, the centre of the Ijesha kingdom immediately before Ilesha. Ogun is said to have camped at Ipole (Ilaje), and when it was deserted for Ilesha, to have pronounced a curse:

> *ǫni pe Ilaje l'oko, ko ni irin ǫna Ogun ye*
> whoever calls Ilaje a mere farm, will not enjoy roads cleared by iron.

(S.A. Ataiyero, *A Short History of the Ijeshas, Part I* (Ilesha, 1978), p. 103).

28 Abiola, Babafemi and Ataiyero, *Itan Ilęsa*, chap. 8.

29 *Itan Ilęsa*, chap. 12, lists Ado, Ara, Ido, Ila, Otun, Ondo, Ijero and Igbajo.

30 Thus Chief D. Oyewumi the *Risinkin*, interview, 22 July 1974.

31 The Makinwa family of Atorin village and Anaye quarter thus trace descent from an Efon man (B.B. Makinwa, interview, 28 July 1979; the family has prepared a typewritten history, and genealogy and *oriki* are also set out in a printed pamphlet, *Ipade Ǫmǫ Ile Makinwa*). As described in chap. 3, p.46, *ǫmęsę* were the sons of substantial chiefs in both Ilesha and subordinate settlements, who were required to be sent to the *Afin* on their father's death. It thus implies that Efon was then firmly under Ilesha control.

32 For details, relating to Efon, Itaji, Oye, Akure, and Aramoko, see Peel, 'Kings, titles and quarters. Part II', *History in Africa* 7 (1980), 248.

33 The 1974 Household Survey produced, from a random sample of nearly 450 households, evidence of some 14 non-titled lineages of non-Ijesha origin. These were from Akure (3), Efon Alaye (3), Ijebu Ode (2), and one each from Ogotun, Ijero, Aramoko, Ado-Ekiti, Ile Oluji, Ondo, and Ife. The dating of these migrations is not easy, but most would have fallen in the eighteenth and early to mid nineteenth centuries. The absence of immigrants from the savannah or Oyo areas is striking.

34 K.V. Elphinstone, *Gazetteer of Ilorin Province* (London, 1921), p.11.

35 On the chronology of these Nupe wars, Peel, 'Kings, titles and quarters, Part I', 140–1. Cf. Law, *Oyo Empire*, pp. 264–5.

36 This is suggested by the links between Igangan, a town founded about this time in southern Ijesha, an area rich in kola, with titles and cults (*Arapatę*; Obalogun) associated with the Nupe wars. One of the founding lineages of Igangan claims descent from Ila Orangun in Igbomina: S.A. Saraibi, *Itan Kukuru nipa Isędalę Ilu Igangan* ('Short History of the Foundation of Igangan', Ilesha(?), n.d.), interview with Igangan chiefs, 9 Aug. 1974.

37 This was not earlier than the seventeenth century since Iwara, which has traditions of foundation by Atakunmosa, already existed. Details of the foundation story in Ataiyero, *Short History, Part I*, pp. 91–2, and oral testimony from Pa J.S. Odidi of Ifewara, interview, 24 Aug. 1979.

38 Thus *Ǫwa* Oluodo's offspring were said to have gone to Ife, and it was from here that his descendant Ofokutu was called to rule in the mid nineteenth century (Abiola *et al. Itan Ilęsa*, chap. 27). Again, they tell the story of an arrogant warrior Odidi who, after making trouble in Ilesha, escapes to Ife (ibid., chap. 102).

39 The account of the Ife/Ilesha relationships given here from the Ijesha side is strongly supportive of the speculative but coherent and (to my mind) convincing argument as to Ife's decline but retention of sacred prestige within Yorubaland put forward by R. Horton, 'Ancient Ife : a reassessment', *JHSN* (forthcoming).

40 Meffre to Griffiths, 16 Feb. 1882 in CO/147/149.48. On the commercial significance of the 'eastern road', one of whose branches went through Iperindo, see S.A. Akintoye, 'The Ondo Road, Eastwards of Lagos, *c.* 1870–1895', *JAH* 10 (1969), 581–98.

41 Clarke, *Travels and Explorations*, pp. 125–7: 'at this place every fifth day are collected together several thousand people from all the surrounding country, with their various articles of exchange, and trading is carried on to such an extent in goods – manufactures and provisions – that quite astonish one not acquainted with the commercial spirit of this inferior country. Here may be seen the representatives of nearly all the Yoruba . . . .'

42 Hinderer, 'Report for 1858', in CA 2/049. He comments that, though Ifes and Ijeshas met here for trade, each was prohibited from going further, but the chiefs were tired of this animosity.

43 *Iwe Itan Oko Apara*, ff. 7–9. Omirinmirin was very large, being said to stretch a mile and a half along the road.

44 See pp.83–95.

45 While *loja* (or *oloja*) can mean 'owner of the market', this does not seem to be its basic meaning. The word, as in Ondo, means 'village-head', and many, if not most, such villages headed by a *loja* did not possess markets.

46 '*omo ijoye nlanla Ilesha*'. Johnson (*History of the Yorubas*, p. 217) describes Ogodo, the market town on the Niger where Yoruba and Nupe met, in similar terms: 'nearly all the children of influential Oyo chiefs resided there permanently for the purpose of trade'.

47 On Apomu, see Law, *Oyo Empire*, pp. 121, 219, 274–5. There seems to be an unresolved problem concerning Apomu's antiquity. Law (p. 219) suggests a late eighteenth century date, on the basis of a local king-list; but Johnson (*History of the Yorubas*, p. 156), says that it was Ijesha molesting of Apomu-bound traders which led to the founding of Ede. This he attributes to the reign of an *Alafin*, Kori, who reigned before the exile to Igboho, i.e. pre-1500 (Law, pp. 48–50).

48 '*Nigbati Atukunmosa ri pe ilu on ko kun to bi on ti nfe . . .*', *Itan Ileṣa*, chap. 8.

49 Chief S.A. Ataiyero (youngest son and local historian), interview, 19 Aug. 1974.

50 Peel, 'Kings, titles and quarters. Part I', 130–42; cf. too M.I. Ekundare, *Iwe Itan awon Adugbo Kokan t'o wa ninu Ilu Ilesha* ('History of Every Quarter in Ilesha', Ilesha, 1966).

51 See above, n. 33.

52 Only two examples are known to me. After the uprising against members of the royal lineage in Bilagbayo's reign (mid eighteenth century), the *Loja* of Isolo village is said to have escaped with his people to Ejigbo, where he was made *Asolo* (Ataiyero, *Short History of the Ijeshas, Part I*, p. 40).
Also, the great Mode descent-group at Ondo claims descent from an immigrant from Ilesha, though his ancestor had earlier migrated to Ilesha from Ondo (Awosika Family Association, *Iwe Itan Mode* Ondo, n.d.).

53 Ayibiowu, Omole and Ode.

54 Adimula Agunloye-bi-Oyinbo (i.e. Bepo) to Governor, Enclosure No. 10 in CO 147/149, Despatch 48 (1882).

55 R.C.C. Law, 'The heritage of Oduduwa: traditional history and political propaganda among the Yoruba', *JAH* 12 (1971).

56 Cf. the saying quoted by Abiola *et al.*, *Itan Ileṣa*, chap. 106:

> *A ki fi ile gbogbo han alejo, Ibokun fi ile han Oyo*
> We don't show the whole house to a stranger; Ibokun showed the house to the Oyo.

One note of caution here. As further described (p.263), *Itan Ileṣa* was written specifically to rebut the Oyo historian Johnson, and its immediate political purpose was to get Ilesha out of Oyo Province into what Ijesha considered to be their rightful political position as capital of Ekiti. There may therefore be *some* exaggeration of the contrast with the Oyo. However, the general tenor of their comments is confirmed by other nineteenth-century evidence (see below) and is implicit in the cultural affinities and migratory movements between Ilesha and Ekiti.

57 Quoted from E.L. Lasebikan in T. Hodgkin, *Nigerian Perspectives: a Historical Anthology* (London, 1960), p. 326.

58 As *Itan Ileṣa* puts it in a passage on Ijesha food:

> *ebi ko pa Ijeṣa, o ni on ko jẹ ẹkọ Ọyọ*
> an Ijesha has to be starving before he'll eat Oyo maize-pap

Johnson (*History of the Yorubas*, p. 215) presents the same contrast: when the maize crop failed one year for lack of rain, the Oyo attacked Igbogi, a town in north-west Ijesha, since 'the staple of the Ijeshas being yam and not corn . . . the yam crop does not depend upon the latter rain'.

59 See the verses quoted in E.B. Idowu, *Olodumare: God in Yoruba Belief* (London, 1962), p. 153. Olufon or Ogiyan (i.e. the deity Orisa Onifon) who came to Ilesha from Ifon, in the savannah north-west of Oshogbo, has a taboo on palm-wine. The best palm-wine is from the forest regions. Osun of Iponda, the main Ijesha centre of this river goddess, will not drink maize-beer, however. (I am grateful to Paul Francis for drawing my attention to this reference.)

60 Clarke, *Travels and Explorations*, p. 125.

61 Johnson, *History of the Yorubas*, pp. 20–5: part of his account of Ilesha is presented under the section entitled 'The Ekitis', but he also calls the Ekiti 'quite distinct from the Ijeshas, especially in political affairs' – an odd thing for the historian of Ibadan's war against the Ekitiparapo to say. A (lost) document prepared by *Ọwa* Ajimoko in 1898 (referred to in 'Notes on Yoruba Crowns by A.D.O. Ife', in MSS. Afr. S 1151/6, Rhodes House) contrasts 'the Highlands of Ekitiparapo', in which Ilesha is included, and 'Yorubaland'. Cf. too comments in an editorial, 12 Nov. 1902, in *Lagos Standard*: it refers to 'the common but inaccurate description of Ekiti people down the coast . . . is that they are Ijeshas, but the Ekitis are not Ijeshas while the Ijeshas may not ineptly be styled Ekitis . . . Ijesha is only one of the 16 kingdoms which constitute the Ekiti Confederacy, and it is the contiguity of the Ijesha to the sea which gives them prominence.'

62 D.J. May ('Journey into the Yoruba and Nupe countries in 1858', *JRGS* 30 (1860), 212–33) was expressly disallowed from going to Ado, three or four days to the east, and, like Clarke, was only permitted to go to Ila-Orangun by an indirect route through Ibokun.

63 Akintoye, *Revolution and Power Politics, passim* and esp. pp. 92–4.

64 E.g. Johnson's list, p. 23; cf. too Akintoye, pp. 6–7. None the less, on one occasion during the Kiriji War, the leaders of the Ekitiparapo wrote styling themselves 'sixteen kings of Ekiti': rulers of Ilesha, Otun, Ijero, Ido, Efon, Oye, Ara, Ikole, Ayede, Ibo (=Obo?), Imesi, Ila-Orangun, Ohin, Ire, Apa, Akure, to Secretary, Yoruba·Mission, 24 March 1885, CMS(Y), 1/7 (5).

65 It is significant that whereas the forest regions (including Ife, Ilesha and Ekiti) use the number sixteen (cf. the 16 *odu* of Ifa, and market periodicities of 4, 8 or 16 days), the Oyo legend used the number seven, though the same principle governed their selection: neighbours of close culture. So we have for Oyo (Johnson, p. 15): Oyo itself, Benin, Ila-Orangun, Owu, Ketu, Sabe and Popo – the last four all being to the west or south of Oyo. The number seven itself suggests a reworking of the basic form of the legend under Islamic influence, as it goes with a migration from Mecca rather than an autochthonous origin at

Ife; and seven is the market periodicity of the most deeply Islamic areas of West Africa (Hausa, Kanuri, Manding country).

66 E.g. Ataiyero, *Short History*, p. 104. *Owa* Ajimoko 'Notes on Yoruba Crowns' gave the sixteen kings as those of Ife, Benin, Oyo, Ilesha, Ado-Ekiti, Aramoko, Ijero, Ila-Orangun, Otun, Ido-Ekiti, Ikole, Efon, Alaye, Ogotun, Ise-Ekiti, Akure.

67 Cf. A. Obayemi, 'The Yoruba and Edo-speaking peoples and their neighbours before 1600', in J.F.A. Ajayi and M. Crowder (eds.), *History of West Africa*, vol. I, second edition (London, 1976), pp. 196–263.

68 J. Goody, *Technology, Tradition and the State* (London, 1971).

3 The structure of the capital

1 On Yoruba towns, see P. Wheatley, 'Significance of traditional Yoruba urbanism', *CSSH* 12 (1970); A.L. Mabogunje, *Yoruba Towns* (Ibadan, 1962); E. Krapf-Askari, *Yoruba Towns and Cities* (Oxford, 1969); W.R. Bascom, 'Early historical evidence of Yoruba urbanism', in U.G. Damachi and H.D. Siebel (eds.), *Social Change and Economic Development in Nigeria* (New York, 1973); J.S. Eades, *The Yoruba Today* (Cambridge, 1980), chap. 3.

2 The estimate of the Revd Charles Phillips, travelling to the Kiriji camp, 'Correspondence respecting the War between Native Tribes in the Interior . . .' Cmnd. 4957, 1887, p. 76. They were described as 'scattered in many suburbs' (i.e. quarters). This estimate would seem to be derived from the extent of buildings or ruins, and comparable estimates are provided by Phillips or by his colleague the Revd Samuel Johnson for very many other towns they passed through (e.g. Iwo, Modakeke and Oshogbo 60,000; Ijebu-Ode 30,000; Ibadan 100,000 etc.). At that time the extent of buildings is certain to have shrunk considerably since before the period of the wars. Actual population is likely to have been much lower. In 1898 Ilesha's population was put at only 5,000, with Modakeke's at 20,000, Oshogbo's at 50,000 and Ibadan's at 200,000 (*Lagos Annual Report* for 1899), but this was at a time when steps were being taken to restore Ilesha's population. By 1911 a Methodist missionary's estimate was 35,000, out of a total Ijesha population of 300,000 (A.E. Southon, *Ilesha and Beyond* (London, n.d.), p. 38). What the population may have been before the sack of 1870 is even harder to say. Hinderer in 1858 described Ilesha's extent as like Ibadan but also said at least half of the houses were in ruins ('Journal for 1858', in CMS (L), CA 2/049), while May, having come from Ibadan via Modakeke, described it as larger than any town except Ibadan itself ('Journey in the Yoruba and Nupe Counties in 1858', *JRGS* 30 (1860), 212–33). Is it possible to make any inferences from these scattered guesses and estimates?

The Phillips/Johnson figures of 1886 provide a basis of comparison, expressing extent of building. Ilesha would have been relatively larger earlier, especially than Modakeke which gained population until the 1890s when much of it was dispersed. But even at its height, Ilesha was probably less compact than the Oyo towns which grew up or absorbed many immigrants in the nineteenth century (May, 'Journey', commented on Iwo's compactness), and so its actual population was likely to be down on estimates based on extent of houses. If May was right about its apparent size relative to Modakeke in 1858, and Modakeke was then smaller than it seemed to Johnson in 1880, Ilesha's population in the 1850s is likely to have been above the 25,000 of Phillips's estimate and considerably below the figure of 60,000 given for Modakeke by Johnson. What is impossible to say is whether the ruins spoken of by Hinderer – unmentioned by the other Europeans, May and Clarke, who visited it about the same time – indicate a significant loss of population from an earlier period, or if he was overimpressed by some of the effects of the civil strife common at that time. One can only regret that Clarke, the most generally informative of these early visitors, admitted that he 'could not judge of its size and population' (*Travels and Explorations*, p. 136).

3 Eades, *The Yoruba Today*, p. 43, is mistaken to include Ilesha along with Ibadan, Abeokuta, Oyo, Oshogbo etc. as a town 'either founded during the 19th century or [which]

grew rapidly during it with the influx of refugees from the devastated areas around'. It is likely that some quarters of Ilesha did take in some refugees from communities such as Otaide or Igbogi Oke, destroyed in north-western Ijeshaland in the wars of the 1820s, but the political and residential structure was unchanged and the *rate* of growth does not seem to have greatly accelerated: see Peel, 'Kings, titles and quarters. Part I', 122, 142.

4 See Ivor Wilks, *Asante in the Nineteenth Century* (Cambridge, 1975), pp. 93, 374.

5 For a comparative study of the *afin* of Yorubaland, see G.J.A. Ojo, *Yoruba Palaces* (London, 1966).

6 Further on the quarters, and especially on the sequence of their foundation, see my 'Kings, titles and quarters. Part I', *passim*. A useful printed source on the quarters, fuller than Abiola *et al.*'s *Itan Ileṣa*, is M.I. Ekundare, *Iwe Itan awọn Adugbọ Kọkan t'o wa ninu Ilu Ilesha* (Ilesha, 1966).

7 This, though apparently unusual, is not restricted to Ilesha. N.A.C. Weir, 'Intelligence Report on Ikerre District' (1933; No. 30169, *NAI*), notes it of Ikere in south-eastern Ekiti.

8 Thus Chief D. Gidigbi, the *Ọrunbatọ* (4th) of Ifofin, interview 6 June 1975. The *akata* tree here was an *uṣin* (akee-apple, *Blighia sapida*), 'as the power which is put to establish this quarter' (*gẹgẹbi aṣẹ ti o fi da adugbo yi*). Other *akata*-trees included *agbagba* (plantain, *Musa sapientium*), *iroko* (African teak, *Chlorophora excelsa*), *ayan* (satinwood, *Distemonanthus* spp), *oṣe* (baobab, *Adansonia digitata*), *ọṣiṣẹ* (Senegalese coral tree, *Erythrina senegalensis*).

9 Ijoka is said to have been founded by a man of Itaji, which is usually assumed to be the Ekiti town of that name (e.g. Obayemi, 'Yoruba and Edo-speaking peoples before 1600', in J.F.E. Ajayi and M. Crowder, eds., *History of West Africa*, vol. 1, second edition, London, 1976, p. 253). However Chief Aduroja the *Lẹjọka* (interview, 20 August 1974) said Itaji was a village near Ilesha. There is also a quarter of Ibokun called Itaji to this day and a saying there which seems to suggest Ijoka drew population from there, perhaps an aspect of Ilesha's displacement of Ibokun as the centre of the kingdom:

> *Aisi Lẹjọka n'Itaji, iya l'o njẹ ọmọ Itaji*
> Without the *Lẹjọka* in Itaji, the people there are suffering

(Francis, 'Power and order', p. 33). It is also significant that the major shrine in *Lẹjọka*'s house, Owari, is a strongly autochthonous deity, also worshipped by the *Ọbanla*.

10 On Ereja I am very indebted to Chief J.O. Malomo the *Agbayewa*, many interviews 1974–75; also with the *Alaye*, 22 August 1974.

11 A phrase used for to 'settle' is to 'take rope' (*gb'okun*).

12 Clarke, *Travels and Explorations*, p. 137.

13 Urban structure of Ondo and Ijebu Ode described in P. C. Lloyd, *Yoruba Land Law* (London, 1962), chaps. 5–6.

14 Ibadan particularly: P. C. Lloyd, A.L. Mabogunje and B. Awe (eds.), *The City of Ibadan* (Cambridge, 1967). See too W.B. Schwab, 'Oshogbo – an urban community?' in H. Kuper (ed.), *Urbanization and Migration in West Africa* (Berkeley, 1965). New Oyo seems a mixture of localized lineages, localities tributary to great chiefs, incorporated villages, bound together under titles reconstituting (in part) the upper reaches of the political system of Old Oyo: J. Macrae Simpson, 'Intelligence Report on the Oyo Division of Oyo Province', 1938, MSS. Afr. S.526, Rhodes House Library, Oxford.

15 Descriptive details in many intelligence reports in National Archives, Ibadan.

16 It may be that titles were more fixed in a well-established town with a complex title structure like Ilesha. Karin Barber suggests they were a good deal more fluid in a small and politically more peripheral town like Okuku, which had many ups and downs in the last century ('How man makes God in West Africa', *Africa* 60, 1981).

17 This reconstruction of the system's development is set out more fully in Peel, 'Kings, titles and quarters. Part II'.

18 See above, pp. 21–2. The *Ogboni* in Ilesha should not be confused with the *Ogboni* cult, as that exists in Oyo, Abeokuta and elsewhere. Such an *Ogboni* cult does not exist in Ilesha except as a secret society of fairly modern introduction and no formal political role. However, symbols shared by the two kinds of *Ogboni* (e.g. earth, iron, elderhood) suggest there may be a link. Does the *Ogboni* cult have its origins merely in the *iwaręfa* titles of ancient Yoruba communities, such as the Ijesha *Ogboni* are? The issue is further discussed in 'Kings, titles and quarters. Part II', 230–1, 249.

19 He was the first to see the *Qwa* when he awoke and had domestic duties like settling disputes between the royal wives; he was the channel for reports from subordinate towns to the *Qwa* and had a tribunal of his own for district cases (Ode-Yunrin); he represented the *Qwa* on ceremonial occasions which the *Qwa* could not attend and played the main role in the installation of all chiefs: Chief J.A. Babatope the *Qdǫle*, interview, 27 Aug. 1974.

20 Such as Owaluse, Atakunmosa and Oluodo; for fuller details see my 'Kings, titles and quarters', Part II, 236.

21 For these figures I am indebted to Chief S. Akinola the *Sawę*, interview, 17 June 1975. He had preserved records of them and, as an active local politician from the late 1930s until taking his title in the late 1950s, had campaigned for the revision of these differentials. I suspect the figures are somewhat biased in favour of the positions of *Qbanla* and *Risawę*, relative to other chiefs, since the then holders of these titles, Ogedengbe and Adedeji, were particularly influential individuals.

22 P. C. Lloyd, 'The political structure of African kingdoms', in M. Banton (ed.), *Political Systems and the Distribution of Power* (London, 1965), pp. 99–100, summarizing the argument of his earlier 'Sacred kingship and government among the Yoruba', *Africa* 30 (1960).

23 For a title to be 'under' another, does not mean it belongs to the same lineage. The lineage of the *Salǫtun*, for example, has a quite distinct tradition of origin to that of *Ogboni*. (Unfortunately, Chief *Salǫtun* had no account as to how his title came to be under the *Ogboni*: interview, 26 Aug. 1974.) However, since *Salǫtun* claims his ancestor migrated from the eastern Ijesha town of Erin, and the *Ogboni* is *onile* of Erin-Oke, I suspect the relationship arises from an original patron/client tie between them. Later it meant that the *Salǫtun* conferred with the *Ogboni* regularly, the *Ogboni* played a role in successions to the *Salǫtun* title and represented the *Salǫtun* and his people at the centre. *Salǫtun* took on some of the ritual character of the *Ogboni*. Thus, in accord with the *Ogboni*'s role as mediator between Palace and Town, it is to the *Salotun*'s house that the *Qwa* goes at Iwude Ogun, after the mock battle between the *Ęlęgbaji* and *Qmǫdeǫwa*, to change his dress and re-emerge as legitimate ruler of the whole town.

24 Chief *Ęminiwa*, interview, 24 July 1974.

25 Chief S. Akinola the *Sawę*, interview, 30 May 1974.

26 My information on *onile*-ships, gathered partly from chiefs at the centre and partly from district communities, is not complete and may contain some inaccuracies. *Qbanla* had Erin-Odo, *Ogboni* had Erin-Oke, Omo via Erin, Ajubu, Idominasi, Igogo, Ibodi, Iyemogun, Araromi, Itagunmodi, Alaba; *Qbaodo* had Erinmo. *Qdǫle* had Ijebu-jesha, Ifewara, Iloba, Ada and other of the old northern 'lost territories', and small villages on Road IV; *Risawę* had Ilerin, Irogbo, Ikoromoja, Ere, Esun, Idoko, Isaobi, Imosan, Ileki, Odoiju, Erinburo, Amuye – mostly small places not far from Ilesha (Ilerin, Irogbo and Ikoromoja were also claimed by *Agbayewa*); *Arapatę* had Ibokun, Ilare, Ilase, Igangan. *Lęjǫka* had Imesi-Ile, Ijeda, Owena, Iloko, Iwaraja, Ijimo; *Loro* had Ipetu-Ijesha, Esa-Oke and -Odo, Iwoye, Otan-Ile, Ilowa, Idoka, Etioni, Oke Osin, Oshu, Ajido and some of the old northern towns (perhaps Igbajo); *Lejofi* had Ikeji, Ibala, Iregun, Oke-Awo and Oke-Omo and a cluster on 'his' road VI – Iwikun, Irode,

Ilota, Iyinta, Iwara, Igbigbon, Imobi. Several other chiefs had one each (e.g. *Salosi* – Ilawun, *Lẹmodu* – Igbadae, *Salọtun* – Imogbara, *Ẹṣira* – Ipoye), and *Babaileoke*, in the nineteenth century, seems to have had several on Road VII (see also p. 283, n. 27).

27 This is neatly exemplified in the case of Ogotun, a town in that band of western Ekiti periodically but impermanently dominated by Ilesha. Chief D. Oyewunmi the Risinkin (interviews, 22 July, 11 Sept. 1974), who claimed no other *onile*-ships, said that Ogotun was 'his' – a relationship created by the 'Ogotun War' of 1861–62, when *Risinkin* Akinluyi took a detachment from the Ijesha forces then attacking Efon Alaye under *Lọkiran* Oruru, and captured Ogotun. The relationship cannot have lasted long and was soon quite notional, but was perhaps the kind of thing which might be reactivated later, or would have endured if Ogotun had been permanently incorporated in the Ijesha kingdom.

28 Chief J.O. Malomo the *Agbayewa*, interview, 4 Dec. 1974.

29 Ipoye on Road IV, for example, gave 30 yams, of which their *onile*, Chief *Ẹṣira*, retained 5: *Bale* of Ipoye, interview, 7 July 1975. Ilaa, also on Road IV gave 20 yams and 4 bushmeat (*Alaa* and chiefs, 30 June 1975). The small communities like Isolo gave 5 yams each at Ogun and Ifa, and 4 bushmeat (*Asọlọ* and chiefs, 8 July 1975). Iponda, on the Oshun, sent fish. In addition to these material offerings, different rural communities were required to perform labour-service, making sure each year that a particular part of the walls or buildings of the *Afin*, assigned to them, was in good repair. This too was part of *iwisin* ('service').

30 *Lagos Standard*, 13 Dec. 1905, especially the report entitled 'Second Interview of the Messengers from Ilesha with the Ekiti-parapo Society'. The Councillor accused of not supporting the *Ọwa* was Peter Apara. See further pp. 98–106.

31 One other kind of payment was mentioned by elderly informants as having once existed: *owo ọsẹ* (literally, 'week money'). This was levied through quarters and household heads, not strictly weekly but as occasion required during the campaigning season to provision the army on the authority of a general meeting (*Ajọ Ijeṣa*) at the *Afin*. Levies were made according to the strength of the quarter, in cowries: 4,000 (*ẹgbaji*) for the *Ẹlẹgbẹ/Ẹlẹgbaji* quarters; 2,000 (*ẹgbẹwa*) for the *Ọmọdeọwa* quarters; 1,000 (*ẹgbẹrun*) for some other smaller units.

32 According to P. J. Meffre, a 'Brazilian' Ijesha trader, in the valuable document 'Towns destroyed by the Ibadans in the Ijesa County' (1882) in CMS (Y), 1/7, 5 (*NAI*).

33 Thus the Revd D.B. Esan, son of *Lejofi* Esan, interview, 23 Feb. 1974.

34 Cf. A.G. Hopkins (ed.), 'A report on the Yoruba, 1910' [a document prepared for the British authorities by six educated Yoruba, of whom one – C.A. Sapara-Williams – was of Ijesha origin], *JHSN* 5 (1969), 76: slaves captured in war are delivered by the war-chiefs to the *ọba*, who 'causes such redistribution as he considers suitable'. On Yoruba slavery in general, the indispensible work is O. Oroge, 'The institution of slavery in Yorubaland, with particular reference to the nineteenth century' (unpublished Ph.D. thesis, Birmingham, 1971). Also useful is B. Agiri, 'Slavery in Yoruba society in the nineteenth century', in P. E. Lovejoy (ed.), *The Ideology of Slavery in Africa* (Beverly Hills, 1981), pp. 123–48.

35 See pp. 93–4. A saying relates to this time:

> *ẹniti a bi n'ile ti a ko bi l'oko, ẹru ni nṣe n'Ileṣa*
> anyone we know in the town but not in the farm, is held to be a slave at Ilesha

Superficially this is puzzling, since most slaves were used in agriculture. But what it means is that, at a time when Ilesha was flooded with many strange people claiming to be Ijesha sons returned from abroad, you could only tell the real ones if they had links with a village, which urban slaves would not be expected to.

The hypersensitivity about slave descent is graphically described in a report by Mojola Agbebi (son of D.V. Agbebi, the pioneer CMS agent at Ilesha and later himself active as an evangelist for the Independent Baptist Church in the Niger Delta) in the *Lagos*

Standard, 16 April 1902. Agbebi claimed that at this time the doctrine was 'once a slave, always a slave', and contrasted Ilesha with New Calabar 'converting them into citizens and incorporating them into the body politic'. Still, this was an exceptional period in Ilesha's history.

36 As argued in my 'Kings, titles and quarters. Part II', 236–42.

37 Implicit here is a distinction between two senses in which 'class' is used by Marxists: (i) as an analytical category denoting those agents who stand in an identical relationship to the 'means of production' or the key resources in any social formation, and (ii) as a real social stratum, possessing various other characteristics derived from its members' common relationship to the means of production which is perpetuated through time and gives rise to a distinct class identity. The perennial, and hitherto unsolved, problem of Marxist sociology has been to specify the relations which hold between these two senses. As I have argued elsewhere ('Inequality and Action: the Forms of Ijesha Social Conflict', *CJAS* 14 (1980), 473–82), class relationships in sense (i) may be said to exist in Ilesha along several axes, wherever expropriation of surplus labour takes place. The existence of concrete social classes, sense (ii), is another matter.

38 Traditions regarding this title are confused. The present *Babaileoke* (interview, 13 Sept. 1974) flatly denied its characterization as a slave and an *abobaku* (one to die with his master), which Abiola *et al.* (*Itan Ileşa*) give, as well as all other elderly informants whom I asked about the matter; and was highly sensitive to definitions of his office which reduced him to being a mere agent of the *Qwa*, rather than an officeholder with his own preroga-tives. In fact *Babaileoke*'s position has virtually collapsed in recent years. The present holder (whose father had held the title earlier), was installed in 1941 and was influential until *Qwa* Ajimoko II's death in 1956; and his eclipse is generally put down to the antagonism to him of *Qwa* Ogunmokun, whose candidature he strongly opposed.

   On other points, Chief *Babaileoke*'s account agreed with Abiola's – on special intimacy with the *Qwa* (he is *Ajiroba*, 'one who awakens the king', and *Oju Qba*, 'the King's Eye') – and strongly suggests a replication of the *Qdole*'s original function. It is significant that *Ajiroba* has more recently been given as a personal title to Yesufu Onigbogi, who rose to influence as *Lotun Emeṣe* – head of the *emeṣe* at the inner court Ode-Odu – at the Palace in the time of *Qwa* Ajimoko II, becoming, in fact, a sort of unofficial *Babaileoke* (Chief Y. Onigbogi, interview, 11 Sept. 1974).

39 See further chap. 5, pp. 79–81.

40 J.D.E. Abiola *et al.*, *Itan Ileşa*, chap. 17, and Chief S.A. Ataiyero, *Short History of the Ijeshas*, Part I, chap. 19.

41 Quoted to me by Canon R.A. Fajemisin (born 1896, of royal descent on both his father's and his mother's sides), interview, 7 August 1979.

42 On the debate about apparent regional variation in Yoruba kinship norms, see Eades, *The Yoruba Today*, pp. 49–59.

43 Oroge, 'Institution of slavery in Yorubaland', chap. 3; also R.J.M. Clarke, 'Agricultural Production in a Rural Yoruba Community' (unpublished Ph.D. thesis, London, 1979), chap. 3. See further chap. 5, pp. 81–6.

44 A contemporary impression of Ijesha, compared with Oyo, housing, is in Clarke, *Travels and Explorations*, p. 137.

45 Mr O. Siyanbola (Fafisibe's grandson), interview, 12 Sept. 1974.

46 Mr M.F. Adegbohungbe (secretary to *Qwa* Ajimoko II and member of the Oluodo family), interview, 2 June 1974; members of the Fajemisin family (grandsons of the *Loja Iwoye*), 20 Dec. 1973.

47 Thus, from a neo-classical position, Hopkins, *Economic History of West Africa*, p. 21: 'the most important economic unit in virtually all West African societies was, and still is, the household'. Compare, on the other hand, the 'domestic mode of production' of the marxisant substantivist, Marshall Sahlins, *Stone Age Economics* (London, 1973).

48 On economic roles of women I am especially indebted to Chief (Mrs) D.O. Ayoola the
    Arişe, interview, 8 August 1979, and Chief (Mrs) H.O. Fajuyitan the *Yeyerisa*, interview,
    11 July 1979.
49 These were the mothers of all men in the 1974 Survey born before 1920, being 294 women
    in all. Of those reported as traders (n=182), 88 were further unspecified, 6 dealt in cloth,
    19 in kola, 18 in foodstuffs, 51 (17% of the total) in cooked food. 14% (n=40) were
    reported as merely 'housewives' or as 'accompanying husband to farm'; these, I suspect,
    were mostly the younger women or women who died while still in an early stage of their
    careers.
50 In Ilesha there was no tradition of men weaving, as there was (on a different kind of loom)
    in Oyo towns.
51 For example *Ile Ọmọyọ*, at Anaye quarter, named after one wife of *Loro* Atakan (Mr J.
    Awomolo, residing there, interview, 18 Dec. 1974); or the lineage which meets at the
    house of Chief E.A. Ariyo, *Lọja Ibala* and hence a recognized *ọmọba*, which is called after
    Orisagbejo, who was one of the wives of Ariyo's father, an *Adominasi* (Chief E.A. Ariyo,
    8 July 1975).
52 Chief S.O. Ogedengbe the *Alatorin*, interview, 19 July 1979.
53 For example, male members of *Ogboni* lineage could bear the name Lasore and females
    the name Molore. *Loro* members of both sexes often bear names compounded with the
    element *Ekun*- (e.g. Ekundare, Ekunbiyi, Ekunfuluke); they have two distinctive cults,
    Ogun Ijamo, brought by the first *Loro* from Ondo, and Orisa Asalu, said to come from the
    first *Loro*'s mother.
54 P.C. Lloyd, 'Conflict theory and Yoruba kingdoms', in I.M. Lewis (ed.), *History and
    Social Anthropology*, pp. 36 ff., 53–4.
55 See, for example, p. 79 as regards *Ọdọle*; p. 213 as regards *Risawẹ*; p. 283, n. 35 as regards
    Şọrundi. In 1963–66 the *Ọwa*-ship itself was very strongly contested by an acknowledged
    'son of a daughter' of *Ọwa*, who was the *preferred* candidate of one agnatic segment of the
    royal house, against another very closely related segment; see p. 241.
56 For example the *Lejofi* title has, since the 1840s, been filled by two or three each of the
    descendants of Alaka and Esan as well as some others. The lineage of *Ọbanla* Ojege (a
    late seventeenth or early eighteenth century *Ọbanla*) has included *Ọbanla* Ogbolu (late
    eighteenth century?), *Ọbaodo* Obojo (mid nineteenth century) and *Ọbanla* Onigbogi
    (early twentieth century). *Risinkin* Oyewumi (interview, 11 Sept. 1974), who was
    paternally of this family, was connected by his mother to two earlier *Risinkin*, his
    grandfather Aniiri, and uncle Abudibagiri. Lineages of this kind seem more limited to the
    descent line passing through successive title-holders and their very close kin than is the
    case with titled lineages like *Ọdọle* or *Loro*, which ramify to produce many segments
    whose members are only remotely linked to a holder of the lineage's title.
57 There have been four quite different representations of the royal lineage, produced at
    different political conjunctures in the twentieth century: see Peel, 'Kings, titles and
    quarters. Part I', 127–30.

4 Town and district

1 Both pairs of terms are used in Abiola *et al.*, *Itan Ileşa*, the latter being title of chap. 83.
   Tile toko ('town-interest, district-interest') was used as a slogan to express the unified
   interests of the kingdom during the agitation which preceded the Riot of 1941; see chapter
   9 below.
2 Thus *Itan Ileşa*, in its summary of the title-system of Ilesha, describes the six senior title-
   holders as *mẹta ni ile* (i.e. *Ọbanla, Ogboni* of Ilesha and *Ọbaodo*), *mẹta l'oko* (i.e. the
   Ogboni of Ibokun, Ijebu, and Ipole): 'three from the house, three from the farms'. In 1952
   there was a vehement debate between educated political leaders from Ilesha and district

towns like Ibokun over Ilesha's claims to represent an undivided interest of *ile/oko*: *WAV*, 12 Sept. 1952, discussed further below, p. 214.

3 Lloyd, *Yoruba Land Law*, pp. 54–8.

4 In CMS(Y), 1/7(5).

5 For example it lists as separate settlements several places – Aguja, Obanifon, Ajido – whose inhabitants moved into Oshu in the reign of *Qwa* Ofokutu, probably during the early 1840s, and which now exist only as quarters of Oshu. For a fuller account see Peel, 'Kings, titles and quarters, Part I', *History in Africa* 6 (1979), 120–1, 147.

6 Otaide (mentioned in Meffre's 'Towns destroyed by the Ibadans . . .') on the banks of the Oshun somewhere west of Oshogbo, was the major site and name of this war (called Ota-onde in *Itan Ileṣa*, chap. 101). Most precise details in Apara, *Iwe Itan Oko Apara*, f. 11, who dates it to *c*. 1822. The war is also recalled in the oral traditions of Ilorigbon and other villages on Road IV, collected by my assistant Mr J. A. Ojo, July–Aug. 1975.

7 For example, the territory of Ibokun, stretching about 10 miles in one direction and 2–4 in the other, contains over 60 such hamlets. Nearly all Ibokun farmers live in the town, while nearly all the hamlet population is tenants: Francis, 'Power and Order', chapter 3.

8 Most of the data on the Muroko villages was ably collected by Mr J.A. Ojo (of Oke Ese quarter, Ilesha, and, through his mother, of Isaobi village in the research area), June – Aug. 1975.

9 Mr Asaolu of Abebeyun (grandson of Famogbiyele, the diviner), interview, 7 July 1975.

10 *Lǫja* of Oke Awo and chiefs, *Qlǫmǫ* by himself, interviews, 25 July 1975.

11 *Alaa* and chiefs, interview, 30 June 1975. The name is said to be taken from Ilara near Akure, where Atakunmosa stopped on way back from Benin. No *onile* except for the *Bajimǫ*.

12 *Asaobi* and chiefs, interview, 14 July 1975. When asked if Isaobi was an *ilu*, the chiefs cried out with one voice: *ilu naa ni o*! 'Indeed it's a town!'

13 Various interviews with all the *Lǫja*, June–Aug. 1974.

14 Interviews: *Qlǫsin* and chiefs, 14 July 1975; *Balę* of Ipoye, 7 July 1975; *Lǫyin* and elders of Ilorigbon, July 1975.

15 Obanla lineage would appear to be that of *Qbanla* Ojege, a great eighteenth century chief, and perhaps the most notable non-titled lineage in Ilesha. While nowhere near as large as the large titled lineages, I regularly come across references to it: e.g. Apara claimed to be connected to it. *Iwe Itan Oko Apara*, ff. 75–7, says his own lineage belonged to Odo Esira where all his kin (*ibatan*) lived, and that '*wǫn tan si* [were related to] *Qbanla Ojege*'.

16 Cf. the account of the foundation of Erinburo village by *Risawę* Turton (the *onile*) in ILE DIV 1/1, 1195 (*NAI*). An Ilesha chief, the *Rawa* of Egbeidi, asks his patron the *Risawę* for land, and is sent to *Qwa*, who directs him to Babarake the founder of Igangan, who points out a place. The *Loye* of Igangan later showed Gureje Thompson the land at Etioni, while the Itaapa settlers were shown theirs by *Lǫja-Odo* at Iwara.

17 Francis, 'Power and order', chap. 2, suggests that in the vicinity of Ibokun, the dominant political form in the locality was a 'village confederation' rather than a capital with subordinate settlements. Significantly the *Oro* cult survives here as an organ of control, though not elsewhere in Ijesha.

18 Two locally printed histories contain much collected tradition of such larger communities as Ibokun, Ipole, Ijebu, Ifewara, Ipetu, Esa-Oke, Iperindo, Ibodi: J.A. Oni, *A History of Ijeshaland* (Ilesha, 1973), and Ataiyero, *Short History*. My assistant Dr Julian Clarke also collected many village-histories on Road VI as far as Ifewara and Igangan, and on Road VII and its branches as far as Ipole and Etioni.

19 Ataiyero, *Short History*, p. 102, attributes Odo's foundation to *Qwa* Oluodo (i.e. seventeenth century), and describes Iperindo as being founded from it, with help from a powerful hunter from Ede. Iperindo's later foundation seems plausible, though the *Tirimi* and chiefs of Iperindo (interview 20 Aug. 1979) now claim an Ife origin and represent the

Tirimi as one who accompanied Obokun on his quest to get the sea-water to cure his father's blindness. This does look rather like the revision of tradition to support modern communal advancement.

20 Iwoye, Esun, Ere were all ruled by *Lǫja* of the Ilesha dynasty; Ilawun has its own chiefly dynasty but the *Salosi*, of Ijamo quarter in Ilesha, has much land and influence there.

21 Erin considers its founder to be a woman who came from Ife with a powerful fetish, *Iro*, now associated with the god of the famous waterfall at Erin, whose waters are taboo to the *Ǫwa*. However, relations with Ilesha were close, representation lying through the *Ǫbanla*, and the Erin people have the task of coming to Ilesha and ritually sweeping the *Afin* before a new *Ǫwa*'s coronation to prevent him having a short reign.

Ipetu has affinities with towns to its south and east, and has always claimed an Ife origin. See S.M. Ogunjulugbe, 'Chief Loro and Ipetu Town', *WAV*, 2 July 1952, for an Ipetu version of the history, though it goes too far in saying it was only British overrule which gave the *Loro* rights as *onile*.

On Imesi, W. Ojo, 'Folk-history of Imesi Ile', *Nigeria Magazine* 42 (1953), and historical statement by the *Ǫlǫja*, in letter to Resident of Oyo, 6 Aug. 1914 in OYO PROF 1/ 10/14 (*NAI*): Imesi-Ile is an Ekiti town from which Okemesi, in Ekiti Division, is a breakaway.

22 See S.O. Adedeji, *Brief History of the Owa of Ijeshaland Chieftaincy Title* (Ibadan, 1957).

23 Arojojoye II (*Ogboni* of Ijebu-jesha) in his *Itan Kukuru fun Iṣẹdalẹ Ilu Ijẹbu-jeṣa* (Ilesha, n.d.), p. 6, says Ilesha and Ijebu-jesha together founded Iwoye, and that the *Ogboni* looked after five of Atakunmosa's children there when he travelled to Benin. The first *Lǫja Iwoye* was the *Ǫwa*'s daughter.

24 On Igangan, S.A. Saraibi, *Itan Kukuru nipa Iṣẹdalẹ Ilu Igangan* (Short History of the Foundation of Igangan; Ilesha, n.d.); also Chief Aribilola II, *Loye* of Igangan, interview, 31 July 1979.
On Ifewara, Pa J.S. Odidi, interview, 24 Aug. 1979 and the brief account of *Ǫǫni* Aderemi of Ife in letter to Local Government Adviser, 5 Sept. 1957 in ILE DIV 1/2, 1909/14 (*NAI*).

25 Chief S.A. Ataiyero, the *Aṣireyun*, interview, 11 Dec. 1973. There are some villages – e.g. Ipaula (VII) and Eyinta (VI) – whose Ijesha inhabitants claim to be all *ǫmǫba* and members of the same segment, in this case Oluodo, from which their *Lǫja* is drawn. It seems very likely that a good proportion of them must be the descendants of slaves settled here by an *Ǫwa* of this line.

26 See pp. 46–7.

27 Oroge, 'Institution of slavery in Yorubaland', pp. 132 ff. Cf. the useful theoretical discussion in S. Miers and I. Kopytoff (eds.), *Slavery in Africa* (Madison, Wisconsin, 1977), pp. 32 ff., esp. p. 37: 'the "slaves" of second and later generations became more deeply embedded in the structure of the master lineage . . .'.

28 See pp. 47, 51.

29 Mr Alake Ogedengbe (head of the lineage) and S.L. Ogedengbe, interview, 9 April 1974, and Chief S.O. Ogedengbe, *Alatorin*, 19 July 1979. Also valuable on Atorin history was Mr B.B. Makinwa, interview, 28 July 1979. Mr Makinwa possesses a typescript history, *Iwe Itan Atorin*, prepared by his father who was styled *Alatorin* too (1959–65).

30 On the context, see p. 91.

31 Sometimes rather misleadingly called *olori* ('head') in Southern Ijesha villages.

32 Chief S.A. Ataiyero, interview, 11 Dec. 1973.

33 Correspondence in ILE DIV 1/1, 842/7: Odo-Iju.

34 'Minutes of Proceedings of Board of Inquiry which went to Itagunmodi on Sat. 13 Feb.

1954 to investigate about the Chieftaincy Dispute of *Ḷọja* of Itagunmodi', under Chief Agunlejika, *Ḷọja* of Oke Ibode. This was a Native Authority document, which I was kindly shown by Mr M.I. Ekundare.

35 The *Risa* had the role of welcoming the new *Ḷọja*. See description and photographs of installation in an anonymous article, 'Loja of Itagunmodi', in *Nigeria Magazine* (1971), 14–31. This concerns Chief (Dr) J.A. Fajemisin, successor to the man installed in 1954.

36 M.O. Abe to Editor, *WAV*, 21 June 1952.

37 Chief E.A. Adesuyi, the *Alẹki*, 23 Dec. 1974.

38 The Fajemisin family, recognized as *ọmọba* (see n. 3, p. 310), claim descent from Oluodo via Okunkolu, *Ḷọja Ipọnda* and later *Ḷọja Iwoye*. In the *Chieftaincy Declarations* of the Western State of Nigeria (Ibadan, n.d.), determined in 1960, six ruling houses, presumably parts of a local lineage, are designated. A critical point in the title's evolution may have been reached in 1952, when the *Ọwa* is reported to have told the Iwoye people to choose their own *Ḷọja* (*WAV*, 7 July 1952).

39 *Awara* and chiefs, interview, 8 Sept. 1979. For an Ilesha version, Adedeji, *Brief History*, which identifies Ajila and Abereogun.

40 See, for example Philip Abrams, 'Towns and economic growth' in P. Abrams and E.A. Wrigley, *Towns in Societies* (London, 1978).

41 Road IV was named after Muroko market. Gbohunekun in the Ekundare lineage history (p. 68 above) sold bushmeat he had caught at Odogbo market. A woman kola-trader figures in the foundation story of Odo-Iwara (*Ḷọja-Odo*, interview, 10 Aug. 1979).

42 Cf. K. Hopkins on Roman towns in Abrams and Wrigley, *Towns* pp. 72–3.

43 Francis, 'Power and Order', pp. 34–5.

44 Details of *Ọtẹ Ẹlẹrun* tantalizingly brief in Abiola *et al.*, *Itan Ileṣa*, chap. 103. Atundaolu, 'Short traditional history . . .' in *Lagos Weekly Record*, June–July 1901, dates it to 1834–36.

5   An age of revolution?

1 Above, chap. 3, pp. 48–9.

2 See especially below, chap. 9, pp. 194–5; also pp. 253–4.

3 Sigismund Koelle in *Polyglotta Africana* (1854) had an 'Idsesa' informant – he recorded it as a distinct language – and said there were 'a great many' Ijesha in Freetown.

In 1890 the ship 'Biafra' was expected from Brazil with repatriates (Enclosure 5 in CO 879/33, No. 399, 41) and in 1894 over 50 'Brazilian' Ijesha, more than those with English names, were among signatories to a document requesting Ogedengbe's return from exile (Enclosure 2 in CO 879/41, No. 475, 16: Carter to Ripon, 28 July 1894).

4 Law, *Oyo Empire*, pp. 280ff.

5 The 'Pole war': Johnson, *History of the Yorubas*, p. 222.

6 Thus *Iwe Itan Oko Apara* ('History of Apara's Farm'), ff. 7–9, based directly on the recollections in 1919 of Peter Apara, whose family farmed in this area. Apara got further details from *Ọwa* Ajimoko who was captured at Omirinmirin in the Ali War, named after the Ilorin commander.

7 Abiola *et al.*, *Itan Ileṣa*, chap. 106. A 'last Ibokun war' is referred to by H. Atundaolu, 'Short traditional history of the Ijeshas', *Lagos Weekly Record*, 15 June–27 July, which might be the same one, except that it is attributed to a different *Ọwa*. On the revival of Benin power up to northern Ekiti in the early nineteenth century, see S.A. Akintoye, 'The North-eastern Yoruba Districts and the Benin kingdom', *JHSN* 4 (1968), 547–52.

8 Abiola *et al.*, *Itan Ileṣa*, chap. 104, though they misdate it. Atundaolu places it in 1856–57. Pa J.S. Odidi, the leading local historian of Ifewara (typescript based on an account given to the Revd Marc Schiltz, 22 Nov. 1973) dates the war to 1852–54 and attributes the kidnapping to Ifes who had settled in Ifewara after their own town was destroyed. He says

that Ilesha even asked for help from Ogunmola of Ibadan. In the end Ifewara was destroyed and remained desolate till the late 1890s.

9 On Ibadan's rise, see various works by Bolanle Awe, especially 'The rise of Ibadan as a Yoruba power in the nineteenth century' (unpublished D. Phil. thesis, Oxford, 1964), and 'Ibadan: its early beginnings', in A.L. Mabogunje, P.C. Lloyd and B. Awe (eds.), *The City of Ibadan* (Cambridge, 1967).

10 On the Oshu war, Johnson, *History of the Yorubas*, p. 293. For an extended synthetic treatment of Ibadan's move eastwards (to which my account is greatly indebted), Akintoye, *Revolution and Power Politics*, chap. 2.

11 On Ibokun, 'now a small and miserable [town] which seems to have much enjoyed the attention of the marauding powers, having been twice destroyed during the last three or four years': D. J. May, 'Journey', 212–33. On the *ajẹlẹ* system, see B. Awe, 'The Ajele system: a study of Ibadan imperialism in the Nineteenth Century', *JHSN* 3 (1964), 47–71.

12 May, 'Journey'; Clarke, *Travels and Explorations*, pp. 125 ff.; D. Hinderer, 'Journal for 1858' in CMS, CA 2/049. Hinderer describes the town wall, 15 feet high and 6 feet thick, joined by wooden scaffolding to tall trees some 10 feet behind it and with a ditch in front, 20 feet deep. He left the town by a short road to Ife, usually prohibited to all but Ijesha, from which the farms were concealed by thick forest. At the frontier-post of Itagun, both Ijeshas and Ifes were mutually stopped from entering one another's territory.

13 Akintoye, *Revolution and Power Politics*, pp. 56–7. These wars are also attested by Ijesha sources which Akintoye does not cite: Atundaolu's 'Short traditional history . . .' under *Ọwa* Ponlose (1852–66), and oral tradition in the families of the two leading Ijesha chiefs involved: *Lọkiran* Oruru (J.D.E. Abiola, *Itan Ileṣa*, chap. 112, and Mr A.D. Abiola, Oruru's great-grandson, interview, 12 March 1974) and *Risinkin* Akinluyi (Chief D. Oyewumi the *Risinkin*, interview, 11 Sept. 1974).

14 Johnson, *History of the Yorubas*, pp. 368–71, 377–83.

15 My best informant on these struggles was Chief J.O. Malomo, the Agbayewa, who was instructed by his uncle George Malomo, son of a late nineteenth century *Agbayewa*. George Malomo was used as an informant by J.D.E. Abiola and the other authors of *Itan Ileṣa*. Otherwise, much oral tradition, unused in *Itan Ileṣa*, exists among the chiefs' descendants.

16 On Danaija, Mr J.O. Olojo of Egbeidi (great-grandson), interview, 8 Jan. 1975, and Chief *Agbayewa*, 29 Aug. 1974. On Alaka, Mr J.O. Falaye of Ijofi (grandson and *olori* of his lineage), interview, 21 Aug. 1974.

17 Gbegbaaje's violent death, unmentioned in the local printed histories, was mentioned by Chief E.A. Adesuyi the *Alẹki* (grandson and senior descendant of *Ọwa* Bepo, Gbegbaaje's son), interview, 23 Dec. 1974. Chief *Agbayewa* said the *Risawẹ* and the *Ogboni*, Ayobiodu, were also killed in this coup.

18 Chief *Agbayewa*, interview, 29 Aug. 1974. Ariyasunle is sometimes said to have been only linked to the *Ọdọle* lineage through his mother – his father being *Ogboni* Omopupa – though his agnatic descendants insist he was linked through his father (Mr Jeje Odole, interview, 27 Aug. 1974). However this may be, Ariyasunle's descendants are considered fully eligible to take the title today and it is agreed that his mother was a very rich and powerful woman.

19 Clarke, *Travels and Explorations*, pp. 134–5, was most 'impressed with the noble and disinterested bearing of this superior man' calling him 'The Prime Minister'. Hinderer referred to him by another of his names: Akoli (i.e. Okanle).

20 Ataiyero, *Short History*, Part I, p. 44.

21 On Ogedengbe's origins the earliest source appears to be an article highly critical of him, in the *Lagos Weekly Record*, 14 Oct. 1893. Other sources include Abiola *et al.*, *Itan Ileṣa*, chap. 114, and Messrs Alake and S.L. Ogedengbe (grandson and head of lineage; son), interview, 9 Apr. 1974. Useful secondary studies are B. Awe, 'Ogedengbe of Ilesha: an

Introductory Note', University of Lagos School of African and Asian Studies, Staff Seminar Papers 1968–69, pp. 161–93; also G.O. Ilori, 'Chief Ogedengbe of Ilesha: a biographical study', B.A. Dissertation, Dept of History, University of Ibadan, 1974.

22 These details of Ariyasunle's downfall from Chief D. Oyewumi, the *Risinkin*, interview, 11 Sept. 1974. Chief Oyewumi, then aged *c.* 70, was a convincing informant and full of details about the genealogical connexions of many of the warriors. His paternal grandfather Onigbogi was one of Ogedengbe's *ipaiye* and himself son of *Qbaodo* Obojo, one of the great chiefs before 1870; his maternal grandfather Aniiri was a *Risinkin* in the 1860s.

23 Jeje Odole (Ariyasunle's great-grandson), interview, 27 Aug. 1974.

24 R.S. Smith, in J.F.A. Ajayi and R.S. Smith, *Yoruba Warfare in the Nineteenth Century* (Cambridge, 1964), pp. 17–18; Law, *Oyo Empire*, p. 284.

25 Mr S.A. Arimoro (son of the warrior Arimoro, another *ipaiye*), interview, 12 Aug. 1974.

26 S.A. Akintoye, 'Economic background of the Ekitiparapo', *Odu* 4 (1968), 30–52; B.A. Awe, 'Militarism and economic development in nineteenth century Yoruba country: the Ibadan Example', *JAH* 14 (1973), 65–77; more generally, A.G. Hopkins, *An Economic History of West Africa* (London, 1973), pp. 142–7.

27 At one time Ogedengbe served as 'war-boy' to Jalaga the *Babaileoke*, otherwise 'Baekure the great slave chief who ultimately escaped to Oshogbo' (*Lagos Weekly Record*, 14 Oct. 1893). In Chief Oyewumi's view (see n.22) *Babaileoke* was one of the four most important chiefs at one time. It may be significant that the villages and towns of which *Babaileoke* was *onile* were all on Road VII, which acquired its strategic importance only in the nineteenth century: Idado, Odo, Iperindo, Ipaula, Ilaye, Odogbo, Ajido, Ayigbiri. A number of settlements of royal slaves (so under *Babaileoke*'s direct authority) were sited in the neighbourhood of Iperindo in the nineteenth century: Ido, Itape, Aasa, Ikorun, Okunrun-mundun (*Tirimi* of Iperindo and chiefs, interview, 20 Aug. 1979).

28 E.g. at Ara, the combined age-grades were called *ipaiye* and headed by an *Oloripaiye*, apparently the equivalent of the Ijesha *Loriqmo*; at Ikere the young warriors, led by the *Igbqran*, were also *ipaiye*: Intelligence Reports (CSO 26), Nos. 29834 on Ara, 29799 on Ikere, *NAI*.

29 S.A. Arimoro, interview, 12 Aug. 1974.

30 On *ologun* households, see E.A. Oroge, 'The institution of slavery in Yorubaland' (unpublished Ph.D. thesis, Birmingham, 1971), chap. 3. The best recent discussion of their organization in relation to economic production is Julian Clarke, 'Households and the political economy of small-scale cash crop production in South-western Nigeria', *Africa* 51 (1981). Though much of Clarke's description relates to Okeigbo, the material is more widely typical, since Okeigbo was, like Ibadan, a community created by the war conditions.

31 See above, p. 45.

32 Johnson, *History of the Yorubas*, p. 381.

33 On one foray as far as Ekiadolo, a few miles short of Benin itself, according to the sons of Fariogun Fajemisin (who went on the raid himself), interview, 26 Dec. 1973. This was 1878.

34 Heavy tributes were paid four times a year, and *Qwa* Bepo had to pay 25 bags of cowries, 20 baskets of kola and a slave before he could be installed (*c.* 1875). He was forbidden to have drums beaten in his honour at the ceremony. He also had to send levies of troops to serve with the Ibadan armies. Adimula Agunloye-bi-Oyinbo (i.e. Bepo) to Governor of Lagos, Enclosure No. 10 in Despatch No. 48, CO 147/149 (1882).

35 At least, this has often been alleged in twentieth century title disputes, often with persuasive circumstantial detail. For example, it is said that after the ninth *Sqrundi* was taken as a slave in 1870, the title fell vacant until filled by one Agbara, formerly a village-chief at Ijemba on Road VII where *Qwa* Bepo's wives used to get firewood and peppers. Agbara used to give lodging to the *Qwa*'s head *emese* Apelidiagba on his way to Iperindo. Thus Chief Bakare the *Sqrundi*, interview, 25 July 1974.

Bepo had some chiefs with him in his quarters at Esa during the Kiriji War, helping him 'to direct and given counsels to their war-chiefs': Bishop Phillips to Moloney, 4 May 1886, in CMS(Y) 1/77(5), *NAI*. Which chiefs these were is not known. In 1894, Bepo's successor was supported by a strange miscellany of title-holders (*Ogboni, Bajimọ, Bakure, Lejofi, Lẹmodu* and *Bamura*), which suggests a very patchy title-system indeed (Enclosure No. 1 in Carter to Ripon 28 July 1894, in CO 879/41, No. 475, 16).

36 By 1877, there were so many Ijesha slaves in Ibadan that in whole districts of the city Ijesha dialect predominated (Oroge, 'Institution of Slavery in Yorubaland', pp. 175ff.). From Ibadan many Ijesha slaves were sold to Abeokuta or Ijebu. It was said that the Ijesha furnished most slaves on Ijebu farms, Ijebu depending on Ibadan for the supply – 'if the Ibadans ceased to catch slaves, the Jebus must cease to import them': Rowe, 'Memorandum on the War' (1883), in Great Britain, *Correspondence respecting the War between Native Tribes in the Interior* ... C.4957 (1887).

37 S.A. Akintoye, 'The Ondo Road, eastwards of Lagos c. 1870–95', *JAH* 10 (1969).

38 See Akintoye, *Revolution and Power Politics*, chap. 3, for an excellent detailed account.

39 Ibid. pp. 80–2. It began as a Christian prayer group known as 'the Ijesha Association'.

40 My account is again largely dependent on Akintoye, *Revolution and Power Politics*, chap. 5, supplemented with some specifically Ijesha traditions.

41 J.P. Haastrup (member of the Lagos Ekitiparapo Society and sometime *Ọwa* Bepo's messenger) to Lt Governor Griffiths, 16 Feb. 1882, in CO 147/149, No. 48.

42 See for example G.W. Johnson on behalf of Ogedengbe to Seidu Olowu, a Lagos trader, 30 May 1890, in CO 879/33, No. 399: Ogedengbe asks for guns, cloth, cartridges, umbrellas and medicine, and suggests that Olowu get himself a farm at Ayesan, obviously to be worked by slaves – 'he will get plenty of men for you to work there'; and also ivory.

43 The Revd D.B. Esan (son of the warrior Esan, who was made *Lejofi* in 1898), interview, 23 Feb. 1974. The tobacco came in wooden casks which needed to be cut and shaken before distribution, hence one of his *oriki*: *ojaja a fi idi apa jalẹ*, 'one who cuts and shakes tobacco down'.

44 Akintoye, *Revolution and Power Politics*, pp. 143–6.

45 A. Millson to Knutsford, enclosure in CO 879/33, No. 399.

46 Cf. his remarks about the Ibadan leader, Latosa the *Kakamfo* in 1882: 'Kakanfo is no crowned king. Ibadan is a city of refuge for all ruffians. I believe crowns were placed on all the heads of us kings and by God and not by Kakanfo who are daily in the habit of taking them off our heads ...' (Adimula Agunloye-bi-Oyinbo to Governor of Lagos, enclosure No. 10 in Despatch No. 548, CO 147/149, 1882).

47 Ogedengbe used slaves captured in his famous raid on Iyayu, in Akoko, to collect tolls at several places, including Esa-Oke and Iwara (on the important route through Okeigbo to the Lagoon). Iwara was long known as Iwara-Ayunbo, after the name of this man. Chief S. Akinola the *Sawẹ*, interview, 18 July 1975.

48 Just after the war Ogedengbe was sharply attacked in the *Lagos Weekly Record*, 14 Oct. 1893, as the 'unproclaimed king of the Ijeshas [who] sways the sceptre of Ijesha-land, elbowing royalty into a corner'. It also refers to 'his thousand wives, by and through whom he procures exorbitant fines and indemnities'. See further chap. 6, pp. 91–2, 97–8, 107.

49 Akintoye, *Revolution and Power Politics*, pp. 125–7, 201–2.

50 On Ejinrin, see Rowe's 'Memorandum on the War' (1883). Ejinrin was a large 8-day market, all-purpose except for the slaves, which were sold at Ijebu Ode.

51 For example, the warrior Gidigbi (later *Ọdọle*; a daughter of his was one of Bepo's wives) had a wife Okunre, a woman big enough to have her own establishment at Ibo-

sinrin quarter, who sold the slaves he captured and supplied him with ammunition: Chief E.A. Adesuyi (Okunre's great-grandson), interview, 23 Dec. 1974.

Or consider the nexus revealed in CO 147/149, No. 48 (1882), enclosures 2 and 7. The head of Okeigbo, Aderin *Ọọni*-elect of Ife, calls especially to see *Ọwa* Bepo's emissaries, Messrs. Haastrup and Meffre, as they pass through. Meffre is said to be a kinsman of Takuro, the head of Ayesan, and allusion is made to Aderin's 'Ijesha friends in Lagos'. In Feb. 1882 a niece of Aderin's, Mama Wolo, travelling with Haastrup and Meffre, has her goods seized by agents of the *Ọṣemawe* of Ondo at Igbindo, and is only saved from enslavement by Meffre's intervention.

52 See chap. 8. pp. 152 ff.
53 *Iwe Itan Oko Apara*, ff. 7–9; Clarke, *Travels and Explorations*, pp. 125–7.
54 CMS G3 A2 (1894), 134: Bp Phillips' Report.
55 Other such names include *Owopetu, Olowoyẹyẹ, Oriowo, Arowolo, Arowosafẹ, Owotumi, Anifowoṣe, Aṣimolowo, Olowoyọ, Arowobusoye, Owolabi, Olowofoyeku, Olowolagba*. These names do not belong to the two categories of 'real' names – *abiṣọ* and *amutọrunwa* – which Yoruba receive at birth, but are more of the order of nicknames acquired or assumed in the course of life.
56 See Akintoye, *Revolution and Power Politics*, pp. xviii–xx.
57 This point well argued in terms which apply to Ilesha by Clarke, 'Households.'
58 Thus Chief J.M. Ajayi-Obe the *Lẹmodu* (grandson of Obe), interview, 1 Jan. 1974. His household included around 75 slaves at his death and they hailed his eldest son as *arọle* (successor to his house, as at Ibadan; cf. Johnson, *History of the Yorubas* p. 327). Some of his old warriors protested at the installation, but the chiefs had their way.

6 The Ijesha 'protected'

1 The first European visits of 1857–58 seem to have occurred in response to feelers originally put out by the Ilesha authorities. Around 1855 the Revd C.A. Gollmer, senior CMS missionary at Lagos, received a highly complimentary message from the *Ọwa*, asking him 'to come and see him and to bring white men with you to live with him': C.A. Gollmer, 'On African Symbolic Messages', *Journal of the Anthropological Institute of Great Britain and Ireland* 14 (1885), 172–3.
2 May, 'Journey', 212–33.
3 D. Hinderer, 'Journal for 1858', in CA2/049 (CMS, London).
4 Enclosure 10, in CO 147/48 (1882). Joseph Pythagoras or Ademuyiwa Haastrup claimed to belong to the royal house of Ijebu Remo, but he was maternally an Ijesha from Ilasc and took his surname from F.K. 'Daddy' Haastrup, who became *Ọwa* in 1896 and who had paid for his education in Lagos. He later retired from Ijesha affairs to become involved in his Lagos auctioneer's business and the politics of Remo: brief life history in *Lagos Standard*, 14 Oct. 1903, also Carter to Ripon, 28 Feb. and 20 Dec. 1894, in CO 879/41 and several references in E.A. Ayandele, *The Missionary Impact on Modern Nigeria 1842–1914* (London, 1966). Meffre had closer Ijesha links, returning home in 1866 from slavery in Brazil (Johnson, *History of the Yorubas*, p. 369).
5 J.P. Haastrup to *Ọwa*, 7 June 1886, in C.4957 (1887).
6 C. Phillips, 'Report on Second Visit', 28 June 1886, C. 4957, and 30 July 1886 in CMS(Y) 1/7 (5), and A. Millson to Knutsford, 30 March 1890. Enclosure 1 in Despatch 27, in CO 879/33 No. 399, also Akintoye, *Revolution and Power Politics*, chap. 7.
7 Treaties reproduced in Akintoye, *Revolution and Power Politics*, pp. 236–42.
8 For example, Fariogun Fajemisin, the later President of the Farmers Association; interview with his sons, 20 Dec. 1973. The father of another respondent, Pastor J.A. Ibidapo (interview, 1 Aug. 1974) took part as a mercenary in the French force which captured Abomey, also in 1892.

9 On Ibadan's incorporation C.H. Elgee, *The Evolution of Ibadan*, (Lagos, 1914). G.D. Jenkins, 'Government and politics in Ibadan', in P. C. Lloyd, A.L. Mabogunje and B. Awe, eds., *The City of Ibadan* (1967), and 'Politics in Ibadan' (Northwestern University, unpublished Ph.D. thesis, 1965), chaps. 3–6.
10 *Lagos Annual Reports*, 1899.
11 CO 879/41, No. 475, especially Carter to Ripon, 28 July 1894, and CSO 1/1, 14, Carter's letters of 19 June 1894 and 23 Aug. 1894; also *Lagos Weekly Record*, 14 Oct. 1893, editorial: 'Chief Ogedengbe of Ilesha'.
12 *Lagos Weekly Record*, 17 Feb. 1894.
13 On the foundation of Okeigbo, see R.J.M. Clarke, 'Agricultural production in a rural Yoruba community' (unpublished Ph.D. thesis, London, 1979), pp. 63–78.
14 G.W. Johnson (Ogedengbe's secretary) to Seidu Olowu, 30 May 1890, in CO 879/33, No. 399.
15 'Kings and the heads of the smallish towns in the Yoruba country are usually appointed from motives quite apart from the capacity to rule – indeed mostly from their weakness of character and susceptibility of being ruled by the elders. Almost invariably there is some one man amongst the elders who is really paramount in the town and who gives the law to the King or Bale ... always a man of substance [who] possesses power by the number of his slaves and his bags of cowries. The King on the other is absolutely dependent upon the charity of the Elders and of the People ... [the *Qwa*] is of the familiar stamp. ..' (Carter to Ripon, 23 Aug 1894 in CSO 1/1, 14); and 'if a man is king, he should govern and not be governed... I know nothing more degrading than the position of an unsupported king' (Carter to Ripon, 28 Feb. 1894, CO 879/41).
16 Interview with Alake Ogunleye Ogedengbe (son of Ogedengbe's eldest son and head of the family) and S.L. Ogedengbe, 9 Apr. 1974. See too CO 147/96 (1894): 'Death of the Owa'.
17 On *Qwa* Ajimoko's personal background, I am indebted to interviews with Messrs J. Adetumi Haastrup and M.F. Adegbohungbe, 2 June 1974, and Chief E.A. Haastrup the *Lumobi*, 2 Aug. 1974. They said he was taken from a farm near Oke Ibode; the oral tradition from Ajimoko's friend Peter Apara, contained within the manuscript history *Iwe Itan Oko Apara*, ff. 7–9, says from Omirinmirin market, which was nearby.

    Ajimoko must have derived his unusual surname from a Danish-born missionary of the CMS, Niels Christian Haastrup, who served in Sierra Leone between 1841 and 1849 (I am grateful to Christopher Fyfe for this information).
18 Carter to Ripon, 10 Dec. 1894, in CO 879/41, No. 475. *Lagos Standard*, 27 March 1895. Date of installation from note in Bishop Phillips' Diary, on microfilm in I.U.L.
19 Mr S.A. Arimoro (son) and Alhaji Amokeoja (grandson of one of Arimoro's close followers), both of Egbeidi, interviews, 12 Aug. 1974.
20 The Revd D.B. Esan (son), interview, 23 Feb. 1974. The antagonism went back to Esan's independent attitude towards Ogedengbe – he would not prostrate to him – which he could afford since he had his own supply of guns, which he distributed to his own followers.
21 CO 879/62, No. 627: 'Reports of Two Journeys in the Lagos Protectorate by Governor Sir W. McGregor, 1900', 5–6.
22 IBA PROF 3/6, 'Resident's Travelling Journal, 1897–99', for 19 Aug. 1897.
23 Ibid. 30 Aug. 1897, speaks of 'young men who return from other places, principally from Lagos'. Phillips noted the decline of the congregation at Itebu 'as the Ijeshas go home'; letter to Revd J.B. Wood, 18 June 1896, in CMS(Y), 2/2/4.
24 CO 147/129 (1898), vol. I, No. 18, 'Fugitive Slaves at Ilesha'; also 'Resident's Travelling Journal', 19 Aug. 1897.
25 CO 149/5, *Lagos Annual Reports* for 1899, p. 79.
26 *Lagos Annual Report* for 1900–1, pp. 12–19.
27 Thus Resident Fuller, 'Resident's Travelling Journal', 20 Aug. 1897.
28 *Lagos Standard*, 24 Apr. 1895.

29 CO 879/65, No. 635, 'Correspondence relating to Botanical and Forestry Matters in West Africa (1889–1901).' The trade peaked in 1896 when over 3.5 million lbs were exported, but already in 1899 Governor Denton reported to Chamberlain that 'little or no rubber is left in the country to the west of the Owena River' (i.e. the eastern frontier of Ijeshaland beyond Ikeji). The later trade through Lagos (*Annual Reports of Southern Nigeria* from 1906 to 1910) derived mostly from areas well to the east, though Ilesha did see a modest revival in those years. More generally, see R.O. Ekundare, *An Economic History of Nigeria 1860–1960* (London, 1973), pp. 82–3.

30 Cf. Bishop Phillips, *Diary*, 22 Feb. 1899: he goes with an Ijebu, Adekoya, to the *Qwa*'s court, after his loads had been seized by the *Lumobi* of Iwara (a *lǫja* and *Qwa* Ajimoko's son) on the grounds of his trying to evade the toll, apparently of £5. Ijebu traders in rubber largely formed the congregation at Ipetu-Ijesha in those years: R.S. Oyebode, 31 Dec. 1906 in *Annual Letters* (CMS, London). Another Ijebu trader was murdered by a local man near Iperindo: 'Resident's Travelling Journal', 19 Dec. 1898.

31 Ajimoko's secretary Atundaolu later considered rubber-tolls the principal source of public revenue – 'the tolls collected on rubber etc. served to build up the kingdom after 27 years of almost uninterrupted and devastating war' – in 'A Bird's Eye View of the Ilesha Question', *Lagos Standard*, 9 Aug. 1905.

32 'Resident's Travelling Journal', 18 Aug. 1897, 18 Dec. 1898.

33 Ilesha's hegemony over Ekiti was explicitly put down to its being closer to the sea, and hence possessing more direct access to the founts of political and economic power: see editorial, assessing Ijesha–Ekiti relations from an Ijesha standpoint, in *Lagos Standard*, 12 Nov. 1902.

34 CO 879/62, No. 627, 'Report of Two Journeys ... by Sir W. McGregor, 1900', p. 6.

35 *Lagos Standard*, 'The River Onni [sic]', 22 July 1896.

36 Chief S.O. Thompson (grandson of Gureje), the *Qlǫni* of Etioni, interviews, 15 Feb., 24 Dec. 1974.

37 *Iwe Itan Oko Apara* (MS. University of Ife Library), esp. f.15, headed *lile awǫn Qyǫ Oshogbo kuro lori oko*, 'driving the Oyo people of Oshogbo away from the farms'.

38 Akure came near to causing trouble between the authorities of the Lagos Protectorate and those of Southern Nigeria, who saw it as a tributary of Benin. With Benin's defeat, as Sir Ralph Moor put it, 'the Akuri country and people will belong to the Owa of Ilesha': CSO 1/1/18 (1897). The Akure did not take this view, and greatly resented 'Ilesha tricksters' making levies, apparently in the name of the Lagos Government: the Revd E.M. Lijadu, 'Journal of a Tour to the Ekiti Country', in G3 A2, 1896, 41 (C.M.S. London).

39 Secretariat File c 117/1917, 'Notes of Yoruba Crowns by A.D.O. Ife', in MSS. Afr. S 1151 (6), at Rhodes House, Oxford, contains excerpts of correspondence with the *Qwa* on his relations with Ekiti going back to 1896, and refers to a document, 'A Correct Sketch of the Highlands of Ekitiparapo and Yorubaland', prepared by the *Qwa* as a rebuttal (or what the file terms an 'impertinent counterblast') to a survey by Resident Fuller of Ibadan. None the less, the British took from the *Qwa*'s 'sketch' what they wanted.

40 Excerpt of letter No. 125 of 1900, Tucker to 'HCS', ibid. See too *Lagos Standard*, 16 March 1902, reporting the judgment of the Rev. Mojola Agbebi, after visiting Ekiti, that 'the king of Ilesha... seemed in some respects to be as obnoxious to the Ekitis as the Ibadans are to the Ijeshas... in some parts of Ekiti to be styled an Ijesha is to be regarded as an opprobrium'.

41 Tucker, loc. cit., called the *Oniṣe* 'a political prisoner at Ilesha'. On the background see H. Atundaolu, 'Bird's Eye View ...' in *Lagos Standard*, 9 Aug. 1905 and, defending the *Qwa*, 'The Atundaolu Manifesto', by Feyishitan, ibid., 6 Sept. 1905.

42 *Lagos Annual Report* for 1900–1, p. 16. The stereotype is still present in Margery Perham's *Native Administration in Nigeria* (London, 1937), p. 177 and, indeed, is echoed in views of Ijesha character current in Nigeria today: *agidi Ijeṣa* ('stubbornness').

43 E.g. Bishop Phillips (*Annual Letters for 1896*, CMS London, pp. 249–51) who, after detailing all the advantages which derived from Ajimoko's accession, concludes they are 'almost counterbalanced by the detriment which his polygamous example and practice cause to the spiritual growth of the Ilesha church'. By 1900, episcopal nagging on this point had precipitated a significant break between the *Ọwa* and the local CMS of which the Methodists were the gainers.

44 I am especially grateful to the Revd D.B. Esan, who is both by family and profession close to the circle round the *Ọwa*, for details here: interviews 18 and 23 Feb. 1974.

45 On Methodism, G.J.C.C. (Golden Jubilee Celebration Committee), *Fifty Years of Methodism in Ilesha Circuit* (Ilesha, 1948) and F.D. Walker, *A Hundred Years in Nigeria* (London, 1942) chap. 17; on Atundaolu, numerous allusions in the Lagos press referring to his later expulsion from Ilesha (e.g. *Lagos Standard*, 28 Nov. 1900); 16 Aug., 23 Aug., 6 Sept., all 1905) and *Synod Minutes* of Methodist Missionary Society (London), esp. Appendix A for 1902. Atundaolu's origins are not clear, though he claimed Ijesha royal ancestry and was linked with the Faseun family of Ijeda village. He did become the slave of a Christian at Abeokuta and taught himself to read while taking his master's children to school. He was interested in Yoruba herbal and divinatory lore and, after his expulsion, practised 'astrology' in Lagos; and this, with his brief but valuable 'Short History of the Ijeshas' (*Lagos Weekly Record*, June and July 1901), places him in that movement for cultural reintegration and synthesis which flourished among the Yoruba intelligentsia in these years (on which, Ayandele, *Missionary Impact*, pp. 250 ff).

46 'Resident's Travelling Journal', 18 Aug. 1897.

47 According to the Revd D.B. Esan and the Jubilee History, children of Chiefs *Ọdọle, Risawẹ, Saloro, Arapatẹ, Lọkiran, Lejofi, Agbayewa*, and *Lukosin* were sent, at least for a time.

48 References above, nn. 41, 45; also CO 147/175, 'Affairs of Ilesha. . . 1899 to 1905, drawn up by Capt. Ambrose'.

49 Phillips, *Diary*, 19 Feb. 1898.

50 McGregor to Chamberlain, 21 May 1901, in CO 879/58, No. 580, 'Correspondence (1899–1901) relating to the Administration of Lagos and Nigeria', pp. 132–4.

51 The story is told how Ogedengbe confuted the chiefs who argued that Ataiyero was too old and infirm to succeed by having him hidden behind a mat-curtain and, when his critics had made their point, calling out to him: *ẹni abẹ awọn, ṣe on gbọ o?* 'the one behind the curtain, does he hear?' For these details, Chief S.A. Ataiyero (youngest son), interview, 11 Dec. 1973.

52 Phillips, *Diary*, 13 Apr. 1903, reported that Ataiyero complained to him of 'the acts and indignities perpetrated continuously by the *Ọbanla*'.

53 There is a graphic and amusing description of Oke Imo, and how taxing it was to climb it – no exaggeration, I can say from personal experience – in *Lagos Weekly Record*, 3 June 1906. On the *shoulder* of the hill, writes the 'traveller' (surely Jackson, the paper's editor), was an encampment of soldiers and clerks, at the *brow* were officers, court house and recreation facilities, while the *crown* was 'capped by a solitary tent within an enclosure in which lives an Englishman (and a Popo woman) who holds the destiny of Ekitiland in his hands'. Even now, over sixty years after Oke Imo's abandonment, when all that remains of the complex is part of one building serving as a barn for cocoyams, a European can be greeted by children in Ilesha as *oyinbo orioke*, 'European from the hilltop'.

54 For a general background history, see T.N. Tamuno, *The Evolution of the Nigerian State: the Southern Phase, 1898–1914* (London, 1972), esp. chaps. 3–6.

55 CO 147/175, confidential, 'Affairs at Ilesha. . .1899 to 1905. . .', *passim*; *Lagos Weekly Record*, 16 Jan. 1904, 'Ijesha Tribute Scheme'. *Lagos Annual Report* for 1905 said the Owa and chiefs got £139 15s 7¼d only in fees and fines.

288

56 Details of these cases in CO 147/171 (1904), vol. III, No. 357, 'Petition of Owa and Chiefs of Ilesha, 20 June 1904'; CO 147/175, No. 173, 'Ileshan Affairs'; CO 147/178 (1905), vol. V; *Lagos Weekly Record*, 30 Apr. 1904, 4 June 1904, 1 Jan 1905, 'The Truth anent the Imprisonment of the Loro of Ilesha'; again 18 Nov. 1905, 'Trouble at Ilesha'; *Lagos Standard*, 15 Oct. 1902, 'Disquieting News from Ilesha', 10 Aug. 1904; 'Practical Working of Lagos Councils Ordinance', and 16 Aug. 1905.

57 CO 147/175, No. 173; 'Annual Report on Northeast District for 1905', in *Lagos Annual Report* (1905), p. 116.

58 CO 147/175, conf., 'Affairs at Ilesha. . .'.

59 Record of Council Meeting with Govr Egerton and Capt Ambrose on 17 March 1905, in CO 147/174, conf., p. 14.

60 CO 147/171 (1904), vol. III, No. 357.

61 Text of the Address, dated 3 Feb. 1905, in CO 149/45, *Lagos Annual Report* (1905); cf. too article 'Congratulatory Address to Captain Ambrose', in *Lagos Weekly Record*, 28 July 1906, by 'an Ijesha', denouncing Adenibi as the 'head and director of [Ambrose's] political spy system' and attacking the signatories as members of her family or else 'people of no importance'.

62 Council Meetings of 17 and 18 March 1905, in CO 147/175, conf.

63 Ibid., Ambrose to Egerton, 26 Apr. 1905; but the rumour was strenuously denied in *Lagos Standard*, 12 July 1905: 'the curious notion of luxuriant imagination which portrays the chiefs of Ilesha as sitting up all night on 18th last with the intention of poisoning the Owa who was only too glad to entreat Governor Egerton to remove him from them to Benin City . . .'.

64 Reports in *Lagos Standard*, 5 Apr. 1905, 'The Owa's Removal from Ilesha', and *Lagos Weekly Record*, 6 May 1905, 'Deportation and Release of the Owa of Ilesha'.
    At Benin Ataiyero was lodged with Chief 'Basheku', presumably the *Ọbasẹki*, whom Bradbury (*Benin Studies*, p. 89) describes as the 'indispensable instrument of British rule' at this time, and with whom he went to witness the Native Council in operation. See further P. A. Igbafe, *Benin under British Administration* (London, 1979), esp. chap. 4.

65 This sentiment is so pervasive in the Lagos newspapers that it seems superfluous to document it, but see, for example, the rather pathetic lament in *Lagos Standard*, 8 May 1895, that the former closeness of Europeans and Africans in Lagos had passed. For good analyses of the period, see Ayandele, *Missionary Impact*, chaps. 6–7 and P. D. Cole, *Modern and Traditional Elites in the Politics of Lagos* (Cambridge, 1975), chaps. 2–3, and esp. pp. 59–87, which deal with links between the Lagos nationalists and the interior kingdoms.

66 Cf. especially Fox-Bourne (London secretary of the Aborigines' Rights Protection Society) to Lyttelton, Colonial Secretary, 10 Aug. 1905, reviewing the whole Ilesha/Ambrose saga, in CO 147/178 (1905), vol. II.

67 *Lagos Standard*, 12 July 1905, 'Interview between the Owa of Ilesha and Commissioner Ambrose' and 2 Aug. 1905, 'Continuation of the Ilesha Troubles'.

68 Recalled by Mr S. Abiodun-Apara (youngest son of Peter Apara), interview, 1 March 1974. 'Lọya Kirisi' was recalled by other respondents as a powerful friend of Ilesha without their being aware of just who he was. A newspaper article in 1952, celebrating Ilesha notables, actually metamorphosed him into 'Lawyer Crisson' (*WAV*, 31 Oct. 1952). Another verse of the song referred to '*Jejeleko*', which might be 'J.J. *l'Eko* (at Lagos)', or James Johnson, the Asst Bishop of Lagos, who was of partly Ijesha descent and strongly nationalist in sentiment (cf. E.A. Ayandele, *Holy Johnson* (London, 1970)).
    Sapara-Williams came up to Ilesha frequently, and though he hailed from *Ile Ọmọyọ* at Anaye, he used to be put up with Ogedengbe nearby as a sort of state-guest: Pa Joseph Awomolo, head of *Ile Ọmọyọ*, interview, 30 Aug. 1974. Cf. too O. Adewoye, 'Sapara Williams: Lawyer and Public Servant', *JHSN* 6 (1971), 47.

69 *Lagos Standard*, 5 Apr 1905. This is an independent report of the meeting of 17 March 1905, of which a government version appears in CO 147/175; though the detail is different, as well as some of the assessment, the two accounts do not contradict one another factually. Ataiyero went on to name Oba Ibokun, Apara, Orimogunje, 'Derby' as the leaders of disloyalty.

70 Otan and Ipole refused to take part in road-making (*Lagos Annual Report*, 1901–02).

71 Signatories were: I. Adenibi, C.A. Lufadeju, J.A. Haastrup, O.W. Campbell and Subulade, Joannah Ladunni, Abigail Haastrup, Adeline Ogunjembola, Emily Fajoregbe, Agbesonya, Aiwe, Adejugbe Betsy, Ojo Oke Isa, David Ibidapo, Amos Ogunyemi, Oba, John Fanimokun, Bakare Orimogunje, Lawani Lemomu, Seidu Ogun, Abubakare Kanmodi, Fagbewese Olesin, Fowowe, Amodu Isona, Afariogun, Longe, Abe Amodu, Obembe Oja, Akerele Fadaini, Ode Awopetu, Ogidan Osunwusi, Ajai, Israel Derby, Soni. The most puzzling of these names is that of O.W. Campbell, since he is recalled as having been the *Ǫwa*'s clerk, though later dismissed; and the Commissioner had regarded him as an instigator of opposition to Oke Imo. Perhaps he was being diplomatic in thus flattering the Commissioner?

72 J.O.K. Olowokure, 'Christianity in Ijeshaland 1858–1960' (M.A. thesis, Ibadan, 1970), chap. 3, presents an ambivalent picture of Ataiyero's religious policy: he was 'progressive' and granted land for churches, yet was on occasion 'anti-Christian', though clear instances of this in practice are not recorded. It is certainly not unlikely that he shared a popular inclination to blame those who had forsaken the old gods in the event of such epidemics as smallpox in 1911 or influenza in 1918–19 (cf. Oyebode's Report for 1919, in CMS (Y), 2/3/4), and that he did not appreciate it when young men neglected customary obligations or showed overt disrespect to the old religion. The Revd R.S. Oyebode, the leading Anglican parson, (Journal for 1902, CMS London) considered Ataiyero 'a private friend of mine' and always kept on good personal terms; and Ataiyero even attended church on occasion early in his reign (e.g. on Easter Day 1908; Oyebode, 'Journal Abstracts', in CMS London G3A2, 1908, No. 141), though he appears not to have done so later, when he had less need to court favour where he could get it.

73 On the background to Orimogunje and other early Muslims, I am grateful to Alhaji S.A. Olatunji, secretary of the Ilesha Muslim Community, who has compiled a MS. history, *Itan bi Islam de si Ileşa*; interviews, 28 Aug., 5 Sept. 1904. Of the other Muslim signatories the most significant was Seidu Ogun, who is actually considered Ilesha's very first Muslim, and who founded the Okesha mosque on land which he got from *Ǫbanla* Ogedengbe.

74 Thus in the report of the *Lagos Standard*, 5 Apr. 1905.

75 If 'Afariogun' of the address is the same as Fariogun, i.e. Peter Fariogun Fajemisin.

76 *Iwe Itan Oko Apara*, f. 20.

77 Interviews, Messrs E.A. and S.O. Lufadeju (sons), 31 March 1974, and Chief S.O. Thompson (son of J.A. Thompson), 24 Dec. 1974.

78 *Lagos Standard*, 13 Dec. 1905, 'Second Interview of the Messengers from Ilesha with the Ekitiparapo Society'.

79 Mr S. Abiodun-Apara, interview, 8 Feb. 1974.

80 CO 147/175, conf., Council Meeting of 17 March 1905, p. 11.

81 Recalled by Chief S.A. Ataiyero, interview, 11 Dec. 1973. On Dabi's exceptional posthumous celebrity, see Appendix 1; one respondent in the Sample Survey simply said: *o kǫkǫ da ęgbę silę n'ilu* ('He was the first to found a club in the town'). Dabi had been a numberman of Capt. Bower's and never forgot it: we have a brief glimpse of him over forty years later as *Lǫja* of Imogbara – for he was an *ǫmǫba* – 'prostrating like mad' to the ADO on tour: OYO PROF 3, 82/1, Diary of Tour, Ife Division (1949).

82 See 'Interview with the Mohammedans of Ilesha headed by Bakare Orimogunje, 17 March 1905', in CO 147/175.

83 Mr O. Siyanbola (son), interview, 12 Sept. 1974.

84 Recalled by the Revd D.B. Esan, interview, 24 Oct. 1974.

85 Native Court Record Books, collected in Ife University Library, for the years from 1906 (the earliest extent) to 1910 were consulted. See too references to marriage practices and 'dowry rules' in *Lagos Annual Reports* for 1900–01, p. 13, and 1904.

86 *Lagos Standard*, 9 Aug. 1905.

87 Ibid.

88 E.g. Ambrose, writing in CO 149/5, *Lagos Annual Report* for 1905, p. 120. J. Opadina, the catechist at Omofe, wrote asking for a rise in his salary in 1910, alleging Ilesha's 'scarcity of foods' as the reason: CMS (Y), 2/2, 11.

89 *Lagos Weekly Record* 5, 12 Aug., 18 Nov., 2 Dec. 1905, *Lagos Standard* 16 Aug., 15 Nov., 9, 13 Dec. 1905.

90 Thus his *oriki*, recorded in Abiola *et al.*, *Itan Ileṣa*, contain an extensive quotation from that of his great ancestor Atakunmosa, who first established Ilesha's links with Benin around 1600. They also celebrate his fight for his judicial prerogatives: *Agba-ọran yewo bi Olodumare*, 'he who takes cases to examine like Almighty God'!

91 Chief J.O. Malomo the *Agbayewa*, interview, 4 Dec. 1974.

92 *Iwe Itan Oko Apara*, pp. 23 ff. At least, it was Apara's view that behind his chief protagonist Oginni Fade, as well as the village people of Iregun and Idominasi, was the *Ọwa*'s support.

93 Recalled by Mr S. Abiodun-Apara.

94 CO 520/64, No. 567: 'State of Affairs at Ipetu'.

95 OYO PROF 1/10/14, 'Oloja of Oke-Imesi-Ipole'.

96 Cf. J.A. Atanda, *New Oyo Empire*, p. 140, on the anomalous use of the Oyo Court in Ijesha affairs.

97 CO 879/62, No. 627, p. 5. But *Lagos Standard*, 24 Aug. 1904, reports a decision of the Ilesha Council in 1901, presided over by the *Ọdọle* as Regent, asking for Ilesha to be excluded from the Forestry Ordinance 'as we have no reserve forest. Every bit of forest and the land we have is owned by heads of families for the benefit of members.'

98 Cf. enclosures reviewing the sequence of events in CO 520/122, conf. (1913), 'Ilesha: Conduct of Owa and Council'.

99 West African Land Committee, *Minutes of Evidence etc.* (1916), p. 408, evidence of R.E. Dennett.

100 CO 520/122, conf., 22 Feb 1913, and CO 520/123, conf. 17 March 1913.

101 OYO PROF 1/100/132, 'Ilesha and Illa General', OYO PROF 1/759, 'Boundary Ife-Ilesha'. For a useful historical survey of the latter dispute, see O. Adejuyigbe, 'Ife-Ijesa Boundary Problem', *NGJ* 13 (1970), 23–38.

102 WALC, *Minutes*, pp. 457–8, and *Correspondence and Papers*, pp. 166–7.

103 WALC, *Minutes*, pp. 261–70.

104 CO 879/113, No. 1005: 'Correspondence relating to Amalgamation 1914'.

105 CO 520/125, Secret, 30 June 1913, 'Western Province: Jurisdiction Acquired'. Lugard was now seeking to rationalize *post hoc* the control of Ilesha by the British, and was considerably embarrassed by the lack of any treaties other than those of 1886 which recognized Ijesha independence. There never had been a Judicial Agreement.

106 On the setting up of Oyo Province, and the role of Resident Ross in it, see Atanda, *New Oyo Empire*, pp. 128–35.

107 H.L. Ward-Price, *Dark Subjects* (London, 1939), pp. 148–53.

108 OYO PROF 1/144/195: 'Owa of Ilesha'.

109 Ibid., *Ọwa* and chiefs to DO, 26 Aug. 1916, objecting that bad medicines might be put in the *salangas* (a kind of latrine).

110 OYO PROF 2/3, c.195.

111 OYO PROF 1/100/132.

112 Mr S.A. Apara, interview, 18 Dec. 1974. He had a blazing row with Ross, and told his children *pe iku Ogun l'o maa ku* – 'that by an iron death he [Ross] would die' – a prophecy fulfilled, so it was said, by Ross's being killed when a train hit his car on a level-crossing, years later back in England. Ross's letter to Secretary, Southern Provinces, 6 Dec. 1916 (in OYO PROF 2/3, c.195) was minuted that the *Owa* and Council were 'greatly frightened by recent events in Iseyin'. See too J.A. Atanda, 'The Iseyin-Okeiho Uprising of 1916', *JHSN* 4 (1969).

113 *Dark Subjects*, p. 127. Sango is the god of thunder – perhaps he was associated with the destruction of the *Afin* by lightning in 1916.

114 Cf. M. Crowder and O. Ikime, *West African Chiefs* (Ile Ife, 1970), p. xv: 'the mainstay of the continuing authority of chiefs was their judicial role'.

115 Cf. CO 879/58, No. 580, pp. 132–4: Governor McGregor to Chamberlain, 21 May 1901, speaks of two routes being contemplated, via Oyo and via Oshogbo. Ilesha would have been quite out of the way of the obvious route, the one chosen, up the Oshun valley and then north over the watershed to the Niger valley.

116 CO 147/175, p. 13.

117 'Journal of Rev. R.S. Oyebode', G3 A2 (1905) No. 120, CMS London.

118 CSO 26/09723.

7 Cocoa and its consequences

1 OYO PROF 3/986–8/1027, vol. 1, esp. Ward-Price's 'Notes on the Candidates for Owa', enclosure in letter of Grier, Resident Oyo, 8 Apr. 1920, and Ward-Price to Grier, 14 Apr., 25 Apr. 1920.

2 Ward-Price, letters of 13 and 14 Apr. 1920 to Resident. George Adetona Haastrup was a trader at Oshogbo, son of *Owa* Ajimoko.

3 For a good economic history of cocoa, covering Yorubaland widely but focussing on Ibadan, Ondo and parts of Ife Division, see Sara Berry, *Cocoa, Custom*.

4 R. Galletti, K.D.S. Baldwin and I.O. Dina, *Nigerian Cocoa Farmers* (London, 1956), p. 3. This monumental economic survey, based on sample villages throughout the cocoa belt (including two Ijesha villages, Oshu and Oke Ibode), was carried out in 1950–52, and also makes use of the findings of an earlier cocoa survey, conducted by the Agricultural Department in 1948.

5 72% of respondents (324 heads of households) reported that they had some interest in farmland – either as owner–farmers, farmers who rented land or non-farming owners who received some kind of rent. Of these 324, 232 had cocoa on the land they owned or worked, while of these latter, 154 (66%) could give sufficient detail concerning date of planting to be useful. A problem arose in 36 cases (mostly respondents in their 50s and 60s) where respondents said their father had planted but that they did not know when. I have assumed that the fathers of 60-year-olds planted in the 1910s, of 50-year-olds in the 1920s; this had the effect of accentuating trends (a rise up to the 1920s, a drop in the 1930s) already evident without adding this category, and is hardly relevant to the figures for the 1930s or after.

6 For data on prices see Berry, *Cocoa, Custom*, pp. 223–4.

7 Data were: 70-year-olds (born 1900–9): 9 father, 18 self, 9 other senior relative.
                        60-year-olds (born 1910–19): 22 father, 13 self, 6 other senior relative.
'Senior relative' mostly meant *egbon* (senior sibling) or father's father.

8 E.g. Oyo Province Annual Report, 1920, in CSO 21/1617: cocoa prices reached £82 per ton at one point in the season, and 1,329 tons were sent from Oshogbo (of which most must have been Ilesha produce). Ward-Price in 1920 considered 1,000 tons 'a low estimate' for Ilesha's annual production. Reports for 1924–26 (in CSO 26/2 File 127234, vol. 1), note a boom in cocoa-production in 1923 and stressed the mounting wealth of farmers

by 1925. This led to the replacement of the old 6s 0d flat rate of tax for farmers by a graduated tax, such as traders had always paid, in 1927.

9 M. Perham, *Native Administration in Nigeria* (London, 1937), p. 177.
10 Berry, *Cocoa, Custom*, p. 52. On the Christian networks, S.S. Berry, 'Christianity and the rise of cocoa-growing in Ibadan and Ondo', *JHSN* 4 (1968) and J.B. Webster, 'The Bible and the Plough', *JHSN* 2 (1963).
11 In what follows, much data derives from family traditions recounted by the following especially: Chief S.O. Thompson the *Ọlọni*, Messrs E.A., C.A., J.A., Dr J.A. and the Revd R.A. Fajemisin, Messrs S.A., Richard, H.A. and Akin Apara, Mr J.A. Haastrup and late Pa Adegbohungbe, Mr R.J. Kujembola, Chief T.O. Adeyokunnu, Chief J.M. Ajayi-Obe and Messrs E.A. and S.O. Lufadeju (interviews throughout 1973–75).
12 Thus Pa E.O. Ayoola, who (though of *Loro* Lineage at Ilesha) was born at Oshu around 1900, living and farming there till he left home to go to Wesley College Ibadan in 1918 (interviews, 21 Dec. 1973, 17 May 1974).
13 West Africa Land Committee, *Minutes of Evidence etc.* (1916), pp. 457–8.
14 See chap. 5, pp. 85–6.
15 Berry, *Cocoa, Custom*, p. 7.
16 For a comparable study using contemporary survey data see I.H. Vanden Driesen, 'Some observations on family unit, religion and polygamy in Ife Division', *Africa* 42 (1972), 44–56.
17 Mr E.A. Oriowo, born *c.* 1914, of Ilesha descent but brought up at Iperindo, interview, 6 June 1975.
18 Cf. A. Aderemi (*Ọọni* of Ife), 'Iwofa', *Odu* 3 (1956), 16–18; Lloyd, *Yoruba Land Law*, p. 310; Berry, *Cocoa, Custom*, p. 102.
19 A farmer friend of Apara's (not a cocoa farmer but a grower of food crops for the Oshogbo market), nicknamed Baba Ipoye,was reckoned rich with up to 30 pawns; he died in 1928: *Iwe Itan Oko Apara*, f.20.
20 Oyo Province Annual Report, 1921, CSO 26/06027.
21 Galletti *et al.*, *Nigerian Cocoa Farmers*, pp. 347, 206.
22 Ibid., pp. 206–8.
23 Full figures for origins of labourers, as reported in 1974 Survey: Agatu 30%, Oyo Yoruba 21%, local Ijesha 17%, north-eastern Yoruba (Kabba, Ekiti, Akoko etc.) 9%, Igbo 6%, Urhobo 6%, Igbira 4%, other 8%.
24 Galletti *et al.*, *Nigerian Cocoa Farmers*, pp. 136–40.
25 Ibid., p. 150.
26 Ibid., Tables 52 and 54 and p. 149.
27 Ibid., p. 145.
28 This is now the word in regular use throughout the Yoruba area to mean rents paid by farming tenants to landowners (as they were until the Land Use Decree came into effect in 1978). It is not an ancient Ijesha term or concept. The earliest documentary use I have encountered in Ijesha was in 1924, in an agreement between the *Ọwa* and the Ibadan chiefs, regarding payments to be made by the people of Ada and other Oyo towns (then still considered 'tributary' to Ibadan) to the *Ọwa* for being allowed to cultivate land near Ibokun just south of the Divisional boundary (cf. Memorandum of 31 Oct. 1924 and subsequent letters in OYO PROF 3/986–8/1027, vol. I).

   Iṣakọlẹ may be contrasted in its character with two customary Ijesha payments: *iwisin* (*isin*), which were the voluntary 'tributes' in kind and labour owed by village people through their *onile*-chief at Ilesha to the *Ọwa* as political overlord; and *iwifọ*, small annual payments made by those who chose to work someone else's land (often chieftaincy land near Ilesha), made in recognition of the owner's continuing rights. I have been told that *iwifọ* especially meant payments made to a land-owner by those who reaped the oil-palm fruits from his land (from *fọ*, to 'wash', referring to the process of oil extraction).

   The initial novelty of *iṣakọlẹ* was not as an 'economic' rent paid by the user to the owner of a scarce resource, but as a material recognition, through a payment which was obligatory but not necessarily large, of the lack of permanent rights by a user who was a *stranger*. The conditions of this arose as much from the political consequences of colonial rule as from the growing commercial value of land. Previously people who moved into the land of another *ilu* did so either as invaders or as settlers prepared to be politically incorporated, owing *iwisin* to the local ruler. Colonial rule made the former impossible and the latter unnecessary. Because the strangers thus had an economic interest in the land without a political allegiance to the *ǫba* as *onilę*, H.L. Ward-Price (*Land Tenure in the Yoruba Provinces*, Lagos, 1939, pp. 32–3) was right to distinguish between *isin* (*=iwisin*) and *iṣakǫlę* as performing different functions. Lloyd is only apparently inconsistent with this when he argues (*Yoruba Land Law*, p. 217) that '*iṣakǫlę* begins as the enforced payment of the customary annual tribute (*isin*)'. For the context makes it clear that the enforcement he speaks of only became necessary when colonial administrative changes made a chief's erstwhile subjects into strangers. For an excellent account of owner/tenant relations, involving *iṣakǫlę*, in Ijeshaland in the late 1970s, see Francis, 'Power and Order', esp. chaps. 3, 8, 9.

29 These described at length in the manuscript *Iwe Itan Oko Apara* ('History of Apara Farm'), composed around 1939 by J.B. Apara. Ataiyero acted through his son-in-law Oginni Fade, who also established links with some of the Oshogbo claimants and, after 1917, with a new *Ataǫja* of Oshogbo, Latona. At this time the payments were called *agbaębǫ* ('offerings') as well as *iṣakǫle*, and might take the form of labour (*iṣę adehun*) or yams. But it does not appear that such *iṣakǫlę* was clearly separated in concept from the old *isin* which village-people paid the *Ǫwa* through their *onile*; or perhaps it was to disguise his purpose through an appeal to custom that, according to Apara, the *Ataǫja* of Oshogbo put up the tenants to go to the *Afin* at Ilesha saying *Ǫwa ni awǫn yio sin, awon ko sin ǫmǫ Apara mǫ* ('they would serve the *Ǫwa*, not Apara's son any more'). Still, *Ǫwa* Aromolaran did send for the authorities of Ipoye village, and asked them to 'show' the land to the Oshogbo people and say that they should give *iṣakǫlę* to the *Ǫwa* through Chief *Ǫdǫle*. As the *Ǫdǫle* was the customary *onile* for small villages on Road IV and Oyo people in general, this looks no different from customary *iwisin* arrangements, despite Apara's use of the term *iṣakǫlę*, so perhaps the *Ǫwa* was playing his own game: to get the Oyo tenants to 'indigenize' as Ijesha. This was around 1923.

Later, in 1937, according to Apara, a new *Ataǫja* who wanted to 'restore' Oshogbo by getting some of 'its' farmland back at Ido-Osun and on the Ilesha road, gave money to Aromolaran who in return 'taught lawsuit' (*ko ęjǫ*) to the Oshogbo tenants. Apara won, and it is interesting that Aromolaran tried to get him to reduce the 'service' owed by the tenants from 200 heaps (i.e. of yams, here a measure of area) to 100 heaps per month – a clear indication that by then we are dealing with not more than a token recognition of another's ownership. Aromolaran is given a backhanded compliment by Apara for his *ǫgbǫn arekereke* ('guileful astuteness') in all this!

30 I am grateful to Mr Akin Apara, son of J.B. Apara and himself a distinguished lawyer, for showing me copies of leases and further explaining much of their background. The compromise agreement of 1937, for example, made with 28 Oshogbo people who got land for a 3-year period, food crops only being allowed, committed them in these terms: 'each of us should be serving you for your farm area we occupied by hoeing 200 heaps every two months' interval, being six times yearly for each man to work in your farm'. One of them, Sangotara, was nominated headman. The 25-year leases, permitting cocoa, made in 1952, were often with the sons of these original labourers of 1937.

31 Cf. the denunciation of what they called 'shakoleism', then being levied by the *Likurę* (*Lǫja*) of Erinburo, by members of the *Ęgbę Atunluṣe* (Minutes, 9 Dec. 1951). S. K. Ilesanmi insisted that *iṣakǫlę* could only be paid by non-natives, and that 'cutlass, salt and gin' was all that was customarily required from the grantee of new land.

The kind of community where this was likely to happen was a village established well before the cocoa age but in an area where cocoa land might be sought. The established families of the village would, as it were, consider their full membership list closed, and expect newcomers drawn to the new resources to pay *iṣakọlẹ* as an indication of their quasi-stranger status. This happened at Atorin, a village near Erinburo, in the 1920s (Chief S. O. Ogedengbe, *Alatorin*, interview, 19 July 1979).

32 Titles were offered to Peter Apara (*Ọbaodo*, and later *Ọbanla* at Ogedengbe's death in 1910). Apara said he was content with being *Seriki* in the church, and 'could not call on God and then call on an idol' (*Iwe Itan Oko Apara* f.5). C. A. Lufadeju, who had a 60-acre cocoa farm near Oke Ibode, did agree to be *Lọja* of Ibala. J. A. Thompson, according to his son (Chief S. O. Thompson, interview, 10 July 1979), started the process of applying for a title (*Loro*) in 1929, but withdrew when his brothers in Lagos protested ('Do you want to be worshipping idols. . . ?'). Fariogun Fajemisin, being an *ọmọba*, was offered a village-headship, *Waṣare Ijana*; but it was remote from his own farm, and in any case he too was very involved in the affairs of Iloro church.

33 On the Farmers' Association, I am grateful to the officials of the Ijesha Cooperative Produce Marketing Union (its descendant), especially Mr Adewusi, its Secretary, and Chief Adejuwon of Ikiyinwa, its President, who allowed me access to its Minute Book, covering 1926–41; also the Fajemisin family again, and Mr D. O. Aluko-Kupoluyi, Secretary of the Farmers' Association 1931–38. There is also a typescript history, 'Cooperation in Ijeshaland', prepared by O. A. Williams, Secretary of the Cooperative Union (as it then became) from 1939–60, of which Mr Adewusi kindly gave me a copy.

34 Cf. Oyo Province Annual Report for 1923: Ilesha agriculture 'very progressive'. Details of the Cocoa Fermenting Scheme, involving sixteen fermenting houses distributed throughout the Ijesha farms, in Oyo Province Annual Report for 1927 (CSO 26/2 File 12723). Also R. Scott in C. D. Forde and R. Scott, *Native Economies of Nigeria* (London, 1946), pp. 251–72, though this grossly exaggerates the role of the Agricultural Department.

35 *Nigerian Cocoa Farmers*, p. 416.

36 Farmers' Association, Minutes, 21 Nov. 1933.

37 Ibid., 27 June 1937; Aug. 1937 James Ekundare, in Fariogun's absence, leads lobbying of Ilesha chiefs.

38 OYO PROF 3, 82/1, Diary of Tour – Ife Division. The informal tolls being levied on roads built by the 'farmers' cooperative' – a striking token of its quasi-political character – are noted.

39 'The President on behalf of other members asked the Superintendent [of Cooperatives, an Englishman] the cause and remedy of the World Wild [sic] depression. He spoke to the meeting very briefly; told them all they need ... the cause was the Great War 1914–18 during which the British Empire and other nations became a hopeless debtor to the U.S.A., honourable debt it was ... And remedy is to assist the British Empire, by buying British made goods ...' (Minutes, 4 July 1932). Not often one encounters such a terse expression of the economic ideology of Empire, at ground level!

40 Oyo Province Annual Report for 1930: blackpod disease had reduced yields and there was agitation for a reversion to the old flat rate of 8s 0d (a notional 2½% of the average farmer's income) which had been replaced in 1927 by a rate based on the number of trees, still intended to represent 2½% of income. Many farmers felt that this assessment of tax liability was unfair – non-bearing trees being included – and liable to corruption. 'Irregular exactions' by tax clerks were admitted and the prime physical target of the angry farmers was in fact the house at Isona quarter of Gabriel Alo, the head cocoa-tax clerk. ('In those days if you want trouble and are a NA official, put up a building', commented one retired clerk!) At Aromolaran's instance, the rate was reduced from 2s 6d to 1s 0d per 100 trees, which was reckoned nearer the notional 2½% of income.

41 *Ǫwa* Aromolaran himself showed a remarkable personal generosity, though. Sometime in the mid-1930s, the leaders of the settlers on the Etioni road mortgaged their houses as guarantee to the road contractor. When money was short, the contractor foreclosed and sealed up J. A. Thompson's house. Aromolaran had it released and helped Thompson out financially. Chief S. O. Thompson, interview, 10 July 1979.

42 *WAV*, 2 Oct. 1952.

43 Thus Fariogun's son E. A. Fajemisin was chosen in the 1950s as a council representative for Itaapa, later becoming Chairman of Ijesha Southern Divisional Council, but though his family connexions mattered, his career has been as a trader and Chief Clerk with John Holt Ltd. Similarly, Gureje's grandson and J. A. Thompson's son, S. O. Thompson, Bursar of Ilesha Grammar School, became first titled head of Etioni in the late 1960s.

44 *Nigerian Cocoa Farmers*, pp. 185–90.

45 Hence 'shakoleism', noted in 1951, n. 31 above. If anything, it was more pronounced in 1975, with an *Ęgbę Lǫjalǫja* or '*Ǫmǫdodo* District Heads' as an organized pressure-group for their interests.

46 Thus A. O. Famoto, *Alaye Pataki nipa Ǫba Ǫwa Ogunmokun* ('Important Information about *Ǫwa* Ogunmokun', Ilesha, 1960) alleged that farmers from Ede, who had been paying notional *iṣakǫlę* (5 yams, 3 tins oil), were required to pay 13 tins and 25 cwt of cocoa. It is also widely said that it was less Ogunmokun than *lǫja* and *ęmęsę* doing it in his name for themselves.

47 Farmers' Association, Minutes, 20 May 1940; 5 Aug. 1929 and Sept. 1937.

48 See Appendix 1.

49 P.T. Bauer, *West African Trade* (Cambridge, 1954), chap. 2.

50 Ibid., pp. 39–42.

51 There is, among men aged 70 and over, a fairly concordant general view of the character of this trade. For more specific details I am chiefly indebted to the Revd D.B. Esan (b. around 1890), who traded between Ilesha and Oshogbo around 1908–9, interviews 23 Feb., 6 Apr., 24 Oct. 1974, and Chief E.A. Ariyo (b. early 1880s) who did go to Ejinrin, interview, 8 July 1975.

52 *Lagos Annual Report* (1900–1), p. 13.

53 Letter of D.M. Anjorin *et al.* to *Ǫwa*, 10 Apr. 1926 (Fadugba Papers) refers to a ruling in 1921 that traders with 'European shops' should stay away from the market at Ereja. Now Asaolu Osue, E.A. Ariyo and Aluko Ibisan had disobeyed – and others soon followed them.

54 Oral evidence concerning the major inter-war traders as follows: for J.D.E. Abiola, Messrs A.D. and Gabriel Abiola (sons), interviews, 12 March, 16 Apr. 1974, and S.A. Oloke (Abiola's chief clerk 1922–36), interview, 17 Dec. 1974; for J.A. Fadugba, interview with Chief A.O. Fadugba (son), 22 May 1974, and Chief Ṣinlaiye Fadugba (brother), 1 Sept. 1974; for J.F. Longe, interview with Chief (Mrs) D.O. Ayoola (eldest daughter), 6 Dec. 1974; for J.S. Oginni, interview with Mr J.O. Ogunseitan (nephew), 29 Apr. 1974; for Asaolu Osue, interview with Mr S.A. Fafowora (son), 2 Aug. 1974.

55 For a brief contemporary account of the system of trade, see *Report of the Commission on the Marketing of West African Cocoa*, Cmd. 5845 (1938) (The Nowell Report), pp. 84–90. This is broadly consistent with accounts given by local informants, except that the latter lay more emphasis on the importance of credit from the firms than Nowell seems to do (p. 86).

56 Chief J.O. Fadahunsi, interview, 17 March 1974.

57 E.A. Lufadeju, interview, 31 March 1974.

58 Twenty-six names were appended to Fadugba's notice *Ofin fun Owo Ǫkǫ Mǫto* of 22 Sept. 1924.

59 Cf. Ekundare, *Economic History*, p. 145.

60 The Oyo Province Annual Reports chronicle the rise of road transport. In 1920, nearly all trade is rail-borne, mostly going to Oshogbo. 1924 sees 'a great amount of [road] traffic', quite unanticipated by PWD. By 1926 a good deal of produce is noted to be going by road to Lagos, charges being 25–30% cheaper than the railway. In 1927 the temporary abandonment of the Ife–Ondo road is noted with satisfaction, since it would attract traffic from the railway to a road route to Agbabu on the Lagoon, whence to Lagos. But in 1930, so great is the cost advantage of road over rail (around £1 a ton) that it is doubted if 10% of the crop will go by rail.

61 A. Aderemi *et al.* to Abiola, Asaola and Fadugba, n.d. 1925 (*Fadugba Papers*). Aderemi was to become the *Ọọni* of Ife in 1930.

62 Acting DO, Ife, to Fadugba, 2 Oct. 1925 (*Fadugba Papers*): 'I will be interested to learn from you since when the functions of the government have been usurped by your society [i.e. the *Ẹgbẹ Atunluṣe*].'

63 Throughout 1931 the Diary entries are preoccupied with family matters, his shortage of funds and his unsuccessful attempts to keep at least one lorry going; but on 19 June 1932 comes a reference to his cocoa farm: £4 10s 0d is spent on items of sacrifice to make a fruitful season, a very significant expense. The same general observation is made by Berry, *Cocoa, Custom*, p. 84.

64 *Gbanja* (*Cola nitida*) is not the same as the kola used ceremonially in Ilesha (*abata, C. acuminata*), but is a different variety introduced specifically for export to Northern Nigeria. Plantains, while indigenous to the Ilesha forests, were not a major traditional item of diet. Commercial plantain-growing (with the Oshogbo market largely in mind) thus represents a significant innovation.

65 Farmers' income an estimate from the fact that Fajemisin and Thompson are said to have paid £12 and £14 tax respectively. Estimate of Abiola's income from his former clerk, S.A. Oloke.

66 Letter of Resident W.A. Ross, 16 Apr. 1931 in OYO PROF 3/986–8/1027, vol. 1. On chiefly land-sales, see below pp. 204–8.

67 Anjorin's popular nickname, *Balogun Gambari* ('war-chief of the Hausa', one of the four major titles below the Emir at Ilorin), derived either from this or, suggested one informant, because he had a shop at Oshogbo near where Hausa congregated. Ilorin was important as the major centre of the *oṣomaalo* trade and Anjorin won a reputation for the help he gave many Ijesha in those parts.

68 This observation might not be worth making were it not that the study of African traders tends to be so constrained by the concern to specify what needs to be 'corrected' in traders' activities to bring them more in line with the ideal role of a firm-building, capital-reinvesting entrepreneur that has been allocated to them in some overall model of national economic development, that the real motive force of their trade is overlooked. Thus P.C. Garlick, in his instructive *African Traders and Economic Development in Ghana* (Oxford, 1971), finds traders' investment in things outside their enterprises 'apparently paradoxical', and explains them, quite narrowly and arbitrarily, in terms of a 'need for security'. Only as a final throwaway gesture is 'presumably self-esteem' admitted, which would open the door to a full cultural analysis of traders' activities (pp. 110–11).

69 Thus T. Adewole, popularly known as Timo Loja, interview with Chief S. Adewole (son), 30 Aug. 1974. He refused to take his relatives to court over the thefts, and moved into plank-dealing instead, from 1931 to his death in 1967. The same is said of J.S. Oginni.

70 I am grateful to Abiola's former chief clerk, S.A. Oloke, *Apena* of the ROF at Oshogbo, for showing me a copy.

71 Diary, 30 Aug. 1932, *Fadugba Papers*.

72 Ibid., 21 June 1922.

73 Ibid., 6 March 1923.

74 Fadugba *et al.* to *Ọwa* and Chiefs, 16 May 1924.
75 Thus his son, A.D. Abiola, interview, 12 March 1974.
76 Thus his son, Chief A.O. Fadugba, interview, 22 May 1974.
77 Diary, 1 Oct. 1935.
78 A valuable documentary source for what follows is 'The Owa of Ijeshaland's Traditional Rights in the Appointment of Town Chiefs', a highly partisan typed statement of several pages prepared by *Ọwa* Ogunmokun in December 1958 during his confrontation with the chiefs over the then vacant *Ọbanla*-ship. (For this I am very grateful to Chief S. Akinola, the *Sawẹ*, for showing me a copy.) It contains a list of historical examples establishing, its author claims, the *Ọwa*'s prerogatives. Chief J.O. Malomo, the *Agbayewa*, was also generous with additional information concerning several of the contestants, several interviews, 1974.
79 Phrasing is *Ọwa* Ogunmokun's.
80 Asaolu Osue was also a candidate. According to *Ọwa* Ogunmokun, Aromolaran asked the chiefs *kini a fi nsan ọrẹ* ('how do we repay a favour?') and they replied *Ọrẹ in a fi nsan ọrẹ* ('by a favour we repay a favour'); so the *Ọwa* said the good Ogedengbe did Ilesha would be repaid by installing Ogunmoyesin to the title.

8 The discovery of Nigeria

1 E.g. R.L. Sklar, 'The Contribution of Tribalism to Nationalism in Western Nigeria', *Journal of Human Relations* 7 (1960), 407–18.
2 S. Amin, *Modern Migrations in Western Africa* (London, 1974), p. 66.
3 This cannot be said definitely since no migration histories were collected from household members other than heads, and deceased members of the age-groups are anyway excluded. One might suppose the non-heads in the older groups to be less likely to have gone out, since going out provided most of those who did with the resources to build their own houses. There is, however, only slight indication of a rise in the proportion of household heads who had never migrated from the 65–74 group upwards. The proportion of non-head males, by age-group, was as follows: none (85 and over), 14% (75–84), 23% (65–74), 31% (55–64), progressively higher in lower age-groups.
4 These figures are derived as follows. Each age group comprises three categories: the household heads, the absent family members and – the only one about which we do not have direct evidence, though we do know their overall numbers, and their ages – the Ilesha residents who are not heads. The last were assumed to have been equally prone to migrate as the household heads of their age-group, and the appropriate number was added to the known total of past or present migrants in that age-group.
5 Regrettably, the discussion has to exclude women, since (as I only realized when coming to analyse the data) women were grossly underreported in the listing of 'absent family members'. Though the sex structure of Ilesha's resident population is so balanced that it is certain that women are now not much less prone to migrate than men, only 240 female migrants were reported in contrast to 1089 men (18% of the total). Since this disproportion was less marked for younger women (e.g. 30% of those aged 15–24), it may be due in some measure to the women being 'lost' on marriage to their natal households but still omitted from the enumeration of 'absent family members' from their husbands' households.
6 See, for example, the characterization of the *Oṣomaalo* as Ijesha in one of the popular *alarinjọ* dramas analysed by J.A. Adedeji, 'Origin and Form of the Yoruba Masque Theatre', *CEA* 12 (1972), 70–86. The name of a certain kind of Ogbomosho trader, *sandiẹdiẹ* (= 'pay small-small'), mentioned by an ex-*oṣomaalo* as having operated alongside in Ijebu, suggests that variant forms of credit-sale, associated with traders of other origins, also existed.

7 Oginni Odole was son of Gidigbi, the ex-warrior who became *Ọdọle c.* 1896–1919 and traded at Ote via Ilorin. Awe Ajanaku was a son of the pre-1870 warlord *Lẹjọka* Danaija; Ode Abugan's father, Apata Awolero of Chief *Loro*'s family, was a warrior with many slaves living at Oke Iro who died before 1900. Interviews with their respective sons *Ọdọle* J.A. Babatope, 27 Aug. 1974, Mr I.O. Ajanaku, 24 May 1975, Mr I.O. Odeyemi, 17 July 1979.

8 Ages here calculated from 103 cases of ex-*ọṣomaalo* in the larger sample, aged 55 or over, where data was complete.

9 J.S. Eades, 'Enterprise in a migrant community: a study of Yoruba migrants in Northern Ghana' (unpublished Ph.D. thesis, Cambridge 1975), esp. chap. 4, pp. 126, 148.

10 One who did was Mr J. Arimoro (b. 1884) of Egbeidi, son of the great warrior Arimoro, who traded to Ejinrin and then became the first *ọṣomaalo* to open up Ado Odo (Egbado), where he built a house and was the leader of the Ijeshas: interview, 10 Aug. 1974, confirming Asiwaju, *Western Yorubaland* (London, 1976), p. 191.

11 *Ara oko* ('farm person') = rustic, boor, 'bushman'; *ara oke* ('person of up-country') = provincial. That the pejorative meanings of the two terms converge so strikingly (= 'uncouth backwoodsman') is itself suggestive of the dependence of Yoruba power-centres on the coastal points of access to the wider world.

12 For fuller explication of this notion, J.D.Y. Peel, '*Ọlaju*: a Yoruba concept of development', *JDS* 14 (1978), 139–65.

13 On Ijebu see E.O. Akeredolu-Ale, 'Socio-economic Study of Development of Entrepreneurship among the Ijebu', *ASR* 16 (1973) and D.A. Aronson, 'Cultural stability and social change among the modern Ijebu Yoruba' (unpublished Ph.D. thesis, Chicago, 1970).

14 Several interviews with each of the individuals concerned, 1973–75.

15 I am grateful to Mr S. Abiodun-Apara and Chief E.O. Ayoola, alumni of the two institutions respectively, for providing names and details. For St Andrew's (or the Church Missionary Training Institution, as it was known until 1919), see also T.O. Ogunkoya, *St Andrew's College Oyo* (Ibadan, 1979). On educational development more generally, D.B. Abernethy, *The Political Dilemma of Popular Education* (Stanford, 1969), esp. Part I, and A.B. Fafunwa, *History of Education in Nigeria* (London, 1974).

16 See, for example, the *ọṣomaalo*'s usage cited above, p. 153.

17 On the missions' role in language development see J.F.A. Ajayi, *Christian Missions in Nigeria 1841–91*, esp. pp. 126 ff.

18 A good example provided in Ogunkoya, pp. 40–1. Between 1911 and 1917 there was much controversy among the students at St Andrew's over the nickname of Mrs Jones, the Principal's wife, which was *Nne* – the Igbo word for 'mother' – which she had assumed on a trip to the Niger Delta. 'Those students who joined issue in the [college's] magazine felt that a Yoruba name should have been chosen instead of an Ibo one ... The Ibo writers dubbed their opponents as unpatriotic.' Obviously it was the nature of a Nigerian patriotism which was at issue.

19 By 'elite' I mean not so much the concept employed in the theoretical literature (on which cf., say, P.C. Lloyd, *New Elites of Tropical Africa*, London, 1966) but the popular usage in Nigeria, where, pronounced '*ee-light*' and often in the plural, it refers to youthful, educated leaders of opinion, especially those who live away from home but involve themselves in its affairs. On this see further, Peel, '*Ọlaju*: a Yoruba concept of development', *JDS* 14 (1978), 163.

20 *Population Census of the Western Region of Nigeria, 1952* (Lagos, 1953), p. 21. Christians constituted 71.6% of this, Muslims 16.4%. According to the 1963 Population Census, Christians constituted 79%, Muslims 19.1%. Ilesha town is more Christian than the population of Ijesha Division as a whole: the 1963 Census gives 85.8% Christian, 13.4% Muslim for the 'urban' population (i.e. Ilesha itself) and 75.4% Christian, 22.0% Muslim

for the rural population. This contrast is in all probability due to the large number of Oyos who live and farm in the west (e.g. Araromi area) and north of the Division – the Oyo Yoruba being predominantly Muslim; and to the fact that one Ijesha district town of some size, Erin Oke, is mostly Muslim. On why Oyo Yoruba are more Muslim see J.D.Y. Peel, 'Religious change in Yorubaland', *Africa* 76 (1967); and T.G.O. Gbadamosi, *The Growth of Islam among the Yoruba* (London, 1978), chaps. 1–3. My own survey (only of household-heads, it is true, but the rule is for the members of their households to follow their suit) gives a slightly higher proportion of Christians in Ilesha still, but it is confirmed by the figure, based on a survey of around 2,000 households, presented in Oyo State of Nigeria, *Ilesha Development Plan* (1978), p. IV.5: 89% Christians, 11% Muslims for Ilesha town.

21 I.e. that put forward by R. Horton, 'African conversion', *Africa* 41 (1971), and 'On the rationality of conversion', *Africa* 45 (1975).

22 For a study which seeks to complement Horton's perspective, in relation to another Yoruba kingdom, J.D.Y. Peel, 'Conversion and tradition in two African societies: Ijebu and Buganda', *Past and Present*, 77 (1977).

23 For example the cult of Ogun Lade at Ilorigbon off Muroko Road, or Ogun Ijamo whose worship was concentrated among members of *Loro* lineage. On the Ogun cult and its modern adaptability throughout Yorubaland see Sandra Barnes, *Ogun : an Old God for a New Age* (Philadelphia, 1980).

24 The main indigenous masked figures are ones belonging to *Ọlọja* of Ibodi, one with palm- frond covering (not cloth like the typical Oyo-Yoruba *egungun*) said to commemorate Obokun's sea-water exploits and a hunter's masquerade, covered with animal skins, that appears at Obalogun's festival. There is no *egungun* festival as such. A number of compounds round the town are known to have these 'imported' *egungun*, and it was the 'owner' of one of them at Igando who said that those who introduced them did so 'to build up their strength'. The best known of these, Gbogoru, belonged to *Risawẹ* Adedeji. It follows that the confrontations between Christians and *egungun* which occurred early in the century (e.g. incidents reported in Bishop Phillips' *Diary*, 6 March 1901) were confrontations, not between an anti-traditional novelty and an agency of traditional custom, but between two rival new powers.

25 Details in Ib.Min.Agric. 1/173, 8876, 'Sasswood poisoning' (*NAI*). This refers to 25 people poisoned at Erin, 65 at Ikeji, 40 at Odo and Iperindo, and says 'a few years' back' 100 people died at Ikeji.

26 The Revd J.B. Wood, 19 Aug. 1885, in CMS (Y), 1/7 (5) (*NAI*).

27 Mr E.A. Fajemisin (who had it from his father Fariogun, a warrior companion of Ogedengbe's and early Christian convert), interview, 12 Sept. 1974.

28 Main source *Iwe Itan Ọgọrun Ọdun ti Isin Kristi ni Ilẹ Ijesha 1857–1957* (Ijebu-Ode, 1957), compiled by Ilesha District Church Council (Chairman: I.G.A. Jadesimi) – a Centenary History of the Anglican church in Ijeshaland, cited below as *Ọgọrun Ọdun*. Its dates appear to be a little unreliable for the beginnings, since it gives 1856 for Hinderer's first visit, whereas Hinderer's first journey to Ilesha appears to have been in 1858 (see his 'Journal for 1858', in CA 2/049). On Bepo's support, see Olubi to Wright, 24 Apr. 1878, in CA 2/075.

29 *Ọgọrun Ọdun*, p. 11. This does not, of course, mean they were all converts.

30 For Methodism, see a much briefer local history, *Fifty Years of Methodism in Ilesha Circuit, 1898–1948*, compiled by the Golden Jubilee Celebration Committee.

31 The two churches agreed on a division of territory between them, in the district as in Ilesha. The Methodists took the areas round Imesi-Ile, Ijeda, Oshu and on the road to Igbadae and Epe; the CMS the rest. *Ọgọrun Ọdun* gives the following dates for the introduction of Christianity: 1896, Ijebu-jesha, Iperindo, Ibokun, Iwoye; 1898, Ipetu; 1900, Ise, Oke Ibode; 1901, Iwara, Ere; 1902, Igangan; 1903, Iponda; 1905, Ifewara

Ikeji; 1906, Old Ikeji, Ibala, Idoka, Idominasi; 1907, Esun, Odo, Irogbo; 1908, Ilare, Erinmo, Ilerin; 1909, Ikiyinwa; 1910, Ikoromoja; 1911, Odogbo; 1912, Ijemba; 1913, Ijimo; 1914, Idooko.

32 The African Church began services on the verandah of John Haastrup's store at Adeti. Its first minister, the Revd Fisher, was a Badagry man and it seems to have been strong among traders with links in that region, like Asaolu Osue; but it really took off with the adherence to it of J.D.E. Abiola in the 1920s.

33 *Qgǫrun Qdun*, pp. 33–7.

34 '*L'oko ẹru*', used of founding members at Ijebu-jesha and Ibokun, *Qgǫrun Qdun*, pp. 31, 65.

35 Abeokuta is mentioned (*Qgǫrun Qdun, passim*) in the church histories of Ise (the local cocoa-pioneer Daddy Faro had been a slave there), Idooko, Idominasi and Idoka; Lagos at Iperindo, Iwoye (where the founder had been in the habit of trekking eight miles and back to Ilesha to worship with his Christian companions from Lagos), and again Idoka, where an *Iya Eko* rallied the women of the village. Lagoon towns, such as Badagry, Itebu and Ayesan are also mentioned.

It is all summed up by a phrase used of Ijemba (*Qgǫrun Qdun*, p. 60): *ati laipẹ a nri awǫn ti idalẹ de, tiwǫn ti gbagbǫ lǫhun* ('and soon we saw those who had returned from their travels, who had become Christians abroad').

36 Of 59 locations mentioned, we find: Lagos 14, Abeokuta 11, Lagoon towns (Ayesan, Ejinrin, Badagry, Porto Novo) 11, Ibadan 4, Ilorin 3, other places in Yorubaland 13, Gold Coast and outside Nigeria 3.

37 The notion that it was quite natural or appropriate, even within the terms of indigenous thought, for someone who went outside to be a Christian or Muslim, is also suggested by Oyebode's report that some 'heathen' parents had made vows on behalf of two sons abroad that they should be Christians: Annual Letter, 6 Dec. 1901, CMS G3 A2.

38 *Qgǫrun Qdun*, p. 46.

39 Cf., for example, Abernethy, *Political Dilemma* pp. 38–55, or F.K. Ekechi, *Missionary Enterprise and Rivalry in Igboland 1857–1914* (London, 1972). Abernethy points out a certain divergence of interest, within an overall interdependence, of government and missions: the government needed to subsidize the missions, but wanted to limit the amount and raise the quality of the education, while the missions, more in tune with the rising popular demand for education, wanted to spread it as widely at primary levels as they could (ibid., pp. 86–91).

40 Detail from records kept at Otapete School, reported by one of my research assistants, Mr O. Fadipe.

41 Interviews: Mrs R.N. Ludlow, Birchington-on-Sea, 18 May 1977 and Chief (Mrs) H.O. Fajuyitan (first teacher at the Homecraft Centre), 11 July 1979. The girls had their own ideas as to what this should be. Part of the Ludlows' plan was to modernize the Ijesha tradition of female weaving, then beginning to fall into decline. The girls were not interested, this being considered 'old woman's work', and wanted to learn sewing and embroidery instead.

42 An apparently casual phrasing shows how similarly Ijesha might conceive of the spiritual and the worldly/political senses in which external centres of power might be trapped. It was as a 'powerful stranger' (*alejo nla*) that Oyebode was received by the leader of the Christian group at Ipetu (*Qgǫrun Qdun*, p. 34). And a few miles away at Iperindo, it was from a stranger, who appeared to him in a noonday vision, that J.A. Babatope sought spiritual enlightenment – an experience which led to his subsequent involvement with the Aladura (Peel, *Aladura*, p. 67).

43 Instances from *Qgǫrun Qdun*, pp. 57, 72, 65–7, 70, 35–6.

44 Cf. letter from Muslim Representatives to Governor, 20 Feb. 1942, in CSO 26/38421 (*NAI*).

45 For the history of Islam in Ilesha, interviews with Alhaji S.A. Olatunji, secretary of the community, 28 Aug. and 5 Sept. 1974, who referred to a MS. history *Itan bi Islam de si Ileṣa* ('How Islam came to Ilesha'); also Alhaji Amokeoja, the Chief Imam, and leading Muslims such as Alhaji S.A. Famuyide and Alhaji S.A.K. Arowojobe, 1974–75. Ijesha Islam is set within the wider regional context in T.G.O. Gbadamosi, *The Growth of Islam among the Yoruba 1841–1908* (London, 1978).

46 'Diary of an Itinerating Tour in the Ijesha County' (the Revd F.G. Toase), in CMS G3 A2, 1894 No. 171.

47 R.S. Oyebode, Annual Letter, 31 Dec. 1906, in CMS G3A2.

48 Men such as Sunmonu Babasale, or Alfa Kanmodi at Iwere, Alfa Amodu Farise and Salami Basorun at Egbeidi. Several of their sons were very influential and popular as traders – Ali Kanmodi, who traded in Hausaland and was a leading light of the important Muslim social society *Ẹgbẹ Killa* or Farise's son Ali Balogun, the first Ijesha to return from the pilgrimage in 1930.

49 Oyebode, in CMS G3A2.

50 Compare with locations of Christians cited n. 36 above: of 19 locations mentioned by respondents, Lagoon towns (Ayesan, Epe, Badagry) 5, non-Yoruba North 5, Ilorin 3, Ibadan 2, Abeokuta 2, other Yoruba 2. Alhaji Olatunji could identify the place of conversion of 8 out of his 10 'first set' of Muslim leaders: Epe 4, non-Yoruba North 3, Abeokuta 1.

51 E.g. Disu Kanike, a Hausa who was first imam of Okesha, the earliest, but not the central, mosque; or Mallam Uthman, who came from Oshogbo and inaugurated public preaching during Ramadan; or Alfa Abdulayi Akorede, Imam 1914–16, Ijebu on father's side but maternally from Iperindo.

52 Of some 62 cases of movement from one form of world religion to another reported of themselves by 443 household heads, 8 were from Islam to Christianity, 4 from Christianity to Islam. The remainder were intra-Christian movements.

53 Peel, *Aladura*, and R.C. Mitchell, 'Religious protest and social change: the origins of the Aladura Movement in Western Nigeria', in R.I. Rotberg and A.A. Mazrui (eds.), *Protest and Power in Black Africa* (New York, 1971).

54 Recalled by S. Abiodun-Apara (Peter Apara's youngest son, who went to St Andrew's in 1924), interview, 1 March 1974.

55 Hinderer, whose main experience was of Ibadan, commented on his first visit in 1858, that in Ilesha there was less of Ifa, but a great deal of Elegba, 'the devil', and complained that he had to spend the whole night next to one at Ibokun (Journal for 1858, CA 2/049). Toase in 1894, again visiting Ilesha from the Oyo-Yoruba areas, 'for the first time … saw a real idol of the devil' at Oke Obode, and described Ilesha as 'full of idols of the devil, which is the family god' (Diary of Itinerating Tour, G3 A2 [1894] No. 171). All this is not as sensational as it sounds, for by then the mistranslation of 'the devil' by the name of the *oriṣa* Esu had permanently affected missionary (and local Christian) discourse. On the real character of Esu, cf. J.O. Awolalu, *Yoruba Beliefs and Sacrificial Rites* (London, 1979), pp. 28–30.

56 Some documentation in Peel, *Aladura*, pp. 102–3.

57 Cherubim and Seraphim existed before the revival, introduced from Ibadan (where Ijesha are prominent in its membership) in 1927; but their major growth has been since then. Now they comprise 5.4% of the population.

58 A fuller and more informed account of Babatope's relations with the CMS than the one I gave in *Aladura* is to be found in J.O.K. Olowokure, 'Christianity in Ijeshaland 1858–1960' (M.A. thesis, Ibadan, 1970), chap. 4.
    Perhaps the most remarkable case of this kind was that of Pastor J.A. Ibidapo of Ifofin quarter (interview, 1 Aug. 1974; but the details also in a short printed autobiographical leaflet), which touches so many points of the whole course of Christian development. Born

1876 at Odo, he became friendly with the cocoa-pioneer Faro, who introduced him to Oyebode, from whom he received baptism in 1908. Up to his 30s he farmed and collected palm-nuts, but when he became a Christian he went to Ilesha to learn carpentry from Isaac Coker alias Jegede Onigbogi at Ifofin. A vision led him to take up work as an evangelist under the CMS, mostly round Akufo in Ibadan Division. Returning to Ilesha in 1928 he continued preaching, now independently of the CMS, and was swept up into the Revival. 1934 ordained as an Apostolic pastor.

59 In 1974 the *Arojo* himself, Chief Paul Jegede, was an Apostolic Church member, and the cult was managed by an *aworo*, an afflicted person who is 'called' by the *orișa* to her service. The '*Oșun*' at Irojo, said to have been brought in a magical cloth by the *Arojo*'s ancestor, consists of a clear, ever-running spring which wells out of the hillside in the forest a few hundred yards from the cult-house: a most numinous place.

60 Repeatedly I was told in villages that had once had three or four local cults that the most obscure and locally-specific ones had died out '*l'aiye Babalola*'. Significantly, the survival chances of deities of a more pan-Yoruba kind, like Osanyin or Osun, have seemed much better.

9 Remaking the town

1 On Oyo Province, see Atanda, *New Oyo Empire*.

2 The best account of Nigeria's administration and its problems, viewed as a whole and from the centre, with great wit and insight, is I.F. Nicholson, *The Administration of Nigeria 1900–1960* (Oxford, 1969), esp. chaps. 7–8.

3 See Francis, 'Power and Order, chap. 4: 'Courts and Colonialism'.

4 J.T. Laleye, interview, 16 May 1975.

5 De la Mothe to Bowes, 15 March 1929, Handing Over Notes, ILE DIV 1/2, IL 103, Vol. II. He goes on to describe the *Owa* as 'a most intelligent and progressive ruler ... always ready to support any policy which tends to the improvement of his people, amongst whom he enjoys great influence and popularity'. Also Oyo Province Annual Report, 1925, in CSO 26/2, 12723, Vol. III (*NAI*).

6 Ibid.

7 Norcott to Palmer, July 1932, Handing Over Notes.

8 Mackenzie to Schofield, 19 June 1933, ibid.

9 Handing Over Notes for 1937 and 1938, *passim.*

10 Resident Ross to Mackenzie, Ife DO, 10 Nov. 1930, OYO PROF 1, 4894: The *Owa* should not be 'under' Ife and should not be so much 'entirely dependent on newly joined cadets'. The Ife DO should take more direct control. Mackenzie replied that the Ilesha staff then included a clerk, an interpreter, an office boy and two political agents.

11 'Sons of the Soil' to Resident, 16 Apr. 1935, OYO PROF 1, 4894. The makeshift character of the British presence in Ilesha must have been nicely symbolized by the fact that until 1935 the ADO's house at Ilesha was roofed with *gbodogi* leaves only, and not corrugated iron, as many an ordinary *oșomaalo*'s now was (Blenkinsop to Outram, 26 Jan. 1935, Handing Over Notes).

12 Main source for *Ęgbę Atunlușe* at this period is the Minute Book, 1923–28, contained in the papers of J.A. Fadugba (University of Ife Library). These also contain much related correspondence. This was supplemented by interviews with several of the oldest surviving members, especially Pa E.O. Ayoola, who was secretary in 1973–75. There are letters about the 'Ijesha Home Union for Education' in the Fadugba Papers, and the formal union of the Young Ijesha Improvement Society and the Education Society is recorded for 30 Dec. 1923, Minute Book.

13 Thus D.M. Anjorin, 14 May 1924, Minute Book.

14 So a member of St Peter's Isona is asked if he will organize 'our branch in your church', 18 Nov. 1923; the matter of a new Christian *asǫju* is discussed 'to uphold our prestige as Christians', 30 December 1973, Minute Book. For years the meetings were held at Otapete, the most centrally placed church, after services. There was one early Muslim member, Seriki Owoeye, who was made *Baba Ẹgbẹ* of the society and on one occasion (22 July 1928) asked 'to vigour the Musulumi' in fund-raising. But there were no more than one or two Muslims among the 60 deceased and 56 living members whose names are recorded in a pamphlet issued for the 1972 anniversary: *Ajǫdun Ẹgbẹ Atunluṣe*, pp. 12–14. The reason is undoubtedly the strong connexion of modern education and Christian culture, which endured after it was decided that Ilesha Grammar School would be formally a community, rather than a church school: the first three principals of IGS (Doherty, Lahanmi and Akinyemi) were Anglican clergymen, and one of them became a Canon.

Progressive Muslim traders of a similar kind to the *Atunluṣe* activists formed the two leading Muslim societies, *Ẹgbẹ Killa* in the 1920s (Nasiru Giwa, Alli Kanmodi, Bello Arewa) and *Ẹgbẹ Bǫrǫkini*, early 1930s (Bello Dawodu, Sunmola Adeyemi). These were more purely social than *Ẹgbẹ Atunluṣe* and never aspired to speak for the whole community as *Atunluṣe* did. According to Alhaji Olatunji (interview, 5 Sept. 1954) they both had ideas about establishing schools and collected money to that end, but did not know quite how to set about it. This was achieved when two Muslim educational societies, Nawair-ud-Deen and Zumratul Islamiyya, which tended to be linked with *Killa* and *Bǫrǫkini* members respectively, were introduced in the late 1940s. The central concern here was to prevent further erosion of the Islamic body through Christian influence in the educational system.

15 25 July 1924, Minute Book. Ibid., 4 Nov. 1923 Fadugba argued it was 'advisable to perform or make a merryment in the year time [i.e. during the Christmas season when the *oṣomaalo* were home and the great civic ritual-cycle of Ogun was in train] so as to attract the public-people and thereby we can [get] more attendances'.

16 8 Aug. 1924, Minute Book.

17 See above chap. 6, pp. 94–6.

18 'Alaiye [i.e. the *Ǫwa*] wishes us to help about the railroad', 29 January 1928, Minute Book. *The Yoruba News* (on which see p. 181) frequently had editorials which aired *Atunluṣe* views: 'Progress II', 11 Dec. 1925, calling on Ijesha notables to take up the Oni River project, or 'A Contrast', 3 March 1925, which praises the progress made by Ilesha under *Ǫwa* Ajimoko I.

19 The 1972 *Ajǫdun* pamphlet gives Anjorin as first, Abiola as second chairman, Haastrup as first, Fadugba as second secretary. From the Minute Book it appears that both Apara and Fadugba served as secretary, and both Anjorin and Haastrup as chairman on various occasions in 1923–24. Anjorin died in 1926 and Abiola became chairman in 1928. Later a Yoruba style was used: in June 1928, Abiola is *Olori* ('head'), with Longe as *Ǫtun* and Asogbe as *Osi*, while the then treasurer, J. S. Oginni, also has his *Ǫtun* and *Osi* in S.A.K. Ilesanmi and B. Fagbemi; and there is *Aṣipa*, *Bada* etc.

20 Reported by Rosedale, DO Ife, to Resident, Oyo, 13 Oct. 1916 in OYO PROF 1/149, 195, including comments by Lufadeju, *Lǫja* of Ibala, who was on the court.

21 I.e. the quasi-autonomous Egba United Government, which lasted up to 1914, and on which see A. Pallinder-Law, 'Aborted modernization in West Africa? The case of Abeokuta', *JAH* 15 (1974), 65–82.

22 On this, one crucial issue which linked Herbert Macaulay's NNDP with the grievances of the Lagos indigenes, see Patrick Cole, *Modern and Traditional Elites in the Politics of Lagos* (Cambridge, 1975), pp. 98–100.

23 O. Haastrup to Fadugba, 14 July 1923; to *Ǫwa*, 21 Aug. 1923, *Fadugba papers*.

24 O. Haastrup to *Ǫwa*, 18 Sept. 1923. This letter is an eloquent rehearsal of Ijesha

claims in the most traditional language. Did not Arimoro save Ife from the Oyos, he asks, referring to the episode of 1882? Ife was a hereditary possession of three kings, *Qwa* as overload of all the Ekiti chiefs, the *Alafin* of Oyo and the *Qba* of Benin. The formal gifts made by the *Qba* of Benin at festivals conceded the *Qwa*'s equality. Let it not be, he concluded, that 'you cultivate and plough and plant, then you leave the fruit for the *Alafin* and his people to reap, making dance and banquet in his own palace at the expense of Ijesha bloodshed'.

25 Notes for minutes, 23 Nov. 1923, *Fadugba papers*. Their Loyal Address to the Governor on tour, 25 Aug. 1925 asked 'to restore our last kingdom to us which we have lost through ignorance and want of knowledge to realize the pleasure and flavour that are contained in dealing with the European as a whole … that the past might be overlooked and restore our Government back to us having the seat at Ilesha with Resident and other staff, claiming our affinity with the Ekitis again'.

26 O. Haastrup to *Qwa*, 29 Nov. 1923.

27 Minute Book, 27 Jan. 1924, Fadugba is commissioned to write to the Ekitiparapo; 14 May 1924, an Ekitiparapo representative, Olulode, attends.

28 Reported in *The Yoruba News*, 15 Apr. 1924. This was the first time that the common practice of today – giving what were in effect honorary titles to attach them to the town's interest as patrons – occurred.

29 *Ęgbę Atunluşe* funds, collected for the Grammar School, were deposited 'in safe in the Democratic party in Lagos'; Minute Book, 29 January 1928.

30 Several letters in OYO PROF 1/1386, Young Ijesha Improvement Society, e.g. Gribble, Acting DO, to Resident, Oyo, 17 Oct. 1925: the society is a 'nuisance' and its schemes were 'impracticable'.

31 For example, when it was insisted that 'Ilesha must get her province', J.F. Longe sounded a cautious, temporizing note: 'in removing the district commissioner from our soil is God's work and before we can get this back we must pray to God for it and work hard', 27 Jan. 1924, Minute Book.

32 Letter to Resident Ross, 10 June 1925, in OYO PROF 1/1386. Interestingly, one of the signatories was J.B. Apara, whose father Ross had tried to terrorize nine years before. Also 9 June 1925, Minute Book.

33 Ibid., messages about Iwara and Ibokun roads delivered to *Qwa*. On markets, see above chap. 7, p. 142.

34 This project seems to have emerged a little later and was, no doubt, regarded as an easier first step to the longer term aim of administrative reorganization: letter to Resident Ward-Price, 30 Apr. 1934, in OYO PROF 1/1386. The ranking of rulers is still a serious aspect of attempts at communal aggrandisement, as is discussed in A.I.Asiwaju, 'Political motivation and oral historical traditions in Africa: the case of Yoruba crowns, 1900–1960', *Africa* 46 (1976), 113–27.

35 J.A. Fadugba's expression: 27 Jan. 1924, Minute Book.

36 *The Yoruba News*, 20 Jan. 1925.

37 See also above, chap. 8, p. 162.

38 *The Yoruba News*, 13 Jan. 1925, a letter headed '*Ekiti ko si labę Ilesha*' (Ekiti is not under Ilesha); also 20 Jan., 3 Feb., 10 March 1925.

39 O. Haastrup to Fadugba, 14 July 1923, *Fadugba papers*.

40 20 Jan. 1925: '*ęnyin ǫmǫ Ileşa isisiyi ti ę fę tę Ekiti mǫlę patapata nitori oju wǫn ko la to ti nyin*'. He looked to 'the power of God' to enlighten the Ekitis, and there too salvation took the principal form of a secondary school, Christ's School, run by the CMS.

41 O. Haastrup to Owa, 21 Aug. 1928. The flavour of *Awe Kari o*! is perhaps best conveyed by the contemporary (British) English 'cheers, mate!'

42 On developments in Ekiti itself, see Akintoye, *Revolution and Power Politics*, pp. 228 ff., especially as regards the role of the Ekiti Progressive Union.

43 E.g. the Ekiti were typed as 'small boys', labourers on Ijesha cocoa farms in the 1920s (cf. above p. 122), and sometimes pushed towards a lower rung on the produce-buying hierarchy, as when Ekiti traders in 1913 were forced by the *ẹmẹsẹ* to sell their palm-kernels in Ilesha to Ijesha, instead of going on to the European firms in Oshogbo (OYO PROF 1/ 100/132).

44 Cf. Abner Cohen's classic study *Custom and Politics in Urban Africa* (Manchester, 1969) or F. Barth (ed.), *Ethnic Groups and Boundaries* (Bergen, 1969).

45 Syrians came to Ilesha in the late 1920s, setting up shops in Adeti Street, between Itakogun and Ereja. In 1929 they were an 'acute' problem, and had met refusal for more settlement from the *Ọwa* in 1933; in 1937 numbers rose again (4 shops and others arriving) and in 1938 were again 'a thorn in the flesh'. (Handing Over Notes, *passim*. ILE DIV 1/2, IL 103, vol. III). Some time in the 1940s they left for good, apparently having been driven out by various techniques, though it is a subject I found it difficult to get people to be explicit about. However, since the names of several Ijesha shopkeepers of middling size were mentioned in this connexion, it appears that economic rivalry was at the bottom of it.

46 Cf. above, pp. 124–9 and Berry, *Cocoa, Custom*, chap. 4.

47 Norcott to Palmer, July 1932, Handing Over Notes.

48 Dispute reviewed in Craig, ADO Ilesha, to D.O., Ife, 25 Jan. 1930, in OYO PROF 1/ 759, Boundary Ife-Ilesha; and set in a wider context by O. Adejuyigbe, *Boundary Problems in Western Nigeria: a Geographical Analysis* (Ile Ife, 1975), pp. 105–25.

49 'Minutes of Meeting held by Ife and Ijesha representatives to discuss Ife-Ilesha Boundary Dispute', 13 Apr. 1949, in OYO PROF 1/759.

50 The story is not told in the brief history issued in the pamphlet issued in 1974 to commemorate the school's fortieth anniversary, but I have heard it from more than one elderly member of *Ẹgbẹ Atunluṣe*.

51 Nov. 1932, the *Ọwa*'s health improving but he rarely leaves the *Afin* and the Court is unsatisfactory. Nov. 1937, *Ọwa*'s health not good so his 'control of affairs has not been as close as usual'. July, 1939, *Ọwa* has been ill all year so far but is getting better; the Court needs watching. Handing Over Notes.

52 Nigerian Youth Movement members to *Ọwa*, 20 Apr. 1939, *Fadugba papers*.

53 On NYM origins see Baker, *Urbanization and Social Change*, pp. 56–60, and, a lively account by a participant, O. Awolowo, *Awo: an autobiography* (Cambridge, 1960), pp. 113–32.

54 F.I.A. Omu, *Press and Politics in Nigeria 1880–1937* (London, 1978), does not directly deal with the *Pilot*, but considers its emergence to mark a 'new era' in journalism (p. 240).

55 Interview, 21 March 1974. Other early members who provided useful accounts were E.O. Fajuyitan (2 Apr. 1974) and J.O. Fadahunsi (24 Nov. 1973). Unfortunately no records of the local NYM, comparable to those available for the *Ẹgbẹ Atunluṣe* and the *Ẹgbẹ Ọmọ Ibilẹ Ijẹṣa*, have survived.

56 J.R. (Richard) Ogedengbe, a son of the great warrior, was sent to be educated with Sapara-Williams in Lagos.

57 Hadji Smith from Ilase, near Ibokun. He belonged to *Ẹgbẹ Atunluṣe* and was for a while treasurer of the Grammar School. His father, Laneagbe Smith, was a trader, and how he came by his surname I do not know. Smith wore a European suit with a red fez, which was in the style of the modernist Muslims in Lagos who embraced the Ahmadiyyah sect (to which he had belonged). That too set him somewhat apart from the typical Ilesha Muslim, since Ahmadiyyah has never had a foothold in the town. See further, H.J. Fisher, *Ahmadiyyah* (London, 1963).

58 Cf. Awolowo, *Awo*, pp. 121–3.

59 Thus E.A. Fajemisin, interview, 21 March 1974.

306

60 On the Association of West African Merchants see C.E.F. Beer, *The Politics of Peasant Groups in Western Nigeria* (Ibadan, 1976), pp. 224–32.

61 See above, p. 133.

62 See R.J. Southall, 'Farmers, Traders and Brokers in the Gold Coast Cocoa Economy', and R. Howard, 'Differential Protest in an African Protest Movement', both in *CJAS* 12 (1978), and J. Miles, 'Rural Protest in the Gold Coast: Cocoa Hold-ups of 1908–1938' in C. Dewey and A.G. Hopkins (eds.), *The Imperial Impact* (London, 1978).

63 Awolowo, *Awo*, pp. 126–7. See too Oyo Province Annual Report, 1937, in CSO 26/2, 12723, Vol. XIV.

64 Dated 15 April 1940, *Fadugba papers*.

65 ILE DIV 1/2, IL 304: Intelligence Report, Matters Affecting.

66 Ibid. DO to *Qwa* and Council, 18 April 1940.

67 A nice example is 'Ilare History in Brief', dated 18 May 1940, ibid. The *Alarẹ* is the eldest of Oduduwa Olofin's 16 sons, it says, *Qwa* being the youngest. He loved his brother so much in the wars that 'my people diminished both in power and number'. Suddenly we are in the nineteenth century and after a mention of the connexions with Ilare quarter in Ife, the DO is reminded that the *Alarẹ*'s land stretches all the way from the Oshun (where *Qwa*'s stops) to that of the *Qrangun* of Ila.

68 Ekunseitan to DO, 3 Oct. 1940, ILE DIV 1/2.

69 NYM members to *Qwa*, 20 April 1939, *Fadugba papers*.

70 J.B. Akinola to ADO, Ilesha, 20 Dec. 1939, *Fadugba papers*.

71 J.B. Akinola to DO, 3 May 1940, ibid.

72 Late S.O. Ademilola, interviewed with J.O. Opesan and A. Fowowe, 21 Nov. 1974. Mr Ademilola (b. 1892) was the oldest surviving founder of *Ẹgbẹ Qmọ Ibilẹ Ijẹsa*, though Mr B. Ajilore (*Baba Ẹlẹsin*, b. late 1880s), who joined a little later and was also among those imprisoned, interviewed May 1974, was also helpful on the origins of the *Ẹgbẹ*.

73 The first definite written reference to it is as the 'Ijesha Burgesses Society' (as it was known for a while in English) in a letter of E. A. Oke *et al.* to DO, 22 Aug. 1940. But it is clear from two letters of Ademilola to DO, both dated 30 July 1940, that he was then in close touch with J. B. Akinola, who was already expressing the main elements of the *Ẹgbẹ*'s programme.

74 Fadugba to Cardale, ADO, 2 May 1936, reproaching him for 'arrogantly using such words as crazy, fool, swine, famous debtor', and concluding by quoting verse:

> Turn, turn, thy hasty foot aside nor crush that helpless worm;
> The frame they careless look derides, a God alone could form.

75 J.B. Akinola to Chief Commissioner, Western Provinces, 9 July 1940, enclosing copies of earlier letters of 20 Dec. 1939 and 3 May 1940 to the DO. There must also have been a letter to the *Qwa*, since the Chief Commissioner, replying 20 Aug. 1940, complains that its tone 'is not such as is normally used'. He also told him to address himself to the DO, which was what he had been doing.

76 DO to E.A. Oke, 22 Aug. 1940. Oke was a public letter writer, from Igbogi quarter, not to be confused with E.A. Oke, the later police-inspector, of Oke Oye quarter.

77 Minutes of Council Meeting, 10 Sept. 1940, copy in *Fadugba papers*. The authorship is not clear, but presumably it was E.A. Adesuyi, the new clerk. On 7 Nov. 1940 he wrote to the *Ẹgbẹ* complaining of harassment by them: 'Do you know that I have other works besides Minutes of Meetings?'

78 *Qwa* to Fadugba, 10 Sept. 1940; Fadugba to *Qwa* and DO, 12 Sept. 1940. DO gives permission, 2 Oct. 1940.

79 Ademilola to DO, 14 Sept. 1940, referring to an interview on the subject four days before.

80 *Owa* and chiefs to Resident, 16 Sept. 1940.

81 Minutes of meetings on 9 October (*Owa*, Resident, chiefs, representatives of *Ẹgbẹ Atunluṣe*, NYM, Motor Transporters and *Omo Ibilẹ*), 11 Oct. 1940 (public session of the Council), 12 Oct. 1940 (*Owa* and chiefs, with *Ẹgbẹ Omo Ibilẹ* representatives). It was in their capacity as *onile* for district communities that the named chiefs spoke.

82 Minutes of meeting of *Owa* and chiefs with *Ẹgbẹ Omo Ibilẹ* representatives, 7 Nov. 1940. Here the purpose was seen as, in Chief *Arapatẹ*'s words, 'how to stop the confusion in the town'. At first the problem was only about non-natives, he said, but now 'bushes in the districts were being searched'. It can hardly have been very reassuring to suspicious minds that the checking of the Treasury was allowed because many of the chiefs – and the *Owa* – were in the habit of borrowing money from it. This meeting marked a decisive shift in the target of the *Ẹgbẹ*, towards the powerful natives.

83 A document, 'Remarks on Examination of Civil Jurisdiction of Ilesha Native Court', exists in *Fadugba papers*. A few years earlier, the administration had considered the *Odolẹ*'s influence on the Court a bad one (Handing Over Notes, 10 Nov. 1932 in ILE DIV 1/2, IL 103, vol. III), and later again it was felt 'a watch should be kept on interference by senior Ilesha chiefs in cases in outlying courts' (ibid., 20 July 1939).

84 Oke to J. Olulode, Secretary of Lagos Council of Ijesha Societies, 16 Oct. 1940. He was right to be anxious since it was certain that many Ijesha in Lagos would belong to the ROF and might incline to side with the *Ẹgbẹ*'s targets. Significantly some of the Ijesha abroad counselled caution with the campaign against the employment of strangers (Secretary, Ijesha Descendants, Ibadan, to Ademilola, 16 Nov. 1940). 'Bats' has a double meaning here: (i) its ambiguous nature (bird/animal) made it magically powerful in a potentially sinister way and so it suggests the secret powers of the Ogboni; (ii) its dual nature implies lack of moral straightforwardness.

85 At meeting of 7 Nov., cited above, n.82.

86 Document dated September 1941, listing ROF members associated with the NA. In all cases where I have been able to check the attributions (at least as far as opinion goes) they were corroborated. After the Riot *Lẹjoka* Abiola is said to have told the Resident that Ige and other NA employees were among its 70 members: Resident to Secretary, Western Provinces, 6 Feb. 1941 in OYO PROF I/3047–9/3065, vol. I.

87 Very many of these, in Yoruba and English, in *Fadugba papers*.

88 The auditor engaged to look at the accounts, J. Adebayo (Report, 18 Oct. 1940), reckoned the NA received £186 7s 6d in forestry fees from April 1939 to March 1940. The illicit levies of forest guards from villages were estimated by Ademilola at £454, and the lost revenue from trees on which fees were not paid (£3 per tree) were reckoned at £593.

89 E.A. Oke to Senior Conservator of Forests, 13 Nov. 1940; Carterall, Senior Assistant Conservator to Fadugba, 16 Nov. 1940.

90 Again, numerous written notes, *Fadugba papers*.

91 The *Olotan* (of Otan-Ile) also wrote to Fadugba (3 Dec. 1940) that he was told: 'the people in the town did not receive theirs, how much more the people in the districts'.

92 J.O. Shajuyigbe of Ibokun to Fadugba, 20 Sept. 1940.

93 Ijesha Union, Kano, to Fadugba, 18 Nov. 1940. A son of Fariogun Fajemisin's who was a trader there, S.A. Fajemisin, added his voice to this view.

94 This finds an intriguing echo in a phrase used in the Minutes of the mass meeting of *Ẹgbẹ Omo Ibilẹ Ijeṣa* – authorship unknown – held at Lion House on 30 November 1940. The call was for contributions to pay the auditor's fees from everyone, 'wether a capitalist or a villager' (*sic*) – an echo of the new radical nationalist terminology being introduced by the *West African Pilot*.

95 Ibid. Speakers from Ipetu-Ibokun, Ipole, Esa Oke, Ibodi, Iperindo, Erin Odo, Iwar-aja – a total attendance of 3,200 reported.

96 Oke to Ǫwa, 13 Nov. 1940.

97 J.R. Ogedengbe *et al.* to DO, 6 Nov. 1940.

98 DO to Oke, 23 Dec. 1940, said pay vouchers had been found for 13 of the villages which had complained and called many of them 'frivolous complaints'. Oke's reply (24 Dec.) was that no proper investigation of the complaints had been done.

99 Ademilola *et al.* to Ǫwa, 28 Dec. 1940.

100 Main sources for the riot: oral testimonies of S.O. Ademilola and Chief D. Gidigbi, both Ẹgbẹ Ǫmǫ Ibilẹ members afterwards imprisoned; letters of DO, Ife-Ilesha, to Chief Secretary, Western Provinces, 11 Jan. 1941, and to Resident, Oyo, 13 Jan. 1941, both in OYO PROF I/3047–9/3065, vol. I (*NAI*); copies of court records of ten of the prosecutions with references from I/19c/41 to I/29c/41, in *Fadugba papers*.

101 I am grateful to Mr E.A.Lufadeju (interview, 31 March 1974) for providing me with a contemporary list of the damages as assessed. These were (rounded to nearest £): Prince Adeniran £947, Lẹjǫka Abiola £875, *Loro* Falode £308, ROF Lodge £295, G.F. (another son of Ǫwa) £58, S.B. Ige £57, S.O. (Ǫwa's driver) £31, J. Laleye £29, J.F. Longe £23, NA buildings £17, O. (another son of Ǫwa) £12, A. (a produce-examiner) £4. Though much larger amounts of damage were claimed at the trial (e.g. £3,400 for the Lẹjǫka's houses), these figures at least point to the relative attention paid to the rioters' targets.

102 A.D.O. Cox's Final Report on Sources of the Riot, in ILE DIV 1/363, vol. III. I am also grateful for Mr. Cox's oral recollections (interview, London, Nov. 1976).

103 DO Ife to Resident, 22 Feb. 1941; and ibid., 20 Jan. 1941, referring to such movements at Esa Oke, Ijebu-jesha, Iwara, and Oshu. OYO PROF I/3047–9/3065, vol. I.

104 Report in *West African Pilot*, 20 Jan. 1941.

105 Ẹgbẹ Ǫmǫ Ibilẹ Ijẹṣa to Chief Commissioner, Western Provinces, 26 Nov. 1941, in OYO PROF 3/3028.

106 I am grateful to Dr Deirdre La Pin for taping Chief Gidigbi's *itan* of the Riot, and for much advice on the nature of the *itan* as an oral medium. Other examples of Gidigbi's art and a full analysis of the *itan* form are to be found in her thesis: 'Story, Medium and Masque: the Idea and Art of Yoruba Storytelling' (Ph.D. thesis, University of Wisconsin, 1977).

107 *Baekurẹ* is an alternative title for the Ṣalua, which seems to have originally been like *Babaileoke*, a senior slave of the Ǫwa. Latterly it is considered one of the *Alapakur-udu* line (junior palace-chiefs), connected with the worship of Orisa Onifon.

108 See above, pp. 79–81 on Ariyasunle and the *ipaiye*.

109 See record of 'R.v. J.L. Ogedengbe *et al.*' (I/28c/41), to do with the attack on the house of the Ǫwa's son who was a vaccinator. J.L. Ogedengbe was also a vaccinator, whose appointment had ended on 31 December, which seems to suggest a motive. Faleto (J.F.) Ogedengbe was, like Richard, a younger son of the great Ogedengbe, and had been trained by Oyebode and later at St Andrew's College, Oyo. Ogun-moyesin, though a grandson of the warrior, was their senior in age, being a son of Ogedengbe's *daodu* Ogunleye (d. 1910).

110 I first encountered this song when being told by members of the Fajemisin family (20 Dec. 1973) about the exploits of their father Fariogun in the wars. It was sung during Ogedengbe's campaigns around Iyayu in Akoko, on an occasion when his enemies though they had trapped him. Then it had an additional line, *Ǫwǫ tẹ Ogedengbe loni o!*; 'Today Ogedengbe falls into our hands o!'

111 Reported in record of 'R.v.A. Haastrup *et al*' (I/25c/51), dealing with the attack on the NA treasury.

112 Whereas in the passage already quoted, it is quite clearly said that the Ǫwa along

with the chiefs misused his position, later it is said, 'the Ǫwa did not commit excess but his great chiefs' (*Ǫwa o ṣaṣeju s'ilu ṣugbǫn awǫn ijoye nlanla*) and that *Ǫdǫle* Ariyasunle had 'usurped the king's position' (*Oun naa fira supo ǫba*), which implies that the quality of the acts was the same.

113 The phrasing is Chief Gidigbi's.

114 Mr Ademilola identified occupations of leading members as follows: J. Akinola, G. Akinwunmi, J. R. and J.F. Ogedengbe, clerks or ex-clerks; Adeola Haastrup and E.A. Oke, public letter-writers; M. Adedoyin, carpenter; J. Lemodu, bricklayer; J. Jalugbo, Jeje Isare, J. Apoesho, Titus Alo, J.O. Lagunju, traders/produce-buyers; G. Omole, bicycle repairer; J. Ajobo, carpenter; J.B. Oni, farmer; B. Ajilore, ex-*oṣomaalo* and herbalist; E. Bolaji, ex-*oṣomaalo* and chief. Craft-occupations like carpenter and bricklayer were themselves declining in wealth and status from the rather special position they had held when they were linked with the early Christians.

115 For Prince Adeniran's role in UAC, oral evidence from Ademilola (which might have been somewhat biased) was confirmed by Chief J.O. Fadahunsi, who was not involved with the *Ẹgbẹ*; interview, 17 March 1941.

116 See above, p. 110. It is significant that 'the Ekiti system', which J.B. Akinola had proposed for Ilesha, made use of quarter chiefs – but then Ekiti towns were smaller and their hierarchies were less affected by wealth acquired elsewhere in the community.

117 '*Ẹru ati ǫmǫ, talaka ati ǫlǫrǫ, alejo ati ibilẹ*'. Thus Iyalode Olori Awo of Esa Oke, to Fadugba, Nov. 1940.

10 The chiefs and the educated

1 Succession details in OYO PROF 3/986–8/1027, vol. 2 (*NAI*). Also A.L.O. Haastrup (Chapel St Lagos), interview, May 1975; and M.F. Adegbohungbe (Ajimoko II's secretary) and J.A. Haastrup, interviews, 2 June 1974.

2 Ijesha Club, Lagos, to DO, 16 Sept. 1942; and various Ijesha to Resident, 28 Sept. 1942.

3 Other educated contestants included E.G. Lufadeju (Dispenser, European Hospital, Jos), M.O. Aofolaju (Senior Produce-Examiner, Ife), S.A. and R.A. Fajemisin (educated trader, Kano; and Anglican clergyman), E.A. Haastrup (retired postmaster, nephew of Ajimoko I).

4 DO to Resident, 10 Sept. 1942; also interview with Mr H.C. Cox, London, November 1976.

5 Oyo Province Annual Report for 1944 in CSO 26/2, File 127234, vol. XVI (*NAI*). Details of the informal 'Advisory Board' which preceded it in ILE DIV 1/363, vol. III.

6 Reorganization of Ijesha NA Council, OYO PROF 3/3100, vol. 2.

7 Thus the Reorganization Committee's Report on Ijesha Press Affairs, 24 Dec. 1952, set up after the paper ran into a financial crisis at the end of 1952, *Ekundare papers*. The *Vanguard's* shareholders included a good selection of Ilesha's councillors and educated notables, the chairman and principal shareholder being J.O. Fadahunsi. Its initial circulation was 1,000 in Ilesha and 3,000 in Lagos, but this had dropped to under 1,500 in all by the end of 1952. A second series, from 1956 to 1961 was more successful.

8 Oyo Province Annual Report for 1946, in CSO 26/2, File 12723, vol. XVI (*NAI*).

9 Ibid.

10 *WAV* 25–31 Aug. 1958.

11 On the importance of the Local Government Act, see Awolowo, *Awo*, p. 278.

12 See above pp. 162–3, and Peel, '*Ǫlaju*'.

13 *WAV*, 21 June 1952.

14 A typewritten report entitled 'Observations on town planning problems of Ilesha', *Ekundare papers*. This was T.M. Aluko the novelist, though he was then only an engineer. *One Man, One Matchet* (London, 1964) and the other novels, so redolent of Ilesha in the 1950s, were yet to come.

15 On Turton's career, see the handbill or manifesto addressed 'To the electors of Ijesha-land', 23 July 1951, in which he reviews his public services. I am grateful to his son M.D. Turton for showing me a copy.

16 P.C. Lloyd, 'Cocoa, politics and the Yoruba middle class', *West Africa* 1873 (17 Jan. 1953), p. 39, and 'Kings, chiefs and local government', *West Africa* 1875 (31 Jan. 1953), p. 79 and 1876 (7 Feb. 1953) p. 103; also his 'Local government in Yoruba towns' (D. Phil thesis, Oxford, 1958).

17 R.L. Sklar, *Nigerian Political Parties* (Princeton, 1963), pp. 478–9.

18 E.g. J. O'Connell, 'The Political Class and Economic Development in Nigeria', *NJESS* (1966).

19 Details in OYO PROF 3/3100, vol. 2. Not all these people (e.g. C.A. Fajemisin) appear to have eventually served as councillors, but the great bulk did.

20 For the general background, P.T. Bauer, 'Origins of the state export monopolies in British West Africa', *Business History Review* 28 (1954) and Hopkins, *Economic History of West Africa*, pp. 263–7. Local details in what follows derive from interviews with J.O. Fadahunsi, 14 Aug., 14 Sept. 1974; L.O. Omole, 26 Feb. 1975; I.O. Ajanaku, 24 May 1975; S.A. Famuyide, 23 Nov. 1974; C.A. Fajemisin, 16 July 1975.

21 S. Ade Osobu, popular Okesha trader and *Baba Ẹgbẹ* of Iloro Church, was President. Other backers included Ekunseitan and Ajanaku.

22 Reported in Acting Resident to DO, Ife/Ilesha, 25 Sept. 1947, in ILE DIV 1/1, 656 B (*NAI*).

23 See above pp. 127–9.

24 On background to this, OYO PROF 1, 4894: Ilesha Divisional Status and inclusion in Ondo Province (*NAI*). After much local agitation, it was the administrators' conviction that 'Ilesha [is] at the moment a square peg in a round hole' (ADO to Resident, 3 July 1948) which swung it.

25 Minutes of NA Executive Cttee, 5 Dec. 1947, ILE DIV 1/1, 656 B.

26 Details in ILE DIV 1/1, 1183: Chieftaincy Land, Ilesha.

27 Judgment of Resident's Appeal Court, 11 Dec. 1944, ibid.

28 Minutes of NA Executive Cttee, 5 Dec. 1947, 19 March, 16 April, 30 April 1948, ILE DIV 1/1, 656 B.

29 Minutes of NA Executive Cttee, 30 Sept. 1954, *Ekundare papers*.

30 ILE DIV 1/1, 1183.

31 Thus when it was proposed that the lands of hereditary chiefs might be sold if the majority of the 'chieftaincy family' agreed, Chief Ọdọle protested that a chief might not agree with his 'family' (all sections of the lineage) and 'even he could not see the reason why a chief should agree with the members of his family before he could sell portion or portions of chieftaincy land': Minutes of NA Lands and General Purposes Cttee, 30 Nov. 1953, ibid.

32 A splendid example of such chiefly ambiguity is provided by a letter from *Ọwa* and *Ọbanla* to *Ẹgbẹ Atunluṣe* (7 Nov. 1951, ibid.). It said they were prepared to confirm existing sales, except in the special cases of *Ogboni* and *Risawẹ* lands. The chiefs would not sell in future; but if a citizen did buy land and had it surveyed, a successor chief could not claim it back, 'although the purchaser may give yams, palm wine, bush meat or any other present to the chief on the stool when he is making his annual festival. That will promote mutual understanding between them both.' But that kind of custom-ary 'present' was what had been given in the *Ogboni* case and had been interpreted as 'rent', i.e. evidence of no sale. That was just what the literates and traders had been objecting to: the chiefs trying to 'sell' land without relinquishing all rights to future remuneration.

33 *Ọwa* to DO about *Ṣọrundi* title, 15 Nov. 1950, in ILE DIV 1/1 842, vol III: Ilesha chiefs. Also R.S. Omowumi, writing as 'secretary of Sorundi family' to protest about

the land-sales, *WAV* 22 Sept., Oct. 1952. The issue was the more bitter because Omowu-mi's grouping claimed Aogo was not truly of the lineage: Chief Bakare the *Ṣọrundi*, interview, 25 July 1974.

34 E.A. Oke to DO, 16 July 1945, ILE DIV 1/1, 1183.

35 Minutes of Ilesha Urban District Council, 18 July 1955, ibid.

36 This is a most tricky subject on which to get *reliable* information, though almost everyone has something to say about it. The money included discretionary gifts to influential chiefs as judged advisable, the cost of quantities of drinks and finally, when a candidate was acceptable, more money for distribution through the chiefly hierarchy (*owo ahahatan*). There are enormous variations in what different people report: for senior titles (*Ọwa*-ship apart) in the 1970s, I was commonly told by non-chiefs, including some unsuccessful candidates, that thousands of pounds were required, while several chiefs put the figure in hundreds. I incline to think the latter underrepresented the amount, since very high payments are not generally approved. This would be in line with a handful of concrete instances where the circumstantial evidence is strong. Some further instances:

In 1942–43 I.A. Owolabi, then a government clerk, was used by S. Latunji, contesting for *Ogboni*, to take £30 solely to win over *Ọdọle* Ladele, who returned £5 to the messenger for his own. At that rate the title must have cost Latunji several hundreds of pounds in all.

In 1947 one Gidigbi complained he was heavily in debt after having paid well over £100 in customary gifts to be *Bajimọ*: Adeola Haastrup (public letter-writer) to Chief Commissioner, Western Provinces, 30 June 1947, *Fadugba papers*.

Also in 1947 the senior chiefs, virtually *en bloc*, complained to the *Ọwa* about inflation: to become a mere village *Lọja* was now £25–30, instead of the former £5, while for a bigger title, £100–£150 was required for the *Ọwa* and his family alone: *Ọbanla* and other chiefs to *Ọwa*, 8 Apr. 1947, ibid.

37 Chief J.M. Ajayi-Obe (his son), interview, 4 March 1975.

38 I say this notwithstanding complaints voiced in the 1950s that marriage was getting expensive too. It was alleged to rise to £80 in all and the NA tried to establish a level of £25 to cover all costs. One heated correspondent wrote to the *Vanguard* (31 May 1952) to 'beg my Atunluses to warn the hungry and thirsty mothers to reduce the high prices of their daughters like selling articles in the market'. See other comments on the theme, *WAV*, 21 June, 26 Aug., 24 Sept., 14 Dec. 1952.

39 As he protested: 'this matter of heavy demands for chieftaincy stool as alleged [by the chiefs who wrote, as cited n. 36] was not laid down by me as I also was a victim' – *Ọwa* to Chiefs, 5 May 1947, *Fadugba papers*.

40 DO to Resident, 6 Oct. 1942, OYO PROF 3/986–8/1027 vol. 2.

41 Oyo Province Annual Report, 1944, CSO 26/2 File 12723 vol. XVI.

42 Chiefs to *Ọwa*, 8 Apr. 1947, *Fadugba papers*; also ILE DIV 1/1, 1920. The *ẹmẹsẹ* were using the *Ọwa*'s beaded staff (*ọpa ilẹke*) to summon people to the *Afin* to take money from them, and interfered with litigants. There was inflation here too, with much more being demanded than the customary *ẹgbẹwa si ẹgbaji* (6d to 1s 0d).

43 IFE DIV 1/1, 866: details of Sam. Latunji (Tekun)'s career in his letter to *Ọwa*, 26 Feb. 1944.

44 Details in ILE DIV 1/1, 842 vol. III: Ilesha chiefs.

45 *WAV*, 26 Aug. 1952.

46 I have not found written documentation of this, but received a detailed oral account from J.O. Ogunseitan (J.S. Oginni's nephew), interview, 14 Aug. 1979. Though this was from an interested party, the details presented here were agreed on by all other chiefly informants who commented on this, virtually the longest running Ijesha land case.

47 ILE DIV 1/1, 1496 – especially a masterly (and apparently disinterested) summing up by *Risawẹ* Turton, letter to ADO, 8 Jan. 1947.

48 ILE DIV 1/1, 813, vol. II: Egbe Omo Ibile Ijesha.

49 A large file of correspondence on this issue is in the *Fadugba Papers* (Univ. of Ife). In fact Fadugba used his contacts with Ogedengbe Macaulay (son of Herbert Macaulay) in Lagos to raise the issue with the Governor-General: cf. Oged Macaulay to Sir Arthur Richards, 19 July 1944. It even got to the point where a Labour MP (Sorensen) asked a question in the House of Commons about the 'Ijesha peasants'. Significantly, these grievances never played anything like the same role in nationalism in Ilesha as those of clerks, teachers and traders.

50 Main general sources on IPU/IWP, interviews with D.O. Osunloye, its secretary, 30 July 1974 and R.A. Awobiyi, 30 May 1975. Also file ILE DIV 1/1, 2003.

51 J. Ade Turton to DO, 17 Aug. 1947, introducing the society, ibid.

52 ILE DIV 1/1, 2010: Intelligence Reports by NA Police. 1 Sept. 1949 a big open council meeting with IWP representatives at Obokungbusi Hall begs *Qwa* to 'pardon' *Risawę*. 5 Sept., quarrel breaks out again when *Risawę* appears and *Qwa* retires in anger; ADO goes to *Qbanla* to try to patch it up. 11, 20 Sept., the dispute gutters on, the councillors defending the *Risawę*. 26 Sept., still unsettled; the chiefs have brought up the idea to send the *Risawę* to Isaobi village (ritually associated with the title) to have his head shaved except for certain tufts, as this was not done at his installation. The chiefs must have felt this was a particularly condign way of getting at Turton, as he was known to feel some disdain for much of the ceremony (e.g. prostration, visiting shrines) linked with the title.

53 The expression used by a former councillor.

54 As Turton himself put it in his Manifesto (cited n. 15 above): 'I have met the Rt Hon. the Secretary of State for the Colonies and His Excellency the Governor, and sat at tables with Chief Secretary, the Chief Commissioners, North, East and West, the Residents, the District Officers as well as Yoruba and non-Yoruba Obas and Nigerian Doctors and Lawyers, and discussed political and social matters Freely with them.'

55 R.A. Awobiyi for IPU to Ijesha NA, 24 Apr. 1949 and to ADO, 29 Apr. 1949, in ILE DIV 1/1, 1236: Constitution of Nigeria, Revision of.

56 In what follows, unless otherwise noted, correspondence cited comes from ILE DIV 1/2, 867: *Risawę* of Ilesha.

57 Letters of Esudire the *Adegbuwa* (a minor title held by *Risawę* lineage), 13 Oct. 1941, J.R. Turton, 7 Nov. 1941, many members of the *Risawę* family, 15 Nov. 1941.

58 In 1941, Asogbe's people produced no written statement of their genealogical claim. In 1952 his son Olatunbosun Gureje set out the claim in *WAV*, 30 June 1952 and made further points in a biting and ironical attack on 'the doctrine which has received the blessing of the undergraduates of Odo Isida, alias the genuine Gonfirans [i.e. Adedeji's side]', *WAV*, 21 Oct. 1952. The fullest statement, occasioned by a further vacancy in the title in 1975, in a widely circulated letter, S.O. Gureje and others to Council Manager Ilesha, 23 Apr. 1975.

59 Minutes of NA Executive Committee, 13 June 1952. After a difficult beginning, the Committee concluded by removing to the *Qwa*'s chapel!

60 Thus the *Ogboni* of Ijebu-jesha: Minutes of NA Executive Cttee, 23 June 1952.

61 E.g. S.M. Ogunjulugbe, headmaster of Iloro School, asserting Ipetu's independence in an article 'Chief Loro and Ipetu Town', *WAV*, 2 July 1952. Further rejoinders and ripostes, ibid. 7 July, 15 July, 24 July, 8 Sept., 19 Sept., 22 Sept., 3 Oct. On Oshu, *WAV*, 29 July; Erin and Omo 13 Aug.; Ibokun 12 Sept.

62 Thus S.O. Thompson, 13 May, A. Aofolajuwonlo, 28 May, the Revd D.B. Esan, 14 May 1952, all *WAV*.

63 *WAV* leader, 19 June 1952; J.S. Ogunjobi, ibid., 14 July 1952.

64 Thus J. Adetunji, *WAV*, 11 July 1952.

65 *WAV*, 12 June 1952.

66 *WAV*, 6 Aug. 1952.

67 *WAV*, 13 June 1952.
68 Thus Chief Gabriel Esho the *Lufoṣan*, interview, 6 Sept. 1974.
69 *WAV*, 27 May 1952; see too on the ITPA, file ILE DIV 1/1, 2003. E.A. Oke – known as an 'ogbigbo politician' after the song sung during the 1941 Riot – later split from ITPA and organized his own rival grouping in opposition to it. Also, interview with M.I. Ekundare, secretary of ITPA, 23 Dec. 1973.
70 See Appendix 1. For further details on Ilesanmi I am indebted to Chief S. Akinola the *Sawẹ*, who lives just round the corner in Ijamo and knows much about his background.
71 Thus Chief S. Akinola, interview, 7 Aug. 1979.
72 Minutes of *Ẹgbẹ Atunluṣe*, 9 Dec. 1951.
73 This appears to have been the first *documented* occasion, at least since the beginning of the colonial period, in which Ilesha's women through their chiefs under the *Ariṣe* acted as a distinct pressure group in the general affairs of the town: cf. *Ariṣe* and her chiefs to Resident and DO, 11 April 1953, criticizing the intervention of the district people in Ilesha affairs and supporting Asogbe. In explanation of this, the present *Ariṣe*, Chief (Mrs) Dorcas Ayoola (interview, 15 Aug. 1979) stressed the excellent links Asogbe had with the women: 'he had famous women, both wives and daughters, who traded for him'. One of them, Ibidun, a kola trader, was very influential among the women of the town, though not a chief.
74 DO to NA Exec. Cttee, 25 June; also to the *Ọwa*. The *Ọwa* replied on June 26 that he wasn't contemplating it, and on 28 June he wrote that he was going ahead.
75 Reports of the installations, *WAV*, 30 June 1952.
76 Chief J.O. Fadahunsi, interview, 24 July 1979. 'Singing proverbial songs, likely to incite mob hysteria', was how *WAV*, 2 July 1952, put it – a clear allusion to the *Ogbigbo* song of the 1941 Riot.
77 *WAV*, 2 July 1952.
78 Minutes of Special Cttee, 19 Aug. 1952. It comprised four chiefs (*Ọdọle and Lẹjọka, Ogbonis* of Ibokun and Ijebu) and six councillors (Ibironke, Famuyide and Fagbulu, plus three from the districts). Fadahunsi was absent in UK on other business for much of this phase.
79 Council of Lagos Ijesha Societies to DO, 11 Sept. 1952.
80 *Ọwa* to DO, 23 Jan. 1953.
81 ITPA to Resident, 29 Jan. 1953.
82 Minutes of Ijesha NA Council, 22 April 1953.
83 *WAV*, 27 June 1952. Also *Ẹgbẹ Atunluṣe*, Minutes, 17 March 1952: Fadahunsi, supported by J.O. Ogunseitan (President of AG) and E.A. Oriowo (Grammar School teacher, NCNC member), proposes Ijesha National Party 'to act as an opposition party to evil practices in any colour or form'. Asogbe was also a member of *Ẹgbẹ Atunluṣe*, and the society was thus divided and immobilized by the dispute over the *Risawẹ* title (Minutes, 1952 *passim*).
84 S.A.K. Ilesanmi and M.I. Ekundare to DO, 16 March 1953, saying they had no confidence in Fadahunsi (NCNC), Ajayi-Obe (NCNC), Omole (AG), Layinka (AG), Saliu (i.e. Famuyide, NCNC), Opebiyi (?), Fajuyitan (AG), Fagbulu (AG), Ibironke (NCNC).

11 Party politics

1 On which see M.J. Dent, 'A minority party – the UMBC' in J.P. Mackintosh, *Nigerian Government and Politics* (London, 1966) and F.O. Anifowose 'The politics of violence in Nigeria: a case study of the Tiv and Yoruba areas' (Ph.D. thesis, Manchester, 1973).
2 For the origins of the parties nationally, the best sources are still J.S. Coleman, *Nigeria: Background to Nationalism* (Berkeley, 1960) and Sklar, *Nigerian Political Parties*.

3 Oral evidence on NCNC from many interviews with Chief J.O. Fadahunsi, Chief J.M. Ajayi-Obe, M.I. Ekundare, E.A. Fajemisin, Alhaji S.A. Famuyide, I.O. Odeyemi, E.A. Oriowo, R.A. Awobiyi, O. Siyanbola, B.B. Makinwa, L.O. Omole, 1973–75, 1979.

4 See above, p. 211. In the *Fadugba Papers* there is a document by Oged Macaulay, 'Memorandum on the Divisional Centralization of Ijesha and Ekiti Lands', and it was Macaulay who raised with the Governor Fadugba's campaign to get the farmers compensated for damage done by gold mining (copies of several letters on this by Macaulay also in *Fadugba papers*).

5 On Lagos, Baker, *Urbanization and Political Change*.

6 In this it had been preceded by the highly successful Ibo State Union. Cf. Awolowo, *Awo*, pp. 168, 171–2.

7 Minutes of NA Executive Committee, 16 Apr. 1948. At the next meeting, 11 May, Fadahunsi suggested it was for the *Qwa* to use his initiative to welcome the *Ęgbę*: ILE DIV 1/1, 656B, *NAI*

8 This account given by C.A. Fajemisin, an AG member, interview, 16 July 1975.

9 According to L.O. Omole (interview 26 Feb. 1975), who later moved from NCNC to AG, the Owo conference was only attended by S.A. Fajemisin (a trader at Kano) and I.F. Opesusi (a public letter-writer, contractor and public figure, but not a major local opinion leader at Ilesha).

10 This account synthesized from accounts by D.D. Layinka (teacher, AG member in 1950), interview, 31 Oct. 1974, and by Fadahunsi.

11 Account of this election mainly from oral testimony of Chiefs S. Akinola and J.O. Fadahunsi, and R.A. Awobiyi.

12 Post, *Nigerian Federal Election*, p. 435.

13 B.J. Dudley, *Instability and Political Order: Politics and Crisis in Nigeria* (Ibadan, 1973), p. 56.

14 On *ilu* see above pp. 31, 55. '*Ijǫba*', despite deriving from *ǫba* ('king'), does not mean 'kingdom' as a total political entity but rather the governing institutions, and specifically nearly always the regional or federal government.

15 An expression used by Dudley, *Instability*, p. 56. This formulation (and the related notion that there is a definite givenness in the 'primordial ties' which underlie politically organized groups) seems vulnerable to the objections which Dudley himself brings to Post's concept of 'communal' choice.

16 In the 1959 election, for example, the NPC got over 90% of the poll in well over a dozen constituencies in the North, while the NCNC managed polls like 96% in Nsukka N. or Owerri N.E.; the highest Yoruba/AG polls were 79% in Ekiti N.W., 75% Ijebu Remo, 76% Ogbomosho S., and more usual majorities were in the 50s and 60s (data in Post, *Nigerian Federal Election*, pp. 451 ff.).

17 See A.R. Zolberg, *Creating Political Order: the Party States of West Africa* (Chicago, 1966).

18 E.A. and C.A. Fajemisin, interviews, 21 March 1974 and 16 July 1975 respectively.

19 Minutes of IUDC Management Committee, 8 Sept. 1960; Mrs Mabel Aluko, interview, 17 Aug. 1979. One might add that G.O.E. Aduroja (*Lęjǫka* Abiola's paternal half-brother) was AG, and that Mrs Aluko's mother (Abiola's wife) was first cousin of Mr O. Siyanbola, NCNC candidate.

20 E.A. and S.O. Lufadeju, interview, 31 March 1974.

21 D.O. Aluko-Kupoluyi, interview, 11 Apr. 1974.

22 Details from Minutes of a meeting of the Sub-Committee appointed to investigate allegation of political activities against Mr J.A. Olaiya (motor-park attendant), 31 July 1961, *Akinola papers*.

23 For AG origins, I am chiefly indebted to interviews with the following: D.D. Layinka, J.O. Ogunseitan, Chief S.O. Thompson, D.O. Osunloye, I.O. Ajanaku, Chief S. Akinola, D.O. Aluko-Kupoluyi.

24 E.g. *WAV* 12–18 Jan. 1957, probably referring to E.A. Oke of Igbogi the former secretary of Ẹgbẹ Ọmọ Ibilẹ. Two Ẹgbẹ leaders – Bolaji the *Risa Ijọka* and S.O. Ademilola – were so strongly identified with NNDP as to have their houses destroyed in 1965–66.

25 An awkward problem arose with the former party affiliations reported in the 1974 Survey of Household Heads. These gave NCNC 31.11%, AG 37.56%, 'no preference' 31.11%, which are quite at variance with actual voting figures in Ilesha for the period. Since, however, 'opposing the Government' (*alatako Ijọba*) was a very common response to the attitude question, 'What things have most held back the progress of the Ijeshas?', being spontaneously given in some 45 instances, it seems reasonable to regard 'no preference' as representing 'NCNC but regretted'. If this is done, the revised NCNC proportion of 62% is in fact very close to the share of the poll that the party won in the elections of 1958, 1959 and 1960 (see Table 11.1, p. 245).

So, assigning 'no preference' to NCNC, we have the following patterns of party preference by the major occupational groups:

	NCNC	AG	
farmers	65%	35%	(n=118)
oṣomaalo	73%	27%	(n=84)
other traders	58%	42%	(n=69)
modern crafts	62%	38%	(n=39)
teachers	42%	58%	(n=31)
clerks	63%	37%	(n=19)

26 See chap. 8, pp. 202–3.

27 D.B. Abernethy, *The Political Dilemma of Popular Education in Southern Nigeria* (Stanford, 1969); A.B. Fafunwa, *History of Education in Nigeria* (London, 1974).

28 I.O. Ajanaku, interview, 24 May 1975. Mr Ajanaku, who has few political illusions, began his remarks by saying he had little interest in politics as such. But from conversations with his Egba friend, Ayo Rosiji (later active in AG), he became convinced that the regional governments would be crucial and that 'in an independent country, business may be in danger if you don't support the ruling party'.

29 *WAV*, 29 May 1952.

30 Both in fact were Andrians. Komolafe founded his own George Burton Memorial Grammar School just outside Ilesha on the road to Ibala, named after the English Principal of St Andrew's, 1919–48, while Akinyemi, after a decade as Principal of Ilesha Grammar School, became the first old boy of St Andrew's to be its Principal, 1965–69.

31 Details of polling in ILE DIV 1/1, 2384/7: Election Results, Federal and Local.

32 On local government changes more generally, see R.E. Wraith, 'Local Government', in Mackintosh, *Nigerian Government and Politics*, pp. 200–67.

33 ILE DIV 1/2, IL 2356/9: Local Government Elections: Results, 1955.

34 These were Orinkiran/Itakogun, Isida/Esira/Agbede, Ereja, Idifi/Idio, U. Ifofin, L. Igbogi, Isokun, Iloro, Itisin/Ilemo, Iroye, Ayeso, U. Okesha, U. Egbeidi, Odo Iro, New Street. These were the only wards listed in the file. I cannot say why the others should be missing or if they would show a different pattern.

35 For example the AG had teams of their notables to do campaign tours throughout the entire district, organized by the seven roads (ILE DIV 1/1, 2386: Action Group). The NCNC did much less by way of public campaigning, though they did make a provocative parade before AG members' houses, with a coffin in which a palm-tree was laid.

36 Alhaji S.A.K. Arowojobe, interview, 29 Aug. 1974.

37 S.B. Farodoye to NCNC Secretary, 5 March 1955, ILE DIV 1/1, 2356: Local Elections.

38 See above n. 34.

39 J.O. Fapohunda for ITPA, c/o Ilesanmi's, to District Officer, 21 Sept. 1954 in ILE DIV 1/ 1, 2356.

40 B.B. Makinwa, interview, 28 July 1979.

41 O. Siyanbola, interview, 19 Aug. 1974.

42 Lẹmọṣọ and quarter-people to Electoral Officer, 14 Dec. 1954, ILE DIV 1/1, 2356.

43 M.I. Ekundare, interview, 22 Dec. 1973.

44 Ijesha Progressive Union, Ibadan, to Local Government Adviser, 28 April 1958, in ILE DIV 1/2/842–12: Obanla Chieftaincy.

45 Opening of NCNC Secretariat, 12 Nov. 1955, in ILE DIV 1/1, 2010: Intelligence Reports by NA Police.

46 Sklar, *Nigerian Political Parties*, chap. 9 and especially p. 478. See further my criticism in 'Inequality and action: the forms of Ijesha social conflict', *CJAS* 14 (1980), esp. 492.

47 On Adelabu and Ibadan see the very fine study by K.W. J. Post and G.D. Jenkins, *The Price of Liberty: Personality and Politics in Colonial Nigeria* (Cambridge, 1973).

48 Emergency Meeting on Lejofi Chieftaincy, 30 March 1958, in ILE DIV 1/1, 2010.

49 Post and Jenkins, *Price of Liberty*, p. 169, and Jenkins, 'Politics in Ibadan' (Northwestern University Ph.D. thesis, 1955), chap. 14.

50 *WAV*, 31 May 1958.

51 Intelligence Report on NCNC meeting, 18 June 1955, ILE DIV 1, 2387.

52 Ibid. On this occasion the NCNC found it necessary to defend C.O. Komolafe, the federal member for Ijesha, from the charge of having stopped a railway line coming to Ilesha – a rather nice case of pure mythic stereotype, with echoes back to 1905.

53 Minutes of Iwara Local Council, 11 May 1955 attended by the Hon. Komolafe, ILE DIV 1/2, 1909/11.

54 See figures for produce and import prices, and constructed price indices in Gavin Williams, *Inequalities in Rural Nigeria* (Occasional Paper, School of Development Studies, University of East Anglia, 1982).

55 Minutes of Ijesha NA Executive Committee, 21 May 1954, *Ekundare papers*. They were subject to taxation in Ibadan and Oshogbo, and in Abeokuta and Ijebu provinces. At first the proposal was for salaried women (i.e. teachers and nurses in the main) to be taxed, then the larger and much harder-to-tax body of women traders.

56 G.O. Orewa, *Taxation in Western Nigeria* (London, 1962), pp. 119–20.

57 ILE DIV 1/2. Rating, Ijesha Division.

58 Thus D. A. Ariyo – 'Awo does not know the rich and poor men in each division' – at an AG meeting, 10 September 1955, in ILE DIV 1/1, 2010.

59 'Tax Payers Association', mostly AG names, c/o E.A. Oke of Igbogi to DO, July 1956 attacking the tax increases as illegal, accompanied in the files by a disclaimer by Ilesanmi, Ekundare and other NCNC-ers, all of the former ITPA, in ILE DIV 1/1, 2003.

60 The system described in Minutes of Ijesha Division NA Council, Ekundare papers. This led to what Orewa describes as a 'phenomenal improvement made in Ijesha Division . . . mainly due to the cooperation of tax payers in bringing potential evaders to light', pp. 119–20.

61 D.O. Oguntoye, C.A. Fajemisin, E.O. Ayoola, J.O. Ogunseitan.

62 Thus Councillor Fasugba, Minutes of Ilupeju Local Council, 6 Aug. 1957, in ILE DIV 1/2, 1909/16. See too *WAV*, 12 April 1958: 'the loan business became one of the materials for organizing the AG in this Division'.

63 Minutes of Ilesha UDC, 4 March 1959.

64 E.g., in the names of small contractors for roads in Minutes of Ijesha NA Executive Cttee, 25 June 1954, one can identify both NCNC names (D.A. Asagidigbi, Adeniyi Haastrup, J.F. Esho, J.K. Dare, J.M. Makinwa) and AG names (S.O. Aduroja, S.A. Fafowora, D.O. Famogbiyele). Later, according to one of these men (Chief D.A. Asagidigbi, interview, 29 Aug. 1974), the successful contractor had to pay a kickback which went into NCNC funds, analogous to the proportion of their official salary which NCNC councillors agreed to pay. Asagidigbi said that for every 5s he was paid, 1s 3d was for NCNC finances.

65 Memorandum submitted by the Members of Opposition of the IDC on the Mismanagement of the Council's Finances (1960; typescript signed by J.O. Lawanson – AG organizing secretary, *Ọbanla* Ibironke and four others). Copy in private papers of Chief S. Akinola.

66 Much correspondence on these themes in ILE DIV 1/2, Rating: Ijesha Division.

67 Main sources for the contest: *WAV* from Oct. 1956; OYO PROF 1/1027 vol. III: Owa of Ilesha; and CB/141/15/1: Owa-Obokun of Ijeshaland (in the Ministry of Local Government).

68 *WAV* 10–16 Nov., 8–14 Dec., 1956.

69 This expression was one rebutted by Lufadeju himself, in letter to the secretary of the Div. Council, 12 Feb. 1957. The sum of £7,000 is also mentioned here. OYO PROF 1/ 1027, vol. III.

70 Ibid., cf. Minutes of a Meeting of Atakunmosa Royal Family at Daddy Fadaka's, in OYO PROF 1/1027. Lufadeju claimed descent from *Ọwa* Obara, a ruler of the early nineteenth century whose notional descendants constitute one of the largest blocs of *ọmọba* in Ilesha (the 1974 Survey found 24% of *ọmọba* claimed Obara descent). Obara's descendants are now considered to belong with Ataiyero, Agunlejika, Ponlose etc., in 'Bilagbayo Ruling House'. Lufadeju's father, the *Lọja Ibala*, had set down his descent in a letter (8 April 1920, in OYO PROF 3/986–8/1027 vol. I) and I was shown a copy of the same letter by his surviving sons (interview, 31 March 1974).

While it is all part of the tactics of chieftaincy contests to deny the legitimacy of rivals as true descendants, and it can be done most readily with descendants of the more distant rulers, the grounds for this rejection look especially thin: (1) The legitimacy of Lufadeju senior was implicitly accepted by *Ọwa* Ataiyero (also of Bilagbayo) when he made him *Lọja Ibala*, and *Ọwa* Ajimoko II also included his name in 'Atakunmosa Ruling House', letter to DO, 12 Sept. 1955, in OYO PROF 1/1027, vol. III. D.A. Ariyo, whose father was the current *Lọja Ibala*, also defended his claim (ibid., 26 Jan. 1957). (2) No one thought to throw this charge against him when C.A. Lufadeju contested in 1920 and Gbadebo in 1942, when neither was a very strong runner. (3) It was alleged at the public meeting of 20 Jan. by Daddy Fadaka (an elder of Bilagbayo branch) that Ataiyero made Lufadeju senior (who was a carpenter) a *Lọja* as a reward for having made a wooden carriage for him to travel to Benin in 1905. This is a clever touch but historically quite fallacious: Ataiyero went in a hammock provided by the Governor (above p. 100).

71 *WAV*, 10 Nov., 1 Dec., 8 Dec. 1956. S.A. Ataiyero was headmaster of the Anglican Modern School, Isona, and energetic leader of Muroko Local Council: 'those who are very close to the easy going gentleman said he is very respectful'. Oginni: 'his personality is very commanding and his influence is very wide not only among the Africans that matter but also within the Europeans of note'. Oginni's uterine descent from his royal grandfather was not denied; he was still the representative of a group of Ataiyero descendants who went back to one wife of *Ọwa* Ataiyero's. S.A. Ataiyero, the youngest of the late *Ọwa*'s sons, sprang from another wife. (Chief S.A. Ataiyero, interview, 19 Aug. 1974).

72 S.A. Ogundiya, interview, 9 March 1974. Mr Ogundiya was secretary of the Council of Lagos Ijesha Societies, 1949–57.

73 *WAV*, 3 May 1958: Ogunmokun declares in an official visit to the Ilesha mosque that 'it was the members of the NCNC that led him to the prominent position he was in . . .'. Other NCNC notables closely related included E.A. Oriowo, councillor and committee chairman, whose mother was Ogunmokun's first cousin (interview, 12 April 1975) and S.O. Akinbolagbe, produce-buyer and councillor for Odo village, who is 'a cousin somehow' of Ogunmokun and grew up in the same locality near Odo (interview, 25 July 1979); Akinbolagbe's strong support for Ogunmokun, against the better judgment of other party leaders, noted in *WAV*, 23 March 1957.

74 The 'Biladu Ruling House' which now figures as one of four Ilesha ruling houses in the Chieftaincy Declaration, embracing Ogunmokun and his near kin and another line claiming

descent from *Qwa* Bilajara, was constructed after Ogunmokun's accession and gazetted, under his influence, in 1961. Ogunmokun was installed as *Luwarǫ* (*Lǫja* of Iwaro) after his nomination as *Qwa* to meet the demand of custom that an *Qwa* be a *Lǫja* first.

75 Johnson, *History of the Yorubas*, pp. 384–6. See p. 253.
76 Cf. Mackintosh, *Nigerian Government and Politics*, chap. 12.
77 This was the subject of a heated debate in the Council on 8 August 1958 (*WAV*, 13 Sept. 1958): AG members saying the Council's intervention was 'untraditional', NCNC saying that they represented the voice of the people.
78 Correspondence in ILE DIV 1/2, 842–12.
79 'The Owa of Ijeshaland's Traditional Rights in the Appointment of Ilesha Town Chiefs' (Dec. 1958), *Akinola papers*.
80 Minutes of Meeting of Chiefs, 22/23 Jan. 1959.
81 This story I was told by an NCNC notable who had it from his brother, a chief. Another chief of AG sympathies, who would have been in a position to know, said he knew nothing of it. However, he would have been strongly motivated to deny it and on balance I am inclined to believe the story.
82 M.I. Ekundare, interview, 23 March 1974; *WAV*, 1 Oct. 1958.
83 *WAV*, 4/11 July 1959; Chief J.O. Fadahunsi, interview, 8 Dec. 1973.
84 Minutes of Ilesha UDC, 5 Dec. 1959; *WAV*, 19 Sept. 1959.
85 Detailed results for the Urban and Southern councils in *WAV*, 28 June 1958, no detailed results for Northern.
86 Results of 1959 Federal Election, broken down by polling station for Urban, Northern, Southern areas, in *WAV*, 19 Dec. 1959.
87 Minutes of *Ęgbę Atunluşe*, 16 Oct. 1960. These were in the possession of the secretary, Mr E.O. Ayoola, to whom I am grateful for allowing access.
88 Ibid. 20 Sept. 1960. Aderogba, the Chairman, was an AG sympathizer, and there was conflict from a rush of new members, all of NCNC affiliation, who were suspected of having it in mind to dismiss the Revd Akinyemi, the AG candidate who was Principal of Ilesha Grammar School.
89 Mackintosh, *Nigerian Government and Politics*, chap. 12. AG won 80 seats, NCNC and allies 44. Ijesha results:

Ilesha Urban East:	O. Olaitan (NCNC) beat L.O. Omole (AG)
Ilesha Urban West:	B. Olowofoyeku (NCNC) beat D.O. Osunloye (AG)
Ijesha Rural North:	S.T. Adelegan (AG) beat B.O. Orioke (NCNC)
Ijesha Rural South:	J.O. Fadahunsi (NCNC) beat G. Aromolaran (AG)

90 Minutes of Ilesha UDC, 15 Aug. 1960. Other accusations included depriving chiefs of their rights, turning the *Afin* into a party secretariat, scheming at the division of Ijesha-land into three parts. The nature of the 'idolatry' is not clear, but was said to have involved sacrificing a black cow at the open market, or so Councillor Amokeodo alleged indignantly, 'to the disgust of the majority of his subjects'.
91 Minutes of Ilesha UDC (Management Committee), 5 Nov. 1960.
92 Speech of Sogbein, Minister of Works to IUDC, 7 Aug. 1959. Particular attention was also given to some roads in the district, such as from Ilesha to Imesi and Ifewara.
93 All the seven names whose party affiliations I could identify among some 24 small contractors (Minutes of IUDC, 27 March 1961) were AG or had been NCNC but changed.
94 See, for example, Mackintosh, *Nigerian Government and Politics*, chap. 10, K. Post and M. Vickers, *Structure and Conflict in Nigeria 1960–1966* (London, 1973).
95 Minutes of Ilesha UDC, 15 Sept. 1962.
96 Minutes of Ilesha UDC, 3 Apr., 14 May, 18 July, 13 Nov. 1963.
97 Minutes of Ilesha UDC, 6 Apr. 1964.
98 *Daily Times*, 11–12 March 1964.

99 His adhesion was announced on 14 March 1964; and according to the *Daily Times* declared: 'after the fullest consultation with the chiefs and people of Ijeshaland ... I hereby announce I had been mandated by my own people ... to join the young and virile party ... with the blessing of all Ijeshas'.

100 This account of these intra-party manoeuvres entirely depends on oral testimony. The most valuable witness I found to be Alhaji S.A. Famuyide, interview, 15 Aug. 1979.

101 E.g. Minutes of Ilesha UDC, 6 Feb. 1964, antagonism between Amokeodo and Owolabi on one side, and Oriowo and Ekundare on the other, about councillors' sitting fees.

102 Minutes of Ilesha UDC, 3 Apr. 1963.

103 R.A. Awobiyi, interview, 31 May 1975.

104 Esho was generally known by the fearsome nickname *Jojoagbo* or 'ram's beard' – 'because he was very strong and difficult to hold'.

105 37 names, in Minutes of Ilesha UDC, 19 May 1964.

106 B.B. Makinwa (Chairman of the Health Committee), interview, 1 Aug. 1979. This sort of thing was severely reprobated by M.A.K. Esho, the Council Chairman.

107 New council of 43 names in Minutes of Ilesha IUDC, 22 May 1965. They now included a doctor and a lawyer, but also several names of people expressly said to have been an inactive as possible.

108 E.g. *Daily Sketch* 13 Dec. 1965: 'If you go to Ilesha which had always been voting for the NCNC in the past; throughout all the exertions of the Ijesha people ... and throughout their sacrifice, they did not have any place in the Government ... on this occasion Ijesha people, for the first time, have reason to be proud for the banner of this region today is an outstanding Ijesha man [i.e. Fadahunsi]. There are Ministers who are sons of Ijeshaland, there are many members of Boards and Corporations who hail from Ijeshaland. Certainly the Ijesha people are not ingrates'.

109 Quoted by M.I. Ekundare, interview, 9 May 1975.

110 Quoted by Chief S. Akinola, interview, 17 June 1975.

111 Reported *West African Pilot*, 6 Apr. 1964.

112 Quoted by I.O. Odeyemi, interview, 17 July 1979.

113 D.D. Layinka, interview, 31 Oct. 1974.

114 *Daily Times*, 29 Dec. 1964, Ijesha results:

North:	C.O. Komolafe (NNDP)	5647	S.O. Ige (AG)	5537
South:	J.A. Ajayi (NNDP)	3898	S.O. Akinbolagbe (NCNC)	3319
Urban:	I.O. Ajanaku (NNDP)	7543	J.O. Ogunbiyi (NCNC)	2247

115 On party thugs very useful is F.O. Anifowose, 'The Politics of Violence in Nigeria' (Ph.D. thesis, Manchester, 1973), esp. chap. 8. The author is evidently Ijesha and conducted interviews with such UPGA leaders as A. Onibokun, C.A. Fajemisin, Akindele Ojo (Famoto), S.O. Akinbolagbe. There is much very convincing data on the training and deployment of thugs, and of the rise of the UPGA response to NNDP pressure. I found my own evidence entirely consistent with Anifowose's account.

116 *Daily Sketch*, 8 Oct. 1965.

117 *West African Pilot*, 22 Oct. 1965.

118 *Daily Sketch*, 5 Nov. 1965.

119 *West African Pilot*, 2 Nov. 1965, *Daily Sketch*, 5 Nov. 1965.

120 *Daily Times*, 9 Nov. 1965: The women refused to disperse before tear-gas and responded with sticks to a baton charge, singing war-songs mentioning Fadahunsi, Olowofoyeku and Akintola. *Daily Sketch*, 12 Nov. 1965.

121 *Daily Sketch*, 7 Oct. 1965 (Irogbo), *W.A. Pilot*, 2 Nov. 1965 (Isaobi), *Daily Times*, 2 Nov. 1965 (Etioni).

122 Details in Anifowose, pp. 304 ff.

123 During the fracas of April 1964, the Nigeria police had actually intervened to restrain NNDP thugs in the presence of Akintola. The Local Government Police served as an arm of whoever controlled the local council and the regional government, until they were effectively intimidated by popular anger orchestrated by UPGA.

What happened to conscientious officers of the Nigeria Police is exemplified in the case of Mr E. A. Oke, an Ijesha, who was removed from his post as DC at Oshogbo (which included Ilesha) to a nominally superior but powerless post in charge of police training at Ibadan, eventually leaving the service on 31 Dec. 1965 (interview, 9 July 1979).

124 In one night 40 houses are said to have been destroyed, and some 160 in all.

125 Thus Chief Fadahunsi himself put it (interview, 24 July 1979). He would have escaped popular rejection if he had resigned when the NCNC called on him to do so after the October election. He was still involved in attempts to get the arrested UPGA notables out of prison on 10 Jan. 1966.

126 R.A. Awobiyi, interview, 31 May 1975.

127 B.B. Makinwa went to Ilorin, and eventually it was his Okesha quarter people who told him to come back as he would be safe, 1 Aug. 1979.

128 *Daily Sketch*, 28 Jan. 1966.

129 It was Chief J.M. Ajayi-Obe, NCNC politician and grandson of the great warrior Obe, who in discussing the *ipaiye* commented 'they were just like the party thugs of our day'.

130 'We are afraid if Ọwa Odigbadigba [Ogunmokun's ancestor] history is not repeating itself', *WAV*, 27 Sept. 1958; also in his pamphlet *Igba Ijọba ti Ọwa Ogunmokun lori Ilẹ Ijesha* ('The time of Ogunmokun's reign over Ijeshaland'). See above p. 82.

131 Chief S.O. Ogedengbe, interview, 19 July 1979.

12 The present and the past

1 On the disturbances in general, see Western State of Nigeria, *Report of the Commission of Inquiry into the Civil Disturbances which Occurred in Certain Parts of the Western State in December 1968* (Ibadan, 1969) – i.e. The Ayoola Report. Also, Beer, *Politics of Peasant Groups*. On the situation in Ijesha I am indebted to comments by Mr Justice Olu Ayoola, author of the Report and himself an Ijesha, interview, May 1975.

2 On the political economy and history of this period in general, see K. Panter-Brick (ed.), *Soldiers and Oil* (London, 1978), especially the contributions by Rimmer and Turner; A.H.M. Kirk-Greene and D. Rimmer, *Nigeria since 1970* (London, 1981), Gavin Williams, *Nigeria: Economy and Society* (London, 1976), esp. pp. 1–54, and G. Williams and T. Turner, 'Nigeria', in J. Dunn (ed.), *West African States: Failure and Promise* (Cambridge, 1978).

3 Most conspicuously P.C.W. Gutkind, 'The view from below: political consciousness of the urban poor in Ibadan', *CEA* 14 (1974); for a fuller critique of Gutkind's argument, see my 'Inequality and action: the forms of Ijesha social conflict', *CJAS* 14 (1980).

4 The 27 members comprised 9 teachers, 9 traders or contractors, 5 lawyers or senior professionals, 3 clerks, 1 unknown; their former political allegiance were 14 NCNC, 12 Action Group, 1 unknown. For this breakdown I am grateful to Mr M.I. Ekundare (himself a member), interview, 5 Dec. 1974.

5 Minutes of Chieftaincy Committee of Ijesha Southern Local Government Council, 11 May 1971.

6 Interviews with Messrs E. A. Oriowo, A. O. Fadugba and E. O. Ayoola, active members of the three bodies respectively.

7 Minutes of Ijesha Planning Council (Chairman: D.A. Aderogba, also of *Ẹgbẹ Atunluṣe*. Secretary: J.O. Famuyiwa, an Ijesha civil servant at *Ibadan*), 9 March 1966. Of the 55 people who attended its first meeting, 24 lived at Ilesha, 12 at Ibadan, 9 at Lagos, 3 at Ife, others at Akure, Ado, Owo, Ikare.

8 I am grateful to Mr S.A. Ogundiya, Secretary of the Ijesha Self-Help Economic Development Committee, set up originally by the Ijesha Planning Council in 1968, for details here;
interview, 27 Feb. 1975.

9 See 'Report of the Ad-Hoc Committee on States Creation', set up by the Ijesha National
Affairs Council. I am again grateful to Mr Ogundiya for showing me a copy of this Report.

10 The elections took place in five stages (federal senators, federal representatives, state
assembly-men, state governors and federal president). The poll was much lower in the first
round than in succeeding ones, mainly because of memories of how dangerous voting used
to be. UPN majorities were even more massive in the larger, later polls than in the first
round, when they were impressive enough – in Atakunmosa II (one part of the old Ijesha
Southern District, including Etioni and Iperindo) rising from 97% in the first round to
99% in the third. In Ilesha I, UPN got 98% in the third round.

11 The NPN (several of whose adherents had been among those elected to the Ilesha Council
in 1976, the first elections for over a decade, but held when parties as such were outlawed)
had grown from a circle of people many of whom had been active in the Esquire Society,
and also *Ijeṣa Parapọ*, a body linked with the wider movement for an Oshun State, active
1977–78. Its key figure was C. O. Komolafe, Ijeshaland's first federal representative
(1954), who had belonged to Akintola's NNDP government before 1966. However, two of
the NPN candidates in 1979 had been UPGA (ex-NCNC) in the 1965 election: O.
Siyanbola and S.O. Akinbolagbe. None the less, NPN was widely felt locally to be NNDP
reincarnate. For details of party emergence in 1978–79 I am chiefly indebted to several
interviews with Messrs R.A. Awobiyi and S.A. Famuyide (UPN), A.O. Fadugba and
S.O. Akinbolagbe (NPN), July-Aug. 1979.

12 See above chap. 6, p. 112.

13 E.g. R. Cohen, *Labour and Politics in Nigeria* (London, 1974), A.J. Peace, *Choice, Class
and Conflict: a Study of Southern Nigerian Factory Workers* (Brighton, 1979), R. Sandbrook and R. Cohen, *The Development of an African Working Class* (London, 1975), esp.
chapters by Lubeck, Remy and Peace.

14 Peace, *Choice, Class and Conflict*, s.v. ethnicity. P.L. van den Berghe, *Power and
Privilege in an African University* (London, 1973).

15 M. Schiltz, 'Rural–Urban Migration in Iganna' (unpublished Ph.D. thesis, London, 1980),
p. 97.

16 Thus the Oxford English Dictionary.

17 A classic study is L. Bohannan, 'A Genealogical Charter', *Africa* 22 (1952). For a survey
of typical views, see J. Vansina, *Oral Tradition* (London, 1973), pp. 12–14. The *fons et
origo* is Malinowskian functionalism.

18 Minutes of Young Ijesha Improvement Society (*Ẹgbẹ Atunluṣe*), 14 May 1924, *Fadugba
papers*. The outcome, of course was *Itan Ileṣa* (1932), by J.D.E. Abiola, S.O.S. Ataiyero
and J.A. Babafemi.

19 For a documented instance of very much this kind of thing, see 'Ilare History in Brief', 18
May 1940, in ILE DIV 1/2, IL 304, *NAI*.

20 Max Weber, *Economy and Society*, ed. G. Roth and C. Wittich, (Berkeley, 1978), vol. II,
pp. 927–93.

21 Two recent studies which have greatly influenced my thinking on the role of tradition and
history are Edward Shils, *Tradition* (London, 1981) and J.W. Burrow, *A Liberal Descent:
Victorian Historians and the English Past* (Cambridge, 1981).

Appendix 1: Let us now praise famous men: a historical popularity poll

In the 1974 Sample Survey of Household Heads, respondents were asked, as the last question of all, to name those people whom they thought had been most 'notable' (*gba-jumọ*) during their lifetimes, both in Ilesha as a whole and in their quarter. The purpose of the question was to counter that bias towards literates and title-holders which must be a danger in my study that starts from documentary sources of a markedly political emphasis, to elucidate Ijesha values of personal achievement and social worth, and to provide myself with a kind of prosopographical index to guide the collection of personal reminiscences.

Respondents were not limited in how many names they might mention, though between 5 and 10 was the norm. The total of individuals mentioned was nearly 300, of whom 142 were mentioned at least three times. The distinction between those famous in the town and in the quarter was not strictly observed, and some declined to pick out individuals in the quarter: *gbogbo wa l'o ni bakanna*, 'we're all the same', said one. Both deceased and living people were mentioned. Obviously a certain bias in who was mentioned arises from the age structure of the respondents: dividing them into four quartiles, one was up to age 48, one was between 49 and 61, one was between 62 and 74, one was those aged 75 and over. *Far* most often mentioned were the two richest men then living in Ilesha, the trading and transport magnates L. O. Omole and I. O. Ajanaku, and several respondents merely characterized contemporary 'notables' as *awọn olowo*, 'the rich'. As regards deceased people, it seems that those with a life-span roughly covering the period 1880–1950 were most likely to be in the minds of respondents who were themselves predominantly old men, born 1910 ± 15 years. It is worth noting that, of the 'top 30' of deceased people mentioned, about 7 or 8 were completely or virtually unknown to me after a year's research, focussed chiefly on the documents.

Names of those people, deceased at the time of enquiry, who were mentioned at least 10 times by respondents, in order of their 'popularity', as follows:

1. J.A. Fadugba   d. 1949. Literate trader, active in *Atunluṣe, Ọmọ Ibilẹ Ijeṣa. O ja fun wa* ('He fought for us'), explained one respondent.

2. J.D.E. Abiola   d. 1949. Big trader, author of *Itan Ileṣa*, active in *Atunluṣe, Lẹjọka.*

3. Ogedengbe   d. 1910. Ilesha's great war-leader.

4. J.F. Longe   d. 1956. Big trader and Christian *asọju* on the Native Court. *Atunluṣe* member.

5. S.A.K. Ilesanmi   d. early 1960s. Shopkeeper, *Atunluṣe* member, *Baba Ẹgbẹ* of Seraphim Society, leader of Tax Payers Association. *Ọmọluwabi* ('a gentleman').

6. *Ọwa* Ogunmokun   d. 1963.

323

7. Ode Abugan	d. 1944. Trader to Ejinrin, later to Ekiti. Popular patron of younger traders.
8. S.A. Adeniran (Isokun)	d. 1956. Eldest son of *Ọwa* Aromolaran. Big transporter in the 1930s.
9. Oginni Sofe	d. late 1930s? Former Ejinrin trader, later had scales for produce at the market and a lorry. Just 'jolly and talkative', and generous with loans.
10. Aluko Dugbe	d. early 1950s? Trader, had one of earliest iron-roofed houses. *Baba Ẹgbẹ* of Okesha Mosque and active in *Ọmọ Ibilẹ Ijẹṣa*.
11. D.A. Afilaka (Anaye)	d. 1938. Shoemaker and trader. Popular in his *ẹgbẹ* and very hospitable.
12. J.R. Turton	d. 1952. Powerful *Risawẹ* on retiring from secretariat post in Lagos. 'He numbered all our houses in Ilesha.'
13. J.J. Ibironke	d. 1973. Big produce-buyer and transporter. Active in NYM and NCNC. *Ọbanla* from 1959.
14. T. Adewole (Okesha)	d. 1967. Trader (planks) and *oṣomaalo* patron (*Ẹgbẹ Amuludun*). So generous that 450 pieces of cloth presented at his funeral. Known as 'Timo Loja'. *Atunluṣe* member.
15. D.O. Agbeja (Ijoka)	d. — ? Substantial trader and transporter. Later *Ọlọja* of Ibodi.
16. *Ọwa* Aromolaran	d. 1942.
17. Asaolu Osue	d. 1958. Ejinrin trader, later shopkeeper and lorry-owner. *Atunluṣe* member.
18. Olowookere Olorunnisomo (Iloro)	d. 1974. Popular and generous trader.
19. Arimoro	d. 1898. Ogedengbe's warrior-companion.
20. Fariogun Fajemisin	d. 1954. President of Farmers' Association, pillar of Iloro Church.
21. Dabi of Orinkiran	d. early 1950s. *O kọkọ da ẹgbẹ silẹ* – 'he was first to found a society [of the modern kind, for young men]'. Tailor, trader, died as *Lọja Imọgbara*.
22. Aluko Olowo Ijero	d. 1931. 'Rich man from Ijero', where he sold cloth. Built one of first storey-houses (1915–16) and patronized the *oṣomaalo*.
23. James Oginni	d. 1949. Enlightened trader, later chairman of *Ẹgbẹ Atunluṣe*.
24. D.M. Anjorin	d. 1926. 'Balogun Gambari'. Patron of the traders of the 1920s, leading founder of *Atunluṣe*.
25. Olesin Isona	d. —? Popular trader.
26. J.F. Olojo (Egbeidi)	d. 1964. Trader and lorry owner in 1920s–30s. *Atunluṣe* member.
27. Jegede Ogboni (Ereja)	d. —? Son of *Ogboni* Fapohunda. Trader and lorry-owner, in 1920s–30s. *Atunluṣe* member.
28. Alege Lewere (Iwere)	d. —? Popular trader of 1920s. Contested *Loro* title in 1929.
29. J.A. Babalola	d. 1959. The great *Aladura* prophet of 1930. Virtually the only non-Ijesha mentioned.
30. S.A. Osobu	d. 1960s? Trader (shop in Okesha), and lorry-owner. President of Ilesha Transport Company and *Baba Ẹgbẹ* of Iloro Church.

324

31. B. Ajilore (Iroye)   d. 1974. 'Baba Elesin'. Trader and medicine dealer. Contested *Loro* in 1929. Active in *Ẹgbẹ Ọmọ Ibilẹ Ijẹṣa*

Those people with the name of their quarter in brackets after their name received at least a third of their 'votes' from residents of their quarter, though a good degree of such local notability was evident in most cases. It may seem odd that Prince Adeniran should appear higher up the list than his father *Ọwa* Aromolaran, who was the main source of his standing and himself both powerful and very highly regarded; but I can only suppose that many of the more elderly respondents, who would be most likely to name Aromolaran, took the view that an *Ọwa* is out of the ordinary run, not to be reckoned as *gbajumọ* against other men.

Appendix 2: Methods and sources

1. PRIMARY SOURCES: NON-DOCUMENTARY

Fieldwork was conducted in Ilesha between September 1973 and August 1975, and again during July and August, 1979. Throughout 1973–75 I was lecturing full-time at the University of Ife (just over twenty miles away) and, except for some longer periods during the vacations, my visits to Ilesha, while frequent, were mostly for a day or a few hours at a time. Apart from attendance at a variety of ceremonies and public functions, fieldwork was mostly focussed on an extended series of interviews, beginning with obvious figures of contemporary public importance and men who, to judge from local documentary evidence, had played a substantial role in public affairs over the preceding few decades or were the close relatives of such men. The interviews ranged both over their public roles, and over their social backgrounds. As the research proceeded, the range of these interviews increased, eventually extending to well over a hundred individuals in Ilesha, of whom about a third were chiefs. In over twenty cases, several substantial interviews were conducted over the period of research – in some cases extending up to a dozen hours of discussion in all. These were with especially significant figures in Ilesha's recent history, or with people exceptionally informed about or interested in Ijesha oral traditions, both of the early twentieth century or the remoter past. Some of these men – Chief S.A. Ataiyero the *Aşireyun* or Chief J.O. Malomo the *Agbayewa*, for example – are widely recognized in the town as *ǫpitan* (historians). As I was also working on documentary sources throughout both periods of research in Nigeria, 1973–75 and 1979, it was possible to return to these key informants as occasion required to seek clarification, extra information and verification of points raised by the documents. Particular informants are noted, as appropriate, in the footnotes.

The 1974 Sample Survey
During the long vacation of 1974, when I was living in Ilesha, a random sample survey of households with male heads was carried out, using eight Ijesha student interviewers. A random sample of 500 households was selected, stratified by quarter, and some 443 questionnaires were completed. As the survey had the public support of the *Qwa* and chiefs, to whom its purpose was explained at one of their Saturday meetings at the *Okemęsę* courtyard of the *Afin*, the rate of overall non-response was remarkably low, less than 2%, though the fullness of response on some questions was not high. The questionnaire took up to two and a half hours to complete and covered the following topics:

(*a*) personal history and social characteristics of the respondent
(*b*) social characteristics of other occupants of the house
(*c*) social characteristics of absent family members
(*d*) details of parentage, lineage, siblings, family cults and history of the respondent
(*e*) details of farmland owned or used by the respondent

326

(*f*) respondent's attitudes to social change, as gauged by answers to a number of open-ended questions

This survey – and I do not know of a similar one having been undertaken to provide data for the reconstruction of social history – had great merits as well as some severe defects. On the positive side it provided invaluable information, not to be got in any other way, about many aspects of the past, especially as regards the phasing of economic and cultural change. It also enabled gross observations about the political structure of the town to be made concrete in mass-quantitative and distributional terms. It was considerations of both time and money which led to the initial decision to use the same survey to collect personal and family histories, *and* data about household composition and migration. This was, in principle, a mistake, and some of the latter data was so incomplete as to be unusable. Related to this is the undoubted male bias of the survey design – *mea maxima culpa!* – compounded by the fact that I had to use male interviewers, as no women Ijesha students applied. Partly this followed from the political interest of the main study, since the formal political sphere is so strongly male-dominated; partly it followed from an assumption that men must be the key informants in the investigation of a predominantly patrilineal system of access to land and title; partly, there was the practical problem that a separate female-oriented interview-form would need design-ing for women respondents or the minority of household-heads who are women. When these deficiencies were realized, it was again the constraints of time and money which ruled out an effective remedy. The distinct historical experience of women, therefore, does not receive adequate treatment in this book, though it has been written in the constant awareness of the problem. May others do better in future!

Iroye and Omofe Surveys
During the Christmas vacation, 1974–75, surveys were undertaken to collect a limited body of information relating to all the houses in two of Ilesha's quarters: when and by whom existing houses were built, and the lineage/residence antecedents of the residents.

Oṣomaalo Survey
When it became clear that so large a proportion of the sample of household heads had been *oṣomaalo* (39%), a further, more detailed survey of a smaller sub-sample of them (34 in all) was conducted, also in the Christmas vacation, 1974–75. The interviews were mostly conduc-ted by two of the same student interviewers who had worked on the earlier household survey. They did not use a standard questionnaire form but were guided by quite a detailed schedule of questions, designed to produce a fairly structured account of the *oṣomaalo*'s career. The early interviews I conducted myself, in the students' presence, and later I sat in on a handful of interviews conducted by them.

Rural Surveys
In June–August 1975, and again in July–August 1975, surveys were carried out in the rural areas, to investigate the character of different kinds of rural settlement and subordinate town. Data was collected from the chief(s) or senior resident(s) principally on traditions of origin, nature of local chiefship, local cults, political links with Ilesha, locally dominant families, introduction of cocoa, local practice as regards tenants, *iṣakọlẹ* etc., presence and origin of such modern facilities as churches, schools, markets, maternity centres etc. These interviews were partly carried out by myself and partly by research assistants, according to a schedule of questions. Information was collected on over 90 substantial settlements, with particular concentration on an area of the Muroko Road (IV), and on the area to Ilesha's south, along Roads VI and VII. In addition a research student linked with the project, Paul Francis, conducted an excellent detailed study of Ibokun and its environs to the north of Ilesha (Road III) during 1978–79 (for details of his thesis, see p. 332).

Methods and sources

2. PRIMARY SOURCES: DOCUMENTARY

A. Government archives

National Archives, Ibadan
The most important single documentary source, comprising the records of the colonial administration in Nigeria, at colony-wide, provincial and divisional levels. No records seem to have survived from when Ilesha was the capital of the North-Eastern District, up to 1913. Most papers were from Oyo Province (OYO PROF) and Ife Division (IFE DIV), and, from 1948, Ilesha Division (ILE DIV). These records go up to 1956, and are particularly full for the late 1940s and early 1950s. IBA PROF 3/6 also largely deals with Ilesha, as do some files from the specialist departments, such as Ib.Min.Agric. 1/163, though these were not systematically worked through. Also important are papers from the Colonial Secretary's office in Lagos (CSO series), especially for Intelligence Reports and Provincial Annual Reports.

Public Record Office, London
For the period up to 1914, this was the richest documentary source, often covering local affairs in the greatest detail. The relevant series are CO 147, CO 149, CO 879 (Lagos Protectorate) and CO 520 (Southern Nigeria).

Council Offices, Ilesha
Here are available Ijesha Urban District Council Minutes and other records dating from the reorganization of Ijesha local government in 1958 until the suspension of local government in 1966, and also Minutes of the Management Committee of the Ijesha Southern Local Government Council from 1973. Documents from before 1958, particularly those of Ijesha Divisional Council, do not seem to be available in the Council Offices, but copies of the Minutes of the Council and many of its Committees may be found in the Ibadan Archives (IFE DIV and ILE DIV), and still exist in the possession of several former councillors (see under C below).

Ministry of Local Government and Chieftaincy Affairs, Ibadan
Here I was given access to a number of open files dealing with chieftaincy matters.

University Library, Ife
Two items consulted here:
Record Books of Ilesha Native Court (contained within the full archive of customary records of Western Nigeria), consulted for the period 1906–10.
Proceedings of the Oyo State Chieftaincy Review (Ademola Commission), vol. I, held at Ilesha, 11 Jan. 1977.

Rhodes House Library, Oxford
MSS. Afr. S. 1151 (6), various documents relating to the period *c* 1895–1917.

B. Church archives

Church Missionary Society, London
Archives now deposited in Birmingham University Library. Papers of all missionaries likely to have visited or worked in Ilesha (Hinderer, Vincent, Allen, Olubi, Phillips, Oyebode) were consulted, in the two series headed CA2 (up to 1880) and G3 A2 (1880 onwards), up to 1914.

CMS Papers, National Archives, Ibadan
Local papers with the heading CMS (Y), running from 1882 to *c.* 1912. These included the very important document 'Towns destroyed by the Ibadans in the Ijesha County', by P.J. Meffre (1882). Also Papers and Diaries of Bishop Charles Phillips.

Methodist Missionary Society, London
Though not nearly as informative as those of the CMS, the Synod Minutes, consulted for the years between 1900 and 1910, did shed light on the affairs of the Revd Hezekiah Atundaolu.

Miscellaneous, Ilesha
Preachers' books and records of church schools consulted at several churches and schools in Ilesha.

C. Private papers

Fadugba papers
A source of cardinal importance for the history of Ilesha. Preserved in several cardboard boxes, they were in the possession of J.A. Fadugba's son, Chief A.O. Fadugba, who has generously deposited them in the Library of the University of Ife. The main items of interest in the papers are:
Minute Book and miscellaneous correspondence of the Young Ijesha Improvement Society
    (*Ẹgbẹ Atunluṣe*), 1923–28
Diaries, kept irregularly between 1923 and 1935, and other personal documents
Correspondence, records of meetings, petitions, transcripts of court proceedings, and other
    documents relating to *Ẹgbẹ Ọmọ Ibilẹ Ijeṣa*, 1939–43.
Correspondence on other public topics, mostly to do with chieftaincy and the struggle to
    compensate farmers for damage done by gold-miners, 1942–49.

Apara papers
Various documents in the possession of the sons and grandsons of Peter Apara, of two kinds:
A manuscript of up to 126 pages, entitled *Iwe Itan Oko Apara* ('History of Apara's Farm') in the possession of Mr Richard Apara, of which a photocopy is now deposited in the University of Ife Library. It contains much material about the nineteenth century derived from the testimony of Peter Apara in 1919, as well as a significant case study of a most unusual kind in the agrarian history of the early twentieth century.
Miscellaneous leases, tenancy agreements etc., in the possession of Mr Akin Apara of Ibadan.

Akinola papers
In the personal possession of Chief S. Akinola, *Sawẹ* of Ilesha, active in public affairs since the early 1940s. These included Minutes of Council meetings and a variety of other documents relating to local affairs between 1952 and 1961. Of particular value was a document composed by *Ọwa* Ogunmokun entitled 'The Owa of Ijeshaland's Traditional Rights in the Appointment of Ilesha Town Chiefs' (1958).

Ekundare papers
A similar collection of papers in the possession of the late Mr M.I. Ekundare of Ifofin quarter, Ilesha.

Ẹgbẹ Atunluṣe
Minute Book, covering 1941–48 and 1950–73, in the possession of the secretary, Chief E.O. Ayoola.

Ijesha Cooperative Produce Marketing Union
Minute Book of the Farmers' Association, 1926–41. Also typescript history 'Cooperation in Ijeshaland', by O.A. Williams, Secretary of the Cooperative Union, 1939–60.

Miscellaneous

A variety of other documents, mostly relating to very recent history, were shown me by individual Ijesha, such as Chief Sir Odeleye Fadahunsi, Chief S.A. Ogundiya, Alhaji S.A. Famuyide, Mr M.D. Turton and others.

D. Newspapers

These provided significant evidence at four distinct periods.

Lagos Weekly Record 1891–1903, Lagos Standard 1895–1910

Though published at Lagos, both papers were edited by men of radical sympathies and good connexions with the interior, so they are an indispensable complement to the impression of Ilesha conveyed in government records.

The Yoruba News 1924–33

Published at Ibadan, this newspaper was the mouthpiece of enlightened sentiment in the main Yoruba towns of the interior.

West African Vanguard. First series 1952–53, second series 1956–61

Published at Ilesha, one of the few Yoruba towns to have a newspaper of its own, it is full of local social information. In its first phase, it expressed the viewpoint of the educated, irrespective of party, and in its second, it was a vehement organ of the local NCNC. A Yoruba edition, *Irawọ Obokun* (Star of Obokun) was published in tandem with it.

1964–66

Three newspapers were consulted over this period, for which few other documentary sources were available: *Daily Sketch* (published in Ibadan, mouthpiece of the UPC/NNDP Western Regional Government), *West African Pilot* (Lagos; organ of NCNC and UPGA), *Daily Times* (Lagos; without definite party affiliation).

E. Printed official documents

Great Britain, *Correspondence respecting the War between the Native Tribes in the Interior and the Negotiations for Peace conducted by the Government of Lagos*, C. 4957, 1887.
    Further correspondence respecting the War between the Native Tribes in the Interior and the Negotiations for Peace conducted by the Government of Lagos, C. 5114, 1887.
Lagos, *Annual Reports* 1889–1905.
Southern Nigeria, *Annual Reports* 1904–13.
West African Lands Committee, *Minutes of Evidence* 1916.
    Papers and Correspondence 1916
Great Britain, *Report of the Commission on the Marketing of West African Cocoa* (Nowell Report), Cmd. 5845, 1938.
Nigeria, *Population Census of the Western Region of Nigeria 1952, 1953*.
Western Nigeria, *Western Nigeria Statistical Bulletin, 1959–1967*
Nigeria, *Population Census of Nigeria*, 1963.
Western State of Nigeria, *Western State Chieftaincy Declarations*, issues for Ijesha South Division and Ijesha North Division, n.d.
Report of the Commission of Enquiry into the Civil Disturbances which occurred in certain parts of the Western State of Nigeria in the month of December 1968 (Ayoola Report), 1969.
Oyo State of Nigeria, *Ilesha Development Plan*, 1978.

F. Other printed primary sources

These fall into three categories: first-hand reports by European visitors and residents; local histories; and miscellaneous local pamphlets.

330

(i)

Clarke, W.H. *Travels and Explorations in Yorubaland (1854–1858)*, edited by J.A. Atanda. Ibadan, 1972.

May, D.J. 'Journey in the Yoruba and Nupe Countries in 1858', *J. Roy.Geog.Soc.* 30 (1860), 212–33.

Southon, A.E. *Ilesha – and Beyond! The Story of the Wesley Guild Medical Work in West Africa*. London, n.d.

Ward-Price, H.L. *Dark Subjects*. London. 1939.

(ii)

Abiola, J.D.E. *Ọrọ Wura: Iwe Oniranti awọn Agba, Amọna awọn Ewe, lati 1822 de 1938* [Golden Words : a Book to jog the memory of the Old, Guides of the Young, from 1822 to 1938]. Oshogbo, 1939.

Abiola, J.D.E., Babafemi, J.A. & Ataiyero, S.O.S. *Itan Ileṣa* [History of Ilesha] Ilesha, 1932.

Adedeji, S.O. *Brief History of the Owa of Ijeshaland Chieftaincy Title*. Ibadan, 1957.

Arojojoye II, *Ogboni* of Ijebu-jesha. *Itan Kukuru fun Iṣẹdalẹ Ilu Ijẹbu-jeṣa* [Short history of the Foundation of Ijebu-jesha]. Ilesha (?), n.d.

Ataiyero, S.A. *A Short History of the Ijeshas, Part I*. Ilesha, 1977.

Atundaolu, H. 'A Short traditional history of the Ijeshas and other hinterland tribes', serialized in six parts in *Lagos Weekly Record*, June–July 1901.

Ekundare, M.I. *Iwe Itan wọn Adugbọ Kokan t'o wa ninu Ilu Ilesha* [History of all the quarters of Ilesha]. Ilesha, 1966.

Golden Jubilee Celebration Committee. *Fifty Years of Methodism in Ilesha Circuit . . . 1898–1948*. Ilesha, 1948.

Ilesha District Church Council. *Iwe Itan Ọgọrun Ọdun ti Isin Kristi ni Ilẹ Ijesha 1857–1957* [History of a Hundred Years of Christianity in Ijeshaland]. Ijebu-Ode, 1957.

Ojo, W. 'Folk history of Imesi-Ile', *Nigeria Magazine* 42 (1953), 98–117.

Oke, M.O. *Itan Ilẹ Ijeṣa* [History of Ijeshaland]. Ibadan, 1969. The great bulk of this is in fact a plagiarism of Abiola, Babafemi and Ataiyero, *Itan Ileṣa*.

Oni, J.O. *A History of Ijeshaland*. Ilesha (?), n.d.

Saraibi, S.A. *Itan Kukuru nipa Iṣẹdalẹ Ilu Igangan* [Short History of the Foundation of Igangan]. Ilesha, n.d.

(iii)

The little printing-presses which abound in towns like Ilesha generate a vast volume of ephemeral printed material, much of which is of interest to the social historian. Hardly any of it, except some of the local histories just listed, finds its way into libraries, and what comes into the hands of the field-researcher does so almost fortuitiously. Of greatest interest are family or individual histories (though few of these are produced), political pamphlets, pamphlets issued by parties to chieftaincy disputes, and (a very large category) orders of service for funerals and anniversaries, which often contain historical sketches of the individuals or societies involved. The following items are the tip of an iceberg:

Ajọdun Ẹgbẹ Atunluṣe [Anniversary of the Improvement Society]. 1972.

Biography of Pastor Joshua Ajayi Ibidapo. n.d.

Chief Sir Odeleye [Fadahunsi] is 80. 1981.

Ekundare, M.I. *Important and Relevant Information on the Vacant Stool of Chief Loro of Ilesha*. n.d. (*c.* 1964).

Famoto, A.O. *Alaye Pataki nipa Ọba Ọwa Ogunmokun* [Important Information about Ọwa Ogunmokun], Ilesha, 1960

Igba Ijọba ti Ọwa Ogunmokun lori Ilẹ Ijesha [The Time of Ọwa Ogunmokun's Reign over Ijeshaland]. Ilesha, 1961.

Ijesha Students Union, *Minutes of 18th Annual Conference Rally at Ifewara*, 1955.

Minutes of 19th Annual Conference Rally at Oke Bode, 1956
Minutes of 20th Annual Conference Rally at Old Ikeji, 1957.
Ilesha Grammar School, *Fortieth Founder's Day Anniversay Celebrations*, 1974.
Ipade Ọmọ-ile Makinwa ... [Meeting of Members of Makinwa Lineage], 1966.

3. SECONDARY SOURCES

Two categories of material are listed below: works solely or specifically devoted to the Ijesha; and a selection of other works on the Yoruba or Nigeria which I have particularly drawn upon in the study. No attempt has been made to list all relevant works on the Yoruba, or comparative and theoretical materials.

(i)
Anon. 'Loja of Itagunmodi', *Nigeria Magazine* (1971), 14–31.
Awe, B. 'Ogedengbe of Ilesha: an introductory note', University of Lagos School of African and Asian Studies, Staff Seminar Papers 1968–69, 161–93.
Francis, P.A. 'Power and order: a study of litigation in a Yoruba community' [Ibokun]. University of Liverpool, Ph.D. thesis, 1981.
Ilori, G.O. 'Chief Ogedengbe of Ilesha: a biographical study', University of Ibadan, Dept. of History, B.A. dissertation, 1974.
Olowokure, J.O.K. 'Christianity in Ijeshaland 1858–1960', University of Ibadan, M.A. Thesis, 1970.
Peel, J.D.Y. '*Ọlaju*: a Yoruba concept of development', *JDS* 14 (1978), 135–65.
  'Kings, titles and quarters: a conjectural history of Ilesha. Part I, The traditions reviewed', *History in Africa* 6 (1979), 109–35.
  'Kings, titles and quarters ... Part II, Institutional Growth', *History in Africa* 7 (1980), 225–55.
  'Inequality and action: the forms of Ijesha social conflict'. *CJAS* 14 (1980), 473–502.
Trager, L. 'Yoruba markets and trade: analysis of spatial structure and social organization in the Ijeshaland marketing system', University of Washington, Ph.D. thesis, 1976.

(ii)
Abernethy, D.B. *The Political Dilemma of Popular Education in Southern Nigeria*. Stanford, 1969.
Adedeji, J.A. 'Origin and form of the Yoruba masque theatre', *CEA* 12 (1972), 70–86.
Adejuyigbe, O. *Boundary Problems in Western Nigeria: a Geographical Analysis*. Ile-Ife, 1975.
Ajayi, J.F.A. & Smith, R.S. *Yoruba Warfare in the Nineteenth Century*. Cambridge, 1964.
Akintoye, S.A. 'Economic background of the Ekitiparapo', *Odu* 4 (1968), 30–52.
  'The Ondo Road, eastwards of Lagos, *c.* 1875–1895', *JAH* 10 (1969), 581–98.
  Revolution and Power Politics in Yorubaland, 1840–1893: Ibadan Expansion and the Rise of Ekitiparapo. London, 1971.
Anifowose, F.O. 'The politics of violence in Nigeria: a case-study of the Tiv and Yoruba areas', University of Manchester, Ph.D. thesis, 1973.
Atanda, J.A. *The New Oyo Empire: Indirect Rule and Change in Western Nigeria 1894–1934*. London, 1973.
Awe, B.A. 'The Ajele system: a study of Ibadan imperialism in the nineteenth century', *JHSN* 3 (1964), 47–71.
  'Militarism and economic development in nineteenth century Yoruba country', *JAH* 14 (1973), 65–77.

Ayandele, E.A. *The Missionary Impact on Modern Nigeria 1842–1914: a Political and Social Analysis*. London, 1966.

Beer, C.E.F. *The Politics of Peasant Groups in Western Nigeria*. Ibadan, 1976.

Berry, S.S. *Cocoa, Custom and Socio-economic Change in Rural Southwestern Nigeria*. Oxford, 1975.

Clarke, R.J.M. 'Households and the political economy of small-scale cash-crop production in South-western Nigeria', *Africa* 51 (1981).

Dudley, B.J. *Instability and Political Order: Politics and Crisis in Nigeria*. Ibadan, 1973.

Eades, J.S. *The Yoruba Today*. Cambridge, 1980.

Ekundare, R.O. *An Economic History of Nigeria 1860–1960*, London, 1973.

Galletti, R., Baldwin, K.D.S. & Dina, I.O. *Nigerian Cocoa Farmers*. London, 1956.

Gbadamosi, T.G.O. *The Growth of Islam among the Yoruba 1841–1908*. London, 1978.

Hopkins, A.G. *An Economic History of West Africa*. London, 1973.

Horton, R. 'Ancient Ife: a reassessment', *JHSN*, forthcoming.

Johnson, S. *The History of the Yorubas*. Lagos, 1921.

Kirk-Greene, A.H.M. & Rimmer, D. *Nigeria since 1970*. London, 1981.

La Pin, D. 'Story, medium and masque: the idea and art of Yoruba story-telling', University of Wisconsin, Ph.D. thesis, 1977.

Law, R.C.C. *The Oyo Empire, c. 1600–1836*. Oxford, 1977.

Lloyd, P.C. *Yoruba Land Law*, London, 1962.

'The traditional political system of the Yoruba', *SWJA* 10 (1954), 366–84.

'Sacred kingship and government among the Yoruba', *Africa* 30 (1960), 221–38.

'Conflict theory and Yoruba kingdoms', in I.M. Lewis (ed.), *History and Social Anthropology*. London, 1968.

Nicholson, I.F. *The Administration of Nigeria 1900–1960*. Oxford, 1969.

Mackintosh, J.P. *Nigerian Government and Politics*. London, 1966.

Obayemi, A. 'The Yoruba and Edo-speaking peoples and their neighbours before 1600', in J.F.A. Ajayi and M. Crowder (eds.), *History of West Africa*, Volume I (2nd edn.). London, 1976.

Ojo, G.J.A. *Yoruba Culture: a Geographical Analysis*. London, 1966.

Orewa, G.O. *Taxation in Western Nigeria*. London, 1962.

Oroge, E.A. 'The institution of slavery in Yorubaland', University of Birmingham Ph.D. Thesis, 1971.

Peel, J.D.Y. *Aladura: A Religious Movement among the Yoruba*. London, 1968.

Post, K. *The Nigerian Federal Election of 1959*. London, 1963.

Post, K. & Jenkins, G.D. *The Price of Liberty: Personality and Politics in Colonial Nigeria*. Cambridge, 1973.

Sklar, R.L. *Nigerian Political Parties*. Princeton, 1963.

Tamuno, T.N. *The Evolution of the Nigerian State: the Southern Phase, 1898–1914*. London, 1972.

Williams, G. *Nigeria: Economy and Society*. London, 1976.

Inequalities in Rural Nigeria. University of East Anglia, School of Development Studies, Occasional Paper, 1982.

Index

Index

340

Index

344

Index

Wesley Guild Hospital, *see* hospitals
West African Lands Committee, 109
West African Pilot, 184
West African Vanguard, 198–9, 214, 235
Western Nigeria: Government of, 199,
228–30, 236–7, 242; as political unit,
224; crisis of (1962–66), 246–7, 250–3
Western Nigerian Development Corporation
(WNDC), 203, 239, 247
Western Nigerian Broadcasting Corporation
(WNBC), 251–2
widow-inheritance, 52, 104
Williams, D., 22
Williams, O. A., 229
Wilson, G. and M., 1
witchcraft, 165, 173
Witt and Busch, 112, 131
wives, 77, 80–1, 85, 94, 106, 120; *See also*
marriage, women
women: and household, 46–50; occupations
of, 50, 278; as eponyms of lineages, 51;

in trade, 85, 133, 216, 314; and tax, 238;
in politics, 225–6, 251–2
woodcarvers, 35, 74

Yagba, labourers, 122
Yegbata, 54
'Yoruba', meaning 'Oyo', 153, 162
Yoruba, northern (savannah), 129–30, 156–8
Yoruba consciousness, 147,,161–2, 220–1,
223–4, 228, 258, 263, 299
Yoruba ethnography, 8–11, 55–6
Yoruba language, 162
Yoruba News, 181
youngmen: as dependent category, 44, 46,
49–50, 81, 153; challenge to elders,
104–6, 111–12, 114, 118; in modern
politics, 211, 248–9. *See also ipaiyẹ,*
loriọmọ

Zik's Athletic Club, 220, 225